The Beauty of the Primitive

The Beauty
of the Primitive

Shamanism and the Western Imagination

ANDREI A. ZNAMENSKI

OXFORD
UNIVERSITY PRESS

2007

OXFORD
UNIVERSITY PRESS

Oxford University Press, Inc., publishes works that further
Oxford University's objective of excellence
in research, scholarship, and education.

Oxford   New York
Auckland   Cape Town   Dar es Salaam   Hong Kong   Karachi
Kuala Lumpur   Madrid   Melbourne   Mexico City   Nairobi
New Delhi   Shanghai   Taipei   Toronto

With offices in
Argentina   Austria   Brazil   Chile   Czech Republic   France   Greece
Guatemala   Hungary   Italy   Japan   Poland   Portugal   Singapore
South Korea   Switzerland   Thailand   Turkey   Ukraine   Vietnam

Copyright © 2007 by Oxford University Press, Inc.

Published by Oxford University Press, Inc.
198 Madison Avenue, New York, New York 10016

www.oup.com

Library of Congress Cataloging-in-Publication Data
Znamenski, Andrei A., 1960–
The beauty of the primitive : shamanism and the Western imagination /
Andrei A. Znamenski.
   p. cm.
Includes bibliographical references and index.
ISBN 978-0-19-517231-7
1. Shamanism.   2. Shamanism—Russia—Siberia.   I. Title.
BL2370.S5Z53 2007
201'.44—dc22   2006020524

9 8 7 6 5 4 3 2 1

Printed in the United States of America
on acid-free paper

Who is the Drummer who beats upon the earth-drum?

Who is the Drummer who makes me to dance his song?

—Hartley B. Alexander, *God's Drum and Other Cycles from Indian Lore* (1927)

Preface

In the summer of 1998, I was working in south-central Alaska among the Athabaskan Indians, exploring their past and present spiritual life. In addition to visiting several remote villages, my research took me farther to Anchorage, where some Athabaskans live. When my trip was nearing its end, in the downtown of this large metropolitan center, I ran across two interesting persons by chance and talked with them almost half a day. Let us call them Jim and Caroline. Both of them are deeply interested in the Native American and Siberian indigenous spiritualities that they call shamanism. In fact, our mutual interest in "tribal" religions was the spark that ignited the conversation. What intrigued me was that not only were they interested in the topic but that they also tried to live those spiritualities, selecting from them those things they could use in their own lives.

Both Jim and Caroline are Caucasians of middle-class background with northern European ancestry. Jim is a real estate agent, and Caroline works in the University of Alaska health system. They are highly educated people, voracious readers, and very tolerant of other cultures, experiences, and religions. They are also what one might call metaphysical dreamers with antimodernist sentiments, but, at the same time, they struck me as cosmopolitan people who are more open to science and the modern world than, for example, some members of mainstream religious denominations. Another attractive feature of their thinking is the way they strive for natural harmony. To them, the sacred is present in nature rather than in a force called "God" that inflicts apocalyptic horrors on those who do not follow one "true" path. Jim and Caroline shared with me the difficulties they have experienced trying to adjust their earth-based philosophy, which they associate with so-called tribal religions, to their Judeo-Christian backgrounds. During our meeting, Jim also talked at length about how shamanic practice helped him to overcome his alcohol addiction, which eventually made him a firm enthusiast of this ancient spiritual technique. Caroline invited me to visit a local Unitarian church to take part in its shamanic drumming session and to observe how they "do things." In turn, I shared with them what I was doing and stories about places I was visiting.

This Anchorage meeting was my first serious introduction to the growing number of Western spiritual seekers who are trying to recover what they describe as ancient, tribal spirituality (which they frequently call shamanism) to resolve modern spiritual problems. Today, shamanic practices, usually in combination with other spiritual techniques, are booming in the West. Seminars, workshops, and retreats invite people to master the basics of shamanism. There is also a large body of literature on the topic and several specialized magazines with thousands of subscribers.

The word *shaman* comes from the Tungus (Evenki) *šaman* or *xaman*, which one can roughly render as "agitated," "excited," or "raised." The Evenki, one of the indigenous groups in Siberia, use this term to refer to their spiritual practitioners of both genders. In the most generic sense, the shaman is a spiritual practitioner who, in the course of a ritual session, using a drum, a rattle, hallucinogens, or other devices, enters an altered state (sometimes also called a trance) in order to establish contact with spiritual forces in the other world. The goal of this spiritual encounter is to secure the help of spiritual beings that populate this otherworldly reality to resolve a problem, cure a patient, correct a misfortune, or predict the future. Mircea Eliade, a historian of religion and the author of a book considered to be a shamanology classic, described shamanism as "archaic techniques of ecstasy" and viewed it as the earliest form of religion.[1] Although many scholars now believe that the "ecstasy" (altered state) is not a necessary attribute of shamanism, for many Western seekers, this is one of the basic pillars of this spiritual practice.

At the same time, since the eighteenth century, when the word *shaman* was introduced into Western usage, it has meant different things to various people. For example, in the eighteenth century, Russian tsars treated shamans as exotic clowns, whom they added to the throng of court jesters. The Enlightenment explorers of Siberia considered shamans to be jugglers who duped their communities and who should be exposed. If one had described the ecstatic behavior of the shaman during a ritual séance to a classical Freudian scholar sometime in the early twentieth century, the analyst might have exclaimed, "This is a psychotic!" On the other hand, if one shows the shaman in action to current Jungian scholars, they might say that this is the process of active imagination, the acquisition of one's essence. To many members of current nature communities in Europe and North America, the shaman is a carrier of high spiritual and ecological wisdom capable of curing Western civilization. Some spiritual seekers are convinced that shamanism is another name for Native American spirituality. Others use the word simply as a synonym for animism and paganism. For some eco-feminist writers, who believe that matriarchy ruled the world in "primal times" and that the first shamans on the earth were women, shamanism describes feminine spiritual power. Finally, many current spiritual seekers see the shaman simply as a person who stays in touch with spirits. As such, the word is used very loosely to describe people who earlier were known under such names as the "medicine" man or woman, "sorcerer," "conjurer," "magician," "witch doctor," and "spiritualist."

Contemplating what makes shamanism so alluring to some Westerners, I began to look into the cultural and intellectual sources of this attraction. The hundreds of books published on the topic of shamanism since the 1960s alone make this an attractive area for exploration. Even before I finished my Athabaskan Indian research, I had begun to read the literature and engage people like my Anchorage acquaintances Jim and Caroline in discussions. Two other projects sustained and expanded my interest in the new topic. Work on an anthology of the Russian writings on Siberian indigenous spirituality and then on a reader of major Western writings on shamanism[2] helped me to place the literature on shamanism and the popular interest in this phenomenon in the context of Western intellectual and cultural history. Working on these projects, I eventually began posing for myself the following questions: how was the expression *shamanism* introduced into Western usage? How have Western perceptions of shamanism changed over time? And why had shamanism, which was the object of a very marginal interest, suddenly attracted attention in the 1960s and 1970s?

These questions have defined the genre and the format of *The Beauty of the Primitive*, which I describe as an intellectual and cultural history. This book, which treats shamanism both as a metaphor and as a living spiritual technique, discusses the evolution of Western perceptions of shamanism from the eighteenth century to the present. It is also a story about those American and European seekers who pursue archaic techniques of ecstasy as spiritual practice. My major characters are mostly Western scholars, writers, explorers, spiritual seekers, and spiritual entrepreneurs with a variety of attitudes toward shamanism. The purpose of the book is to examine these views and experiences and to reconstruct the intellectual and cultural landscapes that influenced their thinking about shamanism. Although I approach their views and experiences seriously, I do not commit myself to judgments about the truth or falsity of a particular scholarly or spiritual path.

At the same time, I do have my personal take on the topic. I do not agree that we can dissociate shamanism and spiritual life in general from their contexts, or what Eliade called the "terror of history." Although our spiritualities

and beliefs do acquire lives of their own, they carry the stamps of our upbringing, the spirit of our time, and our culture. As much as we may desire
it, we cannot escape our history. Therefore, in talking about different perceptions of shamanism and describing neo-shamanic practices, I bring to light
the ways in which people shape the past and present to suit contemporary
tastes. The reader will see how popular cultural trends, as well as ideological
and academic agendas and the life experiences of observers, have molded the
views of shamanism.

The first half of the book deals with scholarly, literary, and travelers'
perceptions of shamanism before the 1960s, when shamanism did not interest anybody except ethnographers and psychologists and when the word
was reserved primarily for the description of indigenous religious practices in
Siberia and western North America. Much of my story in this part of the
volume naturally concerns the literature on Siberia and North America. The
second half of the text deals with the growing appreciation of the shamanism
idiom among spiritual seekers and academics since the 1960s. Here, I also
discuss the emergence of neo-shamanic practices and the current state of shamanism studies. This part of the book is focused mainly on American scholarship and American spiritual communities, not only because neo-shamanism
sprang up and now shines better in the United States, but also because I am
more familiar with the American cultural scene and American writings on the
topic. At the same time, for comparative purposes, I also draw on materials
about neo-shamanism in other Western countries. Furthermore, in my last
chapter, I return to Siberia to explore the fate of the shamanism idiom in its
motherland in the twentieth century.

The premise of this book is that the growing appreciation of shamanism in the West is part of increasing antimodern sentiments, which have become especially noticeable since the 1960s. These sentiments have led many
to discover the beauty of non-Western and pre-Christian European traditions
that lie beyond the Judeo-Christian mainstream culture and that are linked to
the worlds of the spiritual and the occult. Thus, before the 1960s, when belief in such core values of Western civilization as progress, materialism, and
rationalism was at its peak, the interest in non-Western cultures and their
archaic techniques of ecstasy was marginal, limited at best to anthropologists
and a small group of intellectuals with primitivist and esoteric sentiments.
After the 1960s and to the present day, when the lure of those Western values
has dimmed, the attitudes toward non-Western religions have been clearly
colored with a fascination that has acquired mass proportions. The most
visible examples that come to mind are the popular appeal of Buddhism and
Native Americana. The 1960s represent a landmark here.[3] This was a decade
when many Americans and Europeans not only began to scrutinize Western
civilization critically but also to reject what had earlier been considered its

essentials. To some, the very expression *the West* became a curse, associated with colonialism and excessive materialism.

Since the 1960s, in the humanities and the social sciences, the antimodern intellectual shift similarly has led to a greater emphasis on the human, spiritual, and irrational aspects of society's life and to an increasingly reverential attitude toward non-Western "people without history."[4] Where their earlier colleagues had looked for materialistic explanations and the influence of faceless social and economic forces, the new generation of researchers began to see the unique, the individual, and the irrational. Scholars began to more actively bring people into the picture, including groups, experiences, and cultures that had earlier been considered marginal. The increasing use of the expressions *shaman* and *shamanism* can be attributed to that shift in the intellectual climate, which has accelerated since the 1960s.

When speaking of the pursuits of the archaic techniques of ecstasy, some current Western spiritual seekers, scholars, and writers call them *neo-shamanism*. In this book, I use this word along with the conventional term *shamanism*, specifying in each particular case what time period and geographical area I am intending. When discussing neo-shamanism and related spiritual pursuits, many academics also categorize them as *New Age*. This is a broad term that describes Western seekers who oppose, supplement, or go beyond the mainstream Judeo-Christian tradition. "New Agers" stress universal world spiritual traditions, eclectically borrow from the East and the West, and frequently treat their pursuits as a form of spiritual therapy. The expression *New Age* sometimes arouses objections among Western spiritual seekers as a term that refers to a superficial and "flaky" spirituality.[5] Although I think that there is nothing wrong with this expression, I either use this term in quotation marks or occasionally replace "New Age" with a longer but neutral synonym, "mind, body, and spirit."

I also make use of such broad terms as *spiritual seekers* and *unchurched spirituality*. Although very general, the latter expression, introduced by religion historian Robert Fuller, captures the stance of the "New Age" and modern nature movements—"spiritual but not religious."[6] For the descriptions of such practices as neo-shamanism, sociologists also use the expressions *new religious movements* and *alternative religions*. At the same time, I want to note that many "New Age" practices have been in existence for more than thirty years and, therefore, are not new any more. Furthermore, some elements of the "New Age" intellectual perspective have already entered the Western cultural mainstream, which makes one wonder if the word *alternative* is applicable in this case.

Historian Catherine Albanese offers another useful term, "nature religions,"[7] which might even better capture the essence of neo-shamanism. The expression *nature religions* stresses the earth-based philosophy so essential to the many spirituality groups that grew out of Western environmentalism in the 1970s. Moreover, this term allows us to describe such practices as Celtic shamanism, Wiccan shamanism, and other pagan communities, which do not exactly fit the profile of the "New Age"; the latter tends to be eclectic, to borrow from various cultures, and to believe that spiritual knowledge can be delivered through a workshop. Although the "New Age" and modern paganism overlap, pagans more often than not seek to ground themselves in particular cultural traditions and do not strive to construct global spirituality. In neo-shamanism, this pagan trend became especially visible in the 1990s, when many seekers moved away from eclectic reliance on non-Western traditions toward particular European spiritualities. In this case, some modern shamanism practitioners differ from the "New Age" with its emphasis on global and eclectic spirituality. Because such "nature religions" as neo-shamanism are too fluid and impromptu to be called religions, I have slightly changed the Albanese term and use it in my book as *nature spiritualities*. I also use its derivatives, such as *nature community* and *nature communities*. Last but not least, it is essential to remember that neo-shamanism as well as other "New Age" and modern nature movements represent episodes in the history of Western esotericism. As historian of religion Kocku von Stuckrad reminds us, claims to perennial sacred knowledge acquired through extraordinary states of consciousness and invocations of ancient wisdom and nature philosophy are recurring themes in Western cultural history and go back to Gnostic tradition.[8] At the same time, I urge the reader to exercise caution while reading the above-mentioned generalizations. The variety of neo-shamanic (and shamanic) practices makes them too elusive to neatly fit any rigid framework of an academic classification.

I also want to stress that I am not among those academics who look down upon modern Western shamanism as something artificial and imagined in contrast to an ideal, "real" shamanism found, say, among nineteenth-century native Siberians or Native Americans.[9] Neither do I agree with those writers and scholars who portray Western practitioners of shamanism as spiritual colonizers who feed on indigenous spirituality. I equally disagree with those who dismiss these spiritual seekers as hopeless romantics, simply because I am not convinced that being a romantic or a dreamer is a liability. At the same time, I am not a spiritual seeker who experiments with shamanic techniques. I am a sympathetic observer, who does not believe that neo-shamanism, as fuzzy and fluid as it may be, is a spirituality of a lesser caliber than Native American beliefs, Scientology, Catholicism, evangelical Christianity, Wicca, Mormonism, or Hinduism.

Although my book is the first comprehensive attempt to set shamanism studies and neo-shamanism broadly in the context of the Western culture, I do have scholarly predecessors who have covered some aspects of this theme. First of all, I want to acknowledge the contribution of Ronald Hutton. In his

Shamans: Siberian Spirituality and the Western Imagination (2001), he explores perceptions of Siberian shamanism in Russia and the West from the 1600s to the present time. At the same time, Hutton, a historian of modern witchcraft, is more famous for his ground-breaking *The Triumph of the Moon: A History of Modern Pagan Witchcraft* (1999).[10] Although methodologically I benefited more from the second book, I do appreciate his first one; it provides a good discussion of the historiography of Siberian shamanism, both Marxist and non-Marxist. Because Hutton covers this topic well, in my chapter on Siberia, I only briefly address historiography and instead concentrate on the attitudes of Soviet ideologists toward shamanism and on the rise of indigenous neo-shamanism in post-communist Siberia.

Another work that I want to bring to acknowledge is *Shamans through Time* (2000). This anthology, compiled by anthropologists Jeremy Narby and Francis Huxley, samples brief excerpts from scholarly and travel writings on shamanism from the sixteenth century to modern times. I recommend this text as a documentary companion to my book. I would also like to acknowledge research done by historian of religion Kocku von Stuckrad, whose *Schamanismus und Esoterik* (2003) helped me to see better the place of neo-shamanism within modern Western esotericism. I am also pleased to use this occasion to thank this colleague of mine for giving a critical read to the entire manuscript of *The Beauty of the Primitive* and for providing me with good intellectual feedback. Another debt is to *Dream Catchers* (2004) by Philip Jenkins, who has traced the American romance with Native American spirituality from early colonial days to the present. His exhaustive discussion of this topic helped me to better situate the Native American connection to modern Western shamanism.

Finally, in her *Shamanism and the Eighteenth Century* (1992), literary scholar Gloria Flaherty examines Enlightenment perceptions of indigenous spiritualities in Siberia and North America.[11] Particularly, she argues that the fascination with the "beauty of the primitive" came into view during the age of Enlightenment. Indeed, this period gave rise to the concept of the "noble savage" and also enhanced interest in esotericism—a reaction to the excesses of rationalism. Yet, Enlightenment observers remained predominantly skeptical about non-Western nature religions, treating them as a corruption of "higher" classical religions and as natural specimens to be cataloged and classified. Furthermore, despite the obvious fascination of early nineteenth-century Romantic writers with the spiritual and the non-Western, this little altered the dominant Enlightenment skepticism toward "tribal" religions. It was only at the turn of the twentieth century that attitudes toward non-Western spirituality began to seriously change; during that time, the ideas of the Enlightenment, with its focus on modernity, materialism, and rationalism, gradually began to lose their appeal in society. Still, it was sixty more years before faith in Western civilization was shattered, and fascination with non-Western spiritualities, the occult, and the sacred reached mass proportions and eventually entered the American and European cultural mainstream during the 1970s and the 1980s.

The general format of my project—to explore the origin of the shamanism idiom and the history of Western perceptions of shamanism—implies mining a large amount of relevant literature. This has defined the major sources I used for writing *The Beauty of the Primitive*, which are published materials: books, proceedings of shamanism practitioners' meetings, spirituality periodicals, and newspapers. Doing research for the second half of the book, which discusses neo-shamanism, I also relied on my conversations and interviews with academics who do research on shamanism and with spiritual seekers who situate their activities as shamanic. Mostly, these talks were informal conversations and discussions. At the same time, with several of them, I had long formal interviews.

Working on this book, I enjoyed the assistance of many people: scholars, spiritual seekers, editors, and friends. My first debt to acknowledge is to Cynthia Reed, an editor from Oxford University Press, who accepted this book when it was only at the proposal stage and who excused me twice for missing deadlines for the delivery of the manuscript. I am also grateful to anthropologists Douglas Sharon, David Whitley, and Johannes Wilbert for discussing with me their research on shamanism. I would like to acknowledge the help of the spiritual seekers whom I chose to quote in this book. First, my thanks go to the Society of Celtic Shamans and to its informal head, Tira Brandon-Evans. I also extend my gratitude to Eric Perry and Jack Bennett for taking me along on their shamanic journeys and to Deanna Stennett for exposing me to her spiritual therapy based on so-called core shamanism. My special thanks go to transpersonal psychologist and spiritual practitioner Jurgen Kremer, who shared with me his ideas and experiences on how to make oneself more tribal and indigenous within modern Western culture. I also thank Don Wright for involving me in his spiritual sessions centered on the use of replicas of ancient Peruvian whistling bottles and Jan van Vanysslestyne for sharing with me her experiences of bringing Siberian shamanism to North America. I am equally grateful to Wind Daughter, the medicine chief of the Bear Tribe, who generously contributed information about the late Sun Bear. During my travels to southwestern Siberia, I greatly benefited from the help of Mergen Kleshev, my indigenous host and navigator, whom I would like to thank for introducing me to several traditional and newly minted shamanism practitioners in Mountain Altai.

Another debt of gratitude goes to Alabama State University's Department of Humanities, which provided me with a two-year research leave (2002–2004). During this time, I was able to complete the first draft of this book. I would also like to thank the John W. Kluge Center at the Library of Congress and the Slavic Research Center at Hokkaido University in Sapporo, Japan, for granting me visiting fellowships which sustained me during those two years. I would also like to acknowledge the assistance of the American Philosophical Society. Although it already had sponsored my research twice in the past, I want to thank the society's fellowship committee for bestowing on me its grant for the third time, which helped me to complete the work on this manuscript.

In Japan, I especially appreciated the help and collegiality of Koichi Inoue, senior ethnologist from the Slavic Research Center. I am grateful to him not only for our long discussions of Siberian shamanism and neo-shamanism but also for introducing me to the world of *itako*, Japanese female shamans. Here in the United States, I benefited from the help of another senior colleague, Sergei Kan, who kindly shared with me his knowledge of and materials on several characters I discuss in chapters 2 and 3. I also want to thank him for constant moral support during the past few years. When the book was complete, two other close colleagues assisted me in putting the manuscript into good shape. Carolyn Pevey, a sociologist of religion, invested her time in a critical reading of several chapters of the book, which convinced me to make some useful changes in the text. Her help is greatly appreciated. My deep gratitude extends to Jackie Payne, a colleague and a friend from the Department of Humanities, Alabama State University, who edited and proofread this book. I am sure that without her editorial assistance, this text would have been less readable.

My other debts are more personal. I am grateful to my wife, Susan, who perfectly embodies the type of person of whom I write in the second half of this book and whom some scholars describe as "spiritual but not religious." Her readings and experiences brought to my attention sources and cultural outlets that helped me better to grasp the place of neo-shamanism within modern nature, goddess, and eco-feminist spiritualities. Last, but not least, with his passion for the cartoon movie *Shaman King*, my son, little Andrei, introduced me to another manifestation of the shamanism idiom in current Western culture.

Contents

The Beauty of the Primitive

I

Enlightenment and Romantic Writers Look at Shamans

SHAMANS, noun, masc. plural, is the name that the inhabitants of Siberia give to impostors who perform the functions of priests, jugglers, sorcerers, and doctors.

—*Encyclopedie, ou Dictionnaire Raisonné des Sciences, des Arts, et des Métiers* (1765)

Anyone who observed a genuine shaman at the peak of his ecstasy will absolutely admit that he does not deceive, at least at that moment. In reality, he is under the affect [*sic*] of his involuntary and uncontrolled intensely stimulated imagination.

—Ferdinand von Wrangel, Russian-German explorer (1841)

As I mentioned in the preface, the word *shaman* originated from the language of the Tungus (Evenki), one of the Siberian indigenous groups. Russian settlers in Siberia chose this expression and eventually began to apply it to all native spiritual healers. One may wonder why the newcomers came to prioritize this Evenki expression over other indigenous words that described spiritual practitioners. I guess this happened because, unlike other natives, the Evenki reindeer nomads resided literally all over Siberia. Russian and Western explorers encountered pockets of their communities from central Siberia to the coast of the Pacific Ocean. In addition, the Evenki pleased the eyes of explorers with their beautiful clothing and tattoos (see figure 1.1). Eventually, to European travelers, the picturesque Tungus came to symbolize the archetypical Siberian natives. This could be a reason

FIGURE I.I. The Tungus (Evenki), whose settlements were scattered all over east-central Siberia and whose picturesque attire impressed explorers, gave shamanism its name. Johann Gottlieb Georgi, *Das eröfnete Russland, oder Sammlung von Kleidertrachten aller im Russischen Reiche wohnenden Völker* (St. Petersburg, n.p., 1774), plate "Tungus Hunter."

that the newcomers naturally chose the Evenki *shaman* over other tribal definitions as the generic term for all Siberian spiritual practitioners.

At the same time, despite their attraction to particular elements of native crafts and lore, the first explorers, who introduced *shaman* into Western usage, were skeptical about Siberian indigenous spirituality. Driven by the Enlightenment philosophy with its rationalism and skepticism, many eighteenth-century travelers to Siberia were not fascinated with shamanism whatsoever. In line with the dominant rationalist ideas, many explorers denounced it as primitive superstition, which some of them considered a corruption of higher classical religions. The first change of sentiments among educated European observers toward the tribal archaic techniques of ecstasy coincided with the rise of Romanticism, which injected into the writings of travelers and explorers an element of attraction to both the bright and the dark "Gothic" sides of shamanism. In this chapter, in addition to discussing Enlightenment travel writings on Siberia, we will learn about the contribution of Romantic writers and scholars, who laid the foundations of shamanism studies. Among them are such pioneers of shamanology as Orientalist Dorji Banzarov and Finnish folklore scholars and writers. Although inspired by different intellectual and cultural ideals, all of them found tribal spirituality to be attractive and worthy of recording. I will finish this chapter with a discussion of Wilhelm Radloff. One of the prominent representatives of European Romantic Orientalism, this Russian-German linguist and ethnographer pioneered shamanism studies and wrote a book that remained the major source on "classical" shamanism for Western audiences until 1900.

The Birth of the Metaphor: Eighteenth-Century Enlightenment Explorers

Since Russians were the first to use the word shaman to generalize about Siberian spiritual practitioners, some writers mistakenly assume that Russian authors introduced this expression into Western literature and scholarship. In reality, the people who brought the word shaman into Western usage and intellectual culture were the eighteenth-century Germanic explorers and scientists who visited Siberia. They used the word *schaman* to familiarize educated European and American audiences with ecstatic séances performed by native Siberian spiritual "doctors." Many Russian accounts which mentioned shamans existed in manuscripts but remained unknown even to Russians until the late nineteenth century.[1] As a result, Russian-educated people learned about Siberian shamans from original or translated writings of Western explorers of Siberia.

The first published account that widely samples the shamans (*schaman*) from various Siberian communities is *North and East Tartary* (1692) by the Dutch explorer Nicolaas Witsen (see figure 1.2). An Amsterdam mayor, Witsen traveled to Russia in 1664 and 1665 and collected vast data on the geography, resources, and people of Siberia, the area that he and some of his contemporaries called the Tartary.[2]

It is also notable that the image of the Tungus shaman he reproduced in his book showed a man in a fur coat with animal claws, caught in his ecstatic dance. The caption under the picture explained that it was the shaman, the priest of the devil, which mirrored the widespread assessment of tribal spiritual practitioners before the age of Enlightenment. Before the eighteenth century, indigenous spiritual healers in Siberia and beyond were routinely demonized as servants of dark, evil forces. Although in the eighteenth century this attitude framed in Christian phraseology more or less disappeared from secular literature, it remained well represented in the writings of Western missionaries until the twentieth century.

FIGURE I.2. "Tungus Shaman; or, The Priest of the Devil." A drawing from *North and East Tartary* (1692) by Nicolaas Witsen. Courtesy of Tjeerd de Graaf, Nicolaas Witsen Project, Netherlands.

In addition to Witsen, German-speaking explorers were the first to disseminate, design, and shape the content of the expression *schamanism* among educated Westerners. In fact, at the end of the eighteenth and the beginning of the nineteenth centuries, several English and French texts which described Siberian indigenous beliefs preferred to render the word shaman in its original German version: *schaman*.[3] Why was it not Russian but Western explorers who were the first to reflect in print on Siberian spiritual practitioners? Since the times of tsar Peter the Great, Russia, a European peripheral nation that lacked an educated cadre, sought to hire people from Europe, primarily German-speaking scientists, to survey the geography and resources of its frontier areas. These explorers traversed the Siberian wilderness, mapping tundra and taiga forest, searching for mineral resources, measuring temperatures, collecting and recording exotic specimens and antiquities. Along with minerals, plants, and animal species, the eighteenth-century explorers diligently cataloged the ways and manners of indigenous populations, including such "bizarre" superstitions as shamanism.

Daniel Messerschmidt (1685–1735) was one of the first explorers to be hired by the Russians. Like many learned people of the Enlightenment age, the explorer, a physician by profession, was a jack of all trades. During his Siberian expedition, Messerschmidt acted as a naturalist, geographer, Orientalist, and even archaeologist, examining ancient rock art. The scientist attached to himself as an assistant a Swedish army officer, Philip Johann von Strahlenberg, an educated man who was a prisoner of war exiled to Siberia. In his book published in German in 1726, Strahlenberg introduced European audiences to a detailed image of the Siberian drum, which he observed in southwestern Siberia and which he compared with the drums of "Laplanders," the Sámi people from northern Scandinavia. To contemporary Europeans, the latter were classic magicians and sorcerers. Incidentally, Strahlenberg was also the first to report about the hallucinogenic effects of the fly mushroom. At the same time, the way he described this plant did not say anything about its ritual use.[4]

More comprehensive information about shamanism came later, from a team of explorers who surveyed Siberia on the assignment of the Russian Academy of Sciences between 1733 and 1743. The members of the expedition, naturalists Johann Georg Gmelin and George Steller, student assistant Stepan Krasheninnikov, historian Gerhard Müller, and the expedition's recordkeeper, Jacob Johann Lindenau, keenly observed and recorded shamanism. Lindenau, for example, even went as far as to record the texts of the Tungus (Evenki) shamanic chants in the native language with German translations. Another set of detailed records originated from a second academic expedition (1768–1774), which was sponsored by the Russian empress Catherine the Great, one of those European enlightened despots who considered herself a patron of sciences and education. In addition to its head, zoologist Peter Simon Pallas (1741–1811), the expedition included naturalist Johann Gottlieb Georgi, botanist Johann-Peter Falk, and Pallas's Russian student assistant Vasilii Zuev. Published and republished in major European languages, the writings of the participants of these two expeditions established the basic clichés of what Westerners began to call shamanism. These explorers planted in the minds of their readers the view of shamans as either skillful deceivers, simply weird people, or, worse, easily irritated neurotics. Being scientists and collectors, these children of the Enlightenment age were naturally skeptical of indigenous spiritual "delusions."

Georgi and Pallas articulated well this Enlightenment attitude to shamans by coloring their skepticism with dismissive and derogatory expressions. Georgi stressed that Siberian shamans "produce pranks characteristic for the insane and behave as madmen." They "shout," details the explorer, "twist their mouths," and "roar, mumbling various nonsense." All these manipulations, added the ethnographer, are usually produced in darkness and to scare spectators. On his part, describing a typical shamanic séance among the Ostiak (Khanty), Pallas repeated these words almost verbatim: a shamanic session is just "shouting" and "making noise," during which a spiritual practitioner "mumbles nonsense." Observing a séance performed by an Evenki shamaness, Pallas informed his readers that the woman "jumped, posed, grimaced in every way, while hiccupping, murmuring, and cuckooing and finally beginning to act as if she lost her mind." The explorer was not of a high opinion about the moral status of the people he observed: "Usually these shamans are the most cunning people. Through skillful interpretation of their own dreams and other tall tales they achieve a respected status."[5] It is notable that such a contemporary dignitary as the Russian empress Catherine the Great, who liked to position herself as a well-rounded woman of letters, picked up that skeptical and dismissive attitude toward Siberian shamanism. In her play *The Siberian Shaman* (1786), she mocked tribal spiritual practices in the character of shaman Amban-Lai, who is brought by a noble family to St. Petersburg to heal their daughter. In this play, the greedy and unscrupulous swindler manipulates this family's life and fools his audiences with cheap tricks. In addition, the empress used the play to ridicule representatives of her own high society for their eager response to all things esoteric: "You are like shamans. All of you deceive yourself by following imagined rules, and then dupe those who trust you."[6]

Even those eighteenth-century observers who, like the above-mentioned German scholar Müller, a would-be father of Russian history scholarship, came to Siberia specifically to survey geography, antiquities, and the history of the area, looked down at the manifestations of indigenous spirituality. In the northern Altai, among the Shor people, whom he called Tatars and the Teleut, Müller had a chance to observe a shamanistic séance. The whole performance did not impress him: "It suffices for me to say that all of them [séances] are basically similar. Nothing miraculous happens. The shaman emits an unpleasant howling, while jumping about senselessly and beating a flat drum which has iron bells attached inside to intensify the din." Müller stressed that these shamans are miserable deceivers worthy of condemnation: "It does not take long, however, to be convinced of the futility of the farce, of the deceit by those earning their living in this way." Having finished the description of the ceremony, Müller even asked his readers to excuse him for distracting their attention from the body of his main narrative. The explorer explained this digression as his obligation as a diligent observer to record everything he saw.[7]

It is notable that Georgi, a participant in the second academic expedition, approached shamanism with similar reservations. Admitting that he had to provide the full picture of Siberian native beliefs, the explorer nevertheless stressed that he shortened his observations of shamanic "magic and conjuring tricks due to their obvious foolishness" for the fear that a detailed picture of shamanism might offend his readers.[8]

Russian naturalist Krasheninnikov, who became famous for his first complete description of the Kamchatka peninsula, found satisfaction in exposing shamans. Describing the "tricks" of the Itel'men shaman Karyml'acha, whom local natives and Russians kept in high esteem, the explorer told his readers that he had had a good laugh watching how the shaman had "slashed" his guts by cutting a seal's bladder filled with blood that he had hidden under his abdomen. He concluded his observation with a generalization that such cheap tricks would not even qualify shamans to serve as the apprentices of average European magicians or clowns. Pallas and Müller totally agreed with their Russian colleague. The first one wrote that at any European fair Siberian "pocket tricksters" would fail miserably, while the second noted that their "vulgar and miserable tricks" did not match the shows "performed by our wandering magicians." The overall conclusion of the Enlightenment observers was that as second-rate "performers" and "clowns," Siberian spiritual practitioners were good for nothing. Moreover, Johann Gmelin suggested that in order to teach them a good lesson the government should condemn these "mediocre performers" who "cheated their fellows" to perpetual labor in silver mines.[9]

It appears, however, that Russian officials had other plans for shamans. As soon as the word about the exotic appearance of the spiritual doctors and their ecstatic drumming began to reach the imperial court, the Russian royalty sought to make Siberian "magicians" a staple part of court pageants, parades, and entertainment shows that usually sampled the variety of "curiosities" found within the borders of the empire. These types of grand shows, which Peter the Great introduced into court life, were to display the grandeur of the largest surface empire. In the papers of Peter the Great, there is an order that instructs a Siberian governor-general to find from three to four Samoed (Nentsy) shamans and to deliver them to Moscow. Since this administrator was apparently too slow in his search for tribal "magicians," in his second order the tsar sternly reminded him to take the instruction seriously and to bring the shamans to the court promptly "without any excuse." Peter the Great even threatened the official: "If you find some other excuses and do not send the shamans to Moscow, you will be fined." Eventually, in fulfillment of the emperor's order, a small group of common natives, who were not spiritual practitioners, was brought to St. Petersburg and added to the group of court jesters to amuse the tsar's guests.

It is curious that later, in 1722 and then again two years later, Peter still insisted on delivery of a group of "magicians" to his court. Now the emperor contemplated a pageant for which he needed four shamans along with several native families of "tattooed mugs," the nickname Russians used for the Tungus (Evenki), who were famous not only for their splendid clothing but also for picturesque facial tattoos. The most detailed communication was the 1724 emperor's order that instructed the Siberian governor-general to "search with eagerness notwithstanding any expenses" for shamans among various tribes and to bring them together with their "good appropriate shamanic costumes and drums." Also, the administrator was to select the best ones to ship to the court. Zealous officials herded together twenty-five native spiritual practitioners and delivered them to the Russian empire's capital.[10] Empress Ann continued the tradition of court pageants that showed the ethnography and natural curiosities of the empire. For example, in 1740, she threw a mock wedding for her two court jesters. Magnificent in its grandeur, the event involved about two hundred people representing all known tribes of her empire and included people dressed in Tungus shaman costumes. Incidentally, the ritual outfits came from the ethnographic collections gathered during the first and second academic expeditions to Siberia, which were stored in the Imperial Academy of Sciences.

Like the people from the Russian court, Enlightenment explorers did not shy away from using their official credentials to manipulate with shamans as they wished. The travelers similarly ordered local administrators to "deliver" or to "ship" shamans to designated locations, which was natural for the fieldwork methods of that age. The purpose was to observe and scrutinize carefully the primitive magic in order to debunk it. For example, historian Müller widely practiced this type of ethnographic "investigation." In 1738, upon reaching Buryat country, he found out that en route near the town of Irkutsk there lived a famous healer, Lazar Deibogorov. Müller demanded that town officials deliver the shaman to the city. After the officials brought the healer to the scholar, Müller learned that there were two more powerful shamans who, as he heard, "cut and slash themselves with knives during their performances." So the scholar issued another order "to command them, shamans, to go to Irkutsk along with their entire shamanic devices and knives with which they cut themselves." In his desire to dismember shamanic séances and to catch spiritual practitioners in acts of trickery, Müller ordered a Sakha shamaness to perform for him twice in the presence of specially selected witnesses, including Gmelin. After the audience was finally able to expose the spiritual practitioner, Müller forced her to sign a self-exposing testimony that stated that her spiritual work was a fraud. In this document, the shamaness confesses that, "fearing to lose her credentials," she agreed to perform in the hope of deceiving the scientists, but she could not do this because she "was not able genuinely to cut herself without inflicting a wound."[11] Very much like Müller, Pallas ordered shamans to be delivered to him in order to better scrutinize their craft (see figure 1.3). Once, when a Khakass shaman refused to be delivered to the explorer and hid away somewhere, Pallas had his ritual attire, including a robe, and a drum confiscated.[12]

Pallas traveled in the company of an eighteen-year-old research assistant named V. F. Zuev. This youth journeyed part of the route separately from his boss, visiting the Ostiak (Khanty) and Samoed (Nentsy). Zuev's description of the shamans from these two groups heavily affected Pallas's assessment of Siberian spiritual practitioners. Zuev noted that the shamans he met were marked by "madness" and a "sense of fear [puzhlivost]," qualities that he cited as two major signs of their vocation. With stunned surprise, a few times Zuev observed shamanic séances, which he saw as "passions of craze." The youth also became a witness of the incidents of so-called arctic hysteria, when people went "crazy," imitating all of the gestures of surrounding people, having seizures and convulsions, or attacking other persons and wrecking things. To be exact, scholars are still not sure what specifically caused this phenomenon, once widespread in the arctic area. Among possible reasons, they name vitamin deficiency, the detrimental effect of long polar nights on human minds, and the psychological consequences of colonial oppression. What is important for us here is that in Zuev's mind shamanism, with its crazy bodily movements, and arctic hysteria merged into the same pattern of crazy behavior.

FIGURE 1.3. Types of shamans from southern Siberia: a view of an Enlightenment explorer. Peter Simon Pallas, *Puteshestvie po raznym miestam Rossiiskago gosudarstva* (St. Petersburg: Imperatorskaia Akademiia nauk, 1788), 3:345.

Speculating on the origin of the "insane" nature of the Siberians in general, Zuev guessed, "I do not know how we should explain this. It could be their general weakness, gullibility, or simply stupidity. To be honest, I would rather classify this behavior as some sort of illness." Although, according to Zuev, all native Siberians suffered from the hysteria, shamans manifested this illness in its extreme: "When you irritate the shaman too much, he becomes wildly insane. He gallops, rolls on the ground, and hoots. In such moments, the shaman is also ready to hit people around him with what he holds in his hands."[13]

Pallas not only included in his book the speculations of his assistant about the "insane" and "fearful" nature of shamans, but he also expanded them. The naturalist generalized that, based on what he "heard from the other people," the hysterical behavior of Samoed (Nentsy), Tungus (Evenki), and Kamchadal (Itel'men) shamans "developed partially from an irritability of their bodies and excessive strain they place on their minds, and partially from surrounding climate, the specifics of their craft, and the imagination distorted by superstitions."[14] Moreover, solely relying on Zuev's report, the scientist concluded that among the Nentsy and the Sakha the hysteria ("scare") and "madness" reached epidemic proportions; in a state of irritation, the raging "madmen" could kill either themselves or people who accidentally scared them. Later writers on Siberian religions repeatedly referred to Pallas's observations, adding to them their own comments until sometime at the end of the nineteenth century European writers began to routinely associate shamanism with a mental deviation. Eventually, at the beginning of the twentieth century, the link between shamanism and hysteria gradually acquired the status of an academic theory.

Dismissing shamanic practices as miserable and vulgar miracles or diagnosing them as mental ailments, several Enlightenment observers nevertheless tried to explore the origin of these "delusions." Thus, in his *History of Siberia* (1750), Müller speculated if such "perverse teaching" as shamanism sprang up naturally in various localities or originated from a single source? The scholar was inclined to trace the roots of shamanism from the classic Orient. Müller suggested that the cradle of shamanism was India, from where it gradually spread all over Asia, then to Scandinavia, and eventually to native North America. The historian also surmised that the spearheads of this phenomenon were the most ancient inhabitants of India, who had been driven from their country by the "Brahmin" latecomers. By moving out of India, the ancient ones spread themselves over vast areas of Asia, carrying with them their primal religion. While drifting northward and mixing with local people, noted the historian, the ancient Hindu people gradually degenerated, forgot the high wisdom of their ancestors, and developed what later became known as shamanism in its Siberian version with all its crude tricks, like ecstatic dances and drumming. To Müller, the fact that both contemporary northern Asian shamanism and Hindu beliefs were polytheistic pointed to the genetic "Indian connection" in shamanism. The historian also reasoned that if Buddhism had spread from India to Tibet, China, Mongolia, and even to Siberia, nothing prevented us from assuming that shamanism had spread in the same manner from the same source.[15]

Georgi, a contemporary fellow explorer of Siberia, who defined the shaman as the "hermit in possession of all passions," similarly searched for the sources of the ancient faith in the East. Like Müller, he was convinced that shamanism represented a degenerative version of classical "pagan faiths" of a "higher caliber," such as Tibetan Buddhism and Hinduism. At the same time, his generalizations on shamanism were more extensive than the ones of his Enlightenment colleagues. Thus, Georgi found it necessary to include in his four-volume description of all peoples residing in the Russian empire an essay titled "On Pagan Shamanic Order." The explorer also offered his explanation of how in their northward migration those classical faiths might have lost their noble character: "Because of wars, rebellions, population movements, wanderings, the lack of education, and the misinterpretation of tales by stupid and deceiving priestly people, this order [shamanism] was turned into disgusting idol worshipping and blind superstition."[16] To Georgi, the impromptu nature of contemporary inner Asian and Siberian shamanism with its lack of monotheism and any religious dogma was the clear proof of the "degenerative" character of the ancient faith.

Incidentally, the attempt to locate the sources of shamanism in India was not some peculiar hypothesis introduced by Georgi and Müller. Their speculations reflected a popular intellectual stance that was coming into fashion. In the age of Enlightenment, many scholars and writers, especially those who questioned the authority of the Bible and Christianity, turned to India, trying to draw from there the sources of all great religions and civilizations. Later, Romantic writers embraced and expanded this idea.

Out of India: Romantic Orientalism about the Sources of Shamanism

The desire to look for answers in the "Himalaya" became the established scholarly theory in nineteenth-century Orientalism. Commenting on this geographic preference of his Romantic contemporaries, Adolph Erman, a German explorer of Siberia, ironically wrote of an "attempt to establish a mysterious depot for everything which being elsewhere undiscoverable."[17] One of the major spearheads of this intellectual stance became Johann Gottfried Herder (1744–1803), the late Enlightenment thinker and one of the pioneers of early Romanticism. He summarized his intellectual preferences in catchy phrases that sounded like chants: "O holy land [India], I salute to thee, thou source of all music, thou voice of the heart"; and "Behold the East—cradle of the human race, of human emotion, of all religion."[18] Friedrich Schlegel was another prominent Romantic writer and philosopher who promoted the same perception. He invested much time into studying Sanskrit and was among the first to come up with a famous theory that this language of Indian antiquity was the original proto-language shared by both Eastern and Western civilizations. Schlegel also drew historical connections from his linguistic theory. He stressed particularly that the Sanskrit-speaking Aryan nomadic tribes of Caucasian origin, who had conquered India, gave rise to classical Near Eastern, Greek, and Roman civilizations and thus laid the foundation for Western civilization. Later, to describe these Aryan forerunners, scholars and writers coined a special expression: "Indo-Europeans."[19]

To my knowledge, Schlegel was among the first to trace the origin of the word shaman to Sanskrit. In his 1820s works, the philosopher indicated that shaman originated from *samaneans*, a classical antiquity expression that described Buddhist priests in ancient India. Therefore, as Schlegel stressed, *schaman* was a "pure Indian" word. Besides, he remarked, it contained "quite a philosophical sense." In his lectures on world intellectual history, Schlegel speculated on the philosophical meaning of the expression. Draping this meaning in Hindu colors, he interpreted *schaman* as an "equability of mind" that is "requisite to the perfect union with the God." Furthermore, Schlegel was seriously convinced that all Siberian natives used the expression *schaman* as a generic word for their spiritual practitioners. It is possible that he drew this false impression from a superficial reading of the Müller, Georgi, or Pallas books. Moreover, Schlegel stretched out the geography of the word beyond Siberia, insisting that both the "considerable portion of the Tartar races" and northern and even central Asian natives all described their priests and magicians by the word *schaman*.[20]

The philosopher believed that the Buddhist *samaneans*, proto-shamans, were squeezed northward as a result of their conflict with "Brachmans," another ancient Indian "sect." The rest of his story replicated the familiar Enlightenment hypothesis about the northward expansion of shamanism. Repeating the theories of Müller and Georgi, Schlegel argued that, in the process of migration, the "crude nations of Central Asia," which were "sunk to the lowest degree of barbarism and superstition," distorted classical Buddhism. The novelty the philosopher brought to this theory was the linguistic link that was to prove the Indian connection in northern Asian shamanism. In the first half of the nineteenth century, the famous historian of religions Max Müller, who similarly believed that India was the original home of civilized humanity, made this "linguistic method" a staple approach in exploring possible links among various spiritual traditions in ancient times.

Those of Schlegel's contemporaries who worked in the same Romantic tradition and who wrote about shamanism might have differed from each other in details, but the line of reasoning was the same: shamanism is the degenerated northern version of classical Oriental beliefs. All of them took it for granted that the crude natives of northern Asia could not create a religion of their own and simply had to borrow spiritual ideas from civilizations of classic antiquity. For example, a colorful version of the Oriental connection in shamanism was offered by Polish explorer Ludwik Niemojowski. This inquisitive observer, who eagerly sought to witness Siberian shamanic sessions, insisted that "in prehistoric times" shamanism, which he called the "black faith," flourished in the eastern and southern portions of Asia and especially in India. Unlike Schlegel and his predecessors, who never specified the particular center of shamanism in India, Niemojowski boldly pinpointed its "chief seat"—the "Attock" and "Peshawur" areas of India.[21]

Niemojowski portrayed the process of the northern "degeneration" of shamanism as a grand spiritual drama. At first, as he wrote, Brahmanism and Buddhism, which emanated "patience and gentleness," gradually squeezed out adherents of shamanism, the faith "steeped in witchcraft and blood," sending them northward from India to inner Asia and Siberia. Eventually, "the shamans settled in the ice-bound parts of Asia and Europe, some even, reaching the rocky shores of Scandinavia, spread around the White Sea, and the Finn races (Laplanders, Samoieds) have succumbed to their influence; others settled in Siberia, and inoculated the wandering aborigines with their religious ideas."[22] While to the high Oriental civilization on the shores of the Ganges, continued the writer, this religion appeared barbarous, the "primitive races" of northern Eurasia, who lived in a "semi-bestial state" and had no religion whatsoever, found it attractive. As crude as it could be, said Niemojowski, shamanism opened for them a small window to civilization. Unfortunately, as the writer dramatically put it, the severe conditions of the northern areas, especially in Siberia, slowed down the advance toward higher culture and froze in its "pristine rigour" and barbarity the ancient "horrible faith."

In the second half of the nineteenth century, American folklore scholar and mystic Charles Godfrey Leland (1824–1903) offered a peculiarly American version of the Oriental connection in the origin of shamanism. It is notable that, unlike contemporary American writers and scholars, who hardly used the expression shamanism at that time, Leland not only already worked with this word but also accepted the complete historical baggage ascribed to its definition. Most certainly, he absorbed these things during the years of his long schooling and traveling in Germany, whose culture and literature fascinated him very much. Like European Romantic Orientalists, Leland tended to believe that shamanism originated from one source, which certainly was the classic East, the "very ancient common source," as he once put it.[23]

Based on the arbitrary genetic parallels he established between the American Indian mythology of the Eastern United States and the Old World's legends, the writer surmised that shamanism gradually spread from Central Asia to Northern Europe, and then to the Greenland "Eskimo." Later on, the "Eskimo" brought it to the "Wabanaki" Indians of Labrador, New Brunswick, and Maine. Eventually, the "Wabanaki" passed it to the Iroquois, who in their turn carried this faith to the Western tribes. Generalizing about the essence of shamanism, like Niemojowski, Leland gave credit to this primal religion in humanity's religious evolution toward progress. Particularly, Leland pointed out that shamanism was an important step toward an organized religion by taming the excesses of black magic to which people, in his view, clung in earlier times. Leland assumed that shamans created order from chaos by disowning "the darker magic of older days."[24]

Overall, by the end of the nineteenth century, many scholars and writers more or less agreed that the Tungus word shaman originated from the ancient Sanskrit word *sramana* or Pali *samana*, which were common terms for a Buddhist monk in the sacred texts of ancient India. As I mentioned, the linguistic connections invited the relevant cultural and historical links. Although several scholars did continue to question this Indian connection, the majority took it for granted. With slight variations, this interpretation penetrated all standard dictionaries and encyclopedias, which eventually began to register it as an established usage. Thus, the early twentieth-century editions of the German *Brockhaus' Konversations-Lexikon* drew the Siberian shaman from Indian *sramana.* Moreover, *Meyers großes Konversations-lexikon* (1909), which offered the same interpretation, directly referred to the authority of Max Müller and his linguistic method as the source of this interpretation.[25]

Although *The Oxford English Dictionary* offered two alternative versions on the origin of the expression, both of them perfectly fit the assumed Oriental connection. On the one hand, the dictionary suggested that the Tungus shamans should be linked to the Sanskrit *cramana* (ascetic) or Pali *samana*. On the other hand, it is noted that the expression might have penetrated to the Tungus (Evenki) through the Mongolian language, which supposedly assimilated it from the Chinese *sha mén.* If we are to believe the dictionary, in ancient China, the latter word meant "an ordained member of a Buddhist fraternity."[26] In addition, I found several exotic variations of the same presumed Oriental linguistic link in shamanism. Thus, tracing the origin of shaman to the Sanskrit *çámas* (termination, relaxation, and rest), Russian émigré philologist A. G. Preobrazhensky explained in his dictionary of the Russian language (1951) that the expression reached Siberia from Mongolia, and he described a lower class of Buddhist priests who were involved in healing and sorcery.[27]

As early as 1917, anthropologist Berthold Laufer clearly showed that linguistically there was little foundation to keep digging for shamanism's Oriental connection, which was so "tenaciously upheld under the influence of the romantic movement of pan-Indianism." Although the scholar complained that at this time the "ghost of the Indian etymology" haunted "the poor shaman in our standard dictionaries and cyclopedias," some modern reference editions still follow this interpretation, for example, *The American Heritage Dictionary* (1985). Moreover, paying tribute to the old academic tradition, some scholars and spirituality writers still continue to generalize about the genetic Oriental link in inner and northern Asian shamanism and to trace the origin of the word shaman from the Vedic *sram* (to heat oneself), *sramana* (ascetic), or other derivatives that simultaneously bring corresponding Oriental associations. In fact, for some current esotericism writers and spiritual practitioners, this connection provides convenient "scholarly" evidence that allows them to tie shamanism to tantra or to yoga practices. Thus, California anthropologist and shamanism practitioner Larry Peters insists that the shamanic embodiment techniques spread from India to northern Asia and so did the term. Ironically, literary scholar Gloria Flaherty, the author of an interesting book, *Shamanism and the Eighteenth Century* (1992), in which she reveals perceptions of shamanism by the intellectual culture of the Enlightenment, herself fell victim to that linguistic fallacy.[28]

The roots of the persistent desire to set the genetic motherland of shamanism in the classic Orient certainly go back to the enduring intellectual tradition of Romantic Orientalism. I am guessing that it also should be attributed to the influence of Sergei Shirokogoroff (1887–1939), one of the classic scholars of modern shamanism studies. This Paris-educated philologist from Russia, who later turned to ethnography, detected visible spiritual influences of

Tibetan Buddhism in the beliefs of southern Tungus (Evenki). Drawing on these findings, the scholar developed a thesis about southern Siberian shamanism stimulated by Buddhism. Following his intellectual predecessors, he also assumed that, in its turn, the Tibetan tradition might have borrowed the word shaman from India. At one point, Shirokogoroff came up with a special paper where he defended, in his words, "the honour of the family of *sramana* and *saman*" in shamanism studies.[29]

Yet, unlike Enlightenment and Romantic writers, Shirokogoroff never viewed shamanism as an archaic primal religion. The scholar stressed that what he called Tungus shamanism was a religious system that was the result of a spiritual blend between Tibetan Buddhism and Siberian indigenous beliefs in medieval and early modern times. Anticipating current postmodern anthropology, Shirokogoroff preferred to generalize about shamanism as little as possible, restricting himself to Tungus ethnographic materials, and criticized those of his colleagues who dared to draw cross-cultural analogies. At the same time, I think, the scholar exaggerated the influence of Buddhism on Evenki shamanism and naturally drifted toward the Romantic linguistic method. Although Tibetan Buddhism might have stimulated the shamanism of southern Evenki groups—and, more so, Tuvan and Buryat spirituality—I doubt that such Siberian practices as mastering spirits and their calling at will were the result of Tibetan influences as Shirokogoroff tried to convince his readers.[30]

Romantic *Naturphilosophie* and Indigenous Spirituality

The first scholar who attempted to examine shamanism on its own ground without speculating about the Oriental links was the university-educated Siberian native Dorji Banzarov (1822–1855) (see figure 1.4). Coming from the Buryat people and being schooled in Russian universities, at first in Kazan and then in St. Petersburg, he was in a unique position to provide an indigenous perspective on Siberian spirituality. While at Kazan University, Banzarov wrote a master's thesis, "The Black Faith; or, Shamanism among the Mongols" (1846), which provided the first more or less consistent sketch of Siberian and inner Asian shamanism. The essay deals with the beliefs of two related groups, the Buryat and the Mongols. Although grounded in the Enlightenment and contemporary Romantic Orientalist scholarship, Banzarov criticized those of his predecessors who insisted that indigenous Siberian spiritual practices were a "bastardized" version of Tibetan Buddhism. Instead, he pointed to native sources of Siberian and Mongol shamanism. "A closer acquaintance with the subject," wrote the scholar:

> shows that the so-called shamanist religion, at least among the
> Mongols, could not have arisen from Buddhism or any other faith,

FIGURE I.4. Dorji Banzarov (1822–1855), a native Buryat intellectual and one of the first students of shamanism. Dorzhi [Dorji] Banzarov, *Chernaia viera ili shamanstvo u mongolov*, ed. G. N. Potanin (St. Petersburg, n.p., 1891), frontispiece.

that it could have arisen by itself among the people, and that it does not consist of a few superstitions and rites based only on the charlatanism of shamans. The black faith of the Mongols arose from the same source from which were formed many ancient religious systems: the external world, nature, and the internal world, the soul of man.

Essentially, for Banzarov, the human spirit gave rise to shamanism by feeding on local landscapes.[31]

His utterances show that, rather than using the established Indian connection, Banzarov was more inspired by another line of contemporary thought—the philosophy of nature (*Naturphilosophie*). In fact, the ethnographer directly pointed to geographer Alexander von Humboldt as one of his inspirations. One of the chief proponents of this theory, Humboldt drew attention to an intimate link between organic living nature and human beings. Banzarov wrote that the German geographer understood "better than anyone the action of nature on uneducated peoples." Banzarov was also very critical of the eighteenth-century Enlightenment observers who piled the beliefs of all northern Asian groups together in order to draw a picture of generic shamanism. About Georgi's essay

"On Pagan Shamanic Order," which I mentioned above, Banzarov wrote that it was a regrettable attempt to construct a generalized picture of Siberian shamanism by mixing the beliefs and mythologies of Turks, Finns, Mongols, and other peoples. Anticipating the postmodern sentiment dominant in current anthropology scholarship that tries to avoid any cross-cultural generalizations, Banzarov stressed that for research purposes it was more interesting to single out the shamanism of a particular group "with those nuances and details which must have been found among each people."[32] Unfortunately, in his studies of shamanism, Banzarov never went beyond his master's thesis. Torn apart by a cultural clash, feeling alienated from both Russian-educated society and his crude kin, he discontinued his ethnographic studies and eventually drank himself to death.

The Romantic age saw a visible change in the general attitude to non-Western spirituality. I would not say that the overall view of primitive religions moved to a sympathetic treatment. Still, the very intellectual stance of Romanticism, which sought to mute the reigning rationalism and obsession with science, prompted explorers and writers to pay more attention to the spiritual and the mysterious (see figure 1.5).[33] Several travel narratives which deal with native Siberians and describe indigenous shamanism give examples of such changing attitudes. A Baltic German scientist, Alexander von Bunge, who visited the Altai in southwestern Siberia in 1826 in search of plant and mineral specimens, called native shamans skillful "deceivers." At the same time, he informed his readers that, for some unknown reason, he was instinctively drawn to native rituals. Von Bunge noted that, although his formal goal was to collect information about the botany and geology of the area, he frequently made long detours to observe indigenous life and manifestations of native lore. Even when natives did not particularly welcome him, von Bunge tried to attend their gatherings to "witness a festivity," especially when he heard the "captivating sounds of a shaman drum." Not only was von Bunge drawn to native lore, but also in the course of his journey he himself became a "doctor" when word about his successful treatments of several natives spread among local indigenous communities. Moreover, following the locally established rules of the game, von Bunge did not mind accepting the gifts of furs for his healing "séances." The explorer became involved in an exchange of experiences with an Altaian shaman, who came to examine his European colleague and then performed for von Bunge a soothsaying séance using a ram's shoulder blade.[34]

Three more contemporary Siberian travel accounts that mention shamanism illustrate the aforementioned intellectual trend. The first one belongs to explorer Frants Beliavskii (1833) and describes the Khanty and the Nentsy customs. Another one belongs to M. F. Krivoshapkin (1865), who worked as a physician in Khanty country. The third is a book by Ferdinand von Wrangel (1841), a naval commander who explored northern Pacific Rim areas of Siberia and North America and who left to us descriptions of Chukchi shamanism.[35]

FIGURE 1.5. Romantic image of Tungus shamans. A nineteenth-century German lithograph from a Russian album. Fedor K. Pauli, *Description ethnographique des peoples de la Russie* (St. Petersburg: F. Bellizard, 1862), 72–73, plate.

All three authors pay keen attention to folklore, the sublime, and the spiritual. Essential for the intellectual culture of European Romanticism, these elements muted the skeptical Enlightenment attitudes to native spirituality.

Of these books, none better conveys the Romantic attitudes toward indigenous shamanism than Wrangel's travel notes. A Baltic-German baron in the service of the Russian empire, this explorer successfully combined the roles of governmental administrator, explorer, and ethnographer. Incidentally, in addition to his Siberian travel narrative, Wrangel, who was the chief administrator of Russian colonies in North America from 1829 to 1837, published a whole anthology of ethnographic materials on the Yupik, Tlingit, and Athabaskan natives of Alaska and even on California Indians. Like von Bunge, the commander felt the similar unexplainable attraction to ecstatic shamanic rituals, which "create the scene full of horror and mystery, which has captivated me strangely every time."[36] Discussing his encounters with indigenous spiritual practitioners in extreme northeastern Siberia, Wrangel noted that these shamans left on his mind "a long-continued and gloomy impression." He also added, "The wild look, the bloodshot eyes, the labouring breast, the convulsive utterance, the seemingly involuntary distortion of the face and whole body, the streaming hair, the hollow sound of the drum, all conspired to produce the effect." Elaborating on this "Gothic" essence of shamanism, Wrangel remarked that the "gloomy surrounding nature" of Siberia played an essential role in the development of the "mysterious aspirations" of these individuals. As in the case of Banzarov, this utterance was an obvious tribute to the popular *Naturphilosophie.*

Wrangel directly challenged the Enlightenment explorers' assessment of shamans as impostors and clowns:

> Almost all those who up to the present have expressed an
> opinion on the shamans represented them as ill-qualified impostors
> of a crude and vulgar kind, whose ecstasies are nothing more than
> an illusion created to take advantage of people. From the observations
> I made during my journeys in Siberia, I concluded that this judg-
> ment is harsh and unfounded.

He stressed that shamans were "remarkable psychological phenomena" who had nothing to do with trickery and deception. The explorer was convinced that if some native spiritual practitioners did use tricks to deceive members of their communities, they were exceptions and aberrations of the profession. "A true *schaman*," he explained to his readers, "is not a cool and ordinary deceiver, but rather a psychological phenomenon."[37]

In his turn, talking about Nentsy shamans in northwestern Siberia, Beliavskii stressed that the point was not that native doctors performed sleight-of-hand magic tricks, but the respect they enjoyed in their clans. "Simple-minded folk view these raging madmen with tender emotions," he stressed. Describing the character of the people involved in the shamanic vocation, Beliavskii, Wrangel, and Krivoshapkin all portrayed them as creative personalities, who had penetrating minds, strong wills, and ardent imaginations. Wrangel showed that many of them stayed so strongly in their beliefs that they were ready to suffer for their convictions.[38] At the same time, these "native geniuses," as Beliavskii called shamans, were people of "tragic fate" because their artistic and creative talents were unavoidably wasted in the barren northern terrain.

Krivoshapkin, who not only fully shared the Romantic allegories about native geniuses but also directly copied some of them from the Beliavskii text, compared Siberian native youths who were predisposed to shamanism with the tragic characters from the Romantic poems of Alexander Pushkin and Mikhail Lermontov. Krivoshapkin stressed that, not having any other outlets to channel their creativity, these spiritually charged natives attached themselves to practicing shamans, who captivated their attention with unusual behavior.

Eventually, the young native geniuses fulfilled themselves through long vigils, fasting and replicating the craft of their senior colleagues. By constantly imitating the behavior of old shamans, young apprentices developed their sensitivity to such an extreme that, when necessary, they were capable of immersing themselves quickly into the state of a "dream-like ecstasy." To Wrangel, the most skillful candidates who perfected their contemplative skills amid the northern wilderness eventually received the status of genuine shamans and went through an initiation accompanied, as he said, by "many ceremonies, performed in the silence and darkness of night."[39]

The utterances of Otto Finsch, a German geographer who conducted an expedition to western Siberia in 1876, show well the changing attitudes toward indigenous cultures and spiritualities brought by Romanticism. Traversing some of the localities that had been explored by Beliavskii and Krivoshapkin, Finsch on occasion wrote with an irony about particular native spiritual practitioners. Yet, unlike his Enlightenment predecessors, he never slid into denouncing shamanism. He concluded his notes on Siberian indigenous beliefs as follows: "This [shamanism] religion does not have anything immoral. Throughout the centuries, it nourished in the natives their good human qualities. Although some people laugh at and frown upon it, this faith deserves the respect of each educated man, the kind of respect that we should pay to all human beings."[40]

If we look into the intellectual setting for such a change to non-Western spirituality, we should start with such Romantic writers and philosophers as Herder, who was among the first to soften the rationalist attacks of Enlightenment scholars on the "superstitions" of other cultures. In fact, the entire Romanticism project was a movement toward the intellectual rehabilitation of the religious and the spiritual, which earlier Enlightenment writers wanted to dismiss as vestiges of the "dark ages." Herder pointed to the limitations of the Enlightenment and its obsession with reason. The philosopher wanted to validate the role of imagination, emotion, and all aspects of the irrational in human knowledge. In their art, poetry, prose, and, for some, lifestyles, Romantic intellectuals drew attention to things spiritual, mysterious, and what conventional Enlightenment wisdom could consider abnormal or weird. For example, in Herder's eyes, to believe in spirits and to experience spiritual inspiration was natural and beneficial. Acknowledging native superstitions as a religion, he argued against calling their practitioners "deceivers." The philosopher was able to see in the "bestial" and "insane" movements of the shaman the grains of creativity akin to those expressed in the work of artists, poets, and singers.

From Herder's viewpoint, Orpheus, a character from Greek mythology, European skalds and bards, and non-Western spiritual practitioners belonged to the same tribe because all of them were doing spiritual work. Herder pointed out to his contemporaries that classical Greeks had also been savages before their civilization flourished. Moreover, even after they "blossomed," they still were close to nature and, therefore, he reminded, remained "noble Greek shamans [edle griechishe Schamanen]."[41] Bringing together what Pallas, Gmelin, Müller, and other explorers wrote about Siberian religions and adding materials on American Indian and Greenlandic beliefs, the philosopher generalized about shamanism as a universal phenomenon equally characteristic of all peoples at the dawn of their histories. To Herder, the ability of shamans to reach out and captivate their audiences pointed to the "victories of imagination" so much underestimated by earlier writers and some of his contemporaries. The philosopher stressed that the very accounts of the skeptical Enlightenment observers, who always kept wondering why shamans had so much power over native minds, were good indirect proofs of the power of imagination.

Early nineteenth-century Romantic writers who followed Herder not only validated spiritual and visionary experiences but also introduced the view of surrounding nature as an organic animated entity, the stance that manifested itself in the concept of Naturphilosophie. Looking into this and related concepts, in his Schamanismus und Esoterik (2003), German religious studies scholar Kocku von Stuckrad noted that in the books of Romantic writers one can find much of what we see today in the intellectual perspective of neo-shamanism and other nature spiritualities. Thus, anticipating the holistic vision of the world, philosopher Friedrich von Schelling (1775–1854), one of the major spearheads of Naturphilosophie, argued that God was present in nature everywhere. Because nature was an active being of its own, it was irrelevant, wrote Schelling, what people might learn about how to change it. Therefore, to think that people could control the earth was a false assumption. Instead of forcing something on the land and extracting things from it, argued Schelling, people should better learn the ways of nature and live according to them.[42]

Friedrich von Hardenberg (1772–1801), better known under his pen name, Novalis, came up with a similar vision of nature as sacred: "nature would not be nature if it did not have a spirit." This early Romantic fiction writer and poet blurred the border among human beings, plants, and stones, picturing them as parts of one circle of life. As an anticipation of the currently popular spiritual biography genre, in his posthumously published novel, Henry von Ofterdingen (1802),[43] Novalis reflected on his own life, freely blending fictional travel narrative with legends and setting the whole story amid enchanted medieval landscapes. Budding poet Henry, the major character of this book, merges himself with surrounding nature and, almost in a shamanic fashion, goes through visionary experiences.[44] Henry experiences a dream in which he sees a blue flower. The shape of the flower looks like some unknown woman. The intrigued youth is eager to uncover the mystery of the blue flower. Accompanying his mother to Augsburg, where they plan to visit his grandparents, Henry sets out on a journey, which he thinks might help to unveil the mystery. En route, Henry encounters a number of people who immerse him in the world of legends, songs, and fairytales. Ultimately, the search for the blue flower and the final destination are not so important. What is more essential is the journey itself, the way, which turns into a process of spiritual empowerment that allows Henry to transcend the ordinary. Incidentally, Novalis's "blue flower" metaphor acquired symbolic status for contemporary Romantics. The blue flower came to mean the longing for something that was far off, which one could not reach and which in fact was not meant to be reached in order to remain magical and mysterious.

Across the Atlantic, in the first decades of the nineteenth century in the United States, transcendentalism advocated a similar organic approach to nature and spirituality. This American version of Romanticism, which sprang up in New England, served as another intellectual predecessor of the present-day mind, body, and spirit culture. The first names that come to mind when one mentions transcendentalists are Ralph Waldo Emerson and Henry David Thoreau. Although originally transcendentalists drew more on Puritan biblical tradition, later they assimilated many ideas of German Romanticism. For example, Goethe's and Novalis's fiction informed the style of some transcendentalist writers. As von Stuckrad pointed out, in Emerson's famous essay "Nature" (1836), one can easily see parallels with Novalis's earth philosophy, especially in the way Emerson describes the role of the poet, who is endowed with the ability to penetrate the secrets of animated reality.

In their writings, transcendentalists replaced the concept of an anthropomorphic Christian God with the idea of ever-present spirit, about which one can learn by looking into human beings and surrounding nature. Both for German Romantics and their American counterparts, the intuition was an essential tool in approaching the surrounding world. Although Emerson did not go as far as turning nature into something sacred, Thoreau, his contemporary, did. In *Walden; or, Life in the Woods* (1854), describing his beloved Walden Pond and the surrounding landscape, Thoreau literally animates nature. The writer addresses the pond as a human being, calling it a "neighbor" and "great bedfellow." *Walden*, which became an American literary classic, provided an excellent spiritual and textual blueprint for later generations of spiritual seekers.

Another element that links present-day spiritual seekers and the nineteenth-century Romantic writers is the significance that both Thoreau and Emerson attached to dreams and dreaming, which appeared to them as insights into the essence of human nature. Thoreau, for example, wrote that dreams "are touchstones of our characters" and stressed that "in dreams we see ourselves naked and acting out our real characters even more clearly than we see others awake." Celebrating intuition and imagination over pure reason, Emerson added that for the human mind the dream, which tore off the "costume of circumstance," was not only an incredibly helpful tool of self-knowledge, but also a key to the wonder of nature and the universe in its fullest and most real form. He especially appreciated the value of dreaming during waking moments, what today we call "lucid dreaming."[45]

No less important were attempts of transcendentalists to integrate Oriental symbolism into their earth-based mysticism. As far as North America is concerned, transcendentalists became the first to perform this type of intellectual syncretism, although as a spiritual practice it surfaced later when the theosophical movement sprang up in the 1870s. Like many Romantic writers, Emerson, who explored Hinduism, was fascinated with India and integrated Oriental metaphors in his poetry and prose, establishing a tradition of blending non-Western spiritual symbolism with nature-based metaphysics. Thoreau, who was enthusiastic about Buddhism, similarly embraced the dictum: light comes from the East. In addition to the Oriental wisdom, there was also a Native American connection in transcendentalism, although at that time it was not as visible as in the present-day mind, body, and spirit community. For example, Emerson noted that the natural "ignorance" of the American primitives was a blessing: the "simple mind" of the American Indian, who lived a natural life, was not tormented by such problems as original sin, predestination, or the origin of evil.

To Thoreau, who, unlike Emerson, did interact with real Indians, the natives appeared as ideal human beings endowed with the inherent skill to feel nature. In 1841, he wrote in his diary about the nature-bound essence of the Indians: "The charm of the Indian to me is that he stands free and unconstrained in Nature, is her inhabitant and not her guest, and wears her easily and gracefully. But the civilized man has the habits of the house. His house is a prison, in which he finds himself oppressed and confined, not sheltered and protected."[46] If we are to believe one of his transcendentalist friends, Thoreau's last words on his deathbed were "Indian" and "moose." Nobody knows what he actually meant, but the link between nature and the primitive seemed to be obvious.[47]

Incidentally, the modern Unitarian Universalist church, which is rooted in transcendentalism and which is popular with well-rounded, "learned" Americans, is now the major mainstream denomination that actively incorporates many elements of mind, body, and spirit culture, including Native American symbolism, shamanism, and paganism. In the nineteenth century, American Shakers also sought to appropriate Native American symbolism; they insisted that they channeled some of their songs and speeches from the spirits of deceased Indians. In addition to the transcendentalist-Unitarian-Universalist line, Shakers might have also contributed to the modern American tradition of reverence for Native American spirituality, although the fascination with Native American wisdom on a grand scale is certainly a recent phenomenon that entered American life in the 1960s.[48]

Among the nineteenth-century American Romantic writers who sought to appropriate indigenous symbolism for spiritual purposes, the name of Leland stands out. I already mentioned him in relation to the Oriental connection in shamanism. To students of Native Americans, Leland, a folklore writer and mystic, is known more as a collector of Native American (primarily Passamaquoddy and Micmac) tales, which he published in his own free renderings. His major contribution in this field is *Algonquin Legends of New England* (1884), a book that saw numerous reprints. At the same time, Leland became one of the major intellectual fountainheads for the modern Wiccan community. To these people, he is famous for his *Aradia* (1899), a semifictional text that samples gypsy witchcraft folklore.[49] The writer spent a good part of his mature life in Germany, where he fell in love with all things German, including Nordic pre-Christian and medieval folklore. Incidentally, as such, he fits both the European tradition and American intellectual culture. After graduating from Princeton University in 1846, Leland studied in Heidelberg and Munich, where he picked up the ideas of German Romanticism.

Leland was convinced that the spiritual attitude to nature would become an integral part of the Americans if they appropriated the wisdom of indigenous folktales, including those that revealed shamanism, which, in his view, was humankind's first religion. Bringing the revised pieces of Native American folklore to the attention of his compatriots, Leland viewed himself as the messenger of the American Indians' ancient, earth-based wisdom. In doing this, he invoked two stereotypes of the Native American: the Indian as the carrier of timeless spiritual tradition and as the person who maintained intimate relations with nature.[50]

Leland contrasted the Indians' reverence toward nature with non-natives' attitudes:

> The greatest cause for a faith in magic is one which the white man
> talks about without feeling, and which the Indian feels without
> talking about it. I mean the poetry of nature, with all its quaint and
> beautiful superstitions. To every Algonquin a rotten log by the road,
> covered with moss, suggests the wild legend of the log-demon; the
> Indian corn and sweet flag in the swamp are descendants of beautiful spirits who still live in them. And how much of this feeling of
> the real poetry of nature does the white man or woman possess, who
> pities the poor ignorant Indian? A few second-hand scraps of Byron
> and Tupper, Tennyson and Longfellow, the jingle of a few rhythms
> and few similes, and a little second-hand supernaturalism, more
> "accepted" than felt, and that derived from foreign sources, does not
> give the white man what the Indian feels.[51]

Leland occasionally viewed himself not only as a messenger, but also as a practitioner of Native American wisdom. Once he suggested that, like an "Injun," he could hear the voice of the sacred world of nature. We should not separate the Indian and the witchcraft sides of Leland's personality and literary career. Very much like some modern spiritual seeker, immersing himself into the world of American Indian tales and gypsy lore, the writer wove for himself an eclectic spiritual web that became his personal hidden world, the wonderful fairyland, where, in his words, he could "see elves and listen to the music in dropping waterfalls, and hear voices in the wind."[52]

Replicating the efforts of his German teachers, many of whom were working to root Germans in their national soil, Leland sought to plant the spirit of indigenous soil in the hearts of his own compatriots, which would make them truly American. Yet, unlike Germans and other Europeans, as newcomers, Americans had no indigenous soil. Therefore, like many American writers before him and after, Leland was naturally looking at Native American traditions that could provide such an anchor. In one of his essays, he encouraged his fellow Americans to pay more attention to ancient American Indian legends. Although the American Hudson River, as noted Leland, was certainly not the German Rhine River area filled with folklore antiquities, one still could see that "every hill and vale and rock and rivulet around us was once consecrated by all these sweet humanities of the old religion." In fact, he thought that the American Indian lore might be somewhat superior to the European antiquities: "the mythology of the Middle Ages, the quaint wild *mährchen* of Scandinavia and the Teuton and the Celt, while not more attractive from an objective or dramatic point of view, are far inferior to our Algonquin Indian tales in the subtle charm of the *myth*."[53]

Our Early Ancestors: Finnish Ethnography and Siberian Native Spirituality

Like Leland, Finnish linguist and folklore scholar Mattias Aleksanteri [Alexander] Castren (1813–1853; figure 1.6) was concerned about introducing his people to their indigenous folklore and anchoring them in their own native soil. Likewise, he wanted to see them as ancient. As far as shamanism studies were concerned, Castren wanted to stay away from the Oriental connection in Siberian spirituality and ground it in its indigenous land. In this respect, he moved in the same direction as Banzarov. Very much like Banzarov, Castren was not blessed with a long life. Coming out of his 1840s expeditions to western Siberia with his health ruined by tuberculosis, Castren died in his forties. Despite his early death, the scholar was able to amass valuable folklore and ethnographic material that did not lose its relevance despite the work of later ethnographers.

In addition to his linguistic skills, which allowed him to procure ethnographic and folklore information that his Enlightenment predecessors missed, Castren stood out among contemporary students of Siberian cultures because of his intellectual stance. The scholar not only drew folklore and the spirituality

FIGURE 1.6. M. Alexander Castren (1813–1853), a Finnish linguist and folklore scholar, ventured into native Siberia in search of the spiritual and linguistic roots of his nationality. M. Alexander Castren, *Reiseberichte und Briefe aus den Jahren 1845–1849* (St. Petersburg: Buchdruckerei der Kaiserlichen Akademie der Wissenschaften, 1856), frontispiece.

of native populations from their indigenous sources, but he also acted as a sympathetic observer, a stance that, in my view, was rooted in the original goal that drove his ethnographic work. Castren belonged to those intellectuals who actively molded Finnish cultural nationalism. Like many of his colleagues and friends, he hoped that his scholarship might help to instill a sense of national awareness in his compatriots, who had been relegated to the status of subjects of the Russian emperor. We know that all intellectuals driven by nationalist sentiments, directly or indirectly are always preoccupied with searching for the most ancient roots of their budding nations in order to ground their compatriots in particular soil and to make them more indigenous. Such people frequently approach their cultural heritage according to a simple principle: the older the better. Castren, a professor of ethnology at Helsingfors (Helsinki) University, was not an exception in this.

Particularly, Castren wanted to shed more light on early Finnish history. From the very beginning of his academic career, he dreamed about locating the original motherland of the Finnish people ("our early ancestors"), which prompted his quest for common ancient mythological and linguistic roots among all Finno-Ugrian-speaking people. This search took him eastward, first to Sámi (Lapp) country and then to tribal Siberia. One of his favorite scholarly techniques was comparing Finnish mythology and folklore with the contemporary spirituality of related ethnic groups who lived primitive lifestyles and who, he was convinced, "retained the purity of their original tribal characters."[54] About his scholarly mission, which was tightly intertwined with his cultural mission, Castren explicitly said that he "could not pause before finding a connection that links the Finnish tribe to some other larger or smaller groups in the rest of the world."[55]

Given his stance, it was natural that his major work, *Vorlesungen über die Finnische Mythologie* (1853),[56] linked "western" Finnish traditions with "eastern" Finnish elements, which included the Lapp (Sámi) and Ostiak (Khanty) myths and beliefs and the spirituality of related groups. Moreover, the scholar tried to tie to the Finno-Ugrian language family the Tungus (Evenki), the Manchu, and the Turkic-speaking people of the Altai. Feeding his ethnographic imagination with these linguistic speculations, the scholar extended the ancient motherland of the Finns as far as the Altai, an area in southwestern Siberia, on the border with China and Mongolia.[57] The modern Finnish anthropologist Juha Pentikäinen has commented on this linguistic and ethnographic quest of Castren with a bit of irony: "in his eagerness he had found more relatives to Finnish peoples than there really were."[58]

As mentioned above, Castren's intellectual stance was not a personal peculiarity, but a popular mindset characteristic of many of his educated compatriots. Some of them went further, nourishing utopian dreams of a pan-Finnish nation that would include all those of Finnish stock and related groups in northern Russia and Siberia.[59] In all fairness, Castren never went that far, remaining within the limits of the disciplines of ethnography and the humanities. Now, how is all this related to shamanism and to the study of tribal spirituality in general? Trying to establish linguistic and spiritual links with their Asian "kin," Castren and the Finnish ethnographers who followed in his footsteps delved into Siberia and collected tons of ethnographic material on mythology and beliefs, including shamanism. Their practice of drawing wide parallels that transcended cultural and ethnic borders contributed much to the perception of shamanism as a Eurasian phenomenon. Later, such famous visionary scholars as Joseph Campbell and especially Mircea Eliade heavily drew on their data, observations, and conclusions in building their archetypes of universal shamanism.

Like their contemporary German and Russian colleagues, the Finnish ethnographers did not always think highly about the savage daily lives and mores of their Siberian relatives. At the same time, they did feel some spiritual unity with and sometimes even empathy for their tribal kin, who spoke dialects that might have been related to their own and who were similarly doomed to live as subjects of the Russian empire. Overall, Finnish ethnographic records tended to be sympathetic to native Siberians. For example, on occasion, Castren drew attention to a positive social role of Siberian shamans, noting that they helped to maintain the integrity of their communities. The scholar also portrayed indigenous magicians not as passive recipients of the commands of superior spiritual forces but as active practitioners who could saddle these powers. At the same time, Castren phrased this spiritual agency in Enlightenment terms as striving "to conquer nature not only through vigorous bodily movements and incomprehensible words," but also through the mobilization of will power. Therefore, according to the ethnographer, the shamans' "tribal magic" reflected "the protest of the human being against the yoke of nature."[60]

In the wake of Castren's research, regular ethnological ventures into native Siberia in search for mythology, beliefs, and language patterns became an established tradition in Finnish humanities. The quest for the Finnish connection in the Siberian ethnographic wilderness continued unabated from the 1850s to the end of the 1920s, when the Bolsheviks finally closed the area to Western visitors. Driven by the same idea of establishing spiritual and cultural links between the Finns proper and the Siberian Ugro-Finn people (the Khanty, Nentsy, and Evenki), such scholars as Kustaa F. Karjalainen (1871–1919), Artturi Kannisto (1874–1943), Kai Donner (1888–1935), and Toivo Lehtisalo (1887–1962) traversed the vast tundra and forest landscapes of Siberia, collecting and recording ethnographies of their Asian "relatives" and paying a lot of attention to shamanism. Like all cultural nationalists, these ethnographers and folklore scholars were keen to explore the links among the language, myths, and religion.

Following Castren, each of them strived to find his own "good Samoyed professor," usually a native elder, storyteller, or shaman who was shrewd in the native language and folklore and who could immerse him into native spirituality. To make their writings accessible to wider scholarly audiences, they published many of their books and articles in German, the international language of humanities and social sciences in the nineteenth and the early twentieth centuries. European and American authors who wrote on shamanism and Eurasian mythology in the first half of the twentieth century heavily relied on these ethnographies. Among them was the future scholarly celebrity Eliade, who drew not only on their field materials but also on their comparative cross-cultural methodology.

To better illustrate how the Finnish ethnographers worked in the field, let me detail the experiences of Donner, one of those who continued Castren's ethnographic quest. Once, when Donner heard from a Khanty shaman acquaintance a legend about Castren's work among the Ostiak, he was quick to reassure the spiritual practitioner that he, Donner, belonged to the same tribe, which, one can assume, helped him to establish a good rapport with the informant. Donner traveled in Siberia between 1911 and 1913 and observed the Khanty and Evenki. Being well versed in the ethnographic writings of his Finnish, Russian, and German predecessors, Donner came to Siberia with high expectations. Ideal-istically, he hoped to begin observing "archaic" ethnography right away after he got off the train that brought him to western Siberia. What he met at first, however, were only "wretched natives," who had absorbed the worst habits of the surrounding Russian population.

His first encounter with an indigenous other was a native woman who was using a Singer sewing machine to mend clothes. As a well-rounded Eu-ropean intellectual who was accustomed to European conveniences, Donner was at first appalled with the lack of any hygiene. Some of the indigenous dwellings appeared to him as "stinking Augean stables," where people lived "like frogs in marshes."[61] Still, he remained romantically drawn to his distant Siberian cousins. Eventually, the poetic sides of native life, such as beautiful legends, language, and shamanism, coupled with magnificent landscapes overshadowed other impressions that he found unpleasant. Such a stance allowed him not only to close his eyes on many things that upset him in the surrounding life but also to go native, at least for a year, for the purposes of ethnographic participant observation.

Having mastered the basics of local native dialects and moving farther northward to the frozen tundra, the country of the Khanty and the Evenki, Donner eventually received what he craved: a life in a dwelling made of skins, indigenous elders, and plenty of lore. Although the "filth" still occasionally disturbed him, he was able to live side by side with his Siberian relatives for more than a year. During this time, the ethnographer gradually "shed" his old clothing and dressed in furs: "I was dressed as they were, ate as they did, and gave up portions of all my supplies as they did themselves. I spoke their lan-guage and was considered completely as one of their own."[62]

Not without a hidden masochistic pleasure, Donner described how in Russian villages that he and his native friends occasionally visited, he was treated and even abused in the same manner as his Tungus (Evenki) friends. At times, when stunned Russians could not reconcile his Evenki clothing, native speech, and European physique, Donner intentionally played the role of a European who grew up among the natives and pretended that he did not speak Russian. Despite all the hassles of this ethnographic masquerade, the rewards of such experiential living, as Donner stressed, were tremendous. Shamans told him their secrets, storytellers freely narrated their legends, members of households easily shared with him their daily practices. Coloring his scholarship with a heavy dose of Romantic sentiments, Donner exclaimed, "There is a great fascination for a European in steeping himself with the spiritual life of a primitive savage. It requires just as much love as any other task. The results in terms of facts are perhaps not so significant or peculiar, but the knowledge acquired is alive and realistic."[63]

Donner was very sympathetic to shamanic healing and praised the medical skills of Siberian spiritual practitioners. Anticipating the symbolic healing theory, the ethnographer wrote that the people's faith worked miracles: "It often happens that the shaman actually succeeds in curing a sick person with no other means other than the faith which he instills in him [the patient]."[64] Powerful and charismatic shamans whom he met fascinated him as personalities. One of them, named Kotschiiader, especially impressed Donner. He wrote that the man never deceived his kinfolk with magic and "handled the magical drum with amazing seriousness and the pathos displayed in prayers to the gods of his fathers." Delving deeper into this realm of native life, Donner did not mind establishing himself as a "doctor," which brought him more respect from his indigenous hosts. Once, he helped to deliver a baby in a situation when two shamans were helpless.[65]

Donner left to us poetic descriptions of shamanic séances. Remembering one of them, he wrote:

> The evening was quiet and darkness descended. The fire had slowly gone out and the age-old trees of the forest made contours against the starry heavens like large powerful shadows. I had forgotten all that made me a man of civilization; I was thinking neither of Christianity nor of other teachings but rather I was completely involved in childlike admiration of what I saw and heard. I suddenly felt like a child and, as in childhood, I imagined that every object had its spirit, that water and air were populated by mysterious invisible beings who, in inexplicable fashion, ruled the course of the world and the fate of men. In the untouched wilderness and its infinite silence, I was encompassed by the traditional mysticism and religious mysteries through which faith touches so many things.[66]

Many years later, reflecting on his Siberian experiences, Donner noted that he was still under the spell of those mysterious séances; he had become convinced that the shamanic performances helped him to understand how "these children of the wilderness feel and think."

The last from this family of Romantic ethnographers was Uno Holmberg (1882–1949), who conducted field research among the Ket and Evenki people before the Russian Revolution, in 1913 and 1917. His major work, in which the scholar explores cross-culturally Eurasian shamanism as a universal Finno-Ugric-Altaic system, is *Die religiösen Vorstellungen der Altaischen Völker* (*Religious Beliefs of Altaic People*; 1938). Very much like Castren and his successors, Holmberg was convinced that, observing contemporary native traditions of Siberian natives, Finnish ethnographers could see cultural traits that Finns had carried in primal times.[67] It is curious that this scholar is also known under the surname of Harva, which he purposely adopted to stress his Finnish roots. Eventually, Harva-Holmberg established a Finnish school of comparative religion, whose representatives worked with global metaphors and allegories at the expense of particulars. One of his earlier works, *Der Baum des Lebens* (1922), which heavily relied on Siberian materials, dealt exclusively with the tree of life (*axis mundi*), one of these archetypes. To prove that the idea of the center (the world tree) was wired into all mythologies worldwide, the scholar drew numerous cross-cultural parallels among Finnish, Siberian, and Native American folklore and the classical mythologies of the East and Greece. Harva-Holmberg's generalizations about the "world tree," "world mountain," and other archetypes that he found in Eurasian indigenous religions and mythologies were later rounded out in the scholarship of Eliade, who is also considered to be one of the classics of shamanism studies. Thus, in his *Shamanism: Archaic Techniques of Ecstasy* (1964), this celebrated historian of religion gave Harva-Holmberg special credit not only for the cross-cultural approach to shamanism and ancient mythologies but also for disentangling them from culture and history.[68]

Wilhelm Radloff Pioneers Shamanism Studies

Throughout the nineteenth and early twentieth centuries, academic and travel literature in German remained the major source on shamanism in the West. Incidentally, such scholars as Castren and Harva-Holmberg published their major works on Eurasian mythology and religions in that language. As Stephen Glosecki informs us, the term shamanism, in its German version of *schamanism*, began to appear regularly in scholarly and popular literature after the 1870s. Although much of this literature traced the source of this phenomenon to the classic Orient, its contemporary core habitat was set in northern Asia. Shamanism was viewed as a religion of this particular part of the world. At that point, other tribal people were not included in the realm of shamanism. As the *Encyclopedia Britannica* for 1886 informed its readers, shamanism was a religion of "Ural-Altaic groups" of Siberia, such as the Tungus, Mongol, and Turkic-speaking peoples.[69]

At the same time, with the exceptions of the Georgi essay, Banzarov's thin master's essay, and Castren's notes, there was still no special work on shamanism. The first academic who turned from hypothetical speculations on shamanism to comprehensive research and who virtually pioneered shamanism studies was Wilhelm Radloff (1837–1918). Although Radloff has received full credit as one of the first deans of Turkic philology, to my knowledge, nobody has examined his role in shaping shamanism studies. Until the turn of the twentieth century, in addition to ethnographic notes by Castren, his works remained the principal source on shamanism in the West. Moreover, between the 1880s and 1910s, many European encyclopedia entries on shamanism not only referred to Radloff as one of the chief authorities on the topic, but also sometimes exclusively drew on his seminal Siberian ethnography *From Siberia* (*Aus Sibirien*; 1884). For example, the *Encyclopedia Britannica* entry used the southwestern Siberian shamanism observed by Radloff to exemplify the entire phenomenon.[70]

During his university years, Radloff was heavily affected by Carl Ritter, a renowned geographer and historian, who, like his intellectual predecessor Humboldt, paid tribute to *Naturphilosophie* and believed that geographical environments were crucial in shaping human societies. At the same time, under the influence of one of his professors, Wilhelm Schott, Radloff became interested in Oriental studies. In addition to *Naturphilosophie*, he absorbed ideas of contemporary Romantic Orientalism with its emphasis on languages and comparative linguistics. As a result, the young scholar deeply grounded himself in linguistics and philology. It seems that the subtitle to his famous ethnography *Aus Sibirien, Pages from the Diary of a Linguist-Traveler*, was a tribute to this tradition. His university dissertation dealt with Asian religions, which might explain his long-standing interest in indigenous beliefs and shamanism.

By the 1850s, when Radloff was doing his graduate work, scholars had milked such popular research venues as Sanskrit studies and related fields to an extreme, and these areas could not promise any academic opportunities to the young scholar. Following Schott's advice, Radloff tapped languages and the ethnography of the Turkic-speaking populations of inner and central Asia, an area that hardly anybody had looked at seriously for research. Eventually, this project took him to central Asia and Siberia. Thus, Radloff, a German Orientalist scholar, moved to Russia, renamed himself Vasilii Vasilievich Radlov, and later became one of the deans of anthropological scholarship in his new homeland. To some extent, one can compare the role Radloff played for Russian ethnology with the role played by another German, Franz Boas, for American anthropology. Accompanied by his young wife and an interpreter, Radloff, with a fresh doctorate from Jena University, eagerly explored the uncharted linguistic and ethnographic terrain of southern Siberia in the 1860s. His ethnographic letters (1860s), which he later reworked into *Aus Sibirien*, became an anthropological classic for many Russian and Western students of shamanism.

During his first field trips, Radloff, who persistently sought a chance to see a native spiritual practitioner in action, had no opportunity to observe a shamanic séance and accumulated only indirect evidence. At some point, he wrote in his journal in frustration, "Shamans, who could become our sole reliable source in this matter, usually fear to expose their secrets. They always surround themselves with an air of mystery, which is so important in their vocation."[71] Finally, he was able to meet two former shamans who had converted to Christianity. The ethnographer hoped that these spiritual practitioners would dictate to him at least parts of the chants they sang during their sessions. No luck. Instead, one of the shamans responded, "Our former god is already furious at us for leaving him. You can imagine what he can do if he learns that we, on top of everything else, betray him. We are even afraid more that the Russian God might find out how we talk about the old faith. What will save us then?"[72]

The only séances that Radloff was able to record were a short thanks-giving prayer shared with the ethnographer by an Altaian shaman and a ceremony of the spiritual cleansing of a dwelling after a death in a family (see figure 1.7). During the latter rite, Radloff did finally get a chance to enjoy something that resembled a classic Gothic séance about which he had read in the writings of German and Baltic German travelers to Siberia. The cleansing ceremony contained elements of the famous shamanic ecstasy that in the twentieth century became the established scholarly metaphor associated with shamanism. Radloff could hear the shaman's "wild shouts," which were ac-companied by "gigantic leaps." He also saw how, after a fierce dance, the

FIGURE 1.7. A sketch of a shamanic séance made by Wilhelm Radloff during one of his field trips to Mountain Altai in the 1860s. Wilhelm Radloff, *Aus Sibirien: Lose Blätter aus dem Tagebuche eines reisenden Linguisten*, 2 vols. (Leipzig: Weigel, 1884), 2:18–19, plate 1.

exhausted shaman fell to the ground: "This wild scene, magically illuminated by fire, produced on me such a strong impression that for awhile I watched only the shaman and completely forgot about all those who were present here. This wild scene shocked Altaians too. They pulled out pipes from their mouths and sat in a dead silence for a quarter of an hour."[73]

Although the ethnographer had only two accidental encounters with shamanism, through available archival records as well as "hints," "legends, fairy tales, stories, and songs"[74] he received from his native informants, Radloff was able to reconstruct a picture of Siberian native spirituality that far surpassed many contemporary accounts. The scholar was also perceptive enough to notice that shamanism was not an iron-clad doctrine, but a fluid system based on impromptu rituals. He wrote that even with enough data, it was hard to build an exact and typical portrait of shamanism out of the spontaneity and diversity of tribal beliefs. As soon as "we start to describe details of shamanism, contradictory information only distorts the general picture and eventually almost completely destroys it."[75] Unlike many contemporary observers, Radloff placed shamanism on the same level with Buddhism, Christianity, and Islam and stressed, "Shamans are no worse than clerics of other religions." Legitimizing tribal spiritual practitioners in the eyes of his European audience, Vasilii Vasilievich stressed, "Poor shamans are not as bad as they are usually perceived. In fact, they carry the ethical ideals of their people."[76] Such sentiments should be at least partially attributed to the humanistic aspects of the Romantic tradition that shaped Radloff as a scholar and an intellectual. The same tradition might have nourished in him a sense of wonder for primitive beliefs and muted in him Eurocentric attitudes. In this respect, his *Aus Sibirien* belongs to the same body of ethnographic literature as the writings of Wrangel, Finsch, Beliavskii, Krivoshapkin, and Finnish explorers of Siberia. From the 1860s to the 1890s, Radloff's works, which were published in Germany, European Russia, and Siberia, provided a necessary intellectual link that established the topic of shamanism as an integral part of Western humanities and social sciences.

In addition to his linguistic studies and insights into northern Asian spirituality, Radloff became known for introducing into Western scholarship the first full textual record of a shamanic séance.[77] The text represents the prayers, supplications, and utterances of a tribal spiritual practitioner (most probably from the Teleut, the Altai area) during a ritual spring session in honor of Ülgen, a benevolent deity (see figure 1.8). The whole ritual dealt with a ritual horse sacrifice performed by the shaman to solicit from Ülgen an increase of herds and general well-being. During this Ülgen séance, the spirit of the shaman ascended to "heaven" (the upper world) in order to accompany the spirit of the sacrificial horse designated as a gift to Ülgen. Ülgen was one of the chief spirits for a few Altaian clans; other clans never considered Ülgen a major deity. However, by the later nineteenth century, under the influence of missionary

FIGURE 1.8. A shamanic séance in honor of the heavenly deity Ülgen, Mountain Altai, c. 1850s. Published by Wilhelm Radloff in 1884 and used by Mircea Eliade in his book on shamanism, the record of one such ceremony became an example of the classical shamanic séance. Thomas W. Atkinson, *Oriental and Western Siberia* (New York: Harper, 1858), 323.

propaganda, some natives propelled this spirit to the position of the supreme benevolent deity, which Russian Orthodox clerics happily paired with the Christian God. I reconstructed this context of the ritual, which is missing in the Radloff book, based on later ethnographies.

The scholar borrowed the record from an essay of Russian missionary Vasilii Verbitskii and translated it into German for his *Aus Sibirien*. Incidentally, the Russian cleric who published this record in a provincial Siberian newspaper did not observe this séance personally either, but borrowed the record from the archives of the Altaian Orthodox mission. The Radloff book made the Ülgen shamanic session an oft-quoted classic in literature on Siberian shamanism and shamanism in general. In a full or an abridged version, this record was canonized and began its independent journey in the literature on shamanism, from the turn of the twentieth-century writings to Eliade's *Shamanism* (1964). Even authors who do not specifically write on tribal beliefs use the Ülgen séance as a standard example of a generic shamanic session. For example, I encountered a description of this séance as a typical shamanic session in a biography of Carl Jung.[78]

Thus, the annual séance performed by an unknown shaman to a clan deity named Ülgen and recorded by an anonymous Russian missionary sometime between the 1840s and the 1850s acquired universal, pan-tribal proportions.

Although, being a perceptive observer, Radloff pointed out that "not all shamans conducted their sessions in this manner,"[79] the ethnographic imagination of later scholars and writers turned this session into a pan-tribal ritual, a
typical shamanic session, and Ülgen into the supreme deity. For example, to
modern religion scholar Julian Baldick, the séance became "a great religious drama" performed by all Turkic-speaking peoples of southern Siberia to
honor the "supreme god, Bai Ülgen," who, according to folklore scholar Nora
Chadwick, was "the greatest of the gods, who dwells in the highest Heaven."[80]
It appears that the Ülgen record, which described the shamanic journey to the
upper world, was not a small thing in shaping Eliade's perception of classic
shamanism as a spiritual technique dealing with the "flight" to the heavenly
sphere. Unlike native Siberians, who did not prioritize among layers of shamanic cosmos, Eliade believed that the shamanic descent to the underworld
was a later addition to the classic heavenly flight.[81] Well read in Siberian ethnographies, this scholar did note that the specifics of the shamanic séance varied from community to community. Still, seeking to single out cross-cultural
parallels, he used the Ülgen séance to construct the archetype of the shamanic
séance.

2

From Siberia to North America

Regionalists, Anthropologists,
and Exiled Ethnographers

Traditions of other tribes included into the spiritual life of world
civilization will unavoidably benefit everybody.
                    —Siberian regionalist Nikolai Iadrintsev (1882)

By some the term shaman is confined, and perhaps rightly, within
somewhat narrow limits; if I may be pardoned the liberty, I shall
extend rather than restrict the meaning of the term, and shall use it
as applying to that motley class of persons, found in every savage
community, who are supposed to have closer relations with the
supernatural than other men.
                    —American anthropologist Roland Dixon (1908)

At the end of December 1913, Swiss psychologist Carl Gustav Jung
(1875–1961), who seventy years later became one of the intellectual celebrities for many "New Age" and nature communities, had
a dream that profoundly changed his life:

> I was with an unknown, brown-skinned man, a savage, in a
> lonely, rocky mountain landscape. It was before dawn; the
> eastern sky was already bright, and the stars were fading.
> Then I heard Siegfried's horn sounding over the moun-
> tains and I knew that we had to kill him. We were armed
> with rifles and lay in wait for him on a narrow path over
> the rocks. Then Siegfried appeared high up on a crest of
> the mountain, in the first ray of the rising sun. On a chariot
> made of the bones of the dead he drove at furious speed

down the precipitous slope. When he turned a corner, we shot at him,
and he plunged down, struck dead.

Jung interpreted the "savage" as the power of the natural instinct and Sieg-
fried's chariot made of bones as the symbol of how much was sacrificed to the
altar of Western rationalism. This particular dream contributed to Jung's decision to quit contemplating a university career, which he began to consider a useless pursuit of academic intellectualism.[1]

The Jung dream is a good metaphor to describe the sentiments of European and American intellectuals who felt a deep frustration about Western
civilization. In the beginning of the twentieth century, people like Jung were a
minority in a society that still lived by the ideas of progress, Enlightenment, and
academic positivism. Yet, this minority was becoming vocal. The watershed
was the First World War, which like a litmus test confirmed the worst fears
of those who were apprehensive about Judeo-Christian tradition and Western
progress going astray. In *The Decline of the West* (1918), German philosopher
Oswald Spengler summarized these concerns in his vision of civilization's
cyclical development. The scholar stressed that, no matter how vital and triumphant it might be, each civilization eventually entered its "winter," the stage
when it disconnected itself from nature and the sacred and moved fast toward
its apocalypse. Spengler grimly warned his contemporaries that vitality was
leaving the West, and a cold winter night was descending over Euro-American
civilization. The writer envisioned the coming of the new "universal history,"
which would relegate Western Europe to a marginal place in a new history of
humankind.[2] Not a totally utopian prophecy, one might say.

For people like Jung and Spengler, who continued the intellectual tradition of European Romanticism, such apocalyptical visions and critical attitudes
toward the modern West frequently went hand in hand with occult sentiments
and appeals to the values of the ancient ones and of non-Western people, who
appeared to them as carriers of spiritual traits lost by Western civilization. Russian symbolist poet Velimir Khlebnikov expressed well the appeal of the non-
Western in his verse "Venus and Shaman" (1912). The poet juxtaposed the
Siberian shaman, portrayed as a meditating Oriental desert dweller, and Venus, the "European" goddess, who is unbalanced, silly, and changeable. Venus
suddenly finds that she is not in vogue any more and seeks an escape in the
shaman's cave:

> I want to pick up flowers, talk to the trees,
> Get back in touch with the birds and the bees,
> Far from the hum of the pressing crowd,
> Find a place with a rustic temple,
> Hunt for mushrooms, and sing out loud.
> I want to try to follow your example.
> What could be better than a life that's simple?[3]

Furthermore, by the beginning of the twentieth century in the West, primitive man and primitive religion became the objects not only of literary depiction but also of creative emulation, especially in the wake of the First World War.[4] At this time, Euro-American artists, musicians, and writers increasingly began to appropriate and transplant non-Western and pagan symbolism into their oeuvres. The first names that come to mind in this case are the famous abstract artists Pablo Picasso and Wassily Kandinsky. In his search for alternatives to the conventional European styles, the former turned to African primitive art, whereas the latter became fascinated with the symbolism of the Siberian shamanic drum, tree, and journey and incorporated this imagery into his paintings.[5] In the world of letters, D. H. Lawrence with his *Plumed Serpent* (1926) did something similar. With their scandalous ballet performance *The Rite of Spring* (1913), Igor Stravinsky and Sergei Diaghilev shocked Paris audiences with a scene of a pagan sacrifice. Another mover and shaker, Antonin Artaud, who sought to demolish the classic European concept of theater, severely chastised Western culture for falling under the spell of logic and rationalism. Furthermore, arguing that mystical experiences of non-Western primitives would help to expand his perception, in 1936 Artaud ventured into Huichol country in Mexico, where he immersed himself in peyote hallucinogenic sessions: "The rationalist culture of Europe has failed and I have come to the earth of Mexico to seek the basis of a magic culture."[6]

The goal of this chapter is to outline several sources, which, in the intellectual environment that I mentioned above, created cultural precursors for the later rise of a popular interest in such non-Western nature and tribal spirituality as shamanism. I will start with Siberian regionalist writers and ethnographers, who, in their attempt to shape and underline the unique cultural identity of Siberia, looked into indigenous northern Asian archaic traditions. Like their predecessors and teachers, German Romantic writers and scholars, many regionalists were convinced that the cultural light was coming from the East. Siberian shamanic folklore occupied a prominent place in their intellectual quest.

Then, I will move to North America, where we will meet and examine American southwestern regionalists, who similarly worked to ground themselves and their compatriots in soil that was not indigenous to them. Since ethnographic books about Native Americans heavily affected the print culture of modern neo-shamanism in the West, I will also offer several insights into the world of American anthropology and discuss its attempts to capture the traditional cultures of indigenous peoples before their extinction—another project that was informed by German Romantic philosophy. Then, I will show how the shamanism idiom became gradually transplanted from Siberian ethnography to North American ethnology. At the end of the chapter, I will introduce a unique group of people—"exiled ethnographers." In order to maintain their intellectual sanity, some of these dissenters and revolutionaries, whom the Russian tsarist regime relegated to the forests and tundra of northeastern Siberia for their antigovernmental activities in the second half of the nineteenth century, turned to ethnography, exploring the cultures of indigenous Siberians. At least two of them, namely, Vladimir (Waldemar) G. Bogoras (Bogoraz) (1865–1936) and Vladimir (Waldemar) I. Jochelson (1855–1937), banded with American anthropologist Franz Boas and published books that became instrumental in shaping the content of the expression shamanism as it was understood in the West in the first half of the twentieth century.

Ethnographic Fantasies of Siberian Regionalists, 1870s–1920s

A large body of writings on indigenous spirituality, which later shaped our perceptions of shamanism, comes from Russian intellectuals who grew and matured in Siberia, the motherland of the shamanism metaphor. Here again, as in the story about the Finnish ethnographers and folklore scholars discussed in the previous chapter, we will see writers and ethnographers who were preoccupied with their cultural identity. Yet, in this case, it was a regional identity. This story is about Siberian regionalists, a segment of the Russian intelligentsia headed by the writer and folklore scholar Grigorii N. Potanin (1835–1920; see figure 2.1). Intellectually, they were inspired by nineteenth-century German folklore scholarship and by German geographers Alexander von Humboldt and Carl Ritter. The keen interest of the regionalists in Siberian indigenous ethnography and antiquities, including primitive spirituality, was part of their agenda to define Siberia as a region within the Russian empire.

What did people of the nineteenth century know about Siberia? First of all, they certainly knew that this desolate area was a vast frozen land. Second, some were aware that the despotic Russian tsarist regime used it as a dumping ground for both political and common criminals. At the same time, in the second half of the nineteenth century, Siberia entered a period of modernization and became the object of mass colonization. The frozen continent already had its first intellectuals, who mostly grouped around Tomsk University in southwestern Siberia. Thinking about the social and cultural development of their homeland, regionalists were naturally looking at the most "authentic" and ancient cultural values to boost their ideological aspirations.

We know that if such values are missing, they are borrowed or simply invented. In their search for Siberia's authentic identity, regionalists attempted to prove that Siberia was not just a frozen and stigmatized periphery, but a region that culturally and socially was able to stand on a par with European Russia. What and who could provide such proof? Regionalists partially resolved this problem by creating an image of Russian Siberian settlers as rugged individuals, free spirits, and carriers of democratic and nationalistic expectations who could serve as an example for the rest of Russia. Still, Siberian Russians

FIGURE 2.1. Grigorii Potanin (1835–1920), Siberian regionalist and ethnographer. N. Jadrinzew, *Sibirien: Geographische, ethnographische und histori-
sche Studien* (Jena: H. Costenoble, 1886), 68–69.

were new arrivals, and their histories were not ancient enough to serve the
construction of a genuine identity for Siberia.

As in the United States, where for lack of ancient building blocks, the
developing American identity had to rely on elements of Native American culture, Siberian regionalists had to dwell on the indigenous spiritual and material
culture. They used native antiquities and folklore to demonstrate that Siberian
cultural heritage could match or even surpass that of Russia. Seeking to prove
that Siberia was a land with its own rich and unique culture, which was no
less significant than the European Russian tradition, regionalists devoted much
attention to collecting native antiquities and ethnography. In this context, it is
no coincidence that the leader of the regionalists, Potanin, was hardly interested in the ethnography of Russian Siberians. E. L. Zubashev, one of his colleagues, remembered, "The Russian Siberian village drew little attention from
Grigorii Nikolaevich [Potanin], whereas native Siberia was the object of his
most tender feelings."[7]

For example, the location and description of the ancient tombstones of
southern Siberia occupied such regionalists as Potanin, V. A. Adrianov, Nikolai
Iadrintsev, and Dmitrii Klementz, who called these relics of the past "runs,"
drawing analogies with northern European stone relics. Moreover, Potanin insisted that in southwestern Siberia there "still survived remnants of antiquity,

which preceded the earliest ever known civilization."[8] Archaeology was to prove the ancient origin of the indigenous people—the Altaians, Tuvans, and Buryats—and eventually to point to the ancient tradition of Siberia. Along with archaeology, in their search for the cultural uniqueness of Siberia, regional scholars and writers could not bypass shamanism. First of all, because of their skepticism about the official Russian Orthodox Church, an attitude that was characteristic of all members of the contemporary Russian intelligentsia, regionalists were aesthetically more drawn to native spirituality.[9] For example, after his first trip to the Altai in 1880, Iadrintsev, an influential regionalist second only to Potanin, excitedly reported to his friend in Switzerland, "Mores and customs of local savages are extremely interesting. Their religion is shamanism. But what is shamanism? This is pantheism. In a nutshell, the Altai is Greece, where everything is animated: rivers, mountains, stones; here one can hear thousands of legends, and what legends they are!"[10]

When Iadrintsev witnessed a shamanic séance, it produced in him such "an unforgettable impression" that he left a poetic description of the whole session:

> I remember that night when I had to stop at that place. That mysterious beautiful night with thousands of bright stars spread over the awesome mountains full of savage beauty and poetic charm. I saw the shaman in a fantastic costume decorated with rattles and snake-like plaits. Feathers were sticking from his helmet, and in his hands he held a mysterious drum. At first, the shaman circled around the fire. Then he jumped out of the shelter of bark to the open air. My ears still can hear his magnificent howling, his call for spirits, and the wild mountain echo that responded to his invocations.[11]

To another member of the regionalist circle, ethnomusicologist Andrei Anokhin, shamanism appeared as the expressive peak of native singing. He also found that the power of the "shamanic mystery plays" and "prayers" resembled that of Hebrew psalms: "the same incorruptible sincerity that reflects a simple, but deeply sensitive soul, the same metaphors, and the same magnificent pictures of surrounding nature."[12] As significant as it may be, shamanism drew the attention of regionalists not only as an exotic and attractive aspect of native culture. Most important, it appeared to them as the most visible living trait of the ancient indigenous tradition, which they could add to their Siberian cultural project.

Siberian regionalists peculiarly combined their attempts to retrieve the ancient spiritual heritage of Siberia with a vigorous advocacy of modernization and mass colonization of the indigenous periphery. Still, the desire to interweave the native legacy into the Siberian culture added to the regionalist ideology an element of cultural sensitivity. In his seminal book, *Siberia as a Colony* (1882), Iadrintsev underlined the value of each culture, which would attach "unique elements to the future civilization."[13] Stressing that native people's "historical services to Russians in Siberia are not yet appropriately appreciated," he wrote that people could benefit much from the cultures of the indigenous peoples.[14]

Potanin eventually took this cultural relativism to the extreme, subjecting his ethnographic books to one goal: tracing the origin of the entire Judeo-Christian spiritual heritage from an indigenous inner Asian tradition. Drawing arbitrary cultural and linguistic parallels among Hebrew, Russian, early Christian, and European medieval mythologies, on the one hand, and shamanic legends from Mongolia and southern Siberia, on the other, Potanin insisted on their genetic similarity and coined the so-called Oriental hypothesis.[15] What he tried to do was essentially a northern Asian version of the famous Indian connection in Western civilization, the theory popularized by the nineteenth-century Romantic Orientalism. While Romantic writers ascribed the creation of Western tradition to high classical Oriental cultures, Potanin insisted that it was nomadic oral culture in northern Asia that stood at the source of the Judeo-Christian tradition of the occident. As early as 1879, when Potanin was still contemplating his Oriental hypothesis, he already set forth his major thesis: "I am inclined to believe that Christianity originated from southern Siberia."[16] In his folklore and ethnographic studies, the ancestors of the Mongols, Kazakhs, Altaians, Buryats, and the surrounding indigenous communities appear not as nomads who wandered around plundering their sedentary neighbors (the popular contemporary perception) but as cultural heroes who shaped the Western and Near Eastern spiritual traditions.

One of the sound arguments Potanin forwarded in support of his theory was the repeated mass population movements from inner Asia to Europe and the Near East. Indeed, from antiquity to the early Middle Ages, the advancement of people went from the East to the West, not vice versa. Nineteenth-century scholarship did not see in these population movements many creative impulses and considered these nomadic invasions not beneficial but detrimental for the development of people who were on the way. In contrast, Potanin refused to view the inner Asian nomads as destroyers. He took on the European arrogance of contemporary scholars, who put Judeo-Christian blinders on their eyes and did not want to admit the contribution of these "barbarians" to the cultural and spiritual traditions of the West.

Let us take a closer look at how Potanin tried to prove his thesis. For example, in his bulky volume titled *Saga of Solomon*, he drew the origin of the biblical legend about Solomon from the shamanism and mythology of the Mongols. Noting that the Solomon saga includes three central themes, namely, the construction of the temple, the abduction of the wife and her retrieval, and the trials by wise people, he screened Mongol, Hebrew, Slavic, and Anglo-Saxon religious and mythological traditions, searching for materials that might fit these three thematic lines. One of his favorite approaches was the comparative linguistic method that I mentioned in the first chapter, which was popular among Romantic Orientalists. For example, Potanin drew a genetic connection between Tsolmon, the name for Venus in Turkic-Mongol mythology, and the Hebrew name Solomon.

After establishing this and other "links," the writer concluded that the folklore evidence points to the northern Asian origin of the Solomon myth, and he debunked the antiquity of the Bible story. In his view, the Solomon myth penetrated from Asia to the West by the following route. Potanin speculated that after originating in Mongolia, the myth might have gradually drifted to Russia, then moved farther to Byzantium and Italy, and finally to England. Simultaneously, the same myth may have drifted slowly from the nomadic habitats of inner Asia southward to Tibet and India.[17] In a similar manner, he recast the famous biblical legend about the twelve apostles. In this case, he brought together occidental and Oriental stories that contain allusions to twelve individuals and again drew the origin of the entire mythological tradition from the shamanic legends of southern Siberia and inner Asia.

Before Potanin coined his theory, he occasionally allowed himself a dose of self-irony. In one of his 1870s letters, he called his cross-cultural mythological parallels "ethnographic fantasies." Yet, on the whole, he was very serious. In the same letter, Potanin insisted that despite his possible mistakes in particulars, he was right that Turkic and Mongol legends and beliefs were "more ancient than Semitic ones" and that they had given rise to Christianity.[18] Absorbed by his theory, the leader of Siberian regionalism passionately wrote, "Yes, this locality, where we live [southern Siberia] is the genuine motherland of humankind. It was here that the first seeds of Christian legends were planted. Now I am quite sure that the Eden of Adam and Eve was located at the sources of the Irtysh River on the banks of which I was born."[19]

Despite the skepticism of his colleagues from European Russia, Potanin persisted into his final years. Articulating the basics of his Oriental hypothesis for a St. Petersburg scholarly audience in 1911, Potanin continued to insist, "We clearly see that it is the central Asian shamanic legend that lies at the foundation of the legend about Christ, and that the image of Christ himself was shaped according to the image that had existed many centuries earlier in inner Asia."[20] It is clear that trying to raise the cultural significance of Siberia in his own and the public's eyes, Potanin acted as a typical regionalist haunted by an inferiority complex. Thus, his desire to overcome the inequality between the center and the periphery led him to advocate the cultural superiority of the periphery over the center. His colleague, Buddhist scholar Sergei Oldenburg, who was skeptical about the Oriental hypothesis, once noted that Potanin treated folklore studies as Westerners' social obligation to learn from the Asian people.[21]

Mainstream academics in European Russia totally ignored the Oriental hypothesis, a late-blooming Siberian edition of Romantic Oriental scholarship.

Moreover, Eurocentrism, which was reigning supreme in social scholarship at that time, only reinforced negative attitudes toward the Potanin hypothesis. At the same time, in Siberia, Potanin's theory enjoyed popularity and did affect a number of scholars and writers. One of them was Gavriil Ksenofontov, a Sakha native ethnographer, who studied at Tomsk University to become a lawyer and who matured as an intellectual under the heavy influence of Potanin's ideas. After a brief and unsuccessful stint in a short-lived Sakha autonomy demolished by the Bolsheviks in 1918, Ksenofontov wholeheartedly devoted himself to collecting the ethnography of his and neighboring peoples. Eventually, his association with the regionalists led to his arrest and execution in 1938 during the whirlwind of Stalinist purges.

In 1929, Ksenofontov had released a book, *Khrestets: Shamanism and Christianity*,[22] in which he insisted on the similarity between early Christianity and Siberian shamanism and on the special role of inner Asian nomads as cultural heroes. Ksenofontov's approach is more nuanced and sound than the crude parallels drawn by Potanin. Most important, the Sakha scholar successfully avoided the favorite "out of Siberia/Asia" thesis of his predecessor. For Ksenofontov, parallels in mythology did not mean actual genetic connections. Trying to pinpoint the similarities between early Christian traditions and Siberian indigenous beliefs, Ksenofontov drew on the unity of human experience worldwide.

The text of *Khrestets* contained numerous analogies and allusions that served to demonstrate the similarities between northern Asian shamanism and early Christianity. Some of these analogies might appear today as too farfetched. Others sound very plausible. For example, I find attractive his comparison of Jesus Christ with the shaman. There is no doubt, wrote Ksenofontov, that contemporaries viewed Jesus as a folk healer who drove hostile spirits out of individuals just as shamans did. The Gospels describe how Jesus healed the sick, the possessed, the lepers, the deaf, and the blind, and he resurrected the dead. These miracles hardly differ from the ones Siberian indigenous legends ascribe to shamans. Like Jesus, shamans were able to walk on water, feed the hungry, and change the weather. By using his magic, Jesus attracted crowds of common folk. Very much like Sakha spiritual practitioners, Jesus was an honored guest at both weddings and funerals. Ksenofontov stressed that one should distinguish this "folk and primitive Christianity" practiced by Jesus from official Christianity, which later became "infected" by numerous theological speculations and which represents a "branch of ancient philosophy" rather than a form of "natural religion."[23]

Just as in Gospel legends, concluded Ksenofontov, in some native Siberian epic tales, shamans are either born of a holy maiden from a spirit that descended on her or by an old woman, who has a decrepit old husband who is unable to perform intercourse. In legends, shamans are also conceived from the kiss of a dying husband, from a hailstone swallowed by a maiden, from a sun ray, or as a result of amorous relations between a woman and a wolf, a messenger of heaven. Another similarity between shamanic and Gospel legends is the baby Jesus story, whose analogy can be found in a Sakha story about an infant found among cows or about an infant put in a cow crib. In Sakha stories about shamans, there are some episodes that strikingly resemble the Gospel story about a young Jesus who surprises wise elders with his mature mind. Sakha legends also describe how a shaman who is about to be admitted into his vocation is taken to a desolate place in the woods where he fasts, subsisting on water. These legends also refer to shamans who are tempted by spirits, which to Ksenofontov appeared as an analogy for Jesus' temptations in the biblical desert.

It is also important to note that, in the 1920s during his field trips, Ksenofontov collected fascinating, "morbid" tales about the painful initiation of Sakha and Evenki shamans. These stories, which were later translated into German,[24] were extensively used by Mircea Eliade in an English edition of his famous *Shamanism: Archaic Techniques of Ecstasy* (1964). Another modern scholar, mythology writer Joseph Campbell, also heavily relied on that collection of shamanic legends in his *Masks of Gods: Primitive Mythology* (1959).[25] Thus, the legends collected by Ksenofontov, especially the ones about the ritual dismemberment of would-be shamans by spirits and their subsequent resurrection, became classics of shamanism studies.

Incidentally, Ksenofontov similarly cast these materials against Christ's crucifixion and resurrection. Dismemberment usually lasted three days, the scholar reminded us. After this, a shaman is resurrected. Moreover, a resurrected shaman "comes alive" enlightened and "blessed" and with a body that is now able to absorb spirits. Ksenofontov viewed the process of education and initiation of a novice for a shamanic profession by an old shaman as an analogy to the baptism of Jesus by John the Baptist, which triggered Jesus' prophetic mission. Ksenofontov pointed out that among the Buryat actual water ablution is part of a shaman's professional initiation. References in Sakha legends to the miraculous ability of shamans to speak different languages on behalf of the spirits of "alien" shamans might remind Christians of the Pentecost story in which the Holy Spirit descended on the apostles and endowed them with the ability to speak different languages. The Holy Spirit that descended on Jesus in the shape of a white dove becomes an analogy to swans and undefined white birds in Sakha tales about "white shamans." In the shape of birds (crows, loons, hawks), souls of deceased shamans usually flock to a shaman who performs a séance. A more ancient version of the bird spirits is Raven Spirit of Sakha's "black shamanism." Ksenofontov noted that the Gospel dove is nothing less than "retouched, polished and ennobled Raven of the ancient shamanism."[26]

Ksenofontov even revisited the very name of Christ. The scholar refuted the accepted version that the name originated from the Greek word *Khristos*, which means the "anointed one." In his view, one should trace the origin of the name to the Greek verbs "to prophesy" or "to predict," which form the noun *khrestets*, which literally means "the seer" and "soothsayer." Ksenofontov argued that one can see this word in ancient Roman sources about popular Eastern mystery cults. In Roman times, he continued, barbarian magicians and sorcerers were called *khrestets*, which drove him to the conclusion that "Christ" is a later distortion of the word *khrestets*. Thus, summarized the Sakha scholar, the original meaning of modern Greek and Russian *Khristos* (Christ) is simply a sorcerer, a witch doctor, a magician, and a visionary, rather than the "anointed one."[27]

We find a literary version of the Christian analogy for shamanism in *Strashnyi kam* (*Scary Shaman*; 1926) by Viacheslav Shishkov,[28] who started as a regionalist writer and a member of the Potanin circle. The persecutions inflicted on the Altaian shaman Chelbak, the major protagonist of this modernist novel, are compared here with Christ's sufferings. In the novel, which incidentally is based on a real story, an enraged crowd of Russians stones shaman Chelbak to death for performing a shamanic session. Shishkov clearly designed the detailed description of the Russians' escorting Chelbak through a village as a metaphor for Jesus carrying the cross. In their loyalty to the official church, his persecutors betray the idea of genuine Christianity with its compassion. The spirit of the murdered shaman wanders around, gradually drains vitality from his executioners, and finally wipes them out with diseases. The sounds of the shaman drum continue to resonate in the ears of the villagers: "The invisible drum rumbles around. Villagers open their mouths, make the sign of the cross and run away."[29] An old peasant woman, Feodosiia, is the first to realize that what the Russians did was against genuine Christianity and therefore she appeals to the spirit of the dead shaman in a Christian manner, "I am a sinner, I am a sinner, forgive me, father Chelbak."[30]

In addition to their literary and scholarly constructs, regionalists also used shamanic tradition to enhance the public display of Siberian identity. In 1909, Potanin, Anokhin, and Adrianov brought Mampyi, an Altaian shaman from the Katun river area, to the city of Tomsk. Mampyi was to play the core part in an "ethnographic evening" designed to introduce the Tomsk "cultured society" to the samples of Siberian tradition.[31] The native participants in the evening, who represented such tribal groups as the Altaians, Sakhas, Buryats, Tatars, and Khanty, dressed in their traditional garb, displayed scenes from their lives, played native music, and recited short excerpts from their epic tales. These scenes of live ethnography were set against a background of replicated native dwellings, household items, and sacred shrines. Moreover, the walls of Tomsk's hall for public gatherings (*dom obshchestvennogo sobraniia*), where regionalists held the ethnographic evening, were decorated with the skins of Siberian animals. The portrayal of the Siberian landscape was topped by a decoration that depicted a polar night and a huge block of ice.[32]

Large crowds of spectators filled this Siberian house of culture. Members of the public concentrated their attention on Mampyi. Working together to distill the essence of shamanism for a general audience, Mampyi and the regionalists watered down the holistic nature of the "real shamanism" by dividing the shamanic session into several acts for the purposes of display. First, in a "poetic manner," Mampyi described the meaning of shamanism and explained the symbolism of his shamanic costume. Second, the shaman showed how he put on the costume and addressed a fire. Then, in a "whirling dancing manner," Mampyi addressed his ancestor shaman Kanym, the spirit of the Altai, and then Erlik (the deity of the underworld), Ülgen, earth, water, and finally the "foundation of the earth." At the end of the ceremony, Mampyi took off his costume and in a "singing manner" summarized the meaning of the whole ceremony.[33]

The story does not end there. Six days after the ethnographic evening, regionalist archaeologist and ethnographer Adrianov delivered a paper on the basics of Siberian shamanism for a scholarly audience. Serving as a live

FIGURE 2.2a. Siberian shamans on public display. An Altaian shamaness poses for photographer S. I. Borisov (1908); the image was reproduced as a color postcard in the 1910s.

FIGURE 2.2b. Image of a Buryat shaman, black-and-white Russian postcard,
c. 1910s. From the author's collection.

illustration for the presented paper, Mampyi reran the shamanic session he
had performed earlier. That evening, the same paper and session were repeated at the Tomsk Technological Institute, now again for the general public
with the shaman replicating the same session for the third time.[34] Finally, to
reach a yet wider audience, the regionalists duplicated and distributed copies of
Adrianov's paper "Shamanic Mystery Ceremony [kamlanie]." Although he was
out of his tribal setting, during one of these urban sessions, Mampyi so immersed himself in the performance that he entered an actual altered state,
which continued for more than an hour. The organizers had to interrupt him
by force after the curtain already had closed. Inspired by the success of the
Mampyi ethnographic show, Potanin and his friends replicated the public display of Siberian shamanism by inviting indigenous spiritual practitioners
to perform in Barnaul, Irkutsk, and several other cities. The images of Siberian
shamans began to appear on Russian postcards (see figures 2.2a and 2.2b).

No doubt the exotic nature of shamanism and scientific curiosity were among the reasons the Tomsk audience was drawn to Mampyi's "séances." Yet the fact that Potanin and his fellow regionalists accepted Mampyi as an equal, taking him on a tour of the city and sharing with him the results of their scholarly and scientific pursuits, tells us that there was more here than natural curiosity. It appears that the regionalists viewed the native shaman as a person who could add to the developing Siberian culture as a whole. Indeed, during the ethnographic evening in the Tomsk house of culture, the borders between Russians and so-called native others were blurred. In addition to indigenous lifeways, the organizers sampled Russian folksongs accompanied by a balalaika band. Furthermore, the spectators included both Russians and natives who resided in Tomsk.

Mampyi came under intensive psychological and physiological observation while in Tomsk. In the wake of the ethnographic evening, Tomsk-based physician V. V. Karelin presented a special paper on the Mampyi mental state for the members of a local branch of the Russian Imperial Technological Society. Karelin reported that he had tested the shaman before and after his séance, then tested Mampyi again in his neurological clinic, and even, to make the investigation complete, X-rayed the shaman's whole body. What Karelin wanted to convey to his colleagues was that physically and mentally Mampyi was an absolutely normal person without any traces of neurosis and depression.[35] One can consider this a response of the regionalists to the view of shamans as mentally disturbed—a perception that was becoming increasingly popular at the turn of the twentieth century.

Red Atlantis: American Regionalists Learn from the Indigenous Primitive, 1920s–1930s

On the other side of the world, in the United States, a group of writers, artists, and bohemians, who were primarily clustered in the southwestern states, used their own domestic primitives for the similar purposes of anchoring and indigenizing themselves in a soil that was not native to them. Yet, unlike their Siberian counterparts, who had parochial cultural concerns, American regionalists looked at their home Native American archaic tradition, having in mind a broader goal—the creation of cultural and spiritual blueprints for the entire nation.[36]

This growing interest in Native Americana certainly had much to do with the cultural aspirations of Americans, a young nation that was seeking to root itself in North American soil. As early as the 1930s, Jung noticed how Native American symbolism was crawling into the American psyche. Observing some of his U.S. patients, he noted that they frequently manifested unconscious symbols related to the Indians, "just as certain coins of the Union bear an

Indian head." Furthermore, the scholar noted that, in the American hero fantasy, the Indian characters played leading roles. It appears that Jung understood well that it was a natural process: all conquerors are gradually absorbed by the spiritual force of the soil they take over. The famous analyst speculated: "in everything on which the American has really set his heart we catch a glimpse of the Indian." Although the latter might be a slight exaggeration when talking about the United States in the 1930s, it is certainly true about current America. I am not going to expand here on the obvious role of the Native Americans in making American national culture, which is a topic that goes beyond the scope of this book.[37]

Here, I am more interested in another side of this romance with the Indian: the Native American as the embodiment of the values lost by Western civilization in the process of its movement toward modernity. In fact, the image of Native Americans as part of American aesthetics and as the antidote to Judeo-Christian civilization were intimately intertwined. This is shown, for example, in the words of anthropologist and writer Jaime de Angulo, one of the active seekers of American Indian wisdom. In 1925, in a letter to his friend Mabel Dodge Luhan (1879–1962), he stressed the essential need for the Indian symbolism in order both to root American culture and to "tame" modernity:

> The white American *must* preserve the Indian, not as a matter of
> justice or even of brotherly charity, but in order to save his own
> neck. The European can always tie back to his own mother soil and
> find therein the spiritual pabulum necessary to life. But the American, overburdened with material culture, is threatened with self-destruction unless he can find some way to tie himself to his own
> mother soil. The Indian holds that key.[38]

Although the majority of Americans were still tied to individualism and the free market, sentiments like this were gaining popularity in the first decades of the twentieth century. They became especially widespread during the Great Depression, which many people viewed as the end of capitalism and Western civilization.[39]

For some learned Americans, the Indian became a cultural alternative to the ruthless philosophy of Social Darwinism, which informed much of American social life from the Gilded Age to the very end of the Roaring Twenties. In the 1920s, there sprang up a small intellectual movement that looked skeptically at the triumphant economic and commercial activities and subscribed to the notion that "we have the redman as a gift."[40] The image of the Indians as tragic heroes defeated and squeezed out by modernity only enhanced this line of thought. The individuals who sought to invoke primitive values included writers, artists, and ethnographers, many of whom set their creative projects in the southwestern United States. They viewed this region, blessed with gorgeous landscapes, ancient ruins, and exotic native cultures, as a vital cultural resource. Explaining the attraction of the place, a modern nature writer notes, "The American Southwest has a special allure—its beautiful, mysterious landscape is imbued with magical charm and a tangible presence of ancient people."[41] In addition, with its dry and hot climate, the Southwest looked appealing for health reasons. For example, city dwellers with lung problems liked to frequent the area. The first sanatoriums, spas, and resorts were erected here as early as the 1880s. Historian of religion Philip Jenkins writes about this side of the Southwest's allure, "The more invalids migrated to the Southwest, the more this created a mass public for alternative medical treatments, often with a strong occult and metaphysical element."[42] Incidentally, the heavy presence of body, mind, and spirit outlets in present-day New Mexico, Arizona, and California is essentially a continuation of cultural and health projects pioneered in the Southwest in the 1920s and 1930s.

The roots of the cultural primitivism associated with the Southwest can be traced to such early ethnographers as Matilda Coxe Stevenson (1849–1915) and Frank Hamilton Cushing (1857–1900), the explorers of the Pueblo Indians. Stevenson was admitted by the Pueblo Zuni into their secret organizations and ceremonies forbidden for outsiders. Cushing lived among the Indians and wrote captivating popular stories about his experiences. Another important resource is the Norwegian-American explorer and archaeologist Carl Lumholtz (1851–1922), who traversed the southwestern United States and northern Mexico. In his *Unknown Mexico* (1902), he poeticized these localities, describing his journeys to the Tarahumara and Huichol Indians in search of native spiritual and material antiquities. This explorer, who frequently used the term *shaman*, discussed in detail native healing sessions and the use of the peyote cactus and, for a moment, even dreamed about going native.[43] These authors and their successors in the 1920s and 1930s eventually attached to the Southwest an aura of a spiritual paradise that later made it a favorite playground and cultural preserve for both anthropologists and spiritual seekers.

One of the predecessors of these projects was the Taos retreat colony. Established by the New York bohemian millionaire Luhan, it was conveniently located near Taos, a Pueblo Indian village. Luhan viewed it as a "splinter" of ancient society, a place where people were unaffected by the evils of capitalism and modernity and still practiced communal and spiritual life. Explaining the attraction of the place, Luhan once noted that when she heard native singing and drumming at Taos, she felt that here different instincts ruled, and "virtue lay in wholeness instead of in dismemberment."[44]

Her personal philosophy represented an eclectic mixture of occult and Leftist ideas. In her early years, Luhan was interested in theosophy. She also explored Oriental religions, transcendentalism, occultism, and Native American symbolism. At the same time, she was sympathetic to socialism and anarchism and ran a salon that harbored various radical intellectuals. Still, her metaphysical aspirations turned out to be stronger. In 1917, she suddenly left her avant-garde salon life in New York City, which looked boring and sterile, and went to northern New Mexico in order to carve there her small "red Atlantis" amid the picturesque landscapes and native cultures.

Explaining what drove her to Taos in the first place, Luhan noted, "We all need to dream. That is why the Indian thing satisfies me. It is a dream."[45] Part of this dream was drawing to Taos writers, poets, and artists who shared her vision in order to turn the place into a center that would help cure Western civilization from its materialism, individualism, and Eurocentrism. In her letter to John Collier, a social reformer who responded to her call to come to Taos, she outlined the vision of her colony as "a kind of headquarters for the future" and "as a base of operations *really* for a new world plan." She was convinced that, in their social evolution, contemporary Americans were approaching a watershed stage after which they would return to their communal roots and live more spiritually and emotionally fulfilled lives. Like many of her friends, she thought that the Native Americans held the key to this evolutionary door.[46]

In her vision, Luhan certainly jumped ahead of her time. While many American contemporaries still sought the solution of their problems either in materialistic pursuits or class battles, with her spiritual project of what later became known as self-actualization she was definitely a pioneer. Her compatriots did tune themselves to the values she strived for, but it happened much later, in the 1960s and the 1970s. In a striking anticipation of the current fascination with Native American spirituality, Luhan reflected on the spiritual aspects of her living in Taos: "Below us millions upon millions of undamaged Indian souls wait the moment of awakening; they wait until the European element has worn off. They are sleeping while their brothers here in these mountains keep the true fire burning and alive till the morning of emergence."[47]

Part of her retreat from modernity was a marriage to Antonio Luhan, a local Pueblo Indian, who, she thought, would help her to act as "a bridge between cultures." She believed that her new husband's "organic consciousness" added to her intuitive mind would be able to transmit better the wisdom of Indian spirituality to Western people (see figure 2.3). Together, they would bring to Taos various intellectuals and activists to learn from local native communities, which, in her view, were organically linked to surrounding nature. Luhan was flattered to hear that her husband sometimes thought she acted as though she had "some Indian" inside her.[48]

However, Luhan and her friends never thought about going native. The goal was to feed on local indigenous symbolism and cultural philosophy in order to educate the wider society about social and spiritual alternatives, and to enhance their own creativity (see figure 2.4). Thus, writer Mary Austin, who at one point lived in the Taos colony, spiritually linked herself to the Indians and even considered herself one of them. Yet she did not expect her readers to

FIGURE 2.3. Mable Dodge Luhan and Tony Luhan in Taos, New Mexico, 1924. Reproduced by permission of the Huntington Library, San Marino, California.

abandon their comfortable homes for native dwellings nor to accept Indian be-liefs. What Austin, Luhan, and their friends wanted was the transplantation into modern society of the "Indian demeanor" and the Indian connection with the natural world. Essentially, they promoted cultural and aesthetic experiences.[49]

Artist Marsden Hartley, another member of the Taos community, stressed that Native American spirituality and ceremonies were incredible resources for creative inspiration because they surpassed the mainstream cultural drudg-ery. As such, in his view, the Indians were real assets for artists and poets, "for whom they [the Indians] seem to be almost especially created." Inci-dentally, this was one of the reasons that Hartley insisted that society, instead of suppressing, should continue the Indians' "beautiful spectacles." In *The American Rhythm* (1923), the writer Austin challenged classical "Shakespea-rean" standards of contemporary American poetry by bringing to public atten-tion the primitive Native American chants rendered, as she stressed, in her own "fairly liberal translations." In passing, she also noted that the Native

FIGURE 2.4. Bert G. Phillips, a member of the Taos artistic community, with his Indian model. Courtesy Museum of New Mexico, Neg. 40392.

American sacred chants "exhibit an acquaintance with the art of suggestion superior to that practiced by our own psychologists."[50]

The individuals who clustered around Luhan represented an intellectual cocktail of ideas. At the same time, many shared her antimodern sentiments and subscribed to her notion that the Indians possessed superior knowledge that could upgrade contemporary humankind. At various times, her large house accommodated such literary dignitaries as D. H. Lawrence, Willa Cather, Harvey Fergusson, and Jean Toomer. There were many famous and lesser-known painters, sculptors, and photographers: Ansel Adams, Georgia O'Keeffe, Miriam DeWitt, Nicolai Fechin, Laura Gilpin, Marsden Hartley, and Ernest Knee. The place certainly attracted anthropologists, mythology scholars, and social reformers, namely, John Collier, Carl Jung, Jaime de Angulo, Elsie Clews Parsons, and Ella Young. Among others, the Taos colony hosted Aldous Huxley, one of the future spearheads of the psychedelic revolution.

Another important name to note is writer and visionary anthropologist Frank Waters (1902–1995), who became known as the grandfather of southwestern literature. After moving to Taos in 1937 at Luhan's invitation, Waters embarked on a literary career that, in his words, was "built on the premise that man's psyche and the cosmos are related to each other as inner and outer worlds." His particular writings dealt with searching for cultural and spiritual similarities between Pueblo traditions and Eastern religions. Thus, Waters cast the Pueblo Hopi spirituality against his readings on Hindu, Buddhist, and Taoist thought. In all fairness, existing topographical parallels between northern New Mexican landscapes and the inner Asian terrain do invite corresponding spiritual and religious parallels. Incidentally, like Waters, Luhan drew similar spiritual links between the Pueblo religion and Taoism. Moreover, she associated Taos landscapes with the mythical Himalayan kingdom of Shangri-la. An important intellectual influence on Waters was George Gurdjieff, a Russian mystic, about whose works the writer learned from Luhan. Waters also served as a direct intellectual link between seekers clustered around Luhan and the modern countercultural community of the 1960s and the 1970s. His *Masks of Gods* (1950) and *Book of the Hopi* (1963) inspired thousands of spiritual seekers during these decades. For the participants in the counterculture and nature movements, the second book was staple reading along with the famous *Tibetan Book of the Dead*. Waters's books, which continue to be published as paperbacks, are an integral part of the current "New Age" print culture.[51]

On a final note, I want to mention that in the 1960s, the American Southwest again became a mecca for artists, writers, visionaries, and spiritual pilgrims, who capitalized on the intellectual tradition established by such people as Lumholtz, Luhan, de Angulo, Parsons, Austin, and Waters. It appears to be very symbolic that Dennis Hopper, an alternative actor and filmmaker who bought the Luhan house in 1970, established in Taos a small commune and embarked on a movie project named *The Last Movie*. The movie that he shot in a native Peruvian village represents an apocalyptic narrative of the decline and fall of the American empire. The central scene portrays the Indians sacrificing a Caucasian man, played by Hopper himself, in order to reclaim their indigenous land.[52]

In Search of American Indian Traditional Culture: Anthropology of Franz Boas

American anthropology scholarship did not stay away from exoticizing native cultures and contributed much to the impressionistic interpretation of tribal beliefs. After all, both artists and writers, who fed on the symbolism associated with the Indians, and American anthropology scholars pursued the same goal: the retrieval and preservation of passing elements of traditional Indian culture. Pursuing this intellectual project, they downplayed or deleted from the picture the manifestations of modernity in the lives of contemporary Indians.

The person who symbolized this preservationist attitude to Native American tradition is the famous photographer Edward Curtis, who conducted a fascinating ethnographic project between 1907 and 1930. Capturing images of hundreds of Indians with his camera, he treated them as symbols of the passing Romantic and heroic age and, for this reason, asked his models to remove Western clothing and pose in traditional garb amid natural landscapes of rocks, lakes, rivers, and woods. The photographer carried in his wagon pieces of Indian garb that he considered traditional, which he used when his indigenous models did not have the necessary items. If his camera accidentally caught some modern artifacts, Curtis carefully erased them from his prints in order to create a complete illusion of the "Indian reality." To the present day, many generic texts about North American Indians sample photographs from his grand collection.

Contemporary American anthropology scholars approached their ethnographic models with the same sentiments. In fact, some anthropologists themselves have noted that the quest for primitivism is an inherent feature of their scholarship, which naturally brings together people who are skeptical about modernity and those who are fascinated with the non-Western exotic. James Clifford reminds us that by its very nature anthropology is a cultural and artistic enterprise and that "surrealist procedures are always present in ethnographic works, though seldom explicitly acknowledged."[53] Such procedures were certainly present in the writings of Franz Boas, the founder of American anthropology, and his students, many of whom were intellectually grounded in the German Romantic tradition.[54]

Revolting against social evolutionism anchored in Enlightenment reasoning, Boas and his followers moved away from die-hard positivist science simply because in the field of culture, according to Boas, there was no way to establish a direct relationship between cause and effect. Like their colleagues, the primitivist artists, writers, and poets, Boasians were interested in the retrieval and reconstruction of the ideal patterns of timeless traditional Indian cultures rather than figuring out how these cultures or their artifacts evolved in time. To them, Indian cultures were beautiful museum fossils instead of parts of changing complex societies. The utterance of Ruth Underhill, one of the Boasian students, who stressed that she consciously avoided talking about changes in native life in order to underline the beauty of the traditional Indian ways, appears characteristic for the contemporary anthropology profession. Explaining her intellectual stance, she wrote, "I have preferred to use the method of the old men who gave me the poetry and to draw the picture as though all of it were still to be found in the present. The beauty of the ceremony came from the loneliness of the naked figures against the stark desert. Blue jeans, calico dresses, and the waiting automobiles of the whites make them look pathetic."[55] Talking about such authors as Underhill, one current author went so far as to claim, "The Boasian ethnographers, like primitivist poets, created through their writing a world which possesses the virtues lost by modernity."[56]

In contrast to the nineteenth-century evolutionism that graded cultures by their progress toward Western civilization, Boasians viewed all societies as equal and valuable autonomous entities. In his 1902 article, "The Ethnological Significance of Esoteric Doctrines," Boas stressed that scholars should treat sacred tribal doctrines "like any other system of philosophy and [their] study has the same aims as the study of the history of philosophy."[57] This was certainly a humanistic view of human cultures compared to earlier Eurocentric evolutionism. From around 1900 to the 1930s, the increasing popularity of ideas advocated by Boas and his followers eventually produced an intellectual shift in American anthropological scholarship from cultural evolutionism to cultural relativism.

This intellectual stance of the Boasians went back to a line of thought in German humanities articulated by the philosopher Johann Gottfried Herder, the linguist Wilhelm von Humboldt, and later by the anthropologist Theodor Waitz.[58] Boas himself repeatedly stressed his intellectual link to the intellectual tradition of Herder. Like their Romantic predecessors, exploring human society as a collection of autonomous cultures, Boasians placed a large emphasis on language and spirituality or, in other words, on the factors that made cultures distinct. In contrast to the declared objectivity of evolutionism, they were interested in the subjective and intuitive experiences of human beings. A good illustration of this approach is the famous linguistic hypothesis offered by anthropologists Edward Sapir and Benjamin Whorf, who argued that grammar patterns and cultures not only influenced each other but also that a language conditioned the specifics of cultural behavior of peoples.

The general direction of Boasian anthropology, which centered on the retrieval of ideal, precontact, traditional Native American cultures and downplayed the process of intercultural exchange among native groups and between natives and Euro-Americans, encouraged an impressionistic approach to indigenous cultures. Boas treated an impressionistic and intuitive approach to ethnographic material as a necessary element of cultural generalization, which allowed anthropologists to single out and even to enhance traditional elements in native cultures.

In the context of my discussion of shamanism, I would like to draw attention to the Boasian record entitled "I Desired to Learn the Ways of the Shaman." This account is an essential ethnographic source for theory on shamanism, magic, and symbolic healing. Published as a segment of his *The Religion of the Kwakiutl Indians* (1930), this text describes the spiritual adventures of Quesalid, a traditional and primitive Kwakiutl Indian. Quesalid at first does not believe in shamanic "tricks." Moreover, to expose the tricksters, he decides to join their order. The apprentice learns how to hide a little tuft of down in a corner of his mouth and then to bite his tongue or scratch his gums to cover the tuft with blood. Then Quesalid finds out how to throw it out at an appropriate moment in order to present it to a sick person and to his audience as evidence of a disease sucked out from the body of a patient. To his surprise, the people he cures in this manner feel better and even recover. The story ends on a positive note: the young shaman becomes a full-time "tribal doctor" and successfully continues to deliver spiritual medicine to nearby communities.

Boas does not mention that he received this record from George Hunt (1854–1933), an acculturated person of English-Tlingit origin who became one of the chief ethnographic assistants to Boas and other ethnographers who worked among the Kwakiutl people. Moreover, the text is a description of Hunt's own initiation into the shamanic vocation. Hunt, an amateur ethnographer or, as he called himself, a "collector of Indian specimens," at the age of sixteen was initiated into the secrets of the shamanic profession, but he later quit his shamanic occupation because collecting museum objects and working for ethnographers brought him better income.

Anthropologist Harry Whitehead, who recently tracked the biography of "Quesalid," informs us that the actual "conversion" of Hunt to shamanism was more conventional and reminiscent of a classical shamanic call. In this case, Hunt's joining the shamanic vocation did not have anything to do with his alleged wish to expose shamanic frauds. In fact, in the earlier 1897–1900 version of the Quesalid story, which Hunt wrote when he worked with Boas as part of the Russian-American Jesup North Pacific Expedition, the collector of Indian specimens relates how, at thirteen, he fell into a fire and burned himself badly. After this, he suffered fainting and heard ringing in the ears, which continued for ten months. Hunt also stressed, "I had to be held because I acted like someone wild." This is clearly a description of the shamanic call. When he finally recovered, Hunt felt as if he had been visiting another world. His relatives concluded that supernatural powers had entered his body, which eventually persuaded him to join the spiritual vocation. It is unclear why the native ethnographer changed his original story. One can speculate that his reluctance to admit his original belief in shamanism might have something to do with restrictions that the Canadian government imposed on Indian religion at that time. Once, Hunt himself became an object of persecution for performing a traditional ritual.[59]

Boas added to the Quesalid story his own creative spin by couching the record as the testimony of a primitive and traditional Indian. Later scholars took the "I Desired to Learn the Ways of the Shaman" record at its face value as a reluctant conversion of a tribal skeptic to the power of healing magic. Later, famous anthropologist Claude Lévi-Strauss used the account to support his theory of symbolic healing. Humanist psychoanalyst Henri Ellenberger included the same record in his textbook on dynamic psychiatry, a humanistic psychology discipline that sprang up in the 1960s.[60] Thus, the Quesalid account became a small social science classic. In our day, the record has also served as a powerful inspiration for some Western seekers who contemplate becoming spiritual practitioners. This was the case for Leslie Gray, a shamanic practitioner from San Francisco. The story about Quesalid, the Indian doubting Thomas, became pivotal in her conversion from a mainstream rationalist psychologist to a shamanic practitioner.[61]

For several Boasians, the ethnographic imagination became an integral part of their scholarship, which shows again that anthropology is a creative enterprise that stands close to literature. This stance is especially visible in the writings of two influential scholars, Paul Radin and Ruth Benedict, who combined their anthropological occupations with poetry writing. Even Robert Lowie, who in other respects seemed to be a good positivist, as it turned out, was not a stranger to dream experiences. This anthropologist, who extensively wrote on the Crow Indian religion, called himself a "chronic and persistent dreamer." Lowie frequently heard voices and saw visions, and compared them with what he learned from his Native American informants, an exercise that certainly benefited his scholarship. With good reason, he could say, "I can understand the underlying mental and emotional experiences a good deal better than most other ethnologists can, because I have identical episodes every night and almost every day of my life."[62]

It appears that, more than some of his colleagues, Radin treated anthropology as a creative enterprise. Thus, through editing, revising, and merging of the biographies of Jasper and Sam Blowsnake, two Winnebago spiritual practitioners and his major informants, and his own fictional story "Thunder-Cloud," the scholar eventually produced an ethnographic, semifictional autobiography of the Winnebago shaman Crashing Thunder.[63] Radin cast his shaman's spiritual journey along the "road of life" to the "road of spiritland" and back against Dante's spiritual journey, a metaphor familiar to his Western contemporaries. The anthropologist breaks Crashing Thunder's vision into three logical portions, which correspond with the spiritual experiences of the great Florentine. At first, Radin's shaman enters into *via purgativa*, then goes through *via illuminativa* and finally reaches the stage of *via unitiva*. Radin poetically concluded, "So our Winnebago sage emerges from the hidden road to see the stars again and come once more into the air of life."[64] Radin wrote good prose that was tinged with imagination, a tradition that was later continued by such visionary scholars as Joseph Campbell.

A similar type of scholar was anthropologist and poet Ruth Benedict. According to her biographer, even in her doctoral dissertation, "The Concept of the Guardian Spirit in North America," Benedict not only examined the native vision quest phenomenon, but also "attempted to convey to a reader the force of a vision experience."[65] Inspired by her favorite philosopher, Friedrich Nietzsche, in *Patterns of Cultures* (1934), she came up with her famous division of human societies in Dionysian and Apollonian traditions. The first one, in which the writer included the majority of Native American peoples, was famous for various ecstatic rituals such as "shamanic exaltation." In her eyes, the societies she linked to this tradition always tried to go beyond the limits of ordinary reality. They were passionately excessive in their ritual life by using such psychotropic herbs as peyote and *datura* or by tearing their flesh during Sun Dancing. Those who belonged to the Apollonian type of culture, argued Benedict, on the contrary, stayed "cool" within the known map. They avoided disruptive psychological states and stuck to a religion without any orgy, divine frenzy, or vision questing. For Benedict, an example of the second type of society was the Pueblo Indians. Such a choice was natural. After all, like the perspectives of Luhan, Collier, and many other southwestern regionalist colleagues, Benedict's Pueblo's small, red Atlantis embodied the ideal society of harmony.

An interesting example of a collective literary reflection of American anthropologists on the culture of Native Americans is a book project initiated by anthropologist Elsie C. Parsons and titled *American Indian Life* (1922). Parsons, who like Luhan was a wealthy New York bohemian, conducted extensive research among the Taos Pueblo Indians and was closely associated with the members of the Taos retreat colony. For *American Indian Life*, Parsons brought together practically all of the stars of 1920s American ethnology, including Boas, Alfred Kroeber, Lowie, Radin, and Clark Wissler. The goal was to use the format of a fictional essay to show to the public how natives thought. Liberated from the constraints of a formal academic text, the scholars had a chance to indulge themselves in poetic description of the Indians. To a contemporary reviewer, *American Indian Life* proved that "the passionate ethnologist is a first-rate novelist."[66] Centered on native religions, the anthology extensively sampled indigenous spirituality and shamans. Pointing out in the introduction to the volume that this "overproportion is perhaps all for the best," Kroeber noted, "the Indian is, all in all, far more religious than we, and the popular idea errs on the side of ignoring this factor."[67]

Shamanism Goes to North America: The Jesup North Pacific Expedition and Nations of Shamans

Prior to 1900, American ethnographers rarely described Native American spiritual practices as shamanism, assuming that this term was a peculiarly Siberian phenomenon. The most popular words for indigenous spiritual practitioners were "medicine man" and "medicine woman," the expressions originating with French explorers and fur traders, who used the word "medicine" to talk about the activities of native spiritual practitioners in North America.[68] The expression shamanism, with its host of accompanying intellectual associations, had not yet become established usage.

Rather typical in this was Daniel Brinton, who in his 1897 book on primitive religions used the term shamanism only three times, employing it as an occasional synonym for medicine man. In his book on "primitive superstitions," religious scholar Rushton Dorman similarly mentioned the expression a few times only as references to native spiritual practitioners of Alaska and Siberia. Moreover, he explained to his readers that the shaman was a synonym for sorcerer. Likewise, Colonel John G. Bourke, the author of the first comprehensive study of Native American spiritual "doctors" (1892), never applied the term to American Indian spiritual practitioners. It is notable that in assessing Indian medicine men and medicine women, Bourke dismissed them as retrogrades. He went as far as suggesting that officials neutralize them as "major obstacles to the Indian progress."[69]

Besides writer Charles Leland, who was tied to German intellectual traditions, there were only a few scholars who used the term shamanism. Among those few was Boas, the founder of American anthropology. As a German intellectual interested in ethnography, he was most certainly familiar with major writings that discussed the topic of shamanism and could juxtapose Native American spiritual practitioners with their Siberian counterparts. Thus, Boas widely relied on this definition in his 1889 ethnographic report describing the religious practitioners of the Kutenai Indians in British Columbia, whom he had briefly visited a year before.

It is interesting that Alexander Chamberlain, an American folklore scholar who picked up the shamanism expression from Boas, used shaman as a synonym for medicine man, although he did not put the former in quotation marks. This shows that he clearly favored shaman for the description of Native American spiritual practitioners. Another scholar who used the word shamanism was W. J. Hoffman, a German American who worked for the Bureau of American Ethnology (BAE) and who discussed Ojibwa (Anishnabe) Midewiwin sacred societies as shamanic. Two native-born American scholars, Washington Matthews and James Mooney, also frequently used that definition. Matthews, a former U.S. Army physician, was a collector of Navajo (Dine) folklore. Mooney, another BAE ethnologist, who became famous for his research of the Ghost Dance movement, conducted fieldwork among Cherokee spiritual practitioners, whom he described as shamans.[70]

Matthews and especially Mooney were scholars of a humanistic orientation who sympathized with the Indians. It appears that by recasting Native American medicine men and women into shamans, both Matthews and Mooney sought to rehabilitate indigenous spiritual practitioners in the eyes of the reading public. Thus, Matthews thought that his work of collecting Dine folklore might give "some testimony in their [shamans'] favor." Mooney stressed that even "ceremonial religions of the East" could not overshadow Native American spirituality, which is "far from being a jumble of crudities."[71] Moreover, Mooney went far beyond the borders of contemporary objective scholarship by practicing what today we call "activist anthropology." This anthropologist helped to incorporate the Native American Church, whose rituals creatively blended the hallucinogenic qualities of the peyote cactus and Christian ceremonialism. Doing this, the anthropologist hoped to bring all branches of the peyote practitioners together and to give legal protection to the Indian use of peyote.

The major spearhead of the shamanism idiom in American anthropology scholarship was the Jesup North Pacific Expedition (1897–1902), which included Russian and American scholars. The researchers headed by Boas worked on behalf of the American Museum of Natural History (AMNH). In addition to their major goal—collecting ethnographic and archaeological materials for the museum—the expedition was to explore the links between the indigenous cultures of northeastern Siberia and the northwestern coast of North America.[72]

To perform the Siberian part of this research, Boas recruited Bogoras and Jochelson, two ethnographer friends (see figure 2.5) who had years of extensive field experience in Siberia, the area to which the Russian government had earlier banished them for their revolutionary activities. Boas chose them upon the recommendation of Wilhelm Radloff, the Russian-German anthropologist and one of the pioneers of shamanism studies, whom I discussed in chapter 1. Thus, between 1900 and 1902, Bogoras and Jochelson were exploring native Siberian peoples in a new capacity as voluntary anthropologists. After completing his explorations of the Chukchi and the Yupik natives, the former stayed in New York for almost two years, sorting his collections, composing his Chukchi monograph, and writing fiction that reflected his experiences among Siberian natives. Later, back in Russia, Bogoras became one of the leaders of early Soviet anthropology. Jochelson, his partner, moved to the United States in the 1920s and remained there, continuing to work in the AMNH close to Boas and his students.

Published in English as the proceedings of the expedition, Bogoras's book on the Chukchi and Jochelson's on the Koryak[73] introduced into Western scholarship a variety of field materials on Siberian cultures, including shamanism, which both assessed as a form of neurosis sanctioned by indigenous communities. In the wake of the Jesup expedition, which approached the northern Pacific Rim as the interconnected cultural area, ethnologists began more frequently to juxtapose Native American spiritual practitioners against their "classic" Siberian analogies. Eventually, this approach gave rise to the academic metaphor of the "shamanistic complex" that some anthropologists began to use to describe the beliefs of native populations of Siberia and North America.

This extension of the shamanism idiom beyond Siberia became reflected in a public exhibit organized by the AMNH, the academic sponsor of the Jesup expedition. The New York Times Magazine, which in 1904 announced this project in its article "Ancient Religion of Shamanism Flourishing To-Day," stressed that the director of the museum, H. C. Buxton, and his

FIGURE 2.5. Franz Boas with his exiled ethnographer colleagues during the World Congress of Americanists at Göteborg, Sweden (1924). *Left to right*: Waldemar Bogoras, Franz Boas, and Lev Shterenberg. Ia. P. Al'kor, "V. G. Bogoraz-Tan," *Sovietskaia etnografiia* 4–5 (1935): 8.

colleagues were seeking to correct the dismissive attitude toward shamanism on the part of contemporary academics. The goal of the exhibit was to use the extensive collections gathered by Bogoras and Jochelson in Siberia, by Boas on the northwestern coast of North America, and by Carl Lumholtz among the Huichol Indians in Mexico to show that the natives of these areas practiced shamanism.

The *Times* stressed that the habitat of shamanism was northern Asia and western North America. Furthermore, the reporter explained to readers that the shaman was a spiritual practitioner who stood higher than a simple medicine man. Some of the museum's anthropologists might have fed this reporter the idea that the phenomenon of the medicine man represented "a gradual retrogression" from the classical areas of shamanism with their center in Mongolia. Most certainly, the journalist, as always happens with public media, distorted or simplified the views of the interviewed scholars; the article lumped into the realm of shamanism such things as the American Indian potlatch giveaway ceremony and the Chukchi seasonal reindeer sacrifices. Still, the reporter seemed to have captured well the general direction of Boas's, Bogoras's, Jochelson's, and Lumholtz's thinking: a loose interpretation of shamanism as a phenomenon that went beyond northern Asia and included a variety of rituals in addition to the classical shamanic séance. It appears that the journalist also caught well the preservationist attitude of many contemporary anthropologists to indigenous cultures. Stressing that shamanism was equally characteristic of all "primitive races" of all times, the newspaper noted that this "primal religion" had hardly changed since the old Stone Age. "Whatever worship, ceremonies, and festivals he [the tribal person] has acquired according to the needs of environment, his Shamanistic rites are exactly the same everywhere, as they were when Moses broke the golden calf," summarized the reporter.[74]

A British anthropologist of Polish descent, Marie Antoinette Czaplicka (see figure 2.6), eased the introduction of Western readers to Bogoras's and Jochelson's materials by summarizing their writings, along with other exiles' ethnographies and regionalists' ethnographies, in her *Aboriginal Siberia* (1914).[75] When she was writing this particular book, Czaplicka was still an armchair scholar, who had never seen Siberia and its natives. The topics of shamanism and the mental state of Siberian natives occupy the essential part of this book. For many scholars, the Bogoras and Jochelson texts, along with *Aboriginal Siberia*, became reference editions in which they usually looked each time they needed to acquire information about classical shamanism.

Because Czaplicka's book was more compact and accessible than the bulky volumes produced by Bogoras and Jochelson, it became the major comprehensive study on Siberian natives. Czaplicka eventually acquired the status of one of the major experts in the field. *Aboriginal Siberia* complemented and in some cases even replaced Radloff's *Aus Sibirien* (1884) as a standard source on shamanism in the first half of the twentieth century. The fact that she also wrote several encyclopedia articles on the same topic and on Siberian natives in general, in addition to her popular travel book, *My Siberian Year* (1916),[76] might have enhanced that status.

Thus, in the 1880s to 1910s, the *Encyclopedia Britannica* referred to Radloff as the major authority on shamanism; the entire shamanism entry was based on his description of southern Siberian (Altaian) spiritual practices. In the 1940s and 1950s, new editions of this encyclopedia did not mention Radloff, replacing him with references to Czaplicka. As late as 1968, religious scholar Mircea Eliade, the dean of shamanism studies in the 1960s and 1970s, recommended her 1914 work as a major source in the field besides his own book.[77] Later, replicating Czaplicka, a Russian archaeologist of Georgian ancestry, Georgii K. Nioradze (1925) and Swedish religion scholar Åke Ohlmarks

FIGURE 2.6. Marie Antoinette Czaplicka, the author of *Aboriginal Siberia* (1914). From Marie Czaplicka, *My Siberian Year* (London: Mills & Boon, 1916), frontispiece.

(1939) released similar ethnographic digests, only for German readers.[78] Bogoras's and Jochelson's ethnographies and the compilations produced by Czaplicka, Nioradze, and especially Ohlmarks were instrumental in establishing a scholarly perception that shamanism was a psychological phenomenon and that the stronghold of shamanism was among natives of northeastern Asia and northwestern North America.

The particular work that planted the shamanism metaphor in American ethnology was Roland Dixon's paper "Some Aspects of the American Shaman" (1908), delivered as a presidential address to a meeting of the American Folklore Society.[79] Incidentally, Dixon was also a participant in the Jesup expedition. Comparing Native American spiritual practitioners with Siberian shamans, the scholar argued that North American spirituality was more centered on active vision questing and manifested a "democratized shamanism."

In contrast, the Asian spirituality, which was based on the hereditary transmission of shamanic power and trance, appeared to him as more "aristocratic." Regarding this assessment, the religion scholar Åke Hultkrantz perceptively remarked, "In reading Dixon's evaluation of North American shamanism one receives the impression that this was the New World answer to the Old World ideas of the elitist role of the shaman."[80]

Indeed, among many Siberian communities, a simple acquisition of shamanic power by an individual was not enough to become a shaman. The essential prerequisite was hereditary transmission of the vocation in shamanic lineages. In contrast, among many American Indian groups, especially in the Plains area, everybody was expected to be an active seeker of sacred shamanic power. When Siberian native parents learned that their children manifested elements of shamanic behavior, they were frequently petrified and did everything to divert them from shamanism. Plains Indian parents, on the contrary, sent their children to isolated places for vision questing and encouraged them to fast there until spirits took pity on them and sent them supernatural power. The spiritual tradition that stood closest to the classic Siberian shamanism with its hereditary election through the shamanic illness was reported only in western North America.

What Dixon wrote about the democratic nature of American Indian shamanism became an established scholarly trope. In his comprehensive *Primitive Religion* (1937), Paul Radin used that dichotomy between Siberian shamanism proper and democratic American Indian spirituality to contrast two ways of approaching the supernatural. Radin suggested that the first way was the sign of a less-advanced society. He argued that the spiritual world of the "elementary" Siberian people—and, by analogy, of other arctic areas—was full of terror and fear. According to Radin, in these inhospitable regions, people were very susceptible to a belief that fearful spirits truly invaded shamans' bodies and imposed on them the undesirable spiritual vocation. Referring to Bogoras, Czaplicka, and also Dutch anthropologist Knud Rassmusen, Radin wrote about the morbid "neurotic-epileptoid" world of northern shamanism, where candidates to shamanism were petrified of their spiritual calls.[81]

The anthropologist argued that this "Gothic" realm was absent from the open world view of American Indian peoples, whom he viewed economically and socially as more advanced societies. Radin assumed that, in contrast to their Siberian counterparts, egalitarian American Indian communities, which "tolerated individual expression," diluted the morbid nature of primal shamanism by making the supernatural available to everybody. Thus, in his view, the advanced American Indian societies purified the deities and spirits of shamanism, making them more "gentle" and attractive to people.

Although in the 1920s and 1930s, some scholars treated shamans as tribal spiritual practitioners of a higher caliber,[82] many Boasians used the word shaman simply as a synonym for the medicine man or woman. Essentially, one can talk about two overlapping usages. One went back to the expression medicine earlier introduced by French explorers and later adopted by many people writing about American Indian spiritual practitioners. The new term went back to German writings on Siberia. This ambivalence in usage existed until the 1970s, when shamans gradually began to replace the medicine people. In fact, Boasians were themselves the source of that ambivalence. In "Some Aspects of the American Shaman," Dixon invited his colleagues to treat as shamans any spiritual practitioner in every "savage community" of North America.

The incorporation of the Siberian usage with such loose interpretation into North American ethnology posed a question of how to distinguish shamans from the rest of the population. As for California and the Northwest coast, it was relatively clear. As in Siberia, here many spiritual practitioners experienced forceful shamanic calls and joined the vocation involuntarily. Still, in other indigenous societies, especially in the Plains area, any individual could potentially accumulate sacred power through vision questing.

In their comprehensive studies of North American shamanism, two scholars, L. L. Leh and Willard Park, suggested that shamans be distinguished from "lay" people by the degree of sacred power they accumulated through their spiritual exercises. In this case, the shaman became "the individual who, more than the ordinary individuals of his tribe, deals with and influences the supernatural powers."[83] Park admitted that to distinguish shamans from common people by the amount of medicine power was a superficial criterion. Nevertheless, he sided with Dixon and Leh by grouping under the name shamanism "all the practices by which supernatural power may be acquired by mortals." Although Lowie, one of the leading American anthropologists, also had some reservations about the application of the Siberian word, he shared a similar approach. Lowie wrote particularly that strong shamans among North American Indians were simply those fortunate visionaries who accumulated more medicine power than the rest of the people.[84]

Soon, this loose interpretation of the shamanism idea opened a door to the portrayal as shamans not only various sorts of spiritual practitioners but also members of different sacred societies and those who went on vision quests. Based on this broad interpretation, one could argue that all Indians who did spiritual work "shamanized." That is precisely what Marvin Opler did when discussing the Apache Indians, among whom all adult individuals dealt to some degree with sacred medicine. To this anthropologist, the Apache operated as a "nation of shamans."[85]

Reference works and popular scholarly texts reflected the changing views on the geographical expansion of shamanism, from northern Asia to North America. Thus, drawing exclusively on the materials of Radloff, the 1886 edition of the *Encyclopedia Britannica* described shamanism as a regionally bound religion, "which once prevailed among all the Ural-Altaic people and which still lives in northern Asia." In 1911, while still relying on the Radloff discussion of shamanism and defining it as a Ural-Altai religion, the encyclopedia extended the geographical borders of the phenomenon; it vaguely noted, "Properly speaking, however, there is nothing to distinguish shamanism from the religions of other peoples in a similar stage of culture." A 1933 edition of *The Oxford English Dictionary* was more precise about the geography of shamanism. It explained that shamanism was "the primitive religion of the Ural-Altaic peoples of Siberia, in which all the good and evil of life are thought to be brought about by spirits who can be influenced only by shamans; hence applied to similar religions, esp. of North-West American Indians." At the same time, the dictionary, following Castren and Radloff, still singled out the Ural-Altaic cultural realm (the Altaians, Tungus, Ostiak) as the major "habitat" of shamanism; the native North American version appears here only as an offshoot. Several decades later, in 1985, the *American Heritage Dictionary* firmly defined Siberia and North America as the core habitats of shamanism.[86]

The thesis about the "unitary character of Eurasian and North American shamanism" was articulated by Lowie in a special paper on the parallels between Eurasian and North American indigenous beliefs. Among the common features, he pointed to the shaman call in western North America and the ritual of the shaking tent.[87] In fact, similarities not only in religious practices but also in mythology convinced many scholars that shamanism migrated to North America along with the ancestors of the Indians, who moved from Siberia to the New World.

At the same time, to some, the fact of this migration supported by archaeological evidence served as an invitation to revive the search for the original source of shamanism, the intellectual exercise popular with Enlightenment and Romantic writers. E. M. Loeb, for example, stressed that the phenomenon of shamanism "arose once, in one spot" and then radiated over the world, "escaping only the marginal or more primitive peoples." To him, this original motherland was Siberia. Referring to Czaplicka, the anthropologist explained, "If the people who have the shamanism in its most elaborate form were the originators, then Siberia must have been the birthplace of the art. This is certainly the region where people suffer more from nervous diseases, including 'arctic hysteria' than any other known region of the world."[88]

What is interesting about the Loeb thesis is not only his attempt to pinpoint the original motherland of shamanism but also his explanation of why Siberia was the source of shamanism. For contemporary anthropology scholarship, this explanation—northern Asia is the place where "people suffer more from nervous diseases"—was common wisdom that became included in academic books.[89] Like Loeb, many scholars took it for granted that shamanism had something to do with the severe Siberian and northern environment in general, the areas where indigenous people were supposedly prone

to collective and individual hysteria. I will discuss in detail this view of shamanism as a pathological northern phenomenon in the next chapter.

Morbid Landscapes: Shamanism in Siberian Exiles' Writings

In the meantime, I want to introduce the unusual group of people whom I
mentioned in the beginning of the chapter—"exiled" ethnographers, who were
instrumental in shaping that perception of shamanism as pathology. I have
already named two of them: Bogoras and Jochelson. Their link to Western
scholarship was through their participation in the above-mentioned Jesup
North Pacific Expedition and through their subsequent work with Franz Boas,
who was in charge of this scholarly enterprise.

In addition to Bogoras and Jochelson, other prominent exiled intellectuals who wrote about shamans were Isaac G. Goldberg (1884–1939), I. A.
Khudiakov (1842–1876), Dmitrii Klementz (1848–1914), Eduard K. Pekarskii
(1858–1934), Vasilii F. Troshchanskii (1846–1898), Wenceslas Sieroszewski
(1858–1945), Bronislaw Pilsudskii (1866–1918), and Lev Shterenberg (1861–
1927). An intriguing aspect of their biographies is that originally these people
never thought about natives and ethnography. In fact, they hardly had anything to do with scholarly pursuits and academia in general, turning to exploring indigenous lifestyles and customs only during their involuntary "field
experience" in Siberia.

One can guess that the sudden and unexpected encounter with the crude
mores and rough landscapes of Siberia might have insulted the intelligence
of these enlightened Europeans. Under these circumstances, fiction writing
and recording native ethnography could be among the few available outlets to
nourish inquisitive minds in this desolate area. Others pursued such natural
science subjects as geology, botany, and so on. For some, these were the only
ways to remain sane. Sometimes, even these subjects were not always easy to
pursue, because such items as paper and pencils were precious commodities.
From Bogoras's description of his conditions, one learns that occasionally,
when he did not have a pencil, he had to resort to deer blood as a substitute
for ink. While their hardships were difficult, compared to Stalin's later labor
camps, the tsarist exile system looked like a resort. The exiles could meet each
other and travel with the permission of authorities. Popular and scientific
periodicals in European Russia frequently published their notes on the ethnography, geography, economy, population, and geology of Siberia. In any case,
a literary or research career in the exotic setting was always open to those who
wanted to pursue it.

Several exiles who, like Bogoras and Sieroszewski, turned to learning and
writing about Siberian indigenous customs, combined ethnography with fiction writing, considering both to be parts of the same creative pursuit. In fact,

before turning himself into an anthropologist, Bogoras, who lived in exile from 1889 to 1898, at first used Siberian landscapes as a backdrop for his fiction. Even after he became a professional anthropologist, the scholar still felt an urge to continue his fiction writing. Bogoras was strongly convinced that rendering ethnography in the language of fiction was beneficial to anthropological knowledge because it made it attractive. The writer expressed his attitude this way: "Science and art do not interfere with each other, they complement each other."[90] Dmitrii Zelenin, a Soviet folklore scholar who also wrote much on Siberian shamanism, remarked about the intellectual stance of his colleague, "Inside him a fiction writer constantly struggled with a scholar and frequently won. All anthropologists who heard his lectures and talks know about this." In contrast, to Korolenko, a professional fiction writer who was himself a former exile, Bogoras was too tied to the anthropology vocation to be considered a full-fledged writer.[91]

Incidentally, Korolenko, who advocated writing as the most creative way to cope with exile conditions in the northern wasteland, served as an intellectual inspiration for Bogoras and his comrades who wanted to try themselves as writers. Once Bogoras joked that Korolenko should get full credit for establishing a "special literature division" of the "Siberian department of social sciences." Indeed, writing fiction and ethnographies or doing science provided exiles with a good niche that allowed, on the one hand, channeling their own emotions and frustrations and, on the other, distancing themselves from the inhospitable reality. Gradually entering this intellectual niche, Bogoras realized that it was possible to rework the "horrible conditions of life, resembling the lower circles of Dante's hell, into a creative image" and to "approach the polar hell as an observer and a researcher." Eventually, to his surprise, he found out that, even living in Siberia, one could "discover manners and life ways."[92]

Now, a few words about the background of the Siberian exiled ethnographers. These people primarily originated from two groups. They were either participants in the underground, semi-terrorist revolutionary organization Popular Will (Bogoras, Jochelson, Klementz, Pekarskii, Troshchanskii, and Goldberg) or members of the Polish nationalist movement (Sieroszewski, Pilsudskii). While the first sought to overthrow the oppressive tsarist regime, the second fought for the independence of Poland, then a subject area within the Russian empire. Unlike regionalists, the exiled writers culturally and mentally affiliated themselves with the intellectual and social life of European Russia. Although some of the exiles, for example Sieroszewski and Pekarskii, married native women during their exile years and tried at least partially to ground themselves in indigenous life, they still felt alienated from the inhospitable land in which they were forced to live. As soon as an opportunity appeared, either with the expiration of an exile term or with the democratic revolutions in 1905 and 1917, many were glad to return to the mainland, to their former cultural and intellectual milieu.

Their alienation from Siberia notwithstanding, there were factors that might have eased the exiles' interactions with native populations, which put them in a good position as ethnographers compared to short-time visitors. The simple fact that the exiles, by their very status, were marginals already set them aside from Siberian officialdom and from average Russians. Moreover, many of them were ethnic marginals as well. Bogoras, Jochelson, and Shterenberg came from the Jewish pale. Pekarskii, Sieroszewski, and Pilsudskii were Poles. I agree with historian Ronald Hutton, who argues that such marginal status might have helped to create a spiritual bond between the political exiles and the Siberian natives, who were themselves put down by the Russian empire. Incidentally, the indigenous people sharply differentiated between common criminals, who were crude untrustworthy folk, and well-rounded political exiles, who frequently helped natives. At least one short-term visitor, a contemporary observer from Sweden, wrote that the political exiles lived among the natives as equals and friends.[93] Thus, long sentences and peculiar status provided the political exiles with a unique opportunity to dig into native cultures for ethnographic knowledge. Still, unlike Siberian regionalists who viewed native lore as part of their own Siberian tradition and sought to integrate it into their cultural project, the exiles treated native spirituality and ethnography as a distant exotic object set amid morbid landscapes.

Although in their ethnographies, and especially in their fiction, the exiles similarly romanticized shamanism and native life, they tended to sample the grim, diabolic, and Gothic aspects of indigenous spirituality. Being revolutionary dissenters, they sometimes also used shamanic settings to unveil the oppressive conditions of native populations and their "backwardness." This was very different from the approach taken by Potanin, Anokhin, and Iadrintsev, who viewed native shamanism and folklore in bright colors as vital creative traditions that might nourish the entire Siberian culture. My argument is that native backdrops that appear in the exile fiction to some extent mirror the exiles' feelings about the land and people they had to live with. Even in the case of Isaac Goldberg, a revolutionary turned fiction writer who was born, lived in, and eventually was sentenced to Siberia, the exile experience underwrote poetic sentiments he might have developed toward Siberia under other circumstances. Although Goldberg's prose poeticizes the "savages" who live natural life in the wild, their honesty and dignity, his *Tungus Stories* and *The Law of Taiga Forest* deal more with the Darwinian side of the natural "law" of the taiga forest: awesome age-old and savage landscapes and customs of Siberia loom over and literally crush an individual. Goldberg's stories also sample the tragic deaths of natives from epidemics, freezing, and suicides. The landscapes portrayed by Goldberg are grim and inhospitable; this northern desert sucks the person in and does not release.

In the story "Shaman Named Khabiburtsa" (1913), Goldberg portrayed a middle-age Tungus (Evenki) shaman. In the beginning of the story,

Khabiburtsa is shown at the height of his life. He owns tremendous medicine power that can easily stop a rampaging bear. Suddenly, this happy spiritual career is shattered into pieces. Although Khabiburtsa already went through his shamanic illness, he suddenly begins to hear sounds and whispers, which haunt him everywhere. These are helping spirits that somehow got out of his control and try to overpower the shaman. The petrified spiritual practitioner, who cannot tame the revolting beings, runs away and tries to hand them to a neighboring shaman, Kobdel'gi, as a gift. Yet the colleague is not a fool. He senses what is going on and refuses to accept the hazardous present. As a last resort, Khabiburtsa rushes to a Russian village, where an Orthodox priest performs an exorcism session, using icons and the power of St. Nicholas. This remedy does not work either. The end of the story is tragic. Realizing that the spirits are completely out of his control, Khabiburtsa gives a rifle to his wife "just in case." Finally, when the shaman becomes a simple toy in the hands of his rebellious spirits and completely turns into a raving maniac, the scared wife shoots her husband. The scene of the execution is accompanied by the joyful and laughing shouts of the victorious spirits.[94]

The death and dying amid the northern desert as well as the law of the wild are also favorite metaphors of Sieroszewski, a Polish blacksmith who was exiled to Siberia for his participation in the Polish national liberation movement. Like his comrades, Sieroszewski advanced himself in the same "Siberian department of social sciences," nourishing his intelligence by ethnographic pursuits and fiction writing. Everybody who has at least a rudimentary knowledge of Siberian shamanism is familiar with his classic ethnographic notes on Yakut (Sakha) shamans, which Eliade used extensively in his famous book on the archaic techniques of ecstasy.[95] At the same time, not many know that Sieroszewski also wrote ethnographic fiction. I want to look more into these texts, which help to illustrate the exiles' attitudes to Siberian native landscapes.

In Sieroszewski's *On the Edge of the Woods* (1897), the major character, Paul, a clear alter ego of the author, is banished by the tsarist regime to a remote Sakha village, where people, although nice and friendly, "sleep too much and think too little." Paul settles in with the family of an old shaman and immediately files a petition with the authorities, requesting that they remove him from this desolate place at least to a small town. Thus, his life goes by in a futile expectation of a response to his petition. The exile has already read and reread all his books. Time goes by unbearably slowly. Eventually, Paul begins to suffer from insomnia and hallucinates, scaring his native hosts. When Paul is about to go insane, the village is suddenly hit by an epidemic of smallpox. The misfortune wakes him up, and Paul vigorously tries to fight the advancing disease by organizing a quarantine. In the meantime, villagers apathetically prepare to die, assuming that "one cannot escape from his fate." Amid dying and dead people, the old shaman, dressed in his "magic robe" and armed with a drum, makes a last desperate attempt to ward off the advancing illness by performing a séance. However, the spirits of the shaman cannot overpower the mighty "Russian grandma," as natives call the smallpox. Right in the middle of his séance, the shaman suddenly dies of a heart attack. Before Paul can realize what is going on, the defeated spiritual practitioner drops to the ground as if struck by lightning: "The shaman's heart stopped, a small stream of blood was dripping from his mouth, and the dead pupils of the shaman eyes severely stared at Paul."[96]

Although in another Sieroszewski story, "Sacrifice to Gods" (1895), a shaman does not die, he is portrayed as a messenger of morbid spirits who demand that the Tungus (Evenki) people sacrifice their most respected elder. In this particular story, Sieroszewski shows a Tungus community that is haunted by reindeer die-outs and famine. Amid this misery, an elder named Sel'tichan and his family can somehow shield themselves from the maladies and prosper. Moreover, the elder eagerly helps his unlucky kinfolk with food. In the meantime, requested to look into the future of the community, a shaman named Ol'tungab performs a séance, journeys to the other world, and transmits to his audience the "will of spirits": in order to ward off the animal die-out, people have to sacrifice the most prosperous and lucky Tungus.

As in his ethnographic works, in "Sacrifice to Gods," Sieroszewski enjoys detailing the shamanic séance, whose description occupies nine pages, which is almost half of the story. Portraying the Gothic atmosphere of the shamanic divination, the author writes:

> Finally, the shaman slightly trembled and he painfully hiccupped. Trembling and hiccupping gradually increased and turned into real seizing and moaning. Somebody from the audience screamed. An old woman dropped to the ground twisting her body and arching her back. On top of this, a flying black shadow crossed the ground. It was an eagle that soared between the sun and the shaman. Suddenly a piercing scream cut the air. The crowd leaned back like grass pressed by a burst of a wind. Nobody knew who produced the chilling sound, the shaman or the eagle.[97]

The shaman's prophecy divides the natives. The Sel'tichan extended family is ready to fight to save its leader, whereas the rest of the community wants to fulfill the will of the spirits. As in Goldberg's story, the end of "Sacrifice to Gods" is tragic. Despite the protests of his relatives and his own doubts about the sincerity of the shaman, Sel'tichan decides to follow the "law of gods" and publicly stabs himself. When the shaman caringly closes the eyes of the elder with the words "That is how true warriors live and die," the reader is left to guess what actually stirred the human sacrifice. Is it the cunning nature of the shaman? Is it the wicked nature of human beings, who, while in misery, are frequently envious of lucky ones? Or is it the will of the spirits, who want to make sure that in the human world everything is balanced? After all, it does not matter. What matters is the morbid aesthetic of shamanism and the fate of an individual whose life is in the hands of powerful forces that go beyond his or her control.

In passing, I also want to note that one thing struck me about this particular story. Sieroszewski, who all of his exiled life lived among the Sakha natives and hardly encountered any other natives, set the plot of "Sacrifice to Gods" in Tungus (Evenki) country. It is certainly possible that the writer needed to create a popular ethnographic backdrop and, as archetypical Siberian natives, the picturesque Tungus well fit this purpose. Still, there could be another reason. Unlike the stable sedentary and semi-sedentary Sakha, the nomadic Tungus households were more dependent on natural misfortunes. As such, they might have served better to illuminate the major idea that surfaces in the story: the person caught in the grips of powerful natural forces. In this case, the morbid aesthetic of shamanism and the nomadic lifestyles were the forms that helped to better illuminate this line.

At the same time, for other exiled authors, the same shaman-death metaphor could convey an explicit social message. For example, Viktor Vasiliev, who like Sieroszewski did his exile sentence among the Sakha natives, used the idiom of a dying shaman to expose the harmful effects of Russian "civilization" on indigenous peoples, who were rapidly turning into "vanishing natives." In his semifictional essay "Shaman Darkha," which is based on his personal experiences, Vasiliev portrays a Tungus shaman who dies cornered by Christian missionaries.[98] Darkha is a person of tremendous self-sacrifice, using his sacred medicine to help his people. The shaman never refuses to visit the ill, even if they reside far from his home. Although Darkha receives good "fees" for his healing sessions, his vocation does not make him rich. On the contrary, because of the long absences, his household gradually falls apart. On top of everything, his small son dies. Yet Darkha does not complain: "He knew that this was the destiny of all shamans, who were doomed to serve higher forces and constantly interact with spirits, otherworldly beings, for whom worldly pursuits do not matter."

Russian Orthodox missionaries, who try to enforce Christian dogmas on the Tungus, shatter this indigenous landscape. The natives cannot figure out why "people in black robes force them to reject the religion of their ancestors, why they should denounce all spirits and worship only one deity, and to light some 'thick sticks' [candles] and bow to some pictures drawn on boards [icons]." Although clerics confiscate and take away his drum and robe, at first Darkha does not submit. Clansmen make him new paraphernalia and his shamanic powers return. However, fifteen years later, the next encounter with missionaries proves fatal. Although Darkha hides his sacred paraphernalia, this does not help. The clerics find his drum and robe and burn them. The act of burning symbolizes the destruction of shamanic power and indigenous life: "With a hopeless look, old Darkha watched how his things were burning, feeling that along with breaking and warping the skin of his drum, the burning fire was taking away part of his soul, all power of the mighty and glorious shaman who controlled his spirits. What gave sense to his entire life for the past twenty-five years was now passing away."[99] This tragedy breaks the heart of old Darkha, and soon he dies. As someone who himself suffered from the regime, Vasiliev is wholeheartedly sympathetic with the shaman and his faith.

Like the aforementioned exiled writers, Bogoras sampled shamanism and shamans in his ethnographic fiction. In 1902 in the wake of the Jesup expedition, when he was staying in New York City and working on his seminal Chukchi monograph, the anthropologist simultaneously completed his *Eight Tribes*.[100] In a manner similar to Sieroszewski and Goldberg, Bogoras paid attention to the Gothic aspects of shamanism. In fact, in this particular novel, the writer placed the source of shamanic power in a dead corpse, an ethnographic fact he recorded himself.

In *Eight Tribes*, a Chukchi girl named Mami devotes herself to a man she loves. At the same time, Vattan, a shaman's apprentice, wants to win her affection. Unable to charm her, Vattan is ready to commit suicide. Vattuvi, his uncle and teacher, a powerful shaman, talks him out of it and saves the youth by directing him to a strong medicine that works as a love charm. In order to receive this love medicine, at night both the shaman and his apprentice go to a cemetery. Having stripped naked, the uncle and the nephew crawl toward one of the graves on all fours, imitating polar foxes, and dig up a half-decomposed body. Then Vattuvi makes Vattan bite a piece of rotten flesh from the corpse, and they hide it in the young man's medicine bag. Gradually, the medicine begins to radiate love magic. Although the sacred charm proves effective and Mami gives herself to the apprentice, the girl eventually wakes up from the spell. Trying to run away from Vattan, Mami hits her head on a rock and dies. The desperate youth gathers firewood and burns himself and the dead girl in a large pyre.

This ending suggests that Bogoras used the Gothic shamanic setting for a somewhat different goal. Although, like in the case of Sieroszewski and Goldberg, death and dying amid northern landscapes remain an important narrative line in his book, the scholar points to the eventual triumph of humans over morbid spiritual forces. Shrewd and cunning in their creativity, his shamans cannot subdue love driven by its own superior laws—this is the message of the book. With this attitude to indigenous spiritual practitioners, later it would be easier for this ethnographer at first to stamp them as neurotics and then, in Soviet times, to denounce them as parasites that should be eliminated. At this point, we do not part with Bogoras. I will talk more about him and his comrades in the next chapter.

3

Neurotics to Tribal Psychoanalysts

Shamans through the Eyes of Psychology

The shaman is abnormal, neurotic, and epileptic; his functions are based on his abnormal qualities and aggravate these in turn.
—*Encyclopedia of Religion and Ethics* (1920)

The shamanic cure lies on the borderline between our contemporary physical medicine and such psychological therapies as psychoanalysis.

—Claude Lévi-Strauss (1949)

In 1901, sponsored by Franz Boas, Russian ethnographer Waldemar Bogoras, one of the "exiled" ethnographers described in the previous chapter, conducted research among the Chukchi and Yupik natives, the indigenous inhabitants of the northeast of Siberia. Shamanism was an important part of his observations. If we are to believe his accounts, the shamans he encountered were a weird, abnormal, or at least irritable folk. One named Ye'tilin had a nervous tic on his face. Kele'wgi, another spiritual practitioner, once jumped on a Russian merchant with a knife in revenge for unfair trade dealing.

The most memorable was a young shaman named Scratching-Woman, with whom Bogoras maintained ambivalent love-hate and cat-mouse relations. According to Bogoras, this man with elements of behavior that appeared to surrounding people as feminine was irritable to the extreme. The ethnographer had a hard time following his mood swings. Sometimes, Scratching-Woman could be joyful and ready to share the mysteries of his craft with the explorer. At other times, he was cold and aloof, especially when other people were around. For some reason, this lack of desire to converse on spiritual matters in front of other people appeared to the ethnographer as additional evidence of the shaman's nervousness. Scratching-Woman bragged that he could cut himself with a knife and heal the wound in no time. Yet, at the same time, he was sensitive, complaining about pain when the anthropologist tried to apply a plaster to his body. Pressured by Bogoras, Scratching-Woman once reluctantly agreed to perform a shamanic séance. Burning with curiosity, the anthropologist could not resist suddenly lighting a match right in the middle of the ritual, which was supposed to be conducted in total darkness. Furious, Scratching-Woman took away the ethnographer's and his wife's linen that was drying outside. Strangely, the anthropologist ascribed this act of mischievous revenge to the cunning nature of Chukchi spiritual practitioners. On another occasion, Scratching-Woman surprised the scholar by sweating blood. Although Bogoras was convinced that the shaman had played some trick on him, the ethnographer could not figure out how the man did it. When the scholar pressed Scratching-Woman especially hard, the shaman openly mocked Bogoras: "Look at my face. He who tells lies, his tongue stutters. He whose speech, however, flows offhand from his lips, certainly must speak the truth."[1]

Based on his meetings with Scratching-Woman and other indigenous spiritual practitioners, Bogoras came to the following conclusion: "Nervous and highly excitable temperaments are most susceptible to the shamanic call. The shamans among the Chukchi with whom I conversed were as a rule extremely excitable, almost hysterical, and not a few of them were half-crazy. Their cunning in the use of deceit in their art closely resembled the cunning of a lunatic."[2] A year later, the scholar turned to generalizations. He wrote, "Studying shamanism, we encounter, first of all, entire categories of men and women who either suffer from nervous agitation or who are obviously not in [their] right mind or completely insane. It is especially noticeable among women, who are generally more prone to neurosis." The final verdict of the ethnographer on the shamanic vocation sounded as follows: shamanism was a "form of religion that was created through the selection of mentally unstable people."[3]

The Russian anthropologist's description of Chukchi shamans and his generalizations about native spirituality did not pass unnoticed by the outside world. A member of the Russian-American Jesup North Pacific Expedition (1897–1902), Bogoras had his comprehensive ethnography, *The Chukchi*, published in English. That is how the "cunning neurotic" Scratching-Woman became an anthropological classic, the archetype of the arctic shaman. Although Bogoras's insight into the minds of Siberian spiritual practitioners helped to establish the image of the typical shaman, this ethnographer was not the first one to describe shamans as people "on the verge of insanity." When writing his Chukchi monograph, the scholar capitalized on existing Russian writings that already described shamans as neurotics. In many respects, the assessment of shamans as mentally unbalanced people was natural. To the European eye, during their ritual séances, tribal spiritual practitioners manifested unruly behavior or, as nineteenth-century ethnologist John Lubbock put it, worked themselves up into fury.[4] From the end of the nineteenth century through the first half of the twentieth century, writers and academics looked at shamanism through the lens of modern medicine, psychology, and psychiatry. They took it for granted that shamanism represented a culturally sanctioned mental disorder. In order to track the origin of this perception, I will start by exploring the phenomenon called "arctic hysteria."

Arctic Hysteria as Breeding Ground for Shamanism

Eighteenth- and nineteenth-century explorers of Siberia and arctic North America frequently mentioned what appeared to them as extreme nervousness and mental instability of indigenous populations. With a sense of surprise, they described how for no apparent reason some native folk dropped on the ground, arching their backs, singing, or imitating the behavior of others. For example, not infrequently they could observe a woman who, like a zombie, would sit on the ground moving her body back and forth for several hours and murmuring a song. European observers noted that trivial things or movements, such as a sudden exclamation, an unexpected move, a knock, or a bird flying nearby, sometimes easily drove native northerners to what such writers called hysterical fits. To the Western explorers, such scenes looked abnormal. So did incidents of some natives running away to the woods or mountains and remaining there for a few days.

Here is a description of one hysterical fit recorded in 1896 by A. Gedeonov, who lived among the Sakha people in northeastern Siberia:

> It was already late and I decided to go to sleep. Hardly had I closed my eyes than horrible and chilling sounds reached me from a neighboring dwelling. The sounds were rising, so to speak, to a crescendo, their pitch and tempo. Finally, they reached the point when it seemed the chest of the one who was singing would explode. The voice belonged to the woman who was singing in Yakut [Sakha]. At times, she coughed, interrupted her song and resumed it. The power of this horrible singing was increasing. Unable to overcome my fear, I rushed to where the voice was coming from and saw the following picture. On a low bench bed, a woman sat with her hair spread all over her shoulders and chest. Holding her head, she was moving her convulsed body back and forth, left and right like a pendulum. She was sweating heavily, and her chest was rapidly moving. The eyes of the woman were unnaturally wandering around

and large pupils were burning with some dry luster. Occasionally, she interrupted her singing and began to tear apart her clothing, laugh wildly and weep hysterically. The woman's singing, laughing and weeping as well as the appearance of her whole body terrified me so much that I froze in fear. In the meantime, her family acted in a casual manner as if nothing happened and continued their daily chores. They talked, laughed, drank tea, and mended their fishing gear. At that moment, this cold-blooded attitude disturbed me very much. However, a few years later I myself got used to such scenes so much that I slept peacefully accompanied by the hysteric singing of the same woman and in the same dwelling. So I realized that one is capable of adjusting his nerves even to this horrible phenomenon that Russians of the Kolyma River area call shamanism and that the Yakut name menerick.[5]

Note the context in which the common Russian folk, and Gedeonov after them, used the word shamanism. This is one of the keys to my discussion.

Another account that describes similar behavior, but without using the expression shamanism, comes from northern Canada. In 1898, wintering with their ship at Ellesmere Island, the famous polar explorer Robert E. Peary and members of his expedition witnessed an incident that stunned them very much:

> A married woman was taken off with one of these fits in the middle of the night. In a state of perfect nudity, she walked the deck of the ship; then seeking still greater freedom, jumped the rail, on the frozen snow and ice. It was some time before we missed her, and when she was finally discovered, it was at a distance of half-a-mile, where she was still pawing and shouting to the best of her abilities. She was captured and brought back to the ship; and then there commenced a wonderful performance of mimicry in which every conceivable cry of local bird and mammal was reproduced in the throat of Inaloo. The same woman at other times attempts to walk the ceiling of her igloo; needless to say she has never succeeded.[6]

Records like these gave contemporary writers and scholars plenty of material for generalizations about the behavior and character of arctic natives. In 1905, the Danish physician A. Bertelsen surmised that the Inuit of Greenland were predisposed to "impulsiveness, suggestibility, and instability." In a reference book on Eurasian mythology, the Finnish folklore scholar Uno Holmberg casually stated that arctic peoples would seem to be especially inclined to nervous diseases: "The merest trifle scares them, they faint on the slightest provocation or become furious, when they act like maniacs." More recently, in 1972, American psychiatrist Edward Foulks devoted an entire book to the study of this phenomenon that he ascribed to the fact that native northerners did not learn to repress their primary wishes and impulses.[7]

There is no accepted definition in the literature for the aforementioned hysterical behavior, which modern psychiatry explains as a culture-bound syndrome. The most popular term I found is "arctic hysteria." Members of the 1898 Peary polar expedition used the word *pibloktoq*, derived from a distorted Inuit word. Incidentally, modern psychiatric manuals accepted *pibloktoq* as a synonym for arctic hysteria. In the nineteenth and early twentieth centuries, in Russia, some writers called it "Yakut illness" simply because the majority of the accounts of this ailment came from Yakut (Sakha) country in northeastern Siberia. Furthermore, following Siberian native usage, several Russian authors tried to distinguish between so-called regular hysteria and imitation mania described consequently by the Sakha words *menerick* and *emeriak*. The first literally means the "crazy one," while the second is rendered as "the one who agrees."

Ethnographers and explorers also used other tribal definitions in their references to arctic hysteria. For example, describing the imitation mania, the famous student of Evenki (Tungus) shamanism, Sergei Shirokogoroff (1887–1939; see figure 3.1), used the expression "olonism," derived from an Evenki word. However, he did not attach any specific native word to the regular hysteria. Those learned observers who wanted to classify the ailment in the language of positive science used Latin labels. Thus, imitation mania became *chorea imitatoria*, while regular hysteria was cataloged as *hysteria cum demonomania*. For the sake of clarity, in addition to the generic expression arctic hysteria, I will be using *menerick* and *emeriak* because these two words are the most frequently mentioned in ethnographic literature on Siberia. It also appears that arctic hysteria became common public knowledge. At least in late nineteenth-century Siberia, among the Russian and mixed-blood populace, we find a proverbial expression "to marry a woman-hysteric to a *menerick*," which meant to bring together two lousy people who are good for nothing.[8]

Nineteenth-century ethnographers and writers routinely linked arctic hysteria to "female neurosis." Indeed, all ethnographic records inform us that the majority of the hysterics in Siberia and arctic North America were women. These accounts perfectly fit the contemporary Victorian notion that women were emotionally unbalanced people and had a natural tendency for hysteria. In Russia, writers also connected the Siberian ailment to widespread *klikushestvo*, outbursts of a peasant female hysteria in European Russia. Generalizing about hysterical females, many contemporary writers compared them to unruly animals that should be "tamed" and "trapped" to guarantee a successful cure. They prescribed a variety of draconian measures such as applying electricity to the body, administering opium, and bleeding or blistering supplemented by the application of turpentine, mustard, pepper, and strong vinegar. Russian philologist Vladimir Dal', who personally observed a couple of times how "successfully" crude

FIGURE 3.1. Sergei Shirokogoroff, c. 1920. Courtesy Anatoly M. Kuznetsov,
Far Eastern State University, Russia.

Russian peasant folk "cured" *klikushestvo* by publicly flogging affected women,
came to the conclusion that "fear produces a favorable effect on nerves and
brain." In his expert opinion, such "therapy" as flogging could serve as the
best shock cure both for the hysterics of European Russia and for the Siberian
menerick.[9]

One can find the most detailed contemporary description of arctic hysteria
in a book of medical memoirs by physician S. I. Mitskevich. Banished by the
Russian tsarist government to northeastern Siberia, this Marxist revolutionary
and one-time comrade of the infamous Vladimir Lenin, the leader of the Russian
Bolshevik Revolution, did his exile time in the Kolyma River area from 1898
to 1903. In an area devoid of any medical service, local officials appreciated his
skills and appointed Mitskevich the district physician, putting him on official
salary. Thus, unlike many of his comrades, Mitskevich enjoyed relative freedom
of movement. Besides, he married a local Russian girl who had grown up among
the Sakha people, which eased his contacts with the indigenous folk. Attending
to the needs of Russian, Sakha, and mixed-blood patients, Mitskevich had a
chance to observe and record symptoms of arctic hysteria in various localities.

In his book, Mitskevich attempted to construct a picture of how the typical *menerick* hysteria starts and proceeds. In his view, the ailment is usually

triggered by a deep trauma or a misfortune. For example, a woman whose child or husband has died feels sad for several days. She frequently weeps, cannot sleep, and complains about fast heartbeats, headaches, and dizziness. After all this, the physician stresses, the "real" *menerick* hits her; the mind of the woman is blurred, and she begins to experience horrible hallucinations. The woman sees a "devil," a scary person, or some other frightening creature. That is when the patient begins to scream, sing rhythmically, muss her hair, or pound her head on a wall. Then seizures come. The sick one arches her back, a symptom that Mitskevich labeled with the Latin word *opisthotonus*. Finally, her stomach enlarges, which to Mitskevich appeared as "hysterical meteorism." If we are to believe him, during these seizures, the woman frequently demonstrates "lustful postures" and undresses herself.[10]

The second manifestation of arctic hysteria, an imitation mania called by the Sakha word *emeriak*, became a staple ethnographic anecdote from native Siberia. Stories about the Siberian zombie who blindly imitated the movements or voices of nearby people traveled from account to account. Here is how Wenceslas Sieroszewski, a Polish exiled revolutionary turned ethnographer and writer, defined this ailment:

> This disease is something akin to tic and expresses itself in an irresistible inclination to imitate everything that is unusual, surprising and unexpected. Its weak symptoms consist in an unconscious imitation of the heard sounds or calling out the name of the object that has exited the affected one. By means of a gradual irritation, those afflicted with the disease in a higher degree can be brought to an unconscious state during which they lose entire control over themselves and do everything they are told to.[11]

Not infrequently, in northeastern Siberia, Russian travelers entering native dwellings were confused when to the question "What are you doing?" they received in response the same "What are you doing?"[12]

Political exile and writer Z. Schklovsky, while relaxing in a Sakha cabin (yurt) after a long journey, noted the American Indian–like appearance of his host, who had just come back with a fish catch. Being in a romantic mood, he allowed himself to recite loudly from Henry Longfellow's romantic poem *Hiawatha*:

> With hooked fingers,
> Iron-pointed hooked fingers
> Went to draw his nets at morning
> Salmon trout he found a hundred.

To his astonishment, Schklovsky heard somebody behind him repeat the verse. It turned out to be a native *emeriak* woman. Having replicated that verse, she suddenly grabbed a log and attacked the writer's unsuspecting friend, whose spectacles, for some reason, frightened her. After people restrained her, the woman shouted *abas!* (vulva) and began to imitate the movements of those who were in the tent.[13]

The accomplished *emeriak* usually followed any orders and commands they received from people who happened to be nearby. They could easily jump from a roof, breaking their feet. They also could publicly expose themselves or attack somebody with a knife. In the Kolyma area, these imitators frequently became the objects of various crude practical jokes. Local natives and Russians, from small children to the leading people of a town (priests and district police officers), amused themselves by teasing and scaring these poor weaklings. Some people with low self-esteem, in order to reveal how miserable they were, or just to play the role of voluntary clowns, intentionally victimized themselves by playing *emeriak*. As soon as surrounding people noticed a woman was fearful and nervous, they intentionally began to cultivate her imitation behavior until she turned into a full-fledged *emeriak*. Mitskevich described one such potential *emeriak*, a young Tatar woman, a new arrival from European Russia. In a joking manner, she replicated the *emeriak* behavior and, if surprised, exclaimed in Sakha *abas* to the amusement of young men who flirted with her.[14]

As I mentioned, Mitskevich explained both types of arctic hysteria by personal traumas and misfortunes. Of sixteen cases of the ailment that he recorded among Kolyma area women and men, the death of a child or a husband and a serious disease were the most common causes that ignited the bizarre behavior. For example, a native Sakha, Innokentii Taishin, one of these patients, was depressed about his long-lasting syphilis. He began to sing "in a hysterical manner" and soon turned into a *menerick*. When Taishin felt better, his *menerick* symptoms disappeared.[15] It is reasonable to suggest that as the most vulnerable segment of the population, Siberian native women were the first candidates for arctic hysteria. This might explain why relatively few males suffered from this ailment.

Scholars still did not come to agreement about the causes of arctic hysteria. As often happens, the syndrome might be a combination of many factors. The most common and plausible explanation is that the severe northern environment with its cold, lengthy winter darkness and scarcity of food might have triggered such unusual behavior. For example, the explorers who resided among the Inuit people commonly noted a general gloom and depression that increased in the fall season. These moods were especially aggravated in October, during the last weeks of sunlight before people were plunged into the darkness of polar night. Poor hunting enhanced the general melancholy. Dr. Frederick Cook, who spent some time with the Inuit of northern Greenland in the early twentieth century, noted that depression crawled in as the sun waned and disappeared: "The Eskimo unconsciously felt the grim hand of want, of starvation, which means death, upon them." Hence, there was obviously an ecological context for arctic hysteria.[16]

As a Marxist, Mitskevich also linked arctic hysteria to the material conditions of natives, which does make sense. For example, he observed that arctic hysteria was more widespread among impoverished, mixed-blood northern Kolyma people than among the relatively well-to-do Sakha population in southern Kolyma.[17] It is notable that in addition to Mitskevich, both Bogoras and V. I. Jochelson noted the absence of the ailment among the reindeer Chukchi.[18] With their vast reindeer herds and away from the Russian colonial administration, these nomadic pastoralists of the Siberian tundra enjoyed relative prosperity. Such status set them apart from their impoverished indigenous and Russian neighbors residing in the Kolyma River area.[19] In the meantime, all three observers point to the Kolyma River area as the core center of the bizarre behavior. Each year, the Kolyma area inhabitants were haunted by bouts of famine which they treated as an unavoidable evil. In fact, in the 1870s and 1880s, the bands of Chukchi reindeer breeders regularly visited Kolyma settlements, helping starving Russians and mixed-blood folk. Russian authorities officially acknowledged this charity by awarding several Chukchi chiefs imperial medals.

Later scholars also cited nutritional problems as a possible cause. For example, anthropologist Anthony Wallace argued that the whole matter was the lack of vitamins in the diet of native northerners: the low-calcium diet plus the low vitamin D3 synthesis during the dark winter months. Finally, one can suggest that in some cases the hysteria also had something to do with venereal diseases, which were widespread in the Kolyma area, the area that provided the greater part of available accounts of arctic hysteria. It is known that, in its late stage, syphilis causes organic brain disorders, which lead to mental problems and erratic behavior. A good example is the above-mentioned Sakha native Taishin, whom Mitskevich diagnosed as suffering from depression. It is notable that there are no records of arctic hysteria among the current native populations of Siberia and Alaska, who have better diets and access to supplements and medicine.

In the course of her research, the early twentieth-century anthropologist Marie Antoinette Czaplicka found that the odd behavior observers recorded in northern areas could also be found in tropical areas, for example, in the Malay peninsula. Hence, to hold the arctic climate totally responsible for the hysteria was not correct. Still, she did not want to part with environmental determinism. To find an answer, Czaplicka speculated about the influence of extreme climates on people's behavior. Viewed from this angle, hysteria became not the product of the polar cold and night but the result of extreme climates or, as Czaplicka put it, the "hysteria of climatic extremes."[20] In other words, some Siberians "went crazy" because they have extremely cold weather, whereas some Malay people did the same because of the extreme heat. Deep inside, she probably sensed that her interpretation could be an unwarranted speculation. To her credit, Czaplicka came up with a reasonable suggestion: before labeling that unusual behavior as pathology, it would be better to ask the indigenous people themselves what they had to say about their own hysterical fits.[21]

Sergei Shirokogoroff, the famous student of Evenki and Manchu shamanism, began to pose this question to his native acquaintances in southern Siberia. While Czaplicka was putting together her *Aboriginal Siberia* (1914) in England, he and his wife were doing fieldwork among the Evenki people. A cultural relativist, Shirokogoroff dismissed as European fallacies the ecological and economic explanations of the hysteria. What appeared to Westerners as abnormal and bizarre, this ethnographer pointed out, was perfectly normal behavior in the context of the indigenous culture. Speaking against the "medicalization" of arctic hysteria, Shirokogoroff interpreted the fits, many of which he frequently observed himself, as coded messages. In his view, hysterics wanted to convey to the members of their communities important information, hidden wishes, desires, and fears that were not appropriate to reveal in public. Evenki people could not simply expose themselves in front of a whole community, stressed Shirokogoroff. For this reason, they routinely wrapped intimate information in the language of the fit performances. Therefore, concluded the ethnographer, the fit was a convenient form in which to dramatize their fears, expectations, or sentiments. The sudden change in behavior, such as arching the back, dropping on the ground, or convulsing accompanied by singing, immediately drew the attention of a community's members.

Surrounding people usually understood very well the symbolic body and sound language of such unusual performances, stressed the scholar. For example, a girl wanted to marry her beloved one, but circumstances were against the marriage. As a way out, she could turn to a hysterical fit. In the course of her performance, the girl sent signals to the community about her hidden desires. In fact, adds the scholar, such a fit could well be staged in advance through a process of self-excitement, during which the person imagined himself or herself "miserable," the type of behavior that brings to mind a European temper tantrum rather than hysteria.[22]

People who engaged in such hysterical behavior, observed the scholar, never hurt themselves during their seizures. The anthropologist noticed that hysterics frequently opened one or the other eye, watching the effect of their behavior on audiences. Shirokogoroff claimed that the acts of hysteria were always collective events, never performed in solitude. The scholar stressed that although the natives acted their fits, for fellow community members, they were not simply performers but individuals visited by spirits. Criticizing contemporary scholars and writers who, like Mitskevich, viewed arctic hysteria as a disease, the anthropologist suggested that Europeans accept what natives themselves thought about such fits. Since the latter usually referred to the odd behavior as a habit or a custom, Shirokogoroff concluded that arctic hysteria had nothing to do with mental illness.

Physician D. A. Kytmanov, who explored the Evenki natives ten years after Shirokogoroff, confirmed the culture-bound nature of arctic hysteria. In his
essay "Functional Neuroses among the Tungus and Their Relation to Shamanism," he noted that, though erratic and meaningless to the European eye,
the incomprehensible songs of hysterics, their chopped words and phrases
sent meaningful messages to native communities. Kytmanov also drew attention to a striking similarity in body postures of all hysterics he personally
observed. It appeared to him that Evenki *menerick* hysterics followed certain
established blueprints even in minor details. In the beginning, they usually
situated themselves in a traditional position, squatting on the ground. In this
state, they began to vigorously rock back and forth and to sing. The physician
added that the people could stay in this condition for hours. When the hysterics
were tired of singing and swinging, they simply dropped back and lay quietly,
pretending they were asleep, and only occasionally murmuring something.
After the fit was over, all hysterics behaved as if they did not understand what
happened to them.[23]

Some accounts of those who tended to link the native hysteria to the mental state of Siberian natives in fact confirmed what Shirokogoroff said about the
Evenki's hysterics. For example, Jochelson, who was not sure if arctic hysteria
were an illness or autosuggestion, reported an event that he personally witnessed. Once during his field trip, Jochelson stayed in a Sakha house along
with another Russian, a young man who was exiled to Siberia as a common
criminal. Though married, their native hostess became fond of the young man.
When the youth left, she experienced a fit, singing an improvised song that
made her feelings explicit:

> The friend with testicles like wings!
> The stranger-friend from the South, from Yakutsk!
> The friend with supple joints,
> With the handsome face and nice mind!
> I met a friend who is very alert!
> I will never part with him, the friend![24]

In the presence of her husband and children, the woman kept on chanting this
verse for about two hours before she fell asleep. Generalizing about this incident, Jochelson concluded that the event had nothing do with hysteria and
ascribed it to the voice of her subconscious.

Not only individuals but also occasionally entire native bands were caught
in the throes of *menerick* and *emeriak*. The most famous collective frenzy took
place at the turn of the twentieth century in the Upper Kolyma River area
among the Yukagir, impoverished nomads and hunters who were frequently
abused by both Russians and their native neighbors. In the summer of 1899, a
band of the Yukagir came to the Upper Kolyma town and pitched their camp,
intending to purchase salt, lead, and powder. At night, a group of Russian

drunkards suddenly broke into a tent, frightening a Yukagir family. In response, several natives turned to bizarre singing and dancing that quickly
evolved into full-fledged *menerick* behavior. Although the drunks soon left the
camp, the collective fit not only did not stop but also expanded, involving other
members of the band.

Soon one-third of the two hundred Yukagir went "crazy," hopping, dancing, and singing. Some people jumped into the river and stayed there until
their "sane" neighbors dragged them out. Others attacked nearby people with
knives and axes. One old woman was seriously injured during the incident.
Even a few Sakha natives who happened to be staying nearby caught this
malady. The frenzy lasted for four months and then gradually subsided. Yet,
the next summer, the epidemic resurfaced, disabled half of the Yukagir, and
again subsided in the fall. Jochelson adds to this story an important element:
the people who were first to go crazy were several young Yukagir girls, who
uttered "savage sounds," tore their clothes, tried to drown themselves, and
climbed tall larch trees, hiding amid their upper branches.[25] Although the accounts do not tell us exactly what prompted the girls to go *menerick*, one can
assume that one spark that ignited this craze was an attempt of the Russian
drunks to take advantage of them.

Another incident of a collective craze concerned a group of native males
who went *emeriak*. Recorded by the Russian psychiatrist Kashin in 1868, it
became a favorite ethnographic tale that was included in many books on indigenous Siberia and shamanism. Incidentally, Kashin was the one who attached to the *emeriak* disease the Latin label *chorea imitatoria*. The physician
tells us that in the Trans Baikal area, a Russian officer once drilled a para-
military Cossack detachment composed of newly selected Buryat and Evenki
servicemen. Suddenly, instead of responding to the commands of the officer,
the indigenous recruits began to imitate his commands and gestures collectively. When the angry officer began to scream at the natives, they continued to
imitate his shouts.[26] As in the case of the Yukagir natives, this collective craze
could have been a spontaneous psychological defense culturally sanctioned in
the tradition of those indigenous communities.

These two cases of collective frenzy suggest another possible cause for
arctic hysteria: resistance to colonial hegemony. In modern scholarship, when
academics more often than not hold the West responsible for various social
and psychological issues faced by non-Western people, this interpretation becomes popular. Although it is hard to reach definitive conclusions, one may
make an educated guess that, for example, the 1899 collective outburst of
menerick among the Yukagir was an act of symbolic resistance. Witnesses noted
that many Yukagir caught in the seizure were singing in Chukchi, although
nobody in that particular area spoke this language. Since the reindeer Chukchi
enjoyed a quasi-sovereign status and relative economic prosperity within the
Russian empire, to their impoverished and downgraded native neighbors, they

might have represented a symbol of freedom. This might explain the strange singing in the alien language.

The most recent version of the thesis about arctic hysteria as a resistance to colonial hegemony was articulated by Canadian anthropologist Lyle Dick. He examined the link between the presence of the 1898–1909 Peary polar expeditions and the cases of arctic hysteria among the Inuit of Ellesmere Island in northern Canada at the turn of the twentieth century. Dick found that incidents of arctic hysteria sharply increased in the areas visited by the members of the expedition who interfered with the life of the Inuit people. For his exploratory purposes, Peary separated families, placing his Inuit guides and workers under unbearable pressure. Thus, four-fifths of the reported episodes of arctic hysteria happened after natives were removed from their familiar environments or after the separation of families. Moreover, Peary tolerated and in some cases gave license to his companions to coerce indigenous females into sexual relations. Dick suggests that such a practice prompted these women to turn to the bizarre behavior as a psychological defense. The worst case of arctic hysteria took place at Cape Sheridan during Peary's last journey in 1908–1909. That winter, five of the twenty native women Peary encountered went crazy. Therefore, it is reasonable to suggest that at Cape Sheridan, in addition to existing seasonal stresses, the uneven power relations and the sexual abuse aggravated the arctic hysteria.[27]

What Dick has to say about arctic hysteria in northern Canada is also relevant to Siberia. Siberian sources suggest that hysteria was more widespread in the areas where mixed-blood and native populations were impoverished or occupied subjugated status. One example is the Kolyma River area populated by mixed-bloods, political and criminal exiles, and several impoverished native bands. Moreover, the region was one of the centers of the tsarist exile system, where people of influence, usually a district police chief, a Cossack, or a priest, enjoyed absolute power.[28] Travelers' accounts frequently note the extreme fear that the indigenous folk felt toward any officials. Sometimes this fear reached pathological proportions, when natives hid from Russians who appeared to be officials.

In the early 1870s, in Sredne-Kolymsk town, a district police officer developed a habit of crude entertainment for himself. He enjoyed suddenly grabbing local young women from behind and tickling them under their armpits. Nobody dared to challenge this man of power. The officer got used to his "practical jokes" so much that soon almost half of the young women in the town turned either to the imitation mania or to prolonged hysterical laughing. It is notable that the Russian-speaking mixed-blood population of the town called this behavior "shamanizing." Although to the nineteenth-century writer who recorded this episode the whole incident appeared to be an example of an "unintentional hypnosis," it was clearly a psychological reaction to the abusive behavior of the person who was the literal master in this desolate town. One more fact points out that it was a psychological defense. When another police officer in full uniform came to the town for a short visit and then left, the number of hysterical women sharply dropped.[29] At the turn of the twentieth century in the same town, there was another character, the priest Vasilii Berezhnov, who became infamous for his offensive treatment of *emeriak* women. Local women complained to Mitskevich that the priest drove them to fainting fits with his "jokes."[30] The described incidents suggest that there might have been an element of symbolic gender resistance in the acts of the Sredne-Kolymsk females.

The Kolyma area furnished the major part of Siberian records about arctic hysteria. Let us take a closer look at Kolyma country, which appears from ethnographic records to be the center of arctic hysteria. This huge and sparsely populated area, nearly the size of France, lies beyond the Arctic Circle and has the coldest winter temperatures in the world. In the eyes of the Russian tsarist regime, the climatic conditions of Kolyma made it a perfect place for the banishment of political opponents, a practice that was introduced on a wide scale in the 1870s. The isolation and severe conditions set this area apart from the rest of Siberia, which overall is not exactly a nice place to live. The deadliest months, especially for newcomers, are December and January, when the sun does not rise and the temperature fluctuates between −40 and −60 degrees Celsius. Early travelers reported that during the coldest weeks, the locals hibernated, laying all day in their dwellings to conserve energy.

At the turn of the twentieth century, the Kolyma area was the northern part of the Yakutsk district and accommodated only about 6,000 people (see figure 3.2). These were mostly Sakha natives, people of a mixed Russian-native origin, and several Yukagir bands who had lost their reindeer. Annual famine was a routine event. Gedeonov, one of those unfortunate people relegated to this area, described his experiences as a literal nightmare: "To the present day my memory flashes the pictures of life in this depressing land devoid of any hope, the land without past and future. Here mind activities stop and feelings are frozen. Even suffering is gone. What remains is a painful melancholy, so quiet and haunting that one loses any desire to get rid of it." Trying to convey better the idea of the Kolyma landscape, another exile quoted Lord Byron's "Darkness": "Herbless, treeless, manless, lifeless—a lump of death."[31] This was the tundra "lump of death" where Bogoras and the other exiled ethnographers mentioned in chapter 2 did their time.

What I am trying to suggest here is that in their writings, the exiled writers, who themselves most certainly were depressed by the northern landscapes, extended the effect of long and grim arctic winter seasons to the natives. At least, their works show that they indulged in generalizations about the depression, moodiness, irritability, and nervousness of northern natives. In their view, all these factors created a fertile ground for such unusual behavior as hysteria and shamanism. Discussing the character of Sakha

FIGURE 3.2. Map of the Yakutsk district. Quoting Lord Byron, exiled writer Z. Schk-lovsky described the area as "herbless, treeless, manless, lifeless—a lump of death." Z. Schklovsky, *In the Far North-East Siberia* (London: Macmillan, 1916), map appendix.

natives, among whom he spent his exile years, a Polish revolutionary turned ethnographer, N. A. Vitashevskii, portrayed them as people who were nervous literally from cradle to grave. In contrast to their "civilized" counterparts, Sakha children were more "capricious," women were more "quarrelsome," men were more irritable, and old men and women were more "grumpy." Besides, the Sakha in general appeared to him as people who lacked self-control and who were very impatient.[32]

In 1924, his compatriot Stanislaus Novakovsky, who later became a geographer in the United States, took the trouble to summarize all available exiles' accounts of *histeria Siberica*, another Latin name he attached to arctic hysteria. Since many of these records clearly pointed to the landscape and climate as the causes of the fits, he took this interpretation for granted. Novakovsky's article, which was published in the American magazine *Ecology*, was not a small factor in shaping Western perceptions of native Siberia. In addition to rendering the elements usually mentioned in the exiles' writings, such as the polar climate, the monotony of the environment, the poverty of life, and "lack of impressions," Novakovsky painted a generic picture of indigenous northerners' lifestyle as a vicious circle of perpetual mental stresses.

Severe winter, he said, the major source of the hysterical behavior, "strangled man's soul." However, the spring does not bring any relief whatsoever; the drastic transition from one season to another creates conditions in which human souls "find no rest." Neither does summer pacify the native mind and body. During this short warm season, noted the geographer, when living beings are in a hurry to copulate before it gets too cold, native north-erners cannot pursue amorous activities in a normal relaxed pace as people usually do in the West. Paying tribute to popular psychoanalysis, he speculated that this seasonal pressure makes the indigenous folk suffer from extreme sexual anxiety, which weakens their nervous systems. Besides experiencing the sexual tensions, during the short summer, natives have to work night and day, feverishly preparing their winter supplies, wearing out their bodies. As a result, as one might have already guessed, there is "psychic exhaustion" that leads to hysterical fits.[33] Many contemporary students of northern societies took for granted the portrait of native Siberia that Novakovsky drew in his paper. For those who wrote about native northerners, the severe arctic landscapes and arctic hysteria became the backdrops against which they frequently assessed Siberian indigenous cultures.

"Institutionalized Madhouse for Primitives":
Shamanism as Mental Disorder

In 1880, explaining to his readers the meaning of *menerick* (one of the Siberian indigenous words that was used to describe arctic hysteria), the Russian phi-lologist Dal' wrote, "*Menerick* is the one who is possessed by the devil, and the one who shouts, wriggles, rages and usually imitates the voice of some animal. *Menerick* are especially widespread in Siberia and, according to some experts, are related to pagan shamans."[34]

This utterance by the linguist, who was always eager to catch existing usage, clearly shows that by his time, the connection between arctic hysteria and indigenous spirituality was acquiring the status of scholarly truth. Given the established perception that the severe weather made native northerners nervous and agitated, it was easy to conclude that shamans with their ecstatic rituals operated in the same pathological realm. To many contemporary ob-servers, especially to those who were short-time visitors, the bizarre bodily movements and ritual manipulations of the native spiritual practitioners were little different from arctic hysteria. Several authors directly suggested that sha-mans imitated the behavior of the hysterics and simply perfected the art of natural insanity to a professional level. Others added that, by their awesome séances, shamans, who were usually influential communal leaders, sanctioned abnormal behavior in the eyes of the surrounding natives and therefore ag-gravated arctic hysteria.

Consider, for instance, the description of a Sakha shamanic session made by the exiled ethnographer V. L. Priklonskii. The whole scene clearly petrified him and prompted him to speculate about its detrimental effects on the minds of native audiences:

It is hard to say something definitive about the mental state of an audience during the mystery ceremony. I could not read anything special on their faces. Still, about myself I can say that I whole-heartedly wished that the mystery session would be over as soon as possible. Imagine the whole atmosphere one has to deal with: a small cabin with a blazing fire, the fanatic who runs back and forth, two specially selected strong fellows who hardly can keep him from dropping in the fire in his ecstasy or at least from hitting his head, all these wild howling shouts. I doubt that even a person with strong nerves can stand this.[35]

If such long-time explorers as Priklonskii did not venture to look into native cultures for possible explanations of the odd behavior of shamans, short-time superficial observers, who had no time or desire to look into native ethnography, never thought twice about linking arctic hysteria and shamanism. Thus, P. Riabkov, who produced a popular essay on Siberian geography and population in 1882, claimed that Siberian natives suffering from *chorea imitatoria* were shamans. He also used a peculiar expression, "shaman-*menerick*," which implied a direct connection between native insanity and spirituality. In all fairness, this writer openly admitted that he did not know much about arctic hysteria and the religious life of the natives.[36]

The polar explorer Peary was the same type of short-time observer who did not distinguish between a spiritual ritual and arctic hysteria. Once, in 1900, during one of his Canadian arctic journeys, he even disrupted an Inuit shamanic séance for an ailing person, thinking that he dealt again with one of the "Eskimo's" hysterical fits.[37] To European explorers, the intensive fall and winter ritual activities of shamans, who sought to ease the seasonal pressure on the human psyche, hardly differed from outbursts of hysteria that they frequently observed among other natives. Overall, in the minds of many contemporary writers and scholars, the northern landscapes and arctic hysteria clearly became the breeding ground for shamanism.

The earliest elaborate physiological and pathological explanation of shamanic behavior I found is the work of Russian physician M. F. Krivoshapkin (1865). In his notes on the Tungus (Evenki), he stressed that shamanism is an ailment akin to so-called female hysteria, which this writer defined as "hysterical demonomania [*hysteria cum demonomania*]."[38] Still, such perception did not become dominant until the turn of the twentieth century, when the writings of Sieroszewski, Priklonskii, Bogoras, Jochelson, and their exiled comrades firmly established the image of the shaman as a mentally troubled polar magician. By the turn of the twentieth century, observers concluded that shamanism and the hysterical behavior of native northerners were somehow linked together. In any case, they believed that both originated from the severe northern environment that, in their view, naturally bred abnormal personalities. This notion eventually entered all encyclopedias and reference works.

I have a strong suspicion that in linking shamanic behavior to the inhospitable Siberian environment, the exiles and other observers of Siberia, for that matter, not only paid tribute to the contemporary geographical determinism but also might have spilled their own experiences into the ethnographies they produced. Indeed, relegated from the university centers of European Russia to the tundra and taiga forest "desert," devoid of their familiar intellectual climate, and frequently short of even such common items as pencils and paper, these involuntary anthropologists definitely did not feel at home amid the northern wilderness. One can easily detect these gloomy sentiments in exiles' descriptions of Siberian landscapes and native populations.

They are present, for example, in the writings of Priklonskii. The writer singled out the frozen tundra terrain as the force that shapes native spiritual life. Vast and devoid of vegetation, noted this exile, the tundra landscape unavoidably makes an individual feel lonely, grouchy, and irritable. Feeling forgotten by everybody in this desolate land, continued the writer, Siberian natives develop self-absorbed, contemplative personalities prone to mystery and spiritualism. Describing a typical individual from the Sakha, among whom Priklonskii spent his exile years, the ethnographer wrote, "He is always alone with his own thoughts. No wonder that his psychological life is very strained and his fantasy flourishes. He seeks mysterious and mystical experiences. Shamans are the people who fully satisfy these expectations."[39]

N. A. Vitashevskii, his exiled comrade and another writer, devoted a special paper to exploring the connection among the northern environment, "arctic hysteria [menerick]," and indigenous spirituality. Characteristically titled "Toward Primal Psychoneurosis" (1911), this essay argued that during their séances, shamans either imitate the hysterical behavior or directly turn into hysterics. In his view, native apprentices who learn shamanism actually learn to reproduce the arctic hysteria behavior. At the dawn of their history, generalized Vitashevskii, people existed in a state of "total hysteria." Later, at the stage of "advanced shamanism," the hysterical behavior became a monopoly of particular individuals who turned arctic hysteria into a ritual vocation.[40]

A few decades later, anthropologists Paul Radin and Weston La Barre generalized along the same lines about the origin of shamanism. The only difference was that these later scholars replaced the northern environment as the source of shamanic behavior with the general insecurities and dangers of primal living. It is also notable that Vitashevskii believed that the shamanic vocation sprang up from a desire of spiritual practitioners to cure themselves of the mental ailments rampant in primal societies. Their séances reminded him of the behavior of the hysteric who cried out his or her anxiety. In this particular generalization, one can detect the rudiments of the "healed healer" concept, one of the interpretations of shamanism that later became popular in the West.

In his general essay on Evenki ethnography (1922), anthropologist Konstantin Rychkov made an attempt to round out this and other contemporary observations on shamanism as a manifestation of neurosis. We learn from him that shamans, "all of them, without any exception," suffer from hysteria. During their séances, wrote the scholar, shamans reach the "highest level of convulsions," lose consciousness, and rave. He assessed this behavior and the content of shamans' chants as the products of their unbalanced minds. He even wrapped his conclusions in the language of contemporary medical science: the shamanic rituals are the "results of an improper brain function under the effect of shattered nerves."[41]

What also enhanced the perception of shamanism as an offshoot of arctic hysteria was the habit of unlettered Russians and mixed-blood inhabitants in Siberia of frequently calling arctic hysteria "shamanhood" or "shamanizing." For example, about a woman caught in the grips of her hysterical fit, the Kolyma mixed-blood folk would say, "She is shamanizing."[42] Incidentally, unlike the newcomers, native populations never confused spiritual practitioners' vocations and mental ailments, describing them by separate words. Thus, the Sakha natives clearly distinguished between the hysterics, who in their eyes were people possessed and tortured by spirits, and shamans, who called their spirits at will. Contemporary writers, who occasionally did mention this distinction, nevertheless preferred to follow the local Russian usage. A good example is A. Gedeonov, who so colorfully described his horrific encounter with the *menerick* Sakha women. In his 1896 essay for a popular Russian magazine, Gedeonov in passing mentioned that indigenous people never used the expression "shamanizing" to describe "mind ailments." At the same time, he applied this very word to describe arctic hysteria when discussing "fits of shamanism" and "shamanizing women."[43]

While stressing that the Sakha distinguished between mind ailments and the spiritual vocation, physician Mitskevich did the same thing, linking the behavior of the shaman to *menerick*. His rationale for drawing such a connection was simple: "[local] Russians directly say that the sick people suffering from *menerick* fits are 'shamanizing' people." "The picture of ecstasy" in the shamanic séance and the fits of *menerick* patients appeared to him to be identical: "the same rhythms of songs, the same torso movements, the same seizures that follow the ecstasy and the same state of depression and melancholy after the fit." Having linked arctic hysteria and shamanism, the physician admitted that he actually never saw a shaman in his life and noted that he based his generalizations on "what other people say."[44]

The most curious part of his book was a chart that listed fourteen hysterical female patients from the Sakha village of Rodchevo. In addition to their ages and names, the chart mentioned diagnoses. Thus, we learn that among these women, there were twelve patients diagnosed with *menerik*, six with *emeriak*, one with "slight fits," and one with shamanism.[45] Even Jochelson, who, as a self-taught anthropologist, was more knowledgeable about native cultures, put *menerik* people and candidates for the shamanic profession into the same group, calling them "patients."[46] Responding to such assertions, Shirokogoroff, the famous student of shamanism, pointed out that they were "rather a reaction of observers than of natives of these regions." Moreover, he could not resist making an ironic note. Shirokogoroff particularly remarked that to such ethnographers, all Siberian landscapes surely looked abnormal, simply because as Europeans they were accustomed to sunshine, moderate temperatures, city noise, a variety of scenery in the streets, theaters, and good food in restaurants.[47] For the person with money who happened to come to Siberia on his own as a voluntary ethnographer, it might be a cruel remark to make, but it was straight to the point.

Until the beginning of the twentieth century, the generalizations produced by exiled ethnographers about the pathological nature of the shamanic vocation mostly remained within the realm of Russian ethnography. With the publication of the Bogoras and Jochelson ethnographies in English, these assertions entered Western scholarship, where they perfectly merged with popular contemporary psychological theories. The introduction of the exiles' ethnographies into Western scholarship was eased by such summaries as *Aboriginal Siberia* (1914) by the British anthropologist of Polish origin Marie Czaplicka and *Studien zum Problem des Schamanismus* (1939) by a historian of religions from Sweden, Åke Ohlmarks.[48] Both books represent not only good digests of Bogoras, Jochelson, Priklonskii, Vitashevskii, and their comrades, but they also incorporate the ethnographies of Potanin, Anuchin, Ksenofontov, and other Siberian regionalist writers and works of Finnish ethnographers and folklore scholars. Moreover, Ohlmarks links the Siberian materials to native North American ethnology.

Like the exiled ethnographers, in her earlier works, Czaplicka stressed the detrimental influence of cold weather, darkness, and scarcity of food on the social and religious life of Siberian northerners. She, too, at first believed that these factors made native Siberians prone to introspective thinking, hysteria, revelations, divination, and "sexual perversions." The latter could be her reference to the transvestite Chukchi shamans she read about in the Bogoras *Chukchi* book. In her major work, *Aboriginal Siberia*, Czaplicka similarly stated that arctic hysteria lies at the root of the shaman's vocation. However, careful reading of this book reveals that she was not as crude in her assertions as exiled authors or, for example, Ohlmarks, whose scholarship I will discuss below.

For example, Czaplicka stressed that shamans differ from the ordinary hysterical patients, who cannot control the spiritual forces that attack them. Elsewhere, she wrote that pathology is not the essential feature of shamans. However, on the next page, she said that indigenous spiritual practitioners might be pathological personalities.[49] Czaplicka might have sensed that such labels as "pathological" and "normal," which Bogoras, Jochelson, and many other contemporary writers used in discussing native religions, are culture-bound labels. She pointed out that what Westerners viewed as a pathological behavior, from the viewpoint of natives could appear to be normal and vice versa. Although Czaplicka was still an armchair scholar when she was writing her book, she was perceptive enough to figure out that to pile together the ritual activities of the shaman and arctic hysteria did not say anything about the social role of the spiritual practitioner. In one chapter of *Aboriginal Siberia*, she even suggested that for explanations of Siberian indigenous spirituality, one might have to turn to sociology rather than to geography or medical pathology.

In all fairness, she did not articulate her reservations clearly and simply preferred to sample existing ethnographic assessments. It would be better to say that her interpretation of shamanism was inconsistent and ambivalent. I have the impression that those contemporaries who did not read her book carefully or did not pay too much attention to the nuances captured the connection that appeared from the literature Czaplicka reviewed: severe environment = arctic hysteria = shamanism. No wonder Nora Chadwick, an English folklore scholar who was among the first to try to cleanse shamanism from pathological interpretations, criticized Czaplicka for linking shamanism to arctic hysteria, which, strictly speaking, the latter never did.

Unlike Czaplicka, Ohlmarks, the author of the second ethnographic summary, had no reservations about the pathological nature of shamanism. The essence of shamanism appeared to him as the "great hysterical attack which ends with cataleptic collapse, partly the arctic delirium of persecution and spirit-hallucination." In his book, Ohlmarks insisted that "classic" shamanism was a peculiar northern phenomenon developed by "abnormal psychotic individuals" in Siberia and arctic North America. He was convinced that "the great shamanism" could only arise in the severe polar climate with its hysteria-inducing environment. To make his point even more clearly, the scholar attached maps that highlighted the distribution of arctic hysteria in Siberia and North America, with their northernmost areas shown as the zones of the extreme forms of shamanism.

His argument is very simple. In the northernmost tundra areas, weather conditions are most severe. Therefore, in this region, shamanism appears in its pure form, reaching the extreme ecstasy. Farther to the south, the climate is milder, which affects shamanic rituals. Since southern Siberian and subarctic North American spiritual practitioners lack powerful stressors such as polar weather, by default they are devoid of the "psychic abnormality of the great shaman." In order to dramatize their spiritual journeys and maintain the high level of their ecstasy, contended the scholar, the southern shamans have to rely on such supplementary ritual tools as sacred plants (fly agaric mushroom, tobacco, and alcohol) or prolonged drumming and masked dancing. To

Ohlmarks, the only positive social contribution of shamans was the masochistic channeling of collective insanity into their rituals. Drawing on the works of Bogoras, Priklonskii, and Vitashevskii, the scholar viewed indigenous northern societies infected with neurosis and hysteria as fertile human material for the shamanic vocation.[50]

The picture of the development of shamanism he drew in his book was also an ethnographic caricature that mirrored the contemporary Victorian views of women. The fact that the majority of northern hysterics were females, while shamans were people of both genders, gave Ohlmarks an opportunity to pepper his generalizations about the evolution of shamanism with heavily patriarchal sentiments. With their weak, soft, and emotional personalities, asserted the scholar, women only created the precursor of shamanism (arctic hysteria), whereas males actually put these uncontrolled emotions into the language of powerful dramatic performances (shamanic vocation). The majority of the native women, argued Ohlmarks, were doomed to remain "closet shamans"— ordinary arctic hysterics who were unable to regulate their fits. At one point, Ohlmarks exclaimed, "They and only they [males] could raise their stronger mind out of the hysteroid background to the psychically rescuing great shamanic action." If women were good at something, he remarked, it was only in low types of witchcraft, occasional fortune telling, charms, and divination sessions. Ohlmarks insisted that one could rarely find women in the classic shamanism of the polar people, which is simply not true. Contrary to existing ethnographic materials, he also speculated that females either dominated the shamanic vocation or shared it with males in subarctic areas, where the classic shamanism was blurred and corrupted by a milder climate.[51] In all fairness, Ohlmarks only articulated and sharpened the existing intellectual sentiments disseminated in contemporary Russian and Western writings about Siberian and northern indigenous societies.

For Western scholars, the books by Bogoras, Jochelson, Czaplicka, and Ohlmarks that placed the mentally troubled personality of the indigenous spiritual practitioner at the center of debates about shamanism became the major sources for Western scholars of shamanism. In the wake of their works, anthropologists took it for granted that true shamanism was a psychopathological phenomenon related to hysteria.[52] Gradually, the thesis about the mental deviance of tribal spiritual practitioners in northern areas became an established scholarly "truth" and remained dominant throughout the first half of the twentieth century. Such an approach clearly downplayed the social, cultural, and spiritual contexts responsible for the reproduction of shamanic behavior. In the eyes of many scholars, as anthropologist I. M. Lewis metaphorically put it, shamanism became "an institutionalized madhouse for primitives."[53] The most popular diagnoses that scholars issued to shamans were hysteria, neurosis, epilepsy, and schizophrenia. Even those writers who felt that such assessments were superficial agreed that shamanism was a convenient niche for mentally disturbed individuals who experienced problems adjusting to the social life of their communities.

Referring to the Bogoras ethnography, one of the leading American ethnologists, Robert Lowie, defined the shaman as a "neurotic" who represented a "pathological case." In his popular work on the origin of primal religions, Paul Radin stressed that throughout Siberia, the mental instability of spiritual practitioners assumes "pathological proportions." Having read the Czaplicka and Bogoras books, this scholar argued that shamans in this area originated from people suffering from the *menerick* disease.[54]

Interestingly, to explain shamans' pathological behavior, Radin replaced the severe environmental conditions with social and economic circumstances. Mentally unstable people, asserted the anthropologist, best of all reflected the pain, deprivations, and material insecurity so characteristic of the life of primal societies. In their performances, shamans reenacted for the common folk the "drama of man's perpetual struggle for security," the struggle that was always centered on stepping into the unknown and mysterious. Radin wrote, "The neurotic behavior, and the contents of the neurotic-epileptoid consciousness of the shaman thus became representative of the world which the normal man accepted because he himself was conscious of these contrasts in his own life." Overall, the shamanic vocation, stressed the anthropologist, became a niche for neurotic individuals, who were free to select apprentices of the same abnormal caliber. That is how, historically, the blueprints of abnormal behavior became fixed as a religious culture, which later spiritual practitioners, both normal and neurotic, had to emulate to be qualified for the shamanic profession.[55]

In his comprehensive book on the origin of religion, another anthropologist, Weston La Barre, similarly relied on Bogoras and Czaplicka and, like Radin, pointed out that, originally, shamans were recruited from the ranks of the most skilled mentally ill individuals. Interestingly, La Barre also extensively used ethnographic materials collected by Shirokogoroff but never mentioned the critical attitude of this ethnographer to the "shamanism as hysteria" thesis. La Barre believed that all religions in the world started with ecstatic and paranoid self-appointed people who were the best candidates to mirror popular spiritual aspirations. Later, the "normal" folk who aspired to enter the profession had to replicate the ritual practices established by these primal shamans with abnormal psyches.[56]

"Little Hans Totemist": Psychoanalysis and the Shaman

The view of the shamanic vocation as pathology was heavily intertwined with psychoanalysis, which was popular in Western intellectual culture throughout the first half of the twentieth century. The perception of shamanism as a culturally sanctioned insanity perfectly fit the perspective of Sigmund Freud, who believed that religion was nothing less than a form of neurosis or obsession that originated from a sense of infantile helplessness. Such a view of religion originated from his general conception of civilization as neurosis, which is the price humanity has to pay for separating itself from the animal world. Viewed through the prism of classical psychoanalysis, shamanism appears as a social institution that tribal people use to symbolically channel their collective or individual anxieties, primarily of a sexual nature.

Freud's theory of the dream was the cornerstone of the psychoanalytic approach to shamanism. To the psychoanalyst, the fantastic imagery the shaman saw during séances and initiations was the equivalent of a dream experience. In this case, the shamanic séance was a collective analogue to an individual dream. Very much like an individual who spilled his or her concerns and fears into dreams, tribal hunting and gathering societies mirrored their permanent anxieties and insecurities in shamanic sessions—collective dreams. Amid menacing primal landscapes filled with natural calamities, famine, illness, and constant intertribal warfare, shamans symbolically helped to ease tensions and fears. Dreaming together with their shaman and channeling their anxieties into the ecstatic spiritual session, the sick, the starving, and the frightened found at least a temporary solution to their problems.[57]

Psychoanalytically oriented scholars frequently handicapped themselves by sorting their materials to fit particular Freudian clichés and metaphors, the natural fate of all popular ideas. For example, the anthropologist La Barre approached shamans as the paranoid fathers (mothers were ignored for some reason) who protected their communities from supernatural assault. As such, the spiritual practitioners were parental figures to the "frightened and the infantilized." Yet psychologically, added the researcher, shamans themselves resembled children who did not separate themselves from the world and who, through ritual play, hoped to change the world. Overall, in La Barre's view, the shaman acted as a "little Hans totemist" (a reference to one of Freud's classic metaphors), demonstrating "basic infantile and paranoid unmanhood."[58]

In one of his works, Geza Roheim, a Hungarian-American psychoanalyst and folklore scholar, sifted the existing literature on Hungarian, Siberian, and North American shamanisms searching for erotic elements. In his interpretation, the iron pikes, staves, and bullhorns used by Siberian shamans in their performances became symbolic penises, while various openings, passages, and entrances mentioned in the texts of shamanic invocations acquired vaginal characteristics. The scholar certainly could not pass by such direct sexual allusions as large wooden phalluses carved by some Altaian shamans in Siberia, who squeezed them between their legs during annual fertility performances. The analyst also tied the descriptions of shamanic spiritual journeys to other realities to so-called flying dreams. Freud viewed the latter as erection dreams, in which the human body symbolized the penis.[59] In a similar manner, flights of shamanic souls and their penetration into other worlds as well as the intrusion of spirits into the bodies of patients appeared to psychoanalytic scholars as metaphors for intercourse.

A Swiss psychoanalyst, the Reverend Oskar Pfister, attempted one of the first comprehensive discussions of shamanism from the Freudian perspective in 1932. The scholar became intrigued with an ethnographic documentary, *The Mountain Chant* (1928), produced by the American artist and southwestern regionalist writer Laura Adams Armer. The film detailed a Navajo (Dine) healing session that was centered on the use of sand painting, interpretation of dreams, memory backtracking, and communal healing. The movie struck him as full of metaphors that begged to be put into the language of psychoanalysis. Hence, the pastor decided to write a special paper on *The Mountain Chant* as an example of American Indians' "intuitive psychoanalysis."

The major character of the movie, a fifty-year-old Indian, had a terrifying dream in which his children were dead. Remembering that many Native American cultures took dreams as actual experiences in another reality, one could assume how depressed this person was after receiving that message. A spiritual practitioner informed the father that he was to find a shaman-chanter who would sing for him the Mountain Chant to correct the misfortune that had happened in the other world. Finally, the Indian found a chanter, who in turn revealed that when the Indian was a small boy, he probably had seen a sick or dead bear. The chanter also suggested that his patient have one of the Mountain Chants performed to appease the sacred bear. The whole clan came to help with the healing session, which started with the purification of the participants in a sweatlodge and continued for nine days. During these days, under the direction of the healer, male participants made colored sand paintings. After a daily ritual of magic songs, the paintings were destroyed, and their colored sands were poured on the patient. Finally, on the last day, almost two thousand Dine gathered around the patient and his family to sing the concluding verses of the Mountain Chant. After this, the patient recovered from his depression.

The psychoanalytic interpretation of the healing session by Pfister went as follows. The bear symbolized the father of the patient. The Indian, when he was a child, wished his father were dead. Now, when the patient himself became an adult, he began to fear that his own children wanted him to die. Pfister made another assumption: the dream in which the Indian saw his children dead was an unconscious retaliation against his own children. The healing ritual that was to pacify the spirit of the bear became a symbolic reconciliation with the patient's father. The major tools of the symbolic reconciliation were the shaman, who directed the ritual, the community, and the mythology of the tribe.[60]

A modern scholar who can serve as an example of the classical Freudian approach to shamanism is the ethnopsychiatrist George Devereux In the 1930s, he conducted field research among the Mojave Indians of California and eventually defended a dissertation on their sexual life. Based on this and subsequent research, in 1969 Devereux published a book that examined various pathologies of the Mojave personality; shamanism was one of them. Viewing shamans as psychotics who used ritual sessions to save themselves, Devereux insisted that from a psychiatric point of view, shamanism was a "neurotic defense." He was convinced that by rewarding shamans for their fantasizing and erratic behavior, tribal society only prolonged their mental ailments in latent form. Therefore, shamanism appeared to him not as a cure but as a lingering illness. His overall diagnosis of the shamans sounded as follows: "The Mojave shaman of either sex is to be diagnosed either as a borderline case, or else as an outright psychotic." Devereux was so persistent in his thesis about the insanity of tribal shamans that he dismissed as fallacies all views of shamanism that differed from his own. Moreover, he took on those colleagues who wanted to "give the shaman a clean bill of psychological health."[61] Such a radical psychiatric explanation of shamanism eventually prompted Devereux to cast entire native groups that permitted and culturally sanctioned such unbalanced behavior as shamanism as sick societies that bred delirious individuals.

To Devereux, the most convincing fact that shamanism was not good as a permanent curative solution was the ambivalent nature of shamanic power that could easily turn from spiritual healing into spiritual killing with numerous grave consequences to shamans. It is true that in many tribal and pre-industrial communities, the respect enjoyed by spiritual practitioners can easily turn into suspicion and hatred if the shamans' healing sessions or predictions go wrong. Still, these attitudes hardly differ from public attitudes toward mainstream Western physicians, who live under the similar fear of making a professional mistake and becoming the objects of malpractice suits. As for Mojave society, it usually labeled those spiritual doctors who made mistakes as "witches" and pressured them to commit suicide.

His thesis about shamanism as culturally sanctioned insanity notwithstanding, Devereux was good at capturing the dark side of shamanism, which might be a useful antidote for present spiritual seekers who concentrate their attention almost exclusively on the benevolent side of indigenous spirituality. Numerous native oral testimonies the scholar collected show a thin line separating "good" and "bad" shamans. The ambivalent folk attitudes toward shamans and their shaky status in so-called traditional communities might have originated from ambivalent attitudes toward spiritual power, which, in tribal society, is neutral and can go either way. This contrasts with the ironclad Judeo-Christian division between good and evil powers.

No spiritual practitioner in Mojave society felt safe. They were always open to various accusations. For example, if shamans lost several patients in a row or were not skillful enough to predict or cause expected weather changes or to secure hunting luck, the tribal masses could quickly declare them malicious witches. Devereux stressed, "Every shaman is viewed as a potential source of danger, since he can both cause and cure the illness over which he has control. Hence, not even a shaman who has an untarnished reputation as a healer is safe from sudden accusations of witchcraft."[62] No wonder that not many Mojave wished to embrace the vocation of the shaman. Devereux informed us that, psychologically, the candidates for this dangerous vocation were trapped in a double bind. The individuals chosen by spirits to become practicing shamans ran a risk that their powers might go wrong, which would lead to accusations of witchcraft and possible death. At the same time, if the candidates refused to accept the shamanic vocation, the pressure from the unused medicine power could drive them insane.

Several Mojave shared with Devereux stories about how, for no apparent reason, shamans who did no harm to surrounding people suddenly became objects of communal persecution simply because some members of communities ascribed their misfortunes to the evil intentions of spiritual practitioners. As mentioned above, the helpless victims of these accusations frequently turned to suicide as a way out of the situation. Hivsu, one of Devereux's informants, grimly noted, "In times of old I would not have lived this long (56 years). They would have killed me long before this. Shamans seldom lived to a ripe old age. But I would have become a shaman all the same. I could not have helped it." One poor man pressured by his community came to believe that he had bewitched several people. Eventually, the shaman killed himself by purposely lying outside in freezing weather and contracting pneumonia.[63]

I wonder to what extent the Indian stories recorded by Devereux in the 1930s could be considered the descriptions of old and traditional perceptions of shamans. It is common knowledge that, unlike the present-day mainstream culture, in the 1930s Euro-American society demonized indigenous spiritual practitioners. At that time, many Native Americans, as people subjugated by this society, could easily pick up such public sentiments. Furthermore, Indian land dispossession and the cultural assault on native traditions could have undermined the authority and prestige of shamans, whom the common Indian folk might have held responsible for the inability to find a good cure for the pains they felt. This situation was not uncommon for many other tribal societies that had to cope with the rapid advance of Western civilization. At the end of the nineteenth century, several indigenous groups in California began crusading against their shamans, blaming them for all kinds of social and individual misfortunes and occasionally murdering them. The grim observations on the fate of many Mojave spiritual practitioners recorded by Devereux might have reflected the negative stance developed among the Indians in modern times.

For example, among the Miwok Indians, the Mojave's neighbors, there was literally a mass native assault on tribal spiritual practitioners. The Indians hunted down and exterminated shamans, especially those who lost their patients. In 1880, to avoid a fatal end, one poor fellow had to run about three hundred miles from his community and hide in a mountain canyon in the Yosemite Valley.[64] The interviews Devereux conducted with Mojave elders showed that in the 1930s, some individuals who had received shamanic powers in their dreams preferred to go insane by rejecting these powers rather than expose themselves to the hazards of the shamanic occupation. Once Devereux approached a Mojave woman who, as people told him, was nervous in her behavior, which the community interpreted as the manifestation of shamanic powers. The scared woman, in whom the ethnopsychiatrist hoped to find a "budding" shamaness, sent him away with the words, "It is not true at all! I only have a temper."[65]

One of the last prominent students of shamanism steeped in the psychoanalytic tradition was Gerardo Reichel-Dolmatoff (1912–1994). To avoid the perils of Nazism and World War II, this Austrian archaeologist moved to Colombia. In his new homeland, he turned to anthropology and became famous for his studies of the spiritual practices of Amazonian Indians, which were centered on the use of herbal hallucinogens. Reichel-Dolmatoff believed that shamans worked in the realm of the collective unconscious. In his view, they and their patients ingested herbal hallucinogens to unleash the hidden fears and desires of the patients in the form of colorful visions. To him, these visions were simply diagnostic tools, which were couched in the language of religion to unpack the individual and group unconscious.[66]

Although now hardly anyone in shamanism studies remembers psychoanalytic scholars such as Roheim or Devereux, Reichel-Dolmatoff's writings continue to enjoy popularity. The reason is his studies of the ritual use of psychotropic herbs. In the 1960s and early 1970s, this latter aspect of his research drew attention from the American anthropological community. As a result, in the 1970s, for a number of years, Reichel-Dolmatoff worked as a visiting professor at the University of California at Los Angeles (UCLA), which at that time was one of the centers of research in altered states of consciousness.

The major flaw of the psychoanalytic and behaviorist approaches to religion in general is a conviction that humans are exclusively rational beings. From this perspective, all spiritual experiences appear as either pathology or illusion. Instead of looking into the social, cultural, or spiritual role shamans performed for their communities, scholars and writers who medicalized shamanism centered their discussions on the minds of tribal spiritual practitioners. In this scholarship, there was certainly no room for exploring tribal spirituality on its own terms.

To my knowledge, now that psychoanalysis has been driven out from mainstream humanities and social sciences, no scholar approaches shamanism in the classic Freudian style, searching for sexual symbolism. Writers and scholars whose interpretations one can somehow link to psychoanalysis now usually prefer to work within the tradition of the analytical psychology of Carl Gustav Jung (1875–1961). The scholarship of this wayward Swiss disciple of Freud, which merges science and spirituality, is devoid of Freudian positivism. Jung did not attract much attention until the 1960s, when the Western countercultural community rediscovered his writings, which contained a strong antimodern message. Currently, Jung occupies a prominent place in the mind, body, and spirit community, including the practitioners and students of experiential shamanism. Challenging Freud, this Swiss scholar not only dismissed the sexual determinism of his senior colleague, but also argued that in addition to individual unconsciousness, there were archetypes of unconsciousness common to all people. Jung called them the collective unconscious. Introducing this metaphor, the analyst retained the language of modern psychology and, at the same time, effectively parted with the materialist approach of his predecessor by opening a door to the recognition of the spiritual and the sacred.

Sergei Shirokogoroff: The "Psychomental Complex" of Tungus Shamans

One of the few who sought to part with the dominant clinical view of tribal spiritual practitioners while remaining within the realm of the popular psychological approach was Russian ethnographer Shirokogoroff. His scholarship, particularly *Psychomental Complex of the Tungus* (1935), had a profound effect on shamanism studies in the West after the 1960s. Almost all general works on shamanism now mention his name. However, during his time, this ethnographer was a lonely figure among the contemporary students of shamanism. It was not only because Shirokogoroff spent much of his scholarly career in immigrant neighborhoods of Kharbin, China, on the periphery of Western intellectual culture. The chief reason was that his ideas did not fit the format of mainstream scholarship.

In his attempt to grasp the essence of non-Western traditions, Shirokogoroff advocated "insight" and "intuition" as the way of doing ethnography and stressed that "our positive science" did not help much in the anthropological enterprise.[67] Such an intellectual stance might appeal to current students of tribal spirituality who similarly doubt the ability of Western rationalist scholarship to grasp the lifeways of non-Western cultures, but it certainly did not appeal to the representatives of positive science in the 1920s and the 1930s.

Shirokogoroff was also among the first to question the role of an ethnographic field observer, an issue that troubles so much of current anthropology. Thus, he frequently alerted his readers about the manner in which Western ethnographies portrayed the life of non-Western others and warned about numerous Eurocentric biases, which, like mine fields, threatened anthropologists no matter which direction they went. The scholar stressed that to take contemporary ethnographic descriptions of tribal people as "objective" descriptions of "native life" would be naive. Even about the exiled ethnographers, some of whom spent long years among indigenous peoples, the scholar correctly wrote that they suffered from the "superior civilization" complex.

Trained in France as a philologist, Shirokogoroff returned to Russia, where he affiliated himself with the St. Petersburg Ethnographic Museum (Kűnst-kamera). After the First World War, he also worked for a while at the Russian FarEastern University in Vladivostok. However, he spent the most productive years of his career in China, where he moved in 1922. In addition to his interest in Siberian archaeology, indigenous languages, and the Tungus (Evenki) and Manchu spiritualities, the scholar reflected on ethnicity and culture in general. Striving to grasp what makes people an ethnic group (he called it "psycho-mental complex"), Shirokogoroff sought to penetrate the soul and spirit of people he observed. In his generalizations about the ethnic complex, the scholar assumed that human ethnicity was rooted in organic life and human biology. Occasionally, he lapsed into talk about "inborn conditions."

At the same time, he never held human biology to be completely responsible for ethnic behavior and preferred to talk about culturally conditioned behavior.[68] The above-mentioned factors played a significant role in the development of his theory of ethnicity. The scholar approached the latter as an organic entity that went through a stage of high spiritual vitality and then disintegrated in a rationalist decline. Viewed in this context, his negative stance toward the "decadent" and "rationalist" West and sympathies to the rise of the "organic" and "vital" Nazi Germany, sentiments that Shirokogoroff expressed in his 1930s correspondence with a German colleague, Wilhelm Mülmann, should not surprise us.[69]

The linguistic background the scholar acquired during his training in France made him a keen learner of the languages of the people he explored. Shirokogoroff correctly stressed that many bizarre ethnographic stories about tribal peoples and their shamans in particular originated not only in the commitment of Westerners to positive science but also in a simple communication gap. In his time, researchers frequently did not bother to go beyond the basics of the language of a group they came to study and preferred to work through interpreters. Bogoras and Jochelson were not exceptions to this. To help rid himself of the Eurocentric complex and gain insight into Evenki culture, Shirokogoroff studied their language intensively.

Around 1910, Wilhelm Radloff, director of the St. Petersburg Ethnographic Museum, first stirred Shirokogoroff's interest in exploring this group of natives. Radloff suggested that Shirokogoroff turn his attention to either the Evenki, the Samoed (Nentsy), or the Manchu. Eventually, Shirokogoroff chose the first group; the Manchu began to occupy his research later, when he moved to China. Although the Evenki were the most romanticized community of

Siberian natives, nobody had seriously explored their culture. Thus, in 1912, blessed by Radloff, Shirokogoroff departed for the Trans Baikal area in southern Siberia on his first anthropological expedition. The scholar obviously never suffered from a money shortage, for he financed this field trip entirely from his own pocket. His wife, Elizabeth Robinson, was a constant companion and fellow researcher in this and all subsequent expeditions. Working as a team allowed the spouses to probe for male and female perspectives of native cultures they encountered.

At the same time, like many contemporary ethnographers, the Shirokogoroffs were on a quest for samples of traditional indigenous culture. In his reminiscences of their first expedition, Shirokogoroff did not hide that, traveling among sedentary Evenki communities assimilated by the Russians or the neighboring Buryat, he was irritated at first because he was unable to find "pure traditional Tungus." Eventually, in their search for the genuine primitives, the spouses penetrated the depth of the Siberian taiga forest, crossing the Yablonevyi mountain range. Here they finally met several families of traditional reindeer nomads. They returned to the area the next year and for five months wandered with these nomads, gathering ethnographic information and perfecting their language skills. Eventually, Shirokogoroff acquired a fluency in the language that allowed him not only to converse with local shamans, but also to record in detail their "manipulations and methods."[70]

In 1915, during another expedition to the Evenki, who resided near the Mongol border, a wild frontier area, the spouses were accompanied by native guides who turned out to be two local bandits. Although throughout the whole trip, the ethnographers were not exactly sure about their own security, Shirokogoroff was pleasantly surprised that one of them "acted as a little shaman." In the end, Shirokogoroff felt lucky because the two men freely fed him with their own valuable ethnographic information and procured it from other natives. Still, to his frustration, the scholar observed that even in that desolate area, nomadic life was losing its traditional appearance. With disgust, the explorer discovered in a tent of a Tungus chief a gramophone, bottles of Cognac de Martell and champagne, and other, as he put it, "unnecessary objects" that spoiled the primal landscape.[71] Moreover, local shamans freely assimilated Russian saints into their spiritual pantheon.

Like many of his anthropology colleagues at that time, he felt uncomfortable about such corruption of the native culture. Still, the ethnographer eventually overcame this discomfort by following a principle he defined for himself—to accept native culture on its own terms—and it worked well for his scholarship. For example, in his later writings, discussing alien "intrusions" into indigenous beliefs, Shirokogoroff did not search for blueprints of pure and archaic shamanism. Instead, he reasonably surmised that, by its nature, shamanism was an open, eclectic system that accommodated spirits from whatever source they might appear.

During the same year, Shirokogoroff ventured farther southward, to Manchu country, where he impressed local folk with his vast knowledge of the shamanic rituals that he had learned from the Evenki and that he was ready to share with his new hosts. As a result, as the scholar wrote, "I became a kind of specialist, very appreciated among the Manchus, and was elected—a very rare occurrence—into the jury to elect a new shaman."[72] Exchanges of information with Manchu spiritual practitioners immediately opened to the scholar a door to the "Manchu sancta sanctorum," an unlimited access to their sacred knowledge. In a word, Shirokogoroff practiced what today's anthropologists call the participant-observation method.

In the early 1920s, correctly assuming that the psychomental complex of Red Russia would not be the right environment for an intellectual, he made a conscious decision to settle in the Chinese port city of Kharbin. At that time, the city had a vibrant Russian émigré community. Shirokogoroff's subsequent field research naturally shifted southward from the Evenki to the Manchu. *Psychomental Complex of the Tungus*, his seminal book, brings together his earlier ethnographic research in southern Siberia between 1912 and 1917 and some comparative materials on the Manchu culture he observed in the 1920s in northern China. Half of this book deals directly with shamanism.

To Shirokogoroff, Evenki shamanism is not something ancient and archaic. What the scholar meant by shamanism was a mix of local indigenous beliefs and elements of Buddhism that the Evenki people acquired from the Mongols and the Manchu people. He dated the emergence of Evenki shamanism at the eleventh century. The scholar, who observed many Buddhist influences on Evenki culture, subscribed to the Indian connection in Siberian shamanism, at least as applied to southern Siberia. Moreover, he fully shared the views of his Romantic predecessors that the Evenki shaman and Sanskrit *sramana* originated from the same Indian source. Moreover, with his linguist friend N. D. Mironov, Shirokogoroff coauthored a special article in which he defended the "honor" of the *sramana*-shaman interpretation.[73]

At the same time, the scholar avoided crude assessments of his intellectual predecessors, who considered the entire shamanism phenomenon a corrupted form of classical Buddhism that migrated northward. Shirokogoroff preferred to present Evenki shamanism as stimulated by Buddhism and did not extend his generalizations to other indigenous Siberian groups. The scholar pointed out that part of the Evenki shamanic pantheon and some items of their shamans' paraphernalia came from the Buddhist tradition. Thus, Evenki shamans honored images of snakes, which were absent in the Siberian landscape. In their rituals, the spiritual practitioners also appeased a group of spirits called *fuchi*, which originated from the Buddhist pantheon, and used ritual mirrors that came from the same tradition. More questionable were Shirokogoroff's attempts to trace Siberian shaman drums to Tibetan Buddhist musical instruments, and the Evenki shamanic trance to ancient Indian asceticism. Also questionable were his speculative linguistic insights into the shaky link sramana-shaman. In these cases, the Russian émigré ethnographer spoke more as an early nineteenth-century Romantic scholar.

In reference to his concept of southern Siberian shamanism stimulated by Buddhism, it might be more appropriate to say that Shirokogoroff drew attention to the fluid nature of shamanism that readily assimilated alien spirits, no matter from where they came. In addition to the Oriental connection in Evenki shamanism, the scholar also identified Russian Orthodox elements borrowed by the natives.[74] Essentially, the scholar tried to show that shamanism was not a primal religion but a constantly changing mode of thought, natural philosophy, and natural medical practice. As such, it was very eclectic and could freely exist along with other world religions.

Exploring Evenki spirituality, the scholar followed the firm dictum—to accept cultures strictly on their own terms. Following this intellectual stance, Shirokogoroff accepted the reality of native spirits not because he believed in them but simply because the indigenous population he worked with believed in their existence. At the same time, unlike some current experiential scholars, he never went so far as to convert himself to the native spiritual realm. What set Shirokogoroff apart from his contemporary colleagues was his complete dismissal of the popular scholarly notion about the pathological nature of shamanism. He was very critical of the authors who lumped together arctic hysteria, shamanism, and routine mental ailments. Shirokogoroff looked at the works of such writers as the "ethnographic reactions of Europeans" to the cultures of non-Western people and as attempts to cater to the dominant intellectual and cultural sentiments.

The scholar stressed that tribal others suffered from mental ailments no more and no less than people in Western societies. To him, what European observers frequently treated as examples of individual or mass polar psychosis, a breeding ground for shamanic ecstasy, in reality represented culturally sanctioned behavior that sent specific signals to the members of a community. Still, he left unanswered the question of why communities sanctioned these particular types of behavior and not others. Reviewing numerous cases of native hysteria, Shirokogoroff stressed that, in each case, it was a particular message addressed to nearby people.

While the regular hysteria appeared to the scholar to be a meaningful message, the emeriak imitation practice (he called it olonism) served well to discharge pathological energy that might have accumulated in the social life of a community. Shirokogoroff himself observed acts of the imitation mania, usually performed by particular individuals who, the scholar thought, willingly adopted this role. In his book, Shirokogoroff related several incidents when natives intentionally provoked the imitation behavior just, as the ethnographer implied, to let people relax and have a good laugh.

Once the scholar sat in company with an Evenki who was known for this type of behavior and who was eating porridge. Another Evenki, who was sitting nearby, suddenly began to produce movements as if he were rapidly stuffing the food in his mouth. The *emeriak* immediately began to stuff his own mouth with actual food, imitating the behavior of his neighbor. Finally, when he was about to choke, the *emeriak* "woke up" and ran away, accompanied by the laughs of his friends. Later, the scholar carefully observed a knee and eye reflexes of the hysteric and concluded that the man was normal.

A few times, as a practical joke, Evenki friends exposed Shirokogoroff to acts of public masturbation performed by an *emeriak*, who in other respects similarly appeared to be a normal person. One of the men would move his hand as if masturbating in front of this person. In response, the *emeriak* would pull out his penis and immediately produce an erection "to the great satisfaction of all present men and especially women," Shirokogoroff informed us.[75] The ethnographer insisted that, as crude as it may be, in small communities isolated in the taiga forest, such odd behavior "introduces a joyful element of variety" in the life of natives.

Two observations forced Shirokogoroff to change his view of arctic hysteria. First, he noticed that only adult people performed the acts of imitation madness. Somehow, children and old folk did not suffer from this ailment. Second, he saw that when Evenki experienced troubles or crises, all kinds of hysteria were absent from their communities. The ethnographer stressed that when haunted by a famine or epidemic diseases, strangely, natives never went crazy. Instead, they mobilized all their efforts to overcome the crisis. In contrast, as Shirokogoroff observed, hysteria was aggravated when people lived their routine lives in relative comfort. Thus, he noticed that running away to the woods was more popular during the seasons when it was not very dangerous for a person to stay in the wild for several days without food and fire. All these observations went against the contemporary scholarly arguments, which treated native hysteria as pathology.

Essentially, the ethnographer accepted the explanations the Evenki themselves attached to this type of behavior: custom and habit. As a result, the scholar concluded that hysteria was an element of culture rather than a medical pathology. To make the point, Shirokogoroff compared native abnormal behavior with European youngsters' craze to hide in storerooms, cold attics, or restrooms. The ethnographer also sarcastically hinted that to the indigenous peoples of Siberia, such established Western practices as nudism, sexually explicit cabaret dances, or the ecstatic frenzy of left-wing progressive movements, which captivated millions of Westerners in his time, could equally appear to be pathological.[76] This comment would have certainly been a sound observation if he had added to this list of contemporary Western hysteria the Nazi movement, but he never did.

Shirokogoroff believed that the most efficient way of resolving various social and psychological problems in native society was shamanism. To him, native spiritual practitioners were powerful healers who cemented their communities and created order from chaos. The portrait of the shaman the Russian émigré ethnographer drew was of a tribal hero, the backbone of a community, without whom this community fell apart. Later, historian of religion Mircea Eliade incorporated this view of tribal spiritual practitioners in his famous book *Le Chamanisme et les techniques archaiques de l'extase* (1951).

Essentially, Shirokogoroff turned the contemporary pathological approach to shamanism upside down. Where such ethnographers as Bogoras and Ohlmarks saw neurotic tribal magicians who mirrored existing pathologies in their extreme, Shirokogoroff saw heroes who, using the power of minds and spirits, through ritual performances, drained negative pathological energy from their communities. He wrote that the spiritual practitioners acted as "a kind of safety valve" for native societies and as a "necessary biological self-defense of their social organization."[77] Thus, Shirokogoroff stressed that, in case culturally sanctioned hysteria went out of control, shamans could step in to balance the communal behavior. In contrast, those Evenki communities which, for some reason, did not have a shaman, risked descent into complete anarchy.[78] After losing a shaman, they immediately began searching for another one, noted the ethnographer.

Repeatedly stressing that shamans were healthy, the scholar refused to view them either as insane or as projections of collective phobias. Neither did he treat them as the products of an inhospitable environment. His approach to the famous shamanic illness accompanied by seizures, delirium, and other painful mental and physical experiences was the same as to arctic hysteria—a customary behavior that native cultures required of would-be spiritual practitioners. At the same time, he did not explain why native societies prioritized this particular form of behavior. Instead, Shirokogoroff spoke about the social and therapeutic role of spiritual practitioners in their communities, which placed his scholarship closer to modern shamanism studies.

As if anticipating the currently popular nature spirituality sentiments, Shirokogoroff pointed to the practical importance of shamanism, which he assessed as the best self-curing method naturally discovered by the indigenous peoples of Siberia. He also noted that the way European society treated people with "psychic and nervous maladies" left them essentially uncured, while "among the Tungus all these persons would be cured by the shaman's hypnotic influence and would return to their normal activity."[79] Later, in the 1960s, humanistic psychologists used such theses as Shirokogoroff's to revise the concept of mental illness. In 1967, Julian Silverman, one of these scholars and at one point the head of the Esalen Institute, relied on this particular assertion to draw attention to shamanism as a form of spiritual therapy.

Although Shirokogoroff's approach to shamanism occupied a marginal place in contemporary scholarship, there were a few scholars who articulated views similar to his, although from different perspectives. In Britain, folklore scholar Nora Chadwick spoke against the perception of the tribal spiritual practitioners as hysterics. In her now nearly forgotten book *Poetry and Prophecy* (1942), she wrote about the elements of poetic inspiration in primitive trances. Chadwick approached shamans as the "leading intellectuals and creative artists" of primal societies. She pointed out that shamans perfectly controlled their ecstasy and knew exactly what they were doing during their séances, which pointed to their mental health. Incidentally, Chadwick was among the first to introduce the expression "ecstasy" in references to spiritual trances, the usage that Eliade later picked up for his shamanism book. Repeating Shirokogoroff almost verbatim, the folklore scholar stressed that, in addition to incredible creativity, tribal spiritual practitioners manifested tremendous self-discipline, self-control, and strong will. Overall, shamanism appeared to her as "the most democratic of all religions."[80]

Chadwick was also among the first to cast the characters from ancient Nordic folklore against classic Siberian shamanism, a practice that is popular among current shamanism practitioners in the West. She wrote about Odin as the "divine shaman" of the Norse pantheon and stressed that "his affinities are to be sought in northern Asia." In a similar manner, "the cloak of the Irish poets and seers" reminded her of the costumes of the Siberian shamans. Finally, yet importantly, the scholar correctly noted that many of the earlier observations about shamans prioritized male spiritual practitioners and downplayed the role of shamanesses, which certainly betrayed the patriarchal sentiments of contemporary observers.[81]

Even in Soviet Russia, where an ideological crusade against shamans did not become a mandatory political campaign until 1929, some approaches to shamanism resembled the one practiced by Shirokogoroff. The ambivalent Soviet cultural environment of the 1920s was filled with relative pluralism and various social experiments, which today one can describe as countercultural. Intellectuals still could introduce ideas colored in a primitive aesthetic, and ethnographers could travel and collect tales of shamanism. Incidentally, ethnographers gathered much of the most valuable information on Siberian shamanism during that decade.

This might explain the fact that, in contrast to his view of shamanism as an environmentally conditioned insanity, in the 1920s, Bogoras switched to relativism in discussing tribal beliefs. The scholar suddenly began to argue that the shamanic spiritual realm, including flights to heavenly spheres, visions, and dreams, was simply another way of seeing the surrounding world, which was no better and no worse than Western positive knowledge. To support his new argument, the anthropologist employed Albert Einstein's theory of relativity that, at that time, was coming into fashion. In his book *Einstein and Religion* (1923), he quite plausibly suggested that in the context of the Einstein theory, one could treat dreams, spirits, and myths as simply another dimension that could be as real as ordinary reality.[82]

Bogoras stressed that dream experiences played an essential role in the life of tribal people. With passion and wit, he criticized those colleagues who argued that dreams were temporary delusions. He pointed out that those who approached dreaming as a delusion, by default might as well stamp entire non-Western nature religions as insanity, which did not make sense. Since, for people from tribal societies, dreams represented a reality, so be it, concluded this former advocate of the "shamanism as neurosis" theory.[83] The conclusion the scholar drew at the end of his book sounded like one taken from post-modernist experiential anthropology: "phenomena from religious worlds essentially do not differ from other phenomena, both subjective and objective. They have their own dimensions, their own time and represent their own realm, which is independent from our earthly system."[84]

In his new book, one did not see the neurotic Scratching-Woman and other mentally disturbed shamans from his earlier writings. Instead, Bogoras introduced his readers to several "unsolved mysteries" in order to show the power of indigenous shamans. He related a story about his encounter with a Yupik shaman from St. Lawrence Island, Alaska. This old spiritual practitioner, named Assunarak, exposed the Russian anthropologist to a séance accompanied by a miracle that the scholar still could not explain in rational terms. To his credit, he did not try to explain it, following his new relativistic stance.

The shaman covered himself with a red blanket that belonged to the scholar and told Bogoras to hold it tightly. The ethnographer did try to hold it tightly, bracing himself against the frame of the skin dwelling (*chum*), but the rascal was crawling away from him, easily dragging behind both the scholar and the rest of the dwelling along with all its household items. Soon the shaman raised and twisted the entire frame of the *chum*. Skin covers fell, and utensils, plates, and other household items also dropped on the ground with noise, followed by a bucket of water that produced a loud splash. When the scholar loosened his grip, the old shaman resurfaced from under this mess with a giggling remark, "Now, the blanket is mine." Bogoras looked around and noticed with amazement that the dwelling, the plates, the utensils, and the bucket of water were all in order.[85] Being unable to rationalize this incident, the scholar suggested that the best way to deal with such paranormal phenomena was to reconcile oneself to the idea that the metaphysical reality of nature religions did exist according to its own laws. In this realm, he added, tribal folk apparently did tame their spirits as circus people tamed lions and tigers.[86]

Humanistic Scholarship Revisits Shamanism

In addition to Shirokogoroff, one can see the seeds of changing attitudes toward the shamanic vocation in the work of the American medical historian Erwin Ackerknecht. As early as 1943, he criticized scholars and scientists for assessing shamans as pathological personalities. At the same time, not wishing to part with the medicalization of spiritual practitioners in nature religions, the scholar offered an interpretation of the shaman as a healed healer. Ackerknecht argued that shamans were not individuals suffering from nervous diseases but were, in fact, the ones who healed themselves from these diseases. As such, shamans were ideal healers who could better respond to the needs of their patients.[87]

The major change of scholarly attitudes to the spiritual practices in nature religions happened after the famous French anthropologist Claude Lévi-Strauss came up with his landmark articles "Sorcerer and His Magic" (1949) and "Effectiveness of Symbols" (1949), which were reprinted in his seminal *Anthropologie structurale* (1958). Lévi-Strauss portrayed shamans in a favorable light as spiritual practitioners who successfully used symbolic healing (placebo effect) to cure members of their communities. Still remaining within the realm of psychoanalysis, he nevertheless turned upside down the Freudian view of shamans. In contrast to earlier scholars, who had diagnosed shamans as patients suffering from various mental ailments, Lévi-Strauss approached their vocation as a tribal analogue of Western psychoanalysis. The only difference between psychoanalysts and their tribal colleagues, noted the scholar, was that the former listened to their patients, whereas shamans spoke to them.[88] Lévi-Strauss stressed that psychoanalysis, which he called "the modern version of shamanic technique," did not invent anything new. It only recovered some bits and pieces of ancient symbolism without restoring the whole system of spiritual knowledge.[89]

Well positioned in Western humanities and social sciences, Lévi-Strauss, who also was one of the founders of structuralism, validated tribal magic to educated audiences. Calling the primitive spiritual practitioner a hero, Lévi-Strauss stressed, "It is he who, at the head of a supernatural battalion of spirits, penetrates the endangered organs and frees the captive soul."[90] Although, like many contemporary writers, Lévi-Strauss took it for granted that shamans were neurotics, he switched the discussion from shamans' psyches to the healing activities they performed in their communities. The anthropologist was particularly interested in how shamans used existing symbols and mythologies in their curing sessions.

One can summarize his approach as follows. The success of shamanic curing depends on the fact that the patient and the community believe in the reality of the tribal spiritual practitioner's sacred powers. The anthropologist stressed that, if people collectively chose a specific system of emotional and medical healing, it would surely heal them simply because they believed in this system. As an example, Lévi-Strauss plausibly pointed out that psychoanalysis, which heavily infiltrated the 1930s and 1940s intellectual culture, became for many Westerners the same kind of curative mythology.

In his classic discussion of a Cuna Indian shaman's séance for a woman in labor, Lévi-Strauss suggested that, during their healing sessions, shamans engaged metaphors from tribal mythology to effectively ease their patients' pain. In the analyzed episode, a shaman came to facilitate a difficult childbirth. The spiritual practitioner diagnosed that the woman's soul was captured by Muu, the sacred power responsible for the formation of the fetus. To retrieve this soul, the shaman embarked on a journey to the country of Muu and her daughters. The spiritual flight, as happens in many non-Western nature spiritualities, was both external and internal. Muu's way and Muu's adobe were represented by the vagina and uterus of the pregnant woman. The shaman journeyed through these realms and conducted spiritual combat against hostile spirits. In his song, which accompanied this quest, the shaman told the patient and the audience about the obstacles he had to encounter and the great battle with Muu for the woman's soul. The journey to the "dark inner place" was successful. The culprit spirit released the soul, and the woman had a safe delivery.[91]

How does the shaman relieve the sufferings of his patient? To Lévi-Strauss, the shaman's song, which describes his activities and impressions during the journey, is what provides the psychological treatment. In the above-considered case, the spiritual practitioner psychologically manipulates the sick organ through his chant by enacting the tribal myth inside the patient's body. The physical pain is personified. The woman's uterine world becomes populated with fantastic monsters the shaman has to battle. The song meticulously details all these encounters. Thus, concluded the anthropologist, the shaman channels out from the woman's mind the pains that her body cannot tolerate. In other words, the shaman brings to a conscious level the sufferings that linger in her unconscious. That is how relief comes.

Again, the major point here is that the success of healing becomes possible because the person believes in the existing symbols. Lévi-Strauss explained:

> That the mythology of the shaman does not correspond to an objective reality does not matter. The sick woman believes in the myth and belongs to a society which believes in it. The tutelary spirits and malevolent spirits, the supernatural monsters and magical animals, are all part of a coherent system on which the native conception of the universe is founded. The sick woman accepts these mythical beings or, more accurately, she has never questioned their existence.[92]

In order to illustrate the placebo effect of tribal healing, Lévi-Strauss also brought to light the Quesalid record. Later, in the Lévi-Strauss rendering, this ethnographic material became included in various writings on shamanism and symbolic healing and appeared in a psychology textbook. This account, which Franz Boas published as part of *The Religion of the Kwakiutl Indians* (1930), represents the testimony of an Indian named Giving-Potlatches-in-the-World, a traditional primitive native, who at first was skeptical about shamanism but later converted to belief in its healing effects. According to the version published by Boas, this Indian doubting Thomas adopted a shamanic vocation in order to check how local magicians manipulate people: "I desired to learn about the shaman, whether it is true or whether it is made up and whether they pretend to be shamans."[93]

During an initiation stage, senior colleagues lead the apprentice to the house of Cannibal-Dancer hidden deep in the woods. The place, Giving-Potlatches-in-the-World informs us, is a sacred hangout for people who simulate shamanic illnesses in order to enter the shamanic vocation. Spiritual practitioners agree to teach the apprentice their methods, including the simulation of fainting and death. They also show him the place on the body from which the novice can extract a sickness by sucking. The apprentice learns that the sickness that shamans produce for public display during their séances in reality is a bloodied piece of eagle down spit from shamans' mouths after sucking on the sick person's body. The senior colleagues teach Giving-Potlatches-in-the-World that, to produce the blood, he should bite his tongue or suck his gums and hide the eagle down in his mouth before the ritual. Then, during a séance, the down could be "extracted" from the body of a patient and displayed to the public as a "bloody worm," the embodiment of sickness. The apprentice is also instructed to sleep among the graves so that someone will see him there in the morning to let the public know that he is going to become a shaman.

When Giving-Potlatches-in-the-World tries the newly acquired curative skills on surrounding people, to his surprise he discovers that his patients do feel better. The young healer becomes famous as a great shaman and receives a new name, Quesalid. The newly minted spiritual practitioner gradually widens his activities, successfully competing with colleagues who cannot produce such effective symbols of the sickness in the form of a bloody worm. Lévi-Strauss noted that Quesalid's patients recovered because they believed in his powers. To the anthropologist, Quesalid's conversion from a skeptic into a practitioner of shamanism is the best proof of how socially accepted symbols affect the behavior of people who might not necessarily share them.

Indeed, the Quesalid story, as it was published by Boas, is a powerful endorsement of symbolic healing. Later in the course of his anthropological investigation, Harry Whitehead revealed that Quesalid was not a native primitive and skeptic turned shaman but a mixed-blood ethnographer and interpreter, George Hunt, one of the famous Boas's informants. Still, this does not diminish the effectiveness of symbols. Even though Hunt later quit his shamanic vocation, preferring to work for professional anthropologists, in his

youth he did convert to shamanism, though under more traditional circumstances as a result of shamanic illness. Hunt-Quesalid did perform bloody
worm sessions that relieved people from suffering. What is essential here is the
power of a myth shared by the community and a patient and used by tribal
doctors. That is what brings a sense of security and relief to an individual and
to an entire community.

Although still sharing the earlier notion that primitive man was highly
susceptible to various forms of mental disorder, in the 1960s, many authors
clearly began to rehabilitate shamans. In his 1967 paper on shamanism and
schizophrenia, clinical psychologist Julian Silverman (1933–2001) approached
shamans as "healed schizophrenics" and "creative madmen." Silverman became the general manager of the Esalen Institute. This chief center of the human potential movement during the countercultural years in the 1960s and
1970s was among the first in the West to experiment with classical Oriental
and tribal spiritual techniques as forms of therapy. Silverman stressed that
spiritual practitioners in shamanic societies could not only find a cultural niche
in their societies but could also put their talents to the service of their communities. Drawing on the scholarship of Shirokogoroff, the scientist contrasted the attitudes of primal societies to their insane members with the
cruel treatment of such people in Western society, which ostracized and isolated them in asylums. Silverman became one of the first people to weave shamanism into the counterculture. In the summer of the same year when he
published his paper, the psychiatrist conducted a seminar in Esalen titled
"Shamanism, Psychedelics, and the Schizophrenia."[94] The Silverman assessment of shamanism reached public attention through the book *Myths to Live By*
by Joseph Campbell, who used the psychiatrist's paper to contrast the classical
Eastern and tribal spirituality with the Western way devoid of the sacred and
spiritual.[95]

During the same year, in his popular account of the archaic faith of the
ancient hunters, German writer Andreas Lommel came up with a similar argument, pointing out that "shamanism is a mental attitude that comes into
being through the overcoming of a mental illness."[96] Some writers went further, suggesting that shamanic rituals with all their ecstatic movements were,
in fact, replications of the initiation sickness of the shaman. Later, in 1982,
Joan Halifax, a popular mind, body, and spirit writer, neatly developed such
arguments into the theory of shamans as wounded healers. She stressed that,
during their initiations and performing sessions, tribal spiritual practitioners
suffered tremendous physical and moral pain for the sake of their fellow tribal
members. By healing themselves, they eventually came to heal the others. One
current spiritual seeker summarized this thesis about healed healers and
wounded healers: "general rule number one: shamans are often those who
have cured themselves, and in the process have discovered the knowledge that
now allows them to cure others."[97]

The changing views toward tribal spirituality that one can find in the works of Lévi-Strauss, Silverman, Lommel, and Halifax are rooted in the general shift of European and American attitudes toward non-Western traditions, away from Enlightenment rationalism and materialism toward the spiritual and the irrational. I will discuss this intellectual shift, which accelerated after the 1960s and which gave rise to increasing interest in shamanism, in the next two chapters.

4

Power Plants

Psychedelic Culture Meets Tribal Spirituality

"Ah!" breathed Mr. Bath. He took the bottle in his thin, almost transparent fingers and held it up and gazed at it as though it were a long lost friend. Then—quickly—he unscrewed the lid, took a breath, and popped the lid back on again before you could say Jack Robinson! "Oh my!" he whispered. "That smell—why, it takes me back thousands of years! Would you believe it!"

The boys gasped and stared. *"Thousands* of years, did you say, Mr. Bass?" ventured Chuck, thinking surely he had been mistaken.

"Goodness, yes. Why, just one whiff wafted me over the centuries as though they had been nothing."

—Eleanor Cameron, *The Wonderful Flight to*
the Mushroom Planet (1954)

In 1927, while on their honeymoon, investment banker R. Gordon Wasson and his Russian-born wife, Valentina, were taking a stroll in the woods of New York's Catskills Mountains. Valentina suddenly bent and picked up several mushrooms. She stunned her husband by telling him that she was going to eat them. Although Valentina assured Wasson that the mushrooms were edible, he was somehow not convinced. He begged her to leave those disgusting toadstools alone. Wasson went to bed with a feeling that he might not see his wife alive again. The next morning, to his surprise, Valentina, who did cook and eat the mushrooms, had survived.[1]

Intrigued by this experience, both spouses came to the conclusion that their distinct cultural backgrounds had conditioned their different attitudes toward mushrooms. Wasson came from Anglo-Saxon

(Western) culture, which demonizes toadstools and in which even the most enlightened people are apprehensive about them. In contrast, Russian culture appears to be more receptive to the mushroom. Why do some cultures have
deeply seated morbid and frequently unfounded fears of toadstools? Is there
anything to be afraid of? Trying to respond to these questions, Valentina and
Gordon, who had sufficient money and leisure, embarked on their lifelong
exciting quest to explore the role of mushrooms in the histories and folklore of
different cultures. When Valentina died of cancer in 1958, Gordon continued
this quest alone. Eventually, his explorations evolved into research on possible
links between hallucinogenic mushrooms and early religion.

What came out of this research was a small community of scholarship that
brought together people who believed that plant hallucinogens gave rise to human spirituality in archaic times; essentially, Wasson and his colleagues added
a new hallucinogenic dimension to shamanism studies. That "psychedelic
scholarship," which was closely linked to the counterculture of the 1960s,
not only informed the debates about shamanism among academics but also
aroused and fed public interest in shamanism. In the 1960s and 1970s, the
discussions of shamanism in print media that frequently linked it to hallucinogens created the impression that shamanism meant, first of all, experiments
with plant drugs. As a result, for many spiritual seekers, shamanism became
associated with the ritual use of hallucinogenic plants: peyote, morning glory,
mushrooms, tobacco, and others. I found the most recent and the most explicit
expression of this popular sentiment in *Breaking Open the Head* (2002) by
Daniel Pinchbeck. For this second-generation Manhattan bohemian, travel
to the heart of contemporary shamanism means experimenting with plant
psychedelics.

Sacred Mushroom Seeker: Gordon Wasson

A journalist by education and a banker by profession, Wasson (1896–1986) did
not depend on the opinions of academic peers and enjoyed an intellectual
freedom which mainstream scholars can hardly afford. This allowed him to
write and to imagine theories which might have appeared crazy to conventional scholarship. Wasson's books were not confined to any particular academic field but could fit the rubric of anthropology, psychology, history, or
archaeology.

The first urge to see the "sacred mushroom" in action came to Gordon
Wasson as early as the 1940s. In one paper, he read that in remote areas of the
Oaxaca state, Mexican Indians ingested hallucinogenic mushrooms to put
themselves into trances, which gave them visions which they treated as sacred
instructions. These fungi, which the ancient Aztecs called "God's flesh," belong
to the *psilocybe* family (see figure 4.1). The author of the paper, the Harvard

FIGURE 4.1. *Psilocybe mexicana* mushrooms were widely used by the
Mexican Indians in their shamanic sessions. Watercolor by Roger Heim.
Courtesy R. Gordon Wasson Collection, Harvard University Herbaria.

ethnobotanist Richard Evans Schultes, had visited the area in the late 1930s
and collected the mushroom specimen. Yet the ethnobotanist did not participate in any shamanic ceremonies. In 1939, two more researchers visited the
same region and were able to observe how local Indians ingested the mushrooms. In the 1940s, their stories about mind-altering plants did not intrigue
the public and, therefore, went unnoticed. Wasson and his wife wanted to
come to Oaxaca not only to collect *psilocybe* samples and to observe the mushroom divination rites but also to partake in these rituals.

In 1953 and again in 1954, the couple was able to visit Huautla de Jimenez,
a village in the mountains of the Oaxaca state, which is considered the heart of
the Mezatec Indian country. During one of their visits, Gordon and Valentina
observed a mushroom session performed by *curandero* (spiritual healer) Aur-
elio Cassera.[2] However, mere observation was not enough; they wanted to experience the ritual. Their breakthrough came in the summer of 1955, during another expedition to Huautla. This time, their small expedition, which included
Gordon, Valentina, their daughter Masha, and their photographer friend Alan
Richardson, encountered Mezatec shamaness "Dona Maria" (Maria Sabina).
On June 29, Cayetano, a Huautla resident who accommodated the explorers
and whose house later became the site of a landmark shamanic session, took
Wasson and Richardson for a tour of the outskirts of the village in search of
the *psilocybes.* Soon the friends found a large number of the mushrooms. Was-
son noted, "We gathered them in a plasterboard box: the sacred mushrooms

must always be carried in a closed parcel, never exposed to the view of passers-by. They were a noble lot, mostly young, all of them perfect in their moist health and fragrance."[3] In response to the banker's request to meet a local shaman who would help them to try the mushrooms in a ritual setting, Cayetano took the explorers straight to Dona Maria, whom the locals respectfully described as a "curandera of the highest quality [curandera de primera categoria]."

Wasson was fascinated with the intellect and the spiritual aura of the shamaness and referred to her as "a top flight shaman."[4] The first dialogues convinced Wasson that the shamaness was a person of "rare moral and spiritual power, dedicated to her vocation." He felt fortunate that, after a brief conversation, the shamaness volunteered to perform a night mushroom divination ritual for him and his companions. Thus, in the company of Dona Maria and her daughter, the sacred mushroom seekers began two all-night vigils.

On the arranged day, after night fell, the participants in the mushroom vigil gathered in the lower chamber of Cayetano's house. In addition to Wasson and Richardson, there were about twenty-five people present, mostly members of Cayetano's extended family. It was required that the ceremony be performed in complete darkness. Nobody was allowed to leave the house before daybreak and the end of the session. In preparation for the ritual, Wasson and Richardson also fasted all day.

During mushroom sessions practiced in Oaxaca, both clients and shamans usually ingested raw psilocybes and saw visions. While the client scanned the unfolding images, the spiritual practitioner used the mushrooms as a diagnostic tool. Having ingested the mushroom, the curandero entered a trance that opened the door to the world of spirits and, potentially, to the solution of a problem. Sabina explained to Wasson that during the séance, it was not her but the mushrooms that performed the actual healing and talking. To her, the mushrooms were animated "dear little children." Thus, Dona Maria and other curanderos believed that the sacred mushrooms used their bodies as transmitters to report the causes of an ailment or misfortune or to issue instructions on how to solve a problem. Hence, according to their animistic world view, the plants had minds of their own. They could advise, guide, or simply talk to people.

Wasson and Richardson found out that the mushrooms were ingested in pairs, which symbolized male and female sources. Sabina usually consumed thirteen pairs per session, while a patient ate six pairs. Wasson described the moment she handed him six pairs of the mushroom as the culmination of his ethnobotanic search (see figure 4.2). Richardson, whose wife had let him go on this trip on the condition that no "nasty toadstools cross his lips,"[5] could not resist and joined Wasson by also eating six pairs. Usually a person who ingests psilocybe mushrooms begins to feel the hallucinogenic effect of the "mushroom of vision" about thirty minutes later and continues to "see" for five or six hours. After the shamaness swallowed the last mushroom, she made the sign

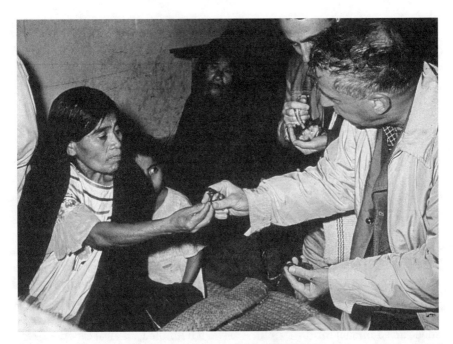

FIGURE 4.2. R. Gordon Wasson receives his ration of *psilocybe* mushrooms from Maria Sabina during her nighttime spiritual séance. Photograph by Alan B. Richardson. Courtesy R. Gordon Wasson Collection, Harvard University Herbaria.

of the cross and was ready to enter the trance. When Dona Maria entered the altered state, she began to dance and chant. Wasson, who came to the shamanic session with a strong desire to fight whatever effect the fungi produced on him, eventually had to submit himself to the will of the sacred mushroom. He also entered an altered state and began to see things. While the *curandera* was tuning herself to spiritual messages from the world of spirits, Wasson and Richardson were observing unfolding visions.

Later, the friends compared their impressions of the session. Although the images they saw differed, there were many similar patterns:

> At first we saw geometrical patterns, angular not circular, in richest colors, such as might adorn textiles or carpets. Then the patterns grew into architectural structures, with colonnades and architraves, patios of regal splendor, the stone-work all in brilliant colors, gold and onyx and ebony, all most harmoniously and ingeniously contrived, in richest magnificence extending beyond the reach of sight, in vistas measureless to man.[6]

To Wasson, these architectural images appeared Oriental, although he could not tie them to any specific tradition. Soon, he saw a bouquet of flowers on the table turn into a car driven by some mythological creatures. Simultaneously, the walls of the room vanished, and they began to flow in a universe stroked by divine breezes. The participants felt they had acquired a "divine mobility that would transport us anywhere on the wings of a thought."[7]

The visions were so vivid that they appeared to Wasson to be more clear and "authoritative" than anything he saw in "mundane reality." To the explorer, the images of various objects he observed in the "other reality" were bright and solid, unlike their blurred and imperfect appearance in "ordinary reality." Wasson compared these solid blueprints with the famous heavenly forms of all earthly things mentioned by the Greek philosopher Plato. The explorer enjoyed the sensation of being in the other reality. Still, he tried to keep the rational part of his brain alert. As Wasson later explained, one side of his mind was enjoying the unfolding visions, while the other was reasoning and observing. Thus, the friends lay in the darkness on their mats, scribbling notes and exchanging whispered comments. He was excited about the divine atmosphere of their small gathering that reminded him of an "agape of early Christians." The fact that they were the first white people to partake of this ancient esoteric ritual, which perhaps went back to "the very dawn of man's cultural history," added an additional thrill.[8] Overall, Wasson felt fulfilled, an ideal experience for any Westerner fascinated with the aesthetics and spirituality of the indigenous primitive.

At the same time, Wasson discovered that Maria Sabina's shamanism was heavily loaded with Roman Catholic symbolism. The shamaness believed that mushrooms grew where Christ spilled his blood on the ground. Wasson also found out that the shamaness was a church member in good standing. While performing her shamanic session for Wasson and his friend, she sat in front of an altar, which had a crucifix hidden in a bouquet of flowers and three lighted candles adorned with Christian images, such as the child Jesus and the baptism in Jordan.[9] Furthermore, at the climax of her séance, the mushrooms pronounced their judgments in the voice of Jesus Christ. This syncretic characteristic of Latin American shamanism was the result of centuries of close Indian-Christian interactions in the area.

Still, Wasson felt that his communication with the world of the sacred through this mushroom session was far more powerful than partaking in any Christian rite. He wrote that, to him, this was genuine communication with the divine: "the Orthodox Christian must accept on faith the miracle of the conversion of the bread and wine into God's flesh and blood. By contrast the sacred mushroom of the Aztecs carries its own conviction: every communicant will testify to the miracle that he has experienced."[10] Indeed, in Dona Maria's session, he did not have to take for granted that bread and wine were Jesus' blood. Mushrooms took Wasson straight into the realm of the sacred by revealing fascinating visions. This ascribed ability of hallucinogens to propel an individual to the realm of the sacred, in contrast to the routine symbolism of mainstream churches, became one of the attractions of indigenous hallucinogenic herbs to Western seekers of alternative spirituality.

For Mezatec spiritual practitioners, as for any other shamans in a tribal setting, mushroom sessions were purely functional: the resolution of a specific problem or the curing of an ailment. Like many Westerners fascinated with the beauty of shamanism, Wasson was more interested in the esoteric and aesthetic side of the "sacred play." For him, the rationale of the shamanic session was a secondary matter. When the explorers approached the shamaness for the first time, Dona Maria naturally asked them about a problem Wasson sought to resolve through this session. Since he had none, Wasson had to quickly come up with a convincing rationale for the séance. An inquiry about their son Peter, who at that time was serving in the army, sounded like a justifiable reason to hold the spiritual session.[11]

After the first mushroom séance, which the shamaness conducted for them on June 29, 1955, Wasson and Richardson participated in another and experienced a second set of visions. In the meantime, Valentina and Masha, who had taken their portion of the toadstools just for curiosity, watched their visions while cozying themselves in sleeping bags outside the house. After the Wassons returned to their New York apartment, they again ingested the mushrooms, trying to learn whether the substance also worked in their urban setting. They were glad to report that some visionary effects were still there. Yet, at the same time, they admitted that those visions were much weaker than those they had experienced in the company of the shamaness.

Wasson continued to experiment with *psilocybe* mushrooms. He had a friend, Swiss chemist Albert Hoffman, whom he asked to isolate the hallucinogenic chemicals of the Mexican toadstool in a lab. Incidentally, this chemist is the one who first synthesized lysergic acid diethylamide (LSD) in 1957. The next time Wasson returned to Oaxaca, he took Hoffman with him. At Wasson's request, he fed Dona Maria his synthetic psilocybin during one of her sacred sessions as a substitute for her magic mushrooms. The chemist explained to the shamaness that it was "the spirit of the mushrooms in the form of pills." The explorer was happy to report that, according to Sabina, there was no difference between the natural mushroom and his extract.

In 1957, Wasson became a celebrity. That year, in *Life* magazine, he published an essay entitled "Seeking the Magic Mushroom," which chronicled his magic sessions with the "mushroom queen" Maria Sabina. Anthropologist Fikes called this paper, which immortalized Wasson, the "best-written and the most widely distributed description of a drug session in modern time."[12] Illustrated with colorful photographs made by his friend Richardson, this piece attracted millions of readers. As a result, many seekers of alternative spirituality turned their attention to indigenous Mexico and farther to South America.

From cultural and literary standpoints, Wasson's encounter with the shamaness was a landmark. This meeting and the subsequent nationwide publicity not only added to the budding psychedelic revolution, but also contributed to the narrative genre of spiritual apprenticeship autobiography that I will discuss in chapter 6. Moreover, one of Wasson's intellectual successors traced the current romance of Western spiritual seekers with Native American spirituality to the meeting of the New York spiritual seekers and the Mezatec shamaness.[13] Although such a statement is certainly an exaggeration, the *Life* article, along with *Black Elk Speaks*, Frank Waters's books about the Hopi Indians, and Castaneda's novels, entered the ranks of those tales of power that have inspired seekers of Native American spirituality and tribal shamanism in general.

Among the seekers stirred at the turn of the 1960s by the Wasson essay was a young Harvard psychology professor named Timothy Leary, future godfather of the psychedelic revolution. Following Wasson's footsteps, Leary arrived in Mexico, where he set up the Harvard Psilocybin Project, involving his colleagues, students, and friends. Among the participants were such celebrities as poet Allen Ginsberg and writer Jack Kerouac. During the same years, UCLA graduate student Carlos Castaneda was contemplating an anthropology career, longing to somehow replicate Wasson's experiences and to find his own primitive shaman, the carrier of herbal hallucinogenic secrets. By the time the United States outlawed psychedelic drugs such as psilocybin in 1966, more than one million people had already tried them.[14]

Whether he wanted it or not, with his *Life* essay, Wasson planted in the popular consciousness the idea that people could travel to an exotic location to find exotic hallucinogens that could unleash extraordinary visions. Gradually, a community of people "mushroomed" around the use of *psilocybes*. Some of them wanted to use the mushroom of vision just to see and nothing else. Others pursued therapeutic goals. In the 1960s, long-haired folks streamed to Oaxaca searching for Sabina or at least for an occasion to ingest the celebrated magic mushrooms. As in many similar cases, public Western pilgrimages to the tribal setting quickly prostituted this native plant that had been hidden from outsiders. Soon, *psilocybe* mushrooms found their way to Mexican peasant markets, where they were openly offered as items of tourist trade. Sabina could not grasp why well-fed and perfectly healthy Westerners were seeking her mushrooms. These people certainly did not look ill to her. Still, the shamaness could not turn away from the persistent outsiders who were desperate to break into the separate reality and who brought cash.

From the late 1960s to the middle of the 1970s, Huautla, residence of Maria Sabina, became the mecca for mushroom pilgrims. The astronauts of inner space besieged the place. The luckiest ones met Maria Sabina or other *curanderos*. The rest of the visitors were simply hanging around. Henry Munn, an anthropologist who visited the village in 1965, remembered hearing Beatles songs on the streets of Huautla. Among the 1960s celebrities, the village attracted leading rock stars such as Mick Jagger, John Lennon, and Peter Townsend, who came to Sabina to conduct spiritual journeys under her guidance. It is quite possible that without Huautla many Americans would have never "turned on, tuned in, or dropped out" in the 1960s. The influx of outsiders disrupted local life to such an extent that the Mexican government closed the village. From 1969 to 1976, police blockaded the road to Huautla to ward off the hippies. Moreover, Maria Sabina herself had to spend some time in jail once for offering the exotic drug to outsiders.[15]

If we are to believe Wasson, Dona Maria once told him that she had visions that someone (read: Wasson and his party) would be coming and taking her centuries-old secret tradition to the wider world. Whether the shamaness said this or not, her entire life was dramatically changed by Wasson's actions. Although the publicity eventually brought her some income and made her own life easier in a material sense, she had to pay a spiritual price. Dona Maria reported that her medicine power was somehow corrupted or, as she put it, "lost in clouds." In the wake of the influx of the "gringo" seekers to Mezatec country, Maria Sabina began to complain, "From the moment when the strangers arrived the 'Holy Children' lost their purity. They lost their strength. They were profaned. From now on, they will serve no purpose. There is no help for it. Before Wasson, I felt that the Holy Children elevated me. I no longer feel so."[16]

Wasson, who quoted these words of hers, was saddened to have been the one who ignited the process of desecration. Yet, perhaps to console himself, the explorer argued that his "discovery" of Sabina was necessary in order to save her knowledge for future generations. Overall, Wasson approached the intrusion of modernity into the islands of archaic spirituality philosophically, stressing the idea that the intrusion was simply inevitable and that discussions of its moral rectitude were pointless.[17]

Although Wasson was very enthusiastic about hallucinogenic toadstools and enjoyed taking mushrooms under the guidance of Maria Sabina, he was reluctant to ride the popular psychedelic spirituality movement of the 1960s and 1970s. Thus, he never fully used the publicity channels opened by the unfolding countercultural revolution. In fact, with his scholastic mind and refined gentleman's demeanor, he was not a good candidate to be a psychedelic spirituality guru. His was the scholarly realm, which brought him the reputation of being a snob in alternative circles. While Leary was promoting the benefits of the counterculture and calling for everybody to enter the other reality, Wasson was advocating caution. He did not want the wider public to be involved in the hallucinogenic experiments in which he himself had participated. After his brief visit to Wasson, during which Leary hoped to find a kindred soul, the flamboyant psychologist was frustrated: "Wasson was opposed to any current use of the mushrooms. Although these fungi had produced all of the great philosophical visions of antiquity, he proclaimed they had no relevance to the modern world."[18]

With irony and skepticism, Wasson talked about people who were "mush-roomed." He also frowned on spiritual pilgrimages to Mexico, which he himself had triggered. Sometimes, he even spoke up against particular spirituality projects that involved hallucinogenic plants. When a dropout community of American *Stropharia* mushroom eaters sprang up near the classical Mayan site Palenque, and the word spread around that ancient and modern Maya in this lowland area ritually used these fungi, Wasson dismissed such utterances as pure nonsense. Much to the frustration of the hallucinogenic plant's seekers, he correctly argued that there was no archaeological or ethnographic evidence that the native people ever used mushrooms in the Maya lowland country.[19]

Mushroom Conspiracy: Sacred Soma, Fly Mushroom, and the Origin of Religion

Wasson did not restrict himself to Mexican field trips probing the magic qualities of the *psilocybe*. He sensed that there was more to it and complemented his field trips to Oaxaca with research of the ethnographic literature, seeking similar mushroom-inspired experiences in other cultures all over the world: China, Indian, Japan, ancient Greece and Rome, Persia, and Siberia. Wasson concluded that Dona Maria's ritual manipulation with her "little children" was not something peculiar to Mezatec Indian tradition. The ritual use of *psilocybe* appeared to him to be a particular case of a universal religious practice that went back to the dawn of human history. In one of his last books, Wasson charac-teristically stressed, "Maria Sabina was The Shaman, the focus for the woes and longings of mankind back, back through the Stone Age to Siberia."[20]

Incidentally, Siberia came to occupy an essential place in Wasson's mush-room theory. Wasson wrote that this area belonged to those few places on earth where modern observers could catch the last living traces of mushroom wor-ship, while in other areas, it was already gone. Specifically, he centered his research on the use by some Siberian natives of fly agaric (*Amanita muscaria*) mushrooms in their shamanic séances (see figure 4.3). What Wasson saw during Dona Maria's séances strikingly reminded him of descriptions of mushroom sessions in arctic Siberia. It seemed that the indigenous Siberians similarly "heard" mushrooms "talk" and, like Dona Maria, received spiritual instructions from the toadstools.

Before going to Mezatec country, the Wassons had already read Jochel-son's and Bogoras's books about the Koryak and the Chukchi people. In fact, the Wassons ranked these ethnographic texts among the major written sources that mention the ritual use of mushrooms.[21] In their descriptions of the life-ways of native peoples of northeastern Siberia, Jochelson and Bogoras, par-ticipants in the Russian-American Jesup North Pacific Expedition (1897–1902), discussed the use of the fly mushroom. Here is how Gordon Wasson

FIGURE 4.3. Several indigenous groups in Siberia used fly mushroom (*Amanita muscaria*) to induce hallucinogenic experiences. Franz E. Köhler et al., eds., *Köhler's Medizinal-Pflanzen in naturgetreuen Abbildungen mit kurz erläuterndem Texte* (Gera-Untermhaus: F. E. Köhler, 1883–1914), vol. 4, plate 7.

described his and his wife's search for comparative analogies in Siberia: "We learned that in Siberia there are six primitive people[s]—so primitive that anthropologists regard them [as] precious museum pieces for cultural study—who use a hallucinogenic mushroom in their shamanic rites."[22]

Let us see what is so special about the Siberian fly agaric that eventually made Wasson place this plant at the center of his scholarship. The mushroom received its academic name, *Amanita muscaria*, from the famous Swedish naturalist Carl Linnaeus. This founder of modern botany remarked that in order to classify this mushroom, he used the Latin word *musca*, which means a "fly." In Sweden, explained the scientist, people used to chop the fly agaric and mix it with milk to kill flies. The *A. muscaria* is a beautiful toadstool with a white solid stem and a bright red cap peppered with white warts. The largest fly agaric can reach nine inches. This fungus usually grows in the pine, birch, and beech forests of northern Eurasia and North America. The psychoactive elements that intoxicate takers of the mushroom include ibotenic acid and alkaloid muscimole. The second compound goes through a human kidney unaltered. That is the reason that the urine of the mushroom taker contains the hallucinogen. When these mushrooms are dried, ibotenic acid converts to muscimole.[23] This might be the reason that the Chukchi and other natives of northeastern Siberia preferred to dry their mushrooms before using them. At the same time, in Western Siberia, people ate them raw or ingested fly agaric broth.

Although some writers consider it weak if compared with the *psilocybe*, ingested in an appropriate dose on an empty stomach, the fly mushroom might be a powerful hallucinogen. Popular novelist Tom Robbins, for example, gave a high score to *A. muscaria*:

> On acid, I felt that I was an integral component of the universe. On muscaria, I felt that I was the universe. There was no sense of ego loss. Quite the contrary: I was a superhero. I wasn't hostile, understand, but felt invincibly strong. Although my biceps are more like lemons than grapefruits, I would have readily accepted a challenge from Muhammad Ali, and even in the sober light of two years after, I believe that I could have given him a good tumble. Euphoric energy was mine aplenty.[24]

To procure the best hallucinogenic effect, fresh mushrooms were sliced vertically in small segments of one centimeter each and heated at 75–80 degrees Celsius, which corresponds to 165–175 degrees Fahrenheit, until dry. The final product was ingested in small pieces. To receive a complete visionary effect and not to overdose themselves at the same time, the Chukchi natives usually did not consume more than five mushrooms at a time; the average dose was three mushrooms. After consuming a full dose of *A. muscaria*, an individual usually falls asleep, and then begins to see and to hear voices and commands. Spirits appear and talk directly with the person. On waking up, one feels energized and revitalized, sometimes to the point of being inspired to run, jump, dance, and be active. Intoxication with the mushroom also changes the size of objects for a taker. The objects might diminish or, on the contrary, increase their size. In indigenous Siberia, among the Chukchi, people believed that the mushroom spirit took an individual to the lower world, to the land of the dead. Frequently, the spirit of the fly mushroom appeared to the native people as a fast-moving power capable of growing in size, crashing stones, and tearing trees apart.

Comparing the ritual use of mushrooms in Siberia, the Americas, and other areas, the Wassons became convinced that hallucinogenic fungi stood at the center of the spiritual lives of ancient people and modern tribal primitives, who maintained the vestiges of the primal mushroom cult. The spouses articulated the first results of their comparative insights in a luxuriously illustrated two-volume work, *Mushrooms, Russia, and History* (1957). Ten years later, Gordon Wasson produced a second book, *Soma: Divine Mushroom of Immortality* (1968), in which he coined the basics of the major thesis that ran through his entire scholarship—that somewhere in the distant past, people came to appreciate the hallucinogenic effects of mushrooms and began to worship them as the source of religious revelation. At the same time, the particular goal of his *Soma* was to prove that the legendary sacred potion soma, whose magic qualities were described in the ancient Indian epic the *Rig Veda*, was, in fact, the fly mushroom.

Scholars ascribe the origin of the *Rig Veda*, which stands as the foundation of the Hindu tradition, to the ancient Aryans. In about the second millennium B.C., moving from the southeastern area near the Caspian Sea, these pastoral people invaded Afghanistan, Pakistan, and northern India, where they mixed with the local Dravidian population The Aryans belonged to the Indo-European language family and spoke Vedic, which is close to classical Sanskrit. The *Rig Veda* is one of the most ancient literary masterpieces written in Sanskrit. Of the more than 1,000 hymns of this epic, 120 deal with so-called soma, a divine drink made of some unknown plant. These particular hymns tell us that in the course of their liturgy, ancient Aryan priests mixed the plant with water, beat out the essence with stones, filtered it, added honey or barley, and drank it before the end of the liturgy.

Before Wasson, scholars had surmised that soma might be some sort of a local plant or, most probably, a metaphor for a magic potion. Comparing the descriptions of soma from the *Rig Veda* with the botanical and hallucinogenic characteristics of the fly mushroom, Wasson found many similarities and concluded that the legendary soma was *A. muscaria*. For example, the *Rig Veda* says that soma grows on mountain heights and in wooded areas. So does the fly agaric. The ancient epic mentions that soma puts people in ecstasy (altered state of consciousness). So does the fly agaric in Siberia.

The "urine link," noted Wasson, was additional evidence of the fly agaric origin of soma. It is known that the hallucinogenic qualities of the fly mushroom do not disappear when passing through the human body and remain in urine. From the travel writings of old explorers of Siberia, Wasson learned that among the Koryak and their neighbors, the Itel'men people, those people who could not get access to *A. muscaria* drank the urine of people who had ingested the mushroom and enjoyed the same hallucinogenic effect. For example, eighteenth-century Russian naturalist Stepan Krasheninnikov, who, incidentally, did not see any connection between the use of fly agaric and shamanism, noted with amusement, "The sedentary Koryak honor the mushroom to such a degree that they do not allow the ones who become drunk on it to urinate on the floor. They collect the urine in a plate, drink and go crazy in the same manner as the ones who ate the mushroom." In a similar manner, his contemporary, German naturalist Johann Georgi, told his readers that Yukagir shamans "take a good drink of urine before entering their ecstasy."[25]

To Wasson, such descriptions perfectly fit the verse he found in the ninth book of the *Rig Veda* that mentions how officiating priests with full bladders urinated soma: "Acting in concert, those charged with the office, richly gifted, do full honor to Soma. The swollen men piss the flowing Soma."

The writer found additional evidence in *Mahabharata*, another famous ancient Indian epic. The tale mentions a holy man named Uttanka who suffers from thirst in the desert. Uttanka meets the god Krishna, who is disguised as a naked filthy hunter. The latter urinates and offers the holy man his urine to quench the thirst. Appalled, Uttanka refuses with indignation. Later, to his frustration, the holy man learns from Krishna himself that he had been offered soma urine. Had Uttanka accepted the urine of the filthy hunter, he would have joined the Immortals.[26]

From these and similar analogies, Wasson drew the conclusion that the Aryans had brought to the Indus Valley the "mushroom cult" that was based on *A. muscaria* and open to everybody. In the course of time, argued the writer, the Aryans mixed with the native people, the Dravidians, and eventually lost their fungi cult. Wasson saw the shamanic use of fly agaric by the Siberians, whom he placed at the fringe of the Aryan civilization, as a last survival of this magnificent ancient cult. The sacred mushroom seeker had to admit that not all native Siberian people used the mushroom; he explained this fact by saying that in the course of history, native Siberians lost much of their ancient fungi cult. Still, Wasson insisted that for those modern natives who did continue to use *A. muscaria*, talking with the magic mushroom represented the central element of their modern beliefs. Any expert in Siberian ethnography will say that this statement is simply untrue. The only area where people frequently used fly agaric for ritual purposes was northeastern Siberia: the Chukchi, Koryak, and Itel'men. Even among these groups, the fungus was applied in combination with other tools of inducing altered states: alcohol, drumming, or chanting.

The Chukchi believed that, despite its marvelous effects, strong shamans did not need any extra device such as *A. muscaria*. They were convinced that fly agaric served the needs of weak shamans, who did not have enough medicine power to catapult themselves to the separate reality. For such people, the mushroom was indeed a handy tool, which, in the words of Chukchi spiritual practitioner Yatargin, "dragged" them to the world of spirits. It is notable that among the Khanty people of western Siberia, in addition to regular shamans, who used a variety of tools to induce altered states, there was a separate group of "fly agaric people." These individuals specialized exclusively in ingesting *A. muscaria* to establish contact with the world of spirits. Incidentally, the Khanty epic storytellers also used fly agaric to boost their energy and to stimulate themselves. To Wasson, all these facts, especially the combination of the mushroom with other tools of reaching altered states, represented a later degeneration of the pure *A. muscaria* worship.

The explorer suggested that the primal religion centered on the mushroom cult was open to everybody. He argued that, "under mushroom," ancient people were able to communicate with the sacred directly, bypassing the priesthood and imagining themselves as incarnations of gods or semigods. Indeed, with such an egalitarian form of worship, who needs priests? Wasson also speculated that, in their search for ideological monopoly, the ancient priesthood and later missionaries from various world religions squeezed out the egalitarian mushroom cult that had existed all over Eurasia. That is essentially how he explained the absence of the ritual use of the fungi in various cultures. For example, Wasson pointed out that in ancient India, priests eliminated the cult of soma; in Siberia Russian colonizers suppressed mushroom wisdom; and in the New World, Catholic friars destroyed or drove underground *psilocybe* users.

It was only natural that later Wasson came to the conclusion that the famous biblical idiom of the forbidden fruit might have been originally rooted in the ancient priesthood's taboo on the ingestion of fly agaric. Wasson also linked the disintegration of toadstool wisdom to the advance of the lettered culture. Knowledge based on rationalized alphabets was incompatible with oral wisdom derived from spontaneous revelations induced by hallucinogenic mushrooms.[27]

Wasson's all-embracing hypothesis about the mushroom origin of shamanism and early religion accommodated all kinds of materials. He mined piles of folklore, archaeological, and ethnographic and literary sources, including hints and offhand remarks of travelers to prove that in primal times the A. *muscaria* mushroom was ritually used all over Eurasia from Scandinavia to the Bering Strait. For instance, in 1975, Wasson accidentally connected with a schoolteacher from Michigan with a master's degree in education, who simultaneously acted as an Ojibwa (Anishnabe) shamaness. To Wasson's joy, the medicine woman informed him that the "Algonquin nation" looked for consultation and advice to fly agaric. In literature he also found a reference to the visionary use of A. *muscaria* by the Athabaskan Indians of the Mackenzie River area in Canada. He used these two facts to link the sacred mushroom complex of Asia to North America.[28]

It is known that fly agaric frequently grows in the shadow of birch trees. Legends of several Siberian natives that somehow mention the birch tree appeared to Wasson to be later references to earlier mushroom worship in Siberia. Particularly, Wasson interpreted these legends as reverence of the birch tree, which he linked to the world tree of Siberian shamans, who, he surmised, saw it as their "cosmic axis" to reach deities. Since the birch tree is the tree of the shaman, and fly agaric grows in the shadow of the birch tree, Wasson suggested that both represented traces of the sacred mushroom cult. Hence, those Siberian communities, which, like the Altaians, worshiped the birch tree rather than A. *muscaria*, were mushroom worshipers anyway, because fly agaric and the birch tree were closely linked.

The hardest task for Wasson was to identify the remnants of mushroom worship in Western and Central Europe, the areas where, for more than a millennium, Judeo-Christian tradition nearly wiped out all traces of pre-Christian beliefs. Still, one could find some circumstantial evidence, argued Wasson. As an example, the writer pointed to a German nursery rhyme, which clearly mentioned fly agaric:

> A manikin stands in the wood
> Stock-still and mute
> He has of purple pure
> A mantle around him.
> Say, who may the manikin be
> Who stands there on one leg?

The children are expected to answer "Happiness mushroom! Fly agaric!" Even the famous episode in Lewis Carroll's *Alice in Wonderland* when Alice encounters a caterpillar sitting on top of a mushroom and smoking carried for Wasson "the flavor of mushroom hallucinations."[29]

Overall, Wasson became convinced that the very idea of the sacred owed its origin to the ritual use of hallucinogenic mushrooms, which, through their mind-altering qualities, eased people's access to the miraculous and the spiritual at the dawn of humankind. In other words, to him, the hallucinogens appeared as "a mighty springboard for primitive man's imagination." In one of his last books, he noted that the magic mushroom allowed practically anyone to see "more clearly than our perishing mortal eye can see, vistas beyond the horizons of this life, to travel backwards and forwards in time, to enter other planes of existence, even as the Indians say, to go there where God is."[30]

Since the mushroom rituals were so closely associated with the realm of the sacred, Wasson suggested abandoning the old expression "hallucinogen" for mind-altering plants and replacing it with a new term—*entheogen*. Wasson and his colleagues believed that the new expression, derived from the Greek word meaning "generating the idea of God," "containing deity," or "the God within," better conveyed the spiritual significance of these plants. This change of terminology stressed that the images produced through the ingestion of the sacred plants were not hallucinations, but the images of genuine alternative universes.

Psychedelic Anthropology

Following Wasson's footsteps, some writers picked up his mushroom theory and continued to search for relevant analogies in other cultures. Like Wasson, several of them accepted *A. muscaria* as the primal spark that generated religious experiences. Others pointed to more powerful toadstools that could similarly serve as candidates for the primal religious "kick." Several current works represent the literal rendering of the Wasson thesis. Writer Reid Kaplan, who discovered *A. muscaria* worship in Scandinavia, draws on archaeological evidence. Having compared engravings on bronze razors found in Danish sites with the rock art of Sweden, he concludes that both portrayed boats containing religious items. The rock art shows a person holding an umbrella-like object. To earlier scholars, it was a sail or a bush used as a sail. For others, it was a symbol of the world tree *Yggdrasil* from Nordic mythology.

Kaplan dismissed those interpretations and suggested that the person depicted on the rock art panel holds the fly agaric mushroom. Referring to the link Wasson established between Siberian use of fly agaric and soma from the ancient *Rig Veda*, Kaplan worked to add Scandinavia to the areas of ancient ritual mushroom use. Kaplan also noted that Scandinavia, with its fertile habitat for various kinds of toadstools, provides an ideal setting for mushroom worship. Last but not least, to the present day, the Swedes maintain a tradition of throwing a toadstool on a bonfire on Saint John's Eve (June 24) to ward off trolls and other evil spirits. Kaplan suggested that this modern tradition is a remnant of the primal shamanic mushroom cult.[31]

Rogan Taylor, another contemporary writer, who searched for evidence of amanita-based shamanism, turned to the familiar character of Santa Claus. Taylor pointed out that Santa's robe of red and white surely mirrors fly agaric colors. Furthermore, the popular image of Santa climbing down a chimney on Christmas Eve could be a modern reminder of the ancient practice of spirits entering through the smoke hole of a Siberian skin dwelling (yurt). The reindeer pulling Santa's sleigh certainly point to reindeer-herding Siberian people, carriers of the ancient mushroom shamanism. Finally, Santa's famous flight through a night sky appeared to Taylor as the classical spiritual flight of the Siberian shaman.[32]

Even glorious Stonehenge did not avoid the mushroom scrutiny that challenged the conventional archaeological view that the site represented an ancient "astronomical observatory." To writer Matthew Calloway, this English archaeological shrine appeared as the "powerhouse that actually summons the sacred mushroom spirits to enlighten and empower people through the creative forces of the Universe."[33] Particularly, Calloway viewed Stonehenge's circular construction as a symbolic replica of the fly agaric cap. Turn the mushroom cap upside down and take off the stem, suggested Calloway, and you will see mushroom gills radiating from the center. Visiting Stonehenge on a sunny day, continued the writer, one will clearly observe how shadows radiate from the site's center. With a bit of imagination, one can certainly see how these shadows resemble the mushroom gills from the underside of the fly agaric cap. At least, that is how Calloway interpreted the famous site. Such a recasting of Stonehenge into a sacramental replica of *A. muscaria* was too much even for those ardent metaphysical scholars who believed in the hallucinogenic origin of European shamanism. One of them even wrote to *Shaman's Drum* magazine, which published the Calloway piece, and advised the editor to be more cautious in the selection of articles.

Agreeing with the general premise of the mushroom methodology, some writers argued that Wasson incorrectly reduced the origin of the sacred to the Siberian fly mushroom and suggested widening the list of hallucinogenic candidates for this role. Steven Leto, a religion historian from Sweden, found an abundant colony of *psilocybe* mushrooms near the ancient site Tofta Hogar. The historian suggested that the mushroom cult in Scandinavia did exist but that it was not exactly centered on fly agaric. Most probably, Scandinavian shamans of old used A. *muscaria* in combination with local species of *psilocybe*, which was a more powerful hallucinogen.

To support his argument, he drew attention to the appearance of Lillvolvan, the famous seeress from the *Saga of Eirik the Red*. The holy woman is portrayed as wearing a blue cloak, which to Leto appeared as an allusion to *psilocybe* stems, which turn blue when touched. The head of the shamaness is crowned with a black-and-white fur cap, which resembles the cap of *Psilocybe semilanceata*. Leto concluded, "So, here we have a woman who is dressed in a manner that can be seen as a Psilocybe mushroom metaphor." In a similar manner, he turned ecstasy-inducing drinks consumed by gods and deities in ancient Scandinavian tales into mushroom potions.[34]

The most outspoken intellectual heir of Wasson was the late radical countercultural philosopher and spiritual seeker Terence McKenna, whom newspapers called the "Timothy Leary of the 1990s." He similarly believed that A. *muscaria* was too weak to serve either as an inspiration for the enchanted soma or as a powerful spiritual boost for human religion. Having personally ingested fly agaric, McKenna, who experimented with various hallucinogens, was not too impressed. Instead of powerful and colorful visions, he saw some vague and blurred images. McKenna speculated that *Psilocybe cubensis*, whose psychedelic effect is far more powerful, could be a better candidate for the role of the sacred mushroom.

Like several other writers, he took Wasson to task for giving undue priority to *Amanita muscaria* and Siberian birches. Particularly, he noted that the *Rig Veda* several times referred to bulls in context with soma. To McKenna, these bull references begged another link—between cow manure and mushrooms; it is known that *Psilocybe cubensis* grow better on cow manure. Still, despite his disagreement with Wasson, McKenna totally agreed with his general thesis and stressed that the "psychedelics are the oldest form of religion."

Furthermore, McKenna stretched the Wasson mushroom thesis to such an extreme that he began to credit toadstools not only for helping to instill the idea of the sacred in human minds but also for igniting the entire human civilization. In his writings, McKenna argued that chemicals contained in *psilocybe* mushrooms might have doubled human brain size and played the role of the "kick starter" for the evolution of consciousness. Viewed from this angle, ancient shamans who used *psilocybe* become the fountainheads of human creativity and civilization. McKenna speculated that by ingesting mushrooms, hunters of the past were able to survive better than their neighbors who did not have access to toadstools.

Hallucinogenic substances civilized people, tamed savage and aggressive instincts in our ancestors, suppressed the uncontrolled expression of human egos, "feminized" them, and enhanced contemplative skills. Overall, McKenna suggested that, in the areas with abundant mushroom colonies, civilizations prospered. In contrast, cultural growth and creatively slowed down in those regions where mushrooms were rare or perished. Essentially, the writer came to consider hallucinogenic mushrooms as a form of organized intelligence. Like many representatives of the mind, body, and spirit community, McKenna was concerned about reshaping rationalistic Western society. He suggested that in order to secure spiritual growth and well-being, people should learn anew the value of the unconscious, which they can do by ingesting plant drugs. In other words, as the alternative to the nuclear mushroom, the metaphor for many evils of modern civilization, McKenna promoted the plant mushroom.[35]

Joan Halifax, one of those who helped to bring shamanism to the attention of modern spiritual seekers, jokingly spoke about the "mushroom conspiracy" that involved "a fascinating network of individuals—young and old, scholar and student, shaman and mystic." "Some of us," she remembered:

> would have the opportunity over the years to meet in the New England calm of Gordon's dining room. Some of us would find ourselves conspiring at meetings. . . . All of us were on the track of the mystery, aware that the mushroom had hidden itself from the Western researcher, historian, anthropologist and archaeologist, and also that it was a key to understanding the traditions of various old shamanic cultures. Moreover, many of us had not only been moved by the ethnographic beauty of those cultures which employed the mushroom as sacrament, but ourselves had also tasted of this mystery and felt a commitment to bringing it to light.[36]

As I mentioned above, scholars and "theobotanists" who followed Wasson did not necessarily accept his reductionist argument that *A. muscaria* or some other toadstool was the very source of the world's primal religion. Along with mushrooms, these people pointed to other possible primal kick starters. It could have been peyote, morning glory seeds, alkaloid vines, or any other known or unknown herbal hallucinogens, which through their magical effects planted the ideas of demons and gods in the minds of our ancestors and thereby gave rise to early religion. Despite the variety of angles of the psychedelic scholarship, its major direction set by Wasson—hallucinogens directed and occupied the core of primal spirituality—resonated well with contemporary countercultural sentiments. Eventually, for some writers, Wasson's thesis about the hallucinogenic nature of shamanism and early religion acquired the status of a solid theory. In her essay "The God in the Flowerpot," psychedelic writer Mary

Barnard summarized the position of these authors on mind-altering herbs: "They are sacred plants, magic herbs or shrubs, magic carpets on which the spirit of the shaman can travel through time and space."[37]

Barnard offered her scenario on how, specifically, sacred herbs could turn the minds of ancient ones to the sacred. Imagine a situation, she wrote, that somewhere in primal times, a starving Native American, whose mind was still clean and devoid of any religious ideas, was wandering somewhere in an arid area of the American Southwest. Desperately searching for food, such a person was ready to try anything, even such unattractive plants as peyote. Ingesting by chance the peyote on an empty stomach, the Indian not only could restore his strength and vitality but also enjoy an incredibly rich vision. This or similar experiences, Barnard suggested, most certainly had a profound effect on dormant human minds. Hence, like powerful engines, mind-altering plants could have triggered the development of the idea of the sacred. Without insisting that her thesis was the only correct answer to the origin of the sacred, the writer nevertheless alerted her readers: "We have to remember that the drug plants were there, waiting to give men a new idea based on a new experience."[38]

Overall, Wasson's scholarship fell on the fertile ground of the psychedelic 1960s and inspired both spiritual seekers and social scholars. Halifax credited him with opening "a big door of perception for scholar and explorer alike." Another admirer wrote with excitement, "His proposal shook the foundation of Western religion and sowed seeds of light that inspired the entheogenic revolution." Although Wasson always distanced himself from engaging popular cultural sentiments, it was clear that his works were among those that set the intellectual background for the psychedelic revolution of the 1960s.[39]

With his lively style, he also helped to popularize the results of the research done by his academically grounded colleagues and friends, such as anthropologist Weston La Barre or the famous ethnobotanist Richard Evans Schultes, whose sophisticated scholarly writings might bore the lay reader. Even such scholarly authorities as Claude Lévi-Strauss and Mircea Eliade made steps to tune their scholarship to the contemporary psychedelic sentiments. Lévi-Strauss, one of the fathers of structuralism, wrote a positive review of the Wasson *Soma* book and offered his own modest generalizations about ritual mushroom use among North American Indians, essentially repeating what Wasson had already said in his works.

With the growing popularity of Wasson's *Soma*, in the early 1970s, Eliade, whose vision of shamanism I discuss in the next chapter, changed his opinion about the role of hallucinogens in shamanism. Poet and writer Robert Graves, who was impressed by Wasson's scholarship, convinced Eliade that there was mushroom use in the Dionysian cults of ancient Greece. Earlier, Eliade firmly believed that the use of mind-altering plants by tribal spiritual practitioners was a later degeneration of pure ancient shamanism; he metaphorically called these substances a "vulgar substitute for 'pure' trance." For Wasson, it was just the opposite: the use of hallucinogens indicated that shamanism was sound and alive, whereas various initiations, rituals, and dance manipulations performed by "pathological individuals" pointed to the degeneration of shamanism. In any case, before he died in 1978, in a conversation with Peter Furst, Eliade remarked that he had become fully convinced that the spontaneous visions and ecstasies induced by sacred plants were archaic experiences and that there was no phenomenological difference between the trances reached by hallucinogens or by other means.[40]

Wasson's insights into the cultural history of the mushroom and the works of his colleagues, especially Schultes and La Barre, along with the growing public interest in tribal plant lore, inspired many scholars and writers to look into the shamanic use of hallucinogenic plants. Assessing the influence of the mushroom theory on his own scholarship as "a journey of discovery," anthropologist Furst, one of the prominent psychedelic scholars at that time, stressed that Wasson stimulated his own interest in the prehistory of hallucinogens and their relationship to shamanism and ecstatic trances.[41] With his multiple contributions to various fields, from modern Huichol ethnography to Mesoamerican archaeology, Furst spearheaded the spread of the shamanism idiom in American anthropology in the 1960s and 1970s.[42]

In 1963, when psychedelic anthropology was making its first steps, on the pages of *Psychedelic Review*, Barnard stressed how this "sexy" topic opened for scholars a large research venue: "The most obvious thread for the ambitious theobotanist to grasp would be the relation of drug plants and intoxicants to shamanism and its characteristic mythology of the disembodied soul." Furst encouraged his anthropology colleagues to be more assertive in promoting hallucinogenic methodology. He noted that anthropologists should not lag behind ethnobotanists and pharmacologists in "this significant field."[43] As a reflection of this scholarly and popular interest, a large number of books and articles on the topic of hallucinogens and shamanism sprang up. An important landmark in this scholarship was a 1970 series of lectures at UCLA on the role of mind-altering herbs in the lives of indigenous peoples. Initiated by Furst, the event brought together major psychedelic scholars, including Schultes, La Barre, Marlene Dobkin de Rios, and Wasson. Last but not least among the participants was Carlos Castaneda, a fresh celebrity writer. The outcome of this event was the book *Flesh of the Gods*, published by a mainstream press.[44]

Those psychedelic anthropologists who believed that hallucinogens were the source of early religion were puzzled by the fact that in the Old World, ritual hallucinogens were less widespread than in the New World. While Asian spiritual practitioners used *A. muscaria* and a few other plants, New World technicians of the sacred were familiar with at least two hundred specimens used for ritual purposes. In 1970, anthropologist Weston La Barre, who is more famous for his comprehensive book on the peyote religion, set out to resolve this ethnological mystery. As a starting point, La Barre used the Wasson assertion that at the dawn of humankind, presumably during the Stone Age period, all societies valued and shared the ecstatic state induced by hallucinogenic plants. Yet, compared to the Americas, Old World history, which was abundant in various social, demographic, and ideological calamities, moved quickly forward. In this whirlwind of history, argued La Barre, people of the Old World lost many of their archaic cultural traits, including ritual hallucinogens.

The anthropologist particularly pointed out that Eurasians gradually lost the knowledge of God's plants under assault from powerful world religions that persecuted and eventually eliminated shamans from ritual life. After thousands of years of religious cleansing, the Siberian fly agaric mushroom stood as the lonely survivor of the dynamic hallucinogenic shamanism of the past. In contrast, stressed La Barre, the inhabitants of the Western Hemisphere, who were shielded by oceans, preserved many features of archaic shamanism, particularly the ritual use of hallucinogens. Viewing the New World as the place where history stopped, La Barre stressed that one could consider the Americas to be a "kind of ethnographic museum of the late Paleolithic-Mesolithic of Eurasia."[45]

Thus, in the Americas, which did not see mass crusades against paganism and witchcraft until the arrival of Europeans, one could find what the Old World had lost in its race toward modernity. No wonder, noted La Barre, that in the Western Hemisphere, shamanism thrived even among high priests of the Aztec empire, which was far from being an egalitarian tribal community. The anthropologist went even further. He suggested that one of the reasons that the Stone Age ancestors of Native Americans migrated from Asia to the Americas was their quest for the hallucinogens that they were losing in Eurasia. Their great respect for mystical ecstasy had allegedly prompted them to cross the Bering Strait to search for new mind-altering herbs to add to their shamanic toolkit. In the course of this journey, speculated La Barre, the Indians stumbled upon the botanical paradise of the Americas, which gave them an excellent opportunity to pursue the archaic techniques of ecstasy without any significant changes.[46]

The psychedelic methodology influenced many humanities and social science scholars who studied indigenous religions and religion in general. One of the most affected fields was Mesoamerican archaeology, where scholars began searching for evidence of ritual use of hallucinogens. Welcoming the expansion of this methodology to the archaeology of ancient Maya, one young anthropologist viewed it in the early 1970s as a "needed kick to conservative Maya scholars, most of whom still view the ancient Maya as calm, benign people" and who would be shocked to learn that the ancient Maya used drugs.[47] In 1974, Dobkin de Rios, an anthropologist who became famous for her pioneering research of *ayahuasca* shamanism, revisited Mayan archaeology from the psychedelic angle.[48] Although there were no direct materials that showed the ritual use of hallucinogens by either ancient or modern Maya, de Rios argued that they had done so. Furnishing circumstantial evidence, the anthropologist asserted that in order to induce their visions, ancient Mayan shamans used not only mushrooms but also toad and water lily products. The impetus to give such psychedelic revision to Mayan religion came to de Rios after she noticed in ancient Mayan sculptures repeated motifs of the mushroom, frog, toad, and water lily.

Since there were no direct references to hallucinogens in Maya culture, de Rios turned to the Wasson argument about the possible priestly suppression of the popular use of plant drugs. Because of this suppression, linked to the rise of political centralization and hierarchy among the Maya, argued de Rios, the hallucinogens retreated underground and eventually disappeared. Hence, the lack of evidence. To the critics of Wasson and de Rios, the thesis about the suppression of mind-altering herbs by ancient priests looked like a convenient attempt to explain the lack of evidence to support the theory of the use of hallucinogens in ancient cultures.

With surprise, the prominent Maya scholar Tatiana Proskouriakoff observed the shamanization of Mayan archaeology that was happening in the 1960s. She felt it necessary to note, "Intuition plays an important role in science, but it should be a strictly private role. It may point a way, but before we are invited to traverse the distance between the signpost and the goal, the path must be carefully surveyed and shown to be free of quicksands."[49] The anthropologist Esther Pasztory was similarly amazed with such revision of the Mesoamerican past. Moreover, she wrote an article that criticized scholars who "populated" Mayan tombs and palaces with shamans. The most stunning experience to her was that this very paper that assailed the shamanization of ancient Maya in fact contributed to the further expansion of the term "shaman" in Mesoamerican archaeology. In frustration, Pasztory had to admit that one could not go against the spirit of the time (zeitgeist): "For most scholars Mesoamerica had 'priests' before 1950 and 'shamans' after. Mesoamerica hadn't changed—we did."[50]

Psychedelic scholarship also became a major source for the revision of the rock art studies that had begun in archaeology in the 1980s. Drawing on ethnographic analogies and the mental experiences of people in trance states, archaeologists who began to call themselves cognitive scholars reinterpreted the rock art produced by ancient and modern tribal peoples. Earlier scholars had explained painted and carved images on cliffs, on rocks, and inside caves worldwide as hunting magic—an applied technique allegedly used by ancient peoples to secure hunting luck. The cognitive scholars challenged this materialistic approach and began to argue that shamans were the people who might have depicted their visionary experiences on rock.[51] In other words, where earlier explorers saw hunting magic, the new generation of researchers found shamans in altered states (figure 4.4). James D. Keyser, an archaeologist with

FIGURE 4.4. Ancient cliff drawings of bighorn sheep in the Coso Range area, California. In the 1980s, many archaeologists began to view such rock art panels as the products of shamans' visionary experiences. Courtesy David Whitely.

the U.S. Forest Service, succinctly summarized this new scholarly attitude to rock art: "It has nothing to do with keeping your belly full. It's keeping your spirit full."[52]

To bolster his argument about the shamanic origin of rock art, David Lewis-Williams, one of the pioneers of the theory, turned to human neurology. He pointed out that rock drawings (various dots, zigzags, parallel lines, and other figures) were strikingly similar to the visionary geometry that people experienced in trances under the effect of hallucinogens or in states of sensory deprivation. Linking the shift in rock art studies to rising countercultural sentiments, California archaeologist Clement Meighan wrote:

> It is no accident that recent years have seen a vast increase in the amount of publication[s] relating rock art to various kinds of drug-induced visions. It is our culture that has been intensely interested and preoccupied with the drug culture during the past 20 years, and it is out of our own minds that the thought comes about prehistoric man's use of drugs and the possible relationship this may have had to rock art.[53]

In a similar manner, other scholars revisited the history of medieval European witch hunts. Earlier scholars saw these events as manifestations of mass delusions. Later, writers began to view them as a product of contemporary social and religious tensions that led to mass psychosis. At the same time, prior to the 1970s, all scholars ascribed medieval descriptions of witches' flights, Gothic sabbaths, and demonic orgies to the morbid fantasies of sadistic inquisitors who tortured bizarre confessions out of the poor victims of witch hunts. It was assumed that these records could not be authentic. In the light of psychedelic anthropology informed by countercultural ideas, these medieval descriptions of witchcraft appeared as an archaic form of European spirituality akin to shamanism.

Michael Harner, the wayward anthropologist and spearhead of shamanism in the modern West, became one of the first to revise the view of the witches' confessions as tall tales.[54] Harner stressed that those authors who wrote about witches and witchcraft either were fascinated with the esoteric side of the topic or concentrated on the brutality of European campaigns against witches. Any child knows fairytales about witches flying on broomsticks and people turning into werewolves. Yet hardly any writer took these flights and shape-shifts at face value, noted the scholar. If one looks at these available records carefully, one will clearly see that witches did fly. The only question is: how did they do it?

To answer this question, stressed Harner, one needs to pay attention to what the records said about hallucinogenic plants. One did not necessarily have to ingest a hallucinogen, like shamans of the Amazon rainforest do, remarked the scholar. Some medieval accounts show that by rubbing mind-altering substances onto their bodies, European witches successfully catapulted themselves into the other reality. The magic ointments were usually alkaloid-rich extracts from hemlock, aconite, belladonna, mandrake, and henbane plants (see figure 4.5), which usually caused hallucinations and erotic dreams. As one fifteenth-century source says, witches rubbed these substances in their armpits and in other "hairy places." In 1960, in an attempt to prove that the witches' flight was possible, German scholar Will-Erich Peukert prepared a mixture of belladonna, henbane, and jimson weed (*datura*) using a seventeenth-century formula and rubbed himself and his associates with this ointment. It appears that his experiment worked, for the research team "fell into a twenty-four hours sleep in which they dreamed of wild rides, frenzied dancing and other weird adventures of the type connected with medieval orgies."[55]

To Harner, who was still a psychedelic anthropologist in the 1960s (he turned away from this scholarship in the 1970s), the broomstick was more than simply a Freudian artifact. Considering the high concentration of nerves and blood vessels in the armpits, the vagina, and other hairy spots, European witches could well have used broomsticks coated with hallucinogenic substances as applicators of the potions to their bodies. In this case, in the "hallucinatory landscapes of their minds," witches indeed might have flown on their broomsticks.[56] Furthermore, witches' flights strongly resemble the classical spiritual journeys of Siberian shamans.

FIGURE 4.5. Henbane (*Hyoscyamus*), one of the powerful hallucinogenic plants. European witches allegedly rubbed it into their armpits and genitals, which allowed them to conduct spiritual flights. Franz E. Köhler et al., eds., *Köhler's Medizinal-Pflanzen in naturgetreuen Abbildungen mit kurz erläuterndem Texte* (Gera-Untermhaus: F. E. Köhler, 1883–1914), 1:11.

Harner also suggested that, because of the hazardous power of European hallucinogens, medieval witchcraft might have been simply a kind of dispersed shamanism, which was different from the classical Siberian template, which united the preparation for the spiritual journey, the altered states, and the divination session in one performance. Hallucinogenic plants are scarce in Europe, hypothesized Harner. Therefore, medieval witches were devoid of opportunity to freely ingest the substances that are widely available to American Indians and that drive an individual to the other reality but not to the point of disabling the spiritual practitioner. For example, the belladonna weed that witches might have applied to their bodies to induce trances and visions is a very powerful substance that causes unconsciousness and even kills in a high dose. This made it impossible to simultaneously experience visions and to perform ritual activities, unlike, for instance, Native American peyote or Siberian mushroom sessions.

Under these circumstances, argued Harner, European witches had to spread their activities over time. The job of bewitching and other ritual activities were reserved for "business" meetings (esbat) during which drugs were

forbidden and witches worked in the ordinary reality. For hallucinogenic experiences, witches used the sabbath, where they encountered demons. Having
ingested belladonna or other mind-altering substances, the witches flew to this
separate reality on their famous broomsticks. Harner suggested that, based
on the powerful nature of European herbal hallucinogens, the European shamanic trance and the ritual became separated.

This assertion prompted Harner to pose another important question. Shall
we always consider the shaman a person who is involved in a trance state and
ritual activities in one experience, as Eliade taught us? If not, surmised the
anthropologist, let us revise and extend the concept of shamanism to include in
this realm such practices as witchcraft that do not exactly fit the classical
framework of shamanism informed by Siberian ethnographies.

"On Some Remarkable Narcotics of the Amazon Valley and Orinoco": Ayahuasca Shamanism

The phrase that I chose as the title for this section comes from a book chapter
in *Notes of a Botanist on the Amazon & Andes* by Richard Spruce, an English
botanist who visited South America in the 1850s. Spruce became one of the
first to compose a comprehensive record of South American herbal hallucinogens in their tribal setting. Before him and for many years afterward, the
mind-altering herbs of Amazonia did not attract too much attention. Explorers
did write about them but never singled them out as something special which
informed entire indigenous cultures. Writers frequently referred to indigenous
plant hallucinogens in passing or relegated this information to sections dealing with native *materia medica*. However, in light of the Wasson mushroom
scholarship and growing psychedelic awareness, the situation changed. Since
the 1960s, the sacred plants of the Amazon rainforest have been the object of
keen research and popular attention. Scholars and astronauts of inner space
have streamed to jungles seeking to experience indigenous rituals that involve
herbal hallucinogens and to detail them in their books.

The most widespread sacred herb ingested by Indian and mixed-blood
shamans and laypeople in the Amazon areas of Peru, Brazil, and Colombia is a
drink that, in appearance, resembles a dark tea. This potion is made of a vine
whose Latin name is *Banisteriopsis caapi*. In 1852, Spruce left the following
description of this plant in his journal: "Woody twiner; stem = thumb, swollen
at joints. Leaves opposite, 6.4 × 3.3, oval acuminate, apiculato-acute, thinnish,
smooth above, appresso-subpilose beneath."[57]

The ritual drink produced from this plant is known under a variety of
names: *caapi, ayahuasca, yage, netema, pinde,* and *nape.* For convenience, I will
be using *ayahuasca,* the expression that seems to be most popular in the
literature. *Ayahuasca* is a word from Quechua, the language spoken by the

Indians in Peru, Ecuador, and northern Chile, and poetically translates as "vine of the dead," "vine of souls," or "vine of the ancestors." Although indigenous spiritual practitioners occasionally cook *ayahuasca* by using only the stem of *Banisteriopsis*, more frequently, they mix the vines with other hallucinogenic plants, which allow them to control the shape and color of the images ignited by the potion. In fact, the expression *ayahuasca* has two meanings. One describes the drink made exclusively from *Banisteriopsis*. The other one is a drink prepared from the mixture of this vine and other mind-altering herbs, whose chemistry is not always familiar to Westerners. The most popular *ayahuasca* recipe is to boil the mixture of the stem of the *ayahuasca* vine (*Banisteriopsis caapi*) with either the leaves of the *chakruna* (*Psychotria viridis*) or *chagropanga* (*Diplopterys cabrerana*).[58]

Spruce, who reported that the Indians he observed used the lower part of the *Banisteriopsis* stem as the major ingredient, left one of the first records of how the sacred potion was cooked:

> A quantity of this is beaten in a mortar, with water, and sometimes with the addition of a small portion of the slender roots of the Caapi-pinima. When sufficiently triturated, it is passed through a sieve, which separates the woody fibre, and to the residue enough water is added to render it drinkable. Thus prepared, its color is brownish-green, and its taste bitter and disagreeable.[59]

Spruce, a detached, positivist Victorian scientist, described the external behavioral "symptoms" of an *ayahuasca* user he observed in the fall of 1852, when he was a guest at a so-called feast of gifts among the Tukano Indians in the Vaupés River area:

> In two minutes or less after drinking it, its effects begin to be apparent. The Indian turns deadly pale, trembles in every limb, and horror is in his aspect. Suddenly contrary symptoms success: he bursts in a perspiration, and seems possessed with reckless fury, seizes whatever arms are at hand, his murucu, bow and arrows, or cutlass, and rushes to the doorway, where he inflicts violent blows on the ground or the doorsteps, calling out all the while, "Thus would I do to mine enemy (naming him by name) were this he!" In about ten minutes the excitement has passed off, and the Indian grows calm, but appears exhausted. Were he at home in his hut, he would sleep off the remaining fumes, but now he must shake off his drowsiness by renewing the dance.[60]

Spruce went to the feast determined to try some *ayahuasca* and at the same time to resist its effects. Indians poured into him so much of the drink that the botanist could hardly stand. To enhance the hallucinogenic effect, his hosts handed him a large cigar. For Spruce, who never smoked, it was more than enough. Fortunately, his friend prepared a cup of coffee that, according to the explorer, eased to some extent the effect of the hallucinogen.

Ingesting this remarkable narcotic is not exactly a pleasant experience. Many people feel nausea. They also vomit and suffer from diarrhea. Their moods switch from euphoria to aggressive excitation. The visions *ayahuasca* takers experience pass rapidly before their eyes and usually turn from gorgeous to horrible and back. They also feel alternations of cold and heat, fear and boldness. *Ayahuasca* also gives a sensation that one's soul has become separated from the body. Frequently, while under *ayahuasca*, people "turn" into various birds or animals and feel that they fly to far-off places and converse with spirits and ancestors. They also see various animals, especially reptiles and feline-like creatures.

To some modern users, the disagreeable taste of *ayahuasca* is exactly what makes it attractive. Daniel Pinchbeck, one of those current spiritual seekers who departed on a spiritual pilgrimage to South America, views the bitter taste of *ayahuasca* as a symbolic antidote to the Western civilization that sugars and pampers people by making everything attractive, tasty, and cozy. Pinchbeck stresses that *ayahuasca* drinkers "vomit and shit, shiver and sweat, and at the same time receive outrageously beautiful visions."[61]

It seems that his point is that one has to suffer for a spiritual reward. Indeed, if we were to believe Western astronauts of inner space, the spiritual rewards of *ayahuasca* ingestion are tremendous, which makes it worth drinking. Reportedly, it provides a vivid "appointment with knowledge." All observations show that *ayahuasca* is far more powerful than Siberian or Mexican mushrooms. In the words of scholar Hans Peter Duerr, this drink seems to be specially designed for flying.[62]

One of the most beautiful descriptions of a spiritual journey sparked by *ayahuasca* can be found in *The Way of the Shaman* by Michael Harner, a book that is considered a classic of modern Western shamanism. Harner underwent this experience in a natural setting during his 1960–1961 stay among the Conibo Indians of the Peruvian Amazon. The anthropologist noted that after ingesting *ayahuasca*, he was exposed to a frightening vision of dragon-like reptiles that took him to the very sources of the original creation and introduced the secret knowledge that was usually reserved only for the dead or for those who were designated to die. He was sure that he was about to die. As Harner metaphorically put it, he felt like the condemned Socrates taking the deadly hemlock amid his Athenian compatriots.[63]

Although terrifying, the experience was enlightening and even liberating because the anthropologist discovered the "way." Despite all the trials and tribulations, the author of *The Way of the Shaman* informs us that this visionary journey ended happily and even pleasantly. Before coming back to the ordinary world, the anthropologist spent some time in the other world flying out into the galaxy, creating marvelous architectural constructions, and even "socializing" with sardonically grinning demons.[64]

The next day, having awakened in a surprisingly fresh and peaceful mood, Harner rushed to his duffle bag, pulled out a tape recorder, and immediately began to narrate his experiences, making sure that nothing was left out. In fact, he felt some sort of fear for his own safety. The fear was understandable. After all, he was the only one who now possessed the secret that the visionary creatures reserved for the dying. Thinking that this esoteric knowledge should be somehow shared with other people, Harner rushed to a nearby evangelist mission, where he detailed his spiritual encounters to two clerics. While Harner was doing his storytelling, the hospitable missionaries occasionally interrupted the anthropologist, reaching for the Bible and pointing out to him the book's verses that directly matched parts of the vision. For example, when Harner told the clerics about a reptile with water coming out of its mouth, the missionaries quickly found a corresponding quote from the Book of Revelation: "And the serpent cast out of his mouth water as a flood."[65]

With a sense of relief, the anthropologist returned to the native village, where a more pleasant surprise was awaiting him. Soliciting an expert opinion from a blind shaman, who frequently visited the spirit world while under *ayahuasca*, Harner shared with him parts of his vision. Stunned by how much the anthropologist had learned during his first journey, the Indian issued his verdict, "You can surely be a master shaman."[66] Overall, the *ayahuasca* journey became for Harner a profound spiritual revelation that convinced him of the reality of spirits and triggered his conversion from an agnostic anthropologist to a practitioner of shamanism. Eventually, he left academia and established the Foundation for Shamanic Studies (FSS), which now works to bring techniques based on indigenous shamanism to Westerners.

Others who went through similar experiences did not see anything sacred in their visions induced by *ayahuasca*. For example, to another student of shamanism, the late Gerardo Reichel-Dolmatoff, an anthropologist who looked at the Amazon indigenous cosmos through the eyes of psychoanalysis, Desana Indians' altered states triggered by hallucinogens were filled with sexual symbolism. Reichel-Dolmatoff observed the *ayahuasca* sessions and ingested the potion himself approximately during the same years when Harner did his fieldwork among the Jivaro and Conibo. In one particular case, Reichel-Dolmatoff concluded that *ayahuasca* visions had something to do with the natives' anxiety about incest.[67] The different perceptions of *ayahuasca* experiences show that everything depends on the intellectual stance of individuals: how they see things, what they expect to see, and especially whether they are ready to see and believe.

By the 1970s, academic and metaphysical students of the Amazon psychedelics came to an agreement that despite the diversity of their cultural settings, people who take *ayahuasca* have essentially similar visionary experiences. It appeared to be another confirmation of what Eliade wrote in his classic *Shamanism: Archaic Techniques of Ecstasy* (1964)—shamanism is a universal human experience that crosses cultural borders. In other words, it does not matter if one is an Indian or a European, the imagery experienced during an *ayahuasca* journey essentially will have the same thematic lines.

Countercultural psychologist from Chile Claudio Naranjo conducted an experiment that tested the imagery that Native Americans and Chileans of European descent experienced after taking the magic potion. He found that at least half of the imagery observed by people was identical. These are usually snakes, dragons, jaguars, or some other kinds of reptiles or predators. Urban elite Chileans who ingested the chemical substance of *ayahuasca* in clinical settings reported that they turned into "balls of energy" and rapidly flew through the sky by becoming winged creatures. They also saw black people and Roman Catholic symbols and felt that they were swirling violently. They also encountered malicious dwarves. At the same time, like their Native American counterparts, the Chileans saw scary panthers and tigers, such reptiles as lizards and dragons, predatory animals, and deep lakes and abysses.[68]

This universal similarity of the *ayahuasca* imagery prompted the Swiss anthropology writer Jeremy Narby to come up with a provocative concept. In his *Cosmic Serpent*, he suggested that the repeated snake-type spiral imagery that both Amazonian shamans and Westerners usually experience after ingesting the *Banisteriopsis* drink is, in fact, the window to the sources of our genetic roots. Narby argued that the spiral reptile imagery of *ayahuasca* visions is nothing less than a distant replica of a human DNA spiral code. In this case, shamanism surely appears to be a deeply archaic phenomenon that takes us not only back to the dawn of human history but straight to the very source of creation.[69]

In traditional settings, among the Indians of the Amazon area, natives use the *ayahuasca* drink on various occasions. First, they believe that the drink purges one's body of unnecessary emotions and feelings. Second, and most important, indigenous shamans drink the potion for diagnostic purposes. Spiritual practitioners take the drink, enter a trance in order to step into unseen realities, and receive relevant information from spirits on how to deal with a particular problem or misfortune. Although the most widespread occasion for the use of *ayahuasca* is spiritual healing, the Indians take the drink on a variety of occasions, for example, initiation ceremonies or funerals. In most cases, both the healer and his patient take the potion. In traditional Amazonian settings, women and prepubescent children rarely ingest the potion. They are only allowed to be present during *ayahuasca* sessions and to observe their effects.

For example, when Desana or Jivaro *ayahuasquero* shamans cure people, they are expected not only to discover the source of an ailment but also to extract the source of this ailment from the body of the patient and to return it to the shaman-sorcerer who inflicted the illness on the patient. Since the effect of *ayahuasca* can be both pleasant and terrifying, the Indians usually ingest the drink in the company of a shaman who can navigate the taker through a spiritual journey by using ritual songs. The effect of the drink on a person depends on many factors—the personality of the user, the atmosphere of the gathering, the properties of the plants, and the dose. In short, the effect of *ayahuasca* is very unpredictable.

Reichel-Dolmatoff stressed that this ambivalent character of *ayahuasca* disturbed the Desana Indians. Hence, the Indians developed various magic spells and songs in hopes of changing the "mind" of the potion in their favor or at least eliminating its most unpleasant effects. The Desana also informed the scholar that the purpose of taking *ayahuasca* was to enter the realm of creation, where the individual could see the creation of the universe, humans, and animals and converse with his clan ancestors. The Indians believed that going through the *ayahuasca* session, the person died and became reborn in the state of wisdom. Such spiritual sessions usually enhanced the beliefs of the Indians, who became convinced that the mythological creatures and deities did exist because they saw them with their own eyes.[70] These utterances made good supportive evidence for the above-mentioned Narby thesis about the *ayahuasca* séances as journeys to the sources of creation.

In addition to indigenous jungle practitioners of *ayahuasca* shamanism, there is a large group of so-called *vegetalistas*, mixed-blood spiritual practitioners, who claim that they receive their knowledge directly from the *ayahuasca* vine and other hallucinogenic plants. Many of these mixed-blood spiritual practitioners operate in a city setting, for example, in Peruvian urban slums. In their healing practices, they rely heavily on Roman-Catholic symbolism and tradition. Thus, these urban spiritual doctors usually seek the source of their patients' troubles in violations of some moral or religious norms. After these shamans partake of *ayahuasca* and see the source of a misfortune, they issue their advice. For example, they could ask an individual to recite a prayer or apologize for misconduct. In this role, urban *ayahuasca* shamans act as analogues of social workers and psychotherapists. There are some *ayahuasca* shamanism practitioners who associate themselves with the Rosicrucians and trace their knowledge both to indigenous Andean cultures and to the old European esoteric tradition. The latter is a good example of a cultural and spiritual blend that encompasses all corners of the world.

After Spruce, the next Westerner who conducted detailed research on Amazon hallucinogenic herbs was the Harvard ethnobotanist Richard Schultes. During the Second World War, he was assigned to the rainforest area to research rubber trees for war needs. In the meantime, on the side, the scientist was searching for information about *Banisteriopsis* and other indigenous psychotropic plants. After the war was over, Schultes continued his explorations (see figures 4.6a and 4.6b).[71]

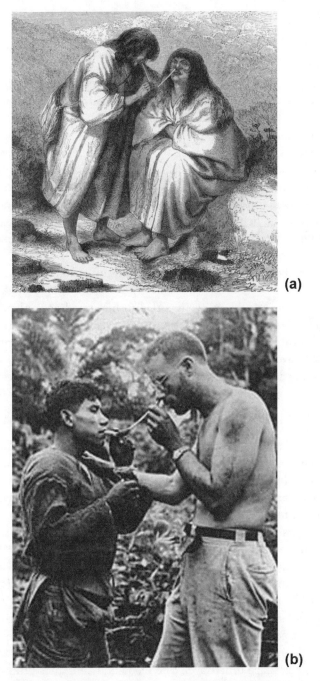

FIGURE 4.6. (a) Amazonian Indians taking tobacco snuff. A nineteenth-century engraving from Paul Marcoy, *A Journey across South America* (London: Blackie, 1872), 2:543. (b) Ethnobotanist Richard Evans Schultes taking tobacco snuff with an Amazonian Indian. Courtesy American Society of Pharmacognosy.

In 1953, while on a field trip in Colombia, he stumbled upon another Harvard alumnus, William Burroughs, a flamboyant literary outlaw and a senior member of Jack Kerouac's literary circle. Kerouac and his friends were among the first to drop out from the Western culture soaked in materialism and tune in to alternative realities, a mindset that became popular later in the 1960s. Burroughs was similarly on a quest for the indigenous vine, only for different purposes. A prolific writer and a spoiled bohemian who lived on trust fund money, Burroughs had wrenched himself through heroin addiction. In addition, during one of his drinking sprees, he had accidentally shot his wife. In 1953, he found a refuge in the Colombian rainforest in the hope that the jungle drink would help him to somehow defeat the addiction and change his life. Burroughs attached himself to the Schultes expedition. The association with the ethnobotanist helped Burroughs to procure twenty pounds of *ayahuasca* and to befriend an Indian witch doctor, who administered the magic drink to him.[72]

With excitement, the writer reported to his friend poet Allen Ginsberg, "Dear Allen. Back to Bogotá. Mission accomplished. I have a crate of Yage [one of the local names for *ayahuasca*] with me. I know how the witch doctors prepare it. I have taken it three times."[73] This jungle companionship between the scientist and the literary spiritual seeker is symbolic. It manifested a close but ambivalent partnership between such researchers as Schultes or Wasson, who simply educated society about hallucinogens, and the coming psychedelic revolution that sought to integrate these hallucinogens into cultural and spiritual life. Incidentally, these ambivalent relations surface in Schultes's reply to Burroughs, who described to the scientist his psychedelic trip as an earth-shaking metaphysical experience. Schultes, a member of the currently extinct tribe of Victorian positivist scientists, brought him down to earth by remarking, "That's funny, Bill, all I saw was colors."[74]

The visions to which Burroughs was exposed during his *ayahuasca* journeys were no less terrifying than what Harner described in *The Way of the Shaman*. During one of his spiritual trips, Burroughs was attacked by flocks of flying snakes and squawking larvae. Eventually, the writer transformed into a large black woman, then into a black man. Then he became a man and a woman at the same time, simultaneously observing a kaleidoscope of Van Gogh–like images. Describing his experiences, the writer wrote to Ginsberg:

> Yage is space time travel. The blood and substance of many
> races, Negro, Polynesian, Mountain Mongol, Desert Nomad, Poly-
> glot Near east, Indian—new races as yet unconceived and unborn,
> combinations not yet realized pass through your body. Migrations,
> incredible journeys through deserts and jungles and mountains. . . . A
> place where the unknown past and the emergent future meet in a
> vibrating soundless hum.[75]

Inspired by these encounters with the sacred, Ginsberg followed his friend and similarly partook of the sacred tea rite in the company of a native witch doctor. The poet claimed that he observed the mystery of creation through the black nostrils of God before being hit by nausea. Although, as in the case of Burroughs, the taste of the drink did not thrill him at all and the unfolding images appeared frightening, his aesthetic sense seemed satisfied: "I began to get high—and then the whole fucking Cosmos broke loose around me."[76] Subsequently, Burroughs and Ginsberg immortalized the magic potion by publishing *The Yage Letters*, a book of their correspondence regarding their quest for the jungle vine.[77] *The Yage Letters* became a cultural and spiritual blueprint for would-be spiritual pilgrims who followed in their footsteps.

Mystical Tourism

Burroughs blazed the trail for thousands of future Americans and Europeans, who in the 1960s and 1970s streamed to South America hoping to ingest the magic potion in order to resolve their spiritual and emotional problems or simply to encounter an exotic setting. In the 1950s, the quest for the rainforest herbal hallucinogen undertaken by Burroughs certainly appeared to be an eccentric venture. Such trips have now turned into a mass pilgrimage that has created a small industry of jungle shamanism that involves Western spiritual seekers, tour operators, and local native and mixed-blood people. For the latter, cooking the magic drink for the tourists and accommodating them brings substantial cash income.

Ayahuasca and other Latin American herbal hallucinogens have become staple products in the marketplace of Western spirituality. Some Westerners who wish to see, to know, or simply, like some of my American friends say, want to try something different, now look for Amazon shamans and ingest the magic potion. People from the United States, Europe, and Japan journey to the jungles and deserts of Latin America to participate in hallucinogen-related rituals. In response to the growing demand, in such countries as Peru, local *ayahuasqueros* have set up jungle retreats and urban healing centers. In many instances, these ventures represent joint enterprises run by North American tour operators with connections in Western "New Age" circles and by local spiritual practitioners. If Burroughs had departed nowadays to the Amazon rainforest to search for the jungle drink to resolve his spiritual problems, he most probably would have booked one of numerous shamanism tours currently offered on-line or in the pages of spirituality print media.

In addition to *ayahuasca*, this spiritual industry now offers many other metaphysical experiences. It could be, for example, an initiation of spiritual seekers into indigenous rituals amid ancient Indian ruins. Sometimes, scenarios of mystic tours include educational programs such as visits to Indian villages, observations of indigenous lore and culture, and learning about local plant and animal life. Still, the ingestion of rainforest hallucinogens remains one of the major components of these ventures. For example, a spiritual enterprise with an exotic name, the Wild Mushroom Traveling Road Show, specializes in catering the jungle's sacred drink to Western spiritual tourists. At the same time, besides drinking *ayahuasca*, its tour program includes the exploration of jungle plants and visits to native villages. Those who feel that they are ready can take part in an all-night *ayahuasca* session with a chanting indigenous shaman. The show is run by Gerry Miller, a Canadian and a graduate of the University of California at Berkeley. He has an art degree and considers himself an expert in hallucinogenic plants. In the summer, when it is too hot to travel to jungles, he and his wife work in their antique store at home in Canada. Yet in the winter, the couple turns all their attention to Amazonia. Their jungle show included a two-week tour up and down the Amazon River and cost $3,600 per person in 1993.[78]

The California-based Four Winds Foundation, another spiritual tour enterprise, similarly offers a variety of cultural and spiritual experiences in addition to *ayahuasca*. Thus, the foundation brings spiritual seekers to Peru to experience ceremonies amid picturesque pre-Hispanic ancient ruins such as Machu Picchu. For example, during one of the foundation's mystic tours to this high-altitude location, ethnographic tourists meditated, observed the sacrifice of a guinea pig whose entrails were analyzed for indication of illness, and went through a trial by fire. The tour also included an initiation of the Western visitors into Peruvian shamanism, an event that took place in a lagoon, which, according to tour organizer Alberto Villoldo, represented an ancient initiation site and an entrance to the spirit world. Mystical tourists stripped themselves naked and threw their personal objects into the water, after which local spiritual practitioner Eduardo Calderon rubbed them with a sword. The ritual was designed as a shamanic rebirth of the participants and their release from the past. Finally, at the end of the ceremony, the initiated were asked to roll in mud, which symbolized their rebirth from Mother Earth. As a result, the overseas spiritual seekers were declared "the new caretakers and healers of the earth."[79]

Peru is one of the most popular destinations for the mystic tours. Some spiritual seekers view the Peruvian Amazon as the Harvard of shamanism. Villoldo, a medical anthropologist from California and simultaneously an "Andean shaman," is one of the most well-known mystical tour operators. His Four Winds Foundation takes groups of Western seekers to work with Peruvian shamans. This travel agent to the spirit world bluntly says, "I charge a lot of money."[80] For a long time, Villoldo worked in partnership with Calderon, a Peruvian *curandero*, artist, and Rosicrucian. According to Villoldo's former administrative assistant, Madrina Denig, in the early 1990s, a three-week shamanic tour run by the foundation cost $30,000, of which Calderon received only $500.[81] At the same time, each year the foundation donates between $40,000 and $60,000 to indigenous people in food and medical assistance.[82] In Peru, there is also a local Lima-based organization, Ayahuasca-Wasi, which offers week-long experiential seminars specially designed to accommodate Western visitors. Along with "Amazonian Shamanism," seminars include meditation and Tibetan philosophy. Some Peruvian spiritual practitioners who work through their agents in North America and Europe charge as much as $10,000 for their shamanic tours.[83]

Opinions about the impact of this mystic tourism on local populations vary. Many scholars and spiritual seekers such as Denig blame North American spiritual entrepreneurs for using indigenous people for profit. Moreover, anthropologist Douglas Sharon, who was the first to "discover" Calderon, uses the expression "culture vultures" to describe people like Villoldo. Some critics also note that the influx of Westerners ruins the traditional setting and profanes indigenous spirituality. The recently deceased hallucinogen writer Terence McKenna wrote with frustration that many jungle shamans were being "destroyed by money, blonde women and invitations to Malibu."[84]

At the same time, foreign and local organizers of spiritual tours stress that their ventures benefit both sides. While Western spiritual tourists feel satisfied experiencing spirituality in the exotic setting, local impoverished economies receive some cash injections. Rivas-Vasquez, a Peruvian philosopher and artist who now runs a permanent *ayahuasca* jungle camp, Yushintaita, which caters to the spiritual needs of visitors from all over the West, points to the benefits of this enterprise for the economy of his community. He stresses that the majority of the surrounding people are happy to see visitors because they bring additional jobs, such as gardening, cooking, and assisting tourists. For example, a group of local women is employed in collecting jungle vines, which he uses to brew his *ayahuasca* medicine. Rivas-Vasquez also uses part of the money he makes during his seminar trips to Europe and North America to organize local cooperatives of farm workers and artists. "Now that they can work, they will be able to eat," summarizes this shaman-intellectual.[85]

Furst, one of those scholars who helped to bring the metaphor of shamanism to American anthropology, tries to put himself in the shoes of those native healers who struggle to survive in the miserable conditions of Latin America, which for many Westerners is hard to imagine. The scholar does not see anything wrong with the desire of indigenous people to benefit from this Western romance with shamanism and tribal spirituality: "If white people want to spend hard cash for a version of shamanism that sounds more genuine because it is in a language they cannot understand, why not derive some modest benefit?"[86]

Alan Shoemaker, an American who runs a mystic tour company called Shamanismo and who specializes in taking tour groups to the Peruvian rainforest, says that when he came to South America for the first time, he thought that *ayahuasca* shamanism was some sort of special spiritual wisdom that had nothing to do with materialistic sentiments. Although his belief in the power of *ayahuasca* visions has not subsided, he is now more down to earth. Today, Shoemaker does not look at Peruvian *curanderos* through romantic eyes:

> I soon learned that most curanderos and ayahuasqueros are trades people who have learned their trade much as one would learn to become a car mechanic or doctor. There is now even a licensing school for curanderos in northern Peru. This is not to say that these curanderos don't have healing powers. I have great respect for most of the curanderos I have worked with. Most healers have a sincere desire to heal, and most are skilled healers. Over the years, I have also encountered some so-called "curanderos" who got into the profession to make money or because there wasn't other work. Cooking *aya-huasca* isn't a difficult task, and memorizing enough icaros [songs] to get through a ritual is simple enough.[87]

Not infrequently in Peru, locals who pose as shamans, *curanderos*, or *aya-huasqueros* do not wait to be approached by Western ethnotourists but take the initiative to reach out to seekers of spiritual wisdom in the hope of making some extra cash. Incidentally, in Peru, some hotels place signs warning Western visitors about local con artists who dress themselves in feathers and beads and pose as *ayahuasca* healers.[88] Don Agustin Rivas-Vasquez, a Peruvian intellectual and *ayahuasca* shamanism practitioner, warns the readers of *Shaman's Drum* about the potential hazards awaiting Westerners in their search for *ayahuasca* spirituality. He points to numerous self-made "instant *ayahuasqueros*" who fill the streets of Lima and Cusco and who come from the ranks of local Indians, mixed-bloods, and even foreigners residing in Peru. These people, he says, "hawk their services and bottles of brew to the unsuspecting hoards of Westerners who flock to Peru in search of exotic psychedelic experiences."

Some of them rush to serve the herbal drink to eager foreigners and do not bother to even learn shamanic chants to give at least a little ethnographic decor to their *ayahuasca* sessions. There are "shamans" who do not know how to cook *ayahuasca*, preferring to buy the ready-made mix from unknown sources. Rivas-Vasquez stresses that, unless a person has established contacts in the area, it is not easy to find a reliable shaman: "Despite the potential legal and psychological risks involved, spiritually hungry Westerners—particularly those who don't speak Spanish—often put themselves in danger of being hustled by enterprising entrepreneurs or being taken advantage of by outright charlatans."[89]

Denig, a shamanism practitioner and a religious science minister from the United States, described several colorful episodes related to her troubles on a bumpy road to indigenous spirituality.[90] A Peruvian anthropologist named

Juan, who advertised himself as a teacher of Andean mysticism, approached Denig, saying that "Master Jesus" ordered him to initiate her into Andean mysteries. The ceremony impressed the woman with its beauty. Three days later, the anthropologist resurfaced with a business offer: "You have been initiated now, Madrina, you can now initiate other people and each time you initiate someone, I have a contract, you will give me $300."[91]

In another unfortunate encounter, a local spiritual practitioner who wanted to strike a partnership with a well-connected Westerner to bring shamanism tour groups to study with him stuck a note on Denig's door, inviting her for a talk. When the intrigued woman came, the "healer" unfolded the details of his spiritual enterprise: she would bring Westerners for a five-day course costing $5,000 per person, after which all participants would be issued papers declaring that they are certified shamans. Denig made a mistake by not dismissing the offer right away. Instead, she mentioned that she could not seal the joint venture without learning how his medicine worked. The "shaman" got her on this. In his zeal to impress the woman with the power of his sacred drink, which was made of the San Pedro cactus, he quickly cooked the potion. Hastily trying to ship the gringa to nonordinary reality, the enterprising man filled the poor woman with a dinosaur's dose of his *remedio*, pouring the drink from a bull's horn into her nose and making her swallow it. "He threw at me everything he could," complained Denig. In the meantime, one of his assistants tried to put Denig in an "appropriate mood" by invoking Gothic images: "You ought to know that there is a powerful green serpent and it is going to consume you."

The final surprise came at the end of the ceremony, when Denig was abruptly asked to pay $1,000 for this demonstration. When the American spiritual seeker refused, the angry "shaman" followed her home, trying to extract the cash. In addition to the above-mentioned troubles, after the "shaman" departed, the musicians who accompanied the ceremony came and began to press her for money as well. The cornered woman had no other choice except to use a weapon from the toolkit of Western civilization by sobering the solicitors with a question, "Money, for what? I did not make a contract with you." About this unfortunate aspect of the economy of jungle shamanism, another American *ayahuasca* user sardonically noted, "Amazonian shamans are the priests, doctors, philanthropists and capitalists of their local economies. We foreign students are the geese supplying the golden nest eggs."[92]

Like many of his colleagues, in the 1980s, when mystic tourists began coming in increasing numbers, Mateo Arevalo, a Shipibo *curandero* from Peru, took advantage of the opportunity to make some extra money and began to cater to visitors from North America and Western Europe who sought wisdom or spiritual healing, or who simply felt passion for exotic places. Arevalo erected jungle lodges for the foreigners and began to run expensive *ayahuasca* retreats.

Moreover, at his home, he now accommodates Western apprentices who come to study shamanism with him for three to six months. Talking about his vocation, the spiritual practitioner stresses, "I am an innovator, adding to my ancestral knowledge. We, the Shipibos, like any other human community—we need to grow and change. We can't just stay the same so that the tourists can stare at the naked Indians in feathers and the anthropologists can treat us like [a] living museum."[93] Arevalo's spiritual venture brings him about $200 each month from his Western apprentices. In addition, he charges $30 per person when he conducts *ayahuasca* sessions for overseas visitors.

Spiritual practitioner Antonio Munoz, his kinsman, in an attempt to use these new opportunities, moved from the rainforest to the capital city of Lima and struck a partnership with a psychotherapist. The two now offer therapy sessions based on modern and traditional techniques, incorporating *ayahuasca* drink into their curative practices. Here, *ayahuasca* serves as a tool of medical analysis prescribed to patients to help them better articulate their fears and traumas. Munoz argues, "Other curanderos need to learn from the science of psychotherapy to better treat our patients. We need to advance, to offer our alternative healing to the whole world."[94]

Such a stance prompts some *ayahuasca* practitioners to rationalize the use of the magic potion in terms of Western science and medicine. For example, explaining to Western audiences the essence of *ayahuasca* healing, Rivas-Vasquez, who provides the magic herb to overseas spiritual seekers, stresses that *ayahuasca* acts as a vitamin that strengthens the immune system and repairs overloaded people's neurons. The spiritual practitioner believes that many drugs contain chemicals that destroy neurons. *Ayahuasca*, as he notes, on the contrary, protects and repairs neurons. Bringing neurons into the picture allows Rivas-Vasquez to draw attention to the potential ecological benefits of *ayahuasca* to modern city dwellers, whose brains are overloaded with information and noise. In addition to the possible psychological effect of the jungle drink, Rivas-Vasquez notes that *ayahuasca* healing is also accomplished through the placebo effect, when the patient firmly believes in the potion's curative power.[95]

To establish a spiritual middle ground with their Western guests who come to South America with a shamanic intent, many spiritual practitioners also tailor their rites to the tastes of these visitors. For example, in Peru, some *curanderos* try to make their ceremonies more traditional by purging them of Christian elements and adding idioms from modern Western esotericism. Thus, although many *curanderos* in Peru used Bibles in their healing sessions, Western spiritual seekers who began streaming to the country in the 1980s viewed the Bible as something that did not belong to indigenous, traditional culture. As a result, some *curanderos* put it away and began to act more "traditionally." Frequently, the healers catering to the tastes of Westerners adopt the expression shaman (*chamán*) with the same goal—to build bridges between them and their Western audiences.[96] Now many Latin American *curanderos* talk about chakras or energy or wrap their séances in the form of therapy sessions, which creates an interesting cultural combination of indigenous, Christian, and "New Age" elements and rituals.

Like its European and American counterparts, current *chamanismo* in Peru puts stress on the benevolent and healing side of shamanism and downplays the dark sides of traditional shamanism, which is usually full of mutual accusations, revenge, retaliation, and the destruction of malicious animals and human beings who are held responsible for various misfortunes. In this new, sanitized, and benevolent version of Amazon shamanism, *ayahuasca* is used for therapeutic purposes. Therefore, it is natural for a modern Peruvian *chamán* to remove magic darts from the body of a patient and yet never return them to their sender, as their traditional counterparts would have done in an act of retaliation.[97]

Sometimes a desire to cater to particular metaphysical demands of Western audiences acquires grotesque forms, as in the case of the Peruvian shaman Calderon. He once had to squeeze rites and ceremonies which were originally designated for a long-time apprenticeship into a short time span to accommodate the interests of an Austrian film crew that came to shoot *Healing States*, a documentary about his work with advanced spiritual students. Although before the event he had informed his apprentices that they had to ingest the drink made of the San Pedro cactus, which contains mescaline, only two times a year, for the filming, the students had to consume the potion each day. As a result, one of the apprentices had a bad reaction and had to be taken from a plane unconscious on the way home to San Francisco.[98]

At the same time, the desire of some Latin American *chamáns* to accommodate Western visitors in every way arouses unwarranted spiritual expectations among the overseas seekers and spiritual entrepreneurs. For example, one mystic tour operator insisted, "The Amazon is being deforested, and the Native Americans are disappearing. Shamanism does not belong to the Indian; they are only the caretakers of that knowledge. The new shamans, according to their prophesies are us, the new caretakers of a vision of ecology, of living in harmony with the earth."[99]

In addition to the Peruvian Amazon, Mexico remains a popular destination for mystical tourists. Besides the lure of the Oaxaca sacred mushrooms, of which I wrote in detail above, spiritual seekers tap peyote lands, the habitat of the Huichol Indians, who are celebrated in the ethnographic literature for their esoteric annual peyote pilgrimages. In the spring and fall, the Huichol usually travel to the highland deserts of San Luis Potosi, an area that is rich in peyote, and retrieve the cacti for their ritual use (see figure 4.7). From the beginning to the end, the whole pilgrimage is accompanied by elaborate rituals, which were colorfully described by anthropologist Barbara Myerhoff in *Peyote Hunt* (1974).

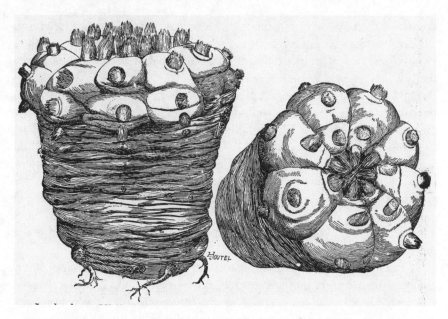

FIGURE 4.7. Peyote cactus (*Lophophora Williamsii*), used by the Huichol and other Native Americans in their rituals, became popular with Western seekers of tribal spirituality in the 1960s and 1970s. Carl Lumholtz, *Unknown Mexico* (New York: Scribner's, 1902), 1:358.

During these pilgrimage seasons, small groups of Westerners come to native villages located along the route and seek Huichol pilgrims, trying to join them. The Indians usually do not mind sharing their peyote rites with outsiders, if the latter show respect to them and pay some cash. Leo Mercado, a thirty-one-year-old potter from Kearny, Arizona, who was able to join the Huichol on their peyote hunt, brought along his family and several friends. For three days, under the guidance of the Indians, they experimented with peyote. However, on the way back, loaded with leftover cacti, they were arrested by Mexican police and spent two months in jail. Despite this misfortune, Mercado remembers with excitement his peyote-generated visionary experience: "You not only see God, you become God."[100]

One organization that caters to the needs of people like Mercado is the California-based Dance of the Deer Foundation, which organizes mystical tours to Huichol country involving not only peyote experiences but a whole range of ritual activities. This foundation, which was one of the first Western centers to promote tribal shamanism, is headed by Brant Secunda, a spiritual seeker, who grew up in an affluent Jewish family in Brooklyn, New York. At age eighteen, he left home and wandered into northern Mexico where he began to apprentice with the Huichol holy man Jose Matsuwa. After twelve years of learning,

Secunda himself became a spiritual practitioner and, simultaneously, a spiritual tour operator. Nowadays, he brings Westerners to the Huichol shamanland and supervises their spiritual training on the spot.

Secunda also claims that the Huichol call him a brother and ask him to perform healing sessions for members of their communities. "Basically I guess you could say I am almost a Huichol," adds the spiritual entrepreneur. Secunda says that he likes to bring his students to Huichol country because "people can see a beautiful culture." Although he is one of the people who draw these Indians into the orbit of global "New Age" culture, Secunda also fears that the different dress styles, different manners, and Western money the mystical tourists bring there might corrupt the purity of Huichol nature with Western materialism.[101]

Europeans and Americans who join tours organized by such spiritual entrepreneurs as Villoldo, Miller, and Secunda have different motives. For some, these rainforest retreats and ingesting hallucinogens in an indigenous setting represent profound spiritual and healing experiences. In a letter to the *San Francisco Chronicle*, Joy Wilder, an alcoholic and drug addict who had tried everything and everywhere, stressed that visions induced by *ayahuasca* finally, for the first time in her life, brought her into a "state of Grace." Reflecting on the dramatic changes the sacred potion produced in her life, she wrote:

> I am a child of the '60s, the consciousness revolution. I am an alumnus [*sic*] of countless 12-step programs, therapy groups, purification diets, meditation practices. I have done my work. But there remains some way in which my core has yet to be touched. And, after just two sessions with ayahuasca, I knew that this was a spirit-energy that could open that last door for me. She [*ayahuasca*] could find the chink in my armor, crack me wide open and let the sunshine illuminate my soul, the spring breeze cleanse the rotting corridors of my mind, and exorcise my disease.[102]

For others, on the contrary, *ayahuasca*, peyote, and mushroom sessions, along with rituals in exotic localities, are just one of many thrilling aesthetic experiences. Jacaeber Kastor, a New York art gallery owner, who was backpacking through Latin America ingesting various native medicines on the way, reflected this mindset when he said, "A lot of us are just middle-class white folks looking for a significant personal experience—we're thrilled to meet strange Indians, and the psychedelics give it a whole further level of excitement and danger."[103]

To a question of a *Calgary Herald* reporter about what drives his clients to join the Wild Mushroom Traveling Road Show Amazon rainforest tours, Miller said, "For some of the people who come along, the trips are sort of vision quests. Others just want to experience the jungle, and look for mushrooms and medicinal plants." For example, among ten spiritual tourists whom Miller brought with him in 1993, only one viewed the whole event as a serious spiritual venture. A playwright by profession, he had joined the tour with the sole goal of ingesting *ayahuasca*, which he viewed as a chance to open a door to the mysteries of primal Stone Age times. The writer noted, "For me, the trip was a life-altering experience. It gives you a chance to travel into prehistory. We visited some villages that were hundreds of miles from civilization, where the people still live in a hunter-gatherer mode." Miller tries in every way to cater to such primitivist expectations of his clients. As soon as the members of his group step on Peruvian soil, they are immediately put onto the boat that takes them directly into jungle wilderness. "By morning," adds Miller, "civilization has been left far behind." Another member of the tour group, a medical transcriptionist, on the contrary, did not know anything about *ayahuasca* and joined the jungle trip simply because she wanted to get away for a while. When an *ayahuasca* ceremony was offered, she decided to try it but just out of curiosity.[104]

Although the accounts of participants in mystic tours are naturally centered on their spiritual and aesthetic experiences (after all, that is what people join these tours for), some of them reveal the firsthand discoveries Westerners can make about life in underdeveloped countries. In addition to spirituality, traveling with a shamanic intent sometimes might prompt mystical tourists to give a critical look to the cultural and social clichés they have absorbed by existing within the cushioned and insulated world of university campuses, metaphysical stores, and healing retreats. In one account, I ran across an interesting side story about how a spiritual pilgrimage to Peru generated a process of genuine discovery of the other and an appreciation of the traveler's home soil.

Pilar Montero, an upper-class Hispanic American from an old aristocratic lineage, and her friend Arthur Colman, an American of Jewish background, joined a shamanic tour group. Guided by two mystical tour operators, Juan Victor Nunez del Prado, a Peruvian anthropologist turned shamanism practitioner after his retirement, and his long-time American apprentice, Elizabeth Jenkins, they ventured into the Peruvian Andes. In a literal sense, for Montero and Colman, the spiritual trip became a journey to another reality: the world of desperate poverty and stagnation. Reflecting on their venture to the Andes, these two Californians and Jungian analysts made the following discovery: "The poverty we saw around us in the Andes accentuated our awareness of the sacredness of the material world we inhabit in California. We clearly realized that it was not just the nature but also our technological superimpositions on it that are the face of God."[105]

5

Shamanism Goes Global

Mircea Eliade and Carlos Castaneda

When the student is ready, the teacher appears.

—Proverb

The increased attention to shamanism in humanities studies and in popular culture since the 1960s is usually associated with two names: Mircea Eliade (1907–1986) and Carlos Castaneda (1925–1998). Eliade, a Romanian-born philosopher and religious scholar, worked for many years as a professor of comparative religion at the University of Chicago. In 1951, while still in Europe, he released *Le Chamanisme et les techniques archaiques de l'extase*, the first grand treatise on shamanism, which became an academic bestseller after its revised translation was published in English as *Shamanism: Archaic Techniques of Ecstasy* (1964). Also an immigrant, Castaneda came to the United States from Peru. Although he failed as a mainstream academic scholar, by publishing an experiential novel, *The Teachings of Don Juan: A Yaqui Way of Knowledge* (1968), he captivated the minds of numerous spiritual seekers and served as an inspiration for many literary emulators. Eventually, Castaneda became one of the informal apostles of the "New Age" community.

The Eliade volume mostly appealed to academics and to those laypersons who were not intimidated by his sophisticated language and numerous endnotes in various languages. In contrast, Castaneda's lively novels formatted as parables took the topic of shamanism to mass audiences. The two books complemented each other, shaping both popular and academic perceptions of shamanism. In this chapter, my goal is not only to detail the contribution of Eliade and Castaneda to shamanology but also to place these writers in the context of a time that contributed to the rise of interest in such practices as shamanism.

Social and Intellectual Setting

The 1960s saw the end of colonial empires, the rise of national liberation movements in the third world, and the resurgence of non-Western "people without history," who had been marginalized by European and American social scholarship. It was also a time of increased distrust of long-cherished ideas of progress, materialism, and rationalism, which constituted the backbone of Western civilization. Many people came to the realization that these values introduced by the Enlightenment not only had exhausted their creative potential but also had been responsible for colonialism and oppression. Intellectuals increasingly began to view Enlightenment positivism as a narrow-minded approach that prioritized science at the expense of other forms of knowledge. Not since the First World War had the prestige of Western civilization fallen so low. By the 1970s, a conviction had grown that Western modernity was a cultural deadlock, a perception that now is part of the intellectual mainstream in Western Europe and North America. To many, the very expression "Western civilization" became meaningless and, at least for some, turned into a curse word. Thus, once enchanted, the West lost its iconic image and became viewed as the major obstacle to human development.[1]

One of the reasons for this change of sentiments could be a gradual shift in the hierarchy of values among middle-class people, from conventional Western values anchored in materialism to a more self-fulfilling life and spirituality. Abraham Maslow, one of the founders of humanistic psychology, described this trend in his famous theory of self-actualization. This celebrity scholar, popular during the psychedelic 1960s, defined the hierarchy of human values as a pyramid. Food and shelter, which were at its foundation, came first. When these were satisfied, then there came the sense of safety. A person who felt safe became concerned about love and belonging. Finally, when these goals were satisfied, people began to strive to express themselves in free and creative ways. The pursuit of spiritual experiences was on the very top of that pyramid of values. It appears that, in the 1960s in affluent Western countries, many people did fill their basic needs and felt the urge to go beyond the mundane materialist aspirations of their parents and grandparents. Maslow assumed that well-educated and materially secure people, unless they were hooked on mainstream materialism and conventional wisdom, were the ones who might reach their highest potential beyond physiological and social needs.[2]

Maslow believed that this self-actualization process would eventually mold a new cosmopolitan personality that could adapt to any culture and at the same time transcend all of them. The bottom line of his philosophy was that the individual could reach what we usually call heaven in this life, not in the afterlife. This and similar visions were certainly a fresh breeze in an intellectual environment that was infected with materialism, behaviorism, and Freudian psychology. To some extent, Maslow's pyramid of changing values helps us to explain why, in the 1960s, materially secure, educated, middle-class people joined communes, experimented with various hallucinogens, participated in the human potential movement, and, eventually, in the 1980s, shaped a nature and alternative spirituality that has now become part of Western culture. The inspiration that the seekers found in non-Western, particularly Asian and Native American spiritual traditions, was an essential part of that self-actualization process.

In the humanities and social sciences, the declining prestige of Enlightenment knowledge led to a growing distrust of academic abstractions and of the grand, all-explaining social and economic schemes, which treated people as pawns in the great game of social and economic forces. Instead, scholars began to put human faces on their subjects and sought to stress human agency. Like their nineteenth-century Romantic predecessors, they began to pay more attention to the roles of the person, culture, and spirituality and became interested in exploring the unique, individual, irrational, and bizarre. Scholars also began to revisit drop-out, drug, and psychic experiences. Earlier dismissed as superstitions and abnormalities, the traditions and knowledge of non-Western others came into the spotlight of Western scholarship. In the human sciences, experiential knowledge acquired high status, and it became a popular practice to live the life of human subjects.[3]

In the 1960s, anthropology moved away from grand cultural and ecological theories and the detached observation of others to experiencing these cultures and exploring how individual natives worked their own societies. Even archaeology, the discipline that by its very nature was locked into studying scarce material remains of the past, did not stay behind. Here, in the 1970s, a new school of thought called cognitive archaeology sprang up. Its adherents called upon their colleagues to use their imaginations to probe the minds and beliefs of the ancient ones. Under these circumstances, an interest in shamanism and altered states of consciousness among tribal peoples was natural.

A profound intellectual shift also took place in psychology, the discipline that became intimately tangled with the self-actualization (human potential) movement and the counterculture. Here, a new scholarship, humanistic psychology, gradually began to replace the dominant psychoanalysis and behaviorism. In contrast to psychoanalysis, which viewed people as actual or potential patients, humanistic psychology, of which Maslow was one of the major originators, approached human beings as healthy individuals. This new scholarship also revisited the concept of mental illness. Humanistic scholars turned their backs to the earlier popular practice of recycling Freudian clichés, and eventually public interest in psychoanalysis declined. What earlier had been treated as abnormal became not only normal but also outstanding and creative. It was only natural that, under these circumstances, attitudes toward such pathological and odd individuals as shamans began to change.

The exploration of alternative realities (altered states) in general and shamanic experiences in particular became the major themes for transpersonal psychology, a new subdiscipline that sprang up in 1969 within humanistic psychology. Transpersonal psychology approached religion and spirituality as valid experiences that carried powerful healing potential. In addition to Maslow's writings, this subdiscipline drew on the intellectual heritage of Carl G. Jung with his stress on archetypes and the transcendent mind; Aldous Huxley, whose famous book *The Doors of Perception* (1954) was one of the intellectual inspirations for the psychedelic revolution; and Alan Watts with his popular works on the psychotherapeutic use of Zen Buddhist techniques.

Scholarly and popular attention to the topic of altered states increased when, in 1969, Charles Tart, a psychologist from the University of California at Davis, published *Altered States of Consciousness*, a textbook that dealt with all kinds of altered states, from dream experiences to nature spiritualities.[4] His major premise was that consciousness is not an unchanged, unified entity but rather parallel, alternating realities. Tart also argued that altered states of consciousness induced by drugs, meditation, dreams, and hypnosis are superior to regular waking states. The book, which was assigned as course reading for psychology classes, soon reached wide audiences. In 1975, the establishment of the California Institute of Transpersonal Psychology (now the California Institute of Integral Studies; see figure 5.1) institutionalized that subdiscipline. Currently, CIIS, an accredited doctoral-level university, is one of a few research centers in the world that study and teach non-Western spiritual practices and Western esoteric techniques from the transpersonal angle.

In the 1960s and 1970s, many alternative scholars and spiritual seekers who approached the personality holistically and who worked to help people develop their emotional and spiritual potentials to their full extent clustered around the Esalen Institute in California, one of the first centers of the self-actualization or human potential movement. Founded in 1962 and supported by countercultural celebrities such as Alan Watts, Aldous Huxley, Carl Rogers, and Maslow, the institute eventually became the mecca of the American counterculture and a testing ground for various alternative spiritualities. It is notable that Esalen was named after the Esselen Indians who once lived in the area and who might have been drawn there by its hot springs. The current institute Web site draws the spiritual connection between the original inhabitants and "the modern Esalen clan—the worldwide family."[5]

Esalen was one of the first countercultural centers to make shamanism part of its experiential curriculum, along with drama therapy, yoga, and various

FIGURE 5.1. California Institute of Integral Studies, San Francisco, is one of the major centers of American esotericism. Photograph by the author.

Asian spiritual techniques. During the 1960s and 1970s, one of the chief managers at Esalen was psychologist Julian Silverman, who wrote a paper in 1967 in which he approached shamanism as a form of spiritual therapy. At the turn of the 1970s, the institute attracted Michael Harner, one of the first to revive shamanism in the modern West. Esalen also lured Carlos Castaneda, who participated in a seminar on shamanism. In the late 1960s and early 1970s, a prominent leader of Esalen programs was Chilean psychologist Claudio Naranjo, who became known for his experiments in urban settings with the South American hallucinogenic vine *ayahuasca* and who eventually set up a metaphysical group of his own. Harner introduced Naranjo to Castaneda, after which the two remained close acquaintances for several years.[6]

Overall, as a backlash to Enlightenment rationalism and materialism, the public interest in such topics as consciousness, spirit, altered states, and paranormal phenomena drastically increased. In countercultural circles, people became convinced of the redemptive power of primal peoples, who were expected to offer curative remedies for modern civilization. Nature spiritual practices that earlier had been stamped as superstition were recast into superperception, and shamans were viewed as tribal analogues of Western psychiatrists, who essentially performed the same functions, working in a different cultural realm.[7]

Mircea Eliade and Archaic Techniques of Ecstasy

Before psychology and anthropology recognized the sacred as an autonomous and valid experience, historian of religion Eliade (see figure 5.2) had already articulated similar ideas in his general books that compared religions and mythologies worldwide. Thus, in his seminal *Shamanism*, he completely parted with pathological and materialistic interpretations of shamanism, exploring it instead as a spiritual experience independent from mental health, culture, and economy. As early as 1946, while still contemplating that book, Eliade wrote in his diary, "I must present shamanism in the general perspective of the history of religions rather than as an aberrant phenomenon belonging more to psychiatry."[8]

A characteristic feature of the entire Eliadean scholarship was his dislike of any approach that placed religion in specific contexts. He was convinced that

FIGURE 5.2. Historian of religion Mircea Eliade (1907–1986). His book *Shamanism: Archaic Techniques of Ecstasy* (1964) became a classic of shamanism studies. Courtesy Special Collections Research Center, University of Chicago Library.

the sacred should be singled out and discussed on its own terms without being reduced to social life, history, economics, or brain function. This method became known as the phenomenological approach. In his shamanism book, Eliade stressed that he looked into "dreams, hallucinations, and images of ascent found everywhere in the world apart from any historical or other 'conditions.'" Intentionally dissociating himself from these "parasites on the religious phenomenon," Eliade noted that his goal was not to ground shamanism in a particular culture, history, or place but to capture its universal nature, "*le côté spiritual*, the symbolism and inner coherence of [it as a] religious ethnological phenomenon."[9]

Eliade was interested in shamanic experience for its own sake and naturally downplayed its mundane aspects. An example was the manner in which Eliade explained the origin of the respect for and reverence of shamans among nonliterate people. Thus, he suggested that tribal spiritual practitioners gained prestige and power not by curing the sick, producing rain, or protecting their communities from aggression, but through surpassing people around them in the amount of sacred power they accumulated. He insisted that this was how ancient and modern elementary societies thought about successful shamans.

Eliade pointed out that modern people, with their secular and materialist mentality, could not comprehend such a mindset:

> For primitive man, donning the skin of an animal was becoming that animal, feeling himself transformed into an animal. We have seen that, even today, shamans believe that they can change themselves into animals. Little would be gained by recording the fact that shamans dressed up in animal skins. The important thing is what they felt when they masqueraded as animals. We have reason to believe that this magical transformation resulted in a "going out of the self" that very often found expression in an ecstatic experience. Imitating the gait of an animal or putting on its skin was acquiring a superhuman mode of being.[10]

Eliade surmised that this superhuman transformation induced in the shaman a euphoric experience ending in ecstasy, which in turn brought spiritual practitioners into contact with the sacred. That was how archaic people consecrated not only animals and animal skins but also the entire world that surrounded them, including trees, mountains, rocks, and rivers.

He approached shamanism as archaic, primal spirituality that sprang up independently among all peoples at the dawn of their history and that allowed them to maintain direct contact with the sacred. Although many scholars now treat his shamanism book as an impressionistic and Romantic treatise, correctly pointing to his factual flaws, we have to give Eliade credit for what he accomplished. With his volume, Eliade rehabilitated spiritual practitioners in nature religions, whom earlier scholars had marginalized as mental deviants, sorcerers, and witch doctors. Placing tribal spiritualities on the same level with so-called world religions, he stressed, "The manifestation of the sacred in a stone or a tree is neither less mysterious nor less noble than its manifestation in a 'god.'"[11]

By the time he began working on his shamanism book, Eliade had already spent three years in India, released a small book on the philosophy of yoga, and become known in Europe as a student of Eastern mythology and religions. Although the scholar was enchanted with the magic and mythology of the Oriental world, he never committed himself to the study of any particular cultural tradition or region. Always a comparative scholar who drew wide cross-cultural parallels, Eliade tried to capture the universal elements in human religious experiences. He appreciated bold and creative synthesis tinged with imagination. For this reason, Eliade treated with deep suspicion the self-imposed topical niches many of his colleagues carved for themselves.[12]

Despite his near-encyclopedic knowledge of all contemporary literature on the topic, Eliade never considered himself an expert on shamanism and tribal people. He saw his own task as a comparative historian of religion as one of uncovering common ancient patterns hidden under the thick layer of "civilization." His insight into the nature of shamanism was part of this effort to decipher these universal archaic patterns. Eliade was fond of the very word *archaic*, which he frequently used as a synonym for the ancient or the primordial. On many occasions, he indiscriminately used this word to describe Stone Age people, classical civilizations, and modern "primitives," all of whom appeared to him to be carriers of primordial wisdom lost by modern civilization.

Thus, according to Eliade, one of the universal elements in shamanism was ecstasy (altered state), which shamans used worldwide to interact with the sacred. Another universal pattern he detected was the shamanic ascent (flight) to the heavenly world. As an example, let us see how Eliade explained the cross-cultural origin of the latter archetype. The scholar began his book on shamanism with an example of the Altaian (Siberia) shaman ritually climbing a birch tree during his séance—the ascent to the heavenly sphere. For the description of the typical shamanic séance, Eliade relied on Wilhelm Radloff's *Aus Sibirien* (1884). If we assume for a moment, said Eliade, that the idea of ascension came from the Oriental tradition, which was in close proximity to the Altai, nothing would prove that Buddhism had planted in the native Altai the ritual of ascension to the sky. One could find similar rituals of ascension to heaven all over the world among people who had nothing to do whatsoever with the ancient Orient. In this case, concluded the scholar, we must assume that the very symbol of celestial ascent is wired into the spirituality of people all over the world. In this case, it "belongs to man as such, not to man as a historical being."[13] In the same manner, Eliade discussed the religious experiences of other ancient and modern people.

Eliade also devoted much attention to another important universal idea, the symbolism of the center (*axis mundi*). Eliade pointed out that manifestations of this symbol could be diverse among various peoples: the shamanic world tree, the sacred mountain, the bridge that Siberian shamans use to access the world of spirits during their spiritual journeys, the smoke hole in a nomadic yurt, the shaman drum or stairs, and temples or sacred towns in more "advanced" civilizations. Still, in essence, all of them conveyed the universal archetypical idea of the center. For example, to Eliade, the fact that the Siberian shamanic drum was made of wood of ritually selected trees pointed to the link with the world tree, which again mirrored the idea of the mystical center.[14]

Eliade also stressed that the shamanic universe worldwide consisted of three levels (another archetypical pattern): the upper, middle, and lower worlds, which are connected by the central axis (the world tree or the sacred mountain). Eliade certainly knew well that shamanic universes varied among different cultures. In his shamanism book, he indicated that, among the Altaians, some people believed that there were seven heavens, while others talked about nine heavens. Still, eager to locate universal patterns, Eliade called such variations later additions that "contaminated" the deeply grounded universal archaic idea of three worlds. Thus, he suggested that the idea of the seven-layered cosmos reached several Siberian indigenous groups through the classical Orient.[15]

On the quest for cross-cultural religious symbolism, Eliade stood close to Jung, another visionary scholar who later became popular in countercultural circles and who shared a somewhat similar vision of the sacred. Although Jung's ideas were grounded in the scholarship of psychology, like Eliade, he was interested in identifying cross-cultural archetypes of spiritual life. Particularly, Eliade became drawn to his Swiss colleague's generalizations about the "universal parallelism" in religious and mythological symbolism worldwide. But Jungian scholarship, for Eliade, was only one of many theoretical inspirations. The particular universal symbols Eliade identified in shamanism entered his scholarship through Finnish folklore scholars who studied Eurasian mythologies, especially historian of religion Uno Harva-Holmberg, who authored the books *Der Baum des Lebens* (*Tree of Life*; 1922) and *Die religiösen Vorstellungen der Altaischen Völker* (*Religious Beliefs of Altaic People*; 1938).[16] Eliade took the archetypical symbolism that Harva-Holmberg found in the mythology and spirituality of Eurasian peoples and extended it to the rest of the world. Another influence came from the ethnographies of Siberian regionalists, who also searched for universal patterns in Eurasian mythology and whose works Eliade knew from German translations.

In "The Formation of North Asian Shamanism," which represents the conclusion to his book on the archaic techniques of ecstasy, Eliade challenged those who believed that shamanism was a regionally based spiritual practice characteristic of northern Asia. Just as Sergei Shirokogoroff found a Buddhist connection in Tungus (Evenki) shamanism (see chapter 3), Eliade acknowledged the link between Tibetan Buddhism and the indigenous beliefs of southern Siberia. Did this mean that Buddhism molded Evenki shamanism, as Shirokogoroff suggested? Eliade did not think so and stressed that Tungus shamanism was "*not a creation of* Buddhism"; he even italicized these words.[17] The scholar wrote that Oriental traditions might have affected the form of Evenki shamanism. After all, their spiritual pantheon did include Buddhist deities. The crux of Eliade's point was that such an influence hardly affected universal archaic patterns of shamanism: the concept of the center, the world tree, the ecstasy, or the celestial ascent to the heaven. Eliade insisted that, despite all of the changes and innovations, the core elements of shamanism, which were deeply ingrained in all archaic cultures, remained the same. Eliade surmised that each shamanism, if cleansed of local cultural traits and alien innovations, would always manifest its universal primal roots.

How can one differentiate between archaic and modern elements in shamanism in this case? Eliade answered this question by using his creative imagination. For example, he somehow assumed that the magic flight of the shaman to the heavenly sphere (upper world) to secure help from celestial beings went back to archaic times, whereas the descent of the shaman to the lower world was a later innovation. The scholar implied that, in archaic times, spiritual forces were divided into good, benevolent deities, which resided in the heavenly sphere, and evil beings, which inhabited the underworld. In reality, many indigenous tribal societies never knew such a division. For example, many eighteenth- and nineteenth-century ethnographic accounts tell us that indigenous peoples of Siberia and North America treated all spiritual forces, no matter where they resided, as neutral. The spirits could become benevolent or evil depending on how well humans appeased them.

In contrast, Eliade's ultimate shaman yearned for flights to the heavens and viewed spiritual journeys to the lower world as descents to hell. The scholar treated these lower-world shamanic journeys as a later innovation layered over the archaic spirituality. Eliade characteristically called them "infernal" travels to the land populated by "demons." Note the use of Judeo-Christian allegories. Following the blueprint of archaic shamanism he built for himself, Eliade suggested that because Evenki shamans devoted too little attention to the ascent to the sky (the archaic technique), their shamanism was "decadent" and, therefore, devoid of classical patterns.[18]

Critics contended that in prioritizing the upper world over the lower world, Eliade betrayed his Christian bias rather than described the actual evolution of shamanism. The biblical metaphors were certainly detrimental to his project of composing a cross-cultural portrait of shamanism, an effort that otherwise might be sound. For example, Eliade linked the very origin of the shamanic vocation worldwide to the idea of the human "fall." He wrote that, from various myths worldwide, we learn that in some unidentified primal time people had lived in a sacred manner in intimate harmony with the natural world. Animals had talked to people, and people had talked to animals. In fact, they had been so close to each other that human beings could turn into animals and then back into human beings. At that paradisaic time, everybody could directly access the sacred.

In "The Yearning for Paradise in Primitive Tradition" (1962), a kind of condensed summary of Le Chamanisme prepared for college students, Eliade noted that as soon as humans broke their intimate connection with "heaven" by separating themselves from the natural world, they lost their easy access to the sacred. At the same time, people immediately began to long for its return, feeling "nostalgia for paradise." Fortunately, noted the scholar, ancient and modern tribal societies were able to stay in tune with the sacred through special mediators—shamans—who helped common folk "to reconstitute the state of primordial man."[19]

Thus, shamans were those few individuals who maintained the original ability of people to talk with sacred animals, to turn into them, and to come back to the ordinary world. All ritual activities of shamans appeared to Eliade as exercises in the mystical reconstruction of the primordial natural state lost by humans. As an example, the scholar used the widespread shamanic practice of imitating the voices of animals. While for many earlier observers, this practice was evidence of shamans' bizarre behavior, to Eliade, such mimicking meant the establishment of "friendship with animals," which led to the acquisition of "animal spontaneity" and eventually advanced the spiritual practitioners "far beyond the general situation of 'fallen' humanity."[20]

Eliade believed that, by using the shamans, tribal people learned how to deal with this original fall and therefore never lost their connection with the natural heaven. In contrast, those societies that stepped on the shaky path of civilization and organized religions experienced a second fall, which proved to be fatal. According to Eliade, the circle of traditional spirituality, represented by myths and shamanic rituals and used to symbolically return people to the state of paradise, became broken. At that point, the spiritual became not only distant and less accessible but also went underground to the level of the unconscious. Eventually, the fall into civilization led people to the swamp of secularism, stressed Eliade. In Western civilization, the sacred was doomed to linger as nostalgia on the level of fantasies, literature, art, music, or social theory. The exception was Christian mystics, whom Eliade considered to be modern versions of shamans. In all other respects, in his view, modern society was not capable of producing any human agents who, like the shamans of old, could spiritually return people to the lost paradise.

Although Christian allegories might have flawed Eliade's scholarship, they might have simultaneously added to the popularity of his books. After all, the biases he spilled into his writings were the biases of an ecumenical visionary scholar open to all kinds of spiritual experiences as long as they fit his

Romantic traditionalism and challenged mainstream Judeo-Christian traditions. Philosopher Douglas Allen, who produced a balanced intellectual biography of Eliade, informed us that the mind of Eliade was affected by a variety of
occidental and Oriental spiritualities. Among them were the Hindu tradition,
mystical Christianity, alchemy, and the nature-oriented Christianity of Eastern
European peasants.

Eliade's scholarship, which layered biblical idioms on his Romantic primitivism, might have looked appealing to modern Western spiritual seekers who
felt at home with all this symbolism. Like Eliade, many of these people came
from the same Judeo-Christian tradition, which they distrusted, and similarly
fed on the variety of non-Western, pre-Christian, early Christian, and Western
esoteric spiritualities. Eliade once noted that all his life he struggled to understand those who believed in particular things: the shaman, the yogi, and the
Australian aborigine along with famous Christian saints such as Meister Eck-
hart or Saint Francis of Assisi.[21] With such a mindset, Eliade certainly never
was a Christian religious scholar, as his critics sometimes depict him. He always criticized mainstream Christian tradition, favoring non-Western spirituality and Western esotericism, which he viewed as carriers of timeless, holistic,
organic, and nonlinear values.

In his vision, the ancient and modern tribal peoples lived myth by periodically abolishing time through sacred rituals, which returned them to the
paradisaic time. In such societies, the whole life moved in a cycle. One can
express this vision with the famous Native American metaphor of the sacred
circle so popular in present nature spiritualities of Europe and North America.
In contrast, surmised Eliade, Western society squeezed the sacred past from its
life and, like an arrow, always headed forward toward progress. Living under a
constant "terror of history," Western people had to pay a high price: meaningless existence, stress, and eventually death. According to Eliade, many contemporary problems essentially originated from a perpetual denigration of the
sacred and spiritual in the Western tradition, which created idols of science
and technology. It was only natural that throughout his career, the scholar remained a stout critic of the Enlightenment tradition with its rationalism, materialism, linear development, and organized Christianity.

There might be two explanations why Eliade came to share such sentiments in the first place, before they became popular in the 1960s. From the
beginning of his career in the 1920s, Eliade was anchored in the tradition of
European Romanticism, particularly in its version that held in high esteem
popular Eastern Orthodox Christianity and organic "soil" spirituality. Not a
small thing was his flirtation with Romanian nationalism. These soil and
nationalist sentiments, usually combined with a distrust of Western Enlightenment tradition, were widespread among many European intellectuals in the
1920s and 1930s. Furthermore, his involvement with the Orient apparently
enhanced his general antirationalist and anti-Western sentiments. In any case,

his world view became relevant at the end of the 1960s, when Western modernity began to lose its intellectual appeal and room opened for antirationalism. This might also help to explain why Eliade eventually acquired the status of a scholarly celebrity in the 1970s.

Eliade explained his keen attention to archaic spirituality by his desire to correct the bias of Eurocentric scholarship, which systematically diminished and ignored archaic myths and beliefs:

> I'm trying to *open* windows onto other worlds for Westerners—
> even if some of these worlds foundered tens of thousands of years
> ago. My dialogue has other interlocutors than those of Freud or
> James Joyce: I'm trying to understand a Paleolithic hunter, a yogi or a
> shaman, a peasant from Indonesia, an African, etc., and communi-
> cate with each one.[22]

Well in tune with many contemporary countercultural seekers in the 1960s and 1970s, Eliade contended that before it was too late, Europeans and Americans should learn from the non-Western other in order to see the surrounding world through the lens of the myth and the spiritual, which would bring people back to the original harmony. He remarked that if we learned, for example, to understand the spirituality of modern Australian aborigines or the spirituality of their counterparts in the Stone Age, this could awaken and tune us to eternal spiritual knowledge. When in 1951 Eliade produced the first French edition of his shamanism book, non-Western spirituality was still the object of a marginal, mostly ethnographic interest. Nevertheless, Eliade prophetically wrote that the fate of European culture depended on dialogue with the non-European spiritual universe.[23] And, sure enough, when Westerners became troubled about their own traditions in the 1960s, they increasingly turned to the non-European traditions.

Eliade repeatedly stressed that although we were condemned to live within Western culture and history, people should master ways to shield themselves against their powers. At least for himself, the writer outlined the following agenda: "My essential preoccupation is precisely the means of escaping History, of saving myself through symbol, myth, rites, archetypes." To Eliade, such a mindset was a fulfillment of a natural human need to go beyond the ordinary realm into the world of dreaming, mythology, and imagination. After all, as he emphasized in his autobiography, "the thirst for the fantastic, for daydreaming, for adventure has remained as unquenched as ever in the soul of modern man."[24]

Since Western civilization had relegated the ancient knowledge to the level of the subconscious, our job would be to reactivate it and bring it to the conscious level. Eliade argued that the first step for Westerners toward the sacred was to learn how to take seriously symbols, metaphors, stories—everything that might bear the remnants of ancient symbols. According to Eliade, such an approach could help to break the spiritual amnesia of Western society and return us to the meaningful life.

Although the scholar always guarded his life from curious outsiders, it appeared from his random remarks that he was not a stranger to spiritual exercises that now might be described as shamanic. As early as the 1930s, when he needed to cope with a problem, the writer would lie on a bed, close his eyes, and propel himself into one of the worlds that fascinated him. At these moments, he sensed that he "had become completely present in one of those extraterrestrial or lost worlds. Then I would begin to live there, to move in a landscape that, to me, seemed entirely real, meeting extraordinary beings who were excited over truly interesting problems."[25]

Although Eliade never cared too much about American cultural and social life in the 1960s, he was sympathetic to the counterculture movement, which he considered to be a good antidote to Western civilization. In 1962, in an anthology, *The Drug Experience* (1961) edited by David Evin, he ran across a description of how mescaline effected mind-altering capabilities. What especially attracted Eliade in that volume was the description of a person who was able to live "outside time" by ingesting peyote. The scholar mentioned in his journal that he "trembled with joy" while reading that record. It is clear from his comment that, in this description, Eliade found the pharmacological confirmation of what he had written about in *Shamanism* and in other essays and books—the possibility of abolishing time and returning to the archaic.[26]

The psychedelic 1960s and new studies on the role of hallucinogens in shamanism forced Eliade to revisit his negative view of mind-altering herbs in shamanism. Originally, he had viewed psychedelic plants as a degeneration of classic shamanism. The scholar believed that true shamanism relied on such tools as drumming, rattling, or chanting to induce altered states. The counterculture and psychedelic scholarship made him recognize that plant hallucinogens were equally as ancient as other tools to enter the nonordinary world.

According to Eliade, another way for modern people to escape profane time and space and return to the mythological was fiction. Eliade was convinced that in modern society, literature played the same role as the myth in archaic society. Once, he called fiction the "residue of mythological behavior" in modern society. Although he admitted that the time spent reading a novel was certainly not the same as the reenactment of a myth by an archaic person, it was still some way to abolish history. Eliade himself was a fiction writer directly involved in the production of this Western version of mythological consciousness.

In his autobiographical notes, he repeatedly talked about himself as a person of the dual vocation—a scholar and a writer. For example, while writing *Shamanism*, he simultaneously worked on a mystery novel, *The Forbidden Forest*. At one point, torn between these two projects, he put aside his research on the archaic techniques of ecstasy and totally devoted himself to the novel.[27] It is also important to note that Eliade began his career as a noticeable figure in the literary world of his native Romania in the 1930s. In all fairness, he was ambivalent about the connection between his scholarship and his literary pursuits. Occasionally, Eliade separated them. At other times, he talked about literature and scholarship as parts of the same creative enterprise, making references to human nature as inherently irrational and refusing to line up with rationalism and positive knowledge.

Although they are formatted as scholarly texts with endnotes and appropriate jargon, Eliade's *Shamanism* and his other texts are not, strictly speaking, conventional academic writings. Injected with a large dose of imagination, they are located somewhere in the middle ground between mainstream scholarship and literature. In his shamanism book, addressed to all contemporaries who are ready to fly on the wings of their imagination, Eliade immersed his readers in the fabulous world populated by gods and magicians and where everything was possible. Here, the dead returned to life; people disappeared and reappeared or turned into animals and vice versa; laws of nature were abolished; and human beings were endowed with the power to freely ascend heavenly heights. As the religion scholar Daniel Noel informed us, there is reason to believe that the literary part of Eliade colored his shamanism book with impressionistic sentiments. I think that the term "visionary scholar" best defines such scholarly writers as Eliade. One might equally apply this expression to some of his friends and colleagues, including Jung and Joseph Campbell.

Although Eliade's popularity among current humanities scholars has declined, his books are still well received in the community of modern Western esotericism. To understand the sources of this popularity, it is important to remember that the scholar sought to reach out not only to academics but also to general audiences that appreciated the world of the spiritual. Thus, contemplating his shamanism book, Eliade especially stressed that he did not want to restrict himself to writing an academic treatise: "It would please me if this book, *Le Chamanisme et les techniques archaiques de l'extase*, would be read by a few poets, dramatists, literary critics, and painters. Perhaps some of them would profit more from the reading of it than would certain orientalists and historians of religion."[28]

In his foreword to the book, Eliade again pointed out that his text was primarily designed for the nonspecialist. Still, writing at the end of the 1940s at the time of reigning positivism and psychoanalysis, the scholar had no illusions about attracting a large audience. In fact, in the foreword he admitted that his descriptions of shamanism and its paraphernalia would most probably leave many readers cold.

Also, he might have sensed that the era of intellectual positivism was coming to its end. Hinting that "things change," Eliade pointed out that the world of modern and ancient archaic peoples was neither less consistent nor less interesting than the contemporary Western world. Moreover, he stressed that any cultivated person who was a true humanist could benefit from learning about non-Western beliefs, "for it has been some time since humanism has ceased to be identified with the spiritual tradition of the West, great and fertile though that is."[29]

Eliade's Legacy: Supporters and Critics

Indeed, times changed. In the 1960s and 1970s, a wide circle of scholars and spiritual seekers who were interested in tapping archaic layers of spirituality welcomed *Shamanism*. Although some current seekers who are interested in shamanism do criticize Eliade for factual flaws, even now, for many of them, his book remains a major text on classical shamanism. The power of Eliade's scholarship is his ability to capture the antirationalist aspirations of his Western audiences and point the direction in which the spiritual seeker might search for alternatives.

In addition to the rehabilitation of nature religions in the eyes of Westerners, his contribution to shamanism studies was to stretch out the geographic borders of the shamanism metaphor. In a sense, he made shamanism go global. His predecessors tended to restrict this phenomenon to Siberia, arctic areas, and western North America. In contrast, Eliade invited scholars to apply this idiom to all non-Western and pre-Christian European beliefs which did not fit the format of organized world religions and in which spiritual practitioners worked in altered states. Since for a long time his book was the major general study in the field, it also set the tone, format, and methodology for many who wrote on the topic in the 1960s and 1970s. Following Eliade, students of shamanism became more interested in exploring its otherworldly and transcendental aspects than its social and cultural contexts, as many present-day academic scholars do.

One of the first to capitalize on the Eliadean approach to shamanism as a universal archaic spirituality was German art writer Andreas Lommel. In *The World of the Early Hunters* (1967), a popular illustrated account of the spiritual world of primordial and modern hunting societies, he sought to grant shamanism "a far wider distribution." Thus, Lommel wrote about "a shadow of Siberia and shamanistic idea[s]" he detected in ancient Greece and other Mediterranean cultures. Viewed from this angle, the legendary Odysseus's descent to the underworld, where the shades were brought to life by blood sacrifices, also appeared to him as an analogue of arctic shamanic legends.[30] Even some anthropologists, many of whom now criticize Eliade and frown upon those who tend to generalize beyond their specific tribe, originally found Eliadean interpretation attractive, at least in the 1960s and 1970s, before it went out of fashion in academia.

Peter Furst, one of the originators of the shamanism idiom in American anthropology, accepted Eliade's premise that shamanism was the world's oldest religion, "the ultimate foundation from which arose all the religions of the world."[31] At the end of the 1960s, he used this approach to revisit Olmec feline sculptures as figures of shamans caught in the act of transformation from humans to animals (see figures 5.3a and 5.3b). Of two major figurines discussed by Furst, "Crouching Figure of a Man-Jaguar" depicts a man kneeling. Another represents a standing were-jaguar. The ferocious faces of both figurines look half-animal and half-human. Furst's predecessors, who speculated that the jaguar might have been a rain deity, linked the sculptures to Olmec rain and fertility rituals. Furst revisited this view, concluding that the sculptures might show ancient shamans caught in the process of transformation into their spirit familiars. The scholar noted that these and other similar-looking figures had a clearly defined dividing line that separated the backs of their heads, which looked human, and the front parts of their faces, which were jaguar-like. Furst speculated that the ancient sculptor might have wanted to show how the human skin gradually peeled away to reveal the jaguar beneath.

(a) (b)

FIGURE 5.3. According to Peter Furst, these figurines, produced by the Olmec Indians (c. 900–300 B.C.), portray jaguar shamans transforming into their spirit familiars. Courtesy Dumbarton Oaks, Pre-Columbian Collection, Washington, DC.

Moreover, the convulsed and ferocious faces of the figurines appeared to the anthropologist as a reflection of the unbearable emotional stress that ancient spiritual practitioners might have felt, moving from ordinary to nonordinary reality. Overall, the feline features one can see in these figures became a "badge of office, the manifestation of the supernatural jaguar qualities inherent in priest or shaman, his spiritual bond and identity with the jaguar."[32]

Moving from the local to the global, Furst stressed that the ritual transformation of shamans into animals was only a particular manifestation of a universal practice. He noted that the motif of the spiritual transformation was a common theme in origin myths all over the world. Drawing on Eliade's scholarship, Furst wrote that when the primal connection between people and animals became broken, the only individuals who were able to retain it were shamans. They continued to journey between the two worlds, periodically reestablishing the mystical solidarity of humans and animals. After Furst, many scholars began to assume that recurring images of were-jaguars on Olmec sculptures and carvings were shamans caught in the stage of transformation. Moreover, by default, academics and popular writers recast many Olmec figurines that depict people in various acrobatic poses as shamans taking postures reflecting the agility of jaguars. It is notable that Furst viewed his revision of the Olmec figurines as an antidote to the established scholarly positivism, which he thought held archaeologists in an intellectual bondage.[33]

Overall, the shamanic idiom became appealing to many archaeologists of Mesoamerica, especially to those who studied Indian art. Like Eliade and then Furst, they became convinced that in traditional society mythology and beliefs survived throughout centuries to an extraordinary extent, which convinced these archaeologists that they can set aside time and history in the exploration of the sacred and the mythological. Archaeologist David Freidel, a student of the ancient Maya, became fascinated with the subject of shamanism during his student years after he read Eliade's *Shamanism*. The book convinced him that shamanism indeed was "a very old, coherent, and broadly diffused mental paradigm." Revisiting Mayan archaeology, Freidel began to look at Mayan art as a reflection of shamanic imagery. Later, the archaeologist and two other colleagues, Linda Schele and Joy Parker, came to a conclusion that several Mayan temple pyramids were symbolic mountains associated with the creation of the world. To them, the pyramids became another version of Eliade's world center (*axis mundi*), which provided access to the upper and lower worlds.[34]

Participating in modern Mayan rituals and projecting them onto ancient Mayan traditions, Freidel and his colleagues sought to prove that "Maya ritual and cosmology has endured for at least two millennia" and that there was an intimate continuity of "Maya reality from the ancient past into the present."[35] To their credit, the writers did not insist that their spiritual rereading of the Mayan past was the best-fit interpretation of that culture. Their major goal was to bring to the picture human agency and spirituality—the aspects that had been neglected by earlier archaeologists. The three archaeologists did not hide that, in their attempt to breathe life into Mayan archaeology, they extensively relied on their imaginations tuned to current spiritual longings. They wrote:

> Because we modern pilgrims are ignorant of the intentions of the original builders, we impress our own meanings and aesthetic values on the Maya monuments, just as we always do when we contemplate masterworks of art from other cultures and other times. And our ignorance is convenient, for it allows free rein to the modern imagination. We see in these ruins what we want to see, be it affirmation of the romantic mysticism of springtime pilgrims, or the practical materialism of many modern scholars who devote [their] lifetime[s] to studying the Maya. We are forced to acknowledge that our perception of the past is always a prisoner of the present. Our reconstruction of the mountains inside the Maya mind is, like the pyramidal mountain restored by a careful archeologist, an interpretation and not the true original.[36]

The scholarship of the late Barbara Myerhoff is another example of the effect of Eliade's writings. Myerhoff, an anthropologist from southern California, is widely known for her beautifully written book on a Huichol Indian peyote pilgrimage (1974).[37] Before she embarked on her fieldwork to Huichol country, she had already formed her opinion about shamans as cross-cultural figures from the Eliade book. Therefore, she naturally searched for universal patterns among the spiritual practitioners she encountered. In her 1976 paper on shamanic equilibrium, she portrayed shamans as the carriers of ancient magic who performed the job of "cosmic undertaking" and repeated almost verbatim the Eliadean thesis about "yearning for paradise": "he [the shaman] brings back knowledge from the shadow realm, thus linking his people to the spirits and places which were once mythically accessible to all."[38]

As for Eliade, for Myerhoff, shamanism was a transcendental phenomenon unrelated to the social and economic concerns of tribal communities. She stressed that shamans occupied prominent positions in their communities because they bridged the realm of human beings with the three-layered cosmos. Discussing the status of the shaman as the person who linked the other world to the world of people, Myerhoff coined the idea of shamanic equilibrium, which further developed Eliade's argument about shamans balancing between the world of people and the world of the sacred. Myerhoff assumed that the major task of shamans in tribal societies was to train themselves to skillfully balance between the opposites they bridged. The anthropologist speculated that the goal of those spiritual practitioners was not to fall into the abyss of the mundane (this world) and, at the same time, to avoid remaining in the state of perpetual ecstasy, which would keep them forever in the other world.[39]

The first live evidence for her equilibrium thesis was one of her California Indian informants, a spiritual practitioner who sometimes liked to stand on one foot and gaze at the horizon. The second was Ramon, a Huichol spiritual practitioner, the major character in Myerhoff's *Peyote Hunt*, who once balanced on one leg for her and Furst by a waterfall after drinking a couple of beers. The latter episode had a funny history. Writer Carlos Castaneda heard this story from Myerhoff and included it in his book *Tales of Power* (1974) as the famous episode of Don Genaro's leaping by a waterfall. Since, in the early 1970s, some scholars still treated Castaneda's books as genuine ethnographies, Furst referred to Castaneda's "informant" Don Genaro arguing that balancing by a waterfall was part of a shamanic tradition of equilibrium. Thus, the fiction writer fed back to two anthropology friends their own story, which they later used to create a small theory.[40]

Myerhoff also expanded on one of the central Eliadean idioms, the human fall from the sacred to the pit of the mundane, by using the famous fairytale "Jack and the Beanstalk." The anthropologist reread the tale as a metaphor of a shamanic journey—the ascent to the heavenly sphere. A poor outsider, Jack noticed that a beanstalk growing from discarded beans now reached the sky. Feeling a call to go up, he climbed the stalk, which Myerhoff interpreted as the Eliadean cosmic center (*axis mundi*), the world pole, or the tree of life. When he was high above, Jack stole riches from a celestial giant. The latter began to chase the culprit. To save himself, Jack quickly climbed down and chopped down the stalk, which meant cutting the "shamanic" tree. By doing this, Jack terminated forever his connection to the supernatural. Down on the earth with his riches brought from heaven, Jack turned into a well-to-do person. Yet by tying himself to the mundane world at the cost of the supernatural, he ceased to be a shaman. Myerhoff concluded that, in this case, the domestic comfort, order, and stability were acquired at the expense of mystery and fantasy.[41] What a wonderful metaphor for the fall of Western man.

Like Eliade, Myerhoff lamented the spiritual decadence of the modern Western world that had lost fantasy and innocence in the process of "maturing." Furthermore, she regretted that Western society did not have shamans, who could have easily corrected the situation and repaired the broken world. At the same time, as a Californian who was witnessing in the 1960s and 1970s the rise of the counterculture and the human potential movement, Myerhoff found it necessary to stress, "Human integration on all levels may yet re-emerge as the goal and the ideal, with the result that shamans will be among us once more."[42]

Some students of medieval Europe similarly found Eliade's scholarship attractive. Thus, applying the Eliadean universal template of the shaman, they revisited the mystical experiences of early Christian saints and ancient Germanic and Scandinavian bards.[43] In *Ecstasies: Deciphering the Witches' Sabbath* (1991), Carlo Ginzburg, a historian of the Middle Ages from UCLA, revisited late medieval European witchcraft as a spiritual practice that fit the blueprint of shamanism provided by Eliade (see figure 5.4). Comparing witches and were-wolves from European medieval folklore with classic shamans from northern Asia, Ginzburg found many cross-cultural parallels. Like Eliade, Ginzburg compared cultures separated by vast geographical spaces and time. In fact, in his essay "Some Observations on European Witchcraft" (1975), Eliade had already pointed to the similarities he had noticed between witches' practices described in European folklore and shamanic trances. Ginzburg went further than his predecessor, implying a genetic kinship among the compared cultures and exploring the common Eurasian shamanic tradition centered on ecstasy and animal transformation. Herodotus's Scythians, modern Evenki from Siberia, and ancient Celtic people became to Ginzburg parts of the same spiritual tradition that stretched from the Pacific Ocean to the Atlantic Ocean.[44]

Reflecting on the ways that the primal "ecstatic cult" could have moved to Europe, Ginzburg hypothesized that Asian nomads might have brought their shamanism to the West, where it was adapted by the Europeans to their

FIGURE 5.4. Witches' flight to a sabbath as a shamanic journey. Historian Carlo Ginzburg and anthropologist Michael Harner recast witches into a European analogue of classical shamans. Drawing from Rudolf Quanter, *Kulturgeschichte des deutschen Volkes* (Stuttgart and Berlin: Union Deutsche Verlagsgesellschaft, 1924), 177.

local beliefs. The historian stressed, "The documentation we have accumulated proves beyond all reasonable doubt the existence of an underlying Eurasian mythological unity, the fruit of cultural relations sedimented over millennia."[45] This thesis sounded like a second edition of the nineteenth-century European Romantic folklore scholarship, which had similarly insisted on the common roots of Eurasian mythology. In the first chapter of this book, I discussed some of these scholars—Finnish folklorists and ethnographers and Siberian regionalist writers.

Ginzburg suggested that medieval witchcraft folklore was a vestige of a pre-Christian ecstatic cult, which Christianity later squeezed from spiritual and cultural life and demonized. For example, Ginzburg stressed that in early medieval texts, werewolves were described either as innocent victims of fate or as benevolent figures. By the middle of the fifteenth century, however, European literature and popular traditions endowed these creatures with their ferocious aspects as devourers of sheep and infants. During the same period, the public began to treat the witch as a malicious creature. That was how, Ginzburg stressed, by the end of the Middle Ages, werewolves and witches eventually acquired their evil features so familiar from modern tales.[46]

Earlier scholars believed that people in the Middle Ages who confessed that they practiced witchcraft often did so under pressure from their fanatical Christian accusers. Ginzburg turned this view around and suggested that we take witches' court testimonies at their face value as reflections of actual spiritual practices. If we did this, asserted the scholar, witches' flying on broomsticks and their shape-shifting into animals, which, to Christian interrogators, appeared to be evidence of pacts with the devil, could be simply manifestations of shamanic practices so familiar from ethnographic descriptions of non-Western nature religions: the spiritual flights and animal transformations of shamans. In this case, continued Ginzburg, the witches' sabbath, the favorite medieval idiom for the description of the diabolical nature of witches, could be a European version of the famous shamanic journey. Indeed, folklore materials collected by the historian indicated that witches who participated in the sabbath went into the beyond and then returned from the beyond—classic examples of the shamanic flight as described by Eliade.

Eliade also had a profound effect on anthropologist Michael Harner, the founding father of neo-shamanism in the West. The intellectual legacy of the Romanian émigré scholar is clearly visible in core shamanism, a psychotherapeutic technique Harner developed by singling out what he viewed as common archetypes of shamanism from all over the world.[47] To some extent, core shamanism became a fulfillment of Eliade's dream about recovering the archaic knowledge for the benefit of modern humanity. Like Eliade, Harner wrote about a time of golden paradise when animals and humans lived in unity, which was subsequently lost. He similarly noted that, after humanity's fall, shamans remained the only people who were able to stay in contact with the animal world. Again, like Eliade, the founder of core shamanism stressed that, despite dramatic historical changes, modern tribal groups living in remote areas still maintained the basics of their shamanic knowledge intact.[48]

In current academic scholarship, the views articulated by Furst, Myerhoff, Ginzburg, and Harner are marginal. The Eliadean cross-cultural and transcendental vision of shamanism does not exactly fit the present-day postmodernist thinking that favors the unique, the different, and the particular and that avoids grand comparisons. Many current anthropologists are usually skeptical of those colleagues who talk about cultural archetypes and draw grand cross-cultural generalizations. One of the reasons for this skepticism is the sources of these generalizations. Are these sources representative enough? Or they are simply accidentally acquired facts filtered through Western eyes? Unsure about drawing broad conclusions, today many anthropologists feel more comfortable restricting themselves to specific cultures and instead letting natives speak up about their own traditions. These scholars argue that such Eliadean concepts as ecstasy, celestial flight, the three world spheres, and the cosmic center (world tree), which he canonized as universal pillars of shamanism worldwide, fall apart when cast against specific non-Western nature beliefs.

In fact, many anthropologists have tried to change or totally discard the very definition of shamanism. This trend began in the 1960s with Clifford Geertz, one of the deans of American postmodernism, who argued that such abstractions as shamanism or totemism, which had been invented by Westerners, were meaningless and only served interested scholars as convenient tools to sort their materials. In an attempt to part with the Eliadean cross-cultural vision of shamanism, anthropologist Mary Atkinson intentionally introduced the plural expression "shamanisms" to underline the fact that tribal spiritual practices were unique and resisted generalization. Archaeologist Robert Wallis picked up the same expression to describe the diversity of spiritual practices of modern neo-shamanism.

More serious concerns have been raised regarding the credibility of Eliade as a researcher. Indeed, as a student of shamanism, Eliade was a perfect example of an armchair scholar—extremely well read in secondary sources, he never observed a single shaman. For anthropologists who consider field experience a prerequisite for any solid insight into the culture of others, this approach discredited his scholarship. Moreover, critics have pointed out that his shamanism treatise contained numerous factual mistakes.[49]

In academia, Eliade's interpretation of shamanism remains more popular with scholars who work in religious and literary studies. It appears that these disciplines more easily accommodate phenomenological and impressionistic visions of shamanism than does anthropology, which is keen on cultural particulars. Siding with Eliade's vision of nature spirituality, literary scholar Stephen Glosecki stressed, "The word shamanism does denote genuine universalistic practices. It is not simply a label used by anthropologists eager to

impose upon tribal societies the magico-religious traits they want to see there."
In a recent work that heavily relies on Eliade's universal interpretation of tribal
spirituality, another literary scholar, Robert Torrance, especially noted that
shamanism is a universal phenomenon that should not be restricted to northern Eurasia and the Americas.[50]

In the wake of the Eliade book, which treated the shamanism idiom very
broadly, scholars and writers gradually began to revisit such old labels as possession, sorceress, magician, and witch doctor, which they had earlier used
to describe tribal spiritual practices. By the end of the 1960s, this dated usage looked anachronistic and begged for change. In these circumstances, the
Eliadean usage proved very attractive. The words shaman and shamanism were
certainly convenient substitutes because they lacked the negative connotations
associated with the above-mentioned terms.[51] Although such popular phrases
as medicine man and medicine woman did survive in academic and popular
writings, since they were tied too much to the North American ethnological
realm, these gender-colored terms did not always look as general and neutral as
shaman to serve as effective descriptions of traditional spiritual practitioners.

Another attraction of the shamanism label was its emphasis on the sovereignty of tribal spiritual practitioners. Eliade's shamans acted as charismatic
heroes who called in their spirit helpers at will and boldly transcended time and
space, establishing contact with the spiritual forces of other worlds. Overall, this
portrayal of the shaman fit the changing attitude toward non-Western cultures,
which reemerged from obscurity in the 1960s and 1970s. A student of African
traditional religions, I. M. Lewis captured well this changing attitude toward
spiritual practitioners in elementary societies: "The shaman is thus the symbol
not of subjection and despondency but of independence and hope."[52]

Lewis became the one who revisited the concept of possession. Widely used
by earlier scholars to describe African spiritual practices, the term implied that
tribal doctors of the "dark continent" were dominated by spiritual forces. Lewis
erased the border between shamanism and possession and came to define the
African medium as "not the slave, but the master of anomaly and chaos." As
a result, he recast African spiritual practitioners as shamans and tied them
to their tribal counterparts in other areas of the world.[53] By doing this, Lewis
extended the Eliadean vision of shamanism to Africa. In his lifetime, Eliade did
not include Africa in his cross-cultural scheme because he did not go so far as to
qualify possession as shamanism. In his comparative study, S. A. Thorpe, a
South African religion scholar, completed the Lewis job by incorporating African spirituality into the field of shamanology by linking Shona and Zulu
spiritual practitioners to their Evenki, Lakota, and Navajo classic colleagues
from Siberia and North America.[54]

Finally, at the turn of the 1970s, Castaneda's bestselling "Don Juan" novels
took the shamanism idiom beyond academia and enhanced the popularity of
the universal cross-cultural interpretation of shamanism pioneered by Eliade.

Although rich, comprehensive, and impressionistic, Eliade's book on the archaic techniques of ecstasy remained a scholarly text. As one spirituality author put it, his shamanism treatise was too dry to reach wide audiences.[55] With Castaneda and his subsequent literary emulators, shamanism moved from the world of scholars into the counterculture and later into nature and "New Age" spiritualities.

Carlos Castaneda: The Making of Don Juan Matus

According to the existing legend, everything began on a hot summer day in the small town of Nogales on the Mexico-Arizona border in 1960. A UCLA anthropology graduate student was sitting at a Greyhound bus station planning to go somewhere to find traditional Indians and write a term paper on the indigenous use of hallucinogenic plants. The search was an attempt to fulfill an assignment of his anthropology professor, who promised to give an "A" to anyone in class who could find and interview a live Indian.

The student was determined to fulfill the assignment and receive his "A." This determination, coupled with his rich imagination, eventually worked. Later, he claimed that he met his Indian at that very station in Nogales. A friend who accompanied the student noticed in a crowd a dark-skinned man, whom he knew slightly as a native knowledgeable about traditional herbs. The friend introduced the indigenous man of knowledge as Don Juan Matus. The graduate student was introduced as Carlos Castaneda. This was the beginning of the famous partnership between the future bestselling author, Castaneda, and his alter ego, the shaman and sorcerer Don Juan. Nobody saw Don Juan, but his spiritual presence affected throngs of spiritual seekers and academics.[56]

Castaneda's term paper dealt with the ritual use of a mind-altering plant called jimson weed (*datura*) (see figure 5.5). Hallucinogenic power plants! There was no better topic to select while the psychedelic 1960s were reaching their peak. It was natural that Castaneda's choice, as his former wife, Margaret, remembered, was "kinky enough to sustain his interest."[57] Later, Castaneda specified that he apprenticed with Don Juan from 1960 to 1972, at first in Arizona and then in the Sonoran Desert in northern Mexico. At the same time, Castaneda's critics pointed out that probably the greater part of his fieldwork was spent within the walls of the UCLA library in intensive reading of the literature on shamanism and hallucinogens.

Margaret remembered that, at first, Carlos did work with several actual Indians. Once, he told her about a Cahuilla native who lived on a reservation near Palm Springs. Most probably, the person he meant was Salvador Lopez, the last well-known Cahuilla shaman, who was famous for his fire-eating performances. Castaneda probably met the spiritual practitioner through Joanie, his girlfriend who lived near the reservation. The Indian might have told the

FIGURE 5.5. Castaneda's term paper that ignited his literary career dealt with jimson weed (*datura*), a powerful hallucinogenic plant used by several Native American tribes in their shamanic ceremonies. Franz E. Köhler et al., eds., *Köhler's Medizinal-Pflanzen in naturgetreuen Abbildungen mit kurz erläuterndem Texte* (Gera-Untermhaus: F. E. Köhler, 1883–1914), 1:23.

future writer about the Cahuilla use of the *datura* plant and other hallucinogens. On other occasions, Castaneda mentioned that he was working with some unidentified Indians who resided in the Colorado River area. Later, when he disappeared from home from time to time, Castaneda told his wife that he went to Mexico to apprentice with Don Juan.[58]

It is likely that the Don Juan character absorbed features of such spiritual practitioners as Lopez, Wasson's Maria Sabina, and a few other shamans Castaneda heard about from his anthropology friends or read about in books. His wife added that the surname that Castaneda picked for his major protagonist might have come from the brand name of a bubbly Portuguese table wine, Mateus, that she and Castaneda liked to drink with their dinners.[59] Nevertheless, until the end of his life, the writer insisted that he did study with Don Juan and that he did his field research in Arizona and northern Mexico.[60] Once, on the back of the title page of his *Tales of Power*, Castaneda even indicated a date of birth of his teacher (1891) and modestly omitted his own. This attempt to give authenticity and sovereignty to his native informant could be one of the mischievous jokes the writer liked to play so much.

Castaneda's power plants paper eventually sparked a magnificent literary career. He not only received an "A" for his work but also expanded the text into a master's thesis. The shrewd financial wizards from the University of California Press, well attuned to the spirit of the psychedelic 1960s, turned it into a bestselling paperback, *The Teachings of Don Juan: A Yaqui Way of Knowledge* (1968). Written in a genre of free-flowing parabolic dialogues, the book described how for a five-year period Don Juan exposed his apprentice Carlos, an anthropology student, to extraordinary reality by way of hallucinogens.

In order not to cage his imagination into a particular cultural setting, Castaneda did not tie his shaman to any specific tradition. On the one hand, Don Juan carried the wisdom of the legendary ancient Toltecs, the native people who resided in northern and central Mexico a thousand years ago. On the other hand, he was portrayed as a multicultural sorcerer with a blurred identity and a mixed cultural background. Castaneda told his readers that Don Juan was a Yaqui by origin, but had to move around a lot and was introduced to many other traditions. About the background of his shaman, Castaneda wrote:

> He never mentioned the place where he had acquired his knowledge, nor did he identify his teacher. In fact, Don Juan disclosed very little about his personal life. All he said was that he had been born in the Southwest in 1891; that he had spent nearly all his life in Mexico; that in 1900 his family was exiled by the Mexican government to central Mexico along with thousands of other Sonoran Indians; and that he had lived in central and southern Mexico until 1940. Thus, as Don Juan had traveled a great deal, his knowledge may have been the product of many influences. And although he regarded himself as an Indian from Sonora, I was not sure whether to place the context of his knowledge totally in the culture of the Sonoran Indians.[61]

Castaneda stressed that it was not his intention to determine Don Juan's precise cultural milieu. More important to the writer was to stress that shamanism and sorcery did not have any borders. One can see the same stance in Castaneda's subsequent books. In an abstract to his Ph.D. dissertation, which he had earlier published as *Journey to Ixtlan* (1972), Castaneda stressed, "The conclusion I have arrived at after years of fieldwork is that sorcery does not have a cultural focus."[62] Indeed, with his blurred and transcultural identity, Don Juan's character could feel at home anywhere: in the Siberian tundra, African savannah, Latin American jungles, and even Los Angeles's cement prairies. This was truly a literary companion to the Eliadean universal shaman.

The particular plot of *The Teachings* was simple. Graduate student Carlos learned how to use three hallucinogenic plants: peyote, jimson weed, and psilocybin mushrooms (*Psilocybe mexicana*). Ingesting these herbs, the writer entered elaborate metaphysical experiments accompanied by mind-altering transformations and shape-shifting. One of these experiments was the famous oft-quoted episode with Castaneda's turning into a crow after smoking a good dose of magic mushrooms under the tutelage of Don Juan:

> He ordered me to wink. He must have repeated this command, and all his other commands countless times, because I could remember all of them with extraordinary clarity. I must have winked, because he said I was ready and ordered me to straighten up my head and put it on my chin. He said that in the chin were the crow's legs. He commanded me to feel the legs and observe that they were coming out slowly. He then said that I was not solid yet, that I had to grow a tail, and that the tail would come out of my neck. He ordered me to extend the tail like a fan, and to feel how to sweep the floor.[63]

In another episode, Carlos ingested peyote and began to hear buzzing sounds and to observe how the eyes of his teacher turned into a bee's eyes.

There is no doubt that the text was released at the right time, when the counterculture public was ready to embrace exotic drugs to heighten its consciousness. The Castaneda book smoothly entered the niche that had already been created by the media popularization of Huxley's mescaline trips, Wasson's mushroom quests, and Timothy Leary's experiments with LSD. Castaneda himself sought to connect his interest in exotic Indian herbs with the mainstream counterculture by approaching Leary in Mexico in 1963 and asking for permission to work with the professor. Carlos tried to intrigue Leary by telling him that Maria Sabina asked him to share some of her secrets with the Harvard scholar. Castaneda even handed the psychedelic guru candles and incense, allegedly the gifts from the shamaness. The future bestselling author explained to Leary that he came to add to the professor's knowledge: "I want to follow in your footsteps. I have learned much from the Indians of Oaxaca and Peru and northern Mexico. I can share their magic with you. We can both become stronger."[64] However, Leary did not appreciate Castaneda's offer and turned him down. It is quite possible that Castaneda indeed encountered Sabina or some nearby indigenous doctors, being one of those numerous spiritual pilgrims who, inspired by Wasson's writings, streamed to Mexico in search of altered states. In any case, Castaneda's first book about the mushrooms certainly appealed to a large group of people, for whom they became the major homegrown drug of choice after marijuana.

Despite the lure of the psychedelic experiences described in Castaneda's first book, *The Teachings* was not only about the ritual use of hallucinogens. Don Juan explained to his apprentice that the mind-altering herbs were not goals in themselves. The whole point was to help Castaneda break away from conventional or ordinary reality and step into the nonordinary realm (separate reality). Don Juan also involved his apprentice in numerous mind games, inviting him to contemplate various verbal parables and to solve philosophical puzzles. In *The Teachings* and all subsequent books, Castaneda portrayed himself as a foolish and naïve Western-educated student who, while learning with Don Juan, tried to shed the vestiges of ordinary reality in order to open himself to the separate reality. In a rare interview, done in 1997 before he died, Castaneda stressed that this was the major thrust of all of the Don Juan sequels: "The goal of Don Juan's shamanism is to break the parameters of historical and daily perception and to perceive the unknown."[65] This narrative line, which challenged the ethics of middle-class America and which dominated all of Castaneda's books, was another element that made his books appealing to countercultural seekers.

Stressing the effect of Castaneda on countercultural audiences at the turn of the 1970s, C. Scott Littleton noted:

> Almost every college or university campus plays host to a hard core of "Castaneda freaks" for whom the "teachings of Don Juan" have become what amounts to a new gnosis—a reflection, perhaps, of the anxieties and yearnings of an age that has become profoundly suspicious of conventional verities, be they scientific or religious.[66]

California Cosmology

Although Castaneda became known as one of the major inspirations for "New Age" culture, he was not interested in the world of spirituality and the occult until the end of the 1950s. Born as Carlos Arana in Peru into the family of a jeweler in the town of Cajamarca, he did not want to spend the rest of his life in his home country, where he did not see much prospect for success. Carlos was convinced that to make something of himself, he needed to emigrate to the United States. When his dream came true, and he stepped on American soil in 1951, the first thing he did was to change his last name to Castaneda—a symbolic act of erasing the old identity and creating a new one.

Castaneda settled in California, where he tried art and sculpture. He also wrote some poetry and short fiction. Still, this did not bring any recognition. English was his second language. Eager to learn to express himself clearly and beautifully in his adopted tongue, he took creative writing classes at Los Angeles City College.[67] Eventually, Castaneda narrowed his ambition to the career of an anthropology professor. Thus, planning to become a man of knowledge, he enrolled at the anthropology department at the University of California at Los Angeles (UCLA) in 1959. He also began dreaming about doing some trailblazing anthropological research that would open the door for publication. At the same time, the constant need to work to survive, the fate of many immigrants, interrupted his creative pursuits. Castaneda did various odd jobs, including working as a cab driver and as a clerk in a liquor store.

He did not care too much about the world of the occult and magic until he read *The Doors of Perception* (1954) by Aldous Huxley, a text that produced a powerful effect on many spiritual seekers of his generation. An Englishman who moved to California in the 1930s, Huxley strived to develop out of Oriental and Western esoteric teachings a philosophy that could become a universal religion. In *The Doors of Perception*, which detailed the author's experiments with mescaline, Huxley argued that this hallucinogen widened human consciousness and therefore benefited people.

For a while, Castaneda became so hooked on the text that he began to treat it as a revelation. Moreover, he began to view its author somewhat as his role model. Although deeply interested in Eastern religions and hallucinogens and opposed to conventional wisdom, Huxley was not an uncombed dharma bum, like some of his contemporaries from the Beat generation. Well-dressed and well-rounded, Huxley seemed to Castaneda the embodiment of a gentleman scholar: urbane, literate, intelligent, and at the same time countercultural. Incidentally, during his student years and at his rare public appearances, Castaneda always showed up in a suit. After he became a celebrity, this conservative appearance amazed his countercultural audiences, who expected to see in him at least something of a sorcerer.

Soon another book, *Sacred Mushroom: The Key to the Door of Eternity* (1959) by Andrija Puharich, captivated Castaneda's attention and replaced Huxley. Among other topics, this text, an offshoot of Gordon Wasson's soma scholarship, discussed how Siberian shamans left their bodies in ecstasy under the influence of fly agaric mushrooms. Finally, after finishing reading another seminal book, Weston La Barre's *The Peyote Cult* (1964), Castaneda was ripe for his own spiritual quest and informed his wife that he was ready to go out and find himself an Indian.[68]

Castaneda's budding interest in alternative spirituality and hallucinogens mirrored the 1950s and 1960s cultural and intellectual environment. There was no better place to explore alternative spirituality interests than California, which was the intellectual forefront of the counterculture and the place where Castaneda settled. In fact, not only that state but also the American West Coast in general were traditionally open to religious and spiritual experiments.

The people associated with the Beat generation and then with the counterculture were all clustered in California and neighboring states. At various times, this state harbored poets Allen Ginsberg and Gary Snyder; writer Jack Kerouac, the informal leader of the Beat generation; and Alan Watts, a former priest turned philosopher who propagated Zen Buddhism among the Western public. Huxley, who came to California in the 1930s, toured the state's college campuses in the 1950s, talking about human potentialities and Oriental religions. In the 1950s and the 1960s, the area began to lure many spiritual seekers who were interested in non-Western spirituality and Western esotericism. Recollecting the experiences of those years, Margaret, Castaneda's former wife, wrote that in the 1960s, UCLA, and California in general, were becoming the "alternative spirituality Mecca." "The whole California coastline was beginning to stir under the influence of an emerging band of psychics and practitioners of extrasensory perception," she wrote.[69]

What later made California the major stronghold of the counterculture was not just the magnetic landscapes and the openness to all kinds of spiritual experiments. Unlike the rest of the West, the state sported an incredible mixture of cultures and people and, most important, middle- and upper-class people who had many resources and much leisure time on their hands to pursue various projects of spiritual self-fulfillment. Of not small significance was the highly developed and well-financed university system. The state universities accommodated a large number of academics and spiritual seekers who were involved in the exploration of nature spirituality, altered states, and experiments with non-Western traditions. Fritjof Capra, Theodore Roszak, Marilyn Ferguson, Lynn White, Gary Snyder, Roderick Nash, Jacob Needleman, and many others were among the countercultural academics and writers who worked in the University of California system and who, in the 1960s and 1970s, laid the foundation for the future body, mind, and spirit culture and ethics. Environmental historian Alston Chase called it "California Cosmology."[70] "The Goddess came consciously into my life after I moved to Berkeley, California, in 1975," uttered spirituality writer Karen Vogel, who, after relocating to the state, found a community of people with whom she was able to partake of female shamanism, goddess rituals, and psychedelics.[71] I am sure that there are many American and overseas spiritual seekers who might have undergone similar experiences after encountering the American West in general and California in particular.

In the 1960s and 1970s, the UCLA anthropology department had many people who were anxious to explore such topics as spirituality, shamanism, and altered states. Many of these scholars were searching for experiential knowledge. In addition to Castaneda, there was another graduate student, Peter Furst, who later became a prominent student of the Huichol Indians and who spearheaded the shamanism metaphor in American anthropology and archaeology. Among the other graduates of this department who held shamanism in high regard were Christopher Donnan, Alana Cordy-Collins, Thomas Blackburn, and Barbara Myerhoff.

The presence at UCLA of such prominent academics as archaeologist Maria Gimbutas, who with her work advanced goddess spirituality in the early 1970s, and historian Carlo Ginzburg, who linked medieval witchcraft to ancient shamanism, adds to the picture of the intellectual milieu. Even nonscholars who expressed an interest in ancient spirituality found their niche on the UCLA campus. In his memoirs, Daniel Statnekov, a former antique collector turned spiritual seeker, remembered that he left the East Coast for California because it was "the American proving ground for new ideas." Through archaeologist Donnan, he received an informal affiliation with the UCLA Museum of Cultural History in order to explore a possible link between ancient Peruvian whistling vessels and altered states.

Archaeologist David Whitley, currently one of the leading proponents of the shamanic interpretation of rock art, who also graduated from UCLA, said, "A lot of people who study shamanism came out of UCLA." When I accepted this statement with a giggle, he added, "It is very true. It is absolutely true. Although I don't remember a course in shamanism, believe me, it was something that was there." When I jokingly provoked him with the question "Maybe the interest in shamanism is somehow related to California proper?" Whitley at first laughed it off, saying, "That is the question I tried to avoid." Then, a moment later, he half-seriously added, "It's got to be more than coincidence that so many people came out of UCLA. When you think about it—they came out of UCLA, they didn't come out of Berkeley. So it is not just California." "So it might be southern California?" I tried to continue our intellectual game, but our conversation somehow strayed off.

The budding UCLA anthropology scholars who became interested in tribal spirituality received their scholarly inspiration from such established professors as anthropologists Gerardo Reichel-Dolmatoff and Johannes Wilbert, both prominent students of Latin American ethnography. Another influence was psychologist Douglas Price-Williams, who was teaching in the anthropology department and researching dreams, shamanism, and altered states. Especially important was the role of the first two, both German-speaking émigré scholars. Reichel-Dolmatoff, an Austrian archaeologist turned anthropologist who moved to Colombia, frequented UCLA in the 1970s as a visiting professor. Although deeply steeped in classical psychoanalytical tradition, the scholar was a marvelous field researcher who produced solid ethnographic works on the shamanic symbolism in Colombian Indian art and the symbolism of shamanic visions. He had extensive field experience and personally ingested ritual hallucinogens and recorded his impressions of these experiences. Incidentally, Reichel-Dolmatoff was among the first to suggest that shamans might have been responsible for much of American Indian rock art.[72]

The influence of Wilbert was both formal and informal through his close interactions with students. A professor of anthropology who came to the United States from Germany and later became the director of the Institute for Latin American Studies, he was famous for his book on the hallucinogenic use of tobacco by Warao Indians.[73] As Wilbert explained to me, his interest in the shamanic use of psychotropic plants was sparked by ethnobotanist Richard E. Schultes, a famous explorer of the plant life of the Amazon rainforest. According to his former students, Wilbert was an excellent educator who taught popular research seminars on Latin American anthropology and shamanism. The professor appreciated his graduate students so much that he invited them to his home for his Latin American seminar, not for brownie points but just for the sake of knowledge. Eventually, the number of participants grew so large that he had to move the meetings to campus. Although Wilbert never prioritized shamanism as his research subject, he spent many years studying tobacco shamanism and apparently served as a role model for his anthropology students. Moreover, some of them shared a story that the professor was himself initiated into tobacco shamanism. When I mentioned this to him, Wilbert laughingly dismissed the story as a tall tale: "I am not a shaman; I simply observed how others were initiated into tobacco shamanism."

The exposure of students to shamanism and shamanism scholarship could have come as well from general courses on California ethnography like the one that Castaneda took with Clement Meighan, for whom he wrote his famous term paper on power plants. Although archaeologist Meighan was not particularly interested in religion, in the course he taught, students got into shamanism by default. As Whitley explained to me: "If you take a course in California ethnography, you are going to be exposed to much shamanism in ethnography, because Californian indigenous cultures were saturated in shamanism." Overall, living in California and studying at UCLA, Castaneda experienced a vibrant intellectual environment that deeply valued spirituality and altered states. This gave him plenty of food for thought and materials for his future books.

"We're All Nothing but Bags of Stories": Castaneda the Postmodernist

Castaneda's *The Teachings*, its follow-ups, *A Separate Reality: Further Conversations with Don Juan* (1971), *Journey to Ixtlan: The Lessons of Don Juan* (1972), *Tales of Power* (1974), and several others, captured the imaginations of millions of readers. They have been translated into seventeen languages and sold about twenty million copies, which made Castaneda an anthropology celebrity whose name was mentioned along with Margaret Mead. His persistent attempts to blur his identity as well as the aura of mystery his admirers cultivated around him only added to Castaneda's attractive image as a writer-sorcerer. After the success of the first book, Castaneda realized that he had finally found his niche. For the rest of his life, the writer continued to produce books which developed the same theme of magical realism and spiritual apprenticeship. He changed settings and brought in new characters. Still, in each book, one could find the same major protagonists, Don Juan and Carlos, and the same message: "there is a reality apart from the ego-bound real world."[74]

Until 1976, when psychologist Richard De Mille published his exposé of Castaneda, many scholars believed that Don Juan was a genuine shaman and sorcerer. Still, perceptive readers noticed right away that something was wrong with Castaneda's ethnographic and natural landscapes. One of the first was R. Gordon Wasson, the world-famous expert on sacred mushrooms, who was surprised that Castaneda smoked mushrooms in a powdered form, a practice that he had never heard of during his extensive explorations in Mexico. Wasson knew well that dried and powdered mushrooms did not even ignite. Hence, he later remarked, "When I first read the book I thought I smelled a hoax."[75] Still, the ethnobotanist was kind enough to give Carlos the benefit of a reasonable doubt. It never struck him that Don Juan actually never existed. Anthropologist David Aberle, the author of a seminal book on the Native American use of peyote, became suspicious of the blurred cultural context of the book, which did not reveal the actual setting of Don Juan.

Later, De Mille and Jay C. Fikes, the major whistle-blowers, cataloged numerous inconsistencies in Castaneda's books. They noted that the creator of Don Juan did not report any native names for the power plants he encountered. The landscapes, flora, and fauna of the Sonoran Desert, where the first book was set, did not match the ones found in the genuine Sonoran Desert in Mexico. For example, the shaman and his apprentice were pestered by animals and insects that do not exist there. Miraculously, Carlos and Don Juan also hiked in 100 degree sweltering heat. Worst, the anthropologist avoided producing field notes of his conversations with Don Juan. There was no way to discover whether Castaneda's sorcerer ever really existed.

Critics also noticed that Castaneda's first books more or less fit the format of an anthropological account and did not use slang. By the end of the 1970s, the anthropology in his new texts was gradually disappearing, giving way to philosophy and Oriental teachings, which the writer peppered with colloquialisms. Don Juan's language went through a dramatic transformation. For example, the shaman freely switched his tribal usage to American slang or suddenly began speaking like a college professor.

When annoying critics were especially persistent in asking Castaneda to reveal to them specifics of Don Juan's practices or the chemical consistency of his magic mushrooms, the writer shielded himself with the walls of metaphysics. Castaneda would simply say that one could not verify the knowledge he received from Don Juan by the standards of Western scholarship: "My presentations have all been descriptions of a phenomenon which is impossible to discern under the conditions of the linear knowledge of the Western world. I could never explain what Don Juan was teaching me in terms of cause and effect."[76] Sometimes, defending himself, the writer simply appealed to spiritual feelings, arguing that to validate shamanic knowledge from the scientific viewpoint would rob the world of its magic.[77]

Critics mentioned another interesting aspect of Castaneda's books. Their plots were all well tuned to the changing aspirations and sentiments of his countercultural audiences. De Mille, the writer who revealed the illusory nature of Don Juan, called Castaneda a Rorschach man, upon whom people projected their sentiments.[78] As a perceptive observer, the creator of Don Juan always shopped around among friends and colleagues for new and fresh ideas, plots, and characters. He immediately caught slight changes in popular culture, wrapped them in beautiful metaphysical garb, and threw them back to his readers. In fact, the writer himself indirectly admitted the shifting nature of his character. In one of his interviews, Castaneda remarked, "For us, Don Juan was there, available always. He didn't disappear. He measured his appearances and disappearances to suit our needs."[79]

For example, in the first book, the plot revolved around Castaneda's pharmacological adventures, which mirrored the sentiments of the psychedelic 1960s. At that point, he ingested hallucinogens and reflected on their effects. Moreover, the mind-altering herbs acquired the status of powerful beings with minds of their own. Mescalito or the peyote plant acted as a teacher and a spiritual guide. Then, in his second novel, *Journey to Ixtlan* (1972), the text that Castaneda defended as his Ph.D. dissertation, "Sorcery: A Description of the World," all drugs suddenly disappeared. Don Juan put hallucinogens aside and opened a new route to spirituality based on esoteric yoga-like meditative techniques and mental exercises.[80]

This was obviously Castaneda's response to the changing social climate at the beginning of the 1970s. By this time, countercultural audiences had become tired of hallucinogens and were gradually turning to "safer" spiritual techniques such as occultism, meditation, and drumming. Simultaneously, the government began indiscriminate attacks on all kinds of hallucinogenic substances. Following this change of sentiments, Castaneda's Don Juan parted with peyote, jimson weed, and mushrooms. The shaman announced to Carlos that once the necessary level of perception was reached, the hallucinogens should be discarded. Moreover, the Yaqui man of knowledge mocked Carlos for not being able to grasp the simple idea that all this mind-altering herb stuff was just another sorcerer's trick he played on Carlos.

In *Tales of Power*, which appeared when the peak of the psychedelic revolution was already over (1974), Carlos asked Don Juan, "Why did you make me take those power plants so many times?" The shaman at first tried to laugh it off: "Cause you're dumb." When Carlos pushed him to explain, Don Juan told his naïve apprentice that the herbs were simply a shock therapy he had used to break the walls of ordinary perception and to ease Castaneda's admission to the nonordinary world. The spiritual teacher told Carlos that, in fact, if they were strong enough, people of knowledge did not need any extra tools to empower themselves. Mental exercises would suffice.[81] Incidentally, during the last years of his life, Castaneda became so paranoid about drugs and psychedelics that he readily banished people from his inner circle on the slightest suspicion that they might have used mind-altering medication. Once, the writer accused one of his female companions of trying to infect him with poisonous energy by having sex with him while she was taking Prozac.[82]

In a similar manner, trying to catch an evolving public mood, in the late 1970s Castaneda began to cater to rising feminist sentiments. Thus, in *Second*

Ring of Power (1978), he introduced female spiritual warriors. Before, Don Juan had preferred male company. Now, while America debated the Equal Rights Amendment, the shaman became surrounded by female disciples. The female dimension that the writer brought to his books also reflected Castaneda's personal change of lifestyle: he surrounded himself with several trusted female "witches," who similarly "apprenticed" at the UCLA anthropology department as graduate students.

Sensitive to the shifting nuances of American cultural life, in the 1990s Castaneda also jumped on the bandwagon of the alternative spirituality workshop movement, which his own books partially helped to inspire. In doing so, the writer stunned his readers by breaking his magic silence and going practical. With the help of the witches Taisha Abelar, Carol Tiggs, and Florinda Donner-Grau, Castaneda established a spiritual corporation, Cleargreen, Inc., and began to teach a system of "magical passes" (body movements) called Tensegrity. While Carlos lectured, his female associates usually demonstrated particular exercises in front of workshop participants. Castaneda argued that these ancient Toltec practices received from Don Juan heightened awareness and increased bodily energy. One of his first Tensegrity workshops took place in 1995. In a high school auditorium, the writer held three days of classes for 250 participants from various countries.

Castaneda's books were tuned not only to the particular realities of American social and cultural life but also to the general postmodernist philosophical thinking that was quickly winning over the minds of the American intelligentsia in the 1960s. This might be another reason that his novels became so popular. The major message of postmodernism was that there is no truth or objective reality and that the world we perceive simply represents our own cultural and social constructs. Don Juan, especially in the later books in which he began to speak as a philosophy professor, repeatedly instructed Carlos that reality was a fiction and that what we referred to with this word was simply a projection of our own cultural and individual experiences. In an interview for *Time* magazine, articulating the philosophy that stood behind his Don Juan books, Castaneda stressed that the key lesson the shaman taught him was "to understand that the world of common-sense reality is a product of social consensus."[83]

If one accepts this approach to the world, as many did, it is certainly fair to say that magic, sorcery, and shamanism are genuine experiences, which are simply different versions of the same creative enterprise as, for example, science. In a similar manner, academic texts can be constructed as art where fact and fiction freely blend with each other. In fact, where some scholars stopped halfway, being apprehensive to unleash their imaginations, Castaneda went to the very end and imagined his ethnographies. After all, Don Juan had taught him that sorcerers could construct and shape their own multiple realities.

Reportedly, the writer would say to people from his inner circle, "We're all nothing but bags of stories."[84]

In this respect, he certainly outdid his UCLA postmodernist teachers. It was probably to them that Castaneda addressed the following mischievous remark in his introduction to the last anniversary edition of *The Teachings*: "I dove into my field work so deeply that I am sure that in the end, I disappointed the very people who were sponsoring me."[85] As a good sorcerer-writer, he simply constructed his imaginary world. Reproduced by the print culture in millions of copies and embraced by numerous admirers, this imagined world did eventually become a reality. When UCLA sociologist Walter Goldschmidt, one of Castaneda's teachers, was endorsing the first Castaneda book as "both ethnography and allegory,"[86] it was not an approval of Castaneda's "hoax," as some later critics mistakenly insisted. It was rather a reflection of the naturally growing tendency within social scholarship and Western intellectual culture in general, which increasingly blurred the border between fact and fiction. As I pointed out at the beginning of this chapter, philosophically, this trend manifested a resurgence of Romantic sentiments in European and American intellectual culture as a reaction to the dominant positivist and rationalist thinking.

In *The Soul of Shamanism*, religion scholar Daniel Noel explored the literary and anthropological sources of the current Western fascination with shamanism and reminded us that such anthropology authorities as Clifford Geertz, Victor Turner, and Claude Lévi-Strauss in different ways erased the border between literature and science and showed that scholarship can be constructed as art. Pointing to this postmodernist rereading of anthropology as art and literature, Noel added that the decision of the anthropology department of the University of California in 1973 to award Carlos Castaneda his Ph.D. for the fictional text that was printed as *The Journey to Ixtlan* was natural and should not surprise anyone.[87]

Wondering how one could receive a Ph.D. in anthropology by making up ethnographic dialogues with an imaginary shaman, De Mille, an author who devoted many years to exposing and debunking Castaneda, was sincerely surprised that scholars did not crusade against what happened at UCLA and that nobody spoke against the decision of his graduate committee to ratify Castaneda's fantasies. Moreover, critic Jay Fikes, who similarly took on Castaneda and his friends Furst and Myerhoff, talked about academic opportunism and a corporate solidarity of scholars, who, he implies, at first endorsed the hoax and then "conspired" to sweep the whole issue under the rug to save anthropology's face.

It appears to me that such critics miss or maybe do not want to see the fact that Castaneda's shamanic texts only mirrored what was already in the air. Castaneda's books were published at a time when scholars began to realize that

it was fruitless to search for "true" or "objective" knowledge. For the most ardent proponents of this approach, it was natural to go a step further to argue
that there was no difference between fact and fiction. It is clear that, after the
1960s, the humanities and social sciences became more accepting of literary
experiments in nonfiction. Castaneda's critics assume that modern anthropology and social scholarship entirely operate as positive science, always relying
on empirical evidence, which is not true. What skips their attention is the deep
postmodern transformation of Western knowledge, which has become more
culturally sensitive, accepting of imagination, and driven by moral considerations rather than by the search for truth.

Castaneda became so hooked on his constructivist philosophy that he
began to practice it not only as an intellectual game but also as a lifestyle, trying,
with a group of admirers, to live his books in ordinary life. The writer enjoyed
confusing people by blurring and constantly altering the details of his own
biography, which to him was apparently a matter of making and remaking
multiple realities. Social reality was constructed anyway—so ran the dominant
thinking. With those whom he admitted to his inner circle, Castaneda became
involved in sorcery games, manufacturing life contexts and settings informed
by the teachings of Don Juan. Castaneda usually called these games "The Magical Theatre of the Real." It was an exciting live play in which he and his
followers changed their names, identities, and goals. In this play, all loyalties,
commitments, and affections were expected to be mocked, shredded, and
dumped.

At his request, a couple of his followers would enact, for example, the roles
of a betrothed couple, and the writer followed up, checking how well they performed their parts in front of their relatives, who usually swallowed the game
as truth. Some of his close admirers burned their birth certificates and acquired new names in order to cut connections with ordinary reality. To erase
their egos, which he treated as a survival of ordinary reality, Castaneda routinely chastised the members of his inner circle in front of others.

The writer and the people who were close to him became so deeply entan-
gled in the web of their fantasies that the whole setting indeed became real and
valid for them. Amy Wallace, a wayward Castanedian, who at one point in her
life had occasionally shared his bed, portrayed the writer as an idealist, to whom
the Don Juan sorcery world became a second reality: "I do not think that Carlos
was a con man who callously sought money and women. I think that he believed in his dream to the last, and did his best to make it come true."[88]

Yet, by chance, Castaneda once became a victim of his obsession with the
reality-as-a-social-construction thesis. In 1970, while still a Ph.D. student but
already a celebrity author, Castaneda accompanied his friend Berkeley anthropologist Michael Harner to the Esalen Institute to assist the latter in a
weekend seminar on shamanism. After the seminar was over, the men joined
other countercultural scholars, who were staying at Esalen, for an interview

session with a San Francisco TV company. During the interview, Castaneda began to expound on his favorite topic that there was no reality and that what one perceived as reality was just a product of social consensus. At one point, the writer threw out a rhetorical question: "How do I know that I exist?" Having heard this, the Gestalt psychologist Fritz Perls, a crude flamboyant character, who was sitting nearby, quickly turned around and slapped Castaneda in the face, obviously to give the writer a sense of reality.[89]

6

Anthropology, Castaneda's Healing Fiction, and Neo-shamanism Print Culture

Suddenly, the anthropologists could see and experience the truth of
shamanic states. They could see spirits, look into people's bodies
with "X-ray" vision, watch people shape-shifting into other forms,
and even take shamanic flights to distant places—activities that
had previously been viewed as metaphors or superstitions.
             —Timothy White, editor of *Shaman's Drum*

Sometimes we just pick up a book and our world is made or un-
made in the reading of that book.
             —Tira Brandon-Evans, Society of Celtic Shamans

Carlos Castaneda's first book, *The Teachings of Don Juan*, and two
subsequent texts were wrapped in the form of anthropological accounts, which gave them credibility. At the same time, Castaneda's
"ethnographies" did not have such formal attributes of anthropological
scholarship as endnotes, bibliographies, or elaborate academic jargon,
which usually scare away the general public. Michael Harner, who quit
the profession of anthropology in order to spearhead shamanic spirituality in the West, noted that most of what scholars wrote was dry as
dust, and he credited the creator of Don Juan with introducing Westerners to the adventure and thrill of shamanism.[1] Coming straight
from the Sonoran Desert, Castaneda's ethnographic accounts could
easily appear to readers to be authentic anthropology (see figure 6.1).
    The fact that Castaneda refused to specify the identity of his
characters brought an intrigue to his plots. Readers of his books were
left free to exercise their imaginations or to look around for cultural

FIGURE 6.1. "Anthropological trickster" Carlos Castaneda, whose novels are still frequently advertised as nonfiction. Photo collage by the author.

and individual parallels with Castaneda's characters and settings. In the long run, as one Castaneda devotee explained:

> It did not matter much to us whether it was ethnography or myth we were reading. Those luminous supernatural beings in that desert landscape—giant spirit moths, the vegetal ally Mescalito, the sorcerer's tentacles that hold Don Genaro to the slippery rocks at the top of the vertiginous waterfall—all were instantly a part of our mindscapes. We were waiting for them as if we needed them, somehow. They broke through into our personal mythologies.[2]

Castaneda and Don Juan became attractive cultural and intellectual models, which inspired at least some spiritual seekers to replicate their experiences. There were reports about people hanging around bus stations in the American Southwest, trying to find Don Juan. Others streamed to the Southwest and farther southward across the Mexican border in hopes of acquiring their own Indian teachers.

Knowing Things by Turning into Them: Anthropology
of Experience and Consciousness

In the early 1970s, not only spiritual seekers but also many scholars took
Castaneda's ethnography and fieldwork at face value. With all seriousness,
they referred to the "impressive evidence" of the altered states and quoted from
The Teachings to support their own generalizations about shamanism and
hallucinogens. My senior American colleagues told me that, in the 1970s,
many instructors who had become captivated by the Don Juan message routinely included *The Teachings* in their anthropology course listings. Several of
them continued to validate Castaneda's scholarship even after the first serious
doubts about his ethnography were made public. One of them wrote, "I have
known him too long and too well to doubt his professional integrity."[3] In
my former home country, Russia, where, for obvious reasons, hardly anyone
is familiar with the Castaneda controversy, there are still several anthropologists who pepper their works with endnotes to the "field studies" of American
scholar Castaneda and his valuable Indian informant Don Juan.

In all fairness, many academics who welcomed Castaneda's books had no
illusions about his ethnography. What attracted them more in these texts was
the overall message. Essentially, Castaneda touched upon a sensitive question,
which deeply concerned the rising postmodernist anthropology: how should
a scholarly observer approach the cultures of others? On the first pages of *The
Teachings*, the writer posed a question: shall we continue to recycle a positiv-
istic "inventory of categories," or shall we approach cultures holistically on
their own terms as integrated systems of knowledge?[4] Castaneda defined his
methodological priorities as follows, "Any phenomenon should be researched
in its own light and in the spirit of its own internal conditions and regulations."
Doing so, the researcher is able to see that "the practical actions of shamans,
viewed as [a] coherent system with its own regulations and configurations"
become "a solid subject for serious inquiry."[5] To put it simply, Castaneda argued that one cannot understand the shamanic world without becoming a
shaman.

In the character of Carlos, scholars, especially those who were researching spiritual culture, saw a colleague who not only declared that truth but who
was actually able to live it. To them, Castaneda penetrated the native mind
by taking it as it was without subjecting this mind to a rationalistic dismemberment. The writer intentionally avoided pigeonholing his Indian shaman
into established academic categories. Instead, Castaneda not only let Don Juan
speak for himself but also became a participant in the sorcerer's world himself. Thus, the writer reached what many anthropologists craved but rarely
could achieve: full participation in rather than observation of rituals. With a

certain amount of envy, C. Scott Littleton, one of those colleagues who took Castaneda's field research at face value, wrote:

> Indeed, this achievement of "full membership" in the world of sorcery as practiced by Don Juan and his friends, which was underscored by Castaneda's famous leap from that central Mexican mesa into [the] frightening albeit seductive realm of *nagual*, is unique in the annals of anthropological fieldwork. While an increasing number of my colleagues are now working closely on [a] one-to-one basis with shamans and curanderos (e.g., Barbara Myerhoff at the University of Southern California and Douglas Sharon at UCLA), none has yet come close to approximating what Castaneda has done.[6]

With a sense of admiration, this anthropologist stressed that, by totally immersing himself in Don Juan's reality, Castaneda himself became a spiritual practitioner.

Many of Castaneda's colleagues appreciated very much that he breathed new life into anthropology scholarship by centering it on human beings instead of on patterns and models. From the observer and the observed, Carlos and Don Juan turned into partners who together produced cultural knowledge. Overall, interested academics began to view his fiction as a useful antidote to existing positivism and behaviorism. Remembering what he enjoyed about the Don Juan sequel most, religion scholar Daniel Noel, who invested many years in studying Castaneda's oeuvre, stressed, "I loved it that an indigenous shaman was constantly getting the drop on a smart graduate-student representative of Western rationality."[7]

What Castaneda rendered in an attractive fictionalized form as "donjuanist thinking" was already brewing in the humanities and social sciences. For example, in anthropological scholarship, researchers began to shift from observing cultures from outside (the "etic" approach) to experiencing them (the "emic" approach). In other words, if scholars wanted to learn about the culture of others, they had to immerse themselves in this culture, striving to become part of it. James Highwater, a Greek-American writer who came to imagine himself as a Native American, captured the essence of this intellectual stance by describing it as "knowing things by turning into them."[8] Commenting on the eager responses of those scholars who welcomed the Don Juan sequels, Barbara Myerhoff, Castaneda's colleague and friend during his graduate years, noted, "They were ready to believe." When psychologist Richard De Mille, the famous debunker of Castaneda, asked her, "And the fact that the Don Juan books are a transparent fraud doesn't invalidate the model?" Myerhoff answered, "No, it doesn't. The model is the same, and the message is needed."[9]

In his conversation with me, Douglas Sharon, Castaneda's acquaintance during his UCLA years, made a similar assessment: "In spite of the fact that

his work might be a fiction, the approach he was taking—validating the native point of view—was badly needed in anthropology, and, as a matter of fact,
I felt it was a helping corrective for the so-called scientific objectivity that we
were taking into the field with us." Considering this intellectual position, it is
equally natural that some scholars continue to call Castaneda's books inno-
vative for anthropology scholarship, commending him for conveying "better
than any other ethnographer" the way that non-Western people perceive the
world within themselves and around us.[10]

As for Castaneda himself, he adopted this method from one of his UCLA
professors, sociologist Harold Garfinkel, who had worked to bring to light so-
called ethnomethodology—essentially another name for the approach mentioned by Myerhoff and Sharon.[11] Garfinkel argued that the truth depended on
a specific culture and ethnic tradition. Today, to many scholars, this assertion
that became part of postmodernist thinking might appear banal but in the early
1960s, such utterances were revolutionary. As applied to anthropology, this
approach is based on the premise that the only legitimate method to explore a
foreign culture is to look at it from inside. From this viewpoint, cultures are only
open to insiders and always remain closed to those who are alien to them.[12]

In the 1960s, American anthropology was gradually moving toward validating the insider's perspective, which became mirrored in the debates between
emic and etic scholars. The first ones, who were also called "ethnoscientists" (or
ethnomethodologists), were ready to immerse themselves in indigenous cultures in order to try to speak in a native voice. The second group was still cling-
ing to traditional positivist and behaviorist methodologies. Sometimes the
debates between these two groups turned into hot disputes. In 1967, during an
American Anthropology Association annual meeting, a brawl broke out in a
bar. A few scholars shouted, calling each other names such as "dirty etic pig!"
and "stupid emic idiot."[13]

Incidentally, for the creator of Don Juan, it took time and effort before he
rid himself of the vestiges of the old rationalistic methodology. When Castaneda was still writing his master's thesis (the future *The Teachings*), ethno-
methodologist Garfinkel made him revise his thesis three times, making sure
that the student would relate his spiritual experiences instead of explain them.
Originally, after his first imaginary peyote session with Don Juan, Castaneda
presented to Garfinkel a text that contained an analysis of his visions. The
professor, as Castaneda remembered, rebuked him, "Don't explain to me. You
are nobody. Just give it to me straight and in detail, the way it happened. The
richness of detail is the whole story of membership." Castaneda spent several
years revising his thesis and then had to revise it again because the professor did
not like that the student slipped into explaining Don Juan's behavior psychologically.[14] Thus, being a good student, Castaneda wholeheartedly embraced
the advice of his senior colleague and created a beautiful text that was full of
dialogues, rich in detail, and, most important, came straight from the "field."

Castaneda surely deserves credit for conveying the newly emerging methodology in an attractive poetic form. His fiction did contribute a great deal to the movement of scholarship away from the dominant conviction that the religion and spirituality of primitives should be studied scientifically as samples of outdated modes of thinking. An anthropologist who embraced both the theoretical message of Castaneda and his ethnography stressed, "We owe him a major debt of gratitude for being out front in the struggle to liberate anthropology from the hyperrationalistic straitjacket it has worn almost since its inception."[15] The Don Juan sequels and the books of authors who worked in the same genre certainly made it easier for scholars to research such topics as shamanism, magic, and the paranormal without provoking ridicule from other colleagues. In the early 1970s, symposiums and panels on these topics became more popular and eventually entered mainstream scholarship. Archaeologist David Whitley, who similarly subscribed to Castaneda's message, told me:

> My reaction to Carlos Castaneda always was: if he made it up,
> he made it up perfectly because everything he talks about Yaqui
> shamanism, I can put in the North American hunters-gatherers sha-
> manism. When I look at it, wow, it is just native California shaman-
> ism. Well, the guy was obviously smart. Whether he is honest or not, I
> don't know, but he was obviously smart. He was a trained anthropol-
> ogist. Whether he deserved his Ph.D. or not is another debate.

Eventually, the most radical proponents of the theoretical message contained in Castaneda's books met together during an annual meeting of the American Anthropology Association (AAA) in Mexico in 1974 and formed the Society for the Anthropology of Consciousness (SAC). Stephan A. Schwartz, one of the founders of SAC, especially stressed that Castaneda's novels were an essential inspiration for the creation of the group.[16] In mainstream anthropology scholarship, there was an ambivalent attitude to Castaneda's oeuvre. On the one hand, it was certainly hard to validate his fiction as anthropological accounts. On the other hand, the methodological message was too attractive and well tuned to contemporary intellectual sentiments to simply be discarded.

In 1978, during the AAA's annual convention, there were two panels dealing with Castaneda. One, which was organized by De Mille, the psychologist who adopted the role of a "Castaneda buster," was critical. Another session, which dealt with experiential anthropology and altered states, balanced the tone of the first panel. Participants in the second session commended Castaneda for making it easier for anthropologists to conduct research on paranormal phenomena and praised him for bringing the spiritual wisdom of other cultures to light. One scholar suggested that the attacks on Castaneda, "a fine, gentle, kindly young man," originated from sheer envy.[17]

An experiential approach to the study of shamanism and religion is currently one of the most popular methods. One can briefly summarize the major intellectual stance of this approach as follows. If a person or group of people insist that they see the otherworldly realm and can describe it, we should accept it as valid and real. This explains the methodological advice which experiential anthropologists give to those scholars who explore the sacred: stay away from rationalizing spiritual experiences. The most radical supporters of the experiential method (anthropology of consciousness) go further and insist that to accept the viewpoints of people one observes is not enough. To them, it is still patronizing and Eurocentric. They argue that, in order to truly understand the spirituality of others, one has to actually merge with their spirituality, accept it, absorb it, and try to live by it. Edith Turner, one of the chief advocates of this approach, insists on a literal conversion to native tradition, which, in her view, allows a scholar to speak from within a culture rather from outside.[18]

Following this dictum, Turner not only personally participated in an African healing session, but also was able, as she said, to see the spirit of an ailment coming out of a patient's back in the form of a large plasma-like gray blob. This was not a symbol or a metaphor, she stressed. To her, this was the revelation: "Then I knew the Africans were right. There is spirit stuff."[19] Doing fieldwork among Canadian native peoples, another anthropologist, Lise Swartz, explored indigenous reincarnation stories and came to the conclusion that reincarnation might occur in reality. Two other scholars, Larry Peters and Robert Desjarlais, went into shamanic trances in Nepal.[20] Robert Wallis and Jenny Blain, an archaeologist and a sociologist from England who share such an approach, have recently extended the going native method to the study of current Western paganism and neo-shamanism. Consciously accepting the reality of spirits, these two scholars became participants in shamanic- and pagan-oriented groups. At the same time, they have successfully combined these spiritual practices with their work as academics.

Proponents of the going native anthropology make a valid point. They stress that, in the study of such religious practices as shamanism, one is either in or out. Outside, scholars can obtain no serious information to nourish research. Wallis correctly stressed, "One cannot sit on the edge and take notes because being present necessitates taking part."[21] Although what Wallis said is certainly true, I am not completely convinced that becoming a true believer facilitates improved insights into spiritual experiences. For example, participating in the 1990s in relevant ceremonies certainly helped me to better understand the popular Christianity of the Athabaskan Indians of Alaska or, more recently, the activities of Western seekers who call themselves Celtic shamans. At the same time, I wonder if one really needs to convert to Christianity or to Celtic spirituality in order to explore these traditions.

Some explorers of the sacred feel uncomfortable about such dancing between mainstream academia and the "reality of spirits"; I am personally convinced that being in the middle ground is precisely what provides the most valuable insights. Anthropologist William Lyon admits that it became hard for him to keep his feet in both worlds. After eleven years of participating in Lakota sacred ceremonies, learning with shaman Wallace Black Elk, and publicizing his spiritual experiences to the Western public, Lyon finally made his choice. He carved a sacred pipe and plunged himself into the realm of the sacred, trying, as he said, to "catch a spirit."[22]

Another good example is Luis Eduardo Luna, a prominent student of the South American ritual hallucinogen *ayahuasca*. He came to Latin America as a conventional researcher, but after twenty-five years of field experience and participation in indigenous *ayahuasca* sessions, he became a shamanism practitioner. Currently, he is an active member of the nature community, organizing spiritual workshops. Reflecting on his transformation, Luna stressed, "In retrospect, however, I can see this development was logical, because from the beginning I had both academic and personal interest in the particular states of consciousness elicited by the ayahuasca."[23]

The best illustration of the conversion of a scholar to spiritual practice is Harner, the person who launched the neo-shamanism movement in the modern West. A prominent student of Jivaro Indians, he turned from participant observation to, as he said, "radical participation" by ingesting *ayahuasca* hallucinogens and taking seriously the visions they induced. The radical participation eventually prompted him to search for a way to replicate shamanic experiences in urban settings. As a result, Harner left academia and became a full-time Western shaman. He also established the Foundation for Shamanic Studies, the first school of Euro-American shamanism. Incidentally, his major book, *The Way of the Shaman* (1980), represents both an anthropological text and a how-to spirituality manual.

Mexican scholar Victor Sanchez, who went through a similar transformation from anthropologist to spiritual practitioner, detailed the whole of his conversion. Sanchez was not so naïve as to believe in the existence of Don Juan. Like many others, he was more attracted to Castaneda by the beauty of his texts: the poetic feelings and "the perennial search for freedom and mystery."[24] The scholar became so involved with the philosophy articulated in the Castaneda novels that he eventually shed his professional identity and other vestiges of Western intellectual garb and turned to a more spiritually enhanced life. Sanchez also established a spiritual workshop, becoming a volunteer propagator of donjuanist thinking. Moreover, he released a practical manual, *Don Carlos*, with a series of exercises on how to remake one's life according to the California sorcerer-writer.

Explaining the sources of his spiritual transformation, Sanchez said that he began his career as a mainstream academic anthropologist. Like many others, he played a regular "scholarship game" by observing and categorizing native others. After a while, he became disgusted with this approach. He began to view himself and his colleagues as "academic conquistadors" who tried to impose ridiculous patterns and models on vibrant native societies. Under these circumstances, the going native approach appeared to him to be a good remedy: "I turned anthropology around, stood it on its head so to speak. I approached the otherness of the Indians, not to transform them but to transform myself, to encounter my unknown face by submerging myself in, what was to me, an alien view of reality." Calling himself a "converted anthropologist," Sanchez says that he gradually embraced native spirituality through intensive reading of Castaneda and subsequent work with actual Native American shamans.[25]

Unlike Harner and Sanchez, the majority of the students of tribal spirituality certainly prefer to remain within the walls of academia, trying to balance the worlds of the ordinary and nonordinary. In her recent book *Nine Worlds of Seid-Magic* (2002), Blain, both a sociology scholar and a practitioner of Nordic shamanism and paganism, vividly described the tension she experiences by trying to stay simultaneously in both realities. For example, as a spiritual practitioner, by way of *seid* (a Nordic divination practice), on her spiritual journey, she traveled to the plains of Midgard, touched the bark of the famous "world tree," Yggdrasil, followed the guidance of the raven, and rode on the wolf's back, feeling his warm soft fur. Moreover, at some point, she herself became a wolf, part of the pack, tracking and killing a stag and tearing its flesh with strong teeth.[26] At the same time, she remained a participant in the academic "sacred circle," teaching social science methods, going to conferences, and publishing scholarly articles.

Personally, I do not see here too much tension, especially in our time, when the humanities and social sciences and campus culture in general can accommodate practically any kind of spiritual and cultural experience or idea, no matter how unusual it might appear. Blain herself pointed to this changing attitude, writing, "It is becoming more acceptable to present aspects of the world—or worlds—in ways that do not lay claim to total 'Truth' or ultimate 'Reality.'"[27] Debunking grand theories and the truths that were considered established, postmodernist thinking opened possibilities for multiple analyses, which in turn opened doors to multiple realities, which for some includes the reality of spirits.

It is clear that current anthropology more readily accommodates experiential and even fictionalized narratives, in contrast to the earlier scholarship that locked itself in the straitjacket of positive knowledge. As an acknowledgment of this tendency, academic presses now accept for publication not only native spiritual biographies, but also accounts of the spiritual experiences of Western practitioners of neo-shamanism.[28] Overall, as Turner informed us, there is much support today for experiential anthropology. Lyon added to this that the number of anthropologists who realize the importance of going native and are "honestly participating in shamanic rituals" is increasing.[29]

It is certainly true. After all, many countercultural projects of the 1960s and 1970s became part of the academic and public intellectual mainstream. In the past, when an anthropologist, for example, went native, his or her academic career was doomed. Now the situation is reversing. Going native is considered an asset and even a requirement. Moreover, those who are still hesitant to move in this direction might run the risk of being viewed as people insensitive to the sentiments of native peoples. Turner alerted us that those scholars who are reluctant to embrace the experiential method and to convert themselves to the religion of the people they explore are "intellectual imperialists," who are no better than the Christian missionaries of old who sought to eliminate pagan beliefs. In a similar manner, Wallis, an archaeologist who went native by embracing the reality of European pre-Christian spirits, stressed that such unreformed scholars suffer from a "colonialist hangover." He also explained to us that they fear sliding into a state of savagery, a concern allegedly ingrained in Western culture.[30]

Tales of Power: The Print Culture of Modern Western Shamanism

The late religion scholar Daniel Noel, who explored the lure of Castaneda's oeuvre, stressed that the books about Don Juan indeed might be a hoax. Yet, it is a very powerful hoax. Moreover, he added that this was a necessary hoax. Why is it so? Here is how Noel explained this. The scholar suggested that the secret of Castaneda's popularity is simple. With his novels, Don Juan's apprentice helped to stimulate the revival of imagination and the spiritual that had been so profaned in the Western world. In modern times, Europeans and Americans have dismissed the power and reality of imagination in general. The major trouble with Westerners is that they constantly dissociate imagination and reality, implying that the first is not real and the second is real, instead of taking the separate reality for granted, as Castaneda did during his apprenticeship with Don Juan.

Like the famous historian of religion Mircea Eliade, Noel noted that literature, mythology, and fairytales remain the last vestige of the spiritual within Western civilization. If spirituality is revived, wrote Noel, it will certainly come from fictional or experiential literature. Viewed from this angle, Castaneda appears to be the creator of a powerful modern myth that helps to breathe the spiritual back into our lives. Therefore, instead of dismissing and debunking Castaneda, Noel viewed his fiction as a good lesson that teaches us to honor our own imagination and dreams, which, in the long run, helps us to return to the spiritual. What Noel tried to say appears to be another version of the old idea that myth can cure the ills of modern Western civilization. Earlier German Romantics and, later, such prominent forerunners of modern Western esotericism as Carl Gustav Jung and Joseph Campbell all insisted that myth would heal Euro-Americans from excessive materialism and rationalism.

Reflecting on the growing Western interest in shamanism and related spiritual practices, Noel also suggested that the current shamanism community essentially sprang up as a bookish phenomenon, an offshoot of the literary culture created by Castaneda and like-minded authors. In other words, neo-shamanism appeared to him to be the result of the intensive reading of fictional, semifictional, and ethnographic books about tribal spirituality and subsequent attempts to reproduce in life what people had read about. With a bit of irony, Noel called the print media, which he thought became the source of the inspiration, "shamanthropology." Current practitioners of shamanism, who insist that their practices are traceable straight to either archaic shamanism or to actual modern beliefs of non-Western elementary societies, certainly disagree with such an interpretation of their activities.

Although Noel did point to an important source of modern Western shamanism, one has to remember that we do not always observe here, as for example in the case of the Wicca religion, the straight pattern: books to spiritual practices.[31] In addition to Castaneda and other inspirational texts, the budding shamanic practices benefited much from the live techniques of the human potential movement in the 1960s and 1970s. After all, Harner, the father of Western neo-shamanism, had extensive field experience in South America and was initiated into hallucinogenic visionary experiences by Amazon Indians before the rise of the countercultural movement. Even though he did not include in his core shamanism much of what he learned from South American indigenous practitioners, Harner subsequently did apprentice with North American Indian spiritual teachers, some of whose techniques he did incorporate into this system.

Also, to reduce inspirational texts of neo-shamanism to Eliade, Castaneda, and anthropology books (shamanthropology) is certainly a simplification. It seems we should talk about the whole body of neo-shamanism print culture, which includes not only Castaneda and Eliade, but also Joseph Campbell, Carl Jung, Native American spiritual biographies and autobiographies, Siberian ethnographies, and early European medieval folklore.

With all these correctives, one can accept the Noel thesis. He drew our attention to the tool that Castaneda used for spiritual recovery. It is not so much through the power of magic herbs described in his first book or through his later Tensegrity seminars, but first of all through the power of his written word that the writer reaches out to us. Most Westerners do not have a chance to observe the shaman in the field or to partake in the exotic rituals described in Castaneda-like books or in actual ethnographic accounts. At the same time, everybody can partake in the written word. In fact, researching relevant books in the UCLA library in order to construct the character of his imaginary sorcerer, Castaneda himself is an example of a person who received spiritual inspiration from the written word.

Harner, a colleague of Castaneda, similarly pointed to the power of the written word in spreading shamanism knowledge in the West. In his classic *The Way of the Shaman*, which he offered as a shamanism manual for modern Westerners, he wrote:

> In Western culture, most people will never know a shaman, let
> alone train with one. Yet, since ours is a literate culture, you do not
> have to be in a professional situation to learn; a written guide can pro-
> vide the essential methodological information. Although it may seem
> awkward at first to learn basic shamanic techniques from a book,
> persist. Your shamanic experiences will prove their own value.[32]

Like Noel, Harner stressed that the "Castaneda hoax" helped to unleash the power of imagination and spiritual works as a necessary antidote to Western rationalism. Shielding the Don Juan sequel from critics, Harner once exclaimed, "I think Castaneda is 110 per cent valid."[33] He admitted that it is possible that Castaneda made up his stories, but it is equally possible that he did it in order to convey a deep truth. Moreover, Harner metaphorically com-pared Castaneda's creative blend of anthropology and fiction with the work of the shaman who tricks his or her clients for their own benefit. Harner said that when Amazonian shamans plan to extract evil darts from the bodies of their patients, they first hide them in their mouths and then "pull" them out, show-ing them to the audience as material proof that the sickness was extracted.[34]

What Noel and Harner said about the intellectual significance of the Castaneda gospel one can equally apply to other fictional and nonfictional writings that awakened Euro-Americans to tribal spirituality. Jurgen Kremer, a transpersonal psychologist from California, called these texts "tales of power" after one of Castaneda's novels. He argued that such writings can help West-erners reconnect themselves with their indigenous roots. To explain how one can accomplish this, Kremer turned to the dictum of postmodernism, which teaches us that the literary text not only does not reflect reality but, in fact, actively shapes it. Kremer suggested that nowadays instead of asking if there is any reality out there, we should ask other questions: "are there consensual realities we want to create? Are these ones we want to participate in?"[35]

Since we live in a narrative reality anyway, surmised the scholar, one certainly should give serious consideration to such tales of power as the nov-els with tribal settings produced by Castaneda, Hyemeyohsts Storm, and Lynn Andrews, which might become powerful tools to mold our own realities. Over-all, Kremer assumed that by acting as engineers of human minds and souls, these writers and like-minded authors promulgate new forms of conscious-ness, which might eventually prompt their readers to shape their own tales of power. Eventually, this might lead to the creation of a new "holographic paradigm" that would be free from excessive rationalism and positivism.[36] Recently, like many other Western practitioners of shamanism, Kremer has added to this body of tales of power early medieval European tales, such as Scandinavian sagas, which carry vestiges of pre-Christian European spirituality and which might better serve to empower Westerners than the texts coming from other cultural traditions or from fictional literature.

Now, let us take a closer look at some tales of power that stirred the imagination of spiritual seekers who searched for tribal wisdom. First of all, Castaneda's novels and books written in a similar format brought to life a spiritual apprenticeship genre that lies somewhere in the middle ground between anthropology and fiction. Although thoroughly milked, this genre is still very much alive. Since the 1960s, in the wake of the stunning success of Castaneda's books, publishers have continued to favor metaphysical experiences in the descriptions of so-called tribal peoples.

Discussing the publishing history of his *Wizard of the Four Winds* (1978), anthropologist Sharon underscored that aspect of the publishing industry. When he was still a graduate student at UCLA, writing a dissertation on his apprenticeship with the Peruvian *curandero* Eduardo Calderon, Sharon was thrilled to receive an advance and contract for a book from Indiana University Press. Yet, eventually, he had to release himself from the contract and turn to another press because the publisher aggressively pushed him to make revisions in order to turn the whole text into an adventure and mystery book. "The bottom line is that they wanted me to write another book like Castaneda's," said the scholar. Recently, Joan Wilcox, a spiritual practitioner who works within the ancient Peruvian tradition, has similarly written that, as an author, she feels pressure from her colleagues and potential publishers to concentrate on otherworldly experiences.[37] She also stressed that experiences with the metaphysical world are what many readers frequently expect in books dealing with shamanism.

The books that belong to the spiritual apprenticeship genre vary in their format and authenticity. A large number of them represent fictional and fictionalized autobiographies. One of the first successful literary emulators of Castaneda was Lynn Andrews, a writer from Berkeley, California, who became what one can call a "female Castaneda." She carved her literary niche by following the premise that to be an Indian and a woman means to carry the same superior moral and ethical ideas. Essentially, this was an attempt to kill two birds with one stone: she capitalized both on Native American and popular feminist spirituality.

Andrews wrote about her learning with Agnes Whistling Elk and Ruby Plenty Chiefs, Canadian Cree medicine women who reside in some unidentified part of Canada. At the end of the first book, *Medicine Woman*, Agnes instructed Andrews to go into the white world to convey the wisdom she learned from the Indians. Incidentally, this narrative line—a Euro-American apprentice coming back to the Western world to teach tribal spiritual wisdom—is standard for many books of this genre.

Andrews's characters essentially acted as feminine recasts of Carlos and Don Juan. Very much like Castaneda, she blurred cultural and geographical settings. In her texts, the Indian culture is a synthetic imagery, a creative trope she used to navigate her readers on the path to "true womanhood." Critics who focus on her lack of ethnographic authenticity are especially angry that, in portraying the Canadian Cree setting, Andrews piled together such diverse and unrelated traditions as those of Plains Indians, the Pueblo, and even the Aztec. Like Castaneda, with the same persistence, the writer has argued that her spiritual experiences really happened.

At the same time, on the wings of her imagination, Andrews has flown much farther than her literary predecessor. To learn about ancient female traditions, she traveled to Yucatan, Nepal, and Australia. In one of her novels, Andrews transplanted herself into medieval England and lived her past life under the name of Catherine. Incidentally, her loyal American Indian teachers, Ruby and Agnes, followed her to Europe and assisted the writer in her time travel.

In addition to the female Castaneda, there has appeared a "Cheyenne Castaneda." This was Charles Storm, a writer from northern California who went by the name of Hyemeyohsts Storm. He came up with a fictional account, *Seven Arrows* (1972), which he formatted as an allegorical ethnography. Storm claimed that he "recovered" an ancient esoteric Cheyenne ceremony called "seven arrows." Like Castaneda's novels, *Seven Arrows* watered down a particular indigenous cultural setting. To Storm, "Cheyenne" is simply a generic metaphor that describes a generalized version of the Plains Indian culture, with Hindu symbolism layered on top. In a similar vein to Andrews and Storm, later spiritual autobiographies have sought to tap new ritual, cultural, and geographic settings. For example, in her semifictional *Entering the Circle* (1996), Russian psychiatrist Olga Kharitidi successfully created a Siberian replica of Castaneda and Don Juan by writing a novel about her apprenticeship with an Altaian shaman in Siberia. Kharitidi's book showed that there is still a large commercial opportunity in this field through the use of new cultural backdrops and localities.[38]

One of the most recent and most peculiar attempts to find a niche in the spiritual apprenticeship genre is *The Shamanic Way of the Bee* (2004) by Simon Buxton, who claimed that he learned his spiritual wisdom from bees by taking the "path of pollen." Buxton argued that he was introduced to this version of shamanism through bee stings on his neck, on the top of his head, and over his third eye. The "bee shaman" also claimed that this "sacramental venom" has induced visionary experiences. Furthermore, Buxton noted that in order to enter altered states, he experimented with nightshade herbs, powerful European hallucinogens.

Playing to the current sentiments of Western practitioners of shamanism, who now more eagerly seek to ground themselves in pre-Christian European spiritualities, Buxton advertised this bee shamanism as a unique ancient form of European shamanism. Like Castaneda, Andrews, and Storm, the author blurred localities, cultures, and dates. This particular case of the experiential genre going wild prompted Timothy White, the editor of *Shaman's Drum*, one of the major periodicals in the Western shamanism community, to chide Buxton for his "fairy tale" and especially for irresponsibly advertising dangerous herbs and methods that the author had probably never used himself. White stressed that a few tall tales based on English folklore will not do any harm and actually might be amusing. However, when the tale is interpreted as authentic ethnography, this might be dangerous.[39]

Finally, there are books that simply clone Castaneda. One of the first texts of this caliber was a jungle fiction, *Wizard of the Upper Amazon* (1971) by Manuel Cordova-Rios and F. Bruce Lamb, which was composed from the digests of earlier published texts. Among other copycats are stories published by two women who belonged to Castaneda's inner circle of witches during the last years of his life. Castaneda claimed that these associates of his apprenticed with Don Juan. The first of these is Taisha Abelar. Like Castaneda, she received her Ph.D. from the UCLA anthropology department and similarly left academia to immerse herself into the world of sorcery.

Abelar's *The Sorcerer's Crossing* (1992) is almost an exact replication of the Castaneda–Don Juan experiences in the same locality (Sonoran Desert), only in a feminine recast. In this book, Abelar told a story of how in the 1960s, somewhere in the mountains near Tucson, Arizona, she met a sorceress. Then she lived with her in Sonora, Mexico. As it turns out, the female magician belonged to the same family of shamans and sorcerers that taught Castaneda.[40] In fact, Abelar came to seriously believe in her own fantasies. Although during the time of her "apprenticeship" in the Sonoran Desert, she was teaching anthropology at a community college, she became convinced that her life in the wilderness was a dreaming reality parallel to her existence in ordinary reality.[41]

Florinda Donner, Castaneda's second associate, received her master's degree from the same UCLA anthropology department and similarly devoted herself to the magic world of Don Juan. While Abelar used the Sonoran Desert as her backdrop, Donner selected for her setting the Amazon rainforest. In her *Shabono* (1982), she described captivating year-long spiritual experiences she allegedly had with Yanomami Indians in 1976 and 1977.[42] As it turned out, during that time Donner never left the United States, doing her graduate studies and simply fictionalizing an account of a woman who lived among these Amazon natives.

Apparently, in order to avoid the headaches they had with inquiries about the validity of Castaneda's dissertation, the UCLA anthropology faculty now took the effort to publish a letter about Donner's work. They expressed surprise at how their full-time graduate student, who never left the walls of the university until the end of 1977, was able to catapult herself into the rainforest and enjoy the jungle experiences among tribal others for the whole year.[43] Although once Donner confessed to a friend, "I tell so many lies I mix myself up," like Castaneda and Abelar, she always insisted on the reality of her experiences. It seems that this attitude fit the life principle that she called "Don Juan's sorceric cloak of confidence." The principle was simple: "stick to your story, and you'll always win."[44]

Many fictional and semifictional tales of power follow a certain pattern. First, the narrator or the author feels overcivilized or experiences a shattering misfortune or a life problem. Then this individual meets an indigenous spiritual teacher who immerses the author in the ocean of spiritual wisdom. The author/narrator embarks on a spiritual quest and goes through stages of an initiation, which are usually accompanied by difficult physical or moral tests, which the candidate usually passes. The end result is usually the total transformation of the apprentice's consciousness. Eventually, the shaman/spiritual teacher tells the candidate that he or she has become a chosen one endowed with certain esoteric wisdom that should be carried to the wider world. After this, the newly minted spiritual practitioner goes into society to help solve the problems of Western civilization, which faces perpetual spiritual and ecological crises. The narrative line of going from the remote non-Western setting to the wider world is essential because it allows an author to link his or her spirituality workshops to a particular non-Christian tribal tradition, which makes such applied spirituality credible.

For example, in her novel *Medicine Woman*, Andrews wrote that after finishing her apprenticeship with Whistling Elk and Plenty Chiefs, two imaginary, multicultural Canadian Cree characters, she wanted to stay in the native wilderness. Yet the shamans decided otherwise by preparing her as a messenger of Indian wisdom to city people. Whistling Elk allegedly reprimanded Andrews (like Castaneda, in her novels Andrews acts under her own name): "You are not Indian. The wilderness does not need you. Where do you think the world needs to be healed but in the cities? It's very easy to be sacred with the trees and the wind. It's very difficult to be sacred on the freeways of L.A." Thus, Andrews reluctantly returned to the cement jungles of Los Angeles and Berkeley and began to heal Westerners.[45]

Nonfictional spiritual narratives set in particular localities and traditions similarly seek to reach out to global audiences and resolve planetary problems. For instance, in her book about an apprenticeship with Peruvian shamans, Wilcox wrote, "I have been given a great gift: to be, in some small and modest way, the conduit for the message of the Q'ero mystics of Peru, to provide the vehicle through which these shamans can speak of their tradition and reach out to a world in need of reminding that we are all spiritual and energetic beings in the Great Web of Being."[46] Another author, Julie Ann Stewart, an

American who went native by turning herself into a Buryat shaman, viewed the southern Siberian shamanism about which she wrote as a tool to touch upon "universal truths that transcend ethnic boundaries."[47] Such utterances are common in these narratives, whose authors present themselves as individuals endowed with the power to deliver sacred knowledge that stirs and heals global consciousness and brings tribal wisdom to urban areas.

The spiritual apprenticeship books certainly vary in their literary quality. On the one hand, we have Castaneda's creatively written prose that became the classic of the genre. There is also the powerful experiential narrative, *The Way of the Shaman* by Harner. *Cosmic Serpent* (1998) by Jeremy Narby is another addition to this genre. In this small book, which is outstanding both in style and concept, the Swiss anthropologist told us that he has noted that many shamanic visions induced by the hallucinogenic drink *ayahuasca* include recurrent images of various reptiles. He has also noticed that these images happen worldwide in other cultures. Most important, in their shape, these reptile images roughly resemble the spiral model of DNA. Using this similarity, he came up with a provocative and creatively crafted thesis that people who experience shamanic visions might travel to the very roots of creation on a molecular level.

In the meantime, there are books that produce an impression of hastily glued patchworks that lack both imagination and literary skills. To be fair, some authors of such texts, for example, Amber Wolfe,[48] do honestly admit that their products represent only "cookbook shamanism," manuals that provide their readers with pocket power. Still, it is hard to exonerate those who claim to reveal high esoteric and healing wisdom received from native spiritual teachers but instead insult the intelligence of their readers with such banalities as this:

> Walking is highly recommended. Most people can do it safely.
> It's not strenuous, but it effectively increases respiration, expands
> lung capacity, stimulates circulation, increases the body's thermo-
> regulatory exchange, maintains good muscle tone, and uplifts the
> spirit all at the same time. You should take a moderately paced walk
> daily.

Or another piece of "wisdom" from the same author: "Thunderclouds create an intensely powerful electricity within them. The power is generated through the explosive reaction between the highly charged negative and positive ions." I took these two passages from *Earthways* by Mary Summer Rain, published by a large American press.[49]

In addition to readable experiential writings of Western spiritual seekers, one should add biographies and ethnographies that come straight from a particular tribal setting. Such narratives carry the powerful aura of authentic indigenous testimonies. For example, for San Francisco shamanism practitioner Leslie Gray, an ethnographic account actually served as a call that triggered her decision to turn to the shamanic vocation. After she read the famous Quesalid record, "I Desired to Learn the Ways of the Shaman" (1930), Gray totally revisited her view of the sacred and spirits:

> My entire life turned around. I realized in a blinding flash that what was called progress—moving from shamanism to mesmerism to hypnotism to Freud and contemporary psychiatry—was not evolution, but devolution. The way this shaman operated was really where the power is. Understanding, interpretation, and analysis were far less powerful than shamanism.[50]

I already discussed the Quesalid record in chapters 2 and 3. Here, I will briefly summarize what is so attractive about this testimony. The account describes how a traditional Kwakiutl Indian, who later receives the name of Quesalid, joins the ranks of shamans. Skeptical about their vocation, he wants to determine whether they are liars. However, after Quesalid learns healing techniques and tries them on people, he notices that they do cure patients. As a result, his disbelief opens a crack, and Quesalid becomes a full-time shaman. Anthropologist Franz Boas published this testimony in 1930 but did not mention that the account belonged not to the traditional Indian, but to George Hunt, a mixed-blood amateur ethnographer of English-Tlingit origin, who assisted Boas in his field research. Hunt was a former shaman who had joined the profession, not out of a desire to validate it, but in a traditional manner after experiencing a shamanic call. Later, he quit the vocation and began to work for anthropologists and then gradually turned himself into a collector of ethnographic specimens.

Later anthropologists, psychologists, and especially spiritual seekers became attracted to the 1930 account because it described the Indian doubting Thomas who converted to the powerful effect of shamanic curing and thereby validated the whole system of traditional healing. The Quesalid story, after it was used by Claude Lévi-Strauss in his famous paper "The Sorcerer and His Magic" (1949), entered the annals of anthropology and ethnopsychology, where it became a classic example of symbolic healing. Henri Ellenberger included the story in his textbook on dynamic psychiatry, *The Discovery of the Unconsciousness* (1970).[51] In rendering the Quesalid story, Lévi-Strauss and Ellenberger sent a message: one can doubt the skills of a particular practitioner of shamanism but not shamanism itself.

One of the most prominent tales of power for modern seekers interested in tribal spirituality is *Black Elk Speaks* (1932) composed by John G. Neihardt. Traversing Lakota country in search of materials for a poem he was working on, this Nebraska poet ran across the Lakota holy man Nicholas Black Elk (1863–1950). During a sickness as a nine-year-old child, Black Elk received a powerful vision, in which he met spiritual forces of the four cardinal directions and eventually received powers to heal and cure from thunder beings who resided in the West. Subsequently, spiritual beings repeatedly showed up and pressured Black Elk, reminding him of their existence. Eventually, the young Lakota realized that his destiny was to become a healer, whose major obligation was to maintain the sacred hoop of life unbroken. The great vision and the pressure from spiritual beings certainly fit the classical model of initiation into the shamanic vocation (shamanic illness). Neihardt befriended the elder and transcribed his life story. By publishing Black Elk's testimony, the poet became one of the fountainheads of the currently popular genre of spiritual biography and autobiography in a tribal setting. Many books of this genre, especially the ones that deal with Native American spiritual testimonies, have replicated the format of *Black Elk Speaks*.

In the 1930s, the reading public of depression-stricken America was more concerned about having bread on their tables and was not yet ready to fully comprehend projects such as Neihardt's. However, in the 1960s and 1970s, in affluent American society, the countercultural movement rediscovered *Black Elk Speaks* as a story containing a powerful spiritual and ecological alternative to Western materialism and rationalism. As a result, the book began to shape the views of many participants in the counterculture and nature movements. Moreover, for some, *Black Elk Speaks* acquired the proportions of a sacred text. It is "the first written record of what has become known as one of the greatest spiritual visions in history," as one of them put it.[52] Stressing the profound effect of *Black Elk Speaks* on his spiritual life, Henry Niese, who himself wrote a spiritual apprenticeship biography, remembered that after he read the book, he "realized for the first time that there is a culture, a body of wisdom, that related to my own experience."[53] Niese became so fascinated with this text that he even promised himself to do his best to mend the "sacred hoop of Indian nations and culture," whose breakdown Black Elk lamented in the end of the book. Incidentally, this ending was a creative addition written by the poet Neihardt, who compiled and edited the narrative.

Contemplating the role of the same book in his intellectual life, Thomas Parkhill, a historian of religion, admitted that, in the 1970s, he would hardly have accepted a complex account of Black Elk's life except Neihardt's *Black Elk Speaks*, which portrayed the Lakota elder as a Native American traditionalist. Parkhill said that this imagery better resonated with his own intellectual and spiritual aspirations in the 1970s than the recently revealed actual biography of the Lakota holy man, who was not only a traditionalist but also a Catholic cat-echist. The scholar stressed that the literary Black Elk helped him to cope with the alienation he felt at the time, when the "hoop" of the troubled American nation was broken in the early 1970s. Thus, the spiritual testimony of the old Lakota prompted him to think about how people could resacralize the modern world.[54]

I am sure that other people who cast *Black Elk Speaks* against the social, cultural, or ecological problems faced by Western society might tell us similar stories. A curious example of the spiritual effect of Black Elk is provided by the psychotherapist Bradford Keeney. For this university professor, the induction into shamanism began not with the text of this book but from the sheer presence of the Black Elk literary spirit. Thus, Keeney reported that he stepped on the shamanic path after he experienced a powerful spiritual vision by passing the University of Missouri's archival storage facility that held the original manuscripts of the conversations between Black Elk and Neihardt.[55]

Incidentally, many modern Native American spiritual biographies and autobiographies follow the format established by *Black Elk Speaks*. In fact, several of them represent spiritual revelations originating from the same Lakota tradition. To many spiritual seekers in the West, the Lakota represent the archetype of the classic American Indian. Since they fiercely resisted the advance of American modernity, the Lakota became the romantic heroes of the lost cause and eventually acquired the image of the Indian highlanders. In addition, they became portrayed as incredibly spiritual people.

The most famous Lakota spirituality narrative that continues the *Black Elk Speaks* genre is *Lame Deer: Seeker of Visions* (1972) by Lame Deer and Richard Erdoes. Interestingly, Erdoes later wrote similar spiritual biography books, at first pairing with Leonard Crow Dog and then with Archie Fire Lame Deer, the son of Lame Deer.[56] Lakota spirituality texts have been also produced by Wallace Black Elk Cow and William Lyon; Pete Caches; Frank Fools Crow and Thomas Mails; Ed McGaa; and Henry Niese.[57] Some of these collaborative texts, for example, the books coauthored by Erdoes, are not designed as spiritual messages to spiritual seekers worldwide. Others, such as the book by Lyon and Wallace Black Elk, on the contrary, carry the message of indigenous spiritual practices to all "Earth people." This stance might fit the tradition of the genre; as Neihardt informed his readers, Nicholas Black Elk directed the story of his vision to all humans.

There are certainly many spirituality texts set in the traditions of other Native American groups. Given the general popularity of North American Indian symbolism in the Western nature community, it is natural that Native Americana fully or partially informs many "New Age" visionary narratives. Quite frequently, these texts, written by both Caucasian authors and people who claim Native American descent, represent a mixture of various Native American traditions with Western metaphysical ideas.[58] They might also blend Native Americana with Oriental and African elements.[59] Alternatively, they might also fuse Native Americana with Christian spirituality[60] or with European medieval folklore.[61] Furthermore, now there are many spiritual narratives that tap other indigenous traditions beyond North America. Thus, there is a large body of visionary literature that draws on the indigenous spirituality of Latin America. There are also several published shamanic autobiographies set in Siberia, the Pacific, and Africa. Recently, many "tales of power" have begun to capitalize on early European folklore, which Western seekers link to pre-Christian times and which they think might better empower them than Native American or other non-Western traditions.[62]

Although some of these texts are grounded in indigenous cultures and describe actual experiences, they frequently cater to the tastes of popular audiences that view particular non-Western societies as carriers of ancient ecological wisdom. The authors and compilers of these books often depict indigenous shamans as the agents of timeless traditional culture. In their rendering, shamanism appears as an archaic spiritual artifact frozen in time and space. For example, in the above-mentioned collaborative text which publicized the revelations of the late Wallace Black Elk, a modern-day Lakota spiritual practitioner, its compiler, anthropologist Lyon, made a puzzling observation:

> North American shamanism is unique in that it has remained relatively untouched by any of the major world religions. This is not the case for the shamans of Europe, Asia, or Africa, where shamanism often takes on Taoist, Christian, or Buddhist motifs. In North America, however, shamanism has remained basically the same for thousands of years. The Native American form of shamanism, rooted deeply in nature and natural elements, is perhaps one of the most pure and powerful forms of shamanism in existence today.[63]

These kinds of statements certainly have a popular appeal. At the same time, they not only contradict the reality but also portray indigenous religion as sort of a Mesolithic fossil incapable of changes.

Shamanism through the Eyes of Mainstream Anthropology Scholarship

A tale of power is not necessarily a novel or a spiritual autobiography set in a tribal tradition. It could be any text, including a scholarly book, provided it responds to the spiritual expectations of Western seekers. For example, many people who are interested in shamanic practices and nature religions in general receive their inspiration from the scholarship of the famous religion scholar Mircea Eliade, the Swiss psychologist and mystic Carl Gustav Jung, and the American comparative mythology writer Joseph Campbell. I have already mentioned in the previous chapter that Eliade's writings, with their antimodern and primitivism messages, were in great demand in the 1960s and 1970s. So was the scholarship of Jung, who worked to marry science and the sacred. Rediscovered during the countercultural years, his writings became an inspiration for transpersonal psychology, a new discipline brought to life at the turn of the 1970s. Campbell was not less famous in countercultural circles. In his books, which continue to enjoy popularity in the modern nature community, he sought to identify common archetypes in the spiritualities of various cultures. The writer also contrasted the Eastern benevolent spiritual tradition to Western corrupt civilization. His popularity was especially boosted in the 1980s when he went on PBS with the program "Joseph Campbell and the Power of Myth."[64] Almost all spiritual seekers in the United States with whom I conversed and who are interested in shamanism, have read at least one book by this writer.

The spiritual practitioner Stephen Larsen explained how, for example, Campbell's *The Hero with a Thousand Faces* (1949) prompted his induction into the world of shamanism. Talking about his state of mind in the 1960s, Larsen described himself as a demythologized, skeptical, half-crazy yet spiritually thirsty youth who, like many of his generation, traded the conventional religion of his parents for positivism. However, Larsen felt a tremendous spiritual void. He thought that his life had lost any meaning and offered nothing except an exhausting struggle for a place on the social and economic ladder. In the early 1960s, by chance, he came across the Campbell book, which spiritually awakened him, helped to balance his mind, and eventually led him to the shamanic path. It appears that, for Larsen, *The Hero with a Thousand Faces* surely became a tale of power, which convinced him that his psychological imbalance was a phenomenon akin to the symbolic shamanic dismemberment that would necessarily result in spiritual restoration.[65]

Those who were particularly interested in Native American religious symbolism received much inspiration from the scholarship of academics who, like Campbell and Eliade, stressed the transcendental aspects of the indigenous nature religions. An example of such a scholar is Åke Hultkrantz, a student of Native American religions from Sweden. Incidentally, in addition to his works on American Indian religions, Hultkrantz is one of the world's authorities on northern shamanism. In his books *Shamanic Healing and Ritual Drama*, *Native Religions of North America*, and *Soul and the Native Americans*, the Swedish religion scholar provided popular overviews of Native American spiritual practices without reducing them to society, economy, and culture.

Hultkrantz did not care about recent scholarly fashions and preferred to work within the old European tradition of a grand narrative. As such, his scholarship went against the currently popular anthropological genre of small case study research. Like Eliade, he refused to reduce religion to its social and cultural context. Instead, Hultkrantz painted with broad strokes over a large cultural landscape. He extended his generalizations from northeastern Siberia to North America and to South America, work that few mainstream scholars in the United States dared to perform.

The Swedish scholar did not hide that he preferred a "humanistic devotion" and an "intuitive process of controlled imagination" to the conventional models of the social sciences. Moreover, Hultkrantz openly admitted his romantic notions and stressed that he "grew up fascinated with Indian lore," especially with the "religious mysteries of American Indian life." He still maintains this romantic attachment to the cultures about which he writes. From the pages of his books, the Native American appears as the steward of the earth, who lives in harmony with the surrounding world. It is natural that his writings are popular among spiritual seekers, both in Europe and North America. His books and public lectures served as an inspiration for the neo-shamanism community in Sweden, whose members frequently appealed to his scholarly authority to back up their spiritual practices.[66]

Intellectually, Eliade, Jung, Campbell, and Hultkrantz stand close to each other because all of these scholars recognized the autonomy of the sacred and did not rationalize religion and mythology. Instead of scrutinizing how particular beliefs changed over time, these scholars explored the timeless archetypes of these beliefs. This approach fits well the expectations of Western seekers of tribal spirituality. Although there is certainly nothing wrong in discussing shamanism or any other spirituality as a cross-cultural category, in present-day academic scholarship, especially among anthropologists, this method is not popular. Those who criticize the generic approach to shamanism do have a point. For example, they stress that one cannot reduce a tribal world view to such universal concepts as the world tree or the three-layered universe, which Eliade and like-minded scholars singled out in their outline of archaic spirituality. Underlining the variety of cultural contexts, many anthropologists now stress that there is no way to narrow them to an abstract perennial shamanism.

This skeptical attitude toward generalizations about shamanism certainly has much to do with the popularity of postmodernist thinking in the current humanities and social sciences, especially in the United States. This line of thought prioritizes the unique and the individual and avoids generalizations. The general message here is that any abstraction is inherently flawed because it never can catch the variety and richness of reality. Furthermore, postmodernist thinking treats ethnographic texts produced by earlier generations of scholars with a deep suspicion, considering them to be collections of the colonial fantasies of Western male explorers and writers. As such, reason the scholars who share this line of thought, these records cannot tell us anything about indigenous societies and their beliefs.

In the 1960s, anthropologist Clifford Geertz, one of the pioneers of that line of thinking and currently one of the intellectual icons of American humanities, debunked the concept of shamanism as an ideal construct, which, in his view, students of religion used to sort their data.[67] Discouraging cross-cultural generalizations, Geertz stressed that shamanism, like any other ethnological abstractions invented by Westerners, hardly withstood scrutiny when applied to particular nature religions in non-Western societies. It is notable that in her comprehensive review essay on shamanism studies (1992), Jane

Atkinson avoided using the term shamanism, preferring the plural shaman-isms. Other scholars picked up this usage in a similar attempt to stress the variety of cultural contexts irreducible to general abstractions.[68]

The anthropologists also stress that what we describe by the generic word shamanism usually exists as an applied spiritual technique for the resolution of particular material and social problems rather than as a tool of an abstract mysticism. Roberte Hamayon, a student of Siberian indigenous religions and one of Eliade's stoutest critics, reminded us that it is essential to keep in mind that this phenomenon represents an integral part of hunter-gatherers' social organization and supports regular life-giving rituals, "destined to ensure the re-production of society and of its natural resources." As early as the 1930s, in his *Psychomental Complex of the Tungus*, Sergei Shirokogoroff stressed that sifting specific traditions in order to single out the generic abstraction as shaman-ism was neither possible nor desirable, simply because one could not divorce the "shamanism complex" from the "larger complex" of cultural and social life.[69]

Anthropology scholars have also noted that it is hard to generalize not only about "universal" shamanism, but also about spiritual practices and prac-titioners on the level of a specific community. Like traditional shamans in non-Western societies, whose healing and performing arts are based on free improvisation, modern-day anthropologists take a polyphonic approach to un-derline that shamanism carries the mark not only of a particular culture but also of an individual spiritual technique. These researchers stress that non-Western nature religions are notoriously fluid. They frequently lack canonized deities and spirits. Different clan groups of the same tribe and individual shamans can have their own deities and can interpret spirits with the same names in different manners.

In her collaborative project that explores Daur shamanism in China, Car-oline Humphrey came up with a theoretical guideline: one cannot reflect on shamanism as a system of knowledge. The description of shamanism is better seen through the eyes of an individual spiritual practitioner set in a particular cultural and social context than in the abstract terms of a tribal or clan sha-manism. Although in this case, the knowledge is bound to be partial, it is this partial nature that allows us to grasp the essence of shamanism. Changing and "dispersive" nature and highly individualized practices are precisely what gives shamanism its unity, stressed the scholar. Humphrey also noted that in the realm of tribal spirituality, the ultimate agency belongs to the individual who "works shamanism," experimenting with available cultural and spiritual mate-rial.[70] Overall, the currently dominant trend in the scholarship of non-Western nature beliefs is to avoid generalizations as much as possible and to place em-phasis on communal or individual spiritual practices.

The studies that examine the polyphonic and individualized character of shamanism seek to unfold tribal spirituality in all its complexity with all of the intruding elements that might appear unrelated to the core of the topic. Thus, anthropologist Michael Brown reproduced and discussed a full version of a healing séance he observed and taped among the Jivaro Indians in Peru. In addition to core elements of the session, one finds in this text a variety of remarks and exclamations coming from the audience that observed and scrutinized the shamanic séance. During the performance, the major protagonist of Brown's essay, shaman Yankush, did not act like Lévi-Strauss's charismatic "tribal psychoanalyst" nor as a spiritual hero who operates with Eliadean cosmic symbols. In Brown's rendering, this particular Jivaro healing séance was an example of an ongoing communal dialogue about spiritual and social power. Far from being an archetypical creator of order from chaos, Yankush appeared as a person filled with insecurities. For example, during the séance, he constantly improvised, trying to safeguard himself from the possible anger of the audience that watched his healing performance and that might easily have turned on him if something had gone wrong with the patient.

Brown is good at showing the ambivalent nature of shamanism, the aspect frequently downplayed by many earlier students of shamanism and by modern Western "New Age" and nature writers. The anthropologist made it clear that in a so-called tribal setting, people can easily recast their benevolent shaman from a tribal hero into a malicious witch. To the audience that observed Yankush, his shamanic session was both dangerous and therapeutic and could go either way. Therefore, Yankush had to perform under constant scrutiny. Moreover, several members of the audience warned him to make sure to use benevolent powers. Trying to protect himself from danger, the shaman sought scapegoats, repeatedly stressing the evil intentions of his colleagues who might have bewitched the woman. Yankush clearly adjusted his chants and spiritual techniques to the changing moods of the spectators. Commenting on this impromptu spiritual performance, Brown suggested that shamanic performances represent "anti-structural worlds," in which shamans and their audiences are like actors in a live play, constantly renegotiating their behavior. For this reason, each healing session illustrates a delicate balance of power between the healer and the community. Essentially, Brown questioned the established ethnological metaphor of the shaman as spiritual hero, the creator of balance and order out of chaos.[71]

This postmodernist view of the shaman as a spiritual anarchist who breaks social order is best articulated in *Shamanism, Colonialism, and the Wild Man* (1987) by Michael Taussig.[72] This physician turned anthropologist explored indigenous *ayahuasca*-based healing practices in southern Colombia. Originally, when he went to Colombia, Taussig did not plan any anthropological fieldwork. A product of the rebel 1960s who was on a quest for a social cause, he arrived in southern Colombia to tend to the medical needs of rural Marxist guerrillas. Gradually, Taussig noticed around him a heavy presence of local spiritual and physical folk doctors, which prompted him to examine this phenomenon more carefully. The research into shamanism that followed merged his Marxist intellectual stance with his interest in healing and curing.

In contrast to Eliade and like-minded authors, Taussig did not portray shamanism as something primal and archaic. Being a Marxist, the scholar traced the origin of the phenomenon in this particular geographic area to the rubber boom period at the turn of the twentieth century, when local Indian labor was ruthlessly exploited by predatory rubber-producing companies. This exploitation reached genocidal levels: companies' agents tortured and murdered Indians. The scholar noted that the colonizers intentionally practiced genocide to keep the native labor under control. Although the rubber boom eventually subsided, the wounded historical memory, heavily infused with fear, remained. The scholar dug deeply into this heart of darkness. He found that the painful experiences of the "rubber days" had penetrated the local collective unconscious and become mirrored in the system of redemptive healing.

Taussig noticed that in southern Colombia, the most powerful and feared were native "wild Indian shamans" in the Amazon jungles down the Putumayo River. Although feared, they were at the same time respected as spiritual doctors who knew their medicine very well. As a result, not only the indigenous folk but also settlers who despised Indians came to seek cures from these shamans. Thus, for these spiritual practitioners, shamanism became a sort of a symbolic liberation. Natives who had been abused by the rubber company in the past "came back" as feared and respected healers.[73]

Taussig's vision of the shaman is of the individual who acts as a trickster-rebel, a kind of an anarchist in Indian garb disrupting the established rules and views. To him, the spiritual session of the indigenous Colombian healer is not something that one can compare with a religious service. It is an impromptu event better compared to Antonin Artaud's theater of cruelty, where chaos, disorder, and anarchy reign and where a happy ending is never guaranteed.

Taussig argued that the whole wisdom of shamans is to provide a stage on which they and those who join them can act out contradictions in society. Like Brown, he stripped shamanism of its heroic and solemn imagery by intentionally bringing into the pictures of *ayahuasca* séances the realities of daily life, including bodily functions, and replicating these sessions in all details:

> Interruptions for shitting, for vomiting, for a cloth to wipe one's face, for going to the kitchen to gather coals for burning coal incense, for getting roots of magical *chondur* from where nobody can remember where they were last put, for whispering a fear, for telling and retelling a joke (especially for that), for stopping the song in mid-flight to yell at the dogs to stop barking, and in the cracks and swerves, a universe opens out.[74]

Taussig wrote that the perception of the shaman as the creator of order from chaos mirrors the romantic notions of the Western imagination rather than the reality of shamanism. The anthropologist pointed out that the very talk about the shamans' mystical trips to the heavenly spheres and their organic unity with their tribes is an example of a "fascist fascination." This is clearly a reference to the scholarship and intellectual background of Eliade, the classic scholar of shamanism studies, who paid tribute to nationalist soil ideology during his early years. The anthropologist simultaneously took on those of his colleagues who associate order with good and disorder with evil. Taussig saw in the anarchy and disorder of Amazon *ayahuasca* spiritual sessions a helpful antidote to the Western "fascist" order, which is rooted in the European Enlightenment with its logic, rationalism, and discipline. According to Taussig, in this spiritual anarchy lies the liberation potential of shamanic sessions. If we are to believe the anthropologist, one of the Putumayo shamans he met directly pointed out to him, "I have been teaching people revolution through my work with plants."[75]

The dismissive attitude of postmodernist anthropology to generalizations about shamanism prompts a critical response from scholars who work in the comparative mythology and religion studies tradition. One of the most prominent representatives of this tradition is Hultkrantz, the Swedish student of Native American religions. Peter Furst, one of those who promoted the use of the shamanism concept in American anthropology and archaeology in the 1960s and 1970s, has similar goals. He stresses that nobody questions the obvious differences among the varieties of shamanisms, which we should explore and record. Still, this does not mean that we must avoid examining shamanism from a cross-cultural perspective as a reflection of a common human *Weltanschauung* (mindset) and common symbols. Furst plausibly argues that the angle from which we approach shamanism is simply a matter of research priorities. Some scholars might want to explore the specifics of shamanism. Others might be more concerned with the fundamentals of shamanism, looking into shamanism as a system of knowledge that seeks to address universal problems of humankind.[76] His and Hultkrantz's positions resonate well with the mindset of those eclectic spiritual seekers who want to pin down the archetypes of perennial ancient wisdom.

7

Toward the Ancient Future

Shamanism in the Modern West

I think this is the great adventure of our age and far more humanly valuable than the "race for space." It is the reclamation and renewal of the Old Gnosis.

—Theodore Roszak, *Where the Wasteland Ends* (1972)

I'm trying to take methods that are thousands of years old and learn how to use them in the 1990s with the problems we have in our culture.

—Sandra Ingerman, shamanism practitioner, Santa Fe, New Mexico

In the United States at the turn of the 1970s, the countercultural revolution, which turned many Americans on to hallucinogens and alternative lifestyles, was on the decline. Many spiritual seekers felt fatigue from the psychedelic and communal experiences and longed for natural, individually oriented spirituality. One of these spiritual seekers was Michael Harner, an anthropologist who, while formally remaining an academic, gradually grounded himself in the countercultural community. Although he had invested much of his earlier career into the study of South American Indian indigenous groups, whose spiritual cultures are saturated with hallucinogens, he purposely moved away from replicating these experiences in Western settings. Instead, Harner searched for alternatives by experimenting with drugless spiritual techniques from native North American, Siberian, and Sámi traditions, which rely more on drumming, rattling, chanting, and guided meditation. Since his thinking resonated well with the sentiments of many spiritual seekers, his workshops began to enjoy popularity.

Eventually, Harner left academia and moved from the East Coast to California in order to devote himself completely to teaching Westerners how to spiritually cure themselves by using "archaic techniques of ecstasy." In 1980, he established the Foundation for Shamanic Studies (FSS), the first school of modern shamanism, which organizes, systematizes, and disseminates archaic knowledge worldwide. Thus, shamanism entered modern Western nature communities. Today, there is a large variety of shamanic groups and individuals in the West. They range from those that seek to ground themselves in particular non-Western traditions to the ones that practice what one can call Wiccan and Celtic shamanism. Moreover, some of these groups and people have nothing to do with Harner and his system of shamanism. At the same time, his *The Way of the Shaman* (1980), designed as a manual for any Westerner wishing to learn shamanic techniques, continues to inspire many people from that community. Since Harner was among the first to spearhead the shamanism idiom in modern Western esotericism, I would like to start this overview of neo-shamanism in Europe and North America with a discussion of Harner's spiritual experiences.

Michael Harner and Core Shamanism

Harner's evolution from a conventional scholar, busily studying Conibo and Jivaro (Shuar) Indians of the Amazon rainforest, into a spiritual practitioner of shamanism was gradual. As he later recalled, the original drive to explore the Amazon indigenous cultures was simply a romantic urge to find a still-unconquered American Indian tribal society: "It was almost a century too late for this opportunity in North America; so I chose South America, and specifically the Jivaro, who were famous for their ability to successfully resist would-be conquerors over the centuries."[1] The anthropologist intended to write an "accurate ethnography" of that indigenous group, which was known for its sensational, morbid practice of "head shrinking."

This gruesome image of the Jivaro originated from the Finnish anthropologist Rafael Karsten, who wrote *The Head-Hunters of Western Amazonas* (1935), the first comprehensive description of these Indians.[2] Karsten described in detail the Jivaro's social and political life, hunting customs, trade, agriculture, language, and material culture. The ethnographer also detailed the effects of the Jivaro mind-altering herbs, which he personally ingested. Still, the Finnish scholar treated all these things more as a backdrop. What he appreciated most was the head-hunting practice, to which he devoted much of his book. He believed that this morbid custom affected all aspects of Jivaro life.

Furthermore, the scholar implied that head hunting and the rituals that sur-round it are the keys to understanding Jivaro society. The decapitation of en-emies and the ritual shrinking of their heads, explained the scholar, is the way to capture the enemies' souls, which reside in their heads and hair. By captur-ing enemies' souls, the Jivaro shield the security of their communities. Thus, the people among whom Harner was planning to do his fieldwork appeared to the outside world to be exotic jungle dwellers immersed in the chilling ritual of shrinking the heads of their enemies.

Harner stressed that, at first, when living among these Indians in 1956–1957, he explored their culture as a whole and did not prioritize their spiritu-ality, including the hallucinogenic brew *ayahuasca* ("the vine of the dead"), a plant drink that the Jivaro ingested under the guidance of a shaman to induce visions. Their shamans offered the anthropologist two opportunities to take the hallucinogen, and each time he backed off in fear of damaging his rationalist mind, "the most important tool I had for my scholarly effectiveness," Harner ironically remarked.[3] In those years, such an intellectual stance was under-standable. In the 1950s, anthropology and Western intellectual culture in gen-eral was still under the spell of positivism and not yet interested in experiential knowledge. Although in 1961, while working among the Conibo Indians of the Peruvian Amazon, the anthropologist tried *ayahuasca*, he still did not make any far-ranging conclusions about the significance of this experience. Indeed, in his 1962 article and his 1963 dissertation, Harner did not say a word about mind-altering herbs.

Harner's appreciation of the rainforest vine came later, during the psy-chedelic revolution. Sometime in the middle of the 1960s, the anthropologist became convinced that scholars, including himself, had underestimated the significance of altered states in affecting indigenous cultures: "I realized an-thropology had underestimated the seriousness of shamanic knowledge and that I had entered a reality far deeper than human culture."[4] His intensive research at the University of California library in Berkeley, which he treated as an attempt "to find kindred spirits, both literally and figuratively,"[5] strength-ened his conviction about the existence of similar spiritual practices all over the world. Like Wasson, Castaneda, Timothy Leary, and many others of his gen-eration, Harner became fascinated with the native hallucinogens, which he began to see as the key to an expanded reality. At that time, he was generally convinced that "the drugs did it" and, like many of his anthropology and psy-chology colleagues, ascribed the origin of religion to ancients' ingestion of hal-lucinogens. Harner stressed that widely publicized experiments with LSD reinforced his view that the bioactive substance contained in hallucinogens was the major tool shamans used to enter altered states.[6]

Instilled with this new awareness, in 1964 he interrupted his library re-search and went back to the Amazon rainforest, with the sole purpose to "give particular attention to the drug's use by the Jivaro shaman."[7] His intention was to attach himself as an apprentice to some indigenous spiritual practitioner from the northwestern part of Jivaro country, the area where local shamans were reportedly especially powerful. Harner boldly approached one of these spiritual doctors, Akachu, and directly asked him to teach him how to work with magic darts, which are central elements of Jivaro shamanism. The Indian longingly looked at the anthropologist's new Winchester and hinted that the gun might serve as a good fee for the magic lessons. The anthropologist gladly handed his gun and cartridges to the shaman. In return, Akachu gave Harner a thick pole made of balsa wood and explained, "This is your magic staff. It will protect you from demons. If you encounter one, throw it at him. It is more powerful than a gun."[8] The anthropologist returned to Berkeley in a new role. Now he was the one initiated into the mysteries of Jivaro shamanism. Committed to learning more about the role of mind-altering plants in shamanism, he visited the Jivaro two more times, in 1969 and 1973, and continued his spiritual apprenticeship. Eventually, by the end of the 1960s, Harner concentrated his research exclusively on native hallucinogenic experiences.[9]

The anthropologist stressed that the mind-altering herbs colored the entire Jivaro culture. For example, he stressed that, among the Jivaro, people began seeking the power of the spirit world as early as childhood. Accompanied by his father, a six-year-old boy would go to a waterfall and persistently pace there beneath the thundering water, trying to induce a sacred vision. If vision did not come, the boy would turn to a spiritual shortcut, chewing the bark of the *datura* plant, the hallucinogen that usually brings the expected images within three to four minutes. Furthermore, Harner informed his readers that the Indians administered mind-altering herbs in weak doses to babies who were only a few days old in order to adjust them to vision questing. The anthropologist also noted that if young boys misbehaved, their parents sometimes gave them herbal hallucinogens—discipline by the power of visions. Even Jivaro hunting dogs, stressed the scholar, were encouraged by their masters to ingest hallucinogens in order to acquire supernatural powers that helped the animals to "see" better.

Sometimes, it is interesting to observe how changing times or scholarly and popular sentiments make us prioritize some themes and downplay others. While Karsten earlier had viewed the Jivaro through the lens of their head-hunting practice, Harner treated them as a nation of shamans steeped in hallucinogenic spirituality. During the heyday of the psychedelic revolution, in a 1968 essay for the popular *Natural History* magazine, Harner recovered and made public the 1960–1961 visionary experiences he had after ingesting *ayahuasca* with his Indian spiritual teachers. The skeptical investigative anthropologist Richard De Mille could not resist an ironic comment: "Harner waited seven years to tell the academic world about his conversation with the true gods."[10]

In this essay, which he later incorporated into his 1980 manual, Harner introduced his readers to the powerful spiritual effect of *ayahuasca*. The anthropologist described his *ayahuasca* journey as follows: "I found myself, although awake, in a world literally beyond my wildest dreams. I met bird-headed people, as well as dragon-like creatures that explained that they were the true gods of this world. I enlisted the services of other spirit helpers in attempting to fly through the far reaches of the Galaxy."[11] After Harner underwent this visionary experience, he shared his sensations with an influential Conibo spiritual practitioner. The indigenous medicine maker, who became impressed with the power of Harner's vision, reportedly predicted that the anthropologist would become a master shaman.

Despite those profound experiences, sometime in the 1970s, Harner realized that what he was learning with Jivaro shamans about entering altered states through the hallucinogens was, in fact, a marginal practice. One can also assume that the waning of the psychedelic revolution in the early 1970s was not an insignificant factor in changing his mind. During that time, American society and culture gradually drifted toward strict antidrug laws. In the 1970s, people realized that there were other, less hazardous ways to achieve expanded reality. More important, there appeared public concern about ecology, healthy lifestyles, and deep spirituality. Overall, there was a thirst for spiritual techniques and experiences that went beyond pharmacology.

It appears that, in the 1970s, Harner began to contemplate how to use the healing potential of shamanism to address the spiritual problems of Western society. As I mentioned at the beginning of this chapter, the lessons of tribal shamanism the anthropologist was going to teach Euro-American audiences came not from the hallucinogenic practices he learned firsthand from the Jivaro. His spiritual blueprints came from the safe methods (drumming or rattling) of the Siberian and Australian medicine people that he read about in ethnographic books or learned from native North American spiritual practitioners with whom he interacted at home.

Tuning himself to the changing sentiments, Harner began to view pharmacological ways of reaching altered states not only as inefficient but also as detrimental. Thus, he pointed out that hallucinogens might unleash confusing imagery, interfere with the concentration necessary for shamanic work, and leave various chemical residues in one's body.[12] Instead, Harner noted that the sound of the shaman's drum supplemented by rattling could produce the same effect as the hallucinogenic snuffs and drinks, but without any negative side effects. The scholar remembered, "I began to experiment with drumming in my personal shamanic work and was pleasantly surprised to find that with the proper techniques and discipline I could go to the same places as with the shaman's psychedelics."[13] Although Harner included in his *The Way of the Shaman* the captivating descriptions of his 1961 visionary experience triggered by the Amazon vine drink, it was mostly a literary exercise. The anthropologist did not recommend his hallucinogenic venture for general emulation. Harner reminded us in that book that one did not have to ingest a hallucinogen in order to plan to turn into a bird or some other animal.[14]

He explained his decision to downplay the role of hallucinogens as a path to altered states by his cross-cultural observations rather than by changing contemporary public sentiments: "I eventually concluded that the Amazonians' use of psychedelics was a minority practice. The much more common method to enter the shaman's altered state of consciousness was monotonous percussive sound, achieved especially through drumming."[15] This certainly is a plausible observation. As early as 1973, in a collection of articles that he edited, *Hallucinogens and Shamanism*, Harner found it necessary to make a brief note that psychedelic agents were only one of the methods for achieving trance-like states, in addition to deprivation, self-torture, and meditation. Harner now insists that he became aware of the marginal place of tribal hallucinogens as early as the middle of the 1960s.[16]

Gradually, by reading ethnographies and studying with indigenous spiritual practitioners who did not use mind-altering herbs, Harner began to shape a system of spiritual techniques, which he called core shamanism. The premise of this system is based on a conviction that, if stripped of its cultural garb, a particular tradition reveals generic cross-cultural practices characteristic for shamanisms all over the globe. In other words, spiritual practices of elementary earth-based societies of all times and of all continents, including pre-Christian Europe, are remarkably similar. In his view, once identified and extracted, the core methods can be used for the spiritual curing of modern Western people. Therefore, Harner centered his teaching strategy on the "distillation and interpretation of some of the millennia-old shamanic methods."[17] Jonathan Horowitz, one of Harner's former students, who now teaches shamanism in Scandinavian countries, elaborated on the techniques of his teacher: "The varnish of culture is skin-deep. These ancient methods lead directly into our innermost world, to the archaic layer which is common to all people." In this case, the task of core shamanism is to "peel off the cultural differences between shamanism in different cultures, and to develop the common core, the fundamentals."[18]

The intellectual source of this approach is the Eliadean vision of shamanism as an archaic cross-cultural spirituality, the original cradle of all beliefs and religions. In *The Way of the Shaman*, Harner credited Eliade for bringing to light the worldwide consistency in shamanic knowledge. Like his intellectual predecessor, the founder of core shamanism is convinced that the ancient way is so powerful and taps so deeply into the human mind that one's culturally colored beliefs and assumptions about reality are essentially irrelevant.[19] Like Eliade, the anthropologist appreciates such recurring cross-cultural symbols as the world tree, the world mountain, and the tunnel. In the same manner, according to Harner, shamans worldwide manifest striking similarities in their spiritual practices, although they are separated by thousands of miles.

It was not coincidental that when critics blamed Castaneda for manufacturing the character of Don Juan as a multicultural "universal shaman" who transcended geographic and cultural borders, Harner defended him. Responding to De Mille, who took on Castaneda for plagiarizing Harner's ethnography, the anthropologist pointed out that there was no plagiarism involved whatsoever. Explaining his position, Harner stressed that shamanic practices were very similar all over the "primitive world."[20] No less important was the fact that Harner's own evolution at the turn of the 1970s, from hallucinogenic to safe shamanism, mirrored the similar change in the Castaneda oeuvre. As we remember, in *The Teachings* (1968), the creator of Don Juan widely sampled the ritual use of hallucinogens (peyote, *datura*, mushrooms), yet the practice completely disappeared in his later novels.

Using spiritual techniques based on drumming and rattling, Harner began to teach interested Westerners shamanic healing and divination. The anthropologist positioned himself as a person recovering archaic knowledge in order to build a better spiritual future. At first, he worked with one or two individuals at a time. Then the number of students increased. By the middle of the 1970s, Harner had already taught workshops for human potential groups at such places as the Esalen Institute in California. Finally, in 1979 in Connecticut, Harner established a nonprofit study center, which later became known as the Foundation for Shamanic Studies (FSS), the first school of shamanism for Westerners. The project turned out to be a success. As a result, in 1987, the anthropologist completely parted with academia to become a "full-time shaman."[21]

Seven years prior to that, he had published *The Way of the Shaman*, one of the sacred texts of the shamanism community in the West. The experiences described in this book provided Western seekers what was missing in Castaneda's novels and in the fiction of his numerous emulators: real natives, real shamans, and real mind-changing techniques. In the same year that he published his manual, the scholar moved his shamanism school from Connecticut to Mill Valley, California. As one of the strongholds of the mind, body, and spirit culture, this area certainly could better accommodate this kind of a spiritual project.

The core ritual item in the Harnerian version of shamanism is the drum. Rationalizing its use as a healing tool, the anthropologist and his associates argue that monotonous drumming can produce changes in the central nervous system and put the person in an altered state. Incidentally, although Harner sometimes uses the expression "altered state," he prefers to talk about the "shamanic state of consciousness." The anthropologist and his associates from FSS point out that drumming in a frequency of four to four and a half beats per second temporarily changes brain wave activity. This facilitates imagery in the human mind and allows people to reach rapidly an altered state, which helps the spiritual practitioner to embark on a shamanic journey.[22]

The founder of core shamanism also stresses that the changes induced by the monotonous drumming build up the resistance of the body's immune system against various diseases. Proponents of the Harnerian version of sha-manism add that no hallucinogen can produce such marvelous effects. The only problem one has to worry about when using the drum is the privacy of one's neighbors. Yet Harner and his associates found a solution. They began to release drumming audio cassettes and CDs, which they advertise as perfect substitutes for actual drumming. This multimedia option that encourages an individual to become his or her own shaman is a truly Western solution framed in the spirit of the Euro-American tradition of individualism.

The activities of the center eventually attracted the attention of thousands of people. Reportedly, the foundation now trains about 5,000 people each year.[23] Many FSS associates and graduates have started their own healing centers and schools. Former students of Harner teach shamanism (see figure 7.1), write books, and lecture all over the United States and Europe. The grad-uates of the core shamanism workshops usually freely use the spiritual tech-niques they learned at FSS to merge with or layer onto their own individual spiritualities. It appears to be one of the goals of the Harner foundation to give spiritual seekers a "spiritual skeleton" on which they should put their partic-ular techniques.

FIGURE 7.1. A scene from a core shamanism workshop in Savannah, Georgia, 2003. Photograph by the author.

One of the most famous shamanism practitioners to apprentice with Harner is Sandra Ingerman, who resides near Santa Fe, New Mexico. She specializes in so-called soul extraction, a creative offshoot of Harnerian shamanism, and runs about forty workshops a year in the United States and beyond. Ingerman is also a prolific spirituality writer. Some FSS graduates turned teachers have moved abroad, carrying Harner's core shamanism to other Western countries. Horowitz, a former anthropologist who similarly apprenticed with Harner, went to Scandinavia, where he now teaches shamanism courses designed along Harnerian lines. Hugo-Bert Eichüller, a social worker and psychotherapist from Germany, after studying with Harner, went back to Nuremberg where he established the Institut für Schamanistische Studien, a German version of the Foundation for Shamanic Studies. Overall, people who have learned Harnerian shamanism and who teach their own groups now work in many Western countries and even in native Siberia, the motherland of shamanism. The foundation has become the major spearhead of shamanic practices in the United States and other Western countries. Despite their different goals and agendas, many spirituality schools and centers, which mushroomed in the 1980s and 1990s and which position themselves as shamanic, directly or indirectly capitalize on the Harner system.

An important component of FSS activities is the preservation of shamanic knowledge on the tribal periphery. It might be a desire of the foundation to somehow pay back indigenous people for the knowledge Western spiritual seekers have digested from their traditions. The foundation responds to the requests of those indigenous groups that ask for help to restore traditional earth-based knowledge undermined by colonization. Again, Harner's associates view this assistance as providing such natives with the skeleton of shamanism knowledge, on which interested natives can put their cultural meat. Thus, such fertilization of a local tradition has helped to enhance the revitalization of shamanic practices in the Tuva republic (Siberia), where native spiritual practitioners blend what has remained from their tradition with the techniques appropriated from Western esotericism.[24]

Critics point out that this project harbors the danger of imposing on native societies the quick-fix version of shamanism constructed for Western audiences. For example, archaeologist Wallis argues that for the restoration of local shamanisms, it is better to use existing native traditions.[25] At the same time, it is not so easy to anchor this politically correct ideal in reality. On many occasions, native people (for example, in the above-mentioned Tuva republic) are themselves interested in cultivating contacts with Harner's foundation and other Western-based "New Age" and nature centers. Moreover, they are ready to receive spiritual feedback from their Western colleagues. Furthermore, in some native societies, for example, in Khakassia (Siberia), where the shamanistic tradition was completely wiped out, one cannot talk about an already-existing tradition. FSS representatives insist that not only Siberians but also some Native American, Sámi, and Inuit people have similarly approached Harner, requesting that he teach them core shamanism to restore their sacred knowledge, which was lost due to conquest and Christianization.

Cast against ethnographic descriptions of nineteenth-century shamanism, Harnerian techniques certainly look different and not so traditional. Still, this does not prevent interested spiritual practitioners in Siberia and other non-Western areas from reading his books and weaving his techniques into their own practices. Non-Western shamanism practitioners who are especially known for their attempts to revive this spiritual practice receive from the foundation an honorary title, "The Living Treasure of Shamanism." For example, such a title was bestowed on Tuvan ethnographer and folklore writer Mongush Kenin-Lopsan.[26]

As I mentioned above, the FSS's associates argue that core shamanism can be conveniently transplanted into any cultural setting as a skeleton around which a person can build his or her own spirituality. Mark Gough, a practicing shaman in Hull, England, who works within Harner's tradition, explained, "You learn these and are then free to put your own cultural or religious identity on top of them." During a workshop that I visited, "American Shamanism 101," Eric Perry, a spiritual practitioner from Savannah, Georgia, repeatedly stressed that the essence of the Harner practices is to remove shamanic techniques and mysteries from their cultural backgrounds. Approaching shamanism not as a religion but as a cross-cultural "spirituality technology," asserted Perry, makes it potentially available for everybody's use, from a Christian true believer to a die-hard atheist.[27] The spirituality developed by Harner integrates not only non-Western earth-based symbols but also the language of Western psychology and psychiatry, particularly psychoanalysis. For example, the neo-shamanic concept of soul loss, which participants of Harner's workshops seek to return, recalls Freud's generalizations about repression and trauma.[28]

In a Harnerian basic workshop, people usually lie on the floor, close their eyes, and try to relax. Accompanied by the intensive monotonous sounds of a drum, they begin to enter the altered state, the spiritual journey to the spirit world. Harner and his associates encourage those participants who have mastered the basics of his core techniques to journey on their own, using drums or earphones and drumming tapes. The spiritual journey usually begins with entering either a passage, or a tunnel, or a cave and then the spirit world. In an introductory shamanism workshop I took with Jack Bennett, a spiritual practitioner from Columbia, South Carolina, who calls himself a firm believer in the Harner method, the spiritual journey started with the following scenario the instructor prepared for us: "Imagine a hole in the ground and here you use your imagination. Go through the hole and try to meet your power animal." The concept of the shamanic journey to otherworldly reality in order to interact with a power animal is central to Harnerian shamanism. During our workshop, Jack kept telling us, "What I do is I journey, and I journey, and I journey, and I journey. Don't tell me about being a shaman and not journey."

Although Harner and those who follow his method insist that the information people learn during those journeys comes straight from spirits, they seem to realize that not everybody in the present-day skeptical world is ready to embrace the reality of spirits right away. In the workshop I just mentioned, the participants were invited to use their imaginations as a first step in order to "smooth" their transition to the spiritual reality. Instructing us on how to start, Jack pointed out, "Journeying is a combination of imagination and allowing whatever will happen to happen." Elaborating on his own experiences, Jack stressed that it took him between twenty and twenty-five journeys, during which he extensively used his imagination, before he began to see spirits and receive information directly from them. Thus, imagination becomes a key to the world of spirits. As core shamanism teacher Horowitz recommends to his students, "Try to switch-off your so-called analytic mind. Try to take your imagination seriously: it is through imagination that the Spirit World makes itself seen to us."[29] Teachers of modern shamanism stress that the whole point is not to turn off one's rational part once or twice but to make this a daily practice, just like exercising.

One of the major goals of Harnerian shamanism is to identify one's own power animal, which acts as some sort of a guardian angel, advises an individual, and shields him or her from misfortunes. In return, people are expected to cultivate a good relationship with the power animal, to visit it on a regular basis through spiritual journeys, to dance with it, and to acknowledge its presence in many other ways. If people forget to maintain contact with the power animal, it might leave temporarily or even forever. In this case, says Harner, the despirited person might get into trouble by falling ill or experiencing various misfortunes. What Harner calls the power animal in existing ethnographic literature is also known as the guardian spirit, spirit familiar, totem animal, or helping spirit.

The images of these power animals and auxiliary spirit helpers that individuals might encounter in their "spiritual holodecks" reflect Western shamanism's fascination with wildlife and all things earth-based. In *The Way of the Shaman*, Harner directly suggested that power animals are "usually wild, untamed species." Among possible candidates, he named cranes, tigers, foxes, eagles, bears, deer, porpoises, and dragons. Dragons, in nonordinary reality, are treated as real beings just as other beasts. Such unattractive domestic animals as hens, pigs, and cows are not eligible for the role of power animal because, as the products of artificial breeding by human beings, they have lost a connection with nature and do not have any power. Harner also stressed that insects never can be power animals.[30] At the same time, the Harner system has allowed cats to enter the spiritual pantheon of core shamanism. Despite their long-time association with human beings, it is assumed that these mysterious creatures still maintain a great deal of autonomy and wildness.

Harner's assortment of guardian spirits significantly narrows the pantheon of reality shamanism that one finds in traditional shamanisms, for example, in classical Siberian spiritual techniques. To my knowledge, in addition to the beings Harner listed in his manual, in Siberia, shamans utilized the help of such unromantic creatures as mosquitoes. Galina Lindquist, who participated in core shamanism workshops in Sweden, found much uniformity in the images of power animals that visited people in their shamanic journeys. Such wild, proud, brave, and beautiful creatures as bears, wolves, eagles, and dolphins are abundant, while such unromantic creatures as skunks and hyenas, which human imagination has endowed with negative features, never became power animals.[31]

In the unpredictable and threatening spiritual pantheon of tribal shamanism, people frequently did not know what to expect from their spirits. In contrast, in core shamanism and in the modern shamanism subculture in general, not only power animals but also all other spirits behave quite benevolently. They never harm people. Harner stressed, "No matter how fierce a guardian animal spirit may seem, its possessor is no danger because the power animal is absolutely harmless. It is only a source of power; it has no aggressive intentions. It only comes to you because you need help."[32] In a similar manner, Timothy White, the editor of *Shaman's Drum*, stressed that his magazine, one of the major periodicals in the community, stays away from publishing articles focused on malevolent and dark aspects of shamanism. He said that he is afraid that such materials might accidentally encourage some to try these dark practices.[33]

Overall, in neo-shamanism, spirits might be gentle or stern, and they might help, taunt, spook, or even perform a spiritual dismemberment of a person. Still, they never hurt one. No matter how scary a shamanic journey is, it always has a happy ending, like an adrenaline-raising movie thriller. Lindquist wrote:

> Even if "they" give you a bitter medicine, it is only for your own good. For example, if, on a journey, the Spirits burn you, eat your flesh or dismember you, this is to rip off obsolete garments pertaining to social masks and to liberate the Self. In the adventure Story genre, everything that happens to you on a journey is a metaphor, as well as the means, of Self-Transformation.[34]

After a successful return from a spiritual journey, its participants, with the help of the workshop leader, other participants, or on their own, see how these spiritual encounters might affect their lives in ordinary reality. Usually the goal of a spiritual journey to the other reality is to secure advice from a power animal about how to fix certain personal problems or cure an illness. The explanation for the benevolent nature of core and other versions of Western shamanism lies in the psychotherapeutic goals of this spirituality, which seeks to unleash the best of human potential.

Harner explained that the shaman does not need to know about the nature of a specific illness. It is enough to make a journey "out there" to the alternative reality, and through contact with spiritual forces, one finds his or her lost power animal and restores it. The restoration of the power animal energizes an individual, strengthens his or her resistance to illness, and helps the person to live a good, happy life.[35] Although Harner insisted that shamanism is not a religion but a method, he noted that it is not enough to believe consciously in the effects of shamanism or in the placebo effect of its practice. One has to embrace the reality of spirits unconsciously without trying to question or explain it. The bottom line of this approach is that by questioning the wisdom of shamanism or by trying to reflect on how effective it might be, one will ruin the whole magic of the spiritual technique. Instead, Harner invites people to immerse themselves in the great unknown and to accept the spiritual realm without explaining its validity in conventional Western terms.[36] To the participants of his workshops who think that they might just imagine the images they see during their journeys to other realities, Harner replies, "Yes, but you must ask yourself why you choose to imagine that particular thing."[37]

Core shamanism and related techniques advertise themselves as a shortcut to spiritual growth, which also resonates well with the mindsets of busy Western audiences. For example, a neo-shamanic manual written by two former students of FSS characteristically "samples ancient techniques that produce immediate results."[38] Jonathan Horowitz, who teaches Harner's core shamanism to spiritual seekers in Scandinavian countries, generalized along the same lines. He stressed that such "democratic knowledge" as tribal spirituality does not require any long introduction and that "it only takes a few minutes to have a shamanic experience."[39] Paula Klempay, a career counselor who learned at FSS, stressed that for those who aspire to partake of shamanism quickly, it is enough to get a tape with drumming music distributed by the foundation, to read Harner's book *The Way of the Shaman* for guidelines, and then to experiment as one wishes.[40] Canadian psychologist Ed Kennedy, another former student of Harner's, who, after apprenticing with the master, established an FSS branch in Thunder Bay, was even more explicit: "I found it's one of the most profound, direct, fastest things that works for the human body. It's a quick fix."[41]

Leslie Gray, a shamanism practitioner from San Francisco, elaborated on that quick approach. She said that the majority of her clients want to regain power to deal better with life situations. At the same time, they are too busy to spend years of their precious time playing the psychoanalysis game, going back and forth digging into their childhood memories. Gray tries to accommodate such desires. In her work, she focuses on people taking present action into their own hands rather than mulling over the past. As an example, she went through the case of a person who approached her when he was passed over for a promotion. The client had never been to a psychotherapist and had no desire to analyze his personality. His goal was to become, as Castaneda would have said, a spiritual predator who is able to receive power to fight for himself at work. To find out how to deal with the situation, Gray conducted a spiritual journey and a divination session for him. Gray stressed that the modern shaman knows very well that current life is fast and hectic and that people frequently must make instant decisions. Therefore, in this hectic environment, according to Gray, shamanism has become a "very quick way of using consciousness, which is not bound by time and place, so you can have immediate access to deeper wisdom and include it in your decision-making."[42]

I would add that urban shamanism is designed not only as a fast access to ancient wisdom but also as a portable and compact technique. A good example is Harner's drumming cassettes and earphones, which can be used by a person to conduct a shamanic journey literally any time and anywhere. In this case, age-old spirituality is always within reach. Crediting this fast and supposedly efficient technique, Gray said, "I use a tape recorder and a tape of drumming with earphones, all of which are portable. You can even use a Walkman. With it, you can be at work and have a decision you need to make, shut the door to your office, lie down on the floor or sit in a chair, close your eyes, turn on the tape to trigger an altered state, and get the answer to a problem."[43]

To support these individualized practices, neo-shamanism appeals to the impromptu nature of traditional shamanism. Indeed, in contrast, for example, to Christianity or Islam, in the past and nowadays the tribal shaman is solely responsible for crafting his or her personal techniques and rituals and does not have to follow any fixed spiritual blueprint. To modern Western seekers, the spontaneity of indigenous spirituality and the lack of corporate unity among tribal doctors appear as inherently anarchistic and reveal the democratic nature of shamanism. Even in Siberia, where native societies especially appreciated inherited medicine power, nothing prevented an individual from receiving this power in another way, provided this person convinced his or her community that it worked. This was more common in the Native American tradition of vision questing, which was accessible to everybody. No wonder that American ethnologists later called the latter practice "democratic shamanism."

Drawing attention to these aspects of traditional spirituality, one of its modern practitioners stressed, "Shamanism is not an elite professional club, open to some and closed to others. Much to the contrary, the indigenous or primal perspective acknowledges that each individual has a unique and viable link with the otherworld, and therefore a gift to give."[44] Moreover, some spirituality writers go as far as directly claiming that non-Western traditional shamanism is spiritual individualism.[45] Obviously, this stance has wide appeal to the Western public, whose tradition is heavily informed by the notions of privacy and individualism. In fact, spiritual individualism is present in all versions of current unchurched spirituality in the West. Some writers have nicknamed this increasingly popular approach to spirituality "sheilaism," after an incident recorded in one famous sociological survey attempted by a group of scholars headed by Robert Bellah. During this survey, scholars inquired of a woman named Sheila Larson what her religion was. She had a hard time responding to the question, pointing out that she picked up a bit here and a bit there and created her own brand of spirituality; she eventually labeled it for the researchers as "sheilaism."[46]

Incidentally, anthropologist Bill Burton from Harner's foundation directly pointed to the American tradition of rugged individualism and personal freedom as a supportive context for the resurgence of shamanism: "No cultural theme is more important to Americans than that of democracy at the level of the individual." Elaborating on this point, he noted that the attraction of shamanic practices is that everyone is free to mold his or her personal spiritual pantheon. Interacting with the helping spirits as their intimate friends, people find a refuge from the isolation they sense in an impersonal mass society and at the same time feel shielded in their spiritual privacy.[47]

In his workshops and writings, Harner repeatedly mentions this individualism factor, explaining that shamanism is a democratic spirituality, where shamans are independent of each other, follow their own spiritual paths, and have no central authority to oversee them. Moreover, he adds that, unlike traditional shamanism practitioners who usually act on behalf of their patients, in core shamanism everyone can act as his or her own priest and doctor, catering to individual needs from soul loss to professional career growth. The founder of core shamanism explained, "In shamanism everyone is his or her own prophet, getting spiritual revelation directly from the highest sources." On another occasion he stressed, "I think that almost everybody is potentially a shaman."[48]

Trying to distill the individualized essence of shamanic techniques for the uninitiated public, Gini Scott, the author of *The Complete Idiot's Guide to Shamanism*, compared the activities of the shamanism practitioner to the work of a film director, who is in complete control of his or her scene. She wrote, "You choose the actors, decide on the setting, give actors a general guideline to follow, and let them improvise. Yet, at any time you can interrupt to redirect and guide the action, and then return to observing again."[49] Overall, in many various modern versions of neo-shamanism, individuals can conduct visionary travels on their own or as part of a group. During these journeys, they freely experiment with spiritual images by entering altered states, creating their own spiritual holodecks, and then populating these realms with various spiritual characters. I think that the Canadian anthropologist Joan Townsend, who surveyed several shamanism workshops in North America, correctly defined neo-shamanism as an "individualist religious movement" in contrast to a "group organized movement" that subjects itself to certain collective standards.[50]

Diversity of Modern Western Shamanism

Although Harner was a pioneer, setting tribal shamanic techniques into a form of Western spirituality, his core shamanism is only one of many versions of shamanism currently found in Western countries. His book and seminars might have helped many spiritual seekers to situate their experiences as shamanism. Still, their particular spiritualities vary considerably and have many other inspirational sources. In fact, not all spiritual practitioners are happy about his version of shamanism. Some, for example, are disturbed by his conviction that shamanic knowledge can be mastered through a workshop. One spiritual practitioner from Savannah, Georgia, Eric Perry, who generally likes the Harner system, is nevertheless concerned about what he sees as the implication of core shamanism: "you are not a shaman unless you have training." Referring to non-Western, traditional, earth-based shamanism, which was devoid of any formal certification process and needed only the approval of a community, Perry once exclaimed, "Black Elk did not have a degree." To people like him, what makes a shamanism practitioner is a personal spiritual revelation. Coaching in the shamanic craft is unnecessary or secondary.

The members of the shamanism community who are critical of Harner also argue that there is no way to digest the abstract core of universal shamanism by stripping off cultural traditions. They stress that shamanism always manifests itself in a particular cultural setting: Lakota, Mongol, Sámi, Jivaro, and so forth. Greywolf, a practitioner of "Druid shamanism" from the United Kingdom, articulated this stance well: "All 'shamanic' practices are responses to local spirits and the natural world, local variations occurring because the practices are painted in the distinctive colors of their native lands."[51] Karen Kelly, the editor of *Spirit Talk*, one of the major shamanism on-line periodicals, echoed the same sentiments: "Firstly my shamanic practice is rooted in my homeland—in the living Earth that I am part of. But it's not simply Nature, but the Nature that surrounds me here in England. I love the deserts of the Southwest, the coastal Rain Forest of Canada, but they are fundamentally alien to me." She said that she listens to the voices of old ones in her own locality, particularly through the ancient stones of Avebury. She stressed that not some distant natives but her local drumming circle is her community, which she needs as a shamanism practitioner. It is notable that for a long time she tried to deny that connection with her native land, but it kept coming back.[52]

Jurgen Kremer, a transpersonal psychologist and spiritual practitioner from California, who for the past two decades has been involved in the recovery of his Nordic indigenous spirituality, is similarly skeptical about the healing potential of Harnerian shamanism. In a conversation with me, he stressed, "Indigenous mind is not generic; it is always specific." Kremer is convinced that a Westerner who goes through brief schooling in such centers as Harner's FSS will remain a cosmopolitan spiritual drifter without any cultural roots. He believes that core shamanism and related techniques are simply attempts to cater to the current yearning for indigenous spiritual knowledge. If not rooted in one's own tradition, these projects are doomed to be abortive.

Instead of playing with generic and universal shamanism, Kremer invites Western spiritual practitioners to be always culturally specific. For example, he suggested that if Northern Europeans ground themselves in the Scandinavian divination techniques of *volva* (female spiritual practitioners in ancient Scandinavia), they automatically bring to life the whole host of cultural associations tied to this expression. The same concerns the word "trance." To Kremer, this word is just another abstract European expression that describes a state in which an individual goes beyond everyday boundaries to the other world. However, the whole picture changes when one uses, for example, the culturally specific Scandinavian word *seidr*. In this case, the individual weaves himself or herself into a particular place filled with culture-bound mythology. According to Kremer, this is a way for European and American spiritual seekers to anchor themselves in their indigenous minds.[53]

Incidentally, such critical remarks about Harnerian shamanism mirror the similar critique of Mircea Eliade by anthropologists who point that the Eliadean universal shamanism is an abstraction that has nothing to do with reality. No doubt, this criticism of the generic cross-cultural vision of shamanism also reflects current postmodern thinking that treats with suspicion all kinds of generalizations and seeks to tribalize and particularize knowledge.

Giving critical scrutiny to the Harnerian version of shamanism, Annette Host, from the Scandinavian Center for Shamanic Studies, made an important observation. She indicated that when we intellectually strip, let us say, Lakota, Nepalese, or Yakut (Sakha) shamanisms of their indigenous garb, we unavoidably wrap the final product in our own cultural outlooks, habits, and biases, even when we do not intend to. Seen from her Nordic European perspective, the shamanism Harner offers appears very much American, "adapted to the American spiritual-fast-food culture," she remarked.[54]

Although she uses her criticism of Harner to prove that core shamanism is wishful thinking, one can turn around her "American spiritual-fast-food culture" thesis. If we take into account the polyglot nature of the modern world and the expanding cosmopolitan culture, whose core is definitely American, we will see that Harnerian shamanism does not look so superficial. It perfectly fits the format of our world as a global village and might look attractive to many people who either belong to hyphenated groups or who simply do not know who they are. Otherwise, how can we explain the fact that his school trains about 5,000 people each year and finds response in the urban jungles of Los Angeles, in Stockholm, in Copenhagen, and even among some indigenous intellectuals residing in Siberian cities? Personally, I would be cautious in dismissing Harnerian shamanism as abstract and unreal. Incidentally, one can equally wonder to what extent Europeans and North Americans who want to anchor themselves, for example, in Celtic or Nordic spiritualities can be considered the legitimate heirs of these traditions.

Let us listen to what Christiana Harle-Silvennoinen, a shamanism practitioner from Finland, who learned with Tuvan (Siberia) shamanism practitioners, has to say about the appeal of the Harner method to the hyphenated people with blurred origins. Although Harle-Silvennoinen seems to have mastered the basic techniques of Tuvan spirituality and has received a Tuvan name and even a red membership card of the professional guild of Tuvan shamans, she still does not feel secure: "I identify myself partially with them, but I do not have the roots culturally, mentally or physically. Perhaps my spiritual roots lie there, but this, I feel, does not give me license to imitate."[55]

As an option, like many current shamanic practitioners in Europe who do not want to be accused of playing "Indian," Harle-Silvennoinen could dress herself in Finnish spiritual garb and safely claim that she became native in her own cultural setting. But can she really do this? It turns out that her polyglot origin does not inspire her to do this either: "And if I won't play Tuvan then what am I? If I dig into my bloodline as far as I can go I find a mix of Swede, German and Welsh. Is that what I am?" Although Harle-Silvennoinen finds a "theological" consolation, pointing out that she practices what her spirit helpers ask her to do, she noted at the same time that the Harner core shamanism is what in fact gives her a basic groundwork: "The seeds were planted, some compost added and just enough rain and sun at the right times. I also realized that what I learned does not necessarily require a trip to Tuva."[56]

There is another problem critics note both regarding core shamanism and also about practicing tribal spirituality in the Western industrial setting in general. Cast against the existing ethnographic literature, the jungle and arctic practices, cozy suburban healing centers, drumming cassettes, and individualized techniques devoid of any particular cultural tradition do not look earth-based. Indeed, for the one who dreams about earth-based tribal shamanism, the products that appear, for example, on the market page of the FSS Web site might not stir romantic and spiritual emotions. Here, in addition to Harner's *The Way of the Shaman*, one finds "mindfolds," CDs, and audio cassettes that serve as substitutes for drums. Those who are interested in genuine drumming can purchase a real drum manufactured of synthetic skin material, which allows one to use it "anywhere anytime in every kind of weather." Moreover, all these products are conveniently packaged into several kits, for beginning, intermediate, and advanced students.[57] When some spiritual seekers who crave holistic and nature-based spiritualities look at these artifacts, they feel that something is missing.

Many spiritual seekers feel that what we call shamanism always existed as a form of local spiritual knowledge set not only in a particular culture but in a

particular soil and landscape. To Loren Cruden, shamanism is a spiritual technique that literally should be anchored in particular earth, streams, animals,
plants, and other elements of the "telephone-less existence." In his turn,
Kremer wrote, "It is quite beyond me to imagine a genuine shaman who is not
grounded in the specificity of the wild and her spirits."[58] To him and to like-
minded people, shamanism transplanted into the cement jungles of the Western megalopolis as a workshop practice does not make sense because it usually
does not lead to a change of lifestyle, away from commercialism and toward the
earth. They do not believe that quick weekend spiritual sessions might change
the consciousness of people. For this reason, Kremer is against the very expression the "urban shaman." He thinks that this term, which is loaded with
modernity associations, simply misleads people who seek to retrieve their own
indigenous mind.

Although the Harnerian version of shamanism has served as a major
inspiration for the practitioners of tribal spirituality, it certainly does not ex-
haust all varieties of modern shamanism in the West. Like the rest of European
and American esotericism, the shamanism subculture is far from homogeneous. The lack of any hierarchy, dogma, or fixed ritual encourages an eclectic
approach to spirituality. Many nature spirituality communities in the West in
general and neo-shamanism in particular view the individual as an independent agent who can shop around and choose at the spiritual market the ideas he
or she likes most. The common approach here is if a spiritual technique works
for one personally, it becomes acceptable. Whether spiritual seekers apprentice
with teachers, participate in workshops, or master shamanism on their own
from books, they usually add their own individual creative spins to the personal
spiritualities that they call shamanism. Most important, shamanism rarely
manifests itself in a pure core form. Frequently, spiritual practitioners weave it
into their existing spiritualities, which they might not even position as shamanism. After all, shamanism is viewed as a spiritual technique.

Frequently, one may find the same people involved in exploring multiple traditions and tailoring their personal spirituality according to their individual or group needs. In this case, any generalizations about the community
of shamanism practitioners will always be rather relative. Anthropologist Galina Lindquist was certainly correct when she described these people as a fluid,
fuzzy community. Archaeologist Robert Wallis, the author of an insightful book
about the British neo-shamans, added that modern Western practitioners
who describe their practices as shamanic are so different from each other that
it is misleading to pile them into the same group. For this reason, he avoids
the generic expression shamanism and uses such words as shamanisms and
neo-shamanisms.[59]

The broad and loose meanings the shamanism idiom has acquired in
modern anthropology, psychology, and religious studies serve well for current
spiritual seekers in the West. As a result, people frequently use this term not

only in the conventional sense of the word as spiritual work in altered states but as a way to situate their spiritual practices as ancient, tribal, and earth-based. Furthermore, people from the Western nature community frequently talk about a shamanic attitude to land or shamanic philosophy, which in other contexts can simply mean a spiritual or ecological attitude toward the earth. Thus, shamanism might mean different things for different people.

In the current unchurched spirituality of the West, there is a variety of groups and individuals who use the expression shamanism to describe their spiritual techniques. These people range from the practitioners of core shamanism and those who find inspiration in a particular non-Western, earth-based spirituality to eco-feminists and participants in the goddess movement. Furthermore, since the 1980s, there is a growing number of pagan and Wiccan people who describe themselves as practitioners of Druid shamanism, Celtic shamanism, and shamanic Wicca.

Strictly speaking, many of these practices resist generalization as purely shamanic because one can equally describe them as pagan, Wiccan, or shamanic. Moreover, the same individual or group can often be simultaneously involved in exploring, experimenting with, and practicing multiple traditions, creating his or her own spiritual blend. This is obvious, for example, in the spiritual resources used by a California group called Hrafner. Its leader, fiction writer Diana Paxson, gradually converted to European pre-Christian spirituality as a result of her work on several novels dealing with characters and events from the Nordic spiritual heritage. At the same time, one of her major inspirations was reading Harner's book *The Way of the Shaman* and participating in his workshop. Still, prior to this, she was already grounded in women's mysteries (goddess spirituality), Kabbalah, and Wicca.

Hrafner mostly draws on Nordic Scandinavian folklore and puts much emphasis on the *seidr* divination—an ancient Scandinavian form of entering altered states for divination purposes that she and her friends learned by reading Nordic sagas. At the same time, members of the group, many of whom have Wiccan backgrounds, do not consider themselves purely shamanism practitioners. Absorbing a variety of spiritual techniques, to which they recently even added Umbanda (an Afro–Latin American practice), Hrafner positions itself as part of a broad pagan network in the San Francisco Bay area.[60] The spiritual profile of this and many other similar groups shows that, unlike scholars who try to classify social and cultural phenomena, the practitioners of nature spirituality are least of all interested in classifying themselves by categories and groups.

The lack of any hierarchy, dogma, or fixed ritual encourages spiritual seekers who experiment with such practices as shamanism to combine eclectic imagery and techniques from various traditions according to their individual tastes. Both those who have schooled themselves in such spiritual centers as Harner's FSS and those who have mastered shamanism on their own add their individual creative spins to shamanic practices. For example, I met spiritual seekers for whom shamanism might appear to be something that represents, let us say, a mixture of Buddhist, Siberian, and Native American symbolism peppered with urban yoga and Jungian analysis. Finally, a growing number of psychotherapists and spiritual counselors, especially those who are trained in transpersonal psychology, use shamanism as a supplementary technique to work with their clients. The rule of thumb here is to select what works well for one personally and discard what does not. A good example is spirituality writer Joan Halifax, who, in addition to Harner, was one of the first to bring shamanism to the attention of the Western educated public. In her personal techniques, she melds Buddhism with shamanism.

Many spiritual seekers purposely stress that their shamanic practices are eclectic and capitalize on several traditions. For example, writer Cinnamon Moon calls herself "a medicine woman with foundation in the teachings of the Plains Indians and the eclectic studies of many other tribes," including elements of Christianity. Another spirituality author, Arnold Mindell, claims that he studied with African, Native American, Australian, Japanese, and Hindu spiritual healers. Drawing on these traditions and on his own psychotherapy practice and experience in conflict resolution, Mindell offers "new shamanism," a system of exercises "based upon a combination of modern psychology and ancient shamanic practice." Flamboyant Donna Henes, who lives in Brooklyn and who defines herself as an "acclaimed urban shaman," samples all kinds of spiritual remedies, from drumming to Reiki and tarot, and laughingly admitted, "I'm a multicultural fashion show."[61]

Even those practitioners who more or less center their spirituality on some particular tradition are eclectic. For example, members of a San Francisco–based group called Wakan dwell heavily on American Indian symbols, particularly the ones that come from the Huichol Indians. American anthropology as well as "New Age" print culture and workshops widely publicized the Huichol spiritual practices, especially their ritual use of peyote, which eventually attracted a number of spiritual seekers. At the same time, the members of Wakan (note that the name comes from Lakota, not Huichol) do not lock themselves into these particular traditions and continue to experiment with other practices.[62] In contrast, another California-based group, the Dance of the Deer Foundation, headed by Brant Secunda, totally devotes itself to exploration of the same Huichol tradition without trying to dilute it with alien elements. Unlike Wakan, the foundation operates as a mystic tour enterprise that takes Westerners directly to Huichol country to apprentice with "real" natives on the spot.

Shamanism as a spiritual therapy also fits well the format of eco-feminism, which approaches women as natural healers who stay in tune with nature, in contrast to the male part of society that seeks to subordinate nature. The premise of eco-feminism is that women stand close to the earth's values and therefore are inherently shamanic people, who will be able to more successfully heal the earth than will males. Moreover, exercising certain doses of imagination, one can relate the subordinated status of women in earlier Western history and the pain it inflicted on the "hidden half" to the ritual sickness and initiation of shamans. Viewed from this angle, women appear as natural shamans. As wounded healers, they rise up to cure the world from patriarchy, rationalism, and materialism.

Roma Morris, a feminist author, argues that many misfortunes, stresses, and life-altering situations (a divorce, a death in one's family, a crisis) that females experience are, in fact, shamanic experiences. The problem is that women, who do not recognize themselves as shamans, simply treat these experiences as misfortunes. By doing this, they miss a chance to use a good spiritual way out that might empower them. Morris and her friend Ginny Black Wolf offer a nine-month shamanic course based on the techniques developed by the famous Wiccan writer Starhawk. A part of the course is a mask-making project, in which women bring to a visual form the pain and suffering coming from the roles society imposes on them. During a shamanic journey, they shed these roles and prepare themselves to embrace new identities. The central part of this ritual drama therapy is burning the masks, which symbolizes liberation from the imposed roles.[63]

The wide variety of Western shamanisms is noticeable everywhere. It is visible, for example, in the choice of tools spiritual seekers use to enter altered states (shamanic state of consciousness) and embark on a shamanic journey. While Harner's followers use drums and rattles, for the followers of the retired psychologist and linguist Felicitas Goodman, musical instruments are only supplementary tools. The major device she and her associates use to immerse themselves into altered states is archaic body postures replicated from ancient figurines and statuettes. There is also a fringe practice, which was pioneered by Daniel Statnekov, that induces shamanic journeys through the replication of the sounds of ancient Peruvian whistling bottles (see figure 7.2). Prior to the 1970s, archeologists believed that pre-Columbian Indians had used these ceramic vessels for carrying water. Challenging this conventional scholarly wisdom, Statnekov and his spiritual followers insist that the major role of these items had been spiritual. Particularly, they are convinced that, if used as whistles, the bottles produce low-frequency sounds that generate altered states of consciousness. Moreover, Gini Scott, the author of the popular *The Complete Idiot's Guide to Shamanism*, informed us that to enjoy a full shamanic experience and to reach the altered states, one actually does not need anything. Drumming and rattling only irritate her and prevent her from stepping into the separate reality. To plunge herself into the altered state, she simply uses creative imagination, guiding her fantasy in a designated direction. Scott claimed that the spiritual holodeck that she constructs using this simple exercise is no less effective than the ones induced by other shamanisms.[64]

FIGURE 7.2. Another way of reaching altered states: blowing into replicas of ancient Peruvian whistling bottles. Courtesy Don Wright.

Despite the variety of their practices, those people who participate in neo-shamanism share some common sentiments. First of all, they recognize the existence of nonordinary reality in addition to the ordinary or mundane reality. This means that these people believe that there is something out there that one can describe as nonordinary reality or separate reality, which is as real as what we perceive in our regular life. If the person is ready to adopt this stance, he or she has to make a second step, to recognize that the spirits who populate this realm are real beings. This is an essential "theological" prerequisite for participation in any school of modern Western shamanism. Belinda Gore, who teaches body posture shamanism, stressed, "Our [spiritual] experiences are not the products of our imaginations or totally a reflection of the personal unconsciousness. While the personal unconsciousness may determine the lens through which we look, the scene itself exists separate from us. We may interact with it, but we do not create it."[65]

Among other essential common sentiments, practitioners of shamanism subscribe to the notion that spirituality should be earth-based, which explains the essential place of environmental ethics in neo-shamanism. Like representatives of other nature religions, practitioners of shamanism are convinced that everything in this world is holistically related. They view the human body as only a small part of this web of natural life. In fact, this stance has already become part of the cultural mainstream in many Western countries.

Another important notion is a negative attitude toward Western civilization, especially to its core elements, Enlightenment and modernity, and, simultaneously, a reverential attitude toward non-Western spiritual traditions and cultures. Many of those who teach and disseminate shamanic practices in Europe and North America argue that from the Stone Age to approximately medieval times, humanity existed in balance with nature and was deeply steeped in spirituality. The Renaissance and Enlightenment reduced the presence of the divine in human life and imposed limitations on human knowledge, excluding everything that was unscientific. They are also convinced that modern Western civilization, which continues to denigrate the significance of the sacred and the spiritual, cages the human mind. Many shamanism practitioners position themselves as people who bring back ancient knowledge to cure modern people from the Enlightenment philosophy.

Sociology of Modern Western Shamanism

During the past years, several scholars have explored neo-shamanism in the West from various angles and in different settings: the United States, Britain, Sweden, and Denmark. Among them are anthropologists Joan Townsend, Galina Lindquist, and Merete Demant Jakobsen; religion scholars Jan Svanberg, Daniel Noel, and Kocku von Stuckrad; archaeologist Robert Wallis, whom I quoted above; and sociologist Jenny Blain. This scholarship gives us an idea of the professional backgrounds, genders, motives, and personal agendas of those who partake of modern shamanism. My composite picture of what I call the sociology of modern Western shamanism is based on the work of the colleagues mentioned above and on my own observations, particularly of a group of people who belong to the Society of Celtic Shamans. I also rely on my formal and informal conversations with shamanism practitioners in California and in the American Southeast, the place where I currently live and teach.

I certainly have no desire to draw a profile of the typical shamanism practitioner nor to point to what specifically brings people to embrace spiritualities that one can describe as shamanic. At the same time, I would like to outline what appears to me to be common features in the intellectual and social backgrounds of people who use the idiom of shamanism. For example, it is noticeable that in the 1980s, many came to this archaic technique of ecstasy through experimenting with hallucinogens and human potential techniques during the earlier countercultural years. For many, shamanism became a natural result of their participation in the environmental and ecological movements that grew in the 1970s. Some of the spiritual seekers who became interested in shamanism came from the ranks of people who tuned themselves spiritually to the Native American spiritual and cultural renaissance in the 1970s or who participated in Leftist and civil rights movements.

Galina Lindquist, who explored Yggdrasil, a group of urban shamanism practitioners in Sweden, found that many members of this fuzzy neo-shamanism community originated from the hippie movement and the Left. Moreover, she suggested that, in the 1980s, many members of the radical Left in Sweden began to drift to alternative spirituality out of their frustration with radical political activism. The people Lindquist interviewed clearly expressed their deep frustration with the rigid authoritarian structure and agendas of the political groups with which they were involved. They had a feeling that instead of a liberation experience, Leftist and ecological political activism subjected individuals to political agendas and suppressed their individuality. Under these circumstances, becoming social introverts by turning to spirituality and the unconscious was a backlash against the unwarranted political and ideological expectations.

Jörgen I. Eriksson, one of those who brought Swedish shamanists together into Yggdrasil, lamented, "There were times when I cursed the time I spent in the Left movement. I asked myself, why could I not discover things in some other simple way? Why did I have to go through the Left to understand? This is what you feel afterwards. Lost time." So, gradually, Eriksson realized that liberation would not be the result of the instant revolt of the wretched of the earth but a long-term process of self-liberation. He rounded out his sentiments as follows:

> I have always wanted to make the world a better place. Now I can see how my inner world corresponded to the outer world, how I could make the world better by making myself a better person. The one presupposed the other. In the Left the idea was that one should repress the personal. The inner Self was not interesting, one should sacrifice the personal for the collective. This is precisely why the Left was full of jerks, awfully unbalanced people, actually.[66]

This statement—the transformation of consciousness as a way to social transformation—mirrors similar sentiments of spiritual seekers in other countries. Like many people from nature spirituality community, Western practitioners of shamanism tend to be liberal-minded people who are very much concerned about social issues and global problems, especially about ecology. At the same time, they ascribe the origin of these problems to a spiritual dysfunction of human beings and seek their resolution through the change of individual consciousnesses. The message here is simple. Instead of trying to change people and society, one should transform one's own mind, body, and spirit. In *The Aquarian Conspiracy* (1980), Marilyn Ferguson, one of the first spearheads of the "New Age," stressed that making a new world means making a new mind. The great "nagual" Carlos Castaneda expressed the same sentiment even better. In his characteristically flamboyant manner, he once uttered, "People talk about revolutions—such crap! First change yourself. Until you've achieved internal revolution, efforts to save the world are meaningless." Deanna Stennett, a graduate of the Harner school and now a shamanism workshop leader, defined her goals as follows: "The miracles that are most needed in our urban jungles are the changes in consciousness and attitude."[67] To all these people, healing begins on the level of an individual mind, then gradually extends to a community and finally to a planetary level.

According to those who seriously subscribe to shamanism as a long-term practice, an essential prerequisite of spiritual healing for Westerners is to learn to step out of the mundane realm and to enter alternate reality, where people can communicate with spiritual beings on a regular basis. It is expected that by doing this, people can expand their consciousness and knowledge beyond the conventional wisdom imposed by their society. The spiritual holodecks that modern Western shamans create during spiritual journeys to these realms become for them grounded and valid human experiences akin to any other experience in ordinary reality. As Harner explained in his classic *The Way of the Shaman*, a person in otherworldly reality may view the experiences in the ordinary world to be illusory. Conversely, to the one in the mundane world, the otherworldly experiences may equally appear to be fantasy. "Both are right, as viewed from their own particular states of consciousness," stressed the anthropologist. He added that much of the prejudice toward the Castaneda books might have arisen from the inability of some people to accept the very idea of the existence of multiple realities. Moreover, Harner suggested treating this prejudice in the field of consciousness as *cognicentrism* similar to the critical manner we approach ethnocentrism among cultures. As modern people learn the value of cultural relativism, they will similarly come to respect cognitive relativism, argued Harner. In his view, one of the ways to correct the situation is to expose more people to shamanic experiences. In this case, they will be able to see for themselves the value of other realities.[68]

The spiritual seekers interested in shamanism point out that, unlike the ancient and tribal ones, who were the masters of altered states, modern city dwellers have become separated from this genetically anchored human need and have to live ecstasy-deprived lives. They are incapable of entering such states. The appreciation of the altered states and the ability of spiritual practitioners to work in these realms are what essentially unite many versions of modern Western shamanism. Goodman and her associates, proponents of a shamanism school that replicates the body postures of ancient figures as a way to induce trance states, stressed that to keep themselves in good spiritual shape, people need to exercise their nervous systems by entering altered states from time to time. They said that the inability of modern society to provide trance experiences to people leads to emptiness that is filled with various forms of addictive behavior, such as the abuse of drugs, alcohol, nicotine, caffeine, and work; excessive sexual indulgence; overeating; and obsessive exercising. Belinda Gore, one of those who teach this body posture shamanism went so far as to suggest that those people who are incapable of altering their consciousness and tuning it to the spiritual realm are psychologically defective.[69]

Such practices as shamanism successfully fill the void created by the increasing disappointment of people with organized mainstream Christianity and other religions. Today, many people are too skeptical to accept the conventional religious doctrines they absorbed as part of their Judeo-Christian upbringing. They are also frustrated about how religious bureaucracies package, advertise, and promote Christianity. In contrast, practitioners of shamanism and related spiritualities advertise their techniques as a return to egalitarian practices, which they link to the primal nature religion that existed before humanity fell into the pit of Judeo-Christian civilization. Comparing the spiritual democracy of ancient shamanism with the hierarchical structure of modern world religions, Harner wrote, "We are now restoring ancient methods to get our own direct revelation, without the need of ecclesiastical hierarchies and politically-influenced dogma. We can find things for ourselves."[70] Sandra Ingerman, one of his close associates, similarly noted, "Shamanism gives you direct revelation, where you can go to the spirits yourself. In a lot of religions, there's a middle person you have to go through. Organized religion has become very bureaucratic, and a lot of people are getting turned off by the bureaucracy."[71]

In *Ecstatic Religion* (1989), anthropologist I. M. Lewis drew our attention to the fact that traditional mainstream Christianity portrays God as a mighty and dominant being. In this world picture, human beings appear to be weak and insignificant. Although it might satisfy people who still live by the notions of religious fundamentalism, this imagery certainly appears patronizing and anachronistic to the educated and skeptical Westerners who hold human agency and individualism in high esteem. Shamanism does not make this mistake. For example, in contrast to conventional Christianity, in shamanism, people can raise themselves to the level of gods by acquiring divine powers. Lewis stressed, "It is by dragging the gods to his own level, as much by soaring aloft to meet them, that the shaman enables man to deal with his deities on an equal or almost equal footing." Therefore, the spiritual message of shamanism is that God is not only with us but also in us.[72]

The lure of the polytheistic nature of shamanism might originate from the same desire to escape the patronizing monotheism of Christianity. Explaining what turned her to "heathen" rituals, Winifred, a spiritual practitioner from England, mentioned as a major reason "the wish to move into a polytheistic religion, because I have always had trouble with the idea of a monotheistic religion. I think polytheistic is much closer to reality as I see it anyway."[73] Historians of religion and some anthropologists note that the rise of popular psychology that began to play the role of a surrogate religion in our secular world also created a space for such psychotherapeutic practices as shamanism. By successfully integrating scientific knowledge (for example, quantum physics, psychology, and anthropology) and the sacred (the "reality of spirits"), shamanism and similar spiritual practices appear attractive to those Westerners who appreciate science but also long for spirituality.

Although shamanic practitioners usually harbor strong negative sentiments toward organized Christianity, they do appropriate a variety of Christian
images and symbols, especially if they can trace them to early and folk Christianity, which they view as pristine and uncorrupted by bureaucracy and civilization. In fact, many of these people view Jesus Christ himself as a master
shaman, who was able to perform miracles just like classical Siberian and Native American spiritual practitioners. In response to the growing popularity of
unchurched spiritualities, some conventional denominations, especially the
ones that are traditionally open-minded and liberal, have begun to accommodate pagan and non-Western symbolism in their practices. For example, in
Seattle, a Church of Unity embraced such practices as chanting in Sanskrit and
Native American vision quests to enhance its popularity in the eyes of pa-
rishioners in a city notorious for its indifference to mainstream Christianity.
Unitarian Universalism, much of whose creed stresses the link between nature
and spirit, is in the forefront of this movement. In this denomination, the romance with nature, the non-Western, and the primitive goes back to Emerson
and Thoreau. Thus, some practitioners of shamanism, neo-paganism, Wicca,
and other nature spirituality groups are simultaneously either members or
friends of Unitarian Universalism or use the facilities of this denomination for
drumming sessions and shamanic healing. John Burciaga, a Unitarian minister in Bethesda, Maryland, argues that now there is a significant subculture
within the ministry, who experiment with various ways of reaching altered
states, including hallucinogens.[74]

In contrast to mainstream denominations or spiritual groups that adhere
to rigid spiritual standards, neo-shamanism does not impose any doctrinal
requirements. In their manual *Urban Shaman*, Jose Stevens and Lena Stevens
wrote, "There exists no dogma, no organization, no special texts, no leaders, no
regulatory board. Anyone can practice its techniques and derive benefit from
its methods."[75] Like many members of modern Western esotericism community, urban shamans are very suspicious of any caste and group loyalties.
Stressing that in his or her ritual practice the shaman is an explorer and an
improviser, modern-day shamanism practitioners are usually very sensitive to
any imposition on their individuality. A long-time spiritual practitioner wrote
that as soon as she begins to hear talk about "other folks" doing shamanism
incorrectly and "us" doing it the "correct" way, she knows that she has entered
another form of institutionalized religion, and it is time to leave such a "sacred
order."[76] With its loose structure and individualized spiritual practices, a neo-
shamanic group, a workshop, or a drumming group is usually amorphous and
short-lived. As such, this antistructure is usually an ideal structure for contemporary middle-class, educated Westerners, who are too skeptical to commit
themselves to group values and who, at the same time, long for collective spiritual experiences.[77]

My impression is that for many people interested in shamanism, it represents a supplementary spiritual technique that they can add to other spiritual practices and beliefs they might already share. To some, shamanism might help to organize their individual mystic experiences. For others, it might remain just an interesting passing experience. I think that Karen Kelly, the editor of the UK periodical *Spirit Talk*, caught well such an attitude to shamanism among nature and neo-pagan communities:

> For me it is useful to compare the difference between practicing shamanic techniques and being a shaman to the difference between practicing meditation and being a Buddhist nun. Hundreds of thousands of people, all over the world meditate. Less of them, and this particularly so in the West, would call themselves Buddhists, follow the Buddhist precepts, try to live in a mindful way. Many simply find meditating a useful way to live more in the present. I count myself amongst these. Fewer still choose to dedicate their lives to seeking Enlightenment, living as monks or nuns. Most shamanic courses teach shamanic techniques—how to journey, how to do a soul retrieval, how to remove intrusions. Most people who I have met on workshops are relatively new to the practice. I have been practicing shamanism for around seven years. I still attend occasional workshops, partly because I enjoy sitting in circle with other practitioners, partly because it is interesting to see what new things you hear when you re-take a course from a different place in your life. Only very rarely do I meet the people I first worked with on courses. Why? Some are working on something else they can add to their healing toolbox, others feel that they have all the tools and techniques they need and now learn directly from their spirits.[78]

I have no doubt that there are many people in nature communities for whom shamanism means a deep, profound, and life-transforming experience. At the same time, I am sure there is an equally large number of people for whom shamanism is one of many spiritualities with which they experiment. There are people who are attracted to this practice simply because it appears to them to be ancient and esoteric. This romantic approach is perfectly natural. Anthropologist Galina Lindquist, one of the first researchers to explore a community of Western neo-shamans, views these spiritual seekers as postmodern romantics. Stressing that they engage in a beautiful "sacred play," she thinks that the aesthetics of shamanism is what mostly attracts Western seekers in this practice.[79]

Blain and Wallis believe that treating neo-shamanism as sacred play trivializes the whole phenomenon. According to these scholars, many people in the modern Western shamanism community do believe in the reality of their spirits and approach their spiritualities as serious sacred practice. At the same time, trying to convince his academic colleagues to take Western neo-shamans seriously, Wallis seems to have gone to another extreme by picturing these spiritual seekers as committed true believers. Thus, he wrote that genuine modern Western shamanism practitioners radically reorient their world views and do not do shamanism for fun and profit.[80] In these utterances, I sense an assumption that having fun or a good time or making a profit have nothing to do with neo-shamanism. I have an impression that, for better or worse, quick, short-term, and lifelong spiritual pursuits—along with fun and profit making and ego trips—are all present among the Western seekers who situate their activities as shamanic.

For some people, the romantic attraction to shamanism might lead to a deeper spiritual experience, or even to the reprogramming of their minds, while for others, it might remain an episode among many others on the way to their self-actualization. Moreover, there are many people for whom both the essence (spirituality) and the form (aesthetics) of shamanism are equally important and cannot be separated. I personally met many spiritual seekers who appreciate both aspects and do not separate them. Finally, there are people who pursue shamanism on a professional basis. In this capacity, they provide to the public what in ordinary language we usually describe as pastoral counseling and psychotherapy. These people run spirituality workshops, retreats, and spiritual tours to "shamanlands" in North America, South America, and northern Asia. For these individuals, the shamanic vocation provides not only spiritual feedback but also generates or supplements their incomes.

Shamanism integrated into the Western market system might serve as a spiritual technique to enhance business and entrepreneurial skills; this particular aspect of neo-shamanism usually disgusts its critics. Heather Campbell from England, who goes by the name Moon Owl, specializes in the shamanic healing of corporations and corporate members using smudging, dancing, drumming, and rattling. For example, on several occasions, Robinsons' drinks and the toy manufacturer Hasbro have solicited her services. A bra manufacturing company, Gossard, hired her to put its staff in touch with nature. In this latter case, Campbell concluded that the bra makers needed to have the company boardroom cleansed from lingering tensions. For this, she used a combination of sage smoke and feathers. Next, Campbell asked the firm's executives to enter the room and dance barefoot to five shamanic rhythms. "Initially, it was as if I had asked them to jump off a cliff," said the shamaness. "But once they got into their stride, the energy in the room quadrupled." Campbell, who charges about £1,000 a day for her services, insists that her clients are always amazed at the answers they get from talking to trees. "I instruct them to ask the tree a simple question, such as, what is the biggest obstacle to prevent this product being the best in its field?" she said. "They find their answers in the first thing that catches their eye. It could be a trail of ants crossing your left foot or five crows landing in the tree you're sitting by."[81]

In her turn, spirituality writer and real estate dealer Lena Stevens explained how she tries to apply shamanic techniques to her business. First, Stevens treats each property with an animated respect, recognizing the surrounding land-scape as alive and part of Mother Nature. Then she conducts a shamanic jour-ney to the separate reality for information about what a particular house has to offer to her client. After this, based on the information she receives from the spirit world, Stevens makes her judgment.[82] Incidentally, her husband and coauthor, psychologist Jose Stevens, teaches corporate members how to fix "fractured companies" and to "guide people to success." He elaborated on the philosophy behind this business shamanism. Invoking the Castaneda creed, Stevens stressed that shamanism is about the accumulation and storage of power. He encourages his clients to hunt aggressively for power, repeating the words of Don Juan almost verbatim: "You're either predator or prey. Learn to be like predators. Learn to stalk power, to observe it, understand it and then pounce on it."

Comparing successful business people with powerful shamans, Stevens pointed out, "If you look at the best leaders in the business world, they are not one-dimensional people. They are multitalented. They are good storytellers; they can lead their corporations through inspirational talks. They are good cer-emonialists. They are powerful warriors and know how to fight a battle. They are men and women of knowledge." Here are several pieces of advice he offers his clients. First, in order to be powerful, they should surround themselves with people who have more power than they do. Eventually, the clients will absorb their power. Second, they should get rid of habits that drain power, such as complaining, whining, and arrogance. Third, they should try to get outdoors each day. Fourth, they should spend time alone in nature up to three days a week and isolate themselves from books, radios, cell phones, and reports.[83] There is no doubt that these spiritual guidelines layer well on such traditional American ideals as individualism, the spirit of enterprise, smooth interper-sonal relationships, and environmentalism.

An extreme example of a person who openly admits that shamanism, for her, is both a business and spirituality is writer Lynn Andrews, the famous promoter of feminine shamanism. She stresses that money making itself rep-resents a spiritual pursuit. Incidentally, she neatly weaves this dictum into her own career. In addition to being a bestselling author, Andrews conducts spiritual counseling. Her rates are quite high. For example, at the end of the 1980s, she received up to ten clients a week and charged them $150 an hour.[84] Although many seekers of tribal spirituality feel disgusted with her ap-proach, she and like-minded people are certainly part of the fuzzy community of Western shamanism.

How do people come to shamanism? To illustrate this, I picked up several portraits of people who integrated shamanic practices into their lives and whose biographies demonstrate the variety of paths to the archaic techniques of ecstasy. In *Shamanic Performances on the Urban Scene* (1997), Lindquist told us about a certain Hedlund, a member of Yggdrasil, a group of Swedish neo-shamans. At an early age, he was widely exposed to ghost stories, which fascinated him. At the same time, he was interested in the sciences and grew up as an atheist. In the 1970s, when radical Left activism was in vogue in his country, Hedlund sided for a while with anarchists and environmentalists. Then, like many people of his generation, he became dissatisfied with the Left and politics in general because of their rigid structure that suppressed the individual. Hedlund wanted to go his own way: "I never liked to hang about in a crowd, with lots of people screaming and the individual disappearing in the mass." Turning inward to his consciousness and further to the unconscious and shamanism became a natural outcome.[85]

Donna Henes, an American urban shaman from Brooklyn, New York, was raised in an observant Jewish family. Her path to shamanism similarly went through the counterculture and political activism. In the early 1960s, at eighteen, Henes moved to New York, where she immersed herself into the world of psychedelics, hanging around with people from St. Marks Place. Then she did a stint in the civil rights and antiwar battles of the 1960s and 1970s, participating in freedom marches in the South. According to her own statement, spiritual revelation struck her in the 1970s when once she placed a piece of Native American weaving on her face. After this, she stepped onto her shamanic path. Now, Henes runs the Mama Donna Tea Garden and Healing Center, which samples the whole range of metaphysical tools, from drumming circles and shamanic counseling to tarot and Reiki. In a pagan and shamanic manner, "Mama Donna" organizes wedding rituals, gives names to newborns, and conducts memorial services and corporate events. The use of the expression shamanism seems to help Henes to better situate and advertise her activities.[86]

Lilian, a spiritual practitioner from Sweden, never participated in any radical agendas. At the same time, she was not a stranger to countercultural print culture. From an early childhood, she was a voracious reader and became versed in all kinds of esoteric philosophies, from Hinduism and Buddhism to Castaneda. Her tribal experience began when she started associating with the Rainbow People, hippie-type groups of Europeans and Americans who since the 1970s have advocated the return to a traditional, earth-based lifestyle. As she stressed, these Rainbow folks initiated her into "Native American spirituality," which, ironically, happened in Norway: "Power songs came strongly, objects were floating in the air, and lots of magical things happened. People saw two Guides behind me, enormous beings, with great wings. These ex-hippies, my first teachers, had told me that I had Power."[87]

For some members of the shamanism community, their inward journey has more to do with personal traumas than with the development of their ideological and cultural tastes. In these cases, phrasing painful experiences through the idiom of shamanism heals mental wounds and builds individual self-esteem. Experiential narratives I read or stories I personally have heard which involve a traumatic experience that sets a person on a shamanic path usually mention reprogramming a human mind from excessive materialism to a spiritually oriented life. Essentially, in such cases, we are dealing with the familiar situation when a life crisis or a misfortune drives an individual closer to the sacred and the spiritual.

Molly Larkin, who collaborated with Creek shaman Bear Heart in narrating his revelations, wrote, "In 1987, I was ready to die. In a twelve-month period, I had lost my business to an unscrupulous partner, filed for personal bank-ruptcy, my lover committed suicide, and, after rebounding into a relationship with an old boyfriend, I was left for a nineteen-year-old receptionist." When the author was ready to commit suicide herself, she met Bear Heart, who radically changed Larkin's life and brought "the clearest answer to finding peace and balance."[88] This particular encounter resulted in the shift of her entire life agenda away from conventional materialistic pursuits. Similarly, for psychol-ogist Bradford Keeney, whose life was disrupted by a devastating divorce and whose university career was ruined by several jealous colleagues, the shamanic path became a helpful spiritual anchor: "In suffering I found no choice but to surrender to a spiritual journey. Having been brought down by the fires of pain, I plunged as deeply as I could into the healing waters of the oldest spir-itual wells. I did not approach any spiritual tradition out of curiosity. I went because life had broken me down and I knew no other place to turn."[89]

Another spiritual seeker, David Lukoff, who is also a psychologist, found that shamanism helped him to cope with his mental problems. In the 1960s, when he was twenty-three, Lukoff dropped out of an anthropology doctoral program and hit the road to find himself, hitchhiking around America and also visiting Mexico and Hawaii. Eventually, like many people of his generation, he reached California, the countercultural beacon. At this point, he heard voices and saw visions, which he could not situate. Lukoff simply thought he was going crazy. Once, a voice told him, "Become a healer." This message prompted him to recast his "insanity" as a traditional shamanic call. As a result, Lukoff immersed himself in the literature on shamanism, reading Eliade's book and the writings of Vilmos Dioszegi, a Hungarian anthropologist who wrote on Siberian shamanism. Simultaneously, he began to apprentice with Sun Bear, Rolling Thunder, and Wallace Black Elk, the first spiritual practi-tioners who positioned themselves as Native American healers on the Amer-ican countercultural scene in the early 1970s. Writer Hyemeyohsts Storm, who writes in the Castaneda genre, and Wallace Black Elk assured Lukoff that his delusions were not a mental illness but a shamanic initiation meant to bring him into communication with spiritual forces. Eventually, Lukoff learned not only how to control his mental states but also how to benefit from them, and he entered the profession of clinical psychology.[90]

A practitioner of Harnerian core shamanism whom I met in Savannah, Georgia, similarly turned to shamanism to put together his soul, which had been shattered by personal traumas and tragedies. A victim of terrible child abuse (his own mother burned his fingers with a cigarette lighter) and a survivor of several near-death experiences, he originally joined a men's ritual group that practiced "male spirituality" in the wilderness, the lifestyle modeled after Robert Bly's Iron John.[91] Among these people, he met several persons who introduced him to Harner's The Way of the Shaman, which prompted him later to take a couple of classes with the FSS. Then, he topped these experiences by a short apprenticeship with a Cherokee medicine man. At one point, the latter instructed him, "Go in the woods, Matt." Thus, Matt went into the woods. There, as he put it, "I prayed my behind off," doing pipe ceremonies and sweatlodges and journeying with a drum, incorporating "Michael Harner's stuff." To the toolkit of his spiritual methods, Matt later also added techniques he learned from a "native woman from the Amazon area." Establishing permanent contact with his power animal, which he found during one of his spiritual journeys, brought peace and stability to his life and anchored him in this and otherworldly reality; the spiritual power animal became his loyal companion, advisor, and comforter.

In contrast to what I have described above, for some Westerners, shamanism becomes a result of their aesthetic quest, which means that spirituality came along with the absorbed aesthetic baggage. Swedish anthropologist Lindquist described the spiritual practitioner and artist Mari, whose original path to shamanism was devoid of colorful spiritual revelations or painful personal traumas. For Mari, everything started with Native American–looking symbolism. While experimenting with unusual materials and colors in her drawings and sculptures, she heard people saying that her work looked Native American and that this was shamanic art. That is how she heard for the first time the expression shaman. Intrigued, Mari turned to books, trying to find out what shamanism was all about. When, in 1982, she heard about a group of people who were interested in shamanism and who were getting together in a Stockholm bookstore, she joined them and became part of Yggdrasil, a Swedish shamanism community.[92]

The road to the shamanic path of Purple Medicine Woman (see figure 7.3), my acquaintance from San Francisco who apprenticed intensively with a Tuvan shamaness in southern Siberia, was similarly at first colored with an intellectual and aesthetic quest. A person of Filipino and Puerto Rican background, she wanted to explore her Asian line. Part of this quest was her railroad trip over inner Asia, which turned her attention to Mongol and Siberian

FIGURE 7.3. American shaman Purple Medicine Woman smudging a Mongolian shaman during a ceremonial gathering in Siberia. Courtesy Debra Varner.

shamanism and eventually to spiritual apprenticeship with a Tuvan shamaness. When a company where she worked went out of business and she lost her job, Purple Medicine Woman decided to devote herself totally to shamanism, both as a spiritual path and as a vocation. Living in San Francisco with its vibrant nature spirituality communities certainly helped her to enter her new vocation, as well as the earlier apprenticeship in the Harner seminars and a master's degree in anthropology she received from the California Institute of Integral Studies—one of the leading centers of American spirituality studies.

In many instances, particular professional backgrounds turn the attention of people to such spiritual techniques as shamanism. The majority of modern practitioners of shamanism in the West come from creative and social service professions. More often than not, they are university students, artists, computer engineers, teachers, humanities and social science scholars, and social and medical workers. To them, we also should add businesspeople. In the latter case, the very nature of their unpredictable ventures usually begs for magical

and metaphysical interference. All of these people are usually voracious readers. They are well educated, and many have university degrees. On the other
hand, among practitioners of shamanism we will rarely see factory workers,
scientists, engineers, or, in other words, people who immerse themselves in the
materialistic professions that are too much grounded in ordinary reality.

Deanna Stennett, who teaches shamanism workshops in the Washington,
DC, area, wrote, "Over the years, my clients, students and fellow participants
have included psychologists, clinical social workers, computer Web designers,
a manager for the mail room at a local university, a novelist, a publisher, a
financial planner, a reimbursement manager for a healthcare company, a li-
brarian, a gastroenterologist, a Catholic nun and a Methodist minister."[93] At
the first North American retreat of which I was a part, organized by the Society
of Celtic Shamans in 2004, I found a psychotherapist from Atlanta, Georgia, a
former nurse from Texas, two artists who were recent graduates of the Savannah College of Arts, a computer engineer from Alabama, a manager from a
Borders bookstore in Philadelphia, and, finally, an African-American house-
wife, who was stationed in the military in Germany and who fell in love with
early European spiritual and cultural traditions. There were also several retired
women, who belonged to the group of Celtic "path masters" and who were
earlier employed in various clerical jobs. The founder of the society is a spirituality writer and an essayist who formerly taught creative writing in British
Columbia, Canada. The only representative of any mundane reality vocation
was the organizer of the meeting, one of the path masters, who was a lab
chemist. Unfortunately, recently she quit the society, but it had nothing to do
with her occupation.

A long-time professional involvement in the exploration of shamanism,
coupled with a welcoming reception of its practices among the public, might
also serve as a catalyst to attempts to replicate such spiritual knowledge in the
Western setting. Harner, the founder of core shamanism, is a vivid example.
Among those who actually teach shamanic practices in workshops and seminars, we see many anthropologists and psychologists, which is natural because
people of these professions directly deal with tribal spirituality and altered
states. Alina Slobodova, a former student of Harner's, who now lives in Moscow, Russia, stressed that she was ripe to embrace core shamanism techniques:
"I was already professionally interested in altered states. I was researching the
psychology of theater performance. When the actor enters his part it is also an
altered state, a creative process."[94]

Lindquist pointed out that the explanation for the large number of creative
and social service professionals in the Western shamanism community might
have something to do with the view of shamanism as entertainment and play.
As I already noted, she believes that the spirit of play is the most distinctive
feature of neo-shamanism. Moreover, as an analogy for shamanic performances

on the urban scene, Lindquist uses children's games. As we know, kids take their play seriously and perform their roles genuinely with their entire body, mind, and soul. When their playtime is over, they come back to their daily routine, only to immerse themselves again in new games with new scenarios next time. When they become bored, children interrupt their play and make up something new, which they play with the same passion. Essentially, to Lindquist, neo-shamanism appears as an "orchestrated context" created through a "live play," in which actors and spectators are mixed and perform together, share emotions and symbols, and establish their own jargon.[95] Some certainly might think that her approach trivializes the whole picture of neo-shamanism. At the same time, to those people from nature community who consider the child mind as the natural mind uncorrupted by civilization layers, her analogy should not look insulting. Indeed, shamanism as a sacred play might bring a necessary element of mystery to the routine of modern Western society, whose members are usually pressured to be deadly serious about whatever they do and to accept once and for all the life scenarios society imposes on them.

Another interesting feature of the Western shamanism community, which we can safely extend to the rest of nature-oriented spiritualities, is its predominantly female population. One can see this trend in a variety of female-oriented spirituality apprenticeship programs, such as Andrews's Sisterhood of Shields. It is also visible in conventional spirituality programs such as, for example, "Indigenous Mind Paths" at Naropa University, Oakland, California, where, in 2003, all nine enrolled students are women. Even a superficial perusal of the gender composition of shamanic workshops and retreats reveals that women far exceed men. Mikael Gejel, one of the leaders of the spiritual network of Swedish urban shamanists, noted that between 70 percent and 80 percent of the people participating in their rituals and activities are women. At the same time, he has noticed that within the same network, the majority of people who write on shamanism are males. Sociological surveys made in Sweden show that more than 80 percent of people interested in the topics and issues raised by nature and pagan print culture are females. On the whole, in Western nature spiritualities, the ratio of women to men is two to one.[96]

We may only speculate about why women are more attracted to alternative spirituality than are men. One guess is that shamanism and related spiritual pursuits might give women more chances for self-realization and self-expression, which they might not find in other walks of life. For example, in *Primitive Passions* (1997), the literary scholar Marianna Torgovnick suggested that the focus the "New Age" culture places on such concerns as relationships and responsibilities look more appealing to women than to men. The emphasis that culture places on psychological healing might similarly respond to the concerns of those women who view themselves as being wounded by male-dominated society and institutions.[97] Incidentally, the latter notion is one of the cornerstones of female spirituality and eco-feminism, intellectual trends that have acquired a special popularity in the United States.

Eco-feminist and female spirituality writers usually link women to the group of others marginalized by a society dominated by white Western males. To these writers, along with Native Americans, African Americans, and many other "wretched of the earth" from the non-Western realm, females, by their social status, are potential healers because they have a firsthand knowledge of suffering. Moreover, some spirituality writers draw conclusions about the healing potential of the woman by simply turning upside down the old Victorian perception of females. They contrast such "inherently female" qualities as their irrationality, organic closeness to Mother Nature, and sensitivity with such "male" characteristics as rationalism, domination, and the cult of violence. For example, Oh Shinnáh, a spiritual practitioner who claims Mohawk-Apache descent and who similarly stresses that shamanism is more popular with women, elaborated in the following manner. She said that woman stands closer to the spirit world because she is a life giver. In contrast, man developed as a hunter and had to take the lives of animals to sustain the lives of people. So women, by default, are endowed with a highly developed intuitive nature, whereas males still have a long way to go to suppress the violent instincts that became ingrained in them through generations.[98]

The basic premise of these assertions is that both society and biology condition women to the role of spiritual healers. Donner-Grau, one of the female witches from the Castaneda inner circle, articulated well this image of the woman as a born shaman. In one of her public lectures, she stressed:

> I wanted don Juan to give me psychedelic drugs—I begged him!—but he refused, saying, "You women don't need the power plants, you're already there." It's nothing for us to dream, to travel in other worlds—we're simply too lazy to do it. And the social order entraps women, robbing them of time for exploration by tying them to bearing and raising children and babying a husband.[99]

The conviction that women are inherent healers attuned to ancient wisdom grew in the 1970s and 1980s and was promoted by the Wiccan writer Starhawk, the late UCLA archaeologist Maria Gimbutas, and female spirituality writer Riane Eisler. In fact, Eisler has acted as a popularizer of Gimbutas's ideas. These authors speculate that, at the dawn of humankind, Europeans lived in an earth-based egalitarian society based on the matriarchy, peace, and cooperation. Then this primal paradise was eliminated by the invasion of so-called Kurgan people from the East, who established a male-dominated society based on warfare and oppression. The latter, they stress, became the hallmark of patriarchal Western civilization. Consequently, these authors encouraged women to tap into their ancient feminine power, which is considered to be the tool of spiritual liberation from Judeo-Christian civilization.

Writer Andrews, the "female Castaneda," has built her entire career on tapping the sources of this feminine power, linking women to Native Americans and, in her subsequent books, to other primitives the world over. This former art dealer seeks to empower her readers by awakening the magicians and shamans in them. In her novel *Medicine Woman*, Andrews described how, after her apprenticeship with two imaginary Indian elders, she became a spiritual warrior and boldly challenged the evil character, the white male shaman Red Dog, who had stolen the marriage basket from her spiritual teachers. The task of Andrews was to retrieve the magic basket, which symbolized the female power stolen by men. By snatching the basket from the evil shaman, the writer restored the balance of power between men and women. Andrews's books became very popular, producing a group of her admirers, some of whom now affiliate themselves with Andrews's esoteric group, the Sisterhood of Shields. The latter gave rise to Andrews's Mystery School in Santa Fe, New Mexico. In a partnership with the University of Natural Medicine in Santa Fe, the school now grants bachelor's, master's, and even doctoral degrees in natural health sciences with a specialization in sacred arts and training. The Mystery School fits the format of a religious studies program, whose graduates enter society as spiritual and pastoral counselors.

Since the 1970s, Western society has gradually opened itself up to various earth-based philosophies, including shamanism. In fact, many elements of nature living and thinking are now parts of the cultural mainstream. Among them are organic gardening, natural foods, and the celebration of Earth Day in the United States. As far as shamanism is concerned, in some cases, it has come to share the niche that earlier belonged to pastoral counseling and psychotherapy. Archaic spirituality has also found its way to Alcoholics Anonymous and to terminally ill patients. Michael Winkelman, an anthropologist from Arizona State University, is convinced that shamanic drumming can help one recover from drug addiction. Furthermore, the National Center for Complementary and Alternative Medicine, a division of the National Institutes of Health, funded a study to determine how shamanism might complement conventional medicine. Nancy Vuckovic, who works as an investigator for Health Research in Oregon, a federal grant recipient, is optimistic about the future of the archaic knowledge: "We're on the road to try and validate shamanism as an alternative medicine."[100]

At the same time, it would be wrong to say that shamanism has already firmly established itself as a widespread form of unchurched spirituality and a therapy. It certainly has not made such inroads in Western society as has Zen Buddhism or such secular religions as yoga or chiropractic. Although people from the "New Age" and nature communities might appreciate shamanism, society in general still views it as a fringe esoteric technique. For example, this attitude clearly emerged during the debates on shamanism on ABC's "Prime Time" show. Discussing Sandra Ingerman's seminars, which help people to communicate with their deceased relatives, medical anthropologist Philip Singer dismissed what she was doing as a blatant fraud. He also did not fail to mention that talking to the dead would cost a person $235.

One viewer, named Reid Hart, who signed up for Ingerman's workshop, challenged the scientist:

> I've attended workshops taught by Sandra and others, and can well say that it might be worth $235 to learn to talk to the dead! Compare that with less than 4 sessions with a psychologist at $70 each. Certainly, these methods can be learned. I've found workshop fees to be reasonable, and the methods effective. Here's a question: If someone gets a benefit from a workshop or a book, then isn't it worthwhile to them? In our culture we have only the accepted medical models available; and they deal with only part of the question. Should not we expand our inquiry into "what is known" beyond this physical reality?

Singer attempted to dismiss this utterance by one phrase: "If such a belief keeps you from being committed to a mental hospital, you are welcome to it."[101] I seriously doubt that Singer would have expressed the same dismissive attitude about yoga or Buddhism, which are now fully embedded in the Western cultural mainstream.

8

Sources of Inspiration

From Native Americana to European
Pagan Folklore

I fearlessly assert to the world, (and I defy contradiction) that the
North American Indian is everywhere, in his native state, a highly
moral and religious being, endowed by his Maker, with an intuitive knowledge of some great Author of his being, and the Universe.
—American artist George Catlin (1840s)

Why seek elsewhere for what exists at home?
—Jean Markale, *The Druids: Celtic Priests*
of Nature (1999)

> The smells of burning sage and cedar fill the air as the
> shaman continues his rhythmic drumming. Everyone in the
> room is silent, lying still on blankets. Soon, the drum is
> accompanied by the voice of a man who hums an unknown
> song, said to be the voice of a summoned spirit. Believers say
> the rhythmic beating of the shaman's drum can take a per-
> son on a journey to meet spirit guides and seek answers to
> questions that have gone unanswered.[1]

This is a scene of a shamanic session performed by Daniel "White
Eagle" Lupinski, a biomedical engineer at the University of Michigan
in Ann Arbor, who also teaches shamanic journeying at the town of
White Lake in Ohio. There is nothing unusual about such sessions,
which since the 1970s have become part of the cultural landscape in
many Western countries. What might be more intriguing are the
explanations which shamanism practitioners, especially from North
America, provide when asked about the origin of their practices.

Let us return to the spiritual practitioner White Eagle with the Polish last name. To a reporter from the *Cleveland Plain Dealer*, who was curious how the engineer became initiated into his spiritual vocation, Lupinski at first situated himself in the environment that made his pursuits possible. Particularly, he stressed that shamanic journeying has recently become popular across the United States because of the rise of interest in American Indian cultures. Detailing how he personally became involved in shamanism, White Eagle added that the interest began fifteen years ago after he read a book about American Indians. After this, for five years he lived on a Navajo reservation "to learn the ways of a shaman, or medicine man." Lupinski eventually completed his training in the archaic techniques by taking classes at Michael Harner's Foundation for Shamanic Studies (FSS). I purposely picked this case of an induction into shamanism through reading about American Indian spirituality and apprenticing with an American Indian teacher because what White Eagle did appears to be rather typical. Like Lupinski, for many people from the neo-shamanism community in North America and Europe, the spiritual path to shamanism began with their interest in Native American spirituality. To many Western seekers, the Native American represents the archetype of the ancient, the ecological, and the spiritual.

The famous mythology writer Joseph Campbell, who was himself involved with Native Americana from childhood, caught well this currently popular perception. He called American Indians the most spiritual people on earth.[2] Sometimes, this popular imagery resurfaces as a Freudianism in the utterances of both Indians and non-Indians. For example, describing how he stepped on the spirituality path after twenty years of worldly materialistic life, the famous Lakota shaman Lame Deer remarked, "My roaming was at an end and I settled down to my only full-time job—being an Indian." By using the word "Indian," Lame Deer meant that he was leaving the world of money making and other materialistic pursuits of the white man and entering the career of a shaman. Madrina Denig is a person of a totally different caliber. A graduate of a ministerial school, she has a mixed origin with some traces of a Cherokee bloodline. Describing how she was inducted into the mysteries of Peruvian shamanism, Denig mentioned in passing, "Because I am part Cherokee, I had grown up with ideas that seem to conform with religious science."[3] The bottom line of both utterances is that being a Cherokee and an American Indian in general means being a spiritually charged person. I am not going now to explore the origin of this stereotype. Other writers have already discussed this in greater detail.[4] In this chapter, I am more interested in how Native Americana, perceived as a source of profound ecological and spiritual wisdom, has contributed to the formation of the neo-shamanism community in the West. I will also discuss the controversy that sprang up from the use of Native American symbolism by American and European spiritual practitioners. Furthermore, my attention is focused on attempts by members of the neo-shamanism community in the West to move away from the Native American dreamlands and toward their own European indigenous spirituality.

Neo-shamanism and Native Americana

Many in the Western nature spirituality community assume that non-Western people, especially those who have maintained in modern times elementary social and political organizations (tribal people), have preserved the remnants of archaic wisdom lost by Western civilization. Tribal spirituality has become the ideal blueprint against which spiritual seekers assess major issues of their own society. Thus, many shamanism practitioners in the West agree that elementary tribal societies lived or still live a collectivist and spiritually rich life and take care of their environment. They also assume that these people are very creative, are gender sensitive, and possess civil courage. Moreover, many believe that Native Americans manifest these ideal features best of all. This conviction that the Native Americans are endowed with superior social values and spirituality strengthened in the 1970s with the rise of environmental movements, which contrasted the earth-based ethics of indigenous peoples with modern Western civilization. Addressing Indian spokespeople who questioned the appropriation of Native Americana by the wider society, one spiritual seeker directly stated, "We woke up and realized that you understand the truth of creation like no other people. You have the truth."[5]

The depiction of the Indian as ecologist and spiritualist reached its peak at the turn of the 1990s on the eve of the 500-year anniversary of Christopher Columbus's arrival in the New World. These years saw the release of a romantic melodrama, *Dances with Wolves* (1991), one of the most powerful mass culture presentations that enhanced the stereotypes I described above. The tremendous popularity of the movie shows that Native Americana and tribal living found an eager response in Western society, which harbors serious doubts about its own civilization. The movie is a story about the retribalization of Lieutenant Dunbar, who, as part of a cavalry unit that is sent to fight the Plains Indians, gradually changes sides. Discovering for himself the wonders of an earth-based lifestyle, Dunbar slowly moves back to the archaic indigenous roots. The whole movie is essentially the process of unmaking Dunbar as a Western man. Incidentally, the retribalization of Dunbar develops under the guidance of Kicking Bird, a Lakota seer and wise man. At first, the lieutenant's hair grows longer. Then he sheds his army clothing and replaces it with Indian buckskins. After this, he sticks a feather in his hair and then begins speaking Lakota. Eventually, Dunbar loses his Anglo name, turning into Dances with Wolves. The movie stirred the sentiments of many Americans and Europeans who long for natural living and harbor negative sentiments against Western civilization. To these people, the film *Dances with Wolves* depicts an attempt to find an authentic way of life that replaces the mode of life that has ruined Western people.[6]

Almost all environmentally aware people or those who are at least a little familiar with the mind, body, and spirit print media know about the speech of Chief Seattle, have read about the wisdom of Black Elk, or have heard about Hopi prophecies. Most probably, they have also run across such metaphors as Mother Earth, the Great Spirit, the four directions, "we are all related," and other symbols that are usually associated with Native Americans. According to a survey conducted in 1989 by *Body, Mind and Spirit*, a spirituality magazine, 22 percent of its respondents had participated in "Native American" spiritual practices or workshops during the previous year. Native American themes occupy a prominent place in the "Spirituality" section of the popular *New Age Catalogue* (1988), which profiles Sun Bear, Black Elk, Carlos Castaneda, and the peyote religion.[7] Native American spirituality, said Mary Ann Winslow, a clerk at the Blue White Rainbow, an Albany, New York, book and crystal shop, "has really gotten into the mainstream. Everyone is getting into sweat lodges, communal circles. We get flyers all the time."[8]

The popularity of the image of the ecological/spiritual Indian in Western countries owes its origin to the dominant position of English-language and American popular culture in the world. In the 1970s and 1980s, in addition to the Castaneda novels, *Black Elk Speaks*, and similar print media coming from North America, traveling spiritual practitioners of Indian and non-Indian origin enhanced the spread of that imagery. That is essentially how Native American symbolism became available to various groups of spiritual seekers, from Canada to Russia (see figure 8.1). Jörgen I. Eriksson, one of the leaders of the Swedish shamanic community, directly points to two sources that served as an inspiration for modern urban shamanism in his country: the American "flood of printed matter" and "Native American" traveling shamans/spiritual leaders.[9]

Swedish anthropologist Galina Lindquist and Jan Svanberg, a religion historian from Finland, explored the map of intellectual routes that led some Swedish spiritual seekers to shamanism. Both of them came to the conclusion that these routes began across the Atlantic in North America. This trajectory concerns not only Native Americana proper, but also core shamanism practices that, as we remember, originated in the United States. In fact, one of the individuals who contributed to the development of the shamanism community in Sweden is an American, Jonathan Horowitz. A student of Harner's, he settled in neighboring Denmark, where he set up the Scandinavian Center for Shamanic Studies, which contributed greatly to the development of a shamanic community in Nordic countries.

Lindquist, who was one of the first to explore a modern neo-shamanism community, detailed the Native American connection in the Swedish community of shamanism practitioners. Before anthropologist Harner came to Sweden

FIGURE 8.1. Russian seekers of Native American spirituality, 1987. Photograph by the author.

and introduced its spiritual seekers to his synthetic cross-cultural version of shamanism, spiritual seekers in that country were already exposed to the spirituality of Rolling Thunder. This former railroad brakeman from Nevada and a traveling spiritual teacher, who billed himself in the early 1980s as a Cherokee shaman, became very popular in Sweden's metaphysical circles. The shamanism community in that country sprang up after Rolling Thunder gave his first seminars in 1982.

Soon, other individuals from the United States, who also positioned themselves as Native American spiritual practitioners, followed him. Among them were Medicine Story, Archie Fire Lame Deer, Richard Deertrack, and Nomad. The last practitioner is an African-American member of the Native American Church who has defined himself as an "African in ethnic origin and Native American in cultural orientation." Among these flying shamans who enthusiastically traveled all over Northern Europe, one name stands out. It is Harley SwiftDeer Reagan, who, like Rolling Thunder, adopted the popular mantle of the Cherokee shaman. According to the people who laid the foundation for the shamanism community in Sweden, in addition to Harner and Rolling Thunder, this particular individual had a strong impact on Swedish seekers of tribal spirituality.[10]

Eriksson explained how an interest in Native Americans prompted him to explore their spirituality and eventually led him to shamanism. In the 1960s and 1970s, he played for a while with then-popular radical Left ideas, beginning as a member of a Maoist group and finishing as a "free socialist." In 1980, as a radio journalist, Eriksson covered the work of the so-called Russell

Tribunal, organized by a European Native American support network in the Netherlands. The tribunal was designed as a permanent forum to scrutinize American Indian policies, especially in the United States. This work exposed Eriksson to Native American political and spiritual activists. The particular event that triggered his conversion to shamanism was reading a book about Rolling Thunder by American spirituality writer Doug Boyd.[11] At that time, Eriksson was not sure about his ideals. Although he wanted to change society for the better, at the same time, he strove to explore his inner world. The spiritual message of Rolling Thunder, who argued that the best politics go through one's own spiritual transformation, helped him to resolve this dilemma. Now all the threads were tied up for Eriksson.

At the same time, the warriors from the Native American movement who came to the Russell Tribunal encouraged Eriksson to search for sacred powers at home instead of following the established fashion, digging into Native American traditions. Thus, Eriksson came to the conclusion that Europeans should recover their own sacred heritage. He began to read about shamanism, searching for possible ancient Nordic links and simultaneously feeding on both Indian and ancient European sources. At the turn of the 1980s, there was already a group of people who were moving in the same direction. In 1982, Eriksson brought eighteen of these people together to Café Vega, where they established a Swedish shamanism group called Yggdrasil with its own magazine; Yggdrasil is the world tree in Nordic mythology.

Eriksson's evolution from Native American to Nordic symbolism mirrors the experiences of his fellow seekers of nature spirituality. At some point between the mid-1970s and the mid-1980s, Swedish urban shamanists heavily grounded their activities in American Indian symbolism. Then they began to debate whether such appropriation of non-native spirituality was the right thing to do. The seekers began to wonder if they would be able to create a valid spirituality by emulating the spiritual practices of an overseas society. Although some of them continued to insist on the use of Native American traditions, others favored native Scandinavian ancient spirituality. Eventually, the voices of the second group prevailed.[12]

Since the origin of neo-shamanism in Western countries is associated with indigenous North America, in its practices and print media, native American Indians play a leading role. Some popular media refer to shamanism as a form of Native American spirituality.[13] The most peculiar example of this stereotype I have ever found is an article published in the *South China Morning Post*. A reporter from this newspaper interviewed a Chinese female intellectual from Hong Kong, who wove into her spirituality Harner's core shamanism and some rituals associated with Native Americans, such as the medicine wheel. The most surprising thing is that neither the reporter nor the shamaness herself mention a single word about the Asian shamanic tradition, which gave birth to the whole metaphor of shamanism. At the same time, the article stresses that shamanism is associated with Native American religions. Some reference works and dictionaries picked up this popular stereotype. Thus, the *American Heritage Dictionary* defines the word *shaman*, first, as "a priest of shamanism" and, second, as "a medicine man among certain North American Indians." Moreover, this popular stereotype spills into scholarship. The anthropologist Peter Furst, a former colleague of Castaneda's during their years at UCLA, wrote that shamanism lies beneath all the world's religions. Yet, as he stressed, among American Indians "it shines through more powerfully than it has been allowed to do elsewhere."[14]

Many neo-shamanism practitioners rely on symbols and artifacts that are usually associated with North American Indians. Among the most popular are vision quests, eagle feathers, hawks, the four directions, the sacred circle, the sweatlodge, drums, dream catchers, and sacred pipes. The spiritual imagery some neo-shamanism practitioners experience on their otherworldly quests is also heavily loaded with Native American symbolism that comes from books, seminars, and spiritual teachers. When I asked Eric Perry, a spiritual practitioner from Savannah, Georgia, who is drawn to the Harnerian version of neo-shamanism, what prompted him to turn to this type of spirituality in the first place, he explicitly pointed to the Native American factor: "Throughout my Kabbalah practices I found myself in touch with spirit guides that appeared to me in indigenous forms that were basically Native American. I did not grow up with the Native American culture or a background. Yet, the things I've learned from these guides are of that culture." After this, he ran across the Eliade book and compared his visions with those of Native American and Siberian practitioners, and it dawned on him, "Gee, these experiences I've been having are shamanic!" Perry added that these spirit beings in Native American form have been his "guiding light" for the past seven years.

When I posed the same question to another acquaintance, a psychotherapist from Atlanta who recently joined the Society of Celtic Shamans, he similarly pointed out that his original interest in shamanism came, as he put it, from "Native American stuff." Particularly, he participated in medicine wheel and sweatlodge ceremonies conducted by people who teach Native American spirituality in the southeastern United States. Another important source was his readings. I was surprised that, unlike many people in the community, he had never heard of the Eliade classic *Shamanism* book. As he specified, his knowledge about shamanism came from popular spirituality texts on Native Americans: *Seven Arrows* by Hyemeyohsts Storm, *The Medicine Way* by Kenneth Meadows, Neihardt's *Black Elk Speaks*, a deck of Indian medicine cards produced by Jamie Sams, and finally *God Is Red* by Vine Deloria, a prominent Native American spokesperson.[15] What is common among all these products, including the Deloria book, is that they present North American traditions in a generic idealized form as an embodiment of the highest spiritual wisdom and contrast it with Judeo-Christian traditions.

Bruce Hawkins, an American spiritual seeker who, like Perry, experienced spiritual revelations colored by Native American symbolism, similarly pointed out that the spark that ignited his interest in nature spirituality was books on Indian history and beliefs. I would like to dwell on his experiences more because they might mirror the experiences of those Americans who came to appreciate Native American spirituality in the 1960s and 1970s, at the time when this country, for the first time in its history, came to deal on a grand scale with the trauma of its past attitudes toward Native Americans. As Hawkins said, his induction into the realm of shamanism was triggered in 1975 by his reading the bestselling *Bury My Heart at Wounded Knee* (1970) by Dee Brown, who presented the history of the American West as perpetual warfare between the Indians and the whites, and Neihardt's *Black Elk Speaks* (1932). Reprinted as a paperback edition in the 1960s and 1970s, the latter book laments the decline of the traditional Lakota ways.[16] Hawkins became emotionally attuned to the tragic history of Native Americans as conquered people and simultaneously interested in their spirituality. During a pilgrimage to battle sites associated with the Indian wars, Hawkins experienced powerful spiritual revelations, which later led to contacts with real Indians, including a brief association with radicals from the American Indian Movement (AIM). To make a long story short, encouraged by his Indian friends, Hawkins began seeking visionary experiences. He ended up by crying out for visions and experiencing out-of-body shamanic soul flights.[17]

Some Euro-American practitioners of shamanism, who downplay the intellectual and cultural environment in which they live and the books they read, are sincerely amazed at how, without any direct contacts with Native Americans, they have become the receptors of Native American spirituality in their dreams and visions. For example, Marcia Lauck, who calls herself "an engineer of inner space" and stresses that she is a typical WASP (white Anglo-Saxon Protestant), was contacted in her dreams by a circle of Native American elders. The elders informed her that they would build a bridge "across which the deep truths and knowledge that shaped their cultures and that were encoded in their ceremonies and medicine bundles, could be introduced into Western Culture for the preservation of the Earth." Lauck, who had never seen an Indian in her life, was stunned by the fact that American Indian elders elected her for that grand mission. Unlike Hawkins, she did not take into consideration that the books she had read and the surrounding metaphysical culture might have affected her imagery. The only sound explanation to her is "theological": the Native American elders entered her mind because of the intervention of divine forces.[18]

Dutch anthropologist Merete Jakobsen, who surveyed several neo-shamanic groups in England and Denmark, related a peculiar story about a native Inuit woman from Greenland, an area that had, in the past, a highly developed shamanic tradition of its own. Raised and educated in Denmark, this woman, a participant in a neo-shamanic workshop, received more inspiration from American Indian philosophy than from her traditional Greenland spirituality. Her spiritual experiences were usually dominated by Native American imagery, which she absorbed from popular American body, mind, and spirit literature that is widely available in Denmark and that is heavily loaded with such symbolism.[19]

My own observations confirm what other authors have written about the Native American connection in the neo-shamanism community, especially in its formative years in the 1970s and 1980s. Among my contacts in the Society of Celtic Shamans (SCS), the majority turned to European nature spirituality after some involvement with Native Americana. Some of them continue to experiment with American Indian symbolism, which they now blend with Celtic practices. For example, before they went Celtic, two SCS path masters from Canada were initiated into the Wolf Clan by Seneca Indian spiritual teachers. Another path master, who is an American, apprenticed for a long time with Hopi teachers in Arizona. Incidentally, she still carries her native name, Lighthawk, and uses in her Celtic rituals a rattle made for her by a Hopi friend, a beautiful piece of work with characteristic Pueblo symbols (see figure 8.2). Lighthawk

FIGURE 8.2. Celtic shaman Lighthawk still uses her Hopi-made rattle, which was acquired when she was pursuing Native American spirituality. Photograph by the author.

explained to me that she could not use this rattle in the Indian setting because in the Hopi culture, such ritual tools were reserved for men only. Yet in
her current Celtic practices, which she designs on her own, there are no restrictions. "In my shamanic travels I can transgress cultures and spaces," she
told me.

American Indian symbolism might serve as a spark that prompts a spiritual seeker to step on the path of spirituality. In addition to Buddhist and Siberian artifacts, the altar of Purple Medicine Woman, my acquaintance from
San Francisco, includes an oil painting of an Indian. Although she positions
herself as a practitioner of Siberian shamanism, she explained to me that this
portrait, placed at the center of the altar, has a mystical power for her because
it somehow triggered her induction into shamanism. Donna Henes, an "acclaimed urban shaman" from Brooklyn who samples the whole range of healing tools, from shamanism to tarot and Reiki, stressed that the light of true
spirituality visited her for the first time when, in 1975, she once placed over
her face a Native American weaving. Mama Donna noted the profound spiritual revelation that she experienced from this contact: "I instantly understood how everything in the world was interconnected."[20] I would like to stress
here that, generally, in the aesthetics of modern Western shamanism, Indian
spirituality rarely manifests itself in a pure form. Normally it comes in combination with other spiritual techniques adjusted to collective or individual
tastes.

One of the first active attempts to weave Native American symbolism into
modern Western esotericism and spirituality was made by the spiritual practitioner Vincent LaDuke (1929–1992), better known as Sun Bear (see figure
8.3). Sun Bear tapped the growing interest in Indian culture and spirituality at
the turn of the 1970s by creating his own spirituality school, Bear Tribe, Inc.
This group merged the traditions of various Indian cultures, contemporary
environmentalism, and rituals personally minted by Sun Bear. He became
especially famous for the introduction of a ritual of the medicine wheel, which
today many Western seekers integrate into their spiritual toolkits. Sun Bear
and his associates traveled widely over North America and Europe spreading
the gospel of Native American spirituality and ecology. The evolution of the
Bear Tribe's projects, from hallucinogens and communes to workshops on
spirituality, mirrors the evolution of Western counterculture in the 1960s and
1970s.

LaDuke, a hyphenated American of German-French-Norwegian-Ojibwa
(Anishnabe) origin, grew up as an Anishnabe on the White Earth Indian Reservation in Minnesota. At fifteen, he became upset that the tribal council did
not accept his advice about the reformation of the economic life of the reservation. The teenager came to the conclusion that "if a prophet couldn't be recognized on his own reservation, it was time to try my own wings." That is how
Sun Bear found himself on the road, traveling all over the United States, briefly

FIGURE 8.3. Sun Bear, the founder of the Bear Tribe, Inc. Courtesy Wind Daughter, medicine chief of the Bear Tribe © www.thebeartribe medicinesociety.org.

living and working at various places. In the 1950s, LaDuke worked on a railroad, at a cemetery, as a cook, and as a woodcutter.

What seems to have triggered his future career as a spiritual teacher and impresario was his stint in Hollywood. Because of his stereotypical Indian appearance, Sun Bear was chosen to play "Indian braves." In fact, the first time he acted as a shaman was in the CBS show "Brave Eagle." LaDuke later remembered that the work in Hollywood was great fun. He enjoyed riding horses and playing an Indian: "Most of us only get to play cowboys and Indians when we're kids. As for me, I was too busy to play then, but now that I've grown up I get to play the same, and get paid for it."[21] Eventually, movie makers began to use him occasionally as a technical director. As an expert Indian, he checked Hollywood Indian garb and native settings for their authenticity. At the end of the 1960s, LaDuke also helped radical anthropologist Jack Forbes to develop a Native American studies program and Indian-related curriculum at the University of California at Davis. Eventually, he found himself teaching Native American philosophy. Unfortunately, his education was limited only to junior high school, and the university administration squeezed him out of the program. LaDuke had to move to an experimental college that was affiliated with the university but was not so strict about credentials. Here he began teaching self-reliance Indian-styled courses. Sun Bear had about seventy students, whom he instructed in how to respect Mother Earth and how to do organic gardening.

The idea to set up a spirituality community, the future Bear Tribe, grew from this particular course. People who clustered around him decided to turn their learning into a lifestyle, which reflected communal sentiments then popular in the Western counterculture. The tribe was finally inaugurated at the end of 1969 on a piece of donated land near Placerville, California. The fact that the camp had no running water or other urban conveniences served as an additional attraction "because it forced people to grow close to the land." Having built shelters, twenty members of the tribe, all white Americans except one Indian from Montana, with Sun Bear as their chief, began to live as "Indians."[22] Soon the news about the tribe and its organic earth-based philosophy spread all over California. In 1971, the tribe already numbered about 200 members who lived in various camps around the state. The Bears grew organic fruits and vegetables and experimented with storing and preserving them. Overall, the LaDuke project was one of those numerous short-lived hippie communes that mushroomed in Western countries in the 1960s and early 1970s.

Soon things in the tribe got out of control. Drug use was rampant. Smoking marijuana, which the Bears called "medicine weed," was very popular. Sun Bear became disgusted with the direction the project took, denounced "those who wanted Timothy Leary's trip," and left for Reno, Nevada, where he turned to publishing.[23] In 1972, he started *Many Smokes*, a spirituality and self-help periodical that publicized earth-based values styled as Native American spirituality. From Reno, Sun Bear eventually moved to the state of Washington. By the middle of the 1970s, he had already dropped the whole idea of building a permanent alternative commune. The influence of the psychedelic 1960s was waning and, along with it, the popularity of communes. Finally, LaDuke found an ideal solution that combined earth-based teachings without committing people to the hazards of communal living. In 1975, he and his associates reestablished the Bear Tribe not as a permanent residential community but as a virtual structure that united Euro-Americans who were scattered all over the United States and who met each other during spirituality seminars and workshops. That is how the Bear Tribe evolved into a group that became an important part of the Western mind, body, and spirit community. In contrast to the goals of the 1960s, Sun Bear radically changed his message. In the 1980s, he argued that his Bear Tribe was not against technology but against the misuse of technology. The motto of the tribe became "not going back to the stone age," but "going to the new age."[24]

Among the new spiritual projects of the Bears was the shaman apprenticeship program centered on the vision-questing program, which included purification sweats and sending people to a mountaintop for one to four days to pray for a vision. Sun Bear and his assistants then interpreted these visions to those who experienced them. He also continued to educate his followers in reverence for all plant, animal, and insect life. There were also workshops on chanting, dancing, drumming, and the use of crystals. The most famous events pioneered by Sun Bear were medicine wheel ceremonies, which attracted hundreds of people.

Sun Bear repeatedly stressed that, although his medicine was Indian-based, it was not static but always changing through an open mixture of various spiritualities from other cultures. What he offered was not a traditional culture-bound spirituality but an incorporation of "whatever my medicine calls for, from everywhere," including elements of rituals from native sacred society Midewiwin, generic pan-Indian sweatlodges, vision quests, and medicine wheels. Hence, he characteristically called himself a "universal medicine man."[25] Although condemned by Indian fundamentalists for the misuse of Indian spirituality, Sun Bear did inspire many people in the Western nature community. It seems that the lack of any rigid system in his teachings, which were keyed to the individual spiritual aspirations of seekers, was the reason for his popularity. After he instructed his students in the basics of natural living and earth-based spirituality, Sun Bear encouraged them to work out their own medicine. The participants in his seminars later became shamanic teachers themselves, going around the United States and beyond on speaking tours and gathering their own groups.

Another example (with a negative flavor) of the appropriation of Native American symbolism for countercultural spirituality purposes is the infamous SwiftDeer. Many Indian spokespeople and Western seekers dismiss him as an aberration and as an example of what a genuine spiritual practitioner should not be. Still, as a historian, I became interested in his career that, to me, manifests in its extreme all of the real or imagined negative features which critics usually ascribe to the "New Agers." In contrast to Sun Bear with his quiet demeanor, SwiftDeer is a flamboyant spiritual "clown," who rode literally any trendy wave of Indian spirituality in the 1970s and 1980s: Castaneda, Sun Dance, sweatlodges. In the cultural cocktail of his Deer Tribe, one also finds conventional metaphysical clichés, Native American spirituality, Buddhism, astrology, the cult of guns, anti-immigrant sentiments, survivalist and militia ethics, and various conspiracy theories.

In the late 1970s, when SwiftDeer was in the beginning stage of his career, he advertised himself in a Swedish shamanism magazine as a Cherokee/Métis shaman, a medicine man, a Rosicrucian, an outstanding healer, and a master in karate and jiu-jitsu with a Ph.D. in humanistic psychology and comparative religion. In addition to these tall tales, SwiftDeer claimed that he was an apprentice of a Navajo shaman, Tom Two Bears Wilson, "also known as Don Genaro from Carlos Castaneda's books." To European spiritual seekers, he also told a tale that he and Castaneda chewed peyote together. According to another story, a Cheyenne medicine man, Storm, a popular fiction writer from northern

California, shared with him his secrets. On one occasion, he claimed that his sacred knowledge came from the society of Twisted Hairs of the Turtle Island, which sheltered itself somewhere in the vicinity of the star Sirius. To potential skeptics, SwiftDeer pointed out, "If you don't believe human beings are descended from the stars, you may have a problem with the history of many cultures." On another occasion, he declared that everything he taught came from a certain Sun Dance council.[26] Having to deal with SwiftDeer's numerous sacred jokes, even those European seekers who were ready to accept him as a Native American shaman began to have second thoughts. Eriksson, a spiritual practitioner from Sweden, stressed that he did learn a lot from Swift-Deer's seminar. At the same time, he was cautious: "I have also kept a critical distance from the man. Have you noticed that this man has an answer to everything? And in some cases he does not know what he is talking about. For example, he says that Odin is a god of lightning. If he makes such mistakes about our heritage, it can be that he is bluffing about other things as well."[27]

While in Europe, he became known as one of the spearheads of the shamanism subculture; in the United States, SwiftDeer scandalized himself by running the so-called Quodoushka practical sex workshops. Much to the outrage of the real Cherokee, SwiftDeer claimed that the workshop was based on ancient Cherokee practices. According to a tale he shared with the participants in his seminars, when he was fourteen years old, an adult Cherokee woman, Phoenix Fire Woman, sexually initiated SwiftDeer. The woman allegedly showed him the art of making love in a Cherokee manner, instructed him about the nine different kinds of vaginas and penises men and women have, and also enlightened him about five levels of orgasm. Not many spiritual seekers in Europe are aware that the Sun Dancing and shamanizing SwiftDeer of the 1980s today is known to his neighbors in Paradise Valley, Arizona, as "Gunnie" Reagan, an active member of the National Rifle Association, a survivalist, and a gun advocate who runs a shooting competition, "Steel Challenge."[28] It appears that SwiftDeer enjoys playing the role of a sacred clown, intentionally antagonizing public sentiments and morality. He definitely learned one of the major rules of Western publicity making: bad publicity is still publicity.

It appears that SwiftDeer does possess a certain charisma that lures some seekers. Porsche Lynn, a participant in his notorious Quodoushka sex seminars, remembered the moment she accidentally encountered SwiftDeer:

> I found in him an amazing, magnetic attraction. I sat down
> with him, and he gave me reflections. I had been kind of living my
> life as a victim, and he called me on it. He said, "You have to fig-
> ure out why you chose these parents, to be birthed into this place
> at this time." Part of me was like, "This guy's full of shit," but he
> said it with such honesty and sincerity that I really had to take it to
> heart.

Another woman, who goes by the name Heather "Moon Owl" Campbell and who studied anthropology at Brown University, was similarly drawn to the personality of "Gunnie" Reagan. After she heard him at a conference in Germany, she "fell in love" with everything he said and "signed up for an apprenticeship immediately." The apprenticeship lasted for seven years and took her from her native Britain to the United States: "We trained hard. We were buried in the ground, we fasted, we sundanced, we sweat-lodged." The culmination of the course was a naming ceremony, during which she received her shamanic name, Moon Owl. After completing the apprenticeship with SwiftDeer, Campbell came back to Britain, where she now works as a shamanic guidance consultant. Her job is to empower corporations and their members.[29]

Spirit Wars: The Indians and "Whiteshamans"

The appropriation of Native American symbolism on a grand scale, and especially the activities of such showmen as "Gunnie" Reagan, are precisely what led to the spirit wars, the contest between American Indian spokespeople and non-Indian spiritual seekers over the use of Native Americana. This is certainly a postmodern tension, which one could not imagine, say, a century ago, when the majority of Westerners simply did not care about tribal beliefs and practices, dismissing them as "primitive superstition." Now, when for both Native Americans and many Western seekers, Native Americana has become an object of veneration, the situation is the opposite.

The most radical American Indian spokespeople, who criticize the use of Indian-related symbolism by the wider society, want Native Americana to be reserved exclusively for the Native Americans. These critics view non-Indian spiritual experiments with native symbols and artifacts as a cultural theft. Moreover, some use stronger language and call this practice a new form of colonialism; first, white people took the land, and now they are ready to steal Indian spirituality. Critics who speak on behalf of the Indians use such strong expressions as "white shamanic neo-imperialism" and "cultural genocide" against Native Americans.[30]

To some extent, such sentiments are a natural backlash on the part of the Native Americans against the zealous and frequently irritating attention of society to all things Indian. At the same time, it is also an understandable concern that the popular adoption by the Western public of the imagery usually associated with American Indians will water down indigenous identity. Indigenous spokespeople, many of whom themselves are uprooted urban individuals seeking to reclaim their traditional identities, want to copyright particular rituals and traditions for themselves to use in cultural construction. For this reason, many of them question the right of the "New Agers" to appropriate Native American spirituality.

The rationale here is very clear. If the surrounding society uses the same symbols, what is left for the Indians? Robert Doren, a detribalized Lakota Sioux from Brule, South Dakota, who now lives in Salt Lake City and runs sweatlodge ceremonies for urban Native Americans, is concerned about the infringement on the Indian tradition. Pointing to ceremonies like the one he conducts, Doren sadly remarked, "It is all we [Indians] have left." Criticizing native spiritual practitioners who do not mind working with non-Indians, Leroy Rattling Leaf, a spokesman for the Lakota, stressed that the more Native Americans share their ceremonies with outsiders, the more they chip away from their native culture: "I think we've lost something because of it. And we can never get it back."[31]

The clash between the Indian preservationists and "New Agers" represents a conflict between two views of identity and spirituality. For the first, the issue is clearly about their individual spirituality. Eclectic seekers, both Indians and non-Indians, claim that spirituality should be designed and shaped according to the individual's desires. It is natural for them to advocate the right to freely experiment with any spirituality in the world and to choose what fits their personal tastes. In contrast, for Native American cultural workers, spirituality is a collective resource that they use to build their shattered identity. Therefore, they view spiritual culture not as a matter of individual choice but as a collective issue. In this context, it is understandable that some Native Americans insist that indigenous communities and their elders must sanction the use of particular ceremonies and objects. Moreover, some Native American spokespeople argue that participation in native rituals should be restricted to those who are Native Americans by blood. An Indian activist, Nancy Butterfield, articulated well this fundamentalist approach in the following words: "Only American Indians who have been chosen by their elders and taught the proper ways to conduct ceremonies—a process that takes years—have the right to practice these traditions."[32]

Indian spokespeople frequently call those who weave indigenous symbols and artifacts into the fabric of the mind, body, and spirit culture "plastic shamans" or "plastic medicine men/women." The assumption here is that the "New Age" rituals are artificial, imagined, and, therefore, not real. By contrast, native ceremonies practiced by Native Americans, especially in such traditional settings as reservations, appear to them to be organic, natural, and real. The most devastating criticism against those Americans and Europeans who emulate specific American Indian rituals was leveled by prominent Native American spokesperson Vine Deloria, Jr., a professor of political science from the University of Colorado. With irony and humor he wrote about those non-Indians who cling to "alleged shamans" as individuals who are ready to "pay hundreds of dollars for the privilege of sitting on the ground, having corn flour thrown in their faces, and being told that the earth was round and all things lived in circles."[33] The crux of the Native American criticism of the "New Age" is that indigenous ceremonies taken out of context and mixed with rituals from other cultures and traditions do not make sense. Drawing on the premise that each religion is somehow mysteriously linked with a specific land or locality, Deloria argues that tribal spirituality is deeply grounded in native communities and, by its very nature, cannot contain a universal message. For this reason, he describes those natives who work with wider audiences as people who betray the values of their respective groups.[34]

The radical writer Ward Churchill, a second prominent critic of "plastic shamans," who also works at the University of Colorado, goes further. Labeling neo-shamanic practices as a meaningless "ritual potluck" devoid of a cultural context, he calls on both whites and Indians to shut down the "New Age" meetings, burn their sweatlodges, impound and return the sacred objects they desecrate.[35] Churchill is so serious about these things and so harsh on those who mess with the imagery associated with Native American beliefs that even fiction writer Tony Hillerman, the author of popular police thrillers that use Navajo (Dine) religion as a backdrop, did not escape his critical eye. In passing, I would like to note that, ironically, Churchill, who positions himself as a native son, a Native American radical activist and a "plastic shamans" buster, was himself busted by his former comrades from the American Indian Movement for "playing" an Indian. According to *Denver Westword*, during an internal squabble in the AIM, several of its leaders began to seriously question the writer's Native American credentials, calling him an "impostor" and a "wannabe" Indian. So far, Churchill cannot produce adequate proof of his American Indian ancestry.[36]

Some radical critics of "plastic shamans" turn the contest over Native American spirituality into a political and economic issue. Lisa Aldred, who views present-day American society through Marxist eyes as divided into the oppressive dominant society and the subjugated indigenous people, believes that any appropriation of Native American culture by whites eventually results in the oppression of indigenous others. Another Marxist author labels spiritual seekers who are drawn to Native Americana as bourgeoisie who are trying to fill their boredom with the pursuit of exotic things. She sarcastically adds that these seekers suffer from "full stomach syndrome."[37]

I do not want to say that the Marxist interpretation of the body, mind, and spirit culture has no point. Certainly, there is a socioeconomic explanation for the rise of mass interest among Europeans and Americans in non-Western traditions. The general increase in affluence in Western countries gave people more leisure time for creative aesthetic pursuits. Here I want to reiterate the famous self-actualization thesis of psychologist Abraham Maslow. What in the 1930s was available to only a few individuals such as Mable Dodge Luhan, who could afford to retreat to Taos, New Mexico, and indulge herself in spiritual pursuits and writing, is clearly accessible to thousands of middle-class Westerners today. What I want to question here is the assumption of the radical critics of "plastics" that the Westerners' interest in Native American cultures and spiritualities is a manifestation of colonialism. In their attempts to reserve Native Americana for the Indians, to sanction what is traditional and what is not, I sense an attempt to freeze religions and cultures in time and space, which, whether one likes it or not, never happens in real life.

At the same time, it is clear that today many Native Americans feel irritated about what they consider to be the mass emulations of Native American traditions. On June 10, 1993, a gathering of about 500 representatives of the Lakota and their kin from the United States and Canada passed a "Declaration of War against Exploiters of Lakota Spirituality."[38] The adoption of the document by this group is very symbolic. In popular Native Americana, the Lakota represent the archetype of the most authentic Indians. Although adopted on behalf of the most "Indian" and romanticized group of Native Americans, the declaration was meant to reflect the sentiments of all Indians. The document outlines a number of offenses against Native American spirituality, including the sale of sacred pipes in stores and the conducting of sweatlodges and Sun Dances not sanctioned by communities. The people who adopted the declaration called for demonstrations, boycotts, and press conferences as ways of taking action. The next year, interested Native Americans formed Warriors of the Sacred Moon on the Trail of the Crow, a group that decided to identify and combat cases of appropriation of Native American symbolism. Another group of Native Americans with similar goals hosts an Internet site where they bust particular "whiteshamans."[39]

On occasion, Native American activists turn to active measures against Indian and non-Indian "plastic" practitioners. For example, in Colorado, AIM activists disrupted a weekend shamanic retreat conducted by the late Sun Bear. In 1993, in Riverside, California, about twenty protesters, also affiliated with AIM, demonstrated in front of the house of Tim Toohey, one of SwiftDeer's apprentices, who ran paid sweatlodge ceremonies in his backyard. In another case, during a talk by writer Storm, the "Cheyenne Castaneda" and author of *Seven Arrows*, American Indian radicals distributed flyers that declared, "Our sacred spiritual practices are not for sale, and if you try to steal them from us, you are guilty of spiritual genocide." In 1990, in a San Francisco Bay area bookstore, protesting Native Americans disrupted public readings by Lynn Andrews, the "female Castaneda," who in her novels milks the topic of female spirituality. The same year, in response to Native American criticism, several booksellers in San Francisco removed from the shelves her classics, such as *Medicine Woman* and *Jaguar Woman*. Sometimes, the Indians protest the use of Native American imagery by such "well wishers" as environmental activists, who frequently appeal to the myth of the ecological Indian without even realizing that Indian preservationists are very sensitive about the public use of this symbolism. In 1990, in San Francisco, twenty Indians gathered to demonstrate against this kind of well-meant appropriation. They carried posters with such words as "Help the owl, but don't help yourselves to our spirituality" and "Do not support spiritual genocide: our culture and land systematically destroyed, now they want our last strength—our spirituality."[40]

Many Indian communities now try to keep outsiders away from their rites and ceremonies. The Hopi Indians, who in the 1960s became the object of persistent countercultural attention and who lived through the hippie invasion, now do not even want to talk with outsiders about their traditions. Not only do they ban photography in their settlements, but they also consider it offensive to take notes in their museum. In 1998, the Lakota tribal government adopted a similar measure. The tribal officials decreed that no aspect of their religion should be taught to non-Indians. Moreover, they listed particular rites forbidden for dissemination or cloning; among them are sweatlodges, Sun Dances, vision quests, and ceremonies that involve sage, tobacco, and animal parts. Moreover, the statute warns: "Any White person or tribal member who knowingly encourages or has non-Indians in any ceremony, Sundance, or Vision Quest as participants will be liable and will be prosecuted in tribal or federal Court for Fraud." This phrasing suggests that there is a certain authentic Indian tradition and that its appropriation or alteration represents a fraud. The documents condemning "plastics" also imply that copyright laws should be extended to the spiritual realm, a claim that is certainly hard to justify.[41]

In order to make sure that native ceremonies stay within their communities, some Native American communities began to restrict their rituals to the individuals who have sufficient Indian bloodlines and who can produce special Indian "roll cards" issued to the members of officially recognized tribes. Specific stipulations vary among various tribes. Some native groups require one-quarter blood to be considered a full-fledged native. It is obvious that, in the United States, the greater part of which consists of hyphenated people of multiple descents, it is hard to stick to this requirement.[42] At the same time, this practice does make sense in the context of the presently dominant ideology of multiculturalism, which cultivates the cultural fragmentation of people by freezing them in their respective ethnic, gender, and cultural niches.

As an example of how a person can get into trouble by stepping into the forbidden territory of Native American symbolism, let us look at the case of Dawn Everhart. Everhart's spiritual practices are based on the cosmopolitan core shamanism of Harner, which does not exactly dwell on any imagery that can be linked to American Indians. Unfortunately, in addition to the core practices, she tried to anchor herself in Native American symbolism. Thus, following the practice popular among some spiritual seekers, she adopted an Indian name, Dances on Water. Everhart also claims that she is $\frac{1}{32}$ Cherokee. In passing, I want to mention that the acquisition of Cherokee identity is a favorite practice among some Western seekers who try to ground themselves in Native Americana. Since historically many Cherokee mixed with Caucasian people, it provides a good opportunity to claim an Indian ancestry. At the same time, Everhart does admit that she never experienced real tribal traditions.

She says that her spiritual techniques come from a medicine man who owns the Metamorphosis New Age Center in Denver and who similarly positions himself as a Cherokee. In addition to Harner, to perfect her spiritual techniques, she apprenticed with other teachers who have written various books on shamanism. Thus, she learned (obviously from Harner) how to make journeys into the spirit world and eventually met her alleged ancestor, a centuries-old Cherokee. Everhart argues that this ancestral spirit became her guide. During one of her spiritual journeys, the ancestor instructed her to go into the wide world to teach classes on the wisdom of shamanism to other people. The spiritual guide even pointed to the college that could accommodate her curriculum. "Go to Colorado Free University," the spirit supposedly said. She did so, and CFU, which is famous for its unusual programs, accepted her as an instructor. That is how she began teaching the eight-hour "Walking the Path of the Shaman" course, charging $45 per person. Although payment was required, she was clearly not after money. Of that sum, she received $9.25, which is far below what an average college teacher makes; the rest went to the university.

Since Everhart taught her students not only how to find their power animals and to locate sacred space but also such sensitive things as the medicine wheel ceremony, which originated from Native American spiritual practices, Dances on Water got into real trouble. Local Native American activists who were especially famous for their campaigns against "plastics" immediately picked up on her as a straw woman because she perfectly fit the profile of the "plastic." CFU was flooded with e-mails that demanded that the school remove the course from the curriculum. An angry protester wrote, "We view it as another opportunity of the white culture to rip off Indian spirituality. . . . If the practice continues, proper NATIVE authorities will be contacted and pressure brought to cease such activities." The university bureaucrats, who apparently did not realize that they were stepping on sacred territory, were so frightened that they immediately canceled not only "Walking the Path of the Shaman" but also, just in case, "Celtic Shamanism," which Everhart was scheduled to teach later and which had nothing to do with Native Americans.[43]

The critical attitude of Native American spokespeople to the appropriation of symbolism they treat as their own makes many spiritual seekers, who receive inspiration from this imagery, feel uncomfortable and insecure. The whole problem of how to better partake of Native Americana without stepping on somebody's toes might strike uninformed people, especially from overseas, as trivial and superficial. Still, that criticism seriously disturbs many members of the Western nature community, especially in North America, where memories of the Native Americans' land and cultural dispossession are still fresh. From time to time, such spirituality periodicals as *Shaman's Drum* or Internet discussion forums dealing with shamanism raise and debate this lingering issue.

In their political sympathies, the majority of the people in Western nature communities tend to be liberal and deeply sympathetic to Native American causes. At least, this is an impression I have drawn from my encounters with neo-shamanism practitioners in the United States. At the same time, they constantly hear the accusations that their "New Age" spiritual practices represent the abuse of beliefs indigenous to the Indians and even a new form of cultural genocide. To cleanse their consciences, some of them feel that the members of nature communities should pay monetary compensation to Native American communities as a partial compensation for the use of indigenous rites and symbols. For example, Timothy White, the editor of *Shaman's Drum*, challenged his readers by donating to nonprofit groups benefiting native people the entire sum he received from Lynn Andrews for running her elaborate ad in his magazine. Chequeesh, a multicultural spiritual practitioner from Berkeley, California, had a similar suggestion. She thought that, in order to feel fulfilled, the one who experiments with Native American religion should find a group of American Indian people "struggling to stay alive, and give money or something back to them."[44]

Trying to justify their spiritual practices, those Euro-American spiritual seekers who draw heavily on Native Americana usually argue that they simply do not have any other choice. Some of them are convinced that their Western civilization is so wicked and corrupt that they cannot find anything inspiring in it. Spirituality writer Cinnamon Moon asked her potential Native American critics, "We can indeed look to our own heritage and culture first, but when that does not hold the answers we are seeking, why should we stop? There was nothing in my ancestry that called to me the way the Medicine Path did." Also addressing her potential critics, Chequeesh generalized along similar lines. She argued that if history elected Native Americans to serve as keepers of the spiritual knowledge, there is nothing they can do about this. The indigenous people are simply destined to share the truth of spiritual wisdom with all other people.[45]

Occasionally, Euro-American spiritual seekers, especially the ones who are desperate to partake of Native American spirituality, masochistically denounce their whiteness in an attempt to merge with nativeness. Thus, in response to the "Declaration of War against Exploiters of Lakota Spirituality," a certain Christopher M. literally pleads, "I am one of those people who are humbly respectful of the Lakota people and the ways the creator has shown them. I am your friend. Even if you declare war on me and reject me for praying to the power that makes the earth in the way you do, I will always be your friend."[46]

To ward off criticism, many spiritual seekers who receive their inspiration from Native Americana simply appeal to metaphysical arguments. They insist that the imagery and particular rituals, which Native Americans might consider their own, come to them not from books or workshops but directly from spirits. The aforementioned Everhart, who got into trouble with the Native American critics of "plastics," stressed, "I don't need Native American permission, because I have communication with my spirit guide, and my information comes from the spirit world, not this world." Josie RavenWing, another Anglo shamaness, similarly holds her spirit guide responsible for giving her a sweatlodge ceremony. Moreover, she posed a metaphysical question to which it will certainly be hard to find a response: whose fault is it if superior beings gave similar ceremonies both to the Indians and Westerners?[47]

Some Western seekers refer to the principles of religious freedom and free choice, two of the cornerstones of Western civilization, which, on other occasions, they assail so much. They point out to their Native American critics that the indigenous people hold no copyright on particular rituals and objects. In her debate with a Native American preservationist, Sunshine Garner, a former participant in Sun Bear's tribal rituals, contrasted the free choice and openness of mainstream Christian denominations with the closed nature of indigenous practices:

> If you were to walk into any church in Tacoma to sing and pray with the people, I know you would be welcome. If you then took a Bible home and read and prayed there, no one would probably say you were stealing their religion. If you then shared with friends what you learned in the church and you prayed together, you would likely not find anyone calling you a plastic Christian or an imitation Bible reader.[48]

Although this is a valid comment, one has to remember that, unlike Christianity with its activist missionary agenda, Native American beliefs do not usually include proselytizing.

Many neo-shamanism practitioners are very sensitive to the criticism of Indian preservationists. Medicine Hawk Wilburn, an author who claims Native American descent, is quite sharp in his response to accusations of misappropriating native spirituality: "If you are afraid that a false form of your religion is going to harm your religion in any way, then there is something wrong with your religion."[49] Another Caucasian spiritual seeker calls the exclusion of people of non-Indian descent from Native American ceremonies racism and segregation.[50] Occasionally, metaphysical groups invite Native American representatives to join them in a healing circle to talk over the whole issue. In 1997, Native American spokespeople were invited to a spirituality conference that specifically dealt with the issue of appropriation. During the last day of the conference, participants happily joined each other in the Dance of the Deer, conducted by the famous "Huichol" Indian shaman Brant Secunda, an American of Jewish background from Brooklyn. Watching how Secunda talked about the dance as "one of our more sacred rituals," one invited Indian sniffed in disgust. Another one approached the ritual more philosophically: "People are hungry for ritual. Even if it's all out of context."[51]

The hazardous situation that currently surrounds the whole matter of Native American spirituality warded many seekers of tribal spirituality off their traditional playground—native North America. Nowadays, many members of the nature community bypass Indian reservations and try to tap new dreamlands, which are still unspoiled by the attention of outsiders and where they can conduct their search safely. Among these final frontiers are Mexico, the Amazon rainforest, and the Peruvian Andes. Since the 1990s, they have added to this list Siberia, the motherland of classical shamanism. Bill Pfeiffer, an organizer of mystical tours to Tuva, explained that one of the reasons he became drawn to this small Siberian republic is an increasing difficulty for Westerners to experience shamanic rituals within North American indigenous cultures. In contrast, he stressed, Western spiritual seekers have discovered that Tuvan shamans enthusiastically welcome outsiders. They are ready to involve the visitors in their rituals, serve them as tour guides, and provide cheap accommodation.[52]

This shift in priorities beyond native North America is reflected in neo-shamanism print media. Thus, White, the editor of *Shaman's Drum* magazine, noted a clear and "unfortunate drop" in the number of submitted articles and books for review that cover indigenous North American spiritual traditions. At the same time, he drew attention to the continuing flow of articles on Amazonian *ayahuasca* shamanism. In fact, the supply of incoming *ayahuasca* materials is so extensive that *Shaman's Drum* has to reject many of them. The editor explained this disproportion by the demeanor of South American indigenous experts. Unlike their overvisited and overexplored North American counterparts, they do not yet feel threatened by the attention of outsiders and are willing to cooperate with Western spiritual seekers.[53]

Cultural and Intellectual Blend, North American Style

The situation with the spread of Indian spirituality in wider society is more complicated than it appears to radical busters of the "plastics." It certainly cannot be reduced to a simplistic dichotomy: Indian preservationists against Caucasian "whiteshamans." The problem here is that many Native American and mixed-blood spiritual practitioners do not share the fundamentalist accusations about others' stealing native spirituality. Many of these people came into the picture in the 1970s and 1980s, when Native Americana was coming into fashion in the United States, Canada, and Europe. The popular fascination with Indian culture and spirituality inspired these shamans, who now could place themselves in the contemporary cultural context by referring to such characters as, for example, Castaneda's Don Juan.[54]

Some of these people were not only ready to work with the wider society but also moved into the mainstream body, mind, and spirit culture and began to promote their own teachings and revelations. For example, Medicine Grizzlybear Lake, an eclectic spiritual practitioner of Seneca-Cherokee origin who converted to Yurok spirituality when he moved to California, tries to reach out to wide audiences: "Our tribal medicines, our power centers upon this earth, our ancient ceremonies, and our spiritual forms of knowledge cry out to be used." He makes it very clear that he does not want to fit the profile of a traditional healer, who is usually pictured as living in a remote part of the reservation "waiting to be discovered by an anthropologist or writer or some kind of psychic researcher."[55]

For example, in the 1970s and 1980s, among the Lakota, the archetypical Indians, a whole host of new medicine men sprang up: Wallace Black Elk, Ed McGaa, Archie Fire Lame Deer, Leonard Crow Dog, and others. They began to travel all over the United States and worldwide, trying to cater to the interest in Indian spirituality. For example, Archie Fire Lame Deer turned himself into a global spiritual traveler and teacher, sharing Lakota spirituality with the Sámi people in Scandinavia, the Ainu in Japan, nature groups in Western Europe, and even running sweatlodges for Indian supporters in communist East Germany before the fall of the Berlin Wall.

Another Lakota spiritual practitioner, Wallace Black Elk, attended to the spiritual needs of many kinds of audiences, from college students to celebrities such as John Denver. Incidentally, like many Native American spiritual practitioners, Wallace discovered his healing gifts during the Native American cultural renaissance in the 1970s. His literary collaborator, anthropologist William Lyon, insisted that when Wallace was five years old, elders discovered in him a gift of shamanic healing. The scholar also argued that Wallace was a spiritual descendant of the famous Nicholas Black Elk from *Black Elk Speaks*. In contrast to Lyon, some Lakota Indians pointed out that he began to position himself as a shaman after the famous 1973 Wounded Knee protest occupation, which not only stirred compassion in white America toward the Indians but also aroused wide interest in Native American culture. For publicity purposes, in order to tie his own image to the image of Black Elk, Wallace changed his original name, Black Cow Elk, to Black Elk. This allowed Wallace to relate himself to his celebrated predecessor for promotional purposes. Indeed, in the *Santa Fe New Mexican*, I ran across material that referred to Wallace as a "traditional Lakota elder and descendent [sic] of the legendary Nicholas Black Elk."[56]

Like Wallace, another Lakota, Crow Dog, similarly adopted the role of a spiritual practitioner during the Indian ethnic renaissance in the 1970s. In fact, he came into the national spotlight as one of the leaders of the 1973 Wounded Knee protest occupation. Likewise, he keeps his door open to people of all races and cultures. Crow Dog strongly disagrees with those of his fellow Lakota who want to reserve indigenous ceremonies for internal consumption. He stressed that there is nothing wrong with the Lakota sharing their beliefs with all races because "in the eyes of the Creator, we are all one." He added, "The Spirit really doesn't care what color you are, as long as you are concerned with carrying on the sacred way."[57] Moreover, some Lakota spiritual practitioners of the older generation share the same attitudes. For example, the much-revered Lakota medicine man Frank Fools Crow was always ecumenical in his approach, catering to the needs of spiritual seekers of all descents. Moreover, going against the grain, he continued to share his spirituality despite the emerging preservationist sentiments among the Native Americans of a younger generation. Fools Crow stressed, "The power and ways are given to us to be passed on to others. To think or do anything else is pure selfishness. We only keep them and get more by giving them away, and if we do not give them away we lose them."[58]

Certainly, cast against the idealized blueprint of traditional Indian spirituality as it was described in old ethnographic books and travel narratives, Western spiritual practices that involve Indian symbolism and artifacts appear to be artificial and nontraditional. Essentially, the critics of "plastic shamans" tend to treat recently invented traditions and communities as imaginary and fictitious. It seems that people sometimes forget that an imagined community does not necessarily mean an imaginary community. As soon as spiritual seekers who choose certain paths invent and imagine their practices through print media, workshops, retreats, or Internet network meetings, they become a community. As such, they are certainly traditional. Archaeologist and shamanism practitioner Wallis sarcastically asked: how much time does it take for a new religious path to turn from invented into traditional? Religion historian Philip Jenkins, who in his book explored in detail the modern American fascination with Native American spirituality and who posed a similar question, stressed that a religion is not less valid because it is recently minted or even contains elements of deceit. As an example, he cited the history of the Mormon Church, whose source was the fertile mind of Joseph Smith. Nor does a religion become less authentic if it borrows from another religion, added the scholar.[59]

Downplaying the fact that essentially all cultural traditions were invented in the distant or recent past and undergo constant changes, the critics of "plastic shamans" draw a line between idealized ancient tribal tradition, which is assumed to be genuine, and later modifications, which, for some reason, cannot be authentic. Eclectic combinations molded by Western spiritual seekers out of European, Hindu, or Native American symbolism, and, especially, placing these combinations in a spiritual "New Age" market might shock people who are used to an interpretation of traditional culture as something aged and remote, but that does not prevent this phenomenon from being part of the cultural landscape of the West. Thus, the literary fantasies of writer Lynn

Andrews, who generated the Sisterhood of Shields, are not too much different from other creation myths, which, for example, gave rise to Michael Harner's core shamanism, theosophy, the Mormon Church, American Shakers, or Lakota spirituality with its White Buffalo Woman. All of these religions and spiritualities were set in their time and place. Some of them sprang up recently, whereas others have existed for centuries. It appears to me that the very debate over what constitutes traditional and nontraditional culture does not make much sense. By its very nature, culture does not stay frozen in time and space as a museum artifact. It is a constantly changing organism. It is especially so in our present-day world, which we frequently describe as a global village, where the rapid exchange of cultural traits proceeds in a geometrical progression. Under these circumstances, there is no clear answer to what exactly constitutes traditional native spirituality.

While Deloria, one of the celebrated Native American spokespeople, thinks that the very fact of crossing cultural borders and mixing the trappings from various religious traditions represents the "bastardization" of Native American traditions,[60] others have a different opinion. Loren Cruden, who conducted a survey of contemporary North American native and non-native spiritual practitioners, stressed, "Culturally and spiritually we are all borrowers anyway," and she wrote that spiritual practitioners constantly feed on each other's medicine. She pointed out, for example, that upon their arrival in the American Southwest, the Navajo adopted many Hopi and Pueblo practices. In fact, many Native American cultures have incorporated both Christianity and "New Age" spirituality into their ceremonies.[61] The argument that cultures develop as monoliths is an intellectual fallacy. Voluntary or involuntary exchanges of spiritual and cultural traits are what always generates the development of societies. Whether we like it or not, we are constantly involved in the process of cultural giving and taking. In cultural and spiritual middle grounds, one can see the emergence of new identities, cultures, and subcultures, a process which defies the sentimental notion of perennial traditional cultures.

Incidentally, some Indians of the older generation did not see any contradiction in blending their Indian spirituality with Christianity, which sometimes does not fit the role ascribed to them by younger Native American activists who came to the cultural and political scene during the 1970s as defenders of traditionalism. For example, Russell Means, a Native American spokesperson, argued that Fools Crow, an influential spiritual practitioner born around 1890 and a symbol of Lakota tradition, was never a Christian. In contrast, in his autobiography, Fools Crow stated:

> I am still a practicing Roman Catholic. I go to Mass once or twice
> a month, and receive Holy Communion whenever I can. My first
> wife did not attend church. My second wife, Kate, whom I married in
> 1958, is also a Roman Catholic, and we attend worship services

together. At the same time, we live according to the traditional religious beliefs and customs of our people, and we find few problems with the differences between the two.[62]

The best examples of spiritual blending are peyotism and the Sun Dance. Peyotism, whose rituals are based on Christian theology, is centered on the generation of sacred visions through the sacramental use of the peyote cactus. This spiritual practice spread from northern Mexico to the American Indians of the western United States at the turn of the twentieth century. For the defeated and demoralized Native Americans, peyote as a hallucinogen provided a pharmacological shortcut to spiritual revelation, which earlier the Indians had reached through vision questing, various acts of physical deprivation, dancing, and drumming. The three men who spearheaded the development of peyotism mirror the intercultural essence of this religion. The first was John Wilson, a mixed-blood person of Caddo-Delaware-French ancestry. Incidentally, he had been a Ghost Dance leader, another syncretic religious movement among the Indians of the American West. Wilson received a spiritual revelation that helped him to compose ritual songs of the peyote movement. The second spearhead was the famous Comanche chief Quanah Parker, another person of mixed-blood origin. When he was terminally ill, and all doctors and medicine men gave up on him, a Tarahumara *curandera* (spiritual healer) from Mexico visited him and offered some peyote tea, which brought Parker back to life. After this, he became one of the most ardent promoters of peyote. The third person who helped to institutionalize peyotism as a new religion was James Mooney, an archaeologist from the Smithsonian Institution. Trying to create a niche in which Indian peyote users could follow their path in peace, the scholar brought together influential peyote leaders, wrote for them a charter, and then had peyotism incorporated as the Native American Church.[63] Commenting on the synthetic nature of this church, American historian of religion Philip Jenkins came to the conclusion that, like the modern "New Age," the indigenous peyotism movement is a classic example of a new religious movement.[64]

The story of the Sun Dance (see figure 8.4), one of the most colorful Indian rituals celebrated in the ethnographic literature about traditional Plains Indians, is another example of a cultural mix adjusted to the changing spirit of the times. Unlike peyotism, which wove Christianity into Native American tradition, the Sun Dance was originally a cultural mutation within the Indian tradition. The ceremony emerged sometime between 1750 and 1800 in the Plains area among the Arapahoe, Cheyenne, and Lakota. Throughout the nineteenth century, it was passed around to other Indians and moved westward. As early as the nineteenth century, the ceremony already represented, as anthropologist Leslie Spier put it, a "synthetic product."[65] The Sun Dance has now become popular both among Native Americans who seek to ground themselves as

FIGURE 8.4. Plains Indian Sun Dance rituals drew the attention of many Western seekers of tribal spirituality. This nineteenth-century drawing by an Indian named George Bushotter shows a scene from a Lakota Sun Dance. James O. Dorsey, "A Study of Siouan Cults," in *Eleventh Annual Report of the Bureau of American Ethnology, 1889–1890* (Washington, DC: Government Printing Office, 1894), 462, plate 48.

Indians and among Western spiritual seekers who want to make themselves more tribal.

In its most generic sense, the rite was designed to fulfill the vows given to supernatural forces and was usually timed to the first summer bison hunt when several related communities came together. Near the center of the camp, a tepee was pitched, where shamans instructed pledgers about the meaning of the ceremony and prepared their regalia. Then the mass of people ceremonially fetched the central pole for the dance lodge, in which pledgers then danced, steadily gazing at the sun. The goal was to enter an altered state in order to communicate with supernatural forces. The pledgers moved themselves into this state through extensive physical deprivation: nonstop dancing that sometimes continued for several days and abstinence from food and drink. Among the Lakota, Cheyenne, and Crow, the Sun Dance always included a required element of self-torture, when vision seekers had the flesh of their breasts and backs pierced and then were tethered to the central pole, around which they danced until the flesh gave away.

The goals and forms of the Sun Dance varied among groups. For example, in some cultures, the self-torture was optional. Moreover, the Kiowa Indians did not accept the very idea of shedding blood during the Sun Dance. While among several groups, the ritual looked benevolent and was centered on spiritual renewal, for others, it was an integral part of warfare culture. For example, in the nineteenth century, among the Crow Indians, the Sun Dance carried an important motif of spiritual revenge. If an Indian suffered the loss of a close relative at the hands of an enemy tribe and could not part with his grief, he turned to the Sun Dance, which helped the individual to secure a necessary vision, the important prerequisite for a successful military venture. Aided by his community, such a person danced and inflicted self-torture until he reached an altered state of consciousness and saw the image of a bleeding enemy. With the general decline of the warfare lifestyle on the Plains, the Sun Dance gradually evolved into a healing ritual. Shamans began to use the Sun Dance gatherings for curing people, prophesying, or changing weather. Wind River Shoshone, who picked up the Sun Dance from the Arapahoe Indians in this benevolent form during the reservation days in the 1880s and 1890s, peppered the rite with Christian symbolism. Ironically, in the 1940s, a Wind River Shoshone spiritual practitioner fed the Sun Dance as a healing ritual back to the Crow, who had dropped the Sun Dance in the 1870s, when bison hunting and warfare declined.[66]

Resurrected in the 1970s, the Sun Dance became a powerful tool of the Native American cultural and spiritual renaissance. Thus, radical activists from AIM frequently used Sun Dance gatherings to deliver their political speeches. Moreover, during that decade, the dance spread to other Native American groups that had never practiced the ritual but whose members came to view the Sun Dance as a symbol of being an Indian. The rite attracted attention not only from Native Americans who wanted to root themselves in Indian soil but also from American and Western European countercultural seekers. In a current version of the Sun Dance among the Lakota Indians, such old elements as sun gazing has disappeared because people consider it detrimental to eyesight. At the same time, flesh piercing has remained. Anthropologist Lyon informs us that today people offer their flesh to spirits during the Sun Dance in order to secure the well-being and happiness of friends and relatives, to promote planetary well-being, or to reconnect themselves with the Wakan (holy) force. These perfectly fit the modern nature spirituality stance. One Lakota spiritual practitioner expressed this modern consciousness-oriented approach to the Sun Dance with one sentence: "People dance in order to better understand themselves."[67]

Lakota spiritual practitioners spread the Sun Dance beyond the Plains country to interested Indians and Caucasians. The spiritual practitioner named

Martin High Bear said that he received a spiritual calling to go to the four directions to bring the dance to a wider world. During his missionary trip, he visited Canada and the Pacific states, and in 1981, he started an annual Sun Dance in Oregon near Mt. Hood. The participants included Caucasian spiritual seekers and northwestern Indians, who had never before practiced the Sun Dance. Two other Lakota whom I mentioned earlier, Wallace Black Elk and Crow Dog, similarly disseminated the Sun Dance both among the interested white public and among Indians who had no such tradition of their own. For example, Crow Dog brought the Sun Dance to the desert lands of the Hopi in Arizona. Ironically, among the twenty-nine participants in the 1990 Indian Sun Dance held at the Pine Ridge Reservation, nearly 90 percent were whites.[68] Still, the postmodern story of the Sun Dance does not end here. The ceremony has moved down beyond North America. A group of Mexican Indians, who Sun Danced with Crow Dog in South Dakota in the 1980s, brought the ceremony back home and began to perform it in a Lakota style. Crow Dog's father ideologically sanctioned this cultural blend by telling his community that he had a vision of tepees lining up from South Dakota all the way to Mexico.[69]

While many non-Indian spiritual seekers benefit from Native Americana, there are many Native Americans who receive their inspiration from the "New Age" community and its print culture.[70] This is especially true of detribalized people of indigenous descent who reside in states with rich traditions of esotericism and nature spirituality. Thus, anthropologist Craig Bates stressed that both the pan-Indian tradition and "New Age" culture shape the spirituality of the modern Miwok Indians, mixed-blood people who reside in California. Moreover, their current spiritual practices include ceremonies received from the Zulu shaman Mutwa, who came from Africa and fascinated some of them with his teachings. The Miwok spiritual seekers make tobacco offerings, do smudging on various occasions, and recite their prayers in English. Responding to the public popularity of Native American spirituality, some have declared themselves shamans. Like many other hyphenated Americans, these Miwok spiritual practitioners are anxious to base themselves in ancient culture and usually claim that they received shamanic powers from their ancestors. Although this new Miwok spirituality clearly gives some urbanized Indians a sense of cultural identity, at the same time, it makes them an integral part of the global "New Age" and nature community. Some elders who still carry vague memories of older practices frown upon this sweatlodge and "rainbow" religion. One of them dismissed the spiritual practices of Miwok neo-shamans with the following utterance: "They lost their whole culture and don't know what the hell they're doing."[71]

The presence of metaphors and ideas from the print media of Western esotericism is also visible in the works of many Native American authors or writers who speak on behalf of Native Americans. For example, Robert Lake, a

California-based spirituality writer of American Indian descent, widely uses concepts of transpersonal psychology, heavily relies on the scholarship of Carl Jung and Bruno Bettelheim, and integrates into his manuals on Native American spirituality numerous Western holistic therapies. Lake came to California in the 1970s to work in the ethnic studies program at Humboldt State University, married a Yurok woman, recast himself into a spiritual teacher named Medicine Grizzlybear Lake, and began to speak on behalf of Yurok and Native Americans in general. Anthropologist Thomas Buckley, who explored the content of Lake's books, noted that his writings essentially reflect the environmental concerns of the wider society and the sentiments of the "New Age" people, who represent the major segment of Humboldt State University students.[72]

One of the best examples of the influence of the mind, body, and spirit culture and scholarship on Native Americans is Lakota writer Dr. Allen Ross, with whom I briefly corresponded at the end of the 1980s. In 1989, he released *Mitakuye Oyasin: "We Are All Related."*[73] Allen stressed that he embarked on the "Indian path" after a landmark meeting with Indian fans from Germany, where he was stationed as a G.I. For many reasons, which for the lack of space I cannot detail here, in Europe Germans stand out as the people who are most attracted to Native Americana.[74] The country has groups and clubs that reenact North American Indian rituals and ceremonies. Ross made friends with one such group, which prompted him to learn more about his own culture and spirituality. After coming back to the United States in 1974, he trod the same route many detribalized American Indians went during the Indian renaissance in the 1970s. He participated in his first sweatlodge ceremony, went on a vision quest, and became part of a Sun Dance circle. Yet, his "red road" did not end there. While learning about indigenous spirituality, Ross began to teach "Philosophy and Native American Beliefs" at the University of Colorado, took a course in Jungian psychology, and discovered profound similarities between Carl Jung's ideas and Lakota philosophy. Eventually, Ross ended up by earning a doctorate in psychology.

In *Mutakuye Oyasin*, Ross not only provided a popular description of Jungian psychology but also looked into parapsychology and brain studies from a "Sioux point of view." Throughout the book, he recast Native American symbolism in the light of particular ideas of Western esotericism. Thus, according to Ross, the Native Americans who stay on the Red Road believe that reincarnation and famous Atlantis represent a body of knowledge that originated from Native America. In the chapter titled with the Lakota phrase *Taka Wakan Skan Ska* ("something sacred is moving"), the writer described the coming of the extraterrestrial. The "blossoming tree" from the famous vision of the Lakota shaman Black Elk became a metaphor for the chakras. Lakota *heyoka*, the contrary sacred clowns, turned out to be masters of telekinesis. Finally, he was convinced that the reverence of the sacred White Buffalo is a manifestation of Taurus worship. Integrating Lakota knowledge into the realm of Western metaphysical scholarship, Ross concluded, "Searching for my roots and my identity, I discovered that the Amerindian traditional rituals were really close to astrology and to the Jungian concept of synchronicity."[75]

There is no doubt that both Native American fundamentalists and Western scholars who are concerned about preserving the authenticity of native cultures will either ignore such works as aberrations or, worse, dismiss them as attempts to appropriate and corrupt American Indian spirituality. Still, somehow I feel uncomfortable when I read that a French anthropologist, who did some fieldwork among the Pine Ridge Lakota, called Ross and like-minded writers "vampire authors" who do not fit the very substance of their indigenous culture and endanger its survival.[76] I have intentionally drawn attention to the Ross book in order to show that its content surely looks bizarre if cast against such classical texts as, for example, *Black Elk Speaks*. Yet this does not make *Mutakuye Oyasin* less Indian or traditional unless one subscribes to the blueprint of the archetypical Indian locked in nineteenth-century culture. The Ross book appears to me as representative of an intellectual globalization of Lakota and Native American spirituality. One can find views similar to those expressed by Ross in the books and articles of other authors who speak on behalf of Native Americans. Obviously, there exists a common cultural and intellectual setting that engages both natives and non-natives and makes such people as Ross the representatives simultaneously of their native cultures and of modern Western esotericism. Incidentally, there are also other Lakota Jungians and Jungians from other Indian cultures, who similarly phrase their spiritualities in familiar Western metaphysical metaphors.[77]

If one compares the philosophical message of "New Age" print media with that of native authors who write on American Indian spiritualities, one will find between them more similarities than differences. Such similarities are natural because both natives and non-natives tap the same line in the Western intellectual tradition, which is grounded in Romanticism, antirationalism, metaphysics, the philosophy of nature (*Naturphilosophie*), and the negative view of modernity. All of them assume that Native American ethics is morally superior to Western culture on every count and share the belief that Indian earth-based values can reshape Western culture.[78]

The most powerful of these common sentiments that transcend cultural and ethnic borders were expressed in the essay "American Land Ethic" (1970) by Native American fiction writer N. Scott Momaday. Stressing that American society should stop polluting the environment and respect Mother Earth, Momaday talked about all Americans and explicitly used the expression "we" without separating people into natives and non-natives: "we Americans need now more than ever before—and indeed more than we know—to imagine who and what we are with respect to the earth and sky. I am talking about an act of the imagination, essentially, and the concept of an American land ethics."[79] The writer directly called on all Americans to learn from tribal wisdom. At that time, people were not yet involved in the contest over the use of Native Americana. Hence, the author could send this message to go and learn from Native Americans. During the same years, Deloria praised Storm's *Seven Arrows* (1972) that, along with Castaneda's books, stimulated public interest in Native American spirituality. Deloria particularly credited Storm for educating Americans about land ethics.[80]

Incidentally, Deloria's major books, *God Is Red* (1973), *The Metaphysics of Modern Existence* (1979), *Red Earth, White Lies: Native Americans and the Myth of Scientific Fact* (1995), and the most recent, *Spirit and Reason* (1999), are vivid examples of that antirationalist and antimodernist line of thought I have described above.[81] Drawing on the writings of Western metaphysical authors, Deloria crusaded against the Enlightenment and frowned upon hard science, logic, and reason. It is notable that he informed his readers that his dissatisfaction with "Orthodox science" began when he read *Worlds in Collision* (1950) by Immanuel Velikovsky. This scholar argued that some miracles described in the Bible were real events initiated by the collision of planets with the earth. Following the popular stereotype of the ecological/spiritual Indian, Deloria portrayed Native American history as an Indian version of the Christian Fall. In his books, pre-Columbian America appears as a paradise populated by nature-loving native people, whose spirituality and earth-based lifestyles were destroyed by corrupt European societies. In a popular brochure dealing with "Native American spirituality," I ran across an assertion that, in fact, it is unimportant whether that paradise really existed or not. What matters is that "it is mystically true—that the story carries power and resonance."[82] Incidentally, reproduced thousands of times in print media, the view of the pre-Columbian Americas as a spiritual and ecological paradise became part of the intellectual mainstream.

Merlin's Call: Western Shamanism in Search of Indigenous European Spirituality

Within Western nature spirituality circles, many people accept the Native American criticism of "plastic shamans" as valid and sound. Although Native Americana continues to enjoy popularity among Western seekers, the controversy over its use has made many of them look for other forms of spirituality that could provide a steadier ground. Overall, currently there is a growing realization that American Indian rites and symbols cannot make non-Indian spiritual practitioners more indigenous. Thus, since the end of the 1980s, the general trend among Western seekers has been to move away from a reliance on Native American symbolism and toward the pre-Christian heritage of Europe. American Studies scholar Dagmar Wernitznig, who with her keen Marxist eye explored what American and European spiritual wannabes have been doing for the past twenty years, informed us in her brochure that the "turning into an Indian" trend is now on a steady decline.[83]

The lingering concerns about incorporating Native Americana occasionally spill into the dreams and visionary experiences of spiritual practitioners. For example, it could be a Native American character or a character from European folklore that visits a seeker and instructs him or her to drop the Indian path and step on the indigenous European road. For Fred Gustafson, a Jungian analyst who received much of his spiritual inspiration from Lakota philosophy, the concern about partaking of Native American spirituality resurfaced in a dream:

> I saw a fine pair of beaded moccasins that were just like the ones I had been looking for. They were light-colored, of a blue-tan tone. I picked them up and saw the price was $40. I knew I already had $20 on me. Money was not the issue though. I needed to see what size they were but could not find the marking for the size. If anything, I was not concerned for the price but I feared they were too large for me.[84]

A Jungian scholar who, like many of his colleagues, looks at the surrounding world through the eyes of dream experience, Gustafson became seriously worried about whether he would be able to live up to the form of the spirituality he had selected.

In the case of John Matthews, who writes much on Celtic shamanism, it was a dream encounter with an Indian shaman named Old Man. Before this, fascinated with Native American spirituality, Matthews devoured *Black Elk Speaks* (1932) and *Book of the Hopi* (1969) by Frank Waters and eventually came to the United States to learn more about the wisdom of the people he liked so much. Matthews explained that during this visit, the Old Man repeatedly visited him in lucid dreams and finally instructed that Matthews must seek his own native shamanism in Britain. After retuning home, Matthews became convinced that the old Celtic mythology he had explored earlier was what represented the last vestige of indigenous shamanism in the British Isles. American spiritual practitioner Frank MacEowan had a similar experience. While participating in a Lakota-style Sun Dance, he became aware of his Celtic ancestors. The ancestors prompted him to seek spiritual wisdom not in Indian country but in the Celtic realm.[85]

Writer Edred Thorsson, a student of Nordic spirituality, stressed that despite their sincere and persistent emulations of non-Western beliefs, Euro-Americans will not be able to find any spiritual authenticity unless they turn to their own traditions. He suggested that ancient Teutonic magic might help

Europeans to recover their "lost souls." The Jungian scholar Daniel Noel similarly pointed out that Western neo-shamans who find inspiration in Native American spirituality or other non-Western culturally bound practices will never feel secure until they turn to their own native sources located in pre-Christian traditions. In *The Soul of Shamanism* (1997), which traces the countercultural, anthropological, and literary sources of present Western shamanism, Noel accepted Deloria's criticism of the "plastics" and alerted readers to the dangers of misappropriating indigenous cultural property. The scholar also used the character of Merlin as a metaphor (archetypical role model) to underline that the Western culture does have images and models that are ancient enough to serve as inspirations and to help shape vital indigenous Euro-American shamanism. Among other candidates for archetypical models of European shamans are Odin, one of the major Nordic deities, Orpheus from Greek mythology, Dr. Faust from European medieval folklore, and several others.[86]

Current versions of Western neo-shamanism increasingly look into European pre-Christian traditions, frequently invoking the symbolism of Celtic and Nordic folklore. Pointing out to his white colleagues the relevance of these traditions, a spiritual practitioner of Native American descent stressed, "The Celts and Teutons with their complex spiritualities, were the 'Indians' of Europe."[87] During his speaking tour of Germany, Churchill, a radical critic of "plastic shamans," similarly alerted his audiences to the fact that "everyone is indigenous somewhere," recommending that his listeners dig for their ancient premodern roots to uncover in themselves Anglo-Saxons, Huns, Goths, and Visigoths.[88] It does not mean that Native American symbolism has been totally discarded. Although in individual spiritual practices, Native Americana might merge with reconstructed pre-Christian European spirituality along with elements picked up from other traditions, the European connection in neo-shamanism is growing to be more visible.

One can see the shifting spiritual priorities, from Native Americana to European ancient folklore, in the utterances of Michael Bromley, a shamanic practitioner and writer from Britain. Like many other seekers of tribal spiritual wisdom, he began his path by tapping American Indian symbolism. He says that he received his current spiritual name, Growling Bear, from a Lakota medicine woman who sensed his "bear energy." Subsequently, Bromley experimented with Indian rituals and artifacts. Yet, in his 1997 book, *Spirit Stones*, Bromley purposely moved away from Indian spirituality, tying himself to his native soil:

> I consider myself a modern-day shaman; I practice a craft
> that is as valid today as when it first began. Unlike most other sha-
> mans throughout the world, I have no shamanic lineage, no conti-
> nuity of father-to-son teaching and understanding of spiritual

teachings and ceremonies. I call myself a Celtic shaman because
the Celts were very old and spiritual people who lived over a vast area
including England. I am English and want to keep my own identity; I do not wish to pretend to be Indian.[89]

Wabun Wund (Marlise James), a writer who, at the turn of the 1970s, fell under the spell of Sun Bear and who later became his wife and one of the leaders
of the Bear Tribe, Inc., came to a similar conclusion. After being for twenty
years on the spirituality path, much of which was informed by Native American
symbolism, she noted, "One thing I learned is that you can't jump cultures. I
learned to accept myself for what I am, a white woman of Welsh-American
heritage, and to take what I learn and make it my own."[90]

One of the first texts that made an attempt to break away from Native
American and other non-Western cultural settings and to chart the European
way for Western seekers is a novel, *The Way of Wyrd: Tales of an Anglo-Saxon
Sorcerer* (1983), by psychologist and writer Brian Bates.[91] Like many texts of the
apprenticeship genre, this text capitalized on Carlos Castaneda's Don Juan
books. Moreover, *The Way of Wyrd* cloned Castaneda's format and even
phrasing. Like Carlos and Don Juan, two major characters of the novel, Wulf
and Brand are involved in numerous mind games. Spiritual exercises that
the sorcerer sets for Brand also look like remakes of the riddles Don Juan
offered to Carlos. Like their literary predecessors, Wulf and Brand demonstrate
superhuman leaps, hunt power plants, lose their souls to predatory spirits, and
interact with "luminous beings." At the same time, one will not find in this
book a Mexican desert, Amazon jungles, or other non-Western settings popular in spirituality print culture in the 1960s and 1970s. The plot of *The Way of
Wyrd* is firmly set in tenth-century Britain and describes the apprenticeship of
a Christian monk, Brand, with Anglo-Saxon sorcerer Wulf. Sent by his supe-
riors to learn about the heathen world view in order to successfully combat it,
Brand goes to a pagan habitat deep in the British woods and attaches himself to
Wulf. However, in the process of his learning, Brand gradually comes to the
realization that the sacred includes not only the Christian God but all of animated nature. As a result, he expands his spiritual consciousness. Without
denouncing Christianity, he comes to embrace paganism. The particular spark
that unleashed Bates's creative fantasy and eventually prompted him to write
this book was an early medieval manuscript that described sacred charms and
healing remedies, whose sources might have been in pre-Christian tradition.

Essentially, by creating a healing fiction grounded in European tradition,
Bates showed that Western seekers can construct their own indigenous spirituality by using imagination even with meager historical and folkloric resources on European pagan traditions. As such, this text certainly became
another tale of power for European and American seekers interested in making themselves more tribal. *The Way of Wyrd* proves the point made by Jean

Markale, a French student of Celtic tradition, who once stressed that "although somewhat battered by centuries of rejection if not outright combat, this [pagan] Western tradition exists and is perfectly youthful and ready to nourish those who are able to ask."[92]

Many neo-shamanism seminars and workshops clearly shifted to rituals and beliefs drawn from Nordic or Celtic mythology, literature, and folklore. As a result, in many Western countries, what is now known as neo-shamanism more often than not feeds on European tradition rather than on Native American or other non-Western symbolism. For example, in Sweden, shamanism practitioners who were originally inspired by Native Americana came to appreciate their own indigenous Nordic shamanic tradition at the end of the 1980s. One of them pointed out that now, in their spiritual journeys to the upper world, his friends would more likely meet Odin than the Great Spirit Wakan Tanka. He also added, "Nordic shamanism lives an independent life again without any need for crutches from the Turtle Island."[93]

For those who situate themselves in the Nordic tradition, the inspiration comes mostly from Scandinavian sagas, from which spiritual practitioners usually single out the ritual of *seidr*. *Seidr* is a séance of ancient Scandinavian divination in an altered state, which appears to Western seekers to be an analogue to the classic shamanic session of Siberia.[94] Another important source is early medieval Old English, Irish, and Welsh poetry and folklore, which serve for the construction of Celtic spirituality or Celtic shamanism. In this case, Druids, Celtic priests, are viewed as analogous to Native American or classical northern Asian shamans. Moreover, some seekers build not only cross-cultural analogues but also try to establish genetic links among the folklore and spirituality of various cultures stretched out over the Eurasian vast spaces, from Siberia to Western Europe. For example, drawing on the Eliade book, French poet and philosopher Markale talks about the unity of Northern European and northern Asian spiritual traditions, which he contrasts with South Asian and Mediterranean traditions.[95]

Modern spiritual seekers who set themselves within the Celtic tradition (see figure 8.5) also see the evidence of altered states in the ancient practice of the "cell of song" that was known in Wales, Scotland, and Ireland until the seventeenth century. To induce creative inspiration, the traditional singers from these areas relegated themselves for a day and a night to a windowless cellar where, with their heads wrapped in cloths, they experienced what we can call sensory deprivation, which triggered altered states and visionary experiences analogous to those of classical shamanism.[96] Archaeological sites and artifacts interpreted as evidence of pre-Christian pagan tradition provide another source for current seekers of ancient European spirituality. For example, such famous English sites as Stonehenge and Averby are spiritually meaningful to many members of nature religions, including neo-shamanism practitioners.

FIGURE 8.5. Celtic shamans receive certificates as path masters during a spiritual retreat in North Carolina, 2004. Photograph by the author.

It is notable that, like the Native American tradition, for some Western seekers, the reconstructed European earth-based traditions embody model spirituality and morality. Thus, in his text, which is widely used as a manual by practitioners of Celtic shamanism, D. J. Conway pointed out to us, "A dynamic, fearless, brilliant people, the Celts learned from all the other civilizations with which they came in contact. For example, legends point to the possible use of yoga techniques and knowledge of the chakras, or light centers, of the astral body." We also learned from him that, compared to their neighbors, the Celts went as far as to grant more rights to their women.[97] One might debate if the Celts truly had all these qualities. What appears to be true here is that the picture drawn by Conway matches closely the current sentiments and expectations of many spiritual seekers.

Unfortunately, in contrast to modern Native American and Siberian ethnographies, which contain plenty of materials to serve as spiritual inspiration, the relevant European records are scarce and heavily loaded with Christianity. The millennia-long dominance of the Judeo-Christian tradition has left little of what had existed prior to this. Transpersonal psychologist Jurgen Kremer, who contemplates how to make European and American minds more tribal, lamented that now there is hardly any visible tradition on which to build a Western nature spirituality.[98] Since Westerners, as he said, were "out of their indigenous mind" for so long, now it is hard to separate pre-Christian spirituality from later Christian layers in existing records. For example, Scandinavian sagas, on which we build our knowledge of ancient Nordic beliefs, were recorded by Christian monks in the thirteenth and fourteenth centuries and were naturally infused with biased attitudes toward pre-Christian traditions. Moreover, as much as some seekers want it, it is hard in these records to peel off the Christian layers from earlier pagan ones simply because the Nordic society the sagas describe (between the ninth and thirteenth centuries) was in a state of transition from paganism to Christianity. Therefore, Judeo-Christian tradition had already made deep inroads into the life of Northern Europeans and set non-Christian spiritual practitioners on the fringe.[99]

For example, in many Scandinavian sagas, pagan spiritual practitioners appear as marginalized figures, sometimes with negative features, which certainly tells us more about contemporary Christian attitudes to the Nordic shamans than about heathen ceremonies. Those writers who transcribed and translated Nordic sagas in the eighteenth and nineteenth centuries further altered the content of these records. Scholar and shamanism practitioner Jenny Blain pointed out that the nineteenth-century translators rendered old Germanic terminology used to describe heathen practices in negative terms. As an example, she gave the poem *Voluspa*, which contains a passage on "women magic," which is open to various interpretations. For example, one of these translations goes as follows:

> Heith she was hight whereto houses she came
> The wise seeress, and witchcraft plied
> Cast spells where she could, cast spells on the mind:
> To wicked women she was welcome ever.

Blain concluded that these might have been the words that were composed, written down, and then translated in different eras, but they can mean different things to different people. As a spiritual practitioner, Blain tries to recover the archaic content of that and other passages. Drawing our attention to the fact that, among many modern tribal people, negative and positive magic were never separated, she translated the text in benevolent terms, adjusting it to the current sentiments of pagan communities:

> Heith she was called when to houses she came,
> Volva well-foretelling, empowering staffs;
> Seid she practiced Seid with thought playing,
> Joy was she ever to despairing women.[100]

Another important thing to remember is that the records that describe archaic European spirituality are scarce and cannot give us a consistent picture of European beliefs in the early Middle Ages. For example, there are bits and pieces of information on and references to the *seidr* practice, but there is only one record that provides a more or less complete description of this divination session. This passage from the *Saga of Eirik the Red*, which is often quoted and frequently reenacted by modern spiritual practitioners, detailed a séance of a divination performed by the ancient Icelandic prophetess (*volva*) who came to Greenland to predict the fate of the local Viking community struck by a famine.[101] Here is an excerpt from this passage that described the appearance of the medicine woman:

> There was a woman there in the Settlement whose name was
> Thorbjorg; she was seeress and was called the Little Sibyl. She
> had nine sisters, all of them seeresses, but now only she was left alive.
> It was Thorbjorg's practice of a winter to attend feasts, and those men
> in particular invited her to their homes who were curious to know
> their fate or the season's prospects. Because Thorkel was the lead-
> ing householder there it was thought to be his responsibility to find
> out when these hard times which now troubles [*sic*] them would
> cease, so he invited her to his home, and a good reception was pre-
> pared for her, as was the custom when a woman of this kind should
> be received. A high-seat was made ready for her, and a cushion
> laid down, on which there must be hen's feathers.
> When she arrived in the evening . . . she was wearing a blue
> cloak with straps which was set with stones right down to the hem;
> she had glass beads about her neck, and on her head a black lamb-
> skin hood lined inside with white catskin. She had a staff in her hand,
> with a knob on it; it was ornamented with brass and set around
> with stones just below the knob. Round her middle she wore a belt
> made of touchwood, and it was [a] big skin pouch in which she kept
> those charms of hers which she needed for her magic. On her feet
> she had hairy calf-skin shoes with long thongs, and on the thong-
> ends big knobs of lateen. She had on her hands catskin gloves which
> were white inside and hairy.

This particular account became a blueprint for many Western spiritual practitioners who seek to ground their techniques in Nordic spirituality and replicate the *seidr* séance. Like Little Sybil, they climb to erected high platforms and perform prophetic sessions accompanied by the drumming and singing of their friends.

The legendary Germanic deity Odin similarly appears as the archetype of the ancient Nordic shaman (see figure 8.6). Particularly, from the *Edda* we learn that he hung on a tree with no food or water for nine days, which appears

FIGURE 8.6. Nordic deity Odin. For many Western spiritual seekers, he is an archetype of the pre-Christian European shaman. Mary E. Litchfield, *The Nine Worlds: Stories from Horse Mythology* (Boston and London: Ginn, 1890), 12–13.

as an act of self-inflicted physical deprivation in order to induce visionary experiences.[102] From the saga, one also learns that eventually Odin received a spiritual revelation—the mystery of eighteen runic spells, which contained the secrets of immortality, self-healing, control over elements, success in love, and winning over one's enemies. Prior to the 1970s, except for a few scholars, hardly anybody assessed this kind of folklore as reflecting shamanic experiences. In the present context, informed by a keen attention to altered states, such records appear to be descriptions of shamanism.

Since references in early medieval records to pagan European practices are not many, it is natural that, in constructing their indigenous spirituality, Western spiritual practitioners rely heavily on their own imaginations. Tira Brandon-Evans (see figures 8.7a and 8.7b), the founder of the North American–based Society of Celtic Shamans, enlightened me about how she screens the available old Irish, Welsh, and Scottish texts for vestiges of pre-Christian traditions. Brandon-Evans stressed that her vision of these records is exclusively her own interpretation, which is not "sacred knowledge" designed

FIGURE 8.7a. Tira Brandon-Evans, one of the path masters in the Society of Celtic Shamans. Photographs by the author.

for emulation by all other SCS members. First of all, in contrast to Conway,[103] the current dean in the field of applied Celtic spirituality, she openly admitted that there was hardly any such thing as Celtic shamanism in the past. Brandon-Evans noted that she and her friends are constructing a new tradition, which they call shamanic and which is based on their rereading of early medieval folklore and on personal visionary experiences, which reveal to them specific rituals and practices. For example, she repeatedly stressed to me that she receives instructions about particular ceremonies from her spiritual advisor, "grandfather Merlin." Hers and her friends' approaches to the old tradition Brandon-Evans outlined as follows: "We are recreating remembering our traditions."

Tira Brandon-Evans also detailed to me how and where she ran across the word "shamanism" for the first time and described her self-induction into

FIGURE 8.7b.

Celtic shamanism. As in the case of many Western neo-shamanism practitioners, there was some Native American connection:

> When I was eleven I read a book about Sequoyah [the famous
> nineteenth-century Indian who invented the Cherokee alphabet], and
> I met there a word "shaman" that was applied to someone who was
> obviously doing what I was doing [a reference to visionary experi-
> ences she had as a girl]. And then I said to myself, "Oh, good, now
> I know what it is called." Then I started going in the [other] world. I
> was looking specifically for an Indian shaman. In the other world,
> I was looking for a guide who was an Indian because I thought
> that the shamans were all Indians. And then the Indian ancestors
> I met in the other world made it clear to me that I had to go and
> find my own tribe. I was not admitted to their circle. And at first, it
> was very confusing to me. I did not understand how all people on
> earth had their guardian spirit.

Sometime in the early 1990s, in a small town's bookstore, Brandon-Evans
stumbled upon a book named *Taliesin: Shamanism and the Bardic Tradition in
Britain and Ireland* by John Matthews:[104] "it did not even have the term 'Celtic
shaman' on the cover, but the instant I saw 'shaman' and the 'bardic tradition' I
went, 'Ah! Oh! Of course!' Before it never occurred to me that shamanism is
completely native and aboriginal to the place, to the tribe." This particular book
and follow-up readings convinced Brandon-Evans that there was the opportunity

to find her native roots or, as she likes to say, to "find our feet." Thus, this literary encounter eventually prompted her to embark on the path of Celtic shamanism. Although the secondary literature written by the members of pagan and neo-shamanism communities is important for her spiritual growth, Brandon-Evans stressed that, for the reconstruction of Celtic shamanism, she prefers to go straight to original sources:

> I am one of these people who if they study something do not like to read what other people have to say about it. I like to read original sources. Of course, I do not have languages. So I have to read them in translations, which means they are filtered. There is a body of literature that conveys Celtic tradition in a diluted Christian form. Still, if you look, you could see.

The sifting of early medieval sources for pagan Celtic elements is a combination of rational thinking and spiritual experiences. Explaining how it works for her, Brandon-Evans said:

> You read and then you think and then you journey. So that is what I do—I read and I contemplate on what I have read and what could that have meant, rationally. All human beings are pretty much the same [the] world over. We all want the same things. The people living in the place we call, for example, the British Isles, in their beliefs about their land would vary from, say, the Altai, because it is a different land. But still it would be about the same basic thing: the earth is our mother. And the sun is a wonderful great thing that gives us life. And the moon is beautiful and mysterious. We live in the same world although not in the same place. So given that, when I read the stories, then I say, "OK, if I've lived then before the Romans came..." And then after I've done that, then I go in the [other] world, and say, "Show me."

That is how, according to Brandon-Evans, particular Celtic rituals and ceremonies descend on her from the otherworld reality.

Describing the otherworld reality she visits on her shamanic journeys in search for particular answers, Tira Brandon-Evans compared it with a beautiful place that has many gates, into which she has to find her own entrance: "It is a process, and it is also subjective. You see, our tradition is broken, and we try to mend it. So, what I discover, see and then contemplate on may be true for others but it may be not. I would never presume to tell anyone that my way of looking at the Celtic tradition is the only way." Despite this personalized approach to her spirituality, some elements of Celtic tradition she found during her spiritual journeys have evolved into established rituals and ceremonies. I noticed, for example, that before doing a water initiation for me, a young shy girl, one of the recently inducted Celtic path masters who have apprenticed with Brandon-Evans, pulled from her pocket a small piece of paper that listed the sequence of the initiation steps. The girl apologized to us for not yet being well versed in the scenario of this ritual, which essentially represented a guided meditation, during which I and another participant, an African-American woman who is interested in Germanic traditions, were taken on a spiritual journey to the "water pool" of wisdom.

In a similar manner, leaders of other pagan and neo-shamanic groups mold their individual spiritual experiences into collective rituals. For example, in her instructional materials for *seidr* journeys, Diana Paxson, an informal leader of the neopagan group Hrafner, expects people to encounter particular Nordic symbols. In her map of the Nordic sacred geography, this fiction writer from the San Francisco Bay area outlined the whole scenario of the spiritual journey, including the details of the magic landscape and the particular characters whom spiritual seekers are expected to encounter. Paxton explained such detailed mapping of the otherworldly reality as an attempt to prompt *seidr* workers to think in terms of cultural symbols from Northern European mythology.

Here is a short excerpt from her long guidelines. The spiritual journey begins in Midgard, a world parallel to ordinary reality. At the center of Midgard, one finds the famous world tree Yggdrasil (see figure 8.8). Then she details:

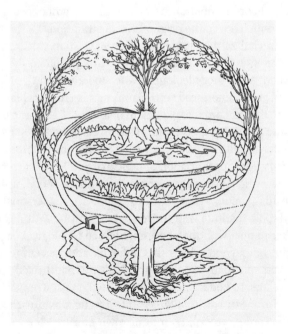

FIGURE 8.8. Yggdrasil, the sacred world tree in Scandinavian mythology, is one of the essential symbols for those Western seekers who pursue Nordic shamanism. J. H. Philpot, *The Sacred Tree; or, The Tree in Religion and Myth* (London: Macmillan, 1897), 115.

The entrance to the underworld lies to the north, where primal ice and fire met to produce the mists of Niflheim. There, beneath
the level of Midgard, lies the well called Hvergelmir, the boiling
cauldron, source of the river Gjöll (roaring, resounding). Here, perhaps is also where we encounter the dog Gram, who must be fed
before the traveler can continue on.

Bean, a spiritual practitioner who partook of this sacred geography, explained
that materials for her manual come not only from the texts of Nordic sagas and
folklore but also from Hilda Davidson's *Gods and Myths of Northern Europe*
(1964), a scholarly book that is very popular in pagan and nature communities.
Although some spiritual practitioners object to such detailed scenarios, which
might ruin the spontaneity and impromptu nature of shamanism, others accept them as a helpful framework.[105]

Those seekers who try to root themselves in native European soil by invoking ancient Nordic symbolism sometimes have to deal with the legacy of the
abuse of this symbolism by the Nazi regime in Germany. It is well known that
in order to mold its ideology, National Socialism widely appealed to Northern
European pagan symbols. For instance, the official symbol of the SS troops was
the oak leaf, which stood for the regenerative powers of nature. The notorious swastika, the core symbol of the Nazi regime, symbolized good luck and
was associated with Thor in the original Nordic tradition.[106] The Nazi ideology
also sought to revitalize the old deities of pre-Christian Northern Europe, advocated the reverence of nature, and strove to link people to their organic soil.
Alfred Rosenberg and other ideologists who stood behind the Nazi Nordic renaissance movement denounced Christianity as a corrupt and false spirituality,
contrasting it to the vital organic paganism of ancient Germanic tribes. Overall,
the Nazi regime cultivated a deep animosity toward the Judeo-Christian tradition and Western civilization in general and harbored strong antimodern
sentiments. This Nazi appropriation of pre-Christian European symbolism has
compromised Nordic spirituality in the eyes of many liberal-oriented people.

Based on his personal experience, Kremer, a transpersonal psychologist
from the Saybrook Institute, reminded us how troubling it might be for the
Western seeker to deal with the above-mentioned ideological baggage. A German by origin, he currently lives in California and was originally drawn to
Native American spirituality and the print culture that thrived around it. Like
many other seekers, to better anchor his spiritual quest, Kremer later began to
move toward European spirituality. Yet, at first, he was unsure about the incorporation of Nordic symbolism into his own spiritual life. A few times, he
grabbed the books of Scandinavian sagas and put them back on the shelf:
"How can I confront my Nordic heritage when the scars inflicted by Nordic
people are so unresolved? Why should I read Norse mythology when Hitler has
abused it so terribly? How can I be German and honest about being German—

when there appears to be nothing in German myth which can nourish me?"[107] Torn by all these doubts, Kremer came to hate the place he was born (Germany) and the education he received (Western Enlightenment curriculum). Still, understanding that there was no way to escape from his heritage, Kremer eventually had to dip into one of the *Edda* poems. Ultimately, he realized that the road to European tribal consciousness would be a long bumpy road because he would have to go through the painful legacy of Auschwitz, past Hitler, past neo-Nazis, past Wotan, past Heidegger, past Jung, and also past Christianization to "whatever may lie beyond."[108]

For some people, the mere mention of European paganism or Odin automatically serves as a red flag, a movement in a dangerous direction. Thus, after White, the editor of *Shaman's Drum*, suggested that Western spiritual seekers follow in the footsteps of Odin, reader Hal Litoff became immediately concerned about the implications of this statement. Litoff pointed out that Odin was a warrior god, which, in his view, contradicted the benevolent nature of modern Western shamanism. He noted that Odin was included in the state religion of Nazi Germany and served as the foundation for the occult practices of Heinrich Himmler's SS. Litoff's particular fear was that following a shaman's path by using such symbols as Odin might be a truly Faustian bargain. In his reply, White noted that Odin was not so much a god of war as first and foremost the god of prophecy. As such, he continued, this deity manifested the Nordic shamanic vision-questing tradition and can be safely restored without bringing back Norse war practices. Interestingly, White used as an analogy the Plains Indians' Sun Dance. Originally linked to the Indian warfare tradition, in the hands of modern Indian and Western spiritual seekers, it evolved into a benevolent ritual of renewal and the continuation of life.[109]

It is notable that, as early as 1936, Carl Gustav Jung, later one of the intellectual icons of the modern esotericism and many nature communities, anticipated such a future countercultural adjustment of Odinism. Reflecting on the active engagement of ancient Germanic symbolism by the Nazis, he stressed:

> Wotan [Odin] must, in time, reveal not only the restless, violent, stormy side of his character, but also his ecstatic and mantic qualities, a very different aspect of his nature. If this conclusion is correct, National Socialism would not be the last word. Things must be concealed in the background which we cannot imagine at present, but we may expect them to appear in the course of the next few years or decades.[110]

Jung also pointed to the venues spiritual seekers might search to recover their indigenous selves. In fact, Jung, whose scholarship is concerned with the retrieval of the archetypes of consciousness, provided direct or indirect intellectual inspiration for many people in Western esotericism, including neo-shamanism. Before Western intellectual culture shifted in the direction of antirationalism, he had already outlined many ideas that later became woven into spirituality practices and print culture. One of the most appealing aspects of Jungian scholarship is the premise that, despite all of the civilized layers, the Westerner essentially remains an archaic man. Jung stressed that, although destructive, the Judeo-Christian tradition did not totally wipe out all routes to the sacred in the West. It simply drove the sacred underground to the realm of the unconscious. Here, spirituality continues to linger in the form of various collective archetypes. According to Jung, the most powerful manifestation of these archetypes is mythology. The way to recover archaic spirituality is to learn how to nourish personal imagination and creative fantasy, which reopen the unconscious. That is how spirituality comes back to one's life.

The manner in which Jung handled non-Western spirituality also offers guidelines which many current spiritual seekers interested in the retrieval of pre-Christian European traditions find useful. Thus, paying tribute to classical Oriental and tribal spirituality, including Native American traditions, the founder of analytic psychology never suggested that non-Western beliefs be emulated or replicated by Westerners as a way to repair a spiritual life profaned by modern civilization. Moreover, Jung discouraged Europeans and Americans from transplanting such practices as Zen Buddhism or yoga to the Western soil. He surmised that, pulled out from their native ground and removed to the Western realm, these practices would become meaningless. The scholar implied that Europeans concerned about their roots should look into their own indigenous spirituality and mythology; the alien tradition can be helpful to situate one's spiritual experiences, but the materials should be indigenous. In 1934, in one of his letters, Jung warned his followers, "The Western road to health must be built upon Western groundwork with Western symbols, and be formed from Western material."[111]

9
Back to Siberia

Adventures of the Metaphor in Its Motherland

I swear by storms and sufferings of the earth,
No more superstitions.
I grew out of them! I got power!
Get out sorcery! Be gone!
Shamanism, be gone!

—Sakha poet Platon Oiunskii,
"Red Shaman" (1925)

One strike of a drumstick at a drum will turn over all your life.
The sick shall be cured, the weak shall be powerful, the unlucky ones
shall catch their luck, the poor shall become rich, an enemy shall
turn into a friend, the unhappy shall recover their happiness, and the
helpless shall be the mighty. Like a deer, the shaman drum will carry
you over all the worlds, where you shall see all your past and
future incarnations, acquire the gift of telepathy, and will be able
to read people's thoughts at a distance knowing in advance if they
bring you good or evil.

—Web site of Altai Academy of Awakening (2004)

We are returning to where we started our intellectual journey—
Siberia. The picture of shamanism in the modern imagination is
not complete without exploring how Soviet Marxism viewed this
phenomenon and what happened with shamanism in its classical
motherland under communism and beyond. In Marxist anthropological theory, shamanism represented one of the early forms of

religion that later gave rise to more sophisticated beliefs in the course of human advancement, a view that Marxism incorporated from its predecessor—
social evolutionism. The premise of Marxism was that eventually, at the highest
levels of civilization, the sacred and religion would eventually die out. Moreover, between the 1930s and the 1950s, to speed up this advancement, the Soviet government unleashed repressions against religions, including Siberian
shamanism. Like any other religion or spiritual practice, to the ideologists of
Soviet Russia, archaic techniques of ecstasy looked detrimental to their grand
project of enforced reprogramming of people's minds according to Enlightenment rationalism, atheism, and positivism. Shamanism became the symbol
of obscurantism and conservatism, which corresponded to Karl Marx's famous
dictum that, by its nature, religion was the "opiate of the people" used by
ruling elites to mask their domination over the laboring masses.

The comprehensive ideological cleansing that lasted two generations terminated the continuity of many shamanic lineages in Siberia. Although the
shamanic world view did not totally disappear, the continuity of its tradition
became seriously undermined. Siberian native spirituality shared the fate of
all religious denominations in Soviet Russia, including Christianity, Tibetan
Buddhism, and Islam. Like these and other religions, shamanism similarly
saw its spectacular return when the sacred, the spiritual, and the occult again
entered Russian life in the 1990s, after the collapse of communism and its
atheistic ideology. The story that follows describes Soviet attempts to theorize
about shamanism using Marxism and the efforts made to eradicate it. This is
also a story about the settings, events, and people that contributed to the return
of shamanism into native Siberian life in the 1990s. I also will place this resurgence of Siberian indigenous spirituality in the context of a global mind,
body, and spirit culture.

Chosen by Social Evolution: Shamanism through Marxist Eyes

Marxist scholarship not only linked religion and spirituality to particular forms
of economic and social life, but also sought to place them on an evolutionary
ladder. This view went back to the nineteenth-century social evolutionism of
John Lubbock, Johann Jakob Bachofen, Lewis Henry Morgan, and Friedrich
Engels. For example, in his treatise *The Origin of Civilization and the Primitive
Condition of Man* (1882), English ethnologist Lubbock characterized shamanism as a stage in the progress of human religions from elementary to advanced
forms. On his evolutionary scale, because it was marked by the worship of spirits, shamanism represented a "considerable advance" compared to such earlier stages as "fetishism/witchcraft" and "totemism," which in his imagination
were centered on the worship of material objects and nature. At the same time,
speculated the scholar, shamanism was not yet developed enough to be called a

"civilized" form of worship, like the next stage, "idolatry," when people began to manufacture images of their ancestors. Incidentally, Lubbock was among the first to generalize about shamanism as a universal phenomenon characteristic of all societies in their primal stage. He stressed that "although the name is Siberian, the phase of thought is widely distributed, and seems to be a necessary stage in the progress of religious ideas."[1]

From the 1930s to the 1980s, Soviet Marxist scholars who absorbed such evolutionist ideas generalized along similar lines. Thus, many Soviet ethnologists were convinced that, at the dawn of human history, everyone was his or her own shaman. Specialized spiritual practitioners, elaborate séances, and shamans proper came later, when societies became more advanced and sophisticated. Explaining the origin of shamanism, an influential Soviet folklore and ethnology scholar, D. K. Zelenin (1936), argued that primordial beliefs at first dealt exclusively with the reverence of nature (pantheism) and solicited various "gifts of nature." At this egalitarian stage, there were no shamans. People did not need special spiritual practitioners to act on their behalf simply because everybody had equal access to spirits. In this democratic spirituality, relations between people and spirits were equal. People did not have to butter up otherworldly beings and behave in a subservient manner to spiritual forces. If hostile demons got out of control, the ancient ones combated or warded them off rather than praying to them. In the Marxist vision, such attitudes mirrored the free, egalitarian nature of the primordial communistic society.

Over time, stressed Zelenin, people who were especially good at extracting illnesses became shamans. Still, they did not form any special group of people. Anybody could be a healer. However, by the end of the New Stone Age, when egalitarian primordial communities began to disintegrate into antagonistic classes, the shamans gradually evolved into a "spiritual aristocracy." This aristocracy eventually adjusted many pre-shamanic myths and rituals to their needs and developed beliefs enacted in humiliating requests addressed to deities. At this point, the scholar imagined, various morbid rituals entered the religious life of people. One of the most important ones was the deification of ancestors/shamans, the "cult of personalities," as another Soviet scholar put it.[2] Moreover, the spiritual pantheon became divided into benign and hostile, major and secondary otherworldly beings. According to Zelenin, this picture mirrored the division of people into elementary classes. Using the established hierarchy among demons, shamans started to use spirits against each other.[3] That is how he explained the origin of the shamanic séance. Generally, to Zelenin and many other Marxist authors, shamanism represented an ideology of a society caught in transition from an egalitarian to a class-based society. As such, in their imagination, shamanism combined elements of the most ancient primal ideology and the ideology that developed in early class society. Viewed from this angle, shamanism appeared to be a historically late form of a primal religion, in which shamans represented transitional figures in a society that was moving away from egalitarian collective worship to a professional priesthood.

Marxist evolutionism gave the same scrutiny not only to shamanism in general but also to particular shamanic paraphernalia. Thus, Leonid Potapov, who studied the Altaian culture, introduced an attractive interpretation of the "bow origin" of the shamanic drum.[4] During their séances, many shamans in Siberia used drums as their symbolic draft animals that carried them to other worlds. At the same time, the scholar noticed that some native spiritual practitioners also used the drums as their symbolic weapons. For example, Altaian shamans hit hostile spirits with arrows shot from their drums, which they viewed as their ritual bows. Drumsticks were also viewed sometimes as arrows. Furthermore, Altaian drums had iron rods for crossbars, which were called *kirysh*, which literally means a "bow string." The iron pendants attached to such rods symbolized arrows. Significantly, the root of the very word "drum" (*jagal* or *cagal*) in the Altaian language points to the bow (*ja, ca,* or *cag*). It is also noteworthy that Potapov met some Altaian shamans who directly called their drums "bows."

In considering how the bow and arrow actually might have become ritual tools, Potapov turned to Marxist economic determinism. The anthropologist stressed that the invention of the bow and arrow advanced ancient tribal economies, which eventually became mirrored in the beliefs of primal society. He speculated that the minds of primal people interpreted in magic terms the miraculous ability of the arrow and bow to kill animals at a distance. That is how, he assumed, these hunting tools became objects of veneration and eventually acquired the status of ritual tools, giving rise to shamanic paraphernalia. Those who used these tools were naturally viewed as carriers of sacred power that secured hunting luck. Skillful archers, who had been in charge of collective clan hunts, might have become the first shamans, speculated Potapov. Particularly, he suggested that these people could have been the first shamans because they most probably controlled the rituals that targeted hunting, the major economic activity in primal society.

While, for Potapov, shamanism sprang up from the needs of early hunting societies, for Zelenin, shamanism originated from the medical needs of ancient communities. In contrast to Potapov, he stressed that historically the first job of shamans was curing. Social and economic functions, such as securing hunting and fishing luck, came later.[5] The most ancient concept of disease, surmised Zelenin, was a perception that an ailment was the intrusion of a hostile spirit in a human body. To cure a sick person meant to extract this spirit from his or her body. Based on this premise, the scholar suggested that sucking the disease from the body of a patient was the most archaic way of curing by the shaman. Placing this healing practice on the bottom of an evolutionary ladder, Zelenin linked sucking to the instinctive animal habit of licking wounds, which, by default, made it primitive. Further speculating about the origin of the practice of "licking-sucking," Zelenin suggested that in archaic times, when people could not reach their ailing spots to lick them, they might have invited their kin to perform this job for them. In this manner, the most skillful lickers could have become the first shamans, surmised the scholar.

The scholar took this interpretation further and used it to explain the "abnormal nature" of shamans; I discussed this once-popular perception of shamanism in chapter 3. Licking and sucking out disease was a dangerous job because, in the eyes of ancient people, wrote Zelenin, a person who helped a sick one transferred this sickness to himself or herself, which could be fatal. Who could safely perform this kind of job? The best candidates, speculated the scholar, were the people who were already sick but not dead. Therefore, the ones who suffered from nervous ailments became a natural choice for the healer vocation. In the eyes of their communities, explained Zelenin, the mentally ill could safely absorb spirits—they were sick anyway. Therefore, continued the scholar, both ancient and modern tribal societies pressured mentally unbalanced people to perform this peculiar work—transplanting into themselves the demons of illnesses from the sick members of their community.[6] The first shamans were not only insane, they were also females, wrote Zelenin. This conclusion was not only because he shared the contemporary conviction that women were more susceptible to hysteria and nervous illnesses than men but also because they bore children. The scholar speculated that, observing pregnant women, ancient people might have viewed them as carriers of "alien bodies." If they could carry these beings inside of them, in the eyes of ancient communities, the females similarly could move into themselves various spirits, which, by default, made them perfect shamans.[7]

Although not shared by all, the blend of the Marxist approach with the concept of shamans as neurotics became popular among some Soviet ethnologists. In addition to Zelenin, Gavriil Ksenofontov, a former Siberian regionalist ethnographer, paid tribute to this thesis in his essay "Cult of Insanity in Ural-Altaian Shamanism" (1928).[8] Like many of his compatriots who learned to "speak Marxist" in the 1920s, Ksenofontov took the trouble to provide an economic explanation for the abnormal minds of shamans. He suggested that the development of native Siberian spirituality depended on periodic shifts in their nomadic economy from reliance on one category of animals to another. The scholar singled out three particular stages in the evolution of the native nomadic economy of northern Asia, which matched three corresponding stages in the development of the shamanic faith. When people lived by hunting, argued Ksenofontov, deities usually manifested themselves as wild beasts. Later, when people turned to a settled life, their deities became more refined and mirrored the images of domesticated animals. Finally, deities acquired human features, which reflected a shift to an economy based on slave labor and the advance of humans to first civilizations. In the most ancient times and among contemporary elementary societies that were still lingering at the first stage, the best ritual "players," wrote Ksenofontov, were mentally unstable people. Among them, no one else could so effectively replicate the behavior of the wild beasts. The ethnographer stressed that when shamans had to play the roles of wild bears, wolves, and other untamed animals, the "insanity of these magicians" reached extreme proportions.

Thus, transmitting from generation to generation a "defective physical structure and shattered nerves," in tribal societies, all shamanic lineages were prone to hereditary mental illnesses. It was especially so in hunting societies, stressed Ksenofontov, because these communities constantly had to deal with wild animals, which provided them with untamed role models. In these societies, shamans remained unfortunate mental wretches, whose ritual séances were in fact the periodic relapses of their inherent abnormal behavior. Among other tribal peoples, who, like his own Sakha people, added Ksenofontov, practiced a settled life and raised stock, shamanism never reached such extreme proportions because here the role model was a peaceful domesticated animal.

It is important to note that V. G. Bogoras, one of those who introduced into Western scholarship the thesis of shamans as mental deviants, was not a stranger to the evolutionary interpretation of shamanism either. Thus, in his 1910 paper on the psychology of northeastern Siberian shamanism, he promoted his neurosis thesis and simultaneously tried to place particular Siberian shamanisms on an evolutionary ladder. Approaching contemporary native Siberian societies as fragments of different stages of human evolution, Bogoras singled out among them the most ancient (egalitarian) and later versions of shamanism. To him, the Chukchi family shamanism, in which all clan relatives acted as shamans, appeared to be the most archaic and egalitarian version of indigenous shamanism. Bogoras contrasted this open spirituality with the elaborate and aristocratic southern Siberian religious practices, in which shamans formed a semiprofessional priestly group responsible for all major rituals. Unlike the Chukchi-type shamanism that frequently assigned leading ritual roles to women, in this "advanced" shamanism, the spiritual life was concentrated in the hands of individual male spiritual practitioners.[9]

Like Zelenin, Ksenofontov, and Bogoras, several Soviet ethnographers of a later generation continued to blend the popular psychological and medicinal interpretations of non-Western nature spirituality with its Marxist assessments. As late as the 1970s and 1980s, such prominent Soviet ethnologists as Sevian Vainshtein, a student of Tuvan shamanism, and Sergei Tokarev, who studied the Sakha and the Altaians, still linked the origin of the shamanic vocation to nervous ailments. For example, in the 1980s, in his textbook on the history of religions, Tokarev stressed, "Shamans were almost always mentally ill, with a propensity for fits of madness." Vainshtein clings to this assertion to the present day. In one of his recent papers, he insisted that "it was only people suffering from visible mental deviations who became shamans; these people carried inherited neurotic reactions, which became entrenched in ritual tradition in the form of so-called shamanic illness."[10]

At the same time, the majority of Soviet anthropologists, for obvious reasons, never accepted the thesis of the inherent insanity of shamans. Digging into the human psyche in order to explain how societies worked contradicted the general message of the Soviet Marxist anthropology—to look for the social and economic roots of each phenomenon. Many Soviet scholars strongly disagreed with the neurosis thesis and assessed shamans as strong-willed individuals who served the rich classes of indigenous societies by manipulating the masses and directing their minds toward "false consciousness."

In all fairness, the works of many Soviet anthropologists of the 1970s and 1980s practiced more nuanced approaches to shamanism, some of which were free of ideological clichés. One of the prominent students of traditional nature religions was anthropologist Vladimir Basilov, who discussed the social and communal role of shamans in Siberian and Central Asia, avoiding the crude economic determinism of his predecessors. Furthermore, in the 1970s, some Soviet scholars completely shed the vestiges of Marxism and picked up alternative theories for the interpretation of shamanism. For example, folklorist Elena Novik, turning away from exploring the social and economic roots of Siberian spirituality, adopted structuralism. Her major thesis is that shamanic séances generally follow one of two major blueprints. The first one is when the shaman retrieves a patient's soul stolen by a hostile spirit. In the second, a shaman extracts the spirit of illness from a patient's body and drives the spirit away.[11]

Moreover, in 1974, E. V. Revunenkova, a scholar who explored the beliefs of both native Siberian and South Asian societies, openly expressed her doubts in the ability of positivist scholarship to grasp the essence of shamanism. It is interesting that Hungarian anthropologist Vilmos Dioszegi, the famous Marxist student of shamanism, expressed the same stance as early as the 1960s. Reflecting on the rich records of shamanic folklore he had accumulated during his trips around Siberia, the scholar wrote, "Science will, no doubt, be able to make use of it. The only question is shall we ever be able to interpret it correctly?" Incidentally, Dioszegi gives us a classic example of a researcher within whom the positivist scholar struggled with the romantic explorer engaged by the aesthetics of shamanism. When, in 1958, for the first time, he heard the chants of the Khakass shaman Kyzlasov, his best ethnographic catch, the scholar remarked, "I have to confess rather embarrassedly, I was immediately impressed by it."[12] This particular utterance caught my attention and made me think about how deeply the wooden stables of Marxist scholarship and Western positive science, for that matter, have distorted the doors of our perception, making people subdue their romantic fascination with the beauty of other cultures as though there is something wrong with this perfectly human aspiration.

Religion of the Oppressed, Useful Esotericism,
or Obstacle to Modernity?

In the literature about Siberian shamanism, there is a mistaken perception that after Soviet communists came to power, they immediately began to eradicate tribal spiritual practitioners as an alien class. This is not exactly an accurate assumption. Strange as it may sound, Siberian "primitives" at first benefited from the demolition of the Russian empire and the Bolshevik revolution. In the immediate aftermath of the 1917 revolution, some Bolshevik theoreticians treated non-Russian nationalities, including indigenous Siberians, as victims of tsarist imperialism. These revolutionaries assumed that the indigenous people should be reimbursed for historical injustices committed against them in the past. Hence, the Bolsheviks initiated what, in current American jargon, one can call affirmative action measures. What enhanced this approach was the revolutionaries' view that all tribal societies were homogeneous egalitarian bands, some sort of primordial proletarians, who did not know the division into the rich and the poor, unlike more "advanced" civilizations.[13] Therefore, at first, communists and their sympathizers rarely crusaded against shamanism, preferring mainstream Christianity as a target for their attacks. In such a climate, practicing shamanists felt relaxed. Moreover, many earlier indigenous converts to Orthodox Christianity found it possible to return to their polytheistic spirituality.

In the 1920s, there were indigenous intellectuals in Siberia, Bolshevik fellow travelers, who argued that shamanism could be a useful tool for ethnonational construction. Some of them portrayed native spiritual practitioners as folk heroes, protectors of the humble and the poor in their communities. A native communist poet from the Sakha people, Platon Oiunskii (1893–1939), portrayed the shaman as an agent of spontaneous popular resistance against oppression and exploitation. In his poetic drama "Red Shaman" (1925), the major character, a Sakha shaman named Kysil-Oiun, acts both as a soothsayer and an activist who stirs the common tribal folk against their oppressors. Thus, conversing with two native laborers, the spiritual practitioner makes them aware of their subjugated status. The drama, which the poet formatted as several shamanic séances performed by Kysil-Oiun, uses Siberian indigenous symbolism to render the basics of Bolshevik ideology. The text starts with the scene of a shamanic confession by Kysil-Oiun. This form corresponds to the traditional humble lamentation style that Sakha shamans and, incidentally, spiritual practitioners in other tribal cultures used for conversing with their deities and spirits on behalf of their people. However, in the poem, the traditional spiritual humility acquires revolutionary proportions and turns, in the lamentation, to the suffering of the popular masses. Addressing otherworldly beings, the red shaman humbly admits that he is not sure if he will be able to head the resistance of his people against oppression:

> Throwing my lot with the poor,
> Will I enflame their hearts with fury
> Will I get through
> To make them fight the cunning and vicious
> I, who is called Red Shaman?
> Breaking deception with my proud wing
> And sending my voice with all my might
> To those in sorrow, weak and timid,
> Will I be able to give these damned and oppressed
> My thoughts—my sharp arrows.
>
> Raising their minds like whirls of smoke,
> Will I turn these slave souls into spears,
> Craving for severe fights
> And seeking revenge?
>
> Will I raise them,
> With their thundering fury,
> To stir the gloomy Middle World
> To enjoy the bloody feast?[14]

In "Red Shaman," the embodiment of all evil is Chief Oros, who rules the middle world. Oros conspires to marry his daughter into the clan of heavenly deities in order to dominate both the middle and upper worlds. The red shaman breaks the plot. He rises to the heavenly sphere and, from there, in the form of a thundering drum engulfed with blue fire, strikes the daughter dead during her wedding ceremony.

Overall, in the 1920s, native shamanism in Siberia, which released itself from such powerful competitors as the Russian Orthodox church, temporarily flourished. During this decade, writers and scholars who wished to explore Siberian indigenous spirituality enjoyed good opportunities not only to collect materials about shamanic practices but also to participate in them. Incidentally, this relaxed environment is one of the reasons that anthropologists and folklore scholars were able to collect so much ethnographic material on shamanism at that time (see figure 9.1). It was in the 1920s that the above-mentioned Sakha ethnographer Ksenofontov gathered his classic stories and legends about Sakha and Evenki shamans and their initiations, materials that later became a shamanology classic. In 1927, Potapov, later one of the stars of Soviet anthropology, did not find it ideologically odd to assist in a ceremony of a shamanic sacrifice that included the strangling of a sacrificial animal. Moreover, in the ambivalent ideological environment of the 1920s, Bogoras, another dean of Soviet anthropology, suddenly began to engage the theory of relativity

FIGURE 9.1. A Khakass shaman. Photograph by N. N. Nagornaia (1928). Such staged romantic images, which were possible in the relaxed environment of the 1920s, disappeared during Stalinism in the 1930s. Courtesy Novosibirsk Regional Museum, Novosibirsk, Russia, fond II-F N2, photograph 2384/149.

in the discussion of Siberian indigenous beliefs, which totally contradicted his earlier views. Before the 1920s, as we remember, he had spearheaded the view of shamans as neurotics. In his 1923 book with the catchy title *Einstein and Religion*, Bogoras argued the opposite. As if anticipating the currently popular intellectual stance, he wrote that the shamanic spiritual realm, including flights to heavenly spheres, visions, and dreams, was simply another world view, a vision no better and no worse than Western positive knowledge. He wrote, "The difference between real and imagined knowledge disappears because the relativity of our being makes pointless any speculations about objectivity."[15]

In the 1920s, the mysteries of shamanic wisdom, along with other Oriental spiritual techniques, aroused the curiosity of the Soviet secret police (GPU), the predecessor of the notorious KGB. One GPU chief, Gleb Bokii, who was a Rosicrucian prior to 1917, continued to express a strong interest in mysticism and esoteric knowledge after the Bolshevik revolution. In the 1920s, seeking to apply occult knowledge to his new vocation, he was on a quest for spiritual techniques that could be used for mind control and reprogramming of people's behavior. For this purpose, Bokii established a "neuroenergetic laboratory" headed by a drop-out medical student and occultist writer, Aleksandr Barchenko, whose spirituality seminars Bokii and some of his colleagues liked to visit. Barchenko was a dreamer and adventurer, who vaguely described himself as a student of "universal rhythm." Like many spiritual seekers of the past and the present, Barchenko believed that dominant rationalism and reason corrupted human knowledge and that to correct the situation, people should look to ancient times, when, in his view, humankind used intuition as a way of learning about the world around them.[16]

Flattered by the attention of his highly positioned friends, Barchenko eventually seduced Bokii by the idea of "Red Shambhala," draping the popular esoteric legend in communist colors. The student of the universal rhythm excited the secret police patrons with stories about secret Oriental knowledge that might have been hidden somewhere in the Tibetan mountains and that, if retrieved, could help to liberate the world from oppression. In his turn, one of Bokii's lieutenants aroused Barchenko's imagination by telling the scholar that his research on "telepathy waves" might become the "crucial weapon in the great proletarian struggle for the control of the planet."[17] Barchenko's insight into the power of shamanism was part of this Shambhala project. Thus, in 1925, using secret police money, Barchenko visited the Altai in southwestern Siberia to learn about local folk utopias and to explore shamanic attire. After his trip, he had some shamanic paraphernalia brought from Altaian museums to Moscow to study the effect of shamanism on the human brain. It is interesting that the confiscation of shamanic objects from the museums was conducted selectively, according to a special secret police list, and did not involve entire collections of ritual objects.[18] One can speculate that Barchenko might have been especially interested in exploring shamanic drums, the major tools of "mind control."

Four years earlier, Barchenko had also been commissioned to conduct an expedition in the Sámi country near the Finnish border. The goal was to explore the *menerick* phenomenon, the outbursts of collective and individual hysteria among native northerners, which, as I showed in chapter 3, contemporary writers frequently linked to shamanism. In reality, the expedition concentrated not so much on *menerick*, but on the exploration of all local manifestations of the paranormal and the magical. Given Barchenko's rich imagination, he populated the northern landscapes he observed with mysteries. Thus, he claimed that his expedition discovered a pyramid-like structure, a gigantic black human figure drawn on a large rock, and a crevice leading deep into the ground that was guarded by some mysterious force that kept the visitors at bay. The explorer also claimed that in the Sámi land, he had discovered a magic island where local shamans for centuries had brought deer horns for ritual purposes.

A follow-up expedition organized by an intrigued explorer, who decided to see for himself the wonders Barchenko witnessed in Sámi country, reported that the pyramid, the figure, and the crevice were natural formations unfortunately devoid of mysteries.

In Sámi country, Barchenko also befriended a shaman named Danilov, who, as the explorer remarked, was able to plunge himself at will into a "cataleptic state" and a "lethargic sleep." Moreover, Barchenko became a participant in a shamanic séance as a patient, turning to a Sámi shamaness in the hope of curing his heart failure. The explorer detailed that the woman lay by his side under the same blanket and through whispering various chants and manipulating a dagger, healed him from the ailment. Upon his return from the expedition, Barchenko fed the imagination of the secret police, describing the Sámi shamans as the descendants of Hyperboreans, the "last magicians of the mysterious ancient civilization that dominated the world in primal times."[19]

It was clear that the strange partnership between the mystic and the secret police could not last forever. After all, his esoteric projects not only failed to secure secret archaic knowledge to benefit the world communist revolution but also totally contradicted the positivist nature of official Marxism. In the 1930s, when the Stalinist regime tightened its totalitarian grip over Soviet society by putting an end to all cultural debates and spiritual experiments, the fates of the neuroenergetic lab, Barchenko, and his secret police patrons who played at magic were sealed. The whole company was arrested, convicted of an anti-communist plot, and promptly executed during the infamous period of the great terror in 1937.

In a similar manner, the attempts of some indigenous Bolsheviks in Siberia to recast shamanism into the religion of the oppressed were doomed because they eventually went against the Enlightenment rationalism of Marxist ideology and its ethos centered on scientific and technological progress. By their very occupation as keepers of spiritual tradition, shamans did not fit the Soviet modernity project. Therefore, it was only a matter of time before the Bolsheviks targeted Siberian indigenous spirituality for total eradication.

Incidentally, the poetic drama "Red Shaman" by Oiunskii, which I discussed above, already reflected the attitude toward shamanism as spiritual conservatism. On the one hand, the red shaman appears as the leader of the spontaneous folk liberation movement. Yet, on the other hand, Oiunskii portrays him as the carrier of age-old superstitions, which cannot complete the liberation struggle. A lonely hero, the shaman is ready to leave the picture to make room for the popular masses, the wretched of the earth, who will take the cause of liberation into their own hands by revolting against the old order instead of relying on magical manipulations. The red shaman puts on his ritual robe, takes his drum, and places a long knife over the drum's cover. Then he blesses the knife that is to become the weapon of the laboring masses who long "to quench its thirst with the blood" of the oppressors. In the final act of the drama, the shaman denounces his vocation and all things mystical, siding with the "mighty reason" prophesied by the "two-legged." Throwing his drum, robe, and sacred items into a fire, he speaks as a converted Marxist, exclaiming that the "world originated from the world itself" and that "there is no god over man."

At the same time, in the 1920s, the Bolsheviks did not yet crusade against shamans and did not label them as enemies of the people. At that time, Soviet writers and scholars mostly criticized them from the position of modernity, routinely portraying Siberian spiritual practitioners as retrogrades who stood in the way of progress. Major critical utterances concerned the issues of medical care, health, and hygiene. One of the crudest stereotypes was the assessment of shamans as "walking germs," people who were allegedly infested with all kinds of contagious illnesses. Newspaper reporter Zinaida Rikhter mirrored this stereotype well when she wrote, "The majority of the shamans are sick with a venereal disease quite widespread among the nomads. These spiritual and body doctors spread the infection and, because of this, they often find themselves in a court."[20]

In a fictional story, "Kamlanie (Shamanizing)" (1931), writer Nikolai Severin dwells on the same imagery to stress the hazardous effects of shamanic healing. The description of ritual paraphernalia serves to underline the unhygienic and detrimental nature of shamanism. Severin's shaman holds in his hands "a dirty drum reminding one of tambourines of gypsy women dancing in beer bars." At the end of the séance, the "dirty shirt of the shaman was all wet with sweat," and over "his face streams of sweat poured mixed with dirt." In another of Severin's fictional books about the socialist transformation of the Altai area, a "menacing shaman" named Chodon comes to heal a sick boy. The spiritual practitioner looks "as predator" at his patient. The eyes of the shaman are blurred as a result of excessive alcohol abuse, stresses the writer. The "silly movements" of the drunken shaman, who performs a séance over the sick boy, the unbearable smell of sweat and tobacco, the eye-piercing nasty smoke from the fire, all lead to a tragic end. Instead of being cured, the sick boy is choked with the suffocating smoke and dies during the séance.[21]

Incidentally, the link that earlier Russian and Western ethnographies established between shamanism and mental illness turned out to be very handy in helping critics to demonize Siberian spiritual practitioners as people detrimental to the mental hygiene of Siberian natives. For example, there were accusations that by their crazy behavior during spiritual séances shamans perpetuated mental illnesses in their communities. Physician D. A. Kytmanov, who explored the Evenki natives in the 1920s and linked shamanism to arctic hysteria, noted that Siberian spiritual practitioners acted as bad role models for the members of their communities. He stressed that by their ecstatic ritual performances, shamans bred potential neurotics, which created a "vicious circle of madness" and resulted in regular outbursts of mass hysteria. Kyt-manov believed that the advance of Soviet modernity into Siberia would nat-urally squeeze out these spiritual retrogrades from social life and stabilize the mental state of isolated indigenous communities. Those remaining youngsters who might still manifest elements of shamanic illness would become patients of psychiatric hospitals, speculated the physician.

In the 1920s Soviet imagination, shamans appeared not only as agents of "traditional ignorance" who blocked the advancement of modern medicine, education, and technology, but also as its pitiful victims. In his book of travel essays, Dmitrii Stonov (1930) described an Altaian shaman as a typical epi-leptic with "feverish, unhealthy luster in small, deeply set eyes," a "high cheek boned puffy face," and "purple shadows around the eyes," with a "pale brown color of the skin." All of these marks told the reader that the indigenous spir-itual doctor was "familiar with moments of epileptic madness, minutes of wild, uncontrolled ecstasy, and creative frenzy." When the shaman tried to smile, added the writer, his smile "turned into an ugly mask."[22] As a result, Stonov pronounced his firm verdict: shamans are "clearly sick individuals suffering from epilepsy." As such, they are "possessed" not with spirits, but "with their own sick fantasies."[23] The assumption was that such people were more vic-tims than culprits. Incidentally, that is how another writer, Sof'ia Zarechnaia, portrayed her major protagonist, the old Buryat shamaness Adai, in her *Black Shamaness* (1929). Adai is not a deceiver, but rather a victim of indigenous traditionalism, who additionally suffers from gender abuse. Repeatedly beaten by her husband, Adai "lost her mind" and eventually turned to shamanizing. Another character, a carrier of communist ideas, feels sympathy for this poor woman.[24]

Anthropologist Bogoras, whom I have repeatedly referenced, had some-thing to contribute to this genre. Picking up this literary line about shamans as pitiful victims of savage ignorance, he made it central in his novel *The Resur-rected Tribe* (1935). At the same time, in addition to a traditional shaman, an obstacle to progress and modernity, the book sampled other popular idioms of the early Soviet communist aesthetic: native women fighting for their libera-tion and rebellious youths crusading against the obscurantism of their ances-tors. Old shaman Chobtagir, one of the major characters, was a leader of a small isolated community of Yukagir, indigenous people residing in northeastern Siberia. Deeply devoted to his spiritual vocation, the old man did not have any other life except a "burning desire to indulge himself in a dance, shamanic howling and vigorous drum beating."[25] In the meantime, hunters could not procure any game, and the community faced starvation. The shamanic séances did not help, either. Eventually women lost their patience (men are shown as passive) and rebel. In response to the old man's bizarre request to sacrifice a deer to appease the spirits in order to return hunting luck, one of the tribal amazons confronted the shaman, "Do not lie, old devil, where will we get deer?

Shamans are deceivers, males are deceivers!" Then other women joined their brave sister and began to chant, "Male shamans are deceivers, male shamans are deceivers."[26] The latter was Bogoras's tribute to the sentiments of female liberation popular in Soviet Russia in the 1920s.

Unlike his contemporary essays about how to reconstruct the life of native northerners, in this book, Bogoras did not yet slip into crude assessments of shamans as exploiters of tribal masses, the stance that became popular in the 1930s. Chobtagir was not a vicious and cunning spiritual doctor. The writer portrayed him as a person who sincerely wanted to help his community. More-over, he was depicted as very genuine in his spirituality. What made him malicious in Bogoras's eyes was the traditional way of life that conditioned the old man's behavior and turned him into a retrograde. The second major pro-tagonist, Kendyk, the shaman's grandson, embodied the native's longing for modernity. In his dream, Kendyk envisioned an "unknown Russian land" with shining roads, red flags, and new hunting guns. Encouraged by the rebellious women, he escaped to a Russian town. Anticipating the coming danger of modernity, the grandfather consulted his spirits. Although spiritual beings in-vited him to fight the Bolsheviks (one of them gave the shaman a knife and said, "Use this to cut and kill"), the old man was torn between his loyalty to the spiritual world and a hidden feeling that the coming changes cannot be stopped. Eventually, the old man chose suicide as a way out.

While Chobtagir was shown as a victim of his traditionalism, Kendyk evolved into an agent of Bolshevik power. Indoctrinated in Bolshevik ideology, powerful, and vigorous, he returned to his remote community to reconstruct it according to communist blueprints. Although in this novel Bogoras did not condemn shamans as class enemies, the ending of the book mirrored the ideo-logical changes at the turn of the 1930s. The elder who succeeded Chobtagir as spiritual leader surrendered all his power to the returning Kendyk and humbly accepted the assigned role of an outsider: the shaman was allowed to remain in the community, but his voting rights were waived. The latter was a direct reference to the routine practice of the disenfranchisement of religious prac-titioners in the Soviet Union since the early 1930s.

Siberian Shamans Become Class Enemies

The Soviet government began applying active measures against shamans at the turn of the 1930s as the construction of the totalitarian regime in the Soviet Union was completed (see figure 9.2). During this decade, a militant collec-tivization and a cultural revolution, which were to inject communism into all segments of society, supplemented the general modernization drive in the country. Before the 1930s, many Soviet propaganda workers in Siberia did not care too much about shamanism, dismissing it as a trivial primitive

FIGURE 9.2. An example of the public campaign against shamanism in the Soviet Union. An anti-shamanic poster encourages the "tribal masses" to expel shamans from their native communities. By G. Khoroshevskii (1931). From the collection of Andrei A. Znamenski.

superstition that would die out on its own and that could not pose any threat, in contrast, for example, to such world religions as Christianity or Islam. The new totalitarian mentality that entrenched itself in the Soviet Union in the 1930s and that sought to flatten all social life according to communist blueprints could not accept such ideological opportunism. Soviet social scholarship, an outgrowth of the dominant communist ideology, responded to the new agenda by demanding the exposure of the class roots of shamanism in order to better eradicate it. Many scholars accepted or had to accept the premise that academic pursuits could not exist "in vain" for their own sake. Assuming that the humanities and sciences always benefited particular social and class interests, Soviet ideologists and scholars stressed that social knowledge should serve the communist cause.

Those scholars who still preoccupied themselves with collecting information on shamanism without thinking how well it would serve the state or laboring classes were assailed as ideological retrogrades. In their works on Siberian indigenous religions, ethnologist I. Kosokov and antireligious propagandist P. Khaptaev took an activist stance and began to speak out against the harmful political effects of the natural disappearance thesis. Both writers called for a militant crusade against the native religion. The new type of anthropologist, argued Khaptaev, must reject the old academic approach that avoided using ethnography for social and political activism: "Modern [Soviet] researchers" he wrote:

> are involved into the study of shamanism not to show to the "learned" academic community of the West and the East that we have shamanism as a manifestation of animism among our small peoples residing in the North, Siberia, and the Far East. Modern researchers study shamanism in order to learn and expose its social roots, its class nature, and its sources, which will make it easier and faster to erase this phenomenon where it still exists.[27]

This new activist approach manifested itself in scholarly attempts to demonize shamans as people who went against the interests of common people—the wretched of the earth. The most popular assessment of Siberian spiritual practitioners was to label them as native clergy who infected the minds of common people with false ideology and thereby served as agents of the rich indigenous aristocracy. Anthropologist and Soviet administrator I. M. Suslov stressed that shamanism was not something trivial but a full-fledged religion responsible for duping the laboring masses. In his atheistic brochure on shamanism, another antireligious propagandist, A. Dolotov, similarly argued that shamanism should be taken seriously as an ideological opponent. Interestingly, in order to show that Siberian shamanism represented an organized religion, this author extensively drew on analogies that regionalist ethnographer Ksenofontov had earlier drawn between Christianity and shamanism.[28]

If shamans were clergy, they were certainly qualified for social restrictions and imprisonment, just like their counterparts from Christianity, Islam, and Buddhism. The ever-present anthropologist Bogoras, who said different things about shamanism at different times, entered the picture again to add his voice to the militant ideological chorus. In 1932, in a popular essay on indigenous beliefs as an obstacle to the socialist reconstruction of indigenous Siberia, the scholar argued that relegating shamanism and Christianity to the same basket as any religion was extremely useful for the purposes of antireligious propaganda. Russian Orthodox Christianity, which many natives had viewed as an alien imposition, never enjoyed much popularity in native Siberia, remarked the anthropologist. Hence, if Soviet propagandists in Siberia would constantly place together the Christian priest and the shaman, native fetishes and Orthodox icons, Christian services and shamanic séances, they would eventually be able to put shamanism down in the eyes of natives. In any case, stressed

Bogoras, such an analogy was always valid, because it would help people to understand that a "religious organization is always counterrevolutionary and serves the interests of dominant classes of exploiters."[29]

In an obvious attempt to flow with the ideological current to preserve his status as a leading Soviet anthropologist, Bogoras developed statements that, in their militancy, far overshadowed similar utterances about shamans by contemporary Soviet anthropologists. In his view, the government should not restrict itself to anti-shamanic propaganda but also apply "strict and determined measures" of administrative punishment that the Soviet atheist state usually practiced in relations with Christian clergy. According to Bogoras, as ideological agents of the well-to-do indigenous interests, shamans were to be "liquidated." While the communist administrator and ethnographer Suslov described shamanic activities simply as detrimental and harmful to indigenous economic and social life, the Bolshevik fellow traveler Bogoras employed much stronger language, labeling shamans "direct wreckers [vreditely]" and calling on Soviet propaganda workers to expose their "antisocial" and "predatory" nature. Abandoning his earlier assertions that all Siberian shamans with whom he was familiar were neurotics, the scholar now stressed that the shamans he knew were reasonable, cunning, and strong-willed people and, therefore, very dangerous.[30]

Bogoras also stated that to concentrate only on the eradication of shamanism was not enough. He stressed that pure propagandistic talks in front of natives about the advantages of a materialistic approach to nature would similarly miss the point. In his view, Soviet authorities were to strive to root out the very soil that bred shamanism: the earth-based spirituality of Siberian people, which animated nature and which conditioned native lifeways and beliefs. To accomplish this, the government was to reshuffle the entire indigenous society by actively planting modern life and demolishing indigenous life. The anthropologist detailed that an "intimate" exposure of indigenous others to publicly performed physical and chemical experiments or to carefully selected films, a greater employment of natives at cannery factories, and their involvement in other machinery-related activities would instill in their minds a rationalist and mechanical mindset and break apart an animistic world view better than any lectures. Incidentally, in the same paper, Bogoras spoke against the anthropological practice of participant observation. He assumed that those scholars who took part in shamanic rituals indirectly validated these harmful practices, which were detrimental to the goals of Soviet communist construction.

It is hard to speculate to what extent the above-mentioned militant views express Bogoras's personal view of shamanism. Like many Soviet scholars since the 1930s, he might have simply lined himself up with the general ideological orthodoxy that was becoming the norm of Soviet intellectual life. Whether this was the case or not, Bogoras's 1932 paper and similar propaganda articles made a convenient case against Siberian spirituality and certainly helped to unleash the governmental campaign against shamans.[31] All in all, by the turn of the 1930s, it was certain that shamanism was ripe for total eradication. Simply to denounce this phenomenon as an obscurantist primitive philosophy that went against progress was not enough. Neither was it sufficient to dismiss indigenous healers as contagious hysterics detrimental to the mental and physical health of the Siberian indigenous masses or as native clergy responsible for keeping the indigenous mind in intellectual darkness.

Since Marxism, especially in its crude Soviet version, frequently turned to economics to explain things, in the eyes of communist ideologists and scholars, it was essential to give shamanism an economic evaluation. The goal was to portray shamans as a class of exploiters who took advantage of poor native masses. Moreover, the Stalinist thesis that parasite classes would escalate their resistance in the process of a movement toward a utopian communist paradise enhanced such an approach to shamanism. To identify the ones who might resist, Soviet bureaucrats began searching for social classes in Siberian indigenous societies, arbitrarily splitting native communities into the "oppressed" and the "oppressors." Unlike their predecessors in the 1920s, Soviet ideologists did not lump any more tribal masses together under the category of primordial proletarians.

In the 1930s, Soviet anthropologists and propaganda workers began to stress that shamans received fees for their fraudulent performances. To them, this was vivid evidence that the spiritual practitioners lived off the working masses. Eventually, the ideologists found a class niche for shamans by categorizing them as native analogues for *kulaks*, a name for well-to-do peasants in the Russian countryside targeted for eradication. In his essay with a characteristic title, "Shamanism and How to Fight It," scholar-bureaucrat Suslov devoted much space to elaborating how shamans accumulate riches and receive fees. To Suslov, the fees were not only in-kind gifts that natives gave to spiritual practitioners for performing healing sessions but also shamans' sharing meals with the families of their patients. Even if native spiritual practitioners were poor, they were bad anyway, simply because, according to Suslov, "the shaman works out mystic ideology, contributes to the wasting of social energy by channeling it into a false direction, which slows down the development of a productive economy."[32] Incidentally, the animal sacrifices that usually accompanied these séances were similarly viewed as destructive to native economies. The conclusion was obvious. As Suslov put it, "The fight against shamanism should become an integral part of class struggle in the North."[33]

Given the lack of clear social divisions in indigenous Siberia, tight kin relations, and numerous vestiges of collective living, it was a hard task to relegate shamans to the class category Marxist ideologists assigned to them. The very fact that many shamans were poor defied the attempts to categorize them as exploiters of the laboring masses. Putugir, an Evenki youth picked up and brought to a large Soviet city for schooling and communist indoctrination, had a hard time grasping the ideological puzzle of the class categorization. When asked in 1930 by his Russian professors to reflect in writing on the religion of his people and to classify shamans by their class status, to the frustration of his teachers, Putugir could not explain why the spiritual practitioners he had personally encountered were humble folk without any riches. Although the written reflections of the youth went into print, they were accompanied by a comment from one of his Russian professors: "Any assertion about the lower social and economic status of shamans should be carefully verified."[34]

Because, in the eyes of the ideologists, shamanism represented an organized religion, and shamans were the class of exploiters, in the 1930s, the Soviet secret police unleashed total and merciless repressions against Siberian spiritual practitioners. I would like to stress that it was not a special ideological campaign that singled out Siberian shamans for eradication. Repressions against shamans were only a minor part of the efforts of the totalitarian communist state to wipe out the sacred and the spiritual from the minds of people and enforce on them the religion of Enlightenment atheism and rationalism. Therefore, shamanism fully shared the fate of Christianity, Islam, Tibetan Buddhism, and other denominations. It is notable that some present-day indigenous elders, when remembering the Stalinist great purges of the 1930s, usually do not distinguish between oppressors and victims as Russians and natives because the entire Soviet Union equally felt the suffocating grip of Stalinism.

Shamans not only were disenfranchised and forbidden to cure people but also were exiled into labor camps. Moreover, frequently both spiritual practitioners and members of their families were ostracized. The spiritual practitioners were declared parasites who lived off the laboring masses and were used as convenient scapegoats, blamed by local authorities for their own economic and political failures. For example, in some parts of Siberia, the governmental campaign of collectivization, which resulted in the mass slaughter of stock, was ascribed to the secret plots of shamans.[35] The regime consciously sought to mobilize public opinion against shamans. Authorities encouraged people to inform on spiritual practitioners who secretly continued their practices. Based on informers' reports, police sometimes arrested natives simply for imitating and mimicking shamans. Occasionally, people were arrested just to fulfill the purge quotas ordered from above. A spiritual practitioner from the Nanai people remembered that in 1937, when the repressions reached their peak: "They did what they wanted! They could write that a person was a shaman and a vermin, and that was that! People came after them from the NKVD [another name for the Soviet secret police], took them and that was that! Shot them!"[36]

Natives of the younger generations, instigated by the regime to revolt against traditions, were especially zealous in persecuting shamans. Overall, the persecutors of the spiritual practitioners were not Russian revolutionaries but mostly local indigenous people, who were inspired by atheistic ideas, a zeal for modernization, and the liberation ethics of the communist state. The policy of demonizing shamans was total and effective and created around them an intolerable atmosphere. Given this stance, it was natural that many natives absorbed anti-shamanic sentiments and maintained them until the end of the 1980s. One should not underestimate the effectiveness of communist propaganda, which became ingrained in the consciousness of many natives. The changing attitudes toward spiritual practitioners were occasionally reflected in folk proverbs and sayings. A Buryat saying capitalized on the perception of shamans as parasites and went as follows: "When a sheep gets lousy, it strays away, / When a man gets useless, he becomes a shaman."

Soviet modernization offered many natives, especially native youth and women, an opportunity to fulfill and advance themselves. Some indigenous elders who now condemn the repressions against shamanism admitted that in Soviet times, they themselves were members of the Young Communist League and stressed that they considered participation in crusades against shamans a heroic deed that allowed them to show off their loyalty to the communist cause. In his conversation with a Russian anthropologist, Nikolai Petrovich, a Nanai native whose mother was a shamaness and who himself, in the 1990s when shamanism came back into vogue, turned into a spiritual practitioner, remembered the 1930s with an element of nostalgia. Moreover, he laughingly confessed:

> I was a kid then, and I was for Stalin! It is very difficult to confess it now, but I have to. So it was! I cannot deny it!... I was brought up in such an atmosphere...! I joined the Communist Youth Union, and then the war started. It was so elating! Do you understand? Sincerely! I was fighting for the [Communist] party. I served seven years in the army, I was educated in the communist spirit. And apart from that, I remembered my childhood and loved my mother. I had dreamed about her.[37]

Under official and mass pressure, many shamans went public, denouncing their vocation. The local press published numerous confessions and self-accusations of shamans. In fear of reprisals for their vocation, many spiritual practitioners rushed to turn their drums in to Soviet officials and tried to keep a low profile. At the same time, some of them made new drums and continued their practices in secret. There were many who did not feel uncomfortable paying their homage simultaneously to communism and shamanism. In fact, anthropologist Boulgakova, who interviewed five such persons among the Nanai, stressed that this type of syncretic mindset was not considered dishonorable. She even insisted that this spiritual blend led to the appearance of a new figure—a shaman-communist.[38]

On the whole, since the 1930s, shamanic practices in the form they existed prior to 1917 either disappeared or sharply declined, going underground and coexisting with Soviet popular culture. I would like to stress that, although many shamanic lineages were disrupted, and the indigenous earth-based phi-losophy was undermined, the shamans of Siberia were never totally wiped out. Russian anthropologists who conducted fieldwork in Siberia in Soviet times occasionally wrote about practicing shamans. During my fieldwork in the Altai in 2001 and 2004, I met two aged spiritual practitioners, one of whom was called by spirits in the 1940s and another one in the 1960s, times when practicing shamanism was detrimental to one's social status. The very stance of Siberian shamanism—that the spiritual craft was imposed on particular individuals by spirits—did not allow people to simply drop this vocation and walk away without serious consequences for their psyche. One can assume that the fear of spirits who, it was believed, could strangle shamans if they quit the profession, prompted some spiritual practitioners to continue their séances in secret despite their formal denouncement of the craft. At the same time, as Dioszegi informed us, there were shamans who approached their ancestors with sacrificial gifts, trying to return the helping spirits they had received after their initiation. Such people hoped that, after sending the spirits away forever, they could turn their backs on shamanism.[39]

Those who continued the spiritual practice had to be inventive to avoid persecution. For example, instead of using drums, the major tools of Siberian shamans in the classical period, spiritual practitioners began to rely on such substitutes as branches and twigs, mittens, bows and arrows, lashes, staves, caps, and other objects. Before the 1930s, these supplementary curative tools occupied a marginal place in indigenous shamanism or were used by begin-ning shamans who were not yet qualified to perform with drums. When the officials made the use of drums unsafe, those secondary tools came to the center of healing practices and replaced the classic paraphernalia. The creative imagination of people went further. Thus, in some areas of native Siberia, shamans began to use pot lids instead of drums, a practice that eventually became traditional. Sociologist Marjorie Balzer, the leading North American ex-pert on Siberian culture and religion, pointed to a creative adjustment of sha-manism to the repressive conditions of Soviet communism. She reported a peculiar example when, in the 1930s, during a curative session, a shamaness named Matriona called her spirits by improvising with a frying pan as a sub-stitute for a drum and a wooden spoon for her drumstick.[40]

There were many other examples of imaginary drums in Soviet Siberia. For instance, for ritual purposes, spiritual practitioners could use images of drums drawn on pieces of material or round hoops. Both could be manipulated silently without attracting attention. In 2001 in Mountain Altai, I encountered a shaman named Krychnakov who used one of these tools. When this man began his spiritual vocation in the 1960s, he used a wooden hoop with ribbons attached to it. To the present day, Krychnakov still uses this ritual item in his curative practice. Others used plain pieces of fabric without any drawings. Incidentally, prior to the 1930s, the act of waving the material as a fringe curative method had its own meaning among the Altaian, Tuvan, and Khakass people. The waving was intended to bring together the master spirits of the locality and to try to ward off the spirits of illnesses. Elders, or any other person, for that matter, could perform this procedure. Under spiritual oppression, such practices as the silent waving of the material gradually came to the center of healing, replacing drumming sessions.

Here is how Tuvan shaman Aldyn Khorel Ondar performed his healing session in July 1975, a time when communism in Russia was still sound. He conducted the shamanic session for prophylactic purposes to help a family, one of whose members was frequently ill. Anthropologist Vera Diakonova, who was present at the event, described it as follows. The shaman and the members of the family gathered around a larch tree, which is considered a shamanic tree. Around the larch tree at the four cardinal directions, the people erected small hearths made of rocks. After this, the shaman Ondar began his séance. Having taken in his right hand a large piece of white material about one meter in length, he stood by the fire made near the tree. Waving the piece of material, the shaman began singing his chants. In a poetic form, Ondar related the life stories of his ancestors and described his spirit helpers. By waving and chanting, the shaman summoned the master spirit of the locality and then sprinkled homemade alcohol in all four directions. The spirit reported to the shaman what would happen to the ailing individual. After the shaman heard the report of the arriving spirit, he sent it off, and finished his séance.[41]

Another interesting phenomenon of the survival of shamanic practices under communism was spreading the shaman's ritual and curative activities among various fringe healers and medicine practitioners, who had always existed on the margin of indigenous society. In other words, the functions of the full-fledged shaman, the object of ideological attacks, were scattered among other spiritual practitioners, who had earlier occupied a secondary place in native society. Again, in such diluted form, it was safer to conduct traditional rituals. Based on her 1983 field research among the Altaians, anthropologist Revunenkova concluded that the profession of the shaman (*kam* in Altaian) indeed went out of use. At the same time, shamanistic ideology did not disappear. Earlier, only shamans had performed all of the major traditional rituals, such as healing, prophesying, and funeral ceremonies. When the Soviet regime eliminated shamans or drove them underground, these functions became shared and spread among minor spiritual practitioners. These auxiliary practitioners gradually took over particular shamanic functions and saved the entire profession.

Thus, traditional clairvoyants called *kosmochi* widened their functions in modern times. At the turn of the twentieth century, they specialized in detecting the spiritual doubles of human beings (*suna*). Yet they were not able to retrieve a *suna* and bring it back, which was a prerogative of shamans. By the 1980s, we already found *kosmochi* endowed with the power of soul retrieval. The *kosmochi* also began to act as mediators between living and dead people, which had also been one of the major jobs of shamans in the past. Moreover, in modern Altaian society, there appeared a new category of people known as "wise ones." In the 1980s, the Altaians directly referred to them as a modern analogue of shamans. The wise ones healed people, removed spells, and prophesied. Unlike other folk healers and clairvoyants, who did not go through any initiation and usually did not experience a spiritual call, the wise ones exhibited elements of sacred behavior as early as childhood, which certainly placed them close to traditional shamans. Sometimes wise ones were also called *kosmochi*, which points to the merging of the functions of shamans and clairvoyants.[42]

As Balzer informs us, the feminization of Siberian shamanism in Soviet times was another strategy for its survival. Prior to 1917, in Siberia, male and female spiritual practitioners were more or less equally represented in the vocation. In the 1930s, high-profile male spiritual practitioners became the first candidates for persecution, which eventually eliminated them from the picture and, with them, much of their esoteric tradition. In the meantime, women took over the vocation on an unprecedented scale.[43] At the same time, this gender shift in shamanism is hardly a peculiar Siberian phenomenon. The feminization of the shamanic profession usually happened in all preindustrial societies that underwent deep modernization or state formation. A good example is *itako* shamanism in Japan, which specializes in communicating with the spirits of the dead and exists exclusively as a female vocation. When I was exploring the *itako* in the Amori prefecture in 2003, I could not find among them a single male. At the same time, historical sources suggest that, in the past, males had been represented in this vocation. We can observe the same situation in Korea, where shamanism is now associated with women.

Shamanism and Indigenous Ethnic Renaissance in Postcommunist Siberia

The decline of Russian communism resulted in a dramatic increase in interest in the spiritual and the religious, a backlash to the seventy years of officially sanctioned atheism. Thus, at the beginning of the 1990s, after traveling all over the world, the shamanism metaphor returned to its motherland, where it soon acquired a mind, body, and spirit of its own, becoming part of a vibrant cultural resurgence of Siberian native communities. Although, as I have mentioned, the vestiges of shamanism survived in Siberia, the totalitarian Soviet state did a "good job" of reprogramming the minds of Siberian natives in the direction of atheism and materialism. When this positive knowledge began to crumble at the end of the 1980s, indigenous Siberians began to search for spiritual and cultural substitutes.

Given the spiritual void produced by the decades of communism and the disruption of many shamanic lineages, the preservation and revival of shamanism in native Siberia means the creation of new knowledge derived from old ethnographic books, European and Russian travel narratives, and the stories of those few elders who might have maintained bits and pieces of their ancient wisdom. First and foremost, one should place the 1990s regeneration of shamanism in the context of the ethnocultural revival of indigenous Siberia. Like many other ethnic groups of the former Soviet Union that were earlier cemented by the communist ideology, Siberian native people felt a need to anchor themselves ethnically and culturally in the new postcommunist world. Under these circumstances, shamanism, wiped out or lingering somewhere on the very fringe of village life or preserved in ethnographic books, entered the toolkit of indigenous cultural workers. These people began to view the shamanism idiom as one of the ways to re-indigenize themselves. Using the expression of anthropologist Eva Fridman, shamanism became a sort of "sacred geography" that helped people to root themselves in their localities, clans, and communities.[44] People who had hidden their shamanic lineages began to come out from the closet and claim their spiritual vocation. Others simply manufactured their shamanic lineages or entered the spiritual craft because, as they say, they felt a calling. For example, in Tuva, one of the Siberian native autonomies, shamanism was propelled to the status of an official religion, along with Tibetan Buddhism and Orthodox Christianity. Reinvented shamanism also occupies a significant place in the cultural milieux of the present-day Sakha and Buryat republics (see figure 9.3).[45]

We know well that in order to build or enhance their ethnic or national sentiments, people frequently appeal to antiquity. In their approach to cultural material that they want to use for these purposes, they follow a simple dictum: the older, the better. Shamanism perfectly fits this profile. Because it appears to be very ancient ("archaic technique of ecstasy"), it is certainly an excellent resource for ethnic and cultural construction. As an indigenous anthropologist from the Buryat, M. I. Gomboeva, phrased it, shamanism is a good way to stir the "ethnopsychological self-awareness" of indigenous Siberians. British ethnologist Piers Vitebsky, a well-known student of Siberian shamanism, told us how in the Sakha republic, indigenous educators turned elements of the shamanic cosmos into a compulsory school curriculum subject, which is designed in the same ethnonational manner. Particularly, the scholar wrote about an administrator from the Sakha Department of Education who lectured to schoolchildren by pointing at a diagram of the indigenous cosmos, detailing

FIGURE 9.3. Modern Buryat shamans during one of their ceremonies. Courtesy Debra Varner.

in what particular spheres specific spirits resided. During such instructive lectures, educators pointed out to children that what they were learning represented their own indigenous knowledge that should be collected and preserved as their cultural heritage. An essential part of this indigenous pedagogy used for ethnic mobilization is a romantic picture of indigenous knowledge as a fixed system of spiritual and moral prescriptions.[46]

I sense this stance—spiritual revival as a planned ethnocultural enterprise—in some stories of modern shamans about their practices. For example, this approach surfaced in the words of Tatiana Kabezhikova, a professional educator turned shamaness. When asked about her most memorable shamanic séance, Kabezhikova related how she was invited by some of her friends from her native Khakassia, a Siberian area in which shamanic tradition was almost totally wiped out, to consecrate a rock named "White She Wolf." Here is the dialogue between the shamaness and Valentina Kharitonova, an anthropologist who interviewed her.

> KABEZHIKOVA   Not far from the Abakan town there is a place with a rock that reminds one of a she-wolf. People call it White She Wolf. Folks who live over there have some sort of a legend about a she-wolf that

had breastfed nine infants. Since all this sounds beautiful and looks attractive, especially now when it became fashionable to revive all this
old stuff, we expected a lot of people to show up the next day for a collective worship. Yet before this prayer, they [the organizers] planned
to invoke the spirit of that white she-wolf.

KHARITONOVA   Was the invocation stipulated in the scenario of this
ceremony?

KABEZHIKOVA   Yes, this was written in the scenario. At the same
time, I learned on my own that I actually needed to go after the spirit
of that she-wolf and retrieve it. Each rock carries specific information.
When I worked for a little while with this rock and established contact
with it, I found out that nobody worshiped this rock for a long time.
So, as they say, the rock was dispirited. So I had to perform the rite.
According to the scenario, several shamans were expected to take part
in this shamanic séance....Many people were present during this
[large] séance for the first time. For many of them it was, I should say,
an awesome experience.[47]

The materials collected by American anthropologist Fridman about the
shamaness I just mentioned similarly pointed to her role as a cultural worker.
Thus, the chief goal of her center for the "shamanic point of view" that Kabezhikova established in Abakan is to educate children in the "old perception
of the world" characteristic for "our ancestors."[48] The center has a folklore en-
semble and revives traditional music and folklore. To make a long story short,
we find in the activities of Kabezhikova and her center the usual toolkit of
people who are concerned about their culture and ethnicity.

If we keep in mind this obvious link between the current revival of shamanism and the indigenous cultural renaissance in Siberia, we will understand better, for example, the desire of the indigenous writer and anthropologist
Mongush Kenin-Lopsan to present his homeland, Tuva, as the birthplace of
genuine shamanism. Thus, this Tuvan cultural worker enlightened us, "Tuva
is the only place on this earth where shamanism survived in its pristine shape.
The Khakass, the Evens and other peoples have shamans, but they lost their
roots. That is why today to study the ancient culture, scholars from all over the
world come to Tuva."[49] Kenin-Lopsan is also proud to carry the title of Living
Treasure of Shamanism endowed on him by Michael Harner's Foundation for
Shamanic Studies (FSS). Moreover, the scholar considers this award to be a
first step toward the recognition of Tuva as the motherland of shamanism, the
official international title he and his associates hope to elicit.[50]

Since much of the living tradition in Siberian shamanism is gone, ethnographic literature represents one of the chief sources about traditional spirituality. The creative use of ethnographic texts by indigenous groups which
want to empower themselves is a common practice in native societies that

have undergone a long period of modernization and colonization. In the same manner, many detribalized Native Americans in the United States unpacked Western ethnographic print media, turning what they could find there into living practices. Indigenous Siberia is not an exception in this case. For example, in the middle of the 1990s, in Chukchi country, which is located in northeastern Siberia, indigenous cultural workers received their inspiration from the writings of Bogoras. Reprinted portions of his classic 1909 Chukchi ethnography were disseminated through local newspapers. Many indigenous teachers and cultural workers either read these materials or used them in their work. Some current shamanism practitioners in Tuva manufactured their tradition in a similar manner. German anthropologist Ulla Johansen surveyed the activities of a "shamanic clinic," one of the spiritual counseling centers in Tuva that sprang up in the 1990s. She discovered that the shamans who work there rely heavily on materials from the local museum and its library. In their search for authenticity, the spiritual practitioners frequent both of them, studying collections and written records and trying to replicate the information they find and designs they see in their practices. Incidentally, the Buryat shamanism practitioners whom she met did the same thing.[51]

Another powerful resource is Russian and Western "New Age" print media, which entered the Russian book market in the 1990s. Incidentally, the ideas picked up from this literature frequently merge with the ethnocultural sentiments I outlined above. For example, the writings of Buryat cultural worker and anthropologist Irina Urbanaeva, who is also an ordained Buddhist nun, benefit from a variety of spirituality authors. Among them we find Georges Gurdjieff, Helena Blavatsky, and Carlos Castaneda. Like her Tuvan colleague Kenin-Lopsan, she wants to prove that the shamanism from her homeland is the most ancient: "Nomadic inner Asia, the motherland of our ancestors, is the region which maintains the most ancient form of esoteric knowledge on the earth." Moreover, Urbanaeva claimed that in inner Asia, one can find elements of "ancient Toltec wisdom," powerfully articulated, she added, by "an Indian shaman Don Juan." The anthropologist also declared that "according to occult data, central [inner] Asia is the region where the spirit of all races had existed." In her utterances, one senses not only cultural nationalism but also a particular source of her inspiration—Blavatsky, who similarly drew the source of sacred knowledge from inner Asia.[52]

To explain why shamans are so important for nourishing ethnic awareness among indigenous Siberians, Urbanaeva's Buryat colleague Gomboeva turned to Carl Jung's classic concept of the collective unconscious and to transpersonal psychology. She argued that in their séances, shamans dig deeply into the archaic memory of an ethnic group by sampling ancient imagery and symbolism, which generate an ethnic unconscious among the members of the group who observe these rituals. It is notable that another Buryat anthropologist, G. R. Galdanova, moved from psychology to human biology, arguing that the current revival of shamanism proves the power and durability of the "genetic code" of the Buryat. To her, shamans are important because they activate and unpack traditional culture, whose blueprints are stored in the genetic memory of an ethnic group.[53]

Let us review several examples of the revival of shamanism by indigenous Siberians in postcommunist Russia. The first example comes from the Itel'-men, the native people of the Kamchatka peninsula. In 1987, cultural workers from this native group established the Council for the Revival of Itel'men Culture, an organization that seeks to retrieve indigenous culture through the reading of early European travel narratives about northeastern Siberia and through conversations with elders. For this purpose, natives periodically conduct reenacting performances in which they recreate scenes from indigenous mythology and the old ways of life. The council has already conducted a few traditional ceremonies. Boris Zhirkov, whom local native residents, with a bit of irony, call "our shaman," is the person who organizes these performances. Zhirkov, a confirmed bachelor who studied ballet in St. Petersburg, lives with his elderly mother. During the aforementioned performances, he sometimes uses a shaman drum, trying to attach more authenticity to the cultural events, although he personally does not consider himself a shamanism practitioner.[54]

One of the most notable examples of the shamanism revival is Tuva, a small republic of 320,000 people in southern Siberia near Mongolia. The Tuvans belong to those few Siberian groups that maintained some visible vestiges of traditional shamanism. At the same time, historically, Tuvan shamanism interacted with and borrowed from Tibetan Buddhism, another major religion in the republic. Until 1944, Tuva was formally an independent nation. In reality, like Mongolia, it was a Soviet colony, which cloned the Stalinist ideology of its elder brother. Along with Buddhism, shamanism was an object of persecutions. Nowadays, Tuva is one of the poorest and most crime-ridden Russian autonomies, which exists mainly on federal subsides. Although the economic activities of Tuva are centered on stock raising, for many residents of the republic, growing and selling cannabis provides a substantial, although illegal, supplement to their meager incomes. In fact, some Western visitors are pleasantly surprised that the "magic herb" sprouts wild and free on the outskirts of Kyzyl, the capital of the republic.

In the 1990s, with the growing tide of ethnic and cultural revival, Tuvan intellectuals and cultural workers banded together to regenerate decaying shamanism. The driving force behind this resurgence was writer and ethnographer Kenin-Lopsan. Known to his friends and associates simply as "professor," a reference to his doctorate in cultural anthropology, Kenin-Lopsan is a colorful character. A child of herders, he claimed that his shamaness grandmother acknowledged his spiritual powers when he was nine years old. During the greater part of his adult life, spent under communism, Kenin-Lopsan was a well-known fiction writer. His novels and stories from that time glorify the advance of Soviet modernity into the life of his people. To his credit, he does not hide his communist past and openly admitted that he remained a member of the Communist party to the very end of the Soviet empire. At the same time, Kenin-Lopsan was a passionate collector of the shamanic folklore of his people. It is notable that he conducted this work before the topic of shamanism became a hot spiritual commodity among his Siberian compatriots. Although the scholar claims a shamanic lineage, he does not perform séances except occasional palm readings. Kenin-Lopsan acted more as a "shaman-administrator," supervising the certification of the ancient faith's practitioners, whom in 1992 he united into an association of Tuvan shamans called Dungur (Shaman's Drum), whose members carry special red shamanic cards as badges of their authenticity.

The association positioned itself as a professional guild of all Tuvan spiritual practitioners. At the same time, by the end of the 1990s, other enterprising individuals in the republic similarly declared themselves shamans and created their own associations or simply began to work on their own. Like the shamans of old, Kenin-Lopsan was not happy about these spiritual competitors. Trying to shield the interests of his professional corporation, the professor denounced non-affiliates as false shamans: "we are the only lawful shamans—and we each have documents proving that we are really a shaman and a member of our organization. There are also some fraudulent shamans and we don't accept them."[55] When a colleague from Germany asked him to specify how his guild protects people from the false shamans, Kenin-Lopsan explained, "We publicize their names on the radio and television, and in papers. We suggest that people not patronize them. We suggest they contact one of our 40 members, who can be identified by their membership card."[56] Moreover, as the self-proclaimed chief of Tuvan shamans, Kenin-Lopsan sought to exercise control over contacts of the association's members with visitors who come to Tuva to explore shamanism. Once he went as far as threatening Ai-Churek, a popular shamaness, to cancel her trip to Italy because she worked with a British film crew without his authorization. The professor explained, "Here we have a hierarchy and we are very strict. Shamanism is more precious than gold in Tuva—and is not to be abused."[57]

The Dungur association was located in a house the Tuva government bought to accommodate shamans. By 2000, the society numbered forty registered shamans and more than one hundred apprentices. Among full-fledged, card-carrying members and apprentices, there were also several Russian and Western spiritual practitioners. The association also ran a shamanic clinic, which opened its doors in 1992 (see figure 9.4). This peculiar facility represented a combination of a spiritual healing center and a hang-out place for all natives, Russians, and foreigners who come to Tuva in search of shamanic knowledge or simply supernatural adventures. Later, several similar clinics were erected in the republic. To a curious visitor from the United States, who

FIGURE 9.4. Shamanic clinic in Tuva, 2003. Courtesy Debra Varner.

pestered the spiritual practitioners employed in the clinic about exactly what they were doing in this building, one of the shamanesses said, "What people really need here is hope. The shaman gives them this."[58]

Upon entering the building, patients met a receptionist to whom they explained their problems and who scheduled appointments and wrote out receipts. On a wall, there were photos of shamans with lists of their specialties and prices. Among them were the extraction of hostile spirits, shamanic funeral ceremonies, fortune-telling sessions, and treatment of regular ailments of the kidneys, backbones, hearts, and bowels. Although sympathetic and open-minded, writer Benedict Allen, who came to Tuva purposely to examine its indigenous spiritual practices, noted a strong commercial element in this project. He wrote about people associated with the clinic, "They simply chose to become *khams* [shamans] because it was convenient—profitable. Not a way of life but a living. In angst-ridden, modern-day Tuva, people were looking for answers—and these neo-shamans were able to provide them, given the right fee."[59]

Each shaman working in the clinic received clients on a daily basis in his or her office. The spiritual practitioners were employed on a rotating basis. After five to six healers worked for a month, a new group of spiritual practitioners replaced them. From time to time, the clinic encouraged visiting Russian, European, and American spiritual seekers to join local shamans to cure local people. Such a cosmopolitan approach to shamanic healing only increased the popularity of the clinic in the eyes of the public. Adjusting their healing practices to the steady flow of clients, who sometimes have to wait in lines, Dungur spiritual practitioners used a conveyer belt method, just like a conventional Western hospital. During their sessions, which usually lasted fifteen minutes, Dungur doctors did not have time to experience such things as the classical shamanic trance in order to conduct a journey to a nonordinary reality. The shamans normally just talked with their clients. They might also have cured patients by laying on hands or by drumbeats. A *Washington Post* reporter who visited the Dungur clinic described his impressions of several shamans' patients he encountered. A couple came to solicit advice regarding a stolen cassette player. They had their suspicions and wanted to confirm them with the shamans. A woman came for help to find a daughter who had gone to work the day before and had not come back home. Another patient came to the clinic with explicit ethnonational sentiments, stressing that he and his wife never went to the Russian doctors because they learned everything they needed to make their lives happy from shamans.[60]

Professional shamanic guilds similar to Dungur sprang up among other indigenous Siberian nationalities and communities. In 1990, Sakha spiritual practitioner and historian Vladimir Kondakov established the Association of Folk Medicine to bring together people who have positioned themselves as practitioners of traditional spirituality and medicine. Another example is the Thundering Drum Association of Buryat Shamans. Founded in 1992 by librarian-turned-anthropologist Nadezhda Stepanova, this spiritual guild united eighty-three shamans. The association included both traditional healers who could somehow prove their shamanic lineages and spiritual practitioners who simply felt a calling to the shamanic vocation. Stepanova, who was the president of the association and a shamanism practitioner, simultaneously taught at the department of ethnology and folklore at the Eastern Siberian Academy of Culture and Arts. Like Kenin-Lopsan, she vigorously cultivated contacts with Western nature communities and markets herself in the West as a practitioner of traditional Buryat shamanism.[61]

Very much like Dungur, the Thundering Drum Association sought to control the dissemination of sacred knowledge in Buryat country. Hence, it is natural that, like their Tuvan counterparts, these newly minted Buryat shamans strove to impose a monopoly on shamanism and contested the right of nonmembers to enter the craft. D. D. Ochirov, one of the members of Thundering Drum, frankly stated, "Our shamanic association was created in order to keep away charlatans from performing rites. Those who want to be qualified as shamans show us their skills and perform rituals. This is an admission requirement, which is necessary to acquire a membership."[62]

I also want to stress that the initial excitement about shamanism in indigenous Siberia characteristic of the early 1990s has now subsided. To many natives who originally became attracted to the archaic spirituality, the whole thing looked like a newly discovered and exciting forbidden fruit. Now, as the Buryat anthropologist Gomboeva lamented, many people have become disinterested in or skeptical of shamanism once again. Moreover, she noted that the future of shamanism in Siberia does not look bright and expressed her regret that her people are turning their attention away from "ethnic self-awareness" to "personal self-awareness."[63] I have the impression that this pessimism might have more to do with her own ethnographic expectations as an indigenous intellectual interested in nourishing cultural nationalism than with the popular sentiments of the Buryat who, after the nationalist sentiments declined, might have begun to treat shamanism as one of many spiritual techniques.

Entering the Circle: Siberian Neo-shamanism and World Esotericism

The upsurge of interest in shamanism in Siberia at the turn of the 1990s should be linked not only to the cultural renaissance of the indigenous people but also to the general rise of the occult and spirituality in the late Soviet Union when the communist ideology was on its deathbed. Particularly, I would like to note the phenomenon of "extrasensory" urban healing popular at that particular time, which manifested itself in public sessions of spiritual healing performed at concert halls, in theaters, and on television programs all over Russia and Siberia. Some native seekers used this nationwide niche to situate and promote their shamanic practices for both native and Russian audiences. Incidentally, to the present day, bringing shamanism practitioners to a theater or a concert stage is one of the favorite ways of popularizing this form of spirituality.[64]

Overall, since the end of the 1980s, with the decline of official atheism and the change of public sentiments toward shamanism, more people in indigenous Siberia began to claim that they had experienced the shamanic call. Many indigenous Siberians who began to position themselves as shamanism practitioners in the 1990s were young or middle-aged people who graduated from colleges and universities. Frequently, they had backgrounds in various creative and humanities professions: anthropology, education, theater, or music. With the rise of interest in the spiritual and the traditional, for such people shamanism became a natural outlet for their creative self-fulfillment. During her visit to Khakassia and Tuva, Canadian folklore scholar Kira Van Deusen was stunned that various singers, philosophers, and musical instrument makers were introduced to her as "shamans." These people not only sampled their spirituality in healing sessions and workshops but also processed this sacred knowledge in lectures, on stage, and in mass media.

Nikolai Ooorzhak-Ool, the fifty-year-old chair of Dungur, an association of Tuvan shamans, came to shamanism from the theater profession. In addition to being a gifted throat singer, he worked as a stage manager, playwright, and actor. Ooorzhak-Ool said that his interest in shamanism was sparked by a small role as a shaman he once played. This prompted him to read more about Siberian indigenous religions and to converse with the remaining elders who still remembered Tuvan shamanism. Thus, for this particular person, the induction into shamanism was an intellectual initiation.[65] At least some of these new post-Soviet spiritual practitioners are not exactly sure about the spiritual roles they have imposed on themselves. During her talks with an American anthropologist, Rosa Nasyk-Dorjou, another Tuvan intellectual who turned to shamanism in the post-Soviet period, stressed that she thinks of herself as a strong healer, but, at the same time, she is plagued by self-doubts. Particularly, Nasyk-Dorjou constantly reflected on the process of her shamanizing, asking herself whether she really sees spirits or if they are merely the product of her own imagination.[66]

The shamans of the new generation are usually voracious readers. Buryat indigenous anthropologist Galdanova noted that these new shamans read ethnographic texts and scholarly works on shamanism, from which they learn "how to do it."[67] Among their professional texts are also the works of European and American spirituality authors. As a result, their practices and usage are loaded with Western "New Age" jargon: "energy," "karma," "chakra," the "astral body," and so on. Thus, people working in one of the Tuvan shamanic clinics informed visiting German ethnologist Johansen that they treated their patients by using the "aura." She also noticed that in their workshop talk, these spiritual practitioners constantly used such expressions as energy and the astral body. The texts of the interviews American anthropologist Fridman conducted with numerous shamanic practitioners among the Buryat and the Tuvans pointed in the same direction.[68]

Those Siberian shamanism practitioners who have the opportunity also try to cultivate their contacts with European and American spiritual seekers and frequently welcome a cosmopolitan spiritual blend. In 1998, during a visit by Tuvan neo-shamans to California to instruct the students of core shamanism, Kenin-Lopsan addressed Harner with the following words, "We think that we'll learn from each other: you from us and us from you. Together we'll work, so that world shamanism will have progress and all of us will prosper together. I think that your shamanism and Tuvan shamanism together is what is called 'world' shamanism."[69] The intention to enter the community of world esotericism was also obvious in the activities of the Tuvan shamanic clinics, which, in addition to the spiritual curing of local people, functioned as mystical tourism centers, catering to the spiritual interests of Western spiritual seekers. Like in the cases of many Latin American *curanderos*, the cosmopolitan aspirations of the indigenous Siberian spiritual seekers and the feedback they receive from Western "New Age" and nature philosophies certainly do not make indigenous Siberian neo-shamanism less authentic than the traditional shamanism of the old times.

Kabezhikova, from the Khakass nationality, is a good example of an indigenous cosmopolitan neo-shaman who borrows widely from both ethnographic texts and Western "New Age" print culture and for whom archaic techniques of ecstasy represent not only a spiritual but also a cultural and intellectual quest. Before the 1990s, under communism, Kabezhikova graduated from a pedagogical university with an educational degree in biology and geography. She linked a call to her spiritual vocation to a serious illness caused by a tick bite. The bites of these insects, which are active in southwestern Siberia, especially in spring, can cause Lyme disease with potentially lethal outcomes. Since the Khakass shamanic tradition was completely erased, there were no elders from whom she could learn. For this reason, Kabezhikova apprenticed with Russian folk healers and with an Evenki shaman. In 1996, she was finally initiated into the profession by a hereditary shaman from Tuva and made herself a costume and a drum. At the end of the 1990s, the newly consecrated shamaness opened a small shamanic clinic in a dormitory in Abakan, the capital of Khakassia.[70]

Her spiritual techniques were informed by intensive reading of Michael Harner and Carlos Castaneda. She regularly met with foreign psychiatrists and anthropologists at her home and also traveled to the West, benefiting from the financial support her Western contacts provided for the revival of shamanism in Khakassia. In her curative methods, Kobezhikova relied on soul retrieval and divination as well as healing through energy channels and chakras. She also ran a mystical tourism project, guiding Russian and Western visitors to sacred sites and power places in her homeland, and she invented various rituals that help these spiritual seekers to reach personal growth and ecological awareness.[71] What she did was essentially the creation of a new shamanism. In this role, she reminded me very much of those detribalized Native Americans in the United States who, to create their tradition, borrowed from their American Indian neighbors or mainstream spirituality culture. In a similar vein, Kobezhikova was little different from those Western seekers who seek to regenerate Celtic or Nordic spiritualities.

For some indigenous neo-shamans, Western spirituality print culture and contacts provide not only feedback but also inspiration. The best example that comes to my mind is Tuvan shamaness Ai-Churek, whose name is poetically translated from Tuvan as Moon Heart (see figure 9.5). This woman was consecrated as a shaman in 1993 by Kenin-Lopsan, the Tuvan anthropologist and writer whom I discussed earlier. That year, in the Tuvan National Theater, Western spiritual seekers affiliated with Harner's FSS performed a public healing session over a native actor with a failing heart. The event was part of the first international shamanism conference in Tuva. Ai-Churek came to see the event as a spectator. Then, joining the impromptu healing session, she left the building as a spiritual practitioner. During the ritual manipulations over the sick actor, trying to involve natives who stood nearby, Kenin-Lopsan suddenly handed her a drum and said, "Drum!" Ai-Churek said that she stepped on the stage and began to drum vigorously. In fact, Ai-Churek became involved in the séance of the public healing so deeply that Kenin-Lopsan had to interfere to bring her back to ordinary reality: "just come down. It is all over. It is all right. Just stop drumming." It is notable that in 1998, during her visit to the United States, Ai-Churek stressed that this particular shamanism conference and the contacts with Harner's associates served her as an inspiration to cultivate her own shamanic skills.[72]

FIGURE 9.5. Tuvan shaman Ai-Churek (Moon Heart) during a nighttime ceremony. Courtesy Debra Varner.

After the performance in the Tuvan National Theater, she decided to become a shamanism practitioner on a permanent basis. In addition to her
regular activities in the shamanic clinic, Moon Heart was constantly on the road
participating in various folk and pop concerts and workshops in the United
States, Germany, France, Italy, and elite clubs of Moscow. In her healing
sessions, Ai-Churek usually used the methods of soul retrieval and massage.
She also cleansed houses, businesses, and offices from hostile spirits, and she
repaired sacred landscapes. Even skeptics who are not exactly thrilled about her
use of Western "New Age" and nature jargon have pointed to the powerful
spiritual effect of her rituals and performances on surrounding people. Writer
Benedict Allen, who came to Tuva to explore local beliefs, was very distrustful
of Moon Heart, especially after she called herself a "child of nature." However,
he eventually came to respect the shamaness for the spiritual work she did in
combating the cynicism and materialism implanted in the minds of her
compatriots during Soviet times.[73]

The example of another Siberian spiritual practitioner, Olga Zaporotskaia,
an Itel'men healer (shamanka) from Kamchatka, shows that the integration of
Western and Russian unchurched spirituality is not always an easy process,
especially if it clashes with mainstream Christianity. Zaporotskaia's spiritual
techniques were based on bits and pieces of information she picked up from
her mother, from reading popular occultist and esoteric materials in Russian
newspapers and magazines, from watching television, and from Russian

Orthodox Christianity. Zaporotskaia was an active member of a local Christian church. In fact, she attributed the origin of her curative skills (the opening of the third eye, she said) to her baptism in 1991. The *shamanka* claims that she can see sickness inside a human being, particularly infected internal organs. However, during the Soviet times, she could not situate this unusual experience. At the beginning of the 1990s, as a result of a long illness that coincided with the resurgence of spirituality and religion in the Soviet Union, she felt her calling.

As she explained, her major healing method was the power of her own biofield (*biopole*). The latter is a popular Russian spirituality idiom, which stands close to what Western spiritual seekers usually call spiritual energy. Zaporotskaia also used the idiom of karma and stressed that she diagnosed people's illnesses by observing their auras. At some point, she absorbed so many ideas from "New Age" print media that she could not reconcile them with her Russian Orthodox faith. As a result, in 1995, constantly questioning both her healing methods and Christianity, she suffered a psychological breakdown. Following the advice of her priest, who called that literature heretical, Zaporotskaia burned all of the "New Age" books she had in her collection in order to stay away from temptation. To Olga Murashko, an anthropologist friend who helped Zaporotskaia to overcome her depression and to reconcile her eclectic practices, the shamaness confessed, "I try to squeeze them [the unchurched spirituality ideas] out from my head, but they keep coming back. Once a woman was moving out, and left me some of the same books I had burned. So now I have these titles again."[74]

Those few aged hereditary shamans who can trace their craft to underground spiritual practices performed during the Soviet times are frequently skeptical about the new healers. During our conversation in the summer of 2004, Toty, an old Altaian shamaness from Mountain Altai, noted to me, "The young ones who suddenly begin to claim that they can 'see,' might put themselves in a grave danger" because many of them ignore the fact that the shamanic gift is transmitted in a particular lineage. At one point, our conversation touched upon Sergei Knyev, an Altaian native.[75] This graduate of a local pedagogical university and failed businessman recently turned to spirituality, trying to position himself as the major Altaian shaman. Talking about his dubious claims, Toty was ironic and bitter at the same time:

> This Knyev is a funny guy. He said at the meeting [that he initiated to bring Altaian spiritual practitioners under his wing] that the master of the Altai descended on him on a white horse and gave him a new name, White Moon. You know, when I heard all this crap, I almost dropped from my chair. Who on earth told him that the spirit master of the Altai converses with human beings? How could it happen? Two or three times, Knyev visited me and invited me

to take part in collective prayers, but I refused. Why should I do
this? What is the point? The world is cruel, and it is hard to fix it. I
don't want to be part of it. Several times, he came and asked me to
teach him. Yet after he said that the master of the Altai talked with
him, I could not trust him. This man gets on my nerves.

Since many of the new indigenous technicians of the sacred cannot link
themselves to shamanic lineages, they are not able to inherit their shamanic skills as was common in the old times. Therefore, they try to somehow
receive their powers from such old-timers as Toty. Alternatively, like the above-
mentioned Knyev, they can simply turn to self-initiation and begin acting as
shamanism practitioners. Again, I mention this not in order to debunk these
people as inauthentic or nontraditional. These novel approaches to shamanic
initiation simply show a natural process of invention of tradition.

As contacts between Siberian spiritual practitioners and Western seekers
increase, the groups cross-fertilize each other (see figures 9.6 and 9.7). One of
the first contacts between Western and Siberian neo-shamans was the partnership between Harner's FSS and the Tuvan cultural workers who clustered
around Kenin-Lopsan and Ai-Churek and who sought to regenerate shamanism in their republic. The spark that ignited this spiritual cooperation was a
trip by people affiliated with the FSS to Tuva in 1993 to enlighten Tuvans about
the rudiments of core shamanism and to participate in the conference that I
mentioned above. Harner and his associates assumed that by bringing their

FIGURE 9.6. Siberian neo-shamanism meets Western neo-shamanism. American
spiritual practitioner Verlinda Montoya builds a sweatlodge during a meeting of Native
American and Siberian shamans in southern Siberia, 2003. Courtesy Debra Varner.

FIGURE 9.7. From California to Siberia. José Argüelles, the father of the Whole Earth Festival and the author of *The Mayan Factor: Path beyond Technology* (1987), during his lecture and workshop tour in southern Siberia. Courtesy Anton Yudanov.

core shamanism to native cultures that have lost much of their spirituality, the FSS would provide a skeleton on which interested natives would layer their cultural meat. This thinking goes back to Harner's vision of shamanism. He argued that, stripped of its cultural husk, in its core, the shamanism of each culture can be reduced to several universal and archetypical techniques that were wired into the minds of people at the dawn of their history.

Siberian shamanic knowledge is now increasingly advertised and offered to Western audiences. More European and American spiritual seekers come to Siberia for brief or long-time apprenticeships. Thus, we have an American woman named Julie Stewart who, after apprenticing with a Cherokee medicine person, went native by turning herself into a Buryat shamaness. Now she is known under the name of Sarangerel. Incidentally, she is not only a practitioner of Buryat-style spirituality but also a writer and scholar. Although some academics might discard her writings because they do not fit the format of mainstream scholarship, I found her book *Chosen by the Spirits* (2001) to be one of the best discussions of Buryat-Mongol shamanism in English. The popularity of the semifictional *Entering the Circle* (1996) by former Russian psychiatrist Olga Kharitidi, who now lives in New Mexico, suggests that there also exists a significant publication and commercial venue in this direction.[76]

Written, formatted, and endorsed especially for the Western book market as a Siberian analogue to Castaneda, *Entering the Circle* blends together the mysterious *Belovodie* utopia,[77] recent discoveries in Siberian archaeology (the famous Altai "Ice Princess" with her attractive tattoo), and the wisdom of Siberian shamans. Moreover, in Seattle there is a group of people who, under the guidance of a visiting native teacher, are learning to master the spirituality of the Ulchi, a small indigenous group that resides in the Russian Far East. Another group from Minnesota, which is linked to Sarangerel, works within the tradition of Buryat-Mongol shamanism. Currently, idioms associated with Siberian shamanism are gradually entering Western "New Age" and nature communities and print media. Some spiritual seekers now layer them over Native Americana, Oriental symbolism, and other more popular versions of unchurched spirituality.

Today, in addition to Hindu, Native American, Buddhist, and Latin American *curandero* teachers, the pool of spiritual instructors traveling in Western countries includes Siberian shamanism practitioners. One of the first to tap the Western market was the Nanai shamaness Mingo Geiker, who in 1994 made a trip to the United States, where she conducted seminars in Seattle. The keen attention that American spiritual seekers paid to her knowledge and the gifts with which they showered her turned her head. After coming back home, she exclaimed, "I have conquered America!" To a friend, she related with excitement how one of the American participants in her seminar kneeled before her. In 1995, a ninety-two-year-old Ulchi native from the Russian Far East, the hereditary shaman Misha Duvan, who was accompanied by his relative, choreography teacher Nadyezhda Duvan, arrived in Seattle where they similarly attracted the attention of the local mind, body, and spirit community. Jan van Vanysslestyne, a psychologist who accommodated them in the United States, became so fascinated with their spirituality that she exclaimed, "This was it. I had found my people."[78]

Those shamans who do not want or do not have a chance to travel abroad sometimes frown upon such sharing of spirituality. Like Native American critics of "plastic" medicine people, they argue that native spirituality should always remain within a community. Some Siberian shamanism practitioners stress that transplanting indigenous knowledge on alien soil upsets the spirits, who eventually inflict various misfortunes on the cosmopolitan spiritual practitioners. For example, a Nanai shaman, Chapaka, attributed Mingo Geiker's quick death to her American visit:

> Mingo died right after she returned home. Having come back, she fell badly ill. Her eyes hurt, she even lost consciousness. That's how [her spirits] punished her! (Her spirits meant: "She was traveling all around chattering and did not give any attention to us!")
> Her own spirits have tortured her to death. Her own spirits! As some

of the shamans go somewhere [to perform], they die. They travel and die. I pity them!

Another Nanai shamaness similarly attributed Mingo's death to her "singing in the shaman way in America."[79] Still, many other Siberian shamanism practitioners continue to travel overseas and to put on performances. So far, they feel well and sound, and their spirits do not seem to be disturbing them.

Epilogue

This book ties the growing popularity of the shamanism idiom and the emergence of neo-shamanism to antimodern sentiments in Western intellectual culture. Since the 1960s, Western academics and spiritual seekers have increasingly questioned the modes of thinking associated with the Enlightenment and, more broadly, with the Western tradition in general. More often than not, this tradition is viewed as devoid of spiritual and ecological values. The romance with the ancient, the primitive, and the occult is a follow-up to the frustration many Europeans and Americans feel about their own civilization.

In some respects, the present rise of antimodernism in the West reminds us of the Romanticism movement in Europe in the early nineteenth century, the first reaction to the advances of the Enlightenment. In fact, much of antimodernism in current humanities and many ideas popular in nature spiritualities can be traced to Romantic writers and philosophers. Like their intellectual predecessors, modern Western seekers and many academics crusade against materialistic science and lament the emptiness of modern Western life, looking to non-European traditions and to European antiquity for spiritual feedback. This line of thought that is critical of modernity has been visibly present in Western tradition since the age of the Enlightenment. However, the antimodern sentiments never reached such large proportions as in the past forty years. Although it has been suggested that these notions, like cycles, rise from time to time in response to popular fatigue with advances in science and technology,[1] there is no indication that the present renaissance of nature philosophy and increasing attention to the spiritual, the irrational, and the tribal will subside in the future. This appears to be the major difference between the revolt against the modern world in the past and in the present.

With the rise of the counterculture in the 1960s and environmental movements in the 1970s, which began to question on a grand scale the values of Western civilization, all old and new spiritual alternatives, which to that moment had existed on the fringes of spiritual and social life, came into the spotlight. By the 1990s, a growing community of people who partook of theosophy, Jungian scholarship, and humanistic and transpersonal psychology and who shared the popular interest in classical Oriental and tribal beliefs produced a consciousness revolution that, to some extent, disarmed a society steeped in materialism and rationalism.[2]

The elements of this consciousness revolution, which in the 1960s were treated as countercultural and alternative, have now entered the mainstream and become forms of collective behavior. At the present time, for many, these forms of behavior define how we pray, eat, sleep, work, spend our leisure time, and fulfill ourselves. They include a sensitive approach to nature, the popularity of organic foods, natural lifestyles, and the emergence of nature philosophy as part of a general culture and political process (for example, the nationwide celebration of Earth Day in the United States and the emergence of Green parties on the Western political scene). The spiritual life of people has become less dogmatic and organized and more individualistic and eclectic as diversity gradually replaces uniformity.[3] It is indicative of this movement that almost 20 percent of Americans now treat with respect the mind, body, and spirit techniques and remedies.[4] The shamanism idiom, which is associated with ancient, spontaneous, individually tailored spiritual activities performed in altered states of consciousness, neatly fits that consciousness revolution.

As I showed in the first and third chapters of this book, prior to the 1960s, not many European and American observers saw the beauty in tribal cultures, which drew only marginal attention. As a manifestation of the primitive world, the word *shamanism* never drew popular attention, being limited to the workshop talk of anthropologists who were researching Siberia and North America. The expression carried a host of negative and antimodern notions, including the bizarre, the irrational, the erratic, and the abnormal. In the 1960s and 1970s, with the general shift in Western intellectual culture away from the Enlightenment tradition, the meanings of the normal and abnormal, the civilized and the primitive were revisited. Precisely because of its antimodern associations, which were now defined as virtuous, the expression shamanism became endowed with positive meaning. Thus, from the odd obscurantist, the shaman became a symbol of wisdom and spiritual redemption. It is not coincidental that, during this time, some American and European academics and writers found the term convenient not only for the description of non-Western nature religions but also for reflecting on spontaneous, irrational, and creative behavior in general. For example, since the 1970s, literature and media increasingly have begun to use shamanism to refer to musicians, artists, writers, and poets who in their creative pursuits go beyond the conventional limits established by contemporary European and American societies.

The aura of the universal and the ancient that Mircea Eliade's classic *Shamanism: Archaic Techniques of Ecstasy* (1964) firmly attached to the word shamanism by default set the term in opposition to the modern. This certainly could not escape the attention of spiritual seekers and academics who were revolting against Enlightenment tradition. The widespread use of psychedelics in the 1960s and the flow of information about the ritual use of psychotropic plants by ancient and modern tribal peoples greatly stimulated public interest in shamanism, especially among those who sought to situate their pharmacological experiences as a spiritual quest. Associated with elementary earth-based societies, which are viewed as stewards of nature, shamanism also carries powerful nature notions that have resonated well with the earth-based ethics that has increasingly molded Western consciousness since the 1970s.

One also should attribute the increasing usage of the word *shaman* to the revision by academics and writers of old terminology that was used to describe non-Western beliefs. During the past forty years, as non-Western nature spiritualities came to occupy an equal place in the family of so-called world religions, such expressions as sorcerers, jugglers, magicians, and witch doctors began to look outdated, betraying the legacy of Eurocentrism and colonialism. As a possible substitute, priest has not qualified, either, because the word is too tied to Judeo-Christian tradition. Presumably, shaman and shamanism do not carry those connotations. The words not only lack any of the above-mentioned biases but are also conveniently devoid of the usage hassles associated with such gender-specific expressions as medicine man and medicine woman; in the Tungus (Evenki), shaman has nothing to do with "man" and is used for the description of spiritual practitioners of both genders.[5]

The fact that the term is of non-Western origin might have added to its attraction. Although culturally linked to the Siberian indigenous group and screened through German and Russian eyes, shamanism is not rooted in any Latin word to be somehow stigmatized as a Western derivative. Hence, the expression can serve well for the description of tribal beliefs all over the world. Even those scholars who do not like to use generic definitions pulled from particular cultural contexts use this term when they need to discuss earth-based spiritual practices across cultures. As an alternative, these academics sometimes use the plural *shamanisms* to stress the variety of spiritual practices. At the same time, in their postmodern desire to get rid of all abstract concepts and paradigms, some anthropology scholars now oppose the term shamanism in principle, replacing it with culturally specific definitions. Despite this hesitance on the part of some anthropologists, the overall use of shamans and shamanism in the humanities, social sciences, and spirituality literature has been on the rise.

In the 1970s, the associations attributed to these words appeared meaningful to Western seekers who wanted to situate their spiritual quests in opposition or as supplementary to the mainstream Judeo-Christian tradition. That is how neo-shamanism emerged as a postmodern spirituality movement well suited for current cultural life. Like many other "New Age" and nature spiritualities, neo-shamanism sprang up in the United States and then spread to other Western countries. For many traditionalists and nature-oriented people, this country, where one can see the fruits of modernity in their extreme, represents the ultimate den of materialism and cosmopolitanism. Therefore, it was natural that, in the 1960s and 1970s, the first spiritual antidotes to modernity blossomed in America. There are certainly cultural prerequisites. Americans are traditionally open to religious experimentation. Since the founding of this country, many people believe that they have the right to choose their own religion or to follow none at all.

The American origin of the "New Age" also explains why Native Americana was held in such great esteem in neo-shamanism, especially in the 1970s and 1980s. Earlier marginalized by modern society as primitive and archaic, in the 1960s and 1970s, Native Americans became for Western seekers a symbol of superior moral and spiritual values precisely because those particular qualities ascribed to them by society had acquired a positive meaning. Some Native American cultural workers and spokespeople are not thrilled about the use of their traditions as a spiritual remedy to cure the ills of Western civilization. Although both Native American and non-native seekers frequently draw on the same intellectual traditions—Romantic nature and primitivist philosophy—they pursue different goals, which leads to a contest over the use of Native Americana. At the core of this dispute are two different approaches to identity. Non-Indian seekers treat spirituality as an individual choice, whereas Native American cultural workers view it as a collective resource to be used to shape their cultural identity. The critical approach of American Indian spokespeople toward the use of Native Americana by the wider society has prompted many Westerners to revisit the form of their spiritual practices. As a result, today, European and American seekers who describe their spiritual activities as shamanic increasingly move away from non-Western traditions. More often than not, they set their spiritual quests in pre-Christian European traditions. The most popular forms of spiritual identity are currently Celtic and Nordic. Still, there are a number of Western seekers who continue to receive spiritual input from non-Western traditions, including Native Americana.

Some academic critics frown on both the experimentation with non-Western symbolism and spiritual practices based on reconstructed pre-Christian European spirituality, considering them superficial and flaky. These critics describe "New Age" and nature spiritual pursuits as "the chic primitivism of a bored affluence" (sociologist Michael Harrington) or the decadent culture of late industrial capitalism (anthropologist Lisa Aldred).[6] Such assertions certainly tell us more about these authors' moral attitudes toward these spiritualities than they explain them. What makes such assessments especially questionable is the view of popular spiritual pursuits as a sign of cultural decline or as a spiritual perversion.

It appears to me that these critics look at the cultural and spiritual life of Western countries through outdated lenses. Unlike the early twentieth century, when the pursuit of the tribal and the ancient was affordable only to a few wealthy bohemians or to a small group of anthropologists and writers, now such spiritual quests are accessible literally to all members of the Western middle class and beyond. Materially secure and with a sufficient amount of leisure time on their hands, many representatives of this growing group of people are naturally more concerned about spiritual matters. Interested in the world beyond their backyards, in their drive to fulfill themselves, they strive to explore themselves and to learn from different cultures. The number of such seekers is increasing. Twisting the Harrington "chic primitivism" phrase around, one may say that many of us (at least in Western countries) sooner or later will eventually become "bourgeoisie" who are bored with material affluence. This bourgeoisie will certainly not be satisfied with the culture and spirituality that suited their parents and grandparents.

The "New Age" and nature spiritualities might appear bizarre to a person immersed in materialism or to an academic who measures cultural and social life by the nineteenth-century Marxist yardstick. There is no doubt that many people coming from underprivileged or third world backgrounds might also find these Western spiritual pursuits to be peculiar. Most probably, they will subscribe to the Harrington quote above. Much of what Western seekers do might appear equally preposterous to Native American fundamentalists or to some scholars who still think that a culture is something old, remote, and frozen in time and space.

The view that the attempts of Western seekers to become tribal are superficial is the most widespread criticism leveled against the "New Age" and modern pagans. Indeed, cast against the ideal traditional culture, their recently invented rituals and creation tales do not look genuine and authentic. Although the attempts of Western seekers to position themselves as the spiritual successors of Native American or, alternatively, Celtic and Nordic traditions will certainly never withstand serious scrutiny, there is no doubt that we are dealing here with a new spiritual movement that has a large number of adherents. Since this is the realm of the sacred, there is nothing illegitimate or superficial in these spiritual quests simply because, in matters of religion, the debate about what represents genuine and nongenuine does not make much sense.[7] For example, the creation story and rituals pioneered by Joseph Smith similarly appeared preposterous to mainstream Christians in the first half of the nineteenth century. Still, nobody will deny that out of his prophecy grew the powerful Mormon Church with hundreds of thousands of followers within and outside the United States. In fact, using the arguments of the critics of emerged or emerging "New Age" and nature spiritualities, one could equally dismiss as inauthentic such American Indian beliefs as, for example, the Handsome Lake Religion or the Native American Church. The first one was the result of the prophecy of Handsome Lake, the early nineteenth-century Indian spiritual leader who blended the Iroquois and Quaker beliefs. The second one was invented at the turn of the twentieth century and merged pan-Indian elements with Christianity.

Unchurched spiritualities that draw on the ancient and the tribal are a visible trait of the present American and European cultural landscape. Many of them have already acquired lives of their own and have many followers. As such, they have certainly become genuine, authentic, and traditional. To those scholars who are ready to explore the phenomenon of the "New Age" and nature spiritualities on their own terms, shamanic practices in the Western urban setting are no better and no worse than rituals of any other natives or non-natives, be they Sun Dancing Lakota, scientologists, Buddhists, or American Southern Baptists.

In this book, I have tried to show that the fuzzy community of neo-shamanism emerged at the convergence of the counterculture/environmental movements, anthropology, psychology, and Native Americana. The 1960s and 1970s counterculture and nature movements, with their reverential attitude toward nature, created a fertile soil for the rise of various earth-based spiritualities. Historian of religion Kocku von Stuckrad, who explored in detail this aspect of neo-shamanism, traced the intellectual roots of neo-shamanism to the nineteenth-century philosophy of nature of the German Romantics, American transcendentalists, and John Muir. The conviction that nature is divine and alive lies at the foundation of many "New Age" and nature spiritualities.

In addition to earth-centered philosophy, anthropology and psychology were two other major spearheads of neo-shamanism. It is no accident that many current teachers of shamanism in the West are people with anthropology or psychology training. Anthropology sprang up in the nineteenth century, primarily as a scholarly enterprise devoted to the exploration of non-Western elementary societies. It was natural that, in the 1960s and 1970s, Western seekers, who came to consider these people an antidote to Western modernity, found in anthropology texts blueprints of ideal spiritual and ethical behavior. Moreover, some anthropologists themselves entered the community of Western esotericism, becoming shamanism teachers and practitioners. The most well-known names are Michael Harner, Edith Turner, and the former long-time editor of *American Anthropologist*, Barbara Tedlock. The label "shaman-thropologists," which historian of religion Daniel Noel attached to such academics, is not completely wrong.

Modern anthropology shares with the "New Age" one important thing: both of them idealize tribal primitives. In fact, the anthropology of consciousness, an offshoot of mainstream anthropology scholarship, advocates conversion to native spirituality as the best way to gain insight into the mindset of the cultural other. Layered onto our politically correct times, the rehabilitation of tribal peoples, which began in the 1960s, quickly turned into the glorification and idealization of these people specifically and of non-Western cultures generally. Driven by moral considerations and anti-Western sentiments, many anthropologists began to silently repress the negative features of tribal living and to exaggerate the positive ones.[8]

The contribution of psychology, especially popular psychology, which has been pivotal for many newly emerged unchurched spiritualities, was no less important. As a manifestation of altered states, shamanism was a natural match for psychology. Yet, as long as psychology remained within the limits of positive science, there was no way to explore this spirituality on its own terms. As a result, for a long time, psychologists considered shamans to be "abnormal." The breakthrough came in the 1960s with the rise of humanistic and transpersonal psychology, which moved away from materialism and behaviorism, revisited the concept of the abnormal, and began to consider the spiritual to be a valid experience. The therapeutic techniques of tribal shamans became a source of knowledge to be utilized for the benefit of Western society. Incidentally, many current shamanic practices in the West exist as programs of short- or long-term spiritual therapy conducted by people trained or at least well read in transpersonal psychology.

Finally, setting neo-shamanic practices broadly within the tradition of Western esotericism, I want to suggest that they belong both to the "New Age" realm and to the modern pagan movement. This originates from the very stance of neo-shamans, who may be either global, local, or both in their spiritual pursuits. Some Western spiritual practitioners of shamanism format their techniques in the "New Age" style. They are eclectics who are oriented toward universal spirituality and who freely borrow from the East and the West. They also believe that spiritual knowledge can be delivered through workshops. Harner's core shamanism and similar spiritual therapies are good examples of such approaches. These seekers assume that there are universal archetypes of shamanism, which are equally characteristic for all cultures (altered states, the shamanic spiritual journey, the three-layered universe, shamanic illness, and others) and which can be learned and replicated in any cultural setting.

At the same time, today the increasing number of shamanism practitioners argues that these features are not necessarily universal, or, if they are, they manifest themselves as local spiritual knowledge intimately linked to a particular cultural and natural landscape. The premise here is that one cannot transplant culturally bounded spiritual practices (shamanisms) to another cultural realm or distill them into a generic shamanism. These spiritual practitioners, who have moved away from the Eliadean vision of shamanism, seek to tie themselves to their own indigenous traditions, a stance they share with many members of modern pagan communities. Interestingly, this sentiment mirrors the similar approach popular among current anthropologists, who view particular nature spiritualities as autonomous cultural traditions that should not be piled together and described by the generic word shamanism. Obviously, such tribalization among both seekers and academics is also a manifestation of the general postmodern approach to knowledge that is described as fluid, dispersed, and culture-bound. Overall, in the modern West, neo-shamanism can exist as a cosmopolitan spiritual therapy that blends elements of many cultures worldwide and as a form of pagan nature spirituality set in a Native American, Siberian, Hawaiian, Celtic, Nordic, or other geographically or culturally specific tradition.

Notes

PREFACE

1. Mircea Eliade, *Shamanism: Archaic Techniques of Ecstasy* (Princeton, NJ: Princeton University Press, 1964).

2. Andrei A. Znamenski, *Shamanism in Siberia: Russian Records of Siberian Spirituality* (Dordrecht and Boston: Kluwer Academic, 2003); *Shamanism: Critical Concepts in Sociology*, edited by Andrei A. Znamenski, 3 vols. (London: Routledge, 2004).

3. On a mass spiritual awakening during this decade, see Robert S. Ellwood, *The Sixtieth Spiritual Awakening: American Religion Moving from Modern to Postmodern* (New Brunswick, NJ: Rutgers University Press, 1994).

4. I borrowed this expression from Eric Wolf, *Europe and the People without History* (1982; reprint, Berkeley: University of California Press, 1997).

5. I want to note that Nevill Drury, a prominent nature spirituality author from Australia who is well versed in shamanism, feels comfortable using this expression in his *The New Age: The History of a Movement* (London: Thames and Hudson, 2004), probably because he could not find a better general phrase to describe this phenomenon.

6. Robert C. Fuller, *Spiritual but Not Religious: Understanding Unchurched America* (Oxford and New York: Oxford University Press, 2001).

7. Catherine Albanese, *Nature Religion in America: From the Algonkian Indians to the New Age* (Chicago: University of Chicago Press, 1990).

8. Kocku von Stuckrad, *Western Esotericism: A Brief History of Secret Knowledge* (London and Oakville: Equinox, 2005), 10–11, 140–141.

9. For the most recent work that is harshly critical of neo-shamanism, see Alice Kehoe's *Shamans and Religion: An Anthropological Exploration in Critical Thinking* (Prospect Heights, IL: Waveland, 2000). Kehoe portrays Western seekers of shamanism as people who are involved in "flaky" activities

that perpetuate racist stereotypes of tribal people as primitives. She also makes a point that the shamanic practices of native Siberians and Native Americans are real, while Western neo-shamanism is not. Ironically, by doing this, Kehoe herself perpetuates the romantic image of tribal societies as carriers of "genuine" and "traditional" culture. She also argues that the shamanism idiom should be reserved for the area it originally described: Siberia and northern North America.

10. Ronald Hutton, *Shamans: Siberian Spirituality and the Western Imagination* (London: Hambledon and London, 2001); Hutton, *The Triumph of the Moon: A History of Modern Pagan Witchcraft* (Oxford: Oxford University Press, 1999).

11. Jeremy Narby and Francis Huxley, eds., *Shamans through Time: 500 Years on the Path to Knowledge* (New York: Jeremy P. Tarcher/Putnam, 2001); Kocku von Stuckrad, *Schamanismus und Esoterik: Kultur- und wissenschaftsgeschichtliche Betrachtungen* (Leuven: Peeters, 2003); Philip Jenkins, *Dream Catchers: How Mainstream America Discovered Native Spirituality* (New York: Oxford University Press, 2004); Gloria Flaherty, *Shamanism and the Eighteenth Century* (Princeton, NJ: Princeton University Press, 1992).

CHAPTER I

1. One of the first known records to mention a shaman character is a manuscript by Russian religious schismatic archpriest Avvakum, whom a Russian tsar banished to Siberia in the 1660s. There, in the 1670s, he wrote his autobiography, in which he recorded his tribulations. Among ordeals he had to deal with as a Christian, the archpriest named a shamanic séance solicited by a local Russian official named Pashkov. The bureaucrat ordered a native spiritual practitioner to predict if a contemplated military attack against the Mongols would be successful. Archpriest Avvakum, *The Life Written by Himself*, translated and edited by Kenneth N. Brostrom (Ann Arbor: University of Michigan Press, 1979), 71. The use of the shamans' services by the Russian official should not surprise. In the seventeenth century and later, in Siberia, local Russian folk, including officials, did not find it appalling to use the services of indigenous shamans.

2. Nicolaas Witsen, *Noord en ost Tartaryen* (1692; reprint, Amsterdam: M. Schalekamp, 1785).

3. See, for example, J. Dadley and Alexander William, *The Costume of the Russian Empire* (London: Bulmer, 1803); Ferdinand von Wrangel, *Narrative of an Expedition to the Polar Sea in the Years 1820, 1821, 1822 and 1823* (New York: Harper, 1841).

4. Philip Johann von Strahlenberg, *An Historical-Geographical Description of the North and Eastern Parts of Europe and Asia* (London: Printed for W. Innys and R. Manby, 1738), 334, 458.

5. Johann Gottlieb Georgi, *Opisanie vsiekh obitaiushchikh v Rossiiskom gosudarstve narodov* (St. Petersburg: izhdiveniem I. Grazunova, 1799), 3:114; Peter Simon Pallas, *Puteshestvie po raznym miestam Rossiiskago gosudarstva* (St. Petersburg: Imperatorskaia Akademiia nauk, 1788), 3, part 1: 306, 82.

6. Ekaterina II (Catherine II, Empress of Russia), *Sochineniia*, edited by Ars I. Vvedenskii (St. Petersburg: Marksa, 1893), 307. For the English translation, see Catherine II, Empress of Russia, *Two Comedies by Catherine the Great, Empress of Russia,*

edited by Lurana Donnels O'Malley (Amsterdam: Harwood Academic, 1998). A detailed analysis of *The Siberian Shaman* can be found in Kocku von Stuckrad, *Schamanismus und Esoterik: Kultur- und wissenschaftsgeschichtliche Betrachtungen* (Leuven: Peeters, 2003), 58–66.

7. J. L. Black and Dieter K. Buse, *G.-F. Müller and Siberia, 1733–1743* (Kingston, Ontario: Limestone, 1989), 85–86.

8. Georgi, *Opisanie vsiekh obitaiushchikh v Rossiiskom gosudarstve narodov*, 113.

9. Stepan Krasheninnikov, *Opisanie zemli Kamchatki* (St. Petersburg: Imperatorskaia akademia nauk, 1786), 2:158–159; Pallas, *Puteshestvie po raznym miestam Rossiiskago gosudarstva*, 105; Aleksandr K. Elert, *Narody Sibiri v trudakh G. F. Millera* (Novosibirsk: Inst. Archeologii i etnografii SO RAN, 1999), 50; Johann Gmelin, "Shamans Deserve Perpetual Labor for Their Hocus-Pocus," in *Shamans through Time: 500 Years on the Path to Knowledge*, edited by Jeremy Narby and Francis Huxley (New York: J. P. Tarcher/Putnam, 2001), 28.

10. *Pamiatniki Sibirskoi istorii XVIII veka*, edited by A. I. Timofeev (1882; reprint, The Hague: Mouton, 1969), 1:240–242; 2:365–367, 436–442.

11. Elert, *Narody Sibiri v trudakh G. F. Millera*, 47, 50.

12. Pallas, *Puteshestvie po raznym miestam Rossiiskago gosudarstva*, 305.

13. V. F. Zuev, *Materialy po etnografii Sibiri XVIII veka* (Moskva: izdatel'stvo Akademii nauk SSSR, 1947), 44.

14. Pallas, *Puteshestvie po raznym miestam Rossiiskago gosudarstva*, 102.

15. G. F. Miller [Müller], *Istoriia Sibiri* (1750; reprint, Moskva: vostochnaia literatura RAN, 1999), 1:532.

16. Georgi, *Opisanie vsiekh obitaiushchikh v Rossiiskom gosudarstve narodov*, 110–111 (for his essay "On Pagan Shamanic Order," see 98–116).

17. Adolph Erman, *Travels in Siberia* (London: Longman, 1848), 2:39.

18. Harry Oldmeadow, *Journeys East: 20th-Century Western Encounters with Eastern Religious Traditions* (Bloomington, IN: World Wisdom, 2004), 21.

19. Arthur Herman, *The Idea of Decline in Western History* (New York: Free Press, 1997), 57.

20. Friedrich Schlegel, *Lectures on the History of Literature* (London: George Bell & Sons, 1876), 114, 139.

21. Ludwik Niemojowski, *Siberian Pictures* (1857; English translation, London: Hurst and Blackett, 1883), 1:174.

22. Ibid., 179.

23. Charles Godfrey Leland, "The Edda among the Algonquin Indians," in *Native American Folklore in Nineteenth-Century Periodicals*, edited by W. M. Clements (Athens, OH; Chicago; and London: Swallow Press and Ohio University Press, 1986), 147.

24. Charles Godfrey Leland, *Algonquin Legends of New England* (1884; reprint, New York: Dover, 1992), 11, 336.

25. "Schamanismus," *Brockhaus' Konversations-lexikon* (1896), 381; (1908), 383; "Schamanismus," *Meyers großes Konversations-lexikon* (1909), 7:689.

26. *Oxford English Dictionary* (1933), 9:616.

27. *Etymological Dictionary of the Russian Language*, edited by A. G. Preobrazhensky (New York: Columbia University Press, 1951), 87.

28. Berthold Laufer, "Origin of the Word Shaman," *American Anthropologist* 19 (1917): 366; "shaman," *American Heritage Dictionary*, 2d college ed. (1985), 1126; Joan Halifax, "Into the Neirika," in *Shamanic Voices: A Survey of Visionary Narratives*, edited by Joan Halifax (New York: Dutton, 1979), 3; Larry G. Peters, *Trance, Initiation & Psychotherapy in Nepalese Shamanism* (Delhi: Nirala, 2003), 7, 13–31; Gloria Flaherty, "The Performing Artist as the Shaman of Higher Civilization," *German Issue* 103, no. 3 (1988): 525.

29. N. D. Mironov and Sergei Shirokogoroff, "Sramana-Shaman: Etymology of the Word 'Shaman,'" *Journal of the North China Branch of the Royal Asiatic Society* 55 (1924): 111.

30. Sergei Shirokogoroff, *Psychomental Complex of the Tungus* (London: Kegan Paul, 1935), 270, 283.

31. Dorji Banzarov, "The Black Faith; or, Shamanism among the Mongols," *Mongolian Studies: Journal of the Mongolia Society* 7 (1981–1982): 56–57.

32. Ibid., 54.

33. For more about how, with their stress on trances, ecstasy, dream states, and nature, Romantic writers laid the foundation for modern earth-based spiritualities, see von Stuckrad, *Schamanismus und Esoterik*, 83–106, 195–221.

34. *Puteshesvie po Altaiskim goram i dzhungarskoi Kirgizskoi stepi*, edited by O. N. Vilkov and A. P. Okladnikov (Novosibirsk: Nauka, 1993), 164, 173–174, 200–201, 203, 216.

35. Frants Beliavskii, *Poezdka k Ledovitomu moriu* (Moskva: v tipografii Lazarevyk instituta vostochnykh iazykov, 1833), 111–122; M. F. Krivoshapkin, *Eniseiskii okrug i ego zhizn'* (St. Petersburg: v tipografii V. Bezobrazova, 1865); Wrangel, *Narrative of an Expedition to the Polar Sea.*

36. Wrangel, *Narrative of an Expedition to the Polar Sea*, 1:136, 286.

37. Ibid., 123, 286.

38. Beliavskii, *Poezdka k Ledovitomu moriu*, 116; Wrangel, *Narrative of an Expedition to the Polar Sea*, 1:285.

39. Krivoshapkin, *Eniseiskii okrug i ego zhizn'*, 315–316; Wrangel, *Narrative of an Expedition to the Polar Sea*, 1:123.

40. Otto Finsch, *Puteshestvie v Zapadnuiu Sibir'* (Moskva: Tip. M. N. Lavrova, 1882), 492.

41. Flaherty, "The Performing Artist as the Shaman of Higher Civilization," 535.

42. Von Stuckrad, *Schamanismus und Esoterik*, 195–205.

43. Novalis, *Henry von Ofterdingen: A Novel*, translated by Palmer Hilty (New York: Ungar, 1964).

44. Kocku von Stuckrad, "Reenchanting Nature: Modern Western Shamanism and Nineteenth-Century Thought," *Journal of the American Academy of Religion* 70 (2002): 784–788.

45. Merle Curti, "The American Exploration of Dreams and Dreamers," *Journal of the History of Ideas* 27, no. 3 (1966): 404–405.

46. *H. D. Thoreau: A Writer's Journal*, edited by Laurence Stapleton (New York: Dover, 1960), 6.

47. Lee Gentry, "Thoreau and the Indian." Available at http://www.vcu.edu/engweb/transcendentalism/criticism/hdt-indian.html (downloaded July 8, 2005).

48. Herman, *The Idea of Decline in Western History*, 136.

49. Ronald Hutton, the well-known historian of modern Western witchcraft and paganism, discussed this part of Leland's career in his *The Triumph of the Moon: A History of Modern Pagan Witchcraft* (Oxford: Oxford University Press, 1999), 141–148.

50. Thomas C. Parkhill, *Weaving Ourselves into the Land: Charles Godfrey Leland, "Indians," and the Study of Native American Religions* (Albany: State University of New York Press, 1997), 91, 96–97.

51. Leland, *Algonquin Legends of New England*, 338–339.

52. Parkhill, *Weaving Ourselves into the Land*, 104.

53. Charles G. Leland, "Legends of the Passamaquoddy," *Century Magazine* 28, no. 5 (1884): 668.

54. Toivo Vuorela, *Ethnology in Finland before 1920* (Helsinki: Societas scientiarum Fennica, 1977), 20.

55. M. Alexander Kastren [Castren], *Puteshestvie v Sibir', 1845–1849* (Tiumen': Y. Mandriki, 1999), 2:52.

56. M. Alexander Castren, *Vorlesungen über die Finnische Mythologie* (St. Petersburg: Buchdruckerei der Kaiserlichen Akademie der Wissenschaften, 1853).

57. Kastren, *Puteshestvie v Sibir'*, 2:52.

58. Juha Pentikäinen, "Northern Ethnography—On the Foundations of a New Paradigm." Available at http://rehue.csociales.uchile.cl/antropologia/congreso/c05 .html (downloaded July 8, 2005).

59. N. V. Shlygina, *Istoriia finskoi etnologii* (Moskva: institut etnologii, 1995), 32.

60. V. G. Bogoraz [Bogoras], "Kastren-chelovek i uchenii," in *Pamiaty Kastrena*, edited by V. G. Bogoraz (Leningrad: iz-vo AN SSSR, 1927), 33.

61. Kai Donner, *Among the Samoyed in Siberia* (New Haven, CT: Human Relations Area Files, 1954), 20.

62. Ibid., 116.

63. Ibid., 117.

64. Ibid., 20.

65. Ibid., 116.

66. Ibid., 69.

67. Uno Holmberg [Harva], *The Mythology of All Races: Finno-Ugric, Siberian* (New York: Cooper Square, 1964), 4:xx.

68. Holmberg [Harva], *Die religiösen Vorstellungen der Altaischen Völker* (Helsinki: Suomalainen Tiedeakatemia, 1938); Holmberg [Harva], *Der Baum des Lebens* (Helsinki: Suomalainen Tiedeakatemia, 1922), 33–51, 133–145; Mircea Eliade, *Shamanism: Archaic Techniques of Ecstasy* (Princeton, NJ: Princeton University Press, 1964), xi.

69. Stephen Glosecki, *Shamanism and Old English Poetry* (New York and London: Garland, 1989), 3; "shamanism," *Encyclopedia Britannica*, 9th ed. (1886), 21:771.

70. Wilhelm Radloff, *Aus Sibirien: Lose Blätter aus dem Tagebuche eines reisenden Linguisten*, 2 vols. (Leipzig: Weigel, 1884); "shamanism," *Encyclopedia Britannica*, 771.

71. Radloff, *Aus Sibirien*, 2:2.

72. Ibid.

73. Ibid., 2:55.

74. Ibid., 2:3.

75. Ibid., 2:14.

76. Ibid., 2:58.

77. Ibid., 2:19–50.

78. V. M. Mikhailovskii, "Shamanism in Siberia and European Russia," *Journal of the Royal Anthropological Society* 24 (1895): 74–78; J. Stadling, "Shamanism," *Contemporary Review* 79 (1901): 93; M. A. Czaplicka, *Aboriginal Siberia: A Study in Social Anthropology* (Oxford: Clarendon, 1914), 298; Eliade, *Shamanism*, 190–197; Nora Chadwick and V. Zhirmunsky, *Oral Epics of Central Asia* (Cambridge: Cambridge University Press 1969), 243–249; J. A. MacCullouch, "Shamanism," in *Encyclopedia of Religion and Ethics*, edited by James Hastings (Edinburgh: Clark; and New York: Scribner's, 1920), 11:442; M. Franz, *C. G. Jung: His Myth in Our* Time (Boston and Toronto: Little, Brown, 1975), 101–102.

79. Radloff, *Aus Sibirien*, 2:52.

80. Julian Baldick, *Animal and Shaman: Ancient Religions of Central Asia* (New York: New York University Press, 2000), 70; Chadwick and Zhirmunsky, *Oral Epics of Central Asia*, 237–238, 245.

81. Eliade, *Shamanism*, 190–198.

CHAPTER 2

1. Marie-Louise Franz, *C. G. Jung: His Myth in Our Time* (Boston: Little, Brown, 1975), 108–109.

2. Oswald Spengler, *The Decline of the West* (1918; English translation, 1926; reprint, New York: Knopf, 1996), 1:427; Arthur Herman, *The Idea of Decline in Western History* (New York: Free Press, 1997), 234, 237.

3. Velimir Khlebnikov, *Collected Works*, edited by Ronald Vroon (Cambridge, MA: Harvard University Press, 1997), 3:140.

4. For more about the Western primitivism movement at the turn of the twentieth century, see Elazar Barkan and Ronald Bush, eds., *Prehistories of the Future: The Primitivist Project and the Culture of Modernism* (Stanford, CA: Stanford University Press, 1995).

5. Peg Weiss, *Kandinsky and Old Russia: The Artist as Ethnographer and Shaman* (New Haven, CT: Yale University Press, 1995).

6. Naomi Green, *Antonin Artaud: Poet without Words* (New York: Simon and Schuster, 1970), 147.

7. E. L. Zubashev, "Grigorii Nikolaevich Potanin: Vospominaniia," *Vol'naia Sibir'* (Prague) 1 (1927): 62.

8. *Pis'ma G. N. Potanina*, edited by A. G. Grum-Grzhimailo (Irkutsk: iz-vo Irkutskogo universiteta, 1989), 3:81.

9. I. R. Koshelev, *Russkaia fol'kloristika Sibiri* (Tomsk: iz-vo Tomskogo universiteta, 1962), 127–128.

10. "N. M. Iadrintsev to Alexandr Khristoforov, 6 December 1883," *Vol'naia Sibir'* 2 (1927): 184.

11. N. M. Iadrintsev, "Altai i ego inorodcheskoe tsarstvo: Ocherk puteshestvia po Altaiu," *Istoricheskii vestnik* 20, no. 6 (1885): 628.

12. Andrei Anokhin, "Shamanizm sibirskih tiurkskikh plemen," Museum of Anthropology and Ethnography Archive, St. Petersburg, Anokhin Papers, fond 11, series 1, file 144, leaf 17 back.

13. N. M. Iadrintsev, *Sibir' kaka kolonia* (St. Petersburg: tip. M. M. Stasiulevicha, 1882), 124.

14. Ibid., 123–124.

15. Potanin articulated his Oriental hypothesis in the following works: *Vostochnie motivy v srednevekovom Evropeiskom epose* (Moskva: tipo-litografiia tovar. I. N. Kushnerev, 1899); *Saga o Solomone: Vostochnie materialy k voprosu o proiskhozhdenii sagi* (Tomsk: izd. Sibirskago t-va pechatnago diela, 1912); *Erke: Kul't syna neba v Sievernoi Azii* (Tomsk: izd. A. M. Grigor'evoi, 1916).

16. Grum-Grzhimailo, *Pis'ma G. N. Potanina*, 3:166.

17. Potanin, *Saga o Solomone*, 2–3, 105.

18. Grum-Grzhimailo, *Pis'ma G. N. Potanina*, 3:80–81.

19. Ibid., 90.

20. Potanin, "Proiskhozhdenie Khrista," *Sibirkie ogni* 4 (1926): 131.

21. Andrei M. Sagalaev and Vladimir M. Kryukov, *G. N. Potanin: Opyt osmyslenia lichnosti* (Novosibirsk: Nauka, 1991), 136.

22. G. V. Ksenofontov, *Shamanizm i khristianstvo* (Irkutsk: tip. Vlast' truda, 1929).

23. Ibid., 128.

24. *Schamanengeschichten aus Sibirien*, edited and translated by A. Friedrich and G. Buddruss (München-Planegg: Barth, 1955), 95–214.

25. Mircea Eliade, *Shamanism: Archaic Techniques of Ecstasy* (Princeton, NJ: Princeton University Press, 1964); Joseph Campbell, *Masks of Gods: Primitive Mythology* (New York: Viking, 1959).

26. Ksenofontov, *Shamanizm i khristianstvo*, 135.

27. Ibid., 135–136.

28. Viacheslav Shishkov, *Strashnyi kam: Povesti i rasskazy* (Moskva and Leningrad: Zemlia i fabrika, 1926).

29. Ibid., 50.

30. Ibid., 44.

31. Zubashev, "Grigorii Nikolaevich Potanin," 62.

32. "Muzikal'naia etnografiia i shamanstvo na 'Sibirskom vechere' v Tomske," *Etnograficheskoe obozrenie* 1 (1909): 134.

33. Ibid., 136.

34. "Shamanskaia misteriia (kamlanie)," *Etnograficheskoe obozrenie* 1 (1909): 138–139; "Kam Mampyi v Tomske," *Etnograficheskoe obozrenie* 1 (1909): 140.

35. "O deistivii kamlania na kama," *Etnograficheskoe obozrenie* 1 (1909): 138.

36. The history of American primitivism centered on Native American cultures from colonial days to the present is discussed in detail in the following works: Helen Carr, *Inventing the American Primitive: Politics, Gender and the Representation of Native American Literary Traditions, 1789–1936* (New York: New York University Press, 1996); Leah Dilworth, *Imagining Indians in the Southwest: Persistent Visions of a Primitive Past* (Washington, DC: Smithsonian Institution Press, 1996); Eliza McFeely, *Zuni and the American Imagination* (New York: Hill and Wang, 2001); and

Philip Deloria, *Playing Indians* (New Haven, CT: Yale University Press, 1998). For the most comprehensive study of the American romance with Indian spirituality proper, see Philip Jenkins, *Dream Catchers: How Mainstream America Discovered Native Spirituality* (New York: Oxford University Press, 2004).

37. For a recent discussion of this topic, see Alan Trachtenberg, *Shades of Hiawatha: Staging Indians, Making Americans, 1880–1930* (New York: Hill and Wang, 2004).

38. Louis Rudnick, *Utopian Vistas: The Mabel Dodge Luhan House and the American Counterculture* (Albuquerque: University of New Mexico Press, 1996), 97.

39. Jenkins, *Dream Catchers*, 18.

40. Marsden Hartley, "Red Man Ceremonials: An American Plea for American Esthetics," *Art and Archaeology* 9, no. 1 (1920): 13.

41. Dennis Slifer, "In the Land of the Horned Gods: Shamanistic Motifs in the Rock Art of Utah," *Shaman's Drum* 61 (2002): 34.

42. Jenkins, *Dream Catchers*, 71.

43. Carl Lumholtz, *Unknown Mexico: A Record of Five Years' Exploration among the Tribes of the Western Sierra Madre, in the Tierra Caliente of Tepic and Jalisco, and among the Tarascos of Michoacan* (New York: Scribner's, 1902), 2:311–347, 356–379, 497. About Cashing, see McFeely, *Zuni and the American Imagination.*

44. George W. Stocking, Jr., "The Ethnographic Sensibility of the 1920s and the Dualism of the Anthropological Tradition," in *Romantic Motives: Essays on Anthropological Sensibility*, edited by George W. Stocking, Jr. (Madison: University of Wisconsin Press, 1989), 220.

45. Sherry L. Smith, *Reimagining Indians: Native Americans through Anglo Eyes, 1880–1940* (Oxford and New York: Oxford University Press, 2000), 193.

46. Rudnick, *Utopian Vistas*, 93.

47. Mabel Dodge Luhan, *Edge of Taos Desert: An Escape to Reality* (1937; reprint, Albuquerque: University of New Mexico Press, 1987), 225.

48. In her memoirs, Luhan portrayed Tony as a seer and a visionary, the embodiment of the Indian wisdom. Although her husband did not mind sharing what he knew about the Pueblo culture with visiting anthropologists and writers, visitors noted that he was more interested in talking about automobiles he enjoyed driving. Writer D. H. Lawrence, one of those who joined the Taos colony, later poked friendly fun at Luhan and her friend Mary Austin (1868–1934) as Indian loving in his play *Altitude*. The play deals with making breakfast at Luhan's mansion. Austin turns each routine cooking chore into a grand spiritual experience. Thus, lighting a kitchen stove appears to her as "homage to the god of fire." When a young Indian maid leaves the room to fetch water, Austin comments, "Don't you notice, the moment an Indian comes into the landscape, how all you white people seem so *meaningless*, so ephemeral?" Rudnick, *Utopian Vistas*, 7, 46–47, 48.

49. Smith, *Reimagining Indians*, 168, 171.

50. Hartley, "Red Man Ceremonials," 11; Mary Austin, *The American Rhythm: Studies of American Songs* (1923; reprint, New York: Cooper Square, 1970), 69, 75.

51. Jenkins, *Dream Catchers*, 138–144; Rudnick, *Utopian Vistas*, 29, 31.

52. Rudnick, *Utopian Vistas*, 29, 90.

53. James Clifford, *Predicament of Culture: Twentieth-Century Ethnography, Literature and Art* (Cambridge, MA: Harvard University Press, 1988), 146.

54. William Adams, *The Philosophical Roots of Anthropology* (Stanford, CA: CSLI, 1998), 306.

55. Carr, *Inventing the American Primitive*, 245.

56. Ibid., 252. For more on Romantic sentiments in anthropology scholarship, see Stocking, "The Ethnographic Sensibility of the 1920s and the Dualism of the Anthropological Tradition."

57. Franz Boas, *Race, Language, and Culture* (1940; reprint, Chicago: University of Chicago Press, 1982), 314.

58. Thomas Eriksen and Finn Nielsen, *A History of Anthropology* (London and Sterling, VA: Pluto, 2001), 23; Adams, *The Philosophical Roots of Anthropology*, 313. On the link between Boasians and the German intellectual tradition, see George W. Stocking, Jr., ed., *Volksgeist as Method and Ethic: Essays on Boasian Ethnography and the German Anthropological Tradition* (Madison: University of Wisconsin Press, 1996).

59. Harry Whitehead, "The Hunt for Quesalid: Tracking Levi-Strauss' Shaman," *Anthropology and Medicine* 7, no. 2 (2000): 161–162.

60. Henri F. Ellenberger, *The Discovery of Unconscious: The History and Evolution of Dynamic Psychiatry* (New York: Basic, 1970), 10–12.

61. Mirka Knaster, "Leslie Gray's Path to Power." Available at http://www .woodfish.org/power2.html (downloaded July 16, 2005).

62. Barbara Tedlock, "New Anthropology of Dreaming," in *Shamanism: A Reader*, edited by Graham Harvey (London and New York: Routledge, 2003), 110–111.

63. Sam Blowsnake, *Crashing Thunder: The Autobiography of an American Indian*, edited by Paul Radin (New York: Appleton, 1926). On how particularly Radin invented his ultimate Winnebago shaman, see Christer Lindberg, "Paul Radin: The Anthropological Trickster," *European Review of Native American Studies* 14, no. 1 (2000): 1–9.

64. Paul Radin, *Primitive Religion: Its Nature and Origin* (New York: Viking, 1937), 166–168.

65. Judith Model, *Ruth Benedict: Patterns of Life* (Philadelphia: University of Pennsylvania Press, 1983), 124.

66. Desley Deacon, *Elsie Clews Parsons: Inventing Modern Life* (Chicago: University of Chicago Press, 1997), 238.

67. Alfred Kroeber, "Introduction," in *American Indian Life*, 14. For this volume, Lowie wrote an essay, "Trial of Shamans"; also see Clark Wissler, "Smoking Star, a Blackfeet Shaman"; and Radin, "Thunder Cloud, a Winnebago Shaman, Relates and Prays," in *American Indian Life*, 41–43, 45–62, 75–80.

68. Norman Bancroft-Hunt, *Shamanism in North America* (Buffalo, NY: Firefly, 2002), 10.

69. Daniel G. Brinton, *Religions of Primitive People* (New York and London: Putnam's, 1897), 65, 218, 232; Rushton M. Dorman, *The Origin of Primitive Superstitions* (Philadelphia: Lippincott, 1881), 370; John G. Bourke, "The Medicine-Men of the Apache," *Annual Report of the Bureau of American Ethnology* 9 (1892): 443–603.

70. Alexander Chamberlain, "Kooteney 'Medicine Man,'" *Journal of American Folklore* 14 (April 1901): 95–99; Walter J. Hoffman, "Pictography and Shamanistic Rites of the Ojibwa," *American Anthropologist* 1, no. 3 (1888): 209–229; Washington Matthews, *Navaho Legends* (Boston: Houghton, Mifflin, 1897); James Mooney, "Sacred

Formulas of the Cherokees," *Annual Report of the Bureau of American Ethnology* 7 (1891): 302–397.

71. Matthews, *Navaho Legends*, 56–57; Mooney, "Sacred Formulas of the Cherokees," 319.

72. On the work of the Jesup expedition and its legacy, see Igor Krupnik and William W. Fitzhugh, eds., *Gateways: Exploring the Legacy of the Jesup North Pacific Expedition, 1897–1902* (Washington, DC: Arctic Studies Center, Smithsonian Institution, 2001); and Laurell Kendall, ed., *Drawing Shadows to Stone: The Photography of the Jesup North Pacific Expedition, 1897–1902* (New York: American Museum of Natural History, and Seattle: University of Washington Press, 1997).

73. Waldemar Bogoras [V. G. Bogoraz], *The Chukchee* (1908–1909; reprint, New York: AMS, 1975); Waldemar [V. I.] Jochelson, *The Koryak* (1908; reprint, New York: AMS, 1975).

74. "Ancient Religion of Shamanism Flourishing To-Day," *New York Times Magazine*, July 17, 1904, 3.

75. Marie Antoinette Czaplicka, *Aboriginal Siberia: A Study in Social Anthropology* (Oxford: Clarendon, 1914). The entire shamanism segment of the book is now in the open domain: "Shamanism in Siberia: Excerpts from *Aboriginal Siberia* by M. A. Czaplicka [1914]." Available at http://www.sacred-texts.com/sha/sis (downloaded July 23, 2005).

76. Marie Antoinette Czaplicka, *My Siberian Year* (London: Mills & Boon, 1916).

77. "Shamanism," *Encyclopedia Britannica*, 9th ed. (1886), 21:771; 11th ed. (1911), 25:798; 12th ed. (1940), 20:454; 13th ed. (1955), 20:454; 14th ed. (1968), 20:343.

78. Georgii [Georg] K. Nioradze, *Der Schamanismus bei den sibirischen Völkern* (Stuttgart: Strecker und Schröder, 1925); Åke Ohlmarks, *Studien zum Problem des Schamanismus* (Lund: Gleerup, 1939).

79. Roland Dixon, "Some Aspects of the American Shaman," *Journal of American Folklore* 21 (1908): 1–12. For an excerpt from this essay, see Jeremy Narby and Francis Huxley, eds., *Shamans through Time: 500 Years on the Path to Knowledge* (New York: Jeremy P. Tarcher/Putnam, 2001), 64–68. A detailed list of American anthropological writings on North American Indian shamanism can be found in Shelley Anne Osterreich, *Native North American Shamanism: An Annotated Bibliography* (Westport, CT: Greenwood, 1989); and Peter N. Jones, "Shamanism in North America: A Comprehensive Bibliography on the Use of the Term." Available at www.bauuinstitute.com/Articles/ShamanismBibliography07–04–05.pdf (downloaded August 29, 2005).

80. Åke Hultkrantz, "The Specific Character of North American Shamanism," *European Review of Native American Studies* 13, no. 2 (1999): 2.

81. Radin, *Primitive Religion*, 161–162.

82. Anthropologist E. M. Loeb suggested that the shaman was "a product of higher cultures" and, therefore, manifested a more advanced religion than the medicine man. The scholar described the latter as a noninspirational shaman or a seer who worked somewhere on the level of natural magic. E. M. Loeb, "Shaman and Seer," *American Anthropologist* 41(1929): 60–61. The above-mentioned *New York Times* report on the AMNH exhibit showed that Loeb was not the only one who shared this view. Later, Mircea Eliade, Underhill, and Hultkrantz tried to distinguish between shamans as experts in ecstasy (altered states) and medicine men/women, who performed

healing without going into an altered state of consciousness or going only into a slight trance. Mircea Eliade, *Shamanism: Archaic Techniques of Ecstasy* (Princeton, NJ: Princeton University Press, 1964), 300; Ruth Underhill, *Red Man's Religion: Beliefs and Practices of the Indians North of Mexico* (Chicago: University of Chicago Press, 1965), 83; Åke Hultkrantz, *The Religions of the American Indians* (Berkeley: University of California Press 1980), 84–102; Åke Hultkrantz, *Shamanic Healing and Ritual Drama: Health and Medicine in Native North American Religious Traditions* (New York: Crossroad, 1992), 18–19. However, the usage these scholars offered had little impact on current scholarly and popular writings, which, especially in the United States, usually follow a broad interpretation of the expression "shamanism."

83. L. L. Leh "The Shaman in Aboriginal North American Society," *University of Colorado Studies* 21, no. 4 (1934): 200; Willard Z. Park, *Shamanism in Western North America* (Evanston, IL, and Chicago: Northwestern University, 1938).

84. Robert Lowie, *Primitive Religion* (1924; reprint, New York: Liveright, 1970), 17, 350; Park, *Shamanism in Western North America*, 10.

85. Quoted from L. Brice Boyer, "Remarks on the Personality of Shamans: With Special Reference to the Apache of the Mescalero Indian Reservation," *Psychoanalytic Study of Society* 2 (1962): 236. To be exact, the first scholar who introduced this "nation of shamans" expression was Lumholtz, the Norwegian-American anthropologist who worked at the AMNH. In his *Unknown Mexico* (1902), he nicknamed the Huichol in Mexico as the "nation of shamans." As I mentioned above, Lumholtz was one of the first to romanticize the indigenous cultures of the American Southwest. Peter Furst, who has promoted the shamanism idiom in American ethnology since the 1960s, picked up that expression from Lumholtz. Peter Furst, " 'The *Maka'kame* Does and Undoes': Persistence and Change in Huichol Shamanism," in *Ancient Traditions: Shamanism in Central Asia and the Americas*, edited by Gary Seaman and Jane S. Day (Niwot: University Press of Colorado, and Denver: Museum of Natural History, 1994), 147–149.

86. "Shamanism," *Encyclopedia Britannica*, 9th ed. (1886), 21:771; 11th ed. (1911), 25:798; "shamanism," *Oxford English Dictionary* (1933), 9:617; "shamanism," *American Heritage Dictionary*, 2d college ed. (1985): 1126.

87. Robert Lowie, "Religious Ideas and Practices of the Eurasiatic and North American Areas," in *Essays Presented to C. G. Seligman*, edited by E. E. Evans-Pritchard et al. (London: Kegan Paul, 1934), 187.

88. Loeb, "Shaman and Seer," 64–65.

89. William Howells, *The Heathens: Primitive Man and His Religions* (New York: Doubleday, 1948), 129.

90. V. G. Bogoraz [Bogoras], *Sobranie sochinenii* (Moskva: Zemlia i fabrika, 1929), 1:15.

91. Bogoraz [Bogoras], *Chuckotskie rasskazy* (Moskva: gos. iz-vo khud. lit-ry, 1962), 15, 17.

92. V. G. Tan [Bogoraz], "Korolenko i sibirskaia shkola pisatelei," in *V. G. Korolenko: Zhizn' i tvorchestvo*, edited by A. B. Petrishchev (Petrograd: Mysl', 1922), 30–31.

93. J. Stadling, *Through Siberia* (1901; reprint, Surrey, England: Curson, 2000), 120.

94. Isaac Goldberg, *Izbrannie proizvedeniia* (Moskva: Khudozhestvennaia literatura, 1972), 67–83.

95. Wenceslas Sieroszewski, "Du chamanisme d'après les croyances des Yakoutes," *Revue de l'histoire des religions* 46 (1902): 204–233, 299–338; William G. Sumner, trans., "The Yakuts: Abridged from the Russian of Sieroszewski," *Journal of the Royal Anthropological Institute* 31 (1901): 65–110.

96. Wenceslas Sieroszewski, *Na kraiu lesov* (St. Petersburg: izdanie L. F. Panteleeva, 1897), 225.

97. Sieroszewski, *Iakutskie rasskazy* (St. Petersburg: tipografia M. Merkusheva, 1895), 151.

98. Viktor Vasiliev, "Shaman Darkha," *Pedagogicheskii listok* 1 (1910): 35.

99. Ibid., 48.

100. V. G. Bogoraz [Bogoras], "Vosem' plemen: Roman iz drevneishei zhizni krainego severo-vostoka Azii," in *Sobranie sochineni V. G. Tana* (St. Petersburg: Prosvieshchenie, 1910), 2:25–195.

CHAPTER 3

1. Waldemar Bogoras [V. G. Bogoraz], *The Chukchee* (1909; reprint, New York: AMS, 1975), 429.

2. Ibid., 415.

3. Waldemar Bogoras [V. G. Bogoraz], "K psikhologii shamanstva u narodov Severo-vostochnoi Azii," *Etnograficheskoe obozrienie* 1–2 (1910): 6.

4. John Lubbock, *The Origin of Civilization and the Primitive Condition of Man: Mental and Social Condition of Savages* (New York: Appleton, 1882), 339.

5. A. Gedeonov, "Za severnym poliarnym krugom," *Russkoe bogatstvo* 158, no. 7 (1896): 91–92.

6. Lyle Dick, " 'Pibloktoq' (Arctic Hysteria): A Construction of European-Inuit Relations?" *Arctic Anthropology* 32, no. 2 (1995): 31.

7. Ibid., 2; Uno Holmberg [Harva], *The Mythology of All Races: Finno-Ugric, Siberian* (New York: Cooper Square, 1964), 4:xx; Edward F. Foulks, *The Arctic Hysterias of the North Alaska Eskimo* (Washington, DC: American Anthropological Association, 1972), 20.

8. Vladimir Dal', *O poveriakh, sueveriakh i predrazsudkakh russkago naroda* (St. Petersburg and Moscow: Volf, 1880), 26.

9. Ibid., 27.

10. S. I. Mitskevich, *Menerik i imyarechenie: Formy isterii v Kolymskom krae* (Leningrad: izd-vo AN SSSR, 1929), 10–11.

11. B. L. Seroshevskii [Wenceslas Sieroszewski], *Iakuty: Opyt etnograficheskogo issledovania* (1896; reprint, Moskva: Posspen, 1993), 247.

12. Gedeonov, "Za severnym poliarnym krugom," 93.

13. Z. Schklovsky [Dioneo], *In the Far North-East Siberia* (London: Macmillan, 1916), 112–113.

14. Mitskevich, *Menerik i imyarechenie*, 38.

15. Ibid., 18.

16. Dick, " 'Pibloktoq' (Arctic Hysteria)," 12.

17. Mitskevich, *Menerik i imyarechenie*, 9.

18. At the same time, this did not prevent Bogoras and Jochelson from linking the shamanism of all Siberian natives to neurosis and arctic hysteria.

19. Waldemar Jochelson [V. I. Jochelson], *The Youkaghir and the Yukaghirized Tungus* (1926; reprint, New York: AMS, 1975), 31.

20. Marie Antoinette Czaplicka, *Aboriginal Siberia: A Study in Social Anthropology* (Oxford: Clarendon, 1914), 323.

21. Ibid., 319, 325.

22. Sergei M. Shirokogoroff, *Psychomental Complex of the Tungus* (London: Kegan Paul, 1935), 253.

23. D. A. Kytmanov, "Funktsional'nie nevrozy sredy Tungusov Turukhanskogo kraia i ikh otnoshenie k shamanstvu," *Sovetskii Siever* 7–8 (1930): 82–85.

24. Jochelson, *The Youkaghir and the Yukaghirized Tungus*, 32.

25. Mitskevich, *Menerik i imyarechenie*, 28; Jochelson, *The Youkaghir and the Yukaghirized Tungus*, 34–35, 38.

26. Quoted from V. L. Priklonskii, "Tri goda v Iakutskoi oblasti," *Zhivaia starina* 4 (1891): 49–50.

27. Dick, " 'Pibloktoq' (Arctic Hysteria)," 17, 19.

28. Mitskevich, *Menerik i imyarechenie*, 6–9.

29. P. Riabkov, "Poliarnie strany Sibiri," in *Sibirskii sbornik*, edited by N. M. Iadrintsev (St. Petersburg: tip. I. N. Skorokhodova, 1887), 41–42.

30. Mitskevich, *Menerik i imyarechenie*, 41.

31. Gedeonov, "Za severnym poliarnym krugom," 98; Schklovsky, *In the Far North-East Siberia*, 5.

32. N. Vitashevskii, "Iz oblasti pervobytnago psikhonevroza," *Etnograficheskoe obozrienie* 58, nos. 1–2 (1911): 222.

33. Stanislaus Novakovsky, "Arctic or Siberian Hysteria as a Reflex of the Geographic Environment," *Ecology* 5, no. 2 (1924): 124–125.

34. Dal', *O poveriakh, sueveriakh i predrazsudkakh russkago naroda*, 27.

35. V. L. Priklonskii, "Tri goda v Iakutskoi oblasti," *Zhivaia starina* 4 (1891): 57–58.

36. Riabkov, "Poliarnie strany Sibiri," 37.

37. Dick, " 'Pibloktoq' (Arctic Hysteria)," 23.

38. M. F. Krivoshapkin, *Eniseiskii okrug i ego zhizn'* (St. Petersburg: v tipografii V. Bezobrazova, 1865), 321, 326.

39. Priklonskii, "Tri goda v Iakutskoi oblasti," 45.

40. Vitashevskii, "Iz oblasti pervobytnago psikhonevroza," 200–201, 206.

41. K. M. Rychkov, "Eniseiskie Tungusy," *Zemlevedenie* 3–4 (1922): 113, 115, 116.

42. Riabkov, "Poliarnie strany Sibiri," 37.

43. Gedeonov, "Za severnym poliarnym krugom," 92–94.

44. Mitskevich, *Menerik i imyarechenie*, 13.

45. Ibid., 21.

46. Jochelson, *The Youkaghir and the Yukaghirized Tungus*, 31.

47. Shirokogoroff, *Psychomental Complex of the Tungus*, 245.

48. Czaplicka, *Aboriginal Siberia*; Åke Ohlmarks, *Studien zum Problem des Schamanismus* (Lund: Gleerup, 1939).

49. Czaplicka, *Aboriginal Siberia*, 169, 253–254.

50. Ohlmarks, *Studien zum Problem des Schamanismus*, 352–353, 354.

51. Ibid., 354–355.

52. Weston La Barre, *The Ghost Dance: Origin of Religion* (London: Allen & Unwin 1970), 318.

53. I. M. Lewis, *Ecstatic Religion: A Study of Shamanism and Spirit Possession* (London: Routledge, 1989), 161.

54. Robert Lowie, *Primitive Religion* (1924; reprint, New York: Liveright, 1970), 242; Paul Radin, *Primitive Religion: Its Nature and Origin* (New York: Viking, 1937), 107.

55. Ibid., 107–110.

56. La Barre, *The Ghost Dance*.

57. Robert F. Kraus, "A Psychoanalytic Interpretation of Shamanism," *Psychoanalytic Review* 59, no. 1 (1972): 27–28.

58. La Barre, *The Ghost Dance*, 70.

59. Geza Roheim, "Hungarian Shamanism," *Psychoanalysis and the Social Sciences* 3 (1951): 154.

60. Oskar Pfister, "Instinktive Psychoanalyse under den Navaho-Indianer," *Imago: Zeitschrift fur anwendung der Psychoanalyse auf die Nature und Geisteswissenschaften* 18, no. 1 (1932): 81–109.

61. George Devereux, *Mohave Ethnopsychiatry: The Psychic Disturbances of an Indian Tribe* (Washington, DC: Smithsonian Institution Press, 1969), 62–63, 285.

62. Ibid., 59.

63. Ibid., 57, 399, 401–402, 412.

64. Craig D. Bates, "Sierra Miwok Shamans, 1900–1990," in *California Indian Shamanism*, edited by Lowell John Bean (Menlo Park, CA: Ballena, 1992), 103–104.

65. Devereux, *Mohave Ethnopsychiatry*, 58–59.

66. Gerardo Reichel-Dolmatoff, *The Shaman and the Jaguar: A Study of Narcotic Drugs among the Indians of Colombia* (Philadelphia: Temple University Press 1975), 201–203.

67. Sergei Shirokogoroff, "What Is Shamanism: Part 1," *China Journal of Science & Arts* 2, no. 3 (1924): 276.

68. Shirokogoroff, *Psychomental Complex of the Tungus*, 262.

69. Wilhelm Mülmann, "S. M. Shirokogoroff: Nekrolog (s prilozheniem pisem, fotografii i bibliografii)," *Etnograficheskoe obozrienie* 1 (2002): 150.

70. Sergei Shirokogoroff, "Ethnological Investigations in Siberia, Mongolia and Northern China: Part 1," *China Journal of Science & Arts* 1, no. 5 (1923): 517.

71. Ibid., 520.

72. Sergei Shirokogoroff, "Ethnological Investigations in Siberia, Mongolia and Northern China: Part 2," 1, no. 6 (1923): 615.

73. N. D. Mironov and S. M. Shirokogoroff, "Sramana-Shaman: Etymology of the Word 'Shaman,'" *Journal of the North China Branch of the Royal Asiatic Society* 55 (1924): 105–130.

74. Shirokogoroff, *Psychomental Complex of the Tungus*, 276–285.

75. Ibid., 248.

76. Ibid., 249, 255, 268.

77. Shirokogoroff, "What Is Shamanism: Part 2," *China Journal of Science & Arts* 2, no. 4 (1924): 369–370; Shirokogoroff, "Ethnological Investigations in Siberia, Mongolia and Northern China: Part 2," *China Journal of Science & Arts* 1, no. 6 (1923): 619–620.

78. Shirokogoroff, *Psychomental Complex of the Tungus*, 255.

79. Shirokogoroff, "What Is Shamanism," 370.

80. Nora Chadwick, *Poetry and Prophecy* (Cambridge: Cambridge University Press, 1942), 56, 58, 61.

81. Chadwick, "Shamanism among the Tatars of Central Asia," *Journal of the Royal Anthropological Institute of Great Britain and Ireland* 66 (1936): 77–78.

82. V. G. Bogoraz-Tan [Bogoras], *Einshtein i religiia: Primenenie kontseptsii otnositel'nosti k issledovaniu religioznikh iavlenii* (Moskva and Petrograd: Frenkel', 1923). This small book was translated into English and published as an article: Waldemar Bogoras, "Ideas of Space and Time in the Conception of Primitive Religion," *American Anthropologist* 27, no. 2 (1925): 205–266.

83. Bogoraz-Tan, *Einshtein i religiia*, 79.

84. Ibid., 114.

85. Ibid., 6.

86. One might agree with Bogoras that there is surely no way to rationalize spiritual experiences. At the same time, one can rationalize one's own scholarship. Exploring his shifting assessments of shamanism, I was asking myself which Bogoras one should trust: the one who in 1910 assessed Siberian shamans as neurotics, or the one who in 1923 approached them as spiritual navigators of parallel realities, or maybe the one who ten years later (see the last chapter of my book) denounced them as parasites who should be eradicated as an alien class. The only explanation of these contrasting assessments is Bogoras's desire to keep his scholarship tuned to dominant academic and ideological fashions.

87. Erwin Ackerknecht, "Psychopathology: Primitive Medicine and Primitive Culture," *Bulletin of the History of Medicine* 14 (1943): 46.

88. Claude Lévi-Strauss, *Structural Anthropology*, translated by Clair Jacobson and Brooke G. Schoepf (New York and London: Basic, 1963), 199.

89. Ibid., 204.

90. Ibid., 199.

91. Ibid., 187–188.

92. Ibid., 197.

93. Franz Boas, *The Religion of the Kwakiutl Indians* (New York: Columbia University Press, 1930), 2:1.

94. Walter Anderson, *The Upstart Spring: Esalen and the American Awakening* (Reading, MA: Addison-Wesley, 1983), 215.

95. Joseph Campbell, *Myths to Live By* (New York: Bantam, 1973), 210–214.

96. Julian Silverman, "Shamans and Acute Schizophrenia," *American Anthropologist* 69, no. 1 (1967): 11.

97. Mickey Hart, "Shaman's Drum: Skeleton Key to the Other Worlds," in *Proceedings of the Seventh International Conference on the Study of Shamanism and Alternate Modes of Healing*, edited by Ruth-Inge Heinze (Berkeley, CA: Independent Scholars of Asia, 1990), 330.

CHAPTER 4

1. R. Gordon Wasson, "Seeking the Magic Mushroom," *Life*, May 13, 1957, 113.

2. R. Gordon Wasson and Valentina Wasson, *Mushrooms, Russia, and History* (New York: Pantheon, 1957), 257–263.

3. Ibid., 288.

4. R. Gordon Wasson, *The Wondrous Mushroom: Mycolatry in Mesoamerica* (New York: McGraw-Hill, 1980), 7.

5. Wasson and Wasson, *Mushrooms, Russia, and History*, 292.

6. Ibid., 293.

7. Ibid., 294.

8. Ibid., 289–290.

9. Ibid., 291.

10. Wasson, *The Wondrous Mushroom*, xviii.

11. Wasson and Wasson, *Mushrooms, Russia, and History*, 296.

12. Wasson, "Seeking the Magic Mushroom"; Jay Fikes, *Carlos Castaneda, Academic Opportunism and the Psychedelic Sixties* (Victoria, BC: Millenia, 1993), 32.

13. Michael Horowitz, "Collecting Wasson," in *The Sacred Mushroom Seeker: Essays for R. Gordon Wasson*, edited by Thomas J. Riedlinger (Rochester, VT: Park Street, 1997), 131.

14. Tim Weiner, "Huautla Journal: The Place for Trips of the Mind-Bending Kind," *New York Times*, May 8, 2002, A4.

15. Joan Halifax, "The Mushroom Conspiracy," in *The Sacred Mushroom Seeker: Essays for R. Gordon Wasson*, edited by Thomas J. Riedlinger (Rochester, VT: Park Street, 1997), 113. Recently, in 2002, Huautla experienced a second hallucinogenic renaissance. Another wave of spiritual pilgrims, who became attracted to a newly recovered hallucinogenic plant called *Salvia divinorum* (a type of sage), has recently flooded the area. Local Indians use the leaves of the plant in their ceremonies during the seasons when the *psylocibe* mushroom is not available. Some of these natives stirred the imagination of spiritual tourists with stories that the new herb was more powerful than the fungi. Weiner, "Huautla Journal," A4.

16. Wasson, *The Wondrous Mushroom*, 222–223.

17. Ibid., 223.

18. Daniel Pinchbeck, *Breaking Open the Head: A Psychedelic Journey into the Heart of Contemporary Shamanism* (New York: Broadway, 2002), 50.

19. Michael D. Coe, "A Vote for Gordon Wasson," in *The Sacred Mushroom Seeker: Essays for R. Gordon Wasson*, edited by Thomas J. Riedlinger (Rochester, VT: Park Street, 1997), 44.

20. Wasson, *The Wondrous Mushroom*, 28.

21. Halifax, "The Mushroom Conspiracy," 112.

22. Wasson, "Seeking the Magic Mushroom," 114.

23. Paul Devereux, *The Long Trip: A Prehistory of Psychedelia* (London: Arkana, 1997), 68.

24. Matthew Calloway, "Stonehenge and Sacred Mushrooms: The Inspiration behind the Circle of Stone," *Shaman's Drum* 58 (2001): 26.

25. Stepan Krashenninikov, *Opisanie zemli Kamchatki* (St. Petersburg: Imperatorskaia akademia nauk, 1786), 2:110; Johann Gottlieb Georgi, *Opisanie vsiekh obitaiushchikh v Rossiiskom gosudarstve narodov* (St. Petersburg: izhdiveniem I. Grazunova, 1799), 3:55.

26. R. Gordon Wasson, *Soma: Divine Mushroom of Immortality* (The Hague: Mouton, 1968), 33–34.

27. Wasson, *The Wondrous Mushroom*, 221.

28. Ibid., 228.

29. Wasson and Wasson, *Mushrooms, Russia, and History*, 194.

30. Wasson, "Seeking the Magic Mushroom," 114; Wasson, *The Wondrous Mushroom*, 28.

31. Reid W. Kaplan, "The Sacred Mushroom in Scandinavia," *Man* 10 (1975): 72–79.

32. Devereux, *The Long Trip*, 69–70, 72.

33. Calloway, "Stonehenge and Sacred Mushrooms," 21.

34. Steven Leto, "Magical Potions: Entheogenic Themes in Scandinavian Mythology," *Shaman's Drum* 54 (2000): 64.

35. Tom McIntyre, "Millennium Witness: Psychedelic Anthropologist Terence McKenna Takes on the Brave New World," *San Francisco Examiner*, October 9, 1994, M12.

36. Halifax, "The Mushroom Conspiracy," 112.

37. Mary Barnard, "The God in the Flowerpot," *Psychedelic Review* 1, no. 2 (1963): 245.

38. Ibid., 246–247.

39. Halifax, "The Mushroom Conspiracy," 114; Calloway, "Stonehenge and Sacred Mushrooms," 23.

40. Peter Furst, "Introduction: An Overview of Shamanism," in *Ancient Traditions: Shamanism in Central Asia and the Americas*, edited by Gary Seaman and Jane S. Day (Niwot: University Press of Colorado, and Denver: Museum of Natural History, 1994), 23.

41. Peter Furst, " 'Vistas beyond the Horizon of This Life': Encounters with R. Gordon Wasson," in *The Sacred Mushroom Seeker: Essays for R. Gordon Wasson*, edited by Thomas J. Riedlinger (Rochester, VT: Park Street, 1997), 76.

42. In the middle of the 1970s, Furst summarized everything that was written by "psychedelic anthropologists" on the topic of shamanism and hallucinogens in his *Hallucinogens and Culture* (San Francisco: Chandler & Sharp, 1976). In this text, designed as a popular read, he described all of the major herbal hallucinogens used by ancient and modern tribal peoples: various types of mushrooms, jimson weed, peyote, tobacco, cannabis, and other less well-known mind-altering substances. Now one can find *Hallucinogens and Culture* in an open domain at http://www.sunrisedancer.com/radicalreader/library/hallucinogensandculture (downloaded July 29, 2005).

43. Barnard, "The God in the Flowerpot," 248; Peter Furst, "Comments," in Marlene Dobkin de Rios, "The Influence of Psychotropic Flora and Fauna on Maya Religion," *Current Anthropology* 15, no. 2 (1974): 154.

44. Furst, " 'Vistas beyond the Horizon of This Life,' " 77.

45. Weston La Barre, *The Ghost Dance: Origin of Religion* (London: Allen & Unwin 1970), 161.

46. Quoted from Furst, "Introduction: An Overview of Shamanism," 19.

47. Nicholas Hellmuth, "Comments," in de Rios, "The Influence of Psychotropic Flora," 155.

48. De Rios, "The Influence of Psychotropic Flora."

49. Tatiana Proskouriakoff, "Comments," in de Rios, "The Influence of Psychotropic Flora," 159.

50. Esther Pasztory, "Nostalgia for Mud," PARI Journal 2, no. 1 (2001). Available at http://www.mesoweb.com/pari/publications/journal/03/mud.html (downloaded July 29, 2005).

51. On the assessment of rock art through the eyes of the shamanism idiom, see David Lewis-Williams, The Mind in the Cave: Consciousness and the Origin of Art (London: Thames & Hudson, 2002); and James L. Pearson, Shamanism and the Ancient Mind: A Cognitive Approach to Archaeology (Walnut Creek, CA: Altamira, 2002). Originally, I planned to include in my book a separate chapter on the use of the shamanism metaphor in archaeology. However, constrained by the specified length of the manuscript, I had to remove this chapter from the final version of the book.

52. Tricia Jones, "Rockin' the Art World: Experts in Prehistoric Stone Art Will Tell Portland Audience about Theories of Shamans' Visionary Imagery," Columbian (Vancouver, WA), September 2, 2002, D1.

53. Quoted from Paul G. Bahn, "Save the Last Trance for Me: An Assessment of the Misuse of Shamanism in Rock Art Studies," in The Concept of Shamanism: Uses and Abuses, edited by H.-P. Frankfort and Roberte Hamayon (Budapest: Akadémiai Kiadó, 2002), 77.

54. Michael J. Harner, "The Role of Hallucinogenic Plants in European Witchcraft," in Hallucinogens and Shamanism, edited by Michael Harner (Oxford: Oxford University Press, 1973), 125–150.

55. Ibid., 131, 139.

56. Mark Plotkin, Tales of a Shaman's Apprentice: An Ethnobotanist Searches for New Medicine in the Amazon Rain Forest (New York: Penguin, 1994), 204.

57. Richard Spruce, Notes of a Botanist on the Amazon & Andes (London: Macmillan, 1908), 2:415.

58. Luis Eduardo Luna, "Ayahuasca: Shamanism Shared across Cultures," Cultural Survival Quarterly 26, no. 3 (2003): 20.

59. Spruce, Notes of a Botanist on the Amazon & Andes, 415–416.

60. Ibid., 419–420.

61. Pinchbeck, Breaking Open the Head, 139.

62. Devereux, The Long Trip, 122.

63. Michael Harner, The Way of the Shaman: A Guide to Power and Healing (San Francisco: Harper & Row, 1980), 4.

64. Ibid., 5.

65. Ibid., 6.

66. Ibid., 8.

67. Gerardo Reichel-Dolmatoff, "The Cultural Context of an Aboriginal Hallucinogen: Banisteriopsis Caapi," in Flesh of the Gods: The Ritual Use of Hallucinogens, edited by Peter Furst (New York: Praeger, 1972), 96, 103.

68. Claudio Naranjo, "Psychological Aspects of the Yagé Experience in an Experimental Setting," in *Hallucinogens and Shamanism*, edited by Michael Harner (Oxford: Oxford University Press, 1973), 176–190.

69. Jeremy Narby, *Cosmic Serpent: DNA and the Origin of Knowledge* (New York: Jeremy P. Tarcher/Putnam, 1998).

70. Reichel-Dolmatoff, "The Cultural Context of an Aboriginal Hallucinogen," 98, 102.

71. For the photographic record of Schultes's explorations in the Amazon, see Wade Davis and Richard Evans Schultes, *The Last Amazon: The Photographic Journey of Richard Evans Schultes* (San Francisco: Chronicle, 2004).

72. Wade Davis and Richard Evans Schultes, *One River: Explorations and Discoveries in the Amazon Rain Forest* (New York: Simon & Schuster, 1996), 151–153.

73. Oliver Harris, ed., *The Letters of William S. Burroughs, 1945–1959* (New York: Viking, 1993), 155.

74. Jonathan Kandell, "Richard E. Schultes: Trailblazing Authority on Hallucinogenic Plants," *New York Times*, April 13, 2001, C11.

75. Martin A. Lee, "Shamanism versus Capitalism: The Politics of the Hallucinogen Ayahuasca," *San Francisco Bay Guardian*, February 19, 2001. Available at http://www.sfbg.com (downloaded November 25, 2003).

76. Allen Ginsberg, "The Yage Letters," in *Ayahuasca Reader: Encounters with the Amazon's Sacred Vine*, edited by Luis Eduardo Luna and Steven F. White (Santa Fe, NM: Synergetic, 2000), 162; Charles Montgomery, "High Tea," *Vancouver Sun*, February 10, 2001, H1.

77. William S. Burroughs and Allen Ginsberg, *The Yage Letters* (San Francisco: City Lights, 1963).

78. Strat Douthat, "Hallucination Ceremony Included in Amazon Tour," *Calgary Herald* (Alberta, Canada), November 13, 1993, D6.

79. Donald Joralemon, "The Selling of the Shaman and the Problem of Informant Legitimacy," *Journal of Anthropological Research* 46, no. 2 (1990): 108–109.

80. Stephanie Schorow, "Sham or Shamanism? The New Age Selling of Earthbased Spirituality Attracts Anger of American Indians," *Boston Herald*, October 15, 1997, O37.

81. Madrina Denig, "Misuse of Psychic Power," in *Proceedings of the Eleventh International Conference on the Study of Shamanism and Alternate Modes of Healing*, edited by Ruth-Inge Heinze (Berkeley, CA: Independent Scholars of Asia, 1994), 180.

82. Schorow, "Sham or Shamanism?" O37.

83. Rachel Proctor, "Tourism Opens New Doors, Creates New Challenges for Traditional Healers in Peru," *Cultural Survival Quarterly* 24, no. 4 (2001): 14–16.

84. Julia Lieblich, "Looking for God on a Psychedelic Drug Trip Obviously Controversial," *Stuart News/Port St. Lucie News* (Stuart, FL), January 31, 1998, D6.

85. Jaya Bear, "Ayahuasca Shamanism: An Interview with Don Agustin Rivas-Vasquez," *Shaman's Drum* 44 (1997): 44.

86. Furst, "Introduction: An Overview of Shamanism," 3.

87. Alan Shoemaker, "The Magic of Curanderismo: Lessons in Mestizo Ayahuasca Healing," *Shaman's Drum* 46 (1997): 39.

88. Proctor, "Tourism Opens New Doors"; Montgomery, "High Tea," H1.

89. Bear, "Ayahuasca Shamanism," 43.

90. Denig, "Misuse of Psychic Power," 182.

91. Ibid., 180.

92. Moira L. MacKinnon, "Stoned in the Jungle: Sylvia Fraser Looks for Truth and Insight among Peru's Shamans," *Hamilton Spectator* (Ontario, Canada), May 24, 2003, M8.

93. Proctor, "Tourism Opens New Doors," 14.

94. Ibid., 14–15.

95. Bear, "Ayahuasca Shamanism," 48.

96. Luna, "Ayahuasca: Shamanism Shared across Cultures," 21.

97. Françoise Barbira Freedman, "The Jaguar Who Would Not Say Her Prayers: Changing Polarities in Upper Amazonian Shamanism," in *Ayahuasca Reader: Encounters with the Amazon's Sacred Vine*, edited by Luis Eduardo Luna and Steven F. White (Santa Fe, NM: Synergetic, 2000), 118.

98. Denig, "Misuse of Psychic Power," 179.

99. Alix Madrigal, "Medicine Wheel Therapist," *San Francisco Chronicle Sunday Review*, September 30, 1990, 9.

100. Kevin Krajick, "Vision Quest," *Newsweek*, June 15, 1992, 62.

101. Alan Morvay, "A Shaman's Journey with Brant Secunda: An Interview," *Shaman's Drum* 20 (1989): 45–46.

102. Joy Wilder, "A New Leaf," *San Francisco Chronicle*, June 4, 2000, 10/Z1.

103. Krajick, "Vision Quest," 62.

104. Douthat, "Hallucination Ceremony Included in Amazon Tour," D6.

105. Pilar Montero and Arthur D. Colman, "Beyond Tourism: Travel with Shamanic Intent," in *The Sacred Heritage: The Influence of Shamanism on Analytical Psychology*, edited by D. F. Sandner and S. H. Wong (New York and London: Routledge, 1997), 237.

CHAPTER 5

1. Arthur Herman, *The Idea of Decline in Western History* (New York: Free Press, 1997), 364–365.

2. Donald Moss, "Abraham Maslow and the Emergence of Humanistic Psychology," in *Humanistic and Transpersonal Psychology: A Historical and Biographical Sourcebook*, edited by Donald Moss (Westport, CT: Greenwood, 1999), 24–37.

3. Theodore Roszak, *Where the Wasteland Ends: Politics and Transcendence in Postindustrial Society* (Garden City, NY: Doubleday, 1972), 332.

4. Charles T. Tart, ed., *Altered States of Consciousness: A Book of Readings* (New York: Wiley, 1969).

5. Eugene Taylor, *Shadow Culture: Psychology and Spirituality in America* (Washington, DC: Counterpoint, 1999), 239.

6. Ibid., 248; Walter T. Anderson, *The Upstart Spring: Esalen and the American Awakening* (Reading, MA: Addison-Wesley, 1983), 223.

7. Timothy Freke and Dennis Renault, *Native American Spirituality* (San Francisco, CA: Thorsons, 1996), 25. For the revision of the tribal spiritual practitioners

during the 1970s, see Henri F. Ellenberger, *The Discovery of Unconscious: The History and Evolution of Dynamic Psychiatry* (New York: Basic, 1970), 3; E. Fuller Torrey, *The Mind Game: Witchdoctors and Psychiatrists* (New York: Ballantine, 1972); R. Warner, "Deception and Self-Deception in Shamanism and Psychiatry," *International Journal of Social Psychiatry* 26, no. 1 (1980): 41–52.

8. Mircea Eliade, *Autobiography* (Chicago: University of Chicago Press, 1990), 18.

9. Mircea Eliade, *Shamanism: Archaic Techniques of Ecstasy* (Princeton, NJ: Princeton University Press, 1964), xiv; Eliade, *Autobiography*, 91.

10. Eliade, *Shamanism*, 459–460.

11. Ibid., xvii.

12. Douglas Allen, *Myth and Religion in Mircea Eliade* (New York and London: Routledge, 1998), 20.

13. Eliade, *Shamanism*, xiv.

14. Ibid., 169.

15. Ibid., 259, 274.

16. Uno Harva [Holmberg], *Der Baum des Lebens* (Helsinki: Suomalainen Tiedeakatemia, 1922); Uno Harva [Holmberg], *Die religiösen Vorstellungen der Altaischen Völker* (Helsinki: Suomalainen Tiedeakatemia, 1938).

17. Eliade, *Shamanism*, 498.

18. Ibid., 500.

19. Eliade, "The Yearning for Paradise in Primitive Tradition," in *The Making of Myth*, edited by Richard M. Ohmann (New York: Putnam, 1962), 86.

20. Ibid., 88, 90–91, 98.

21. Allen, *Myth and Religion in Mircea Eliade*, 121, 123, 135, 221.

22. Ibid., 301.

23. Ibid., 296–297, 301.

24. Ibid., 111–112, 213, 273.

25. Ibid., 215.

26. Mircea Eliade, *No Souvenirs: Journal, 1957–1969* (New York: Harper & Row, 1977), 157.

27. Seymour Cain, "Poetry and Truth: The Double Vocation in Eliade's Journals and Other Autobiographical Writings," in *Imagination and Meaning: The Scholarly and Literary World of Mircea Eliade*, edited by Norman J. Gorardot and Mac Linscott Ricketts (New York: Seabury, 1982), 88–89; Mac Linscott Ricketts, "Mircea Eliade and the Writing of *The Forbidden Forest*," in Gorardot and Ricketts, *Imagination and Meaning*, 105.

28. Eliade, *Autobiography*, 91.

29. Eliade, *Shamanism*, xx.

30. Andreas Lommel, *The World of Early Hunters* (London: Evelyn, Adams & MacKay 1967), 10, 105.

31. Peter Furst, "Roots and Continuities of Shamanism," in *Stones, Bones and Skins: Ritual and Shamanic Art*, edited by Anne Trueblood Brodsky et al. (Toronto: Society for Art Publications, 1977), 21.

32. Peter Furst, "The Olmec Were-Jaguar Motif in the Light of Ethnographic Reality," in *Dumbarton Oaks Conference on the Olmec*, edited by Elizabeth P. Benson (Washington, DC: Dumbarton Oaks Research Library and Collection, 1968), 170.

33. Ibid.

34. David Freidel, Linda Schele, and Joy Parker, *Maya Cosmos: Three Thousand Years on the Shaman's Path* (New York: Morrow, 1993).

35. Ibid., 48, 11.

36. Ibid., 36.

37. Barbara Myerhoff, *Peyote Hunt: The Sacred Journey of the Huichol Indians* (Ithaca, NY, and London: Cornell University Press, 1974).

38. Barbara Myerhoff, "Shamanic Equilibrium: Balance and Meditation in Known and Unknown Worlds," in *American Folk Medicine: A Symposium*, edited by Wayland D. Hand (Berkeley: University of California Press, 1976), 99.

39. Ibid., 102.

40. Jay Fikes described in detail the whole story behind the equilibrium theory. Moreover, he held Myerhoff and Furst responsible for catering to the tastes of countercultural audiences by sensationalizing the shamanic part of the Huichol Indian culture. Jay C. Fikes, *Carlos Castaneda, Academic Opportunism and the Psychedelic Sixties* (Victoria, BC: Millenia, 1993). Furst retaliated by calling such assertions paranoid and similarly questioning Fikes's credibility as a researcher. These mutual accusations eventually sparked a legal battle between the two scholars. For more about this battle, see Simon Romero, "Peyote's Hallucinations Spawn Real-Life Academic Feud," *New York Times*, September 16, 2003, F2.

41. Myerhoff, "Shamanic Equilibrium," 104–106.

42. Ibid., 107.

43. D. F. Melia, "The Irish Saint as Shaman," *Pacific Coast Philology* 18, nos. 1–2 (1983): 37–42; Stephen Glosecki, *Shamanism and Old English Poetry* (New York and London: Garland, 1989).

44. Carlo Ginzburg, *Ecstasies: Deciphering the Witches' Sabbath* (1991; reprint, New York: Penguin, 1992), 213.

45. Ibid., 267.

46. Ibid., 154.

47. It is notable that, before Eliade and Ginzburg linked European medieval witchcraft to shamanism, Harner had already done so in his paper "The Role of Hallucinogenic Plants in European Witchcraft," in *Hallucinogens and Shamanism*, edited by Michael Harner (Oxford: Oxford University Press, 1973), 125–150. At the same time, Harner's take on the topic of witches as European shamans concerned more the possible role of hallucinogens in their rituals. Particularly, the anthropologist suggested that tales about witches' ecstatic behavior and orgies somehow mirrored actual trance states that witches reached by rubbing herbal hallucinogens on their bodies. I have discussed Harner's paper in chapter 4, which deals with psychedelic scholarship.

48. Michael Harner, *The Way of the Shaman: A Guide to Power and Healing* (San Francisco: Harper & Row, 1980), 42, 57, 59.

49. In addition, Eliade became the object of various ideological accusations. I would like to alert readers that they should be treated with caution. Some of them might be valid, considering his intellectual roots in the traditionalist soil movement in Romania in the 1930s. Other accusations appear to be far-fetched. For example, philosopher Kelley Ross has argued that, since the writings of the émigré scholar privileged nonrational "archaic religion," Eliade's scholarship should be linked to the

"neo-pagan amoralism of the Nazis." Mark Sedgwick, *Against the Modern World: Traditionalism and the Secret Intellectual History of the Twentieth Century* (Oxford and New York: Oxford University Press, 2004), 109–117. Recently, anthropologist Barbara Tedlock has unwarrantedly claimed that then-dominant psychoanalysis heavily affected Eliade's shamanism book, which is simply not true. In fact, one of the major goals of Eliade's *Shamanism* was to completely revisit psychological and psychoanalytical interpretations of the archaic techniques of ecstasy. Tedlock also insisted that, under the influence of psychoanalysis, Eliade downplayed the role of female shamans in history. Barbara Tedlock, *The Woman in the Shaman's Body: Reclaiming the Feminine in Religion and Medicine* (New York: Bantam, 2005), 64. It appears that by denigrating the historical role of shamanesses, Eliade simply mirrored the general Victorian sentiments widespread in intellectual and cultural life in the 1940s and 1950s.

50. Glosecki, *Shamanism and Old English Poetry*, 4; Robert M. Torrance, *The Spiritual Quest: Transcendence in Myth, Religion, and Science* (Berkeley: University of California Press, 1994), 139.

51. Harner, *The Way of the Shaman*, 20.

52. I. M. Lewis, *Ecstatic Religion: A Study of Shamanism and Spirit Possession* (London: Routledge, 1989), 169.

53. Ibid., 169, 44.

54. S. A. Thorpe, *Shamans, Medicine Men and Traditional Healers: A Comparative Study of Shamanism in Siberian Asia, Southern Africa and North America* (Pretoria: University of South Africa, 1993).

55. Stephen Larsen, "Foreword," in Bradford P. Keeney, *Shaking Out the Spirits: A Psychotherapist's Entry into the Healing Mysteries of Global Shamanism* (Barrytown, NY: Station Hill, 1994), ii.

56. One can find the most complete collection of materials on Castaneda's life and books as well as critiques of his writings on Corey Donovan's site "Sustained Action." Available at http://www.sustainedaction.org (downloaded August 5, 2005).

57. Margaret Runyan Castaneda, *A Magical Journey with Carlos Castaneda* (Victoria, BC: Millenia, 1996), 83.

58. Ibid., 3, 5, 83; Corey Donovan, "Salvador Lopez: One of Castaneda's Original Informants?" Available at http://www.sustainedaction.org/Explorations/salvador_lopez.htm (downloaded January 27, 2005).

59. Amy Wallace, *Sorcerer's Apprentice: My Life with Carlos Castaneda* (Berkeley, CA: Frog North Atlantic, 2003), 5–6; Peter Applebome, "Mystery Man's Death Can't End the Mystery," *New York Times*, August 19, 1998, E1.

60. Carlos Castaneda, *The Teachings of Don Juan: A Yaqui Way of Knowledge* (1968; reprint, Berkeley: University of California Press, 1998), xi.

61. Ibid., 5.

62. Richard De Mille, *Castaneda's Journey: The Power and the Allegory* (Santa Barbara, CA: Capra, 1976), 71.

63. Castaneda, *The Teachings of Don Juan*, 132.

64. Fikes, *Carlos Castaneda*, 25, 54.

65. Daniel Trujillo Rivas, "Navigating into the Unknown: An Interview with Carlos Castaneda, 1997." Available at http://www.ajna.com/great_teachings/toltec/rivas_interview_castaneda.php (downloaded July 25, 2005).

66. C. Scott Littleton, "An Emic Account of Sorcery: Carlos Castaneda and the Rise of a New Anthropology," *Journal of Latin American Lore* 2, no. 2 (1976): 146.

67. "Don Juan and the Sorcerer's Apprentice," *Time*, March 5, 1973, 43–45.

68. Castaneda, *A Magical Journey with Carlos Castaneda*, 83.

69. Ibid., 39.

70. Alston Chase, *Playing God in Yellowstone: The Destruction of America's First National Park* (Boston: Atlantic Monthly, 1986), 346. I would like to acknowledge Ronald Hutton's *The Triumph of the Moon: A History of Modern Pagan Witchcraft* (Oxford: Oxford University Press, 1999), 350–351, which drew my attention to Chase's book.

71. Karen Vogel, "Female Shamanism, Goddess Cultures, and Psychedelics," *ReVision* 25, no. 3 (2003): 19–28.

72. South African archaeologist David Lewis-Williams developed this hypothesis into a full-fledged theory, which is currently one of the most popular interpretations of ancient and modern tribal rock art.

73. Johannes Wilbert, *Tobacco and Shamanism in South America* (New Haven, CT: Yale University Press, 1987).

74. Castaneda, *A Magical Journey with Carlos Castaneda*, 3.

75. Peter Furst, " 'Vistas beyond the Horizon of This Life': Encounters with R. Gordon Wasson," in *The Sacred Mushroom Seeker: Essays for R. Gordon Wasson*, edited by Thomas J. Riedlinger (Rochester, VT: Park Street, 1997), 79.

76. Rivas, "Navigating into the Unknown."

77. Castaneda, *A Magical Journey with Carlos Castaneda*, 26.

78. Richard De Mille, ed., *The Don Juan Papers: Further Castaneda Controversies* (Belmont, CA: Wadsworth, 1990), 340.

79. "Carlos Castaneda's Comeback," *Skeptic* 4, no. 1 (1996): 16.

80. Carlos Castaneda, *Journey to Ixtlan: The Lessons of Don Juan* (New York: Simon and Schuster, 1972).

81. Castaneda, *Tales of Power* (New York: Simon and Schuster, 1974), 12.

82. Wallace, *Sorcerer's Apprentice*, 141.

83. Castaneda, *A Magical Journey with Carlos Castaneda*, 4; "Don Juan and the Sorcerer's Apprentice," 44.

84. Wallace, *Sorcerer's Apprentice*, 45.

85. Castaneda, *The Teachings of Don Juan*, xii.

86. Ibid., xxi.

87. Daniel Noel, *The Soul of Shamanism: Western Fantasies, Imaginal Realities* (New York: Continuum, 1997), 93. For more about the Castaneda controversy, see Noel, ed., *Seeing Castaneda: Reactions to the "Don Juan" Writings of Carlos Castaneda* (New York: Putnam, 1976); De Mille, *Castaneda's Journey*; and De Mille, *The Don Juan Papers*.

88. Wallace, *Sorcerer's Apprentice*, 397.

89. Anderson, *The Upstart Spring*, 224.

CHAPTER 6

1. Richard De Mille, ed., *The Don Juan Papers: Further Castaneda Controversies* (Belmont, CA: Wadsworth, 1990), 22; Michael Harner, *The Way of the Shaman: A Guide to Power and Healing* (San Francisco: Harper & Row, 1980), xvii.

2. Stephen Larsen, "Foreword," in Bradford P. Keeney, *Shaking Out the Spirits: A Psychotherapist's Entry into the Healing Mysteries of Global Shamanism* (Barrytown, NY: Station Hill, 1994), i.

3. C. Scott Littleton, "An Emic Account of Sorcery: Carlos Castaneda and the Rise of a New Anthropology," *Journal of Latin American Lore* 2, no. 2 (1976): 146.

4. Carlos Castaneda, *The Teachings of Don Juan: A Yaqui Way of Knowledge* (Berkeley: University of California Press, 1998), 6.

5. Ibid., xii.

6. Littleton, "An Emic Account of Sorcery," 148.

7. Sandy McIntosh, "An Interview with Daniel C. Noel." Available at http://www.sustainedaction.org/explorations/an_interview_with_daniel_noel.htm (downloaded July 25, 2005).

8. James Highwater, *Primal Mind: Vision and Reality in Indian America* (New York: New American Library, 1982), 63.

9. De Mille, *The Don Juan Papers*, 348, 354.

10. Yves Marton, "The Experiential Approach to Anthropology and Castaneda's Ambiguous Legacy," in *Being Changed: The Anthropology of Extraordinary Experience*, edited by David E. Young and Jean-Guy Goulet (Petersborough, Ontario: Broadview, 1994), 274, 285.

11. For more on ethnomethodology, see Harold Garfinkel, *Studies in Ethnomethodology* (1967; reprint, London: Polity, 2003).

12. Olav Hammer, *Claiming Knowledge: Strategies of Epistemology from Theosophy to the New Age* (Leiden: Brill, 2001), xv.

13. Littleton, "An Emic Account of Sorcery," 147.

14. "Don Juan and the Sorcerer's Apprentice," *Time*, March 5, 1973, 44.

15. Littleton, "An Emic Account of Sorcery," 152.

16. Stephan A. Schwartz, "Boulders in the Stream: The Lineage and Founding of the Society for the Anthropology of Consciousness." Available at http://www.stephanaschwartz.com/PDF/SAC_history.pdf (downloaded August 5, 2005).

17. De Mille, *The Don Juan Papers*, 132–133.

18. Edith Turner, "A Visible Spirit Form in Zambia," in *Shamanism: Critical Concepts in Sociology*, edited by Andrei A. Znamenski (London: Routledge, 2004), 456; Turner, *Hands Feel It: Healing and Spirit Presence among a Northern Alaskan People* (DeKalb: Northern Illinois University Press, 1996), xxv.

19. Edith Turner, "Reality of Spirits," in *Shamanism: A Reader*, edited by Graham Harvey (London and New York: Routledge, 2003), 146.

20. Turner, *Hands Feel It*, xxv; David E. Young and Jean-Guy Goulet, "Introduction," in *Being Changed: The Anthropology of Extraordinary Experience*, edited by David E. Young and Jean-Guy Goulet (Petersborough, Ontario: Broadview, 1994), 7.

21. Robert J. Wallis, *Shamans/Neo-Shamans: Ecstasy, Alternative Archaeologies, and Contemporary Pagans* (London: Routledge, 2003), 6.

22. Wallace Black Elk and William Lyon, *Black Elk: The Sacred Ways of a Lakota* (San Francisco: Harper & Row, 1990), xxi.

23. Luis Eduardo Luna, "Ayahuasca: Shamanism Shared across Cultures," *Cultural Survival Quarterly* 26, no. 3 (2003): 22.

24. Victor Sanchez, *The Teachings of Don Carlos: Practical Applications of the Works of Carlos Castaneda* (Santa Fe, NM: Bear, 1995), xiv.

25. Unfortunately for Sanchez, his activities became annoying to the very person whose ideas he so eagerly propagated. Castaneda did not appreciate such vigorous attempts to speak on his behalf and nailed down the zealous emulator with a lawsuit for the infringement of his copyrights. In his court statement, the writer stressed that Sanchez's seminars interfered with his own spiritual enterprise, Cleargreen Inc., and diverted potential clients. Castaneda particularly claimed that Sanchez harmed his business interests by illegally replicating on the cover of *Don Carlos* the eagle, desert, and other related imagery which readers traditionally associated with the Don Juan sequels. The shocked Castaneda admirer could not comprehend how the critic of Western rationalism used all of the power of ordinary reality, including one of the most influential Los Angeles law firms, to shield his intellectual property. Corey Donovan, "Background on Castaneda's Lawsuit against Victor Sanchez." Available at http://sustainedaction.org/Explorations/explorations_iii.htm (downloaded August 5, 2005). Still, one should be fair to Castaneda: shamans of old were equally competitive and did not like it when fellow colleagues stole their helping spirits or infringed on their spiritual clientele.

26. Jenny Blain, *Nine Worlds of Seid-Magic: Ecstasy and Neo-Shamanism in Northern European Paganism* (London and New York: Routledge, 2002), 70–78.

27. Ibid., 27.

28. See, for example, Felicitas Goodman, *Where the Spirits Ride the Wind: Trance Journeys and Other Ecstatic Experiences* (Bloomington: Indiana University Press, 1990).

29. Turner, *Hands Feel It*, xxv; William Lyon, *Encyclopedia of North American Shamanism* (Santa Barbara, CA: ABC-CLIO, 1998), xiv.

30. Edith Turner, "Reality of Spirits," in *Shamanism: A Reader*, edited by Graham Harvey (London and New York: Routledge, 2003), 148; Wallis, *Shamans/Neo-Shamans*, xiii–xiv.

31. Ronald Hutton, *The Triumph of the Moon: A History of Modern Pagan Witchcraft* (Oxford and New York: Oxford University Press, 1999).

32. Harner, *The Way of the Shaman*, xii–xiii.

33. De Mille, *The Don Juan Papers*, 22.

34. Ibid., 22.

35. Jurgen W. Kremer, "Tales of Power," in *Proceedings of the Fourth International Conference on the Study of Shamanism and Alternate Modes of Healing*, edited by Ruth-Inge Heinze (Berkeley, CA: Independent Scholars of Asia, 1988), 44.

36. Ibid., 34. See also his "Shamanic Tales as Ways of Personal Empowerment," in *Shaman's Path: Healing, Personal Growth & Empowerment*, edited by Gary Doore (Boston: Shambhala, 1988), 189–199.

37. Joan Wilcox, *Keepers of the Ancient Knowledge* (London: Vega, 2001), xv.

38. Lynn Andrews, *Medicine Woman* (San Francisco: Harper & Row, 1981); Hyemeyohsts Storm, *Seven Arrows* (New York: Harper & Row, 1972); Olga Kharitidi, *Entering the Circle: The Secrets of Ancient Siberian Wisdom Discovered by a Russian Psychiatrist* (San Francisco: HarperSanFrancisco, 1996).

39. Simon Buxton, *The Shamanic Way of the Bee: Ancient Wisdom and Healing Practices of the Bee Masters* (Rochester, VT: Destiny, 2004); Timothy White,

"Fictionalized Autobiographies Can Take Reader on Wild Rides to Nowhere," *Shaman's Drum* 67 (2004): 17.

40. Taisha Abelar, *The Sorcerer's Crossing* (1992; reprint, New York: Penguin, 1993).

41. Amy Wallace, *Sorcerer's Apprentice: My Life with Carlos Castaneda* (Berkeley, CA: Frog North Atlantic, 2003), 389.

42. Florinda Donner, *Shabono: A Visit to a Remote and Magical World in the South American Rainforest* (1982; reprint, San Francisco: HarperSanFrancisco, 1992).

43. Corey Donovan, "A Regine Thal/Florinda Donner-Grau Chronology." Available at http://www.sustainedaction.org (downloaded August 5, 2005).

44. Wallace, *Sorcerer's Apprentice*, 288.

45. Beth Ann Krier, "Making It Big in Shamanism," *Record*, February 11, 1988, E29.

46. Wilcox, *Keepers of the Ancient Knowledge*, xii.

47. Sarangerel [Julie A. Stewart], *Chosen by the Spirits: Following Your Shamanic Calling* (Rochester, VT: Destiny, 2001), x.

48. Amber Wolfe, *In the Shadow of the Shaman* (1988; reprint, St. Paul, MN: Llewellyn, 2003), front matter, 58.

49. Mary Summer Rain, *Earthways* (New York: Pocket, 1990), 42, 29.

50. Mirka Knaster, "Leslie Gray's Path to Power." Available at http://www.woodfish.org/power2.html (downloaded July 16, 2005).

51. Henri F. Ellenberger, *The Discovery of Unconscious: The History and Evolution of Dynamic Psychiatry* (New York: Basic, 1970), 10–12.

52. Bradford P. Keeney, *Shaking Out the Spirits: A Psychotherapist's Entry into the Healing Mysteries of Global Shamanism* (Barrytown, NY: Station Hill, 1994), 8.

53. Henry Niese, *The Man Who Knew the Medicine: The Teachings of Bill Eagle Feather* (Rochester, VT: Bear, 2002), ix–x.

54. Thomas C. Parkhill, *Weaving Ourselves into the Land: Charles Godfrey Leland, "Indians," and the Study of Native American Religions* (Albany: State University of New York Press, 1997), 120.

55. Keeney, *Shaking Out the Spirits*, 8–9.

56. John (Fire) Lame Deer and Richard Erdoes, *Lame Deer: Seeker of Visions* (1972; reprint, New York: Pocket, 1976); Leonard Crow Dog and Richard Erdoes, *Crow Dog: Four Generations of Sioux Medicine Men* (New York: HarperCollins, 1995); Archie Fire Lame Deer and Richard Erdoes, *Gift of Power: Life and Teachings of a Lakota Medicine Man* (Rochester, VT: Bear, 2001).

57. Ed McGaa, *Mother Earth Spirituality: Native American Paths to Healing Ourselves and Our World* (San Francisco: Harper & Row, 1990).

58. Doug Boyd, *Rolling Thunder: A Personal Exploration into the Secret Healing Powers of an American Indian Medicine Man* (New York: Random House, 1974); Carmen Sun Rising, *Rolling Thunder Speaks: A Message for Turtle Island* (Santa Fe, NM: Clear Light, 1999); Sun Bear, Wabun, and Barry Weinstock, *The Path of Power* (New York: Prentice Hall, 1988); Robert "Medicine Grizzlybear" Lake, *Native Healer: Initiation into an Ancient Art* (Wheaton, IL: Theosophical, 1991); Brooke Medicine Eagle, *Buffalo Woman Comes Singing: The Spiritual Song of a Rainbow Medicine Woman* (New York: Ballantine, 1991); Wolf Moondance, *Rainbow Medicine: A Visionary Guide to Native American Shamanism* (New York: Sterling, 1994); Barbara Kerr and John

McAlister, *Letters to the Medicine Man: Apprenticeship in Spiritual Intelligence* (Cresskill, NJ: Hampton, 2002).

59. Arnold Mindell, *The Shaman's Body: A New Shamanism for Transforming Health, Relationships, and Community* (San Francisco: HarperSanFrancisco, 1993).

60. Cinnamon Moon, *A Medicine Woman Speaks: An Exploration of Native American Spirituality* (Franklin Lakes, NJ: New Page, 2001).

61. Ed McGaa, *Rainbow Tribe: Ordinary People Journeying on the Red Road* (San Francisco: HarperSanFrancisco, 1992).

62. There are numerous shamanic spiritual biographies and autobiographies that are set in indigenous Latin America. A large part of this growing body of literature deals with the ritual use of hallucinogenic herbs. See, for example, a shamanic biography centered on the use of *ayahuasca*, Jaya Bear, *Amazon Magic: The Life Story of Ayahuasquero & Shaman Don Agustin Rivas Vasquez* (Taos, NM: Colibri, 2000), or a spiritual autobiography that details the peyote experiences of an American seeker, a member of the neo-shamanic group Wakan, among the Huichol Indians of Mexico, Tom Pinkson, *Flowers of Wiricuta: A Gringo's Journey to Shamanic Power* (Mill Valley, CA: Wakan, 1995). For the first tale of power set in the European pre-Christian tradition, see Brian Bates's novel *The Way of Wyrd: Tales of an Anglo-Saxon Sorcerer* (1983; reprint, Carlsbad, CA: Hay House, 2005). An example of a visionary tale that uses the Hawaiian indigenous setting is Henry Wesselman, *Medicinemaker: Mystic Encounters on the Shaman's Path* (New York: Bantam, 1998). Kharitidi's *Entering the Circle*, a visionary book of fiction, which I mentioned earlier, uses some elements of Siberian shamanism as a backdrop. For a deeper insight of a Western seeker into the Siberian shamanic tradition, see Sarangerel, *Chosen by the Spirits*.

63. Black Elk and Lyon, *Black Elk*, xi–xii.

64. Harry Oldmeadow, *Journeys East: 20th-Century Western Encounters with Eastern Religious Traditions* (Bloomington, IN: World Wisdom, 2004), 109–110.

65. Stephen Larsen, "Foreword," in Bradford P. Keeney, *Shaking Out the Spirits: A Psychotherapist's Entry into the Healing Mysteries of Global Shamanism* (Barrytown, NY: Station Hill, 1994), i–ii.

66. Christopher Vecsey, "Introduction," in Åke Hultkrantz, *Belief and Worship in Native North America* (Syracuse, NY: Syracuse University Press, 1981), x, xix; Jan Svanberg, "Scandinavian Neo-Shamanism: The Contribution of the Academic Study of Religion in Reconstructing Beliefs and Practices of Tradition within Post-Modern Urban Milieus," *Acta Ethnographica Hungarica* 43, nos. 1–2 (1998): 157.

67. Amanda Porterfield, "Shamanism: A Psychological Definition," *Journal of the American Academy of Religion* 55, no. 4 (1987): 725.

68. Jane Monnig Atkinson, "Shamanisms Today," *Annual Review of Anthropology* 21 (1992): 307–330; Wallis, *Shamans/Neo-Shamans*.

69. Roberte N. Hamayon, "Shamanism in Siberia: From Partnership in Superstructure to Counter-Power in Society," in *Shamanism, History, and the State*, edited by Nicholas Thomas and Caroline Humphrey (Ann Arbor: University of Michigan Press, 1994), 77; Sergei M. Shirokogoroff, *Psychomental Complex of the Tungus* (London: Kegan Paul, 1935), 241.

70. Caroline Humphrey and Urgunge Onon, *Shamans and Elders: Experience, Knowledge, and Power among the Daur Mongols* (Oxford and New York: Clarendon, 1996), 2, 5, 360.

71. Michael Brown, "Shamanism and Its Discontents," *Medical Anthropology Quarterly* 2, no. 2 (1988): 102–120.

72. Michael Taussig, *Shamanism, Colonialism, and the Wild Man* (Chicago: University of Chicago Press, 1987).

73. Emily Eakin, "Anthropology's Alternative Radical," *New York Times*, April 21, 2001, B7.

74. Michael Taussig, "Montage," in *Ayahuasca Reader: Encounters with the Amazon's Sacred Vine*, edited by Luis Eduardo Luna and Steven F. White (Santa Fe, NM: Synergetic, 2000), 123.

75. Martin A. Lee, "Shamanism versus Capitalism: The Politics of the Hallucinogen Ayahuasca," *San Francisco Bay Guardian*, February 19, 2001. Available at http://www.sfbg.com (downloaded November 25, 2003).

76. Åke Hultkrantz, "The Meaning of Ecstasy in Shamanism," in *Tribal Epistemologies: Essays in the Philosophy of Anthropology*, edited by Helmut Wautischer (Aldershot, England: Ashgate, 1998), 163; Peter Furst, "Roots and Continuities of Shamanism," in *Stones, Bones and Skins: Ritual and Shamanic Art*, edited by Anne Trueblood Brodsky et al. (Toronto: Society for Art Publications, 1977), 6; Furst, "Introduction: An Overview of Shamanism," in *Ancient Traditions: Shamanism in Central Asia and the Americas*, edited by Gary Seaman and Jane S. Day (Niwot: University Press of Colorado, and Denver: Museum of Natural History, 1994), 5.

CHAPTER 7

1. Michael Harner, "Altered State of Consciousness and Shamanism: A Personal Memoir," in *Materialy mezhdunarodnogo kongressa shamanizm i inie traditsionnie verovania i praktiki*, edited by V. I. Kharitonova and D. Funk, Ethnological Studies of Shamanism and Other Indigenous Spiritual Beliefs and Practices, no. 5, pt. 1 (Moskva: Institut Antropologii i Etnografii, 1999), 69.

2. Rafael Karsten, *The Head-Hunters of Western Amazonas: The Life and Culture of the Jibaro Indians of Eastern Ecuador and Peru* (Helsingfors: Societas Scientiarum Fennica, 1935).

3. Harner, "Altered State of Consciousness and Shamanism," 70.

4. Harner, "A Different Drummer," *Natural History* 106, no. 2 (1997): 50.

5. Harner, "Altered State of Consciousness and Shamanism," 71.

6. Ibid., 72.

7. Harner, "The Sound of Rushing Water," in *Hallucinogens and Shamanism*, edited by Michael Harner (Oxford: Oxford University Press, 1973), 17.

8. Harner, *The Way of the Shaman: A Guide to Power and Healing* (San Francisco: Harper & Row, 1980), 11.

9. Harner, "The Sound of Rushing Water," 17.

10. Richard De Mille, *Castaneda's Journey: The Power and the Allegory* (Santa Barbara, CA: Capra, 1976), 114.

11. Harner, "The Sound of Rushing Water," 16.

12. Harner, *The Way of the Shaman*, 31, 44.

13. Harner, "Altered State of Consciousness and Shamanism," 72.

14. Harner, *The Way of the Shaman*, 60.

15. Harner, "A Different Drummer," 50.

16. Harner, "Altered State of Consciousness and Shamanism," 72.

17. Harner, *The Way of the Shaman*, xv.

18. Galina Lindquist, *Shamanic Performances on the Urban Scene: Neo-Shamanism in Contemporary Sweden* (Stockholm: Department of Social Anthropology, Stockholm University, 1997), 27–28.

19. Harner, *The Way of the Shaman*, xii.

20. Richard De Mille, ed., *The Don Juan Papers: Further Castaneda Controversies* (Belmont, CA: Wadsworth, 1990), 40.

21. Harner, "A Different Drummer," 51.

22. Melinda Maxfield, "The Journey of the Drum," *ReVision* 16, no. 4 (1994): 157–163.

23. Debra George Siedt, "Taking a Journey to a Healthier Place," *Capital* (Annapolis, MD), November 30, 2003, F1.

24. In 1993, in Tuva during a short-lived mass fascination with shamanism and other spiritual fruits earlier forbidden by the Soviet atheistic state, crowds of natives welcomed the foundation associates during their trip to the area. At least part of this enthusiasm one can ascribe to the attempts of Tuva intellectuals to use the nearly extinct shamanism for the purposes of ethnic and cultural nationalism. A natural human curiosity was not a small factor here as well. After all, the Tuva republic was literally isolated from the outside world during communism.

25. Robert J. Wallis, *Shamans/Neo-Shamans: Ecstasy, Alternative Archaeologies, and Contemporary Pagans* (London: Routledge, 2003), 222.

26. I discuss the contribution of Kenin-Lopsan to the revitalization of Tuvan shamanism in chapter 9.

27. "Spiritual Healing," *Hull Daily Mail*, November 8, 2003, 16; Eric Perry, "American Shamanism," lecture presented at the Pagan Pride Day, Unitarian Universalist Church, Savannah, GA, October 17, 2004.

28. Paul C. Johnson, "Shamanism from Ecuador to Chicago: A Case Study in New Age Ritual Appropriation," *Religion* 25, no. 2 (1995): 171, 173.

29. Lindquist, *Shamanic Performances on the Urban Scene*, 74.

30. Harner, *The Way of the Shaman*, 67, 113, 81.

31. Lindquist, *Shamanic Performances on the Urban Scene*, 76.

32. Harner, *The Way of the Shaman*, 67–68.

33. "Letters," *Shaman's Drum* 56 (2000): 10.

34. Lindquist, *Shamanic Performances on the Urban Scene*, 68.

35. Michael Harner, "The Ancient Wisdom in Shamanic Cultures," in *Shamanism: An Expanded View of Reality*, edited by Shirley J. Nicholson (Wheaton, IL: Theosophical, 1987), 9.

36. Ibid., 11–12.

37. Cally Law, "Spirit Level," *Sunday Times* (London), March 21, 1999, Features.

38. Angelique S. Cook and George A. Haw, *Shamanism and the Esoteric Tradition* (St. Paul, MN: Llewellyn, 1992), front matter.

39. Lindquist, *Shamanic Performances on the Urban Scene*, 24.

40. Barbara Clearbridge, "Shamanism Alive and Well in Urban America." Available at http://www.energyworkinfo.com/files/shaman.html (downloaded November 29, 2003).

41. Kim Zarzour, "Witch Doctor Takes You on Trip to Another World," *Toronto Star*, December 1, 1987, G1.

42. Mirka Knaster, "Leslie Gray's Path to Power." Available at http://www.woodfish.org/power2.html (downloaded July 16, 2005).

43. Ibid.

44. Frank H. MacEowan, "Reclaiming Our Ancestral Bones: Revitalizing Shamanic Practices in the New Millennium," *Shaman's Drum* (July–November 2001): 17.

45. Wolf Moondance, *Rainbow Medicine: A Visionary Guide to Native American Shamanism* (New York: Sterling, 1994), 7.

46. Robert Bellah et al., *Habits of the Heart: Individualism and Commitment in American Life* (1985; reprint, Berkeley: University of California Press, 1996), 219–249.

47. Bill B. Burton, "Western Shamanism in a Cultural Context," in *Materialy mezhdunarodnogo kongressa shamanizm i inie traditsionnie verovania i praktiki*, edited by V. I. Kharitonova and D. Funk, Ethnological Studies of Shamanism and Other Indigenous Spiritual Beliefs and Practices, no. 5, pt. 2 (Moskva: Institut Antropologii i Etnografii, 1999), 235–236.

48. Michael Harner, "What Is a Shaman?" in *Shaman's Path: Healing, Personal Growth & Empowerment*, edited by Gary Doore (Boston: Shambhala, 1988), 10; Harner, "The Ancient Wisdom in Shamanic Cultures," 16.

49. Gini Graham Scott, *The Complete Idiot's Guide to Shamanism* (Indianapolis, IN: Alpha, 2002), 182.

50. Joan Townsend, "Modern Non-Traditional and Invented Shamanism," in *Shamanhood: Symbolism and Epic*, edited by Juha Pentikäinen (Budapest: Akadémiai Kiadó, 2001), 257.

51. Wallis, *Shamans/Neo-Shamans*, 85.

52. Karen Kelly, "Editorial," *Spirit Talk* 14 (2001): 24. Available at http://www.shamaniccircles.org/spirit_talk/index.html (downloaded July 29, 2005).

53. Jurgen Kremer, "Seidr or Trance? Toward an Archaeology of the Euro-American Tribal Mind," *ReVision* 16, no. 4 (1996): 183–192.

54. Annette Host, "What's in a Name," *Spirit Talk* 14 (2001): 1. Available at http://www.shamaniccircles.org/spirit_talk/index.html (downloaded July 29, 2005).

55. Christiana Harle-Silvennoinen, "In the Land of Song and the Drum: Receiving Inspiration from Tuvan Shamans." Available at http://www.geocities.com/talkingdrums (downloaded June 20, 2004).

56. Ibid.

57. "The Foundation for Shamanic Studies: Shop Online." Available at http://www.shamanism.org/products/supplies.html (downloaded August 28, 2003).

58. Jurgen Kremer, "Practices for the Postmodern Shaman," in *Proceedings of the Tenth International Conference on the Study of Shamanism and Alternate Modes*

of Healing, edited by Ruth-Inge Heinze (Berkeley, CA: Independent Scholars of Asia, 1993), 39.

59. Lindquist, *Shamanic Performances on the Urban Scene*, 263; Wallis, *Shamans/ Neo-Shamans*.

60. Maude Stephany, "An Interview with Diana Paxson," *Echoed Voices* (November 2002). Available at http://www.echoedvoices.org (downloaded June 20, 2004); Wallis, *Shamans/Neo-Shamans*, 93–94.

61. Cinnamon Moon, *A Medicine Woman Speaks: An Exploration of Native American Spirituality* (Franklin Lakes, NJ: New Page, 2001), back cover; Arnold Mindell, *The Shaman's Body: A New Shamanism for Transforming Health, Relationships, and Community* (San Francisco: HarperSanFrancisco, 1993), xi–xii; Andrew Jacobs, "Happy Borrower from the World's Rituals," *New York Times*, December 25, 1998, B2.

62. John Littleton, " 'With Spirit at the Center': A Postmodern Ethnography of the Wakan Community and Its Earth-Centered Shamanism" (M.A. thesis, California Institute for Integral Studies, 1993), 554.

63. Roma Heillig Morris, "Woman as Shaman: Reclaiming the Power to Heal," *Women's Studies* 24, no. 6 (1995): 573–585. For more on shamanism from a feminist perspective and on the historical role of women as shamans, see Barbara Tedlock, *The Woman in the Shaman's Body: Reclaiming the Feminine in Religion and Medicine* (New York: Bantam, 2005).

64. Scott, *The Complete Idiot's Guide to Shamanism*, 168.

65. Belinda Gore, *Ecstatic Body Postures: An Alternate Reality Workbook* (Rochester, VT: Bear, 1995), 22.

66. Lindquist, *Shamanic Performances on the Urban Scene*, 269.

67. Marilyn Ferguson, *The Aquarian Conspiracy* (Los Angeles: Tarcher, 1980); Amy Wallace, *Sorcerer's Apprentice: My Life with Carlos Castaneda* (Berkeley, CA: Frog North Atlantic, 2003), 169; Deanna Stennett, "Shamanism: Becoming Part of the Whole Web of Life," *Annapolis Capital*, June 13, 2002, A12.

68. Harner, *The Way of the Shaman*, xiii–xiv.

69. Gore, *Ecstatic Body Postures*, 4, 13.

70. Harner, "The Ancient Wisdom in Shamanic Cultures," 15–16.

71. Steve Rabey, "Healing Journeys: Interest in Ancient Tradition of Shamanism Experiencing a Revival," *Hamilton Spectator* (Ontario, Canada), July 8, 1995, B13.

72. I. M. Lewis, *Ecstatic Religion: A Study of Shamanism and Spirit Possession* (London: Routledge, 1989), 184, 170, 183.

73. Jenny Blain, *Nine Worlds of Seid-Magic: Ecstasy and Neo-Shamanism in Northern European Paganism* (London and New York: Routledge, 2002), 13.

74. Julia Lieblich, "Looking for God on a Psychedelic Drug Trip Obviously Controversial," *Stuart News/Port St. Lucie News* (Stuart, FL), January 31, 1998, D6.

75. Jose Stevens and Lena S. Stevens, *Urban Shaman: Tapping the Spirit Power within You* (New York: Avon, 1988), 10.

76. Carol Proudfoot, "Shamanism Is Alive and Well Whether from the Core or the Apple Itself," *Spirit Talk* 14 (2001): 6. Available at http://www.shamaniccircles.org/ spirit_talk/index.html (downloaded July 29, 2005).

77. Merete Jakobsen, *Shamanism: Traditional and Contemporary Approaches to the Mastery of Spirits and Healing* (New York: Berghahn, 1999), 152.

78. Karen Kelly, "Review of Merete D. Jakobsen's *Shamanism* (1999)," *Spirit Talk* 10 (2000). Available at http://www.shamaniccircles.org/spirit_talk/index.html (downloaded July 29, 2005).

79. Lindquist, *Shamanic Performances on the Urban Scene*.

80. Wallis, *Shamans/Neo-Shamans*, 106.

81. Lisa Brinkworth, "Have You No Shaman?" *Sunday Times* (London), March 30, 1997, Features; Lynn Cochrane, "The Shamanic Rights," *Sunday Times* (London), November 5, 2000, Features.

82. Lena Stevens, "Getting to Know Your Environment through Shamanism," in *Proceedings of the Sixth International Conference on the Study of Shamanism and Alternate Modes of Healing*, edited by Ruth-Inge Heinze (Berkeley, CA: Independent Scholars of Asia, 1989), 78.

83. Nancy Salem, "Shamans Offer Secrets to Power, Writer Says," *Albuquerque Tribune*, August 19, 2002, 11.

84. Shari M. Huhndorf, "Going Native: Figuring the Indian in Modern American Culture" (Ph.D. diss., New York University, 1996), 228; Beth Ann Krier, "Making It Big in Shamanism," *Record*, February 11, 1988, E29.

85. Lindquist, *Shamanic Performances on the Urban Scene*, 266.

86. Jacobs, "Happy Borrower from the World's Rituals," B2.

87. Lindquist, *Shamanic Performances on the Urban Scene*, 272.

88. Bear Heart and Molly Larkin, *The Wind Is My Mother: The Life and Teachings of a Native American Shaman* (New York: Clarkson Potter, 1996), ix–x.

89. Bradford P. Keeney, *Shaking Out the Spirits: A Psychotherapist's Entry into the Healing Mysteries of Global Shamanism* (Barrytown, NY: Station Hill, 1994), 17.

90. David Lukoff, "Shamanistic Initiatory Crisis and Psychosis," in *Proceedings of the Seventh International Conference on the Study of Shamanism and Alternate Modes of Healing*, edited by Ruth-Inge Heinze (Berkeley, CA: Independent Scholars of Asia, 1990), 238, 240, 242.

91. Robert Bly, *Iron John: A Book about Men* (Reading, MA: Addison-Wesley, 1990).

92. Lindquist, *Shamanic Performances on the Urban Scene*, 272.

93. Stennett, "Shamanism," A12.

94. V. I. Kharitonova, "Variatsii na temu: Stranstvia po miram psikhicheskoi vselennoi," in *Izbranniki dukhov: Traditsionnoe shamanstvo i neoshamanism*, edited by V. I. Kharitonova, Ethnological Studies of Shamanism and Other Indigenous Spiritual Beliefs and Practices, no. 4 (Moskva: Institut Antropologii i Etnografii, 1999), 265.

95. Lindquist, *Shamanic Performances on the Urban Scene*, 294–296.

96. Svanberg, "Scandinavian Neo-Shamanism," 155; Adrian Ivakhiv, *Claiming Sacred Ground: Pilgrims and Politics at Glastonbury and Sedona* (Bloomington: Indiana University Press, 2001), 176. According to a sociological survey of a 2002 international gathering of 115 American and European practitioners of shamanism at Oracle, Arizona, women represented 84 percent and men 16 percent of participants. Drawing a profile of a "typical attendee," the authors of the survey stress that this is a white woman in her late 40s who works in a helping profession. Peter Bloom, Mary Myers, and Nancy Anderson, "Oracle 2002 Survey Report." Available at www.shamaniccircles.org/2002oraclesharings/OracleReport.pdf (downloaded October 26, 2006).

97. Marianna Torgovnick, *Primitive Passions: Men, Women, and the Quest for Ecstasy* (New York: Knopf, 1997), 180–181.

98. Alan Morvay, "An Interview with Oh Shinnah, a Mohawk-Apache Healer," *Shaman's Drum* Mid-Spring (1989): 21.

99. Wallace, *Sorcerer's Apprentice*, 41.

100. Michael Winkelman, "Complementary Therapy for Addiction: 'Drumming Out Drugs,'" *American Journal of Public Health* 93, no. 4 (2004): 647–651; Debra George Siedt, "Taking a Journey to a Healthier Place," *Capital* (Annapolis, MD), November 30, 2003, F1.

101. "Dr. Philip Singer on Popular Shamanism." Available at http://www .astralgia.com/webportfolio/omnimoment/archives/chats/br112996.html (downloaded September 6, 2005).

CHAPTER 8

1. Leslie Garner Crutchfield, "Shamanic Travelers Can Attain Balance, Teacher Says," *Cleveland Plain Dealer*, December 26, 1995, 5B.

2. Kurt Kaltreider, *American Indian Prophecies: Conversations with Chasing Deer* (Carlsbad, CA: Hay House, 1998), 129.

3. John (Fire) Lame Deer and Richard Erdoes, *Lame Deer: Seeker of Visions* (1972; reprint, New York: Pocket, 1976), 59; Madrina Denig, "Misuse of Psychic Power," in *Proceedings of the Eleventh International Conference on the Study of Shamanism and Alternate Modes of Healing*, edited by Ruth-Inge Heinze (Berkeley, CA: Independent Scholars of Asia, 1994), 178.

4. Philip Jenkins, *Dream Catchers: How Mainstream America Discovered Native Spirituality* (New York: Oxford University Press, 2004), provides a comprehensive discussion of the fascination with Native American spirituality from colonial times to the present day.

5. Christopher F., "Responses to the Declaration of War against Exploiters of Lakota Spirituality" (March 20, 1999). Available at http://puffin.creighton.edu/lakota/ war_8.html (downloaded July 12, 2005).

6. Fred Gustafson, *Dancing between Two Worlds: Jung and the Native American Soul* (New York: Paulist, 1997), 64.

7. Michael York, *The Emerging Network: A Sociology of the New Age and Neo-Pagan Movements* (Lanham, MD: Rowman and Littlefield, 1995), 165.

8. "Indians Battle for Their Heritage," *Times Union* (Albany, NY), May 5, 1994, A1.

9. Galina Lindquist, *Shamanic Performances on the Urban Scene: Neo-Shamanism in Contemporary Sweden* (Stockholm: Department of Social Anthropology, Stockholm University, 1997), 47.

10. "Black Roots of 'Red Indians,'" *Herald Express* (Torquay), July 2, 2003, 12; Lindquist, *Shamanic Performances on the Urban Scene*, 33.

11. Doug Boyd, *Rolling Thunder: A Personal Exploration into the Secret Healing Powers of an American Indian Medicine Man* (New York: Random House, 1974).

12. Lindquist, *Shamanic Performances on the Urban Scene*, 276; Jan Svanberg, "Scandinavian Neo-Shamanism: The Contribution of the Academic Study of Religion

in Reconstructing Beliefs and Practices of Tradition within Post-Modern Urban Milieus," *Acta Ethnographica Hungarica* 43, nos. 1–2 (1998): 155.

13. Doug Blackburn, "For the Love of the Land," *Times* (Albany, NY), May 2, 1999, G1.

14. Kate Whitehead, "Shamanic Reading," *South China Morning Post*, December 14, 2003, 11; "shaman," *American Heritage Dictionary*, 2d college ed. (1985), 1126; Peter Furst, "Introduction: An Overview of Shamanism," in *Ancient Traditions: Shamanism in Central Asia and the Americas*, edited by Gary Seaman and Jane S. Day (Niwot: University Press of Colorado, and Denver: Museum of Natural History, 1994), 3.

15. Kenneth Meadows, *The Medicine Way: How to Live the Teachings of the Native American Medicine Wheel* (London: Rider, 2001).

16. Dee Brown, *Bury My Heart at Wounded Knee: An Indian History of the American West* (New York: Holt, Rinehart & Winston, 1970); and John Gneisenau Neihardt, *Black Elk Speaks: Being the Life Story of a Holy Man of the Oglala Sioux* (1932; reprint, Lincoln: University of Nebraska Press, 1971).

17. Bruce Hawkins, "Shamanic Soul Flight in the Space Age," in *Proceedings of the Eighth International Conference on the Study of Shamanism and Alternate Modes of Healing*, edited by Ruth-Inge Heinze (Berkeley, CA: Independent Scholars of Asia, 1991), 254.

18. Marcia S. Lauck, "Dreamtime and Natural Phenomena," in *Proceedings of the Eighth International Conference on the Study of Shamanism and Alternate Modes of Healing*, edited by Ruth-Inge Heinze (Berkeley, CA: Independent Scholars of Asia, 1991), 107.

19. Merete Jakobsen, *Shamanism: Traditional and Contemporary Approaches to the Mastery of Spirits and Healing* (New York: Berghahn, 1999), 180.

20. Andrew Jacobs, "Happy Borrower from the World's Rituals," *New York Times*, December 25, 1998, B2.

21. Sun Bear, Wabun, and Barry Weinstock, *The Path of Power* (New York: Prentice Hall, 1988), 65.

22. Ibid., 129.

23. Brad Steiger, *Medicine Talk: A Guide to Walking in Balance and Surviving on the Earth Mother* (Garden City, NY: Doubleday, 1975), 169.

24. Sun Bear, Wabun, and Weinstock, *The Path of Power*, 40.

25. Ibid., 44.

26. Lindquist, *Shamanic Performances on the Urban Scene*, 33–35.

27. Ibid., 40.

28. Susy Buchanan "Sacred Orgasm," *Phoenix New Times* (Arizona), June 13, 2002. Available at http://www.phoenixnewtimes.com/issues/2002-06-13/news/feature.html (downloaded August 6, 2005); Bill Bertolino, "E. V. Speed Shooters Aiming Honors in National Competition," *Scottsdale Tribune* (Arizona), August 18, 2003.

29. Buchanan "Sacred Orgasm"; Lisa Brinkworth, "Have You No Shaman?" *Sunday Times* (London), March 30, 1997, Features; Lynn Cochrane, "The Shamanic Rights," *Sunday Times* (London), November 5, 2000, Features; Loudon Temple, "Going Back to Her Roots," *Herald* (Glasgow), May 13, 2000, 19.

30. Dagmar Wernitznig, *Going Native or Going Naïve: White Shamanism and the Neo-noble Savage* (Lanham, MD: University Press of America, 2003), x; Ward Churchill,

Indians Are Us? Culture and Genocide in Native North America (Monroe, ME: Common Courage, 1994), 283–289.

31. Mark Havnes, "Leaders Decry Those Who Dabble in Indian Religion," *Salt Lake Tribune* (Utah), December 13, 1997, Religion:1; Karen Lincoln Michel, "Indians Rap Takeover of Rituals," *Omaha World Herald*, July 22, 1995, 61.

32. Lindquist, *Shamanic Performances on the Urban Scene*, 51; Nancy Butterfield, "New Age Movement Stealing American Indian Ceremonies," *Seattle Times*, April 7, 1990, A15. In his recent book, anthropologist Michael F. Brown provided the most comprehensive and balanced discussion of the legal and moral aspects of the appropriation of Native Americana by the wider society. Michael F. Brown, *Who Owns Native Culture?* (Cambridge, MA, and London: Harvard University Press, 2003).

33. Vine Deloria, Jr., *God Is Red: A Native View of Religion* (1973; new edition, Golden, CO: North American, 1992), 41.

34. Vine Deloria, Jr., *For This Land: Writings on Religion in America* (New York and London: Routledge, 1999), 266; Deloria, *God Is Red*, 43.

35. Stephen Bruner, "Do Earth-Based Ceremonies Belong to Natives Only?" *Shaman's Drum* 51 (1999): 6.

36. Steve Jackson, "Civil Wars: The Fury Flies as Indian Activists Take Aim at Each Other," *Denver Westword*, February 9, 1994, 14.

37. Lisa Aldred, "Plastic Shamans and Astroturf Sundances: New Age Commodification of Native American Spirituality," *American Indian Quarterly* 24, no. 3 (2000): 344; Wernitznig, *Going Native or Going Naïve*, xxxiv.

38. For the text of the declaration, see "Declaration of War against Exploiters of Lakota Spirituality." Available at http://puffin.creighton.edu/lakota/war.html (downloaded August 6, 2005).

39. "Indians Battle for Their Heritage," A1; "New Age Frauds & Plastic Shamans." Available at http://users.pandora.be/gohiyuhi/nafps (downloaded August 6, 2005).

40. Aldred, "Plastic Shamans and Astroturf Sundances," 348; Ricardo Duran, "Group Says Riversider Is Exploiting Indian Ways," *Press-Enterprise* (Riverside, CA), October 24, 1993, B5; Patricia Holt, "Arguing a Writer's Spirituality," *San Francisco Chronicle*, November 5, 1990, F5; Butterfield, "New Age Movement Stealing American Indian Ceremonies," A15.

41. Robert J. Wallis, *Shamans/Neo-Shamans: Ecstasy, Alternative Archaeologies, and Contemporary Pagans* (London: Routledge, 2003), 203.

42. Ibid., 215, 204.

43. Vaishalee Mishra, "Class Dismissed: Following the Path of the Shaman Just Got Tougher at Colorado Free University," *Denver Westword*, August 3, 2000, News.

44. Timothy White, "From 'Selling Medicine' to Giveaway," *Shaman's Drum* Mid-Summer (1989): 4–5; Will Nofke, "Living in a Sacred Way: An Interview with Chequeesh, a Chumash Medicine Woman," *Shaman's Drum* Fall (1985): 17.

45. Cinnamon Moon, *A Medicine Woman Speaks: An Exploration of Native American Spirituality* (Franklin Lakes, NJ: New Page, 2001), 84; Nofke, "Living in a Sacred Way," 16.

46. "Responses to the Declaration of War against Exploiters of Lakota Spirituality, October 13, 1998, to March 28, 1999." Available at http://maple.lemoyne.edu/~bucko/war_8.html (downloaded January 31, 2000).

47. Mishra, "Class Dismissed"; Roberta Louis, "Return to Spirit: An Interview with Josie RavenWing," *Shaman's Drum* 47 (1997): 57.

48. Sunshine Ann Garner, "A Comment to 'The Spiritual Ways of the Native Americans Work Best,'" *Seattle Times*, April 21, 1990, A15.

49. Loren Cruden, *Coyote's Council Fire: Contemporary Shamans on Race, Gender & Community* (Rochester, VT: Destiny, 1995), 60.

50. Bruner, "Do Earth-Based Ceremonies Belong to Natives Only?" 4.

51. Stephanie Schorow, "Sham or Shamanism? The New Age Selling of Earth-Based Spirituality Attracts Anger of American Indians," *Boston Herald*, October 15, 1997, 037.

52. Bill Pfeiffer, "Making Rainbows in Tuva," *Shaman's Drum* 64 (2003): 31.

53. Timothy White, "The Parallel Paths of Shamanism and Mysticism," *Shaman's Drum* 60 (2001): 4.

54. Lowell John Bean and Sylvia Brakke Vane, "The Shaman Experience," in *California Indian Shamanism*, edited by Lowell John Bean (Menlo Park, CA: Ballena, 1992), 18.

55. Robert "Medicine Grizzlybear" Lake, *Native Healer: Initiation into an Ancient Art* (Wheaton, IL: Theosophical, 1991), 9, 196.

56. Steve Jackson, "Sacred Ground," *Denver Westword*, October 19, 1994, 26; William S. Lyon, "The Visions of Wallace Black Elk," *Shaman's Drum* Spring (1987): 37; Avis Little Eagle, "Sacred Pipe Keeper Fears Feds Will Step In." Available at http://users.pandora.be/gohiyuhi/articles/art00086.htm (downloaded July 12, 2005); Stephen Powell, "Whole Planet Lands on Santa Fe's Doorstep," *Santa Fe New Mexican*, June 28, 1996, 58.

57. Michel, "Indians Rap Takeover of Rituals," 61. What especially offends the critics of "plastic shamans" is that people like Wallace and Crow Dog routinely charge substantial fees for introducing Western seekers to their version of Native American spirituality. Justifying this practice, Crow Dog stated, "Long, long time ago, holy men who performed healing ceremonies were given such things as buffalo robes, teams of horses, tepees and other possessions. In today's money, that could be as much as a quarter of a million dollars. If I doctor you and you give me $1,000, that's cheap." Ibid. He is not wrong. For example, in the idealized nineteenth-century old times, among Plains Indians, spiritual practitioners received in-kind payments for their curing sessions. Spiritual visions could also be purchased, and fees were paid by novices for an initiation into such shamanic associations as the Crow Indians' Tobacco Society.

58. Ed McGaa, *Rainbow Tribe: Ordinary People Journeying on the Red Road* (San Francisco, CA: HarperSanFrancisco, 1992), xi.

59. Wallis, *Shamans/Neo-Shamans*, 31; Jenkins, *Dream Catchers*, 248.

60. Deloria, *For This Land*, 281.

61. Cruden, *Coyote's Council Fire*, 16.

62. Damian Costello, *Black Elk: Colonialism and Lakota Catholicism* (Maryknoll, NY: Orbis, 2005), 56.

63. Omer C. Stewart, *Peyote Religion: A History* (Norman and London: University of Oklahoma Press, 1987), 68–96, 219–226.

64. Jenkins, *Dream Catchers*, 252.

65. Leslie Spier, "The Sun Dance of the Plains Indians: Its Development and Diffusion," *Anthropological Papers of the American Museum of Natural History* 16, no. 7 (1921): 460.

66. Robert Lowie, *Primitive Religion* (1924; reprint, New York: Liveright, 1970), 27; Spier, "The Sun Dance of the Plains Indians," 461–462, 495, 519; Åke Hultkrantz, *Belief and Worship in Native North America* (Syracuse, NY: Syracuse University Press, 1981), 243, 258–259.

67. William S. Lyon, "The Sun Dance as a Healing Ritual," in *Proceedings of the Seventh International Conference on the Study of Shamanism and Alternate Modes of Healing*, edited by Ruth-Inge Heinze (Berkeley, CA: Independent Scholars of Asia, 1990), 362.

68. Mary Thunder, *Thunder's Grace: Walking the Road of Visions with My Lakota Grandmother* (Barrytown, NY: Station Hill, 1995), 217; Lyon, "The Sun Dance as a Healing Ritual," 360–362.

69. Thunder, *Thunder's Grace*, 156, 158.

70. Joan B. Townsend, "Western Core and Neo-Shamanism: Trends and Relations with Indigenous Societies," in *Rediscovery of Shamanic Heritage*, edited by Mihaly Hoppal and Gabor Kosa (Budapest: Akadémiai Kiadó, 2003), 324.

71. Craig D. Bates, "Sierra Miwok Shamans, 1900–1990," in *California Indian Shamanism*, edited by Lowell John Bean (Menlo Park, CA: Ballena, 1992), 110.

72. Thomas Buckley, *Standing Ground: Yurok Indian Spirituality, 1850–1990* (Berkeley: University of California Press, 2002), 75–76.

73. A. C. Ross, *Mitakuye Oyasin: "We Are All Related"* (Ft. Yates, ND: Bear, 1989).

74. For a detailed study of the European fascination with Native Americana, see German Dziebel, "Playing and Nothing: European Appropriation of Native American Cultures in the Late 20th Century" (Ph.D. diss., Stanford University, 2006).

75. Ross, *Mitakuye Oyasin*, 229.

76. Daniele Vazeilles, "Shamanism and New Age: Lakota Sioux Connection," in *The Concept of Shamanism: Uses and Abuses*, edited by Henri Paul Francfort, Roberte Hamayon, and Paul G. Bahn (Budapest: Akadémiai Kiadó, 2001), 380–381, 382.

77. Pensy Hawk Wing, "Lakota Teachings: Inipi, Humbleciya, and Yhuwipi Ceremonies," in *The Sacred Heritage: The Influence of Shamanism on Analytical Psychology*, edited by Donald F. Sandner and Steven H. Wong (New York: Routledge, 1997), 193–202; Bobby Lake-Thom (Bobby Grizzlybear Lake), *Spirit of the Earth: A Guide to Native American Nature Symbols, Stories, and Ceremonies* (New York: Penguin, 1997), 42–47.

78. Amanda Porterfield, "American Indian Spirituality as a Countercultural Movement," in *Religion in Native North America*, edited by Christopher Vecsey (Moscow: University of Idaho Press, 1990), 154.

79. N. Scott Momaday, "American Land Ethic," in his *The Man Made of Words: Essays, Stories, Passages* (New York: St. Martin's, 1997), 47.

80. Jenkins, *Dream Catchers*, 168.

81. Deloria, *God Is Red*; Deloria, *The Metaphysics of Modern Existence* (San Francisco: Harper and Row, 1979); Deloria, *Red Earth, White Lies: Native Americans and the*

Myth of Scientific Fact (New York: Scribner, 1995); Deloria, *Spirit and Reason: The Vine Deloria, Jr., Reader*, edited by Barbara Deloria, Kristen Foehner, and Sam Scinta (Golden, CO: Fulcrum, 1999).

82. Timothy Freke and Dennis Renault, *Native American Spirituality* (San Francisco, CA: Thorsons, 1996), 22.

83. Wernitznig, *Going Native or Going Naïve*, 9.

84. Gustafson, *Dancing between Two Worlds*, 79.

85. John Matthews, *The Celtic Shamanism: A Handbook* (Shaftesbury, England: Element, 1991), 6; Frank H. MacEowan, "Reclaiming Our Ancestral Bones: Revitalizing Shamanic Practices in the New Millennium," *Shaman's Drum* (July–November 2001): 15–19.

86. Edred Thorsson, *Northern Magic: Rune Mysteries & Shamanism* (St. Paul, MN: Llewellyn, 1998), xiii; Daniel Noel, *The Soul of Shamanism: Western Fantasies, Imaginal Realities* (New York: Continuum, 1997).

87. Cruden, *Coyote's Council Fire*, 59.

88. Churchill, *Indians Are Us?* 236–237.

89. Quoted in Wernitznig, *Going Native or Going Naïve*, 49.

90. Carole Beers, "Author Tells of Her Spiritual Quest with Bear Tribe Society," *Seattle Times*, February 11, 1991, C3.

91. Brian Bates, *The Way of Wyrd: Tales of an Anglo-Saxon Sorcerer* (1983; reprint, Carlsbad, CA: Hay House, 2005).

92. Jean Markale, *The Druids: Celtic Priests of Nature* (Rochester, VT: Inner Traditions, 1999), ix.

93. Lindquist, *Shamanic Performances on the Urban Scene*, 42.

94. For one of the most complete historical reconstructions of the *seidr* ritual, see Thomas A. DuBois, *Nordic Religions in the Viking Age* (Philadelphia: University of Pennsylvania Press, 1999), 122–138.

95. Markale, *The Druids*, 186–197.

96. Wallis, *Shamans/Neo-Shamans*, 86.

97. D. J. Conway, *Advanced Celtic Shamanism* (Freedom, CA: Crossing, 2000), 5.

98. Jurgen W. Kremer, "Indigenous Science for Euro-Americans," in *Proceedings of the Eleventh International Conference on the Study of Shamanism and Alternate Modes of Healing*, edited by Ruth-Inge Heinze (Berkeley, CA: Independent Scholars of Asia, 1994), 50.

99. Jenny Blain, *Nine Worlds of Seid-Magic: Ecstasy and Neo-Shamanism in Northern European Paganism* (London and New York: Routledge, 2002), 90; Wallis, *Shamans/Neo-Shamans*, 137; DuBois, *Nordic Religions in the Viking Age*, 205–206.

100. Blain, *Nine Worlds of Seid-Magic*, 100, 108.

101. *Eirik the Red, and Other Icelandic Sagas*, edited by Gwyn Jones (Oxford: Oxford University Press, 1961), 133–137.

102. *The Elder of Poetic Edda*, edited by Olive Bray (1908; reprint, New York: AMS, 1982), 103.

103. Conway, *Advanced Celtic Shamanism*, 1.

104. John Matthews, *Taliesin: Shamanism and the Bardic Tradition in Britain and Ireland* (London: Aquarian, 1991).

105. Blain, *Nine Worlds of Seid-Magic*, 39–41.

106. Arthur Herman, *The Idea of Decline in Western History* (New York: Free Press, 1997), 418–419; Wallis, *Shamans/Neo-Shamans*, 134.

107. Jurgen Kremer, "Practices for the Postmodern Shaman," in *Proceedings of the Tenth International Conference on the Study of Shamanism and Alternate Modes of Healing*, edited by Ruth-Inge Heinze (Berkeley, CA: Independent Scholars of Asia, 1993), 43.

108. Ibid., 45.

109. "Letters," *Shaman's Drum* 56 (2000): 10.

110. Carl Gustav Jung, *Civilization in Transition*, translated by R. F. C. Hull (Princeton, NJ: Princeton University Press, 1970), 192.

111. Harry Oldmeadow, *Journeys East: 20th-Century Western Encounters with Eastern Religious Traditions* (Bloomington, IN: World Wisdom, 2004), 100.

CHAPTER 9

1. John Lubbock, *The Origin of Civilization and the Primitive Condition of Man* (New York: Appleton, 1882), 339–340, 347.

2. Ivan A. Manzhigeev, *Buriatskie shamanisticheskie i doshamanisticheskie terminy: Opyt ateisticheskoi interpretatsii* (Moskva: Nauka, 1978), 51.

3. Dmitrii K. Zelenin, *Kult ongonov v Sibiri: Perezhitki totemizma v ideologii sibirskikh narodov* (Moskva: izd-vo Akademii nauk, 1936), 736.

4. Leonid Potapov, "Luk i strela v shamanizme u Altaitsev," *Sovetskaia etnografiia* 3 (1934): 64–76.

5. Zelenin, *Kult ongonov v Sibiri*, 354–355.

6. Ibid., 354, 358–359, 361, 362–363.

7. Ibid., 364–365.

8. Gavriil Ksenofontov, "Kul't sumashestviia v uralo-altaiskom shamanizme," in his *Shamanizm: Izbrannye trudy* (Iakuts: Sever-iug, 1992), 254–265.

9. V. G. Bogoraz, "K psikhologii shamanstva u narodov Severo-vostochnoi Azii," *Etnograficheskoe obozrienie* 1–2 (1910): 9–10.

10. Sergei Tokarev, *History of Religion* (Moscow: Progress, 1986), 89; S. I. Vainshtein and N. P. Moskalenko, "Problemy Tuvinskogo shamanstva: Genesis, izbrannichestvo, effektivnost' lechebnikh kamlanii, sovremennii renessans," in *Shamanizm i rannie religioznie predstavlenia*, edited by D. A. Funk, Ethnological Studies of Shamanism and Other Indigenous Spiritual Beliefs and Practices, no. 1 (Moskva: Institut Etnologii i Antropologii, 1995), 66.

11. Vladimir Basilov, "Chosen by the Spirits," in *Shamanic Worlds: Rituals and Lore of Siberia and Central Asia*, edited by Marjorie Mandelstam Balzer (Armonk, NY: North Castle, 1997), 3–48; E. S. Novik, "The Archaic Epic and Its Relationship to Ritual: From Ritual and Folklore in Siberian Shamanism," in Balzer, *Shamanic Worlds*, 185–236; Novik, "Struktura shamanskikh deistv," in *Problemy slavianskoi etnografii*, edited by A. K. Baiburin and K. V. Chistov (Leningrad: Nauka, 1979), 204–212.

12. Vilmos Dioszegi, *Tracing Shamans in Siberia: The Story of an Ethnographical Research Expedition* (Oosterhout: Anthropological Publications, 1968), 72–73.

13. Yuri Slezkine, *Arctic Mirrors: Russia and the Small Peoples of the North* (Ithaca, NY: Cornell University Press, 1994), 147, 153–154.

14. Platon Oiunskii, *Stikhotvoreiia* (Leningrad: Sovetskii pisatel, 1978), 113–114.

15. V. G. Bogoraz-Tan [Bogoras], *Einshtein i religiia: Primenenie kontseptsii otnositel'nosti k issledovaniu religioznikh iavlenii* (Moskva and Petrograd: Frenkel', 1923), 116.

16. A. I. Andreev, *Vremia Shambaly: Okkultism, nauka i politika v Sovetskoi Rossiii* (St. Petersburg: Neva, 2004), 130–131, 196.

17. Anton Pervushin, *Okkul'tnye tainy NKVD i SS* (St. Petersburg: Neva; Moskva: OLMA-press, 1999), 152.

18. Andreev, *Vremia Shambaly*, 152; Pervushin, *Okkul'tnye tainy*, 175.

19. Andreev, *Vremia Shambaly*, 84; Pervushin, *Okkul'tnye tainy*, 146. Hyperborea is a legendary vanished northern country, whose inhabitants were described by ancient Greek authors as a race of happy people who lived an enjoyable life for 1,000 years.

20. Zinaida Rikhter, *V strane golubikh ozer: Ocherki Altaia* (Moskva and Leningrad: Molodaia gvardiia, 1930), 8.

21. Nikolai Severin, *Tsvetushchee zoloto: Altaiskie ocherki* (Moskva: OGIZ-Molodaia gvardia, 1931), 17, 25; Severin, *Sny Olonga: Altaiskaia povest* (Moskva-Leningrad: gos. iz-vo, 1930), 47.

22. Dmitrii Stonov, *Povesti ob Altae* (Moskva: Federatsiia, 1930), 47.

23. Ibid., 59.

24. Sof'ia Zarechnaia, *Chernaia shamanka: Povest' iz zhizni Buriat* (Moskva: Zemlia i fabrika, 1929).

25. V. G. Tan-Bogoraz [Bogoras], *Voskresshee plemia* (Moskva: Goslitizdat, 1935), 14.

26. Ibid., 22.

27. I. Kosokov, *K voprosu o shamanstve v Severnoi Azii* (Moskva: Bezbozhnik, 1930); P. Khaptaev, "Izuchenie shamanstva na novom etape (po povodu knigi Kosokova)," *Antireligioznik* 12 (1931): 69–70.

28. Innokentii Suslov, "Shamanstvo i bor'ba s nim," *Sovetskii siever* (March 1931): 90–91; A. Dolotov, *Shamanskaia vera* (Moskva: Bezbozhnik, 1930), 30.

29. V. G. Bogoras-Tan [Bogoras], "Religiia kak tormoz sotsstroitel'stva sredi malykh narodnostei Severa," *Sovetskii siever* (January–February 1932): 144.

30. Ibid., 155–157.

31. During the same years, based on the radical reassessments of Siberian beliefs, anthropologist S. Ursynovich composed an anti-shamanism propaganda educational program for the Militant Godless Union, a Soviet public association created to combat religion in all fields of life. In this program, shamans were similarly defined as "counterrevolutionary elements" and shamanism as "anti-Soviet activities directed to the wrecking of socialist construction among the Siberian peoples." S. Ursynovich, "Shamanstvo: Proekt programmy dlia antireligioznogo kruzkha," *Antireligioznik* 11 (1931): 12.

32. Suslov, "Shamanstvo i bor'ba s nim," 91.

33. Ibid., 90.

34. Andrei A. Znamenski, *Shamanism in Siberia: Russian Records of Siberian Spirituality* (Dordrecht and Boston: Kluwer Academic, 2003), 231.

35. P. N. Il'akhov, "Repressii protiv severnikh shamanov (1920–1935)," in *Istoriko-etnosotsial'nie issledovania: Regional'nie problemy*, edited by V. N. Ivanov (Novosibirsk: Nauka, 1998), 91, 94.

36. Tatyana Boulgakova, "Nanai Shamans under Double Oppression," *Pro Ethnologia* (Tartu, Estonia) 15 (2003): 135. Available at http://www.erm.ee/?node=101 (downloaded July 9, 2005).

37. Ibid., 144.

38. Ibid., 147.

39. Dioszegi, *Tracing Shamans in Siberia*, 58–59.

40. Boulgakova, "Nanai Shamans under Double Oppression," 133; Marjorie Mandelstam Balzer, "Ot bubnov k skovorodam: Povoroty syd'by shamanizma v istorii Sakha (Yakutov)," in *Shamanizm i rannie religioznie predstavlenia*, edited by D. A. Funk, Ethnological Studies of Shamanism and Other Indigenous Spiritual Beliefs and Practices, no. 1 (Moskva: Institut Antropologii i Etnografii, 1995), 25.

41. V. P. Diakonova, "Predmety k lechebnoi funktsii shamanov Tuvy i Altaia," in *Material'naia kul'tura i mifologiia*, edited by B. N. Putilov (Leningrad: Nauka, 1981), 145–146.

42. E. V. Revunenkova, "Zametki o sovremennoi terminologii, sviazannoi s shamanizmom u Telengitov," in *Shamanizm i rannie religioznie predstavlenia*, edited by D. A. Funk, Ethnological Studies of Shamanism and Other Indigenous Spiritual Beliefs and Practices, no. 1 (Moskva: Institut Etnologii i Antropologii, 1995), 88–98.

43. Marjorie Mandelstam Balzer, "Shamans as Healers, Rebels and Philosophers: Exploring Cultural Repression and Resilience in Siberia," in *Materialy mezhdunarodnogo kongressa shamanizm i inie traditsionnie verovania i praktiki*, edited by V. I. Kharitonova and D. Funk, Ethnological Studies of Shamanism and Other Indigenous Spiritual Beliefs and Practices, no. 5, pt. 2 (Moskva: Institut Antropologii i Etnografii, 1999), 94.

44. Eva Jane Neumann Fridman, *Sacred Geography: Shamanism among the Buddhist Peoples of Russia* (Budapest: Akadémiai Kiadó, 2004).

45. For more about the present-day renaissance of native shamanism in Siberia, see Marjorie Mandelstam Balzer, "Two Urban Shamans: Unmasking Leadership in Fin-de-Soviet Siberia," in *Perilous States: Conversations on Culture, Politics, and Nation*, edited by George E. Marcus (Chicago: University of Chicago Press, 1993), 131–164; Mihaly Hoppal, "Shamanism in Siberia Today," in *Shamanic Cosmos*, edited by Romano Mastromattei and Antonio Rigopoulos (Venice and New Delhi: Venetian Academy of Indian Studies and D. K. Printworld, 1999), 107–116; Caroline Humphrey, "Shamans in the City," *Anthropology Today* 15, no. 3 (1999): 3–11; Andrei Vinogradov, "'After the Past, before the Present': New Shamanism in Gorny Altai," *Anthropology of Consciousness* 10, no. 4 (1999): 36–45.

46. M. I. Gomboeva, "Etnopsikhologicheskaia identifikatsiia v shamanistskoi praktike aginskikh Buryat," *Gumanitarnii vektor* 2 (1998): 56; Piers Vitebsky, "From Cosmology to Environmentalism: Shamanism as Local Knowledge in a Global Setting," in *Shamanism: A Reader*, edited by Graham Harvey (London and New York: Routledge, 2003), 286, 293; Igor Krupnik and Nikolai Vakhtin, "In the 'House of Dismay': Knowledge, Culture and Post-Soviet Politics in Chukotka, 1995–1996," in *People and the Land: Pathways to Reform in Post-Soviet Siberia*, edited by Erich Kasten (Berlin: Riemer, 2002), 31.

47. V. I. Kharitonova, "Variatsii na temu," in *Izbranniki dukhov: Traditsionnoe shamanstvo i neoshamanism*, edited by V. I. Kharitonova, Ethnological Studies of

Shamanism and Other Indigenous Spiritual Beliefs and Practices, no. 4 (Moskva: Institut Antropologii i Etnografii, 1999), 254–255.

48. Fridman, *Sacred Geography*, 188.

49. Liubov Rak, "Proiti skvoz' ogon'," *Trud*, June 10, 2004, 13.

50. Vasilii Diatlov, "Plesnite koldovstva," *Itogi*, August 30, 2003. Available at http://www.itogi.ru/Paper2003.nsf/Article/Itogi_2003_08_26_12_2832.html (downloaded August 30, 2005).

51. Krupnik and Vakhtin, "In the 'House of Dismay,'" 33; Ulla Johansen, "Shamanism and Neoshamanism: What Is the Difference?" in *The Concept of Shamanism: Uses and Abuses*, edited by H.-P. Francfort, Roberte Hamayon, and Paul G. Bahn (Budapest: Akadémiai Kiadó, 2001), 302.

52. Irina S. Urbanaeva, "Shamanizm Mongol'skogo mira kak vyrazhenie tengrianskoi ezotericheskoi traditsii Tsentral'noi Azii," in *Tsentral'no-aziatskii shamanizm: Filosofskie, istoricheskie, religioznye aspekty, materialy mezhdunarodnogo nauchnogo simpoziuma*, edited by Irina S. Urbanaeva (Ulan-Ude: Buriatskii institut obshchestvennykh nauk, 1996), 48–49.

53. Gomboeva, "Etnopsikhologicheskaia identifikatsiia," 57; G. R. Galdanova, "Buryatskii shamanizm segodnia," in *Materialy mezhdunarodnogo kongressa shamanizm i inie traditsionnie verovania i praktiki*, edited by V. I. Kharitonova and D. Funk, Ethnological Studies of Shamanism and Other Indigenous Spiritual Beliefs and Practices, no. 5, pt. 2 (Moskva: Institut Antropologii i Etnografii, 1999), 272.

54. O. A. Murashko, "Shamanstvo i traditsionnoe mirovozzrenie itel'menov," in *Izbranniki dukhov: Traditsionnoe shamanstvo i neoshamanizm*, edited by V. I. Kharitonova, Ethnological Studies of Shamanism and Other Indigenous Spiritual Beliefs and Practices, no. 4 (Moskva: Institut Antropologii i Etnologii, 1999), 160–182.

55. Benedict Allen, *Last of the Medicine Men* (London: Dorling Kindersley, 2001), 95.

56. Peter Uccusic, "Shamanism Alive and Well: The 1999 Legacy of the First FSS Expedition to Tuva," *Shamanism* 13, nos. 1–2 (2000): 52–53.

57. Allen, *Last of the Medicine Men*, 91–92.

58. "The Professor, the Shaman, and Me." Available at http://www.thunderperfectmind.com (downloaded May 18, 2004).

59. Allen, *Last of the Medicine Men*, 95.

60. David Brown, "Traditional Healing Returns to Tuva," *Washington Post*, July 18, 1995, Z10.

61. For more on Stepanova, see Fridman, *Sacred Geography*, 162–164; and Humphrey, "Shamans in the City."

62. N. L. Zhukovskaia, "Buriatskii shamanism segodnia: Vozrozhdenie ili evolutsia," in *Materialy mezhdunarodnogo kongressa shamanizm i inie traditsionnie verovania i praktiki*, edited by V. I. Kharitonova and D. Funk, Ethnological Studies of Shamanism and Other Indigenous Spiritual Beliefs and Practices, no. 5, pt. 3 (Moskva: Institut Antropologii i Etnografii, 1999), 165.

63. Gomboeva, "Etnopsikhologicheskaia identifikatsiia," 64.

64. Native cultural workers who write scripts for the staged shamanic performances, which usually include dances, ritual songs, and public healing, frequently improvise and do not stick to ethnographic tradition. Such an approach usually does

414 NOTES TO PAGES 353-360

not present a problem for newly minted shamans of the younger generation and especially for actors who pose as shamans. For those few practitioners who started their spiritual vocation prior to the 1980s, before it became fashionable, the innovations pose a serious challenge. Yet, attracted by an opportunity to make money, some old shamans bend to the requirements of stage managers. For example, during an ethnic festival, a Nanai shamaness named Maria Beldy initially refused to bow to the spirit of water and feed the water, which was alien to her tribal tradition. Still, pressured by the organizer of the festival, she acquiesced. Some spiritual practitioners intentionally distort elements of shamanic rituals, chants, and attire to make them inauthentic and thus to relieve themselves from the potential anger of spiritual forces. Tatyana Boulgakova, "Shaman on Stage (Shamanism and Northern Identity)," *Pro Ethnologia* 11 (Tartu, Estonia). Available at http://www.erm.ee/?node=101 (downloaded July 9, 2005).

65. About similar intellectual self-initiations of neo-shamans in the neighboring republic of Altai, see Agnieszka Halemba, "Contemporary Religious Life in the Republic of Altai: The Interaction of Buddhism and Shamanism," *Sibirica* 3, no. 2 (2003): 176.

66. Kira Van Deusen, *Singing Story, Healing Drum: Shamans and Storytellers of Turkic Siberia* (Montreal and Kingston: McGill-Queen's University Press, 2004), 176; Uccusic, "Shamanism Alive and Well," 53; Fridman, *Sacred Geography*, 215, 221–222.

67. Fridman, *Sacred Geography*, 172.

68. Johansen, "Shamanism and Neoshamanism," 300, 302; Fridman, *Sacred Geography*, 164–165, 187, 216.

69. Susan Grimaldi, "Tuvan Shamanism Comes to America." Available at http://www.susangrimaldi.com/docs/tuvamerica.pdf (downloaded July 9, 2005).

70. Fridman, *Sacred Geography*, 187.

71. Van Deusen, *Singing Story*, 171, 174; Fridman, *Sacred Geography*, 187.

72. Grimaldi, "Tuvan Shamanism Comes to America."

73. Van Deusen, *Singing Story*, 171, 174; Allen, *Last of the Medicine Men*, 78–89, 101–102.

74. O. A. Murashko, "Sovremennaia magiko-misticheskaia praktika u Itel'menov," in *Materialy mezhdunarodnogo kongressa shamanizm i inie traditsionnie verovania i praktiki*, edited by V. I. Kharitonova and D. Funk, Ethnological Studies of Shamanism and Other Indigenous Spiritual Beliefs and Practices, no. 5, pt. 1 (Moskva: Institut Antropologii i Etnografii, 1999), 199.

75. For more about Knyev and neo-shamanism in the Altai, see Halemba, "Contemporary Religious Life in the Republic of Altai," 174–177.

76. Sarangerel [Julie A. Stewart], *Chosen by the Spirits: Following Your Shamanic Calling* (Rochester, VT: Destiny, 2001); Olga Kharitidi, *Entering the Circle: The Secrets of Ancient Siberian Wisdom Discovered by a Russian Psychiatrist* (San Francisco: Harper-SanFrancisco, 1996).

77. In a literal translation from Russian, *Belovodie* means the "white water land"; white is the symbol of purity. *Belovodie* is the name of an old Russian peasant utopia, which is now part of Siberian folklore. In the eighteenth and early nineteenth centuries, many peasant serfs from European Russia, primarily schismatic Old Believers who rejected official Christianity, ran away eastward in the hope of finding a promised

land of plenty and free worship. Their imagination placed this utopia roughly within the borders of the present-day Altai. In the early twentieth century, artist and theosophist Nicholas Roerich romanticized *Belovodie* as the Siberian Shambhala. John McCannon, "By the Shores of White Waters: The Altai and Its Place in the Spiritual Geopolitics of Nicholas Roerich," *Sibirica* 2 (October 2002): 167–190.

78. Janet I. Tu, "65th and Divine Blissful Paths Converge on Northeast 65th, Seattle's Metaphysical Center," *Seattle Times*, April 2, 2000, M1.

79. Boulgakova, "Shaman on Stage."

EPILOGUE

1. Dagmar Wernitznig, *Going Native or Going Naïve: White Shamanism and the Neo-noble Savage* (Lanham, MD: University Press of America, 2003), xxiii.

2. Olav Hammer, *Claiming Knowledge: Strategies of Epistemology from Theosophy to the New Age* (Leiden: Brill, 2001), 71–73.

3. Don Lattin, *Following Our Bliss: How the Spiritual Ideals of the Sixties Shape Our Lives Today* (New York: HarperCollins, 2003).

4. Stephen Hunt, *Alternative Religions: A Sociological Introduction* (Aldershot, England: Ashgate, 2003), 133–134.

5. When making references to native Siberians, some gender-sensitive Western seekers try to replace "shaman" with "shamanka" in order to coin a special term to describe female spiritual practitioners in a tribal setting. In reality, the word *shamanka* is a Russian distortion of the Evenki *shaman*—a similar attempt to find a gender-specific word to describe indigenous women involved in shamanic activities. Like shamanism, the word *shamanka* was introduced into Western literature by eighteenth-century German explorers of Siberia, who occasionally included it in the texts of their narratives and in captions that accompanied colorful engravings depicting female spiritual practitioners from native Siberia.

6. Quoted in Steven Charleston, "From Medicine Man to Marx: The Coming Shift in Native Theology," in *Native American Religious Identity: Unforgotten Gods*, edited by Jace Weaver (Maryknoll, NY: Orbis, 1998), 159; Lisa Aldred, "Plastic Shamans and Astroturf Sun Dances," *American Indian Quarterly* 24, no. 3 (2000): 343.

7. Philip Jenkins, *Dream Catchers: How Mainstream America Discovered Native Spirituality* (New York: Oxford University Press, 2004), 247–249.

8. Esther Pasztory, "Nostalgia for Mud," *Precolumbian Art Research Institute Journal* 2, no. 1 (2001). Available at http://www.mesoweb.com/pari/publications/journal/03/mud.html (downloaded August 10, 2005).

Bibliographical Essay

The goal of this essay is not to provide a comprehensive list of all sources that I used when working on *The Beauty of the Primitive*. Here, I single out the most important books and articles, which will orient the reader in the overwhelming literature on shamanism and shamanism studies. I assume that those who are interested in particular issues will go directly to individual chapters' endnotes, which contain complete references to all of the relevant sources used in this book.

Since the time Mircea Eliade had his classic *Shamanism: Archaic Techniques of Ecstasy* published in English (Princeton, NJ: Princeton University Press, 1964), many other authors have attempted to present a similar cross-cultural picture of shamanism. The most recent attempt was made by British anthropologist Piers Vitebsky in *Shamanism* (Norman: University of Oklahoma Press, 2000). His small and lavishly illustrated volume can serve as a good introductory reading on the topic. For the most comprehensive reference edition that taps shamanisms of both ancient and modern peoples from all over the world, see Mariko Namba Walter and Eva Jane Neumann Fridman, eds., *Shamanism: An Encyclopedia of World Beliefs, Practices, and Culture*, 2 vols. (Santa Barbara, CA: ABC-CLIO, 2004).

On the emergence of interest in shamanism in Europe and America as part of the general history of Western esotericism, see a seminal study, *Schamanismus und Esoterik: Kultur- und wissenschaftsgeschichtliche Betrachtungen* (Leuven: Peeters, 2003), by Kocku von Stuckrad. In their popular anthology, *Shamans through Time: 500 Years on the Path to Knowledge* (New York: Jeremy P. Tarcher/Putnam, 2001), anthropologists Jeremy Narby and Francis Huxley illustrate the evolution of the Western representation of shamanism by providing brief excerpts from the works of European and American explorers, writers, anthropologists, and spiritual seekers from the 1500s to the present. Readers who are interested in learning about the variety of viewpoints among present-day anthropologists, psychologists, historians of religion, and spiritual seekers on the topic of shamanism might want to consult *Shamanism: A Reader*, edited by Graham Harvey (London: Routledge, 2003). One can find a more elaborate version of the same story in my three-volume anthology *Shamanism: Critical Concepts in Sociology* (London: Routledge, 2004). This collection of extensive excerpts from relevant works is introduced by my lengthy essay, "Adventure of the Metaphor: Shamanism and Shamanism Studies," which might also serve as a useful reference resource.

The major periodical that brings together humanities and social sciences scholars who write on shamanism is the Hungary-based *Shaman: Journal of the International Society for Shamanistic Research* (http://www.arts.u-szeged.hu/journal/shaman/shaman .html), which has been published since 1993. Although slightly dated, Jane Atkinson's "Shamanisms Today," *Annual Review of Anthropology* 21 (1992): 307–330, still remains a good brief introduction into the historiography of shamanism studies. While scholars in religious studies more or less accept the Eliadean vision of shamanism as a perennial cross-cultural phenomenon, many anthropologists do not share this view. Naturally centered on cultural particulars, they cling more to the postmodern vision of tribal spirituality as culturally specific local knowledge. For this reason, in their discussions of nature religions, some anthropologists either completely avoid the word *shamanism* or prefer to talk about *shamanisms*. In addition to Atkinson's article, which follows this tradition, for a similar postmodern view of tribal spiritualities, see Robert J. Wallis, *Shamans/Neo-Shamans: Ecstasy, Alternative Archaeologies, and Contemporary Pagans* (London: Routledge, 2003). Incidentally, in addition to the above-mentioned *Schamanismus und Esoterik* by Kocku von Stuckrad, Wallis's book is the most detailed study on the emergence and development of neo-shamanism in the modern West. The reader interested in learning more about a critical attitude to the expansion of the shamanism idiom into the humanities, social sciences, and general culture might consult Henri Paul Francfort, Roberte Hamayon, and Paul G. Bahn, eds., *The Concept of Shamanism: Uses and Abuses* (Budapest: Akadémiai Kiadó, 2001).

On the representation of Siberian and Native American shamanisms in the writings of Enlightenment explorers, see Gloria Flaherty, *Shamanism and the Eighteenth Century* (Princeton, NJ: Princeton University Press, 1992). In "Reenchanting Nature: Modern Western Shamanism and Nineteenth-Century Thought," *Journal of the American Academy of Religion* 70 (2002): 784–788, Kocku von Stuckrad explored the nineteenth-century Romantic philosophy of nature as an intellectual prerequisite of modern Western shamanism. For examples of Romantic ethnographies dealing with shamanism, see Dorji Banzarov, "The Black Faith; or, Shamanism among the Mongols," *Mongolian Studies: Journal of the Mongolia Society* 7 (1981–1982): 56–57; Wilhelm Radloff, *Aus Sibirien: Lose Blätter aus dem Tagebuche eines reisenden Linguisten*, 2 vols. (Leipzig: Weigel, 1884); and Kai Donner, *Among the Samoyed in Siberia* (New Haven, CT: Human Relations Area Files, 1954). Although incomplete and eclectic, Elémire Zolla's *The Writer and the Shaman: A Morphology of the American Indian* (New York: Harcourt Brace Jovanovich, 1973) provides several glimpses into the representation of Native American shamanism in American fiction and ethnology. The major work that introduced the shamanism metaphor in American ethnology is Roland Dixon's "Some Aspects of the American Shaman," *Journal of American Folklore* 21 (1908): 1–12.

For an example of how the shamanism idiom was used in Western primitivism at the turn of the twentieth century, see Peg Weiss, *Kandinsky and Old Russia: The Artist as Ethnographer and Shaman* (New Haven, CT: Yale University Press, 1995). On the role of Native Americana in Western primitivism during the same period, see Helen Carr, *Inventing the American Primitive: Politics, Gender and the Representation of Native American Literary Traditions, 1789–1936* (New York: New York University Press, 1996); and Philip Jenkins, *Dream Catchers: How Mainstream America Discovered Native Spirituality* (New York: Oxford University Press, 2004). For debates about the origin of the word *shaman*, see Berthold Laufer, "Origin of the Word Shaman," *American Anthropologist* 19 (1917): 361–371; and N. D. Mironov and S. M. Shirokogoroff, "Sramana-Shaman: Etymology of the Word 'Shaman,'" *Journal of the North China Branch of the Royal Asiatic Society* 55 (1924): 105–130.

On V. G. Bogoras and V. I. Jochelson, the exiled ethnographers who familiarized Western scholars with classical Siberian shamanism, and the Jesup expedition, see Igor Krupnik and William W. Fitzhugh, eds., *Gateways: Exploring the Legacy of the Jesup North Pacific Expedition, 1897–1902* (Washington, DC: Arctic Studies Center, Smithsonian Institution, 2001). *In the Far North-East Siberia* (London: Macmillan, 1916) by Z. Schklovsky, who at some point was himself an exiled explorer, provides a good description in English of the natural, social, and cultural environment that surrounded people like Bogoras, Jochelson, Sieroszewski, and their comrades whom I describe in my book. For examples of the exiled ethnographers' works that refer to shamans, see Waldemar Bogoras [V. G. Bogoraz], *The Chukchee* (1908–1909; reprint, New York: AMS, 1975); Waldemar [V. I.] Jochelson, *The Koryak* (1908; reprint, New York: AMS, 1975); and Wenceslas Sieroszewski, "Du chamanisme d'après les croyances des Yakoutes," *Revue de l'histoire des religions* 46 (1902): 204–233, 299–338.

On the culture of Siberian natives viewed through the eyes of the arctic hysteria thesis, see Stanislaus Novakovsky, "Arctic or Siberian Hysteria as a Reflex of the Geographic Environment," *Ecology* 5, no. 2 (1924): 124–125. For the extreme view of shamanism as a manifestation of the arctic hysteria thesis, see Åke Ohlmarks, *Studien zum Problem des Schamanismus* (Lund: Gleerup, 1939). In *Aboriginal Siberia: A Study in Social Anthropology* (Oxford: Clarendon, 1914), Marie Antoinette Czaplicka articulated a milder version of the same argument. Before the publication of Eliade's *Shamanism* in English in 1964, *Aboriginal Siberia*, which was formatted as a reference ethnography, remained the major source on classical shamanism for North American and British scholars. Sergei M. Shirokogoroff's classical *Psychomental Complex of the Tungus* (London: Kegan Paul, 1935), which was the only major contemporary work that contained a critique of the view of shamanism as neurosis, was written in a sophisticated language and went against the dominant psychiatric interpretation of shamanism and for these reasons, *Psychomental Complex of the Tungus* never enjoyed popularity before the 1960s. On the psychoanalytic view of shamanism, see Robert F. Kraus, "A Psychoanalytic Interpretation of Shamanism," *Psychoanalytic Review* 59, no. 1 (1972): 27–28; Geza Roheim, "Hungarian Shamanism," *Psychoanalysis and the Social Sciences* 3 (1951): 131–169; George Devereux, *Mohave Ethnopsychiatry: The Psychic Disturbances of an Indian Tribe* (Washington, DC: Smithsonian Institution Press, 1969).

The most comprehensive discussion of Robert G. Wasson's intellectual legacy, including his soma scholarship, is Thomas J. Riedlinger, ed., *The Sacred Mushroom*

Seeker: Essays for R. Gordon Wasson (Rochester, VT: Park Street, 1997). Michael Harner, ed., *Hallucinogens and Shamanism* (Oxford: Oxford University Press, 1973), another collection of articles and essays, is a good compact source on psychedelic shamanism. See also Peter Furst, *Hallucinogens and Culture* (San Francisco: Chandler & Sharp, 1976), which describes all of the major herbal hallucinogens used by ancient and modern tribal peoples: mushrooms, jimson weed, peyote, tobacco, cannabis, and other less known mind-altering substances. The book now can be found in an open domain at http://www.sunrisedancer.com/radicalreader/library/hallucinogensandculture. The most recent account of psychedelic shamanism is Daniel Pinchback's *Breaking Open the Head: A Psychedelic Journey into the Heart of Contemporary Shamanism* (New York: Broadway, 2002). On *ayahuasca* shamanism, see Luis Eduardo Luna and Steven F. White, eds., *Ayahuasca Reader: Encounters with the Amazon's Sacred Vine* (Santa Fe, NM: Synergetic, 2000); and Jeremy Narby, *Cosmic Serpent: DNA and the Origin of Knowledge* (New York: Jeremy P. Tarcher/Putnam, 1998).

On the spiritual great awakening in the 1960s and the rise of the "New Age" and nature religions in the 1970s and 1980s, which set the background for the emergence of neo-shamanism, see Theodore Roszak, *Where the Wasteland Ends: Politics and Transcendence in Postindustrial Society* (Garden City, NY: Doubleday, 1972); Robert S. Ellwood, *The Sixtieth Spiritual Awakening: American Religion Moving from Modern to Postmodern* (New Brunswick, NJ: Rutgers University Press, 1994); Michael York, *The Emerging Network: A Sociology of the New Age and Neo-Pagan Movements* (Lanham, MD: Rowman and Littlefield, 1995); Nevill Drury, *The New Age: The History of a Movement* (London: Thames and Hudson, 2004); Catherine Albanese, *Nature Religion in America: From the Algonkian Indians to the New Age* (Chicago: University of Chicago Press, 1990); Robert C. Fuller, *Spiritual but Not Religious: Understanding Unchurched America* (Oxford and New York: Oxford University Press, 2001); Eugene Taylor, *Shadow Culture: Psychology and Spirituality in America* (Washington, DC: Counterpoint, 1999); Walter T. Anderson, *The Upstart Spring: Esalen and the American Awakening* (Reading, MA: Addison-Wesley, 1983). On the rise of transpersonal psychology, one of the major intellectual sources of neo-shamanism, see Donald Moss, ed., *Humanistic and Transpersonal Psychology: A Historical and Biographical Sourcebook* (Westport, CT: Greenwood, 1999).

There is abundant literature on the intellectual life and scholarship of Mircea Eliade, who is considered the classic scholar of shamanism studies. The most useful general account, which helps to explain Eliade's approach to shamanism as perennial wisdom, is Douglas Allen's *Myth and Religion in Mircea Eliade* (New York and London: Routledge, 1998). Unfortunately, we do not have a similar comprehensive account on Carlos Castaneda. There are partisan works that either welcome Castaneda's contribution to esotericism and spirituality or debunk him and like-minded authors as a hoax. *A Magical Journey with Carlos Castaneda* (Victoria, BC: Millenia, 1996) by Margaret Runyan Castaneda, his former wife, and *Sorcerer's Apprentice: My Life with Carlos Castaneda* (Berkeley, CA: Frog North Atlantic, 2003) by Amy Wallace, one of Castaneda's former cohorts, provided some insights into his archaic spiritual techniques. For the works that expose Castaneda's ethnographies, see Richard De Mille, *Castaneda's Journey: The Power and the Allegory* (Santa Barbara, CA: Capra, 1976); Richard De Mille, ed., *The Don Juan Papers: Further Castaneda Controversies* (Belmont, CA: Wadsworth, 1990);

and Jay C. Fikes, *Carlos Castaneda, Academic Opportunism and the Psychedelic Sixties* (Victoria, BC: Millenia, 1993). The latter work also targeted anthropologists Barbara Myerhoff and Peter Furst. Fikes argued that these former Castaneda colleagues courted countercultural audiences by sensationalizing Huichol shamanism. The late religion scholar Daniel Noel, who edited a collection of essays, *Seeing Castaneda* (New York: Putnam, 1976), was less dismissive. In this anthology and in his later book, *The Soul of Shamanism: Western Fantasies, Imaginal Realities* (New York: Continuum, 1997), Noel asserted that Castaneda's fiction has a healing effect on Western culture by promoting the revival of the spiritual and the mythological, which modernity squeezed out from human life. For the impact of Castaneda on anthropology scholarship and on the necessity for students of spirituality to go native, see Yves Marton, "The Experiential Approach to Anthropology and Castaneda's Ambiguous Legacy," in *Being Changed: The Anthropology of Extraordinary Experience*, edited by David E. Young and Jean-Guy Goulet (Petersborough, Ontario: Broadview, 1994), 273–297.

Such books as Castaneda's *The Teachings of Don Juan: A Yaqui Way of Knowledge* (Berkeley: University of California Press, 1968); Hyemeyohsts Storm's *Seven Arrows* (New York: Harper & Row, 1972); and Lynn Andrews's *Medicine Woman* (San Francisco: Harper & Row, 1981) sparked the whole tribal spirituality apprenticeship genre, which now includes more than a hundred experiential novels and which serves as an inspiration for many seekers of tribal wisdom. Although many of these texts usually sample non-Western archaic spiritual techniques, one should add to this list of spirituality novels, for example, Brian Bates's *The Way of Wyrd: Tales of an Anglo-Saxon Sorcerer* (1983; reprint, Carlsbad, CA: Hay House, 2005), which seek to shape the spiritual blueprints of indigenous Western shamanism through the reconstruction of European pre-Christian cultural settings. Furthermore, like in the 1970s and 1980s, ethnographic and folklore texts originating from traditional tribal settings, e.g., John G. Neihardt's famous *Black Elk Speaks* (New York: Morrow, 1932), and the writings of such prominent visionary scholars and writers as Carl Jung and Joseph Campbell who, like Eliade, worked within the phenomenological tradition, continue to inspire many Western practitioners of shamanism.

For comprehensive discussions of the culture, sociology, aesthetics, and spirituality of neo-shamanism communities in Europe and North America, see John Littleton, "'With Spirit at the Center': A Postmodern Ethnography of the Wakan Community and Its Earth-Centered Shamanism" (M.A. thesis, California Institute for Integral Studies, 1993); Galina Lindquist, *Shamanic Performances on the Urban Scene: Neo-Shamanism in Contemporary Sweden* (Stockholm: Department of Social Anthropology, Stockholm University, 1997); Jan Svanberg, "Scandinavian Neo-Shamanism: The Contribution of the Academic Study of Religion in Reconstructing Beliefs and Practices of Tradition within Post-Modern Urban Milieus," *Acta Ethnographica Hungarica* 43, nos. 1–2 (1998): 151–161; Svanberg, *Schamantropologi i gränslandet mellan forskning och praktik: En studie av förhållandet mellan schamanismforskning och neoschamanism* (Åbo: Åbo Akademis Förlag/ Åbo Akademi University Press, 2003); Merete Jakobsen, *Shamanism: Traditional and Contemporary Approaches to the Mastery of Spirits and Healing* (New York: Berghahn, 1999); Jenny Blain, *Nine Worlds of Seid-Magic: Ecstasy and Neo-Shamanism in Northern European Paganism* (London and New York: Routledge, 2002); Robert J. Wallis, *Shamans/Neo-Shamans: Ecstasy, Alternative Archaeologies, and Contemporary Pagans* (London: Routledge,

2003); and Kocku von Stuckrad, *Schamanismus und Esoterik: Kultur- und wissenschafts-geschichtliche Betrachtungen* (Leuven: Peeters, 2003). The above-mentioned scholars either provide balanced (Lindquist, Jakobsen, Svanberg, and von Stuckrad) or sympathetic (Littleton, Wallis, Blain) accounts of neo-shamanism. For a work that is critical of modern Western pursuits of tribal spirituality, see Alice Kehoe's *Shamans and Religion: An Anthropological Exploration in Critical Thinking* (Prospect Heights, IL: Waveland, 2000).

The practical manual *The Way of the Shaman* (San Francisco: Harper & Row, 1980) by shaman-anthropologist Michael Harner, who was one of the fountainheads of neo-shamanism in the modern West, became a classic. Since the 1980s, a large number of similar how-to brochures and manuals have been produced. While some of them have creatively incorporated Harner's method, many others have nothing to do with his core shamanism system whatsoever. Among the essential texts that teach the archaic techniques of ecstasy to modern spiritual seekers are Jose Stevens and Lena S. Stevens, *Urban Shaman: Tapping the Spirit Power within You* (New York: Avon, 1988); Angelique S. Cook and George A. Haw, *Shamanism and the Esoteric Tradition* (St. Paul, MN: Llewellyn, 1992); Arnold Mindell, *The Shaman's Body: A New Shamanism for Transforming Health, Relationships, and Community* (San Francisco: HarperSanFrancisco, 1993); and Gini Graham Scott, *The Complete Idiot's Guide to Shamanism* (Indianapolis, IN: Alpha, 2002). Since its introduction in the 1970s, the shamanism metaphor has become an integral part of Western esoteric discourse by entering a variety of "New Age" and nature spiritualities. For example, it is reinvoked in eco-feminism (Barbara Tedlock, *The Woman in the Shaman's Body: Reclaiming the Feminine in Religion and Medicine* [New York: Bantam, 2005]), in Wiccan tradition (Christopher Penczak, *The Temple of Shamanic Witchcraft* [St. Paul, MN: Llewellyn, 2005]), and in so-called business magic (Richard Whiteley, *The Corporate Shaman: A Business Fable* [New York: HarperBusiness, 2002]).

In terms of spirituality periodicals, the American *Shaman's Drum*, the UK-based *Sacred Hoop*, and the on-line *Spirit Talk* (http://www.shamaniccircles.org/spirit_talk) are the major magazines in English, serving thousands of people interested in the archaic techniques of ecstasy. From 1984 to 1998, many North American spiritual seekers and visionary scholars interested in shamanic techniques gathered for annual conferences in California. The materials of these meetings have been published in fifteen volumes, which reproduce not only the delivered papers but also the texts of commentaries, discussions, and workshop materials. The last volume was released in 1998 as *Phoenix Rising VI: Proceedings of the Fifteenth International Conference on the Study of Shamanism and Alternate Modes of Healing*, edited by Ruth-Inge Heinze (Berkeley, CA : Independent Scholars of Asia, 1998). In addition to the magazines I mentioned above, these proceedings represent invaluable primary sources for any student of the fuzzy culture of modern Western shamanism.

The best discussion of Native Americana as an inspiration for nature and "New Age" communities and individuals is Philip Jenkins's *Dream Catchers: How Mainstream America Discovered Native Spirituality* (New York: Oxford University Press, 2004). What sets this study apart from other works is his approach. Jenkins gives the benefit of the doubt both to Indians who criticize "New Agers" and to non-Indian spiritual seekers who feed on Native Americana. Although poorly researched and written, Dagmar Wernitznig's *Going Native or Going Naïve: White Shamanism and the Neo-noble Savage*

(Lanham, MD: University Press of America, 2003) provides an example of the most recent critique of "white shamans" who experiment with Native American traditions.

The most comprehensive account in English on the history of Russian and Soviet perceptions of Siberian shamanism is Ronald Hutton's *Shamans: Siberian Spirituality and the Western Imagination* (London: Hambledon and London, 2001). The reader interested in learning about Soviet assessments of shamanism as a culturally conditioned spiritual vocation might also consult Vladimir Basilov, "Chosen by the Spirits," in *Shamanic Worlds: Rituals and Lore of Siberia and Central Asia*, edited by Marjorie Mandelstam Balzer (Armonk, NY: North Castle, 1997), 3–48. On the resurgence of shamanism in modern Siberia and the development of indigenous neo-shamanism in this area, see Marjorie Mandelstam Balzer, "Two Urban Shamans: Unmasking Leadership in Fin-de-Soviet Siberia," in *Perilous States: Conversations on Culture, Politics, and Nation*, edited by George E. Marcus (Chicago: University of Chicago Press, 1993), 131–164; Piers Vitebsky, "From Cosmology to Environmentalism: Shamanism as Local Knowledge in a Global Setting," in *Shamanism: A Reader*, edited by G. Harvey (London and New York: Routledge, 2003), 276–298; Jane Neumann Fridman, *Sacred Geography: Shamanism among the Buddhist Peoples of Russia* (Budapest: Akadémiai Kiadó, 2004); Caroline Humphrey, "Shamans in the City," *Anthropology Today* 15, no. 3 (1999): 3–11; Benedict Allen, *Last of the Medicine Men* (London: Dorling Kindersley, 2001); Kira Van Deusen, *Singing Story, Healing Drum: Shamans and Storytellers of Turkic Siberia* (Montreal and Kingston: McGill-Queen's University Press, 2004). For examples of experiential narratives of Western authors informed by the symbolism and spirituality of Siberian shamanism, see Sarangerel [Julie A. Stewart], *Chosen by the Spirits: Following Your Shamanic Calling* (Rochester, VT: Destiny, 2001); and Olga Kharitidi, *Entering the Circle: The Secrets of Ancient Siberian Wisdom Discovered by a Russian Psychiatrist* (San Francisco: HarperSanFrancisco, 1996).

Index